OXFORD HISTORY OF MODERN EUROPE

General Editors

ALAN BULLOCK *and* **F. W. D. DEAKIN**

Oxford History of Modern Europe

THE STRUGGLE FOR MASTERY IN EUROPE 1845–1918

By A. J. P. TAYLOR

SPAIN 1808–1939

By RAYMOND CARR

THE RUSSIAN EMPIRE
1801–1917

BY

HUGH SETON-WATSON

OXFORD
AT THE CLARENDON PRESS
1967

Oxford University Press, Ely House, London W. 1

GLASGOW NEW YORK TORONTO MELBOURNE WELLINGTON
CAPE TOWN SALISBURY IBADAN NAIROBI LUSAKA ADDIS ABABA
BOMBAY CALCUTTA MADRAS KARACHI LAHORE DACCA
KUALA LUMPUR HONG KONG TOKYO

PRINTED IN GREAT BRITAIN

IN MEMORY OF MY PARENTS

ROBERT WILLIAM SETON-WATSON

(1879–1951)

AND

MARION ESTHER SETON-WATSON

(1883–1963)

PREFACE

It is difficult to write the history of another country. The foreigner has not grown up in its physical and mental climate, and he cannot understand them, still less feel them, in the same way as its own people do. He can spend long periods in a foreign land, learn its language, work and live among its citizens, to some extent think as they do, and be accepted as a friend. This is not the same thing as being one of the people of the country, but still it is something. This I have done in several countries, but Russia is not one of them. I have visited Russia briefly, I have known its language for many years, and I have had pleasant contacts with individual Soviet citizens. I might perhaps, if I had been more persevering, have spent much longer periods in this way. However, the most that I could have achieved, and which some persons known to me have indeed achieved, is still far less than what above I have called living among a foreign nation and being accepted as a friend. It has not in fact been possible for many years for a foreigner to live like this in Russia unless he has been willing to turn his back on his own country. There are signs that it may become possible some years hence, that my children's generation may be able to live among Russians as my father's generation were able.

The foreigner is of course writing for his own people, or for peoples whose language is the same as his own. He has to stress at some length points which to a Russian are so obvious that they do not even deserve a mention. He has to put together, and try to make a coherent picture of, many details which are found scattered in many sources; to do this is indeed as important a duty, towards his audience, as that search for new facts in documents which has become the exclusive preoccupation of so many professional historians. British historians have already made substantial contributions to the historical literature on Russia. Besides Sumner and Pares are many lesser names. In recent decades American contributions have been still more impressive—both monographs and general surveys. Nevertheless, there is still room for works in English on nineteenth-century

Russia. It is to the English-speaking public—and not to the expert on specific sectors of Russian history, not even to the specialist in Russian history, so much as to the reader interested in general history—that this work is offered, after much toil and with little satisfaction.

I do not expect that my work will in any way enlighten Russians. Certainly it will teach them no facts. It is just conceivable that the great distance from which I approach the subject may lend some detachment, or that some comparisons that I have made with other lands or periods may have some small marginal value. To any Russian who may read it, I can sincerely say that if I lack the warm feeling that comes from long experience and human contact, at least I do not lack respect for his great nation, or love for his splendid language, or gratitude for the joy which its literature, above all the great Pushkin, has given me.

The period covered begins with the accession of Alexander I and ends with the abdication of Nicholas II. The Revolution and all that followed will, it is hoped, form the subject for another volume in this series by another author. The centre of attention in this book may be described as political and social history—the history of institutions, classes, political movements and individuals. Other aspects are treated marginally.

Systematic description and analysis of foreign policy is the subject of separate volumes in this series. But I have not been able simply to leave out the foreign relations of the Russian Empire, least of all in the age of Alexander I and Napoleon, when internal and foreign policy, war and peace were inextricably connected. Within the general framework of foreign relations, I have perhaps given relatively more attention than is usual to Russian policy in Asia, including the conquest and consolidation of what may be called the colonial empire. Much less space has been given to foreign policy in the last decades, which is generally well known and has in any case been covered by the first volume published in this series.[1] Military events are too lightly dealt with, but I have at least tried to give the reader the basic facts—where the campaigns were fought and with what result—which are so often omitted in modern general historical surveys.

[1] A. J. P. Taylor, *The Struggle for Mastery in Europe 1848–1918*.

The technical aspects of economic history are absent, but there is a very broad overlapping zone between the political, social and economic, which concerns the development of agriculture and industry and the changing pattern of social classes. An economic historian would treat these subjects differently, but I do not think that I have ignored them.

History of literature is another distinct field. But in nineteenth-century Russia literature was so closely connected with political and social history that it often has to be mentioned. There are thus references to the works and lives not only of the most politically minded but also of the greatest creative writers. Arts and sciences are only mentioned in a few bare statements, designed to remind readers that at such and such a time Lobachevsky was developing his mathematics, Chaikovsky composing his symphonies, or Chagall learning to paint.

One aspect which is commonly underrated is the imperial. Russia was a multi-national empire, more than half of whose subjects were not Russians. Clearly a single volume cannot examine in any depth the history of all the non-Russian peoples. But I have devoted a good deal of space to the relations of these peoples with the Russians, and to the development of political movements among them, together with some sketchy references to their social structures and economic development.

By far the most important was the Polish people. It is hoped that a separate volume on Poland will appear in this series, which will do justice to the abundant Polish sources. My own brief sections on Poland are based on very limited study. For the first half of the period I am largely though not exclusively indebted to the two recent books by R. F. Leslie, while for the second half I have used a wider range of less satisfactory works. For the other non-Russian peoples a mixture of a few primary and secondary sources, mostly in Russian but some also in German and Ukrainian, has had to suffice. Any British scholars willing to devote themselves to systematic study of the history of the main non-Russian peoples of the Empire in this period will find a most rewarding use for their talents.

My aim has been to see the period as it was, rather than in terms of what happened after it; to consider policies and personalities in terms of what was possible in their time, rather than to impose on them the standards which are accepted in our own.

It has seemed to me desirable to refrain from giving good and bad marks to the personages of the drama, to dub them 'progressive' or 'reactionary'. Nevertheless, my own preferences may from time to time stand out. I am not ashamed of having preferences, but I have tried not to force them on my readers, and where I have failed I ask their indulgence.

This is not of course the approach of Soviet historical literature. It is based on the 'periodization' of human history, on the development of human society through the slave-owning, feudal and capitalist phases to its culmination in socialism. According to this school of thought, the Great October Socialist Revolution of 1917 is the greatest event in history, dividing it more basically in two than the birth of Christ. For the Russian people is claimed the honour of having made the first successful socialist revolution in history. All Russian history was a preparation for this great event, everything in the past which points towards it should be stressed and everything which led in a different direction should be discounted. Variations on this theme can be found in a good deal of recent Western historical literature on Russia which, starting from a point of view hostile to the Bolshevik Revolution, nevertheless regards it as the overwhelmingly important event, and examines earlier events mainly in order to find explanations of its origin.

I should like to express my respect for much of the work which has been done from these points of view, but I do not share this apocalyptic outlook, in either its hagiographical or demonological version. The Bolshevik Revolution was unquestionably one of the greatest events in all human history. But my narrative stops before it took place, and I have not felt that the purpose of my book should be to explain it. I have tried to give most space, at each stage of my story, to the problems which were at that stage the most important. For this reason I have not given much space to the divisions within the social democratic movement. To explain the actions, theories, and personalities of the many factions involved would require a book in itself; there are many such books already; and whatever their effects after 1917, these factions did not play a very important part in Russian political life before the Revolution. I hope that the author who writes the second volume on Russia in this series will feel free to go back over the period of my volume, in order to explain the background to 1917 by detailed treatment of these earlier Marxist factions. I hope also that he will do justice to the final collapse of the Imperial régime in February 1917, of which I have deliberately given only a bald and superficial summary.[1]

The published primary sources which I have used are more satisfactory on the first half of the period than on the second, but there is certainly plenty of material available in Western libraries. There is no doubt much more in Russian archives. When scholars from this county are admitted to work in Russian archives in the same conditions in which foreign scholars are admitted to archives in Britain, it will be possible to write better books than I, or indeed my generation, can hope to write. In the last decades of the nineteenth century the output of memoirs and of contemporary comment on social problems notably increased. The years after 1905 were an especially fruitful period. Valuable collections of documents, and admirable monographic studies, were published during the first years of the Soviet regime. This was followed by an intellectual ice age of more than twenty years. In the last decade, however, Soviet scholars have done a tremendous work of scholarship in the history of the revolutionary movement and in some branches of social and economic history, for which one must be profoundly grateful. The history of the bureaucracy was for long comparatively neglected, but the admirable works of N. M. Druzhinin and P. A. Zayonchkovsky have done much to fill this gap in recent years. The history of the Church and of religious ideas remains virtually untouched. This is a field of immense importance, of which with deep regret I confess my ignorance, while expressing the hope that pioneers will soon appear.

My work has been made possible by the kindness of many, and I should like briefly to express, however inadequately, my gratitude at least to those who have helped me most.

The Council of the School of Slavonic and East European Studies generously granted me a year's study leave to write the

[1] While this volume was in the press, there appeared the fascinating work of Dr. G. Katkov, *Russia 1917: the February Revolution*. His immense erudition and valuable insights will be indispensable to later authors, whether or not they share his judgements.

bulk of the book, whose preparation had occupied me fitfully for more than ten years. I was awarded a Fellowship in 1963–4 at the Center for Advanced Study in the Behavioral Sciences in Stanford, California, and was a Visiting Fellow for the summer (that is, winter) months of 1964 in the Department of International Relations of the Australian National University at Canberra. My debt of gratitude to Dr. Ralph Tyler and Mr. Preston Cutler at the Center, and to Professor Bruce Miller at the A.N.U. is enormous: in both places the working conditions were ideal, and the kindness and intellectual stimulation of my colleagues unforgettable. I must also thank Dr. Campbell and Mr. Sworakowski of the Hoover Library in Stanford, a rich source of Russian historical materials, for their kind and sustained interest, and the library staff for their unfailing and resourceful co-operation. Not least I must thank Mrs. Dorothy Brothers at the Center and Miss Elizabeth Bennett at the School for their secretarial labours, often in trying conditions. And at all stages my wife has encouraged my efforts and shared my troubles, for which I am eternally grateful.

My debts go beyond this, to those who helped me acquire whatever basic understanding I may have. Sir Bernard Pares, the pioneer of Russian historical studies in England, made me aware of Russia as a child, and kept the interest alive in later years. I owe still more to his son, the late Professor Richard Pares, not so much in the Russian field as in the stimulation given by a brilliant mind and an outstanding tutor. B. H. Sumner's immense knowledge and inexhaustible courtesy I shared with countless others, and shall never forget. Nor shall I forget the inspiration I received at an earlier age from C. E. Robinson and Harold Walker: by treating me as an intelligent adult when I was not, they made it possible for me to try to become one, and assisted the process with all the skill and kindness at their command. My greatest debt is to my father, and it cannot be adequately expressed.

CONTENTS

PART THREE
THE GENDARME OF EUROPE

PART FOUR
THE TSAR LIBERATOR

PART FIVE
THE AGE OF COUNTER-REFORM

PART SIX
FROM REVOLUTION TO REVOLUTION

LIST OF MAPS

NOTE ON DATES, SPELLING, AND MEASURES

DATES are difficult in Russian history, because until 1918 Russia used a different calendar from the rest of Europe. The dates of the Russian (or Julian) calendar were in the nineteenth century twelve, and in the twentieth century thirteen days behind those of the European (or Gregorian). To give both versions of every date would be pedantic, and wearisome to the reader, especially when there is a difference in months and even years. (For instance, '27th December 1837 / 8 January 1838'). To convert all dates into one or the other calendar would probably create as many difficulties as it would solve. The solution I have adopted is to use the Russian calendar in all chapters concerned with internal events in the Russian Empire, and the European calendar in all chapters concerned with foreign relations, including all foreign wars and including the relations between Russia and the Kingdom of Poland. This solution will, I believe, be the most convenient for the reader. The large literature of diplomatic and international history, in various languages, uses European dates, whereas the literature of Russian internal history, the bulk of which is in Russian, uses Russian dates. The reader will find that my system makes comparison and reference to other sources less confusing for him than a uniform system would be. If I have not been completely successful in eliminating inconsistencies and errors, I ask the reader's indulgence.

Spelling also presents difficulties. Proper names from languages which use the Latin alphabet modified by accents or other special signs (Czech, Polish, Croatian, Roumanian, Turkish), have been rendered in the appropriate spelling, unless they are so well known in another spelling as virtually to have become English words. For attempts (not all entirely successful) to explain the pronunciation of these Latin variants, the reader is referred to existing dictionaries and grammars of the languages. In rendering Russian names, and titles or quotations in the Russian language, I have used the accepted transliteration, with certain modifications which seem to me to reproduce the sound more exactly. For these minor foibles, which do not occur very often, and which should facilitate rather than impede the reader's understanding, indulgence is requested. A certain number of Russian names which have become familiar in English are spelt as English words (for instance, Moscow and not Moskva). Some Russian words (for instance, zemstvo) have been for the same reason treated as English words, with English plurals, while others (for instance, *uezd*) have not. The choice has inevitably been arbitrary in marginal cases.

The following are the European metric equivalents of the main Russian measures:

pood (*pud*)	16·3 kilograms
arshin = 28 inches	·71 metres
sazhen'	2·13 metres
verst (*versta*)	1·06 kilometres
desyatina	1·09 hectares

PART I

EIGHTEENTH-CENTURY RUSSIA

I

POLITICAL AND SOCIAL FORCES

The Growth of the Russian State

If Europe is but the westernmost peninsula of Asia, the territory which has come to be known as 'European Russia' is the bridge between the peninsula and the main continental land mass. It stretches between the Arctic ice and the Black Sea, and falls into two main regions, forest and steppe.

From Central Asia, the starting place of so many mass migrations and invasions of the last three millennia, two routes, separated by the Black Sea, lead to the European peninsula. The one goes from Persia through Asia Minor, the other from the Caucasus or the Kazakh steppes across southern Russia. It is with these migrations that the known history of Russia begins, in the steppes to the north of the Black Sea.

The evidence of archaeology, and occasional references in Greek literature, are variously interpreted, and no general agreement among historians, or final proof of one particular hypothesis, is likely. It is, however, certain that there lived in this region, from about 700 to 200 B.C., a people known as Scythians, who were in contact with Greek settlements in the Crimea, themselves based on sea-borne trade. The Scythians had craftsmen whose works in gold are among the greatest achievements of human art. Around the end of the second century A.D. the Goths, Germanic in language, occupied southern Russia, but were driven out by the Huns at the end of the fourth. For the next four hundred years or so various peoples from Central Asia passed through the Russian steppes, and fought each other or the indigenous inhabitants. The most solid political structure established in this period was the state of the Volga Bulgars, based on the middle Volga and its tributary the Kama, which existed until the mid twelfth century.[1]

Meanwhile, around the borderline between forest and steppe, tribes belonging to the linguistic group known as Eastern Slavs had established themselves. They extended their settlement north and east into the forest zone, where they came into contact with various tribes belonging to the linguistic group known as Finno-Ugrian. Yet another factor in the situation were the Norsemen, great traders and travellers, who from Scandinavia explored the southern shores of the Baltic and sailed up the rivers.

After the division between forest and steppe, the second most important geographical feature of European Russia is its river system. In central Russia, within a comparatively small area, are the sources of three great rivers, the Dvina which flows west into the Baltic, the Dnieper which flows south into the Black Sea, and the greatest of the three, the Volga, which flows south-east into the Caspian. The Norsemen soon crossed the watershed and travelled down the Dnieper. Already in the eighth century there was trade between Damascus and Gotland. The Slav state which was growing up around the Dnieper, with Kiev as its centre, profited from the trade with the Arab and Byzantine empires. The relations between Slavs and Norsemen are the subject of continuing controversy. The traditional version of the foundation of the Kiev Russian state—that it was created in 862 by the Norsemen Rurik and his Varangians[2] at the invitation of the Slavs—has been bitterly contested by nationally minded Russian historians, both before and since the creation of the Soviet Union. That Norsemen played some part in the early state of Kiev Rus, and that some upper-class families were of Norse extraction, can, however, hardly be doubted.

[1] A branch of the Bulgars, a people of Turkic language of which little is known, moved westwards and established itself between the Black Sea and the lower Danube. These Bulgars became absorbed by the indigenous Slav population, whose language they adopted, but they gave their name to the country which became known in the ninth century as Bulgaria.

[2] This was the name given by the Byzantine Greeks to Scandinavians who served in the Byzantine army, or as bodyguards to Byzantine emperors. In Russia the use of the word was extended to cover Scandinavians generally.

Kiev Rus became in the tenth century a considerable state, based on the Dnieper valley and controlling part of the Black Sea coast, but extending also eastwards across the steppe and far to the north and north-east into the forest zone. It maintained regular relations with the Byzantine empire, from which it received Christianity, the symbolic date for whose establishment in Russia is 988, the year in which Vladimir, grand duke of Kiev, was converted. The Kiev state was weakened by the constant invasions of Asian peoples across the steppe from the east. It was also weakened by the quarrels between members of the grandducal family, made still more dangerous by the complicated system of succession to princely office. As a result of these internal struggles the centre of power moved from Kiev to the north-east—to Vladimir and Suzdal. In this area the Slavs became mixed with the Finnish tribes, who adopted the Slav language and the Christian religion.

In the thirteenth century occurred by far the greatest of the invasions from Asia, that of the Mongols led by the successors of the formidable Djengiz Khan. The Mongols sacked Kiev in 1241 and subdued the whole of Russia. The empire of Djengiz Khan was divided, and Russia came under the Golden Horde, whose capital was at Saray on the Volga, not far from the present-day city of Volgograd.[1] The ethnic Mongol element in the state of the Golden Horde was never numerous. The people of this state were mostly Tatars, speaking a language of the Turkic group. In the fourteenth century the rulers (khans) of the Golden Horde became Moslems. The khans allowed the Russian princes of central Russia to rule as their vassals, subject to regular payment of tribute and to confirmation of each ruler's succession. During the two and a half centuries of Tatar yoke, the principality of Moscow acquired primacy among the territories of central Russia.

Meanwhile the south-western regions, the Dnieper valley and Kiev itself, passed under the rule of the grand duchy of Lithuania, which was united with the Kingdom of Poland, first by a loose personal union in 1386 and then by complete incorporation in 1569. In the north-west the city-state of Novgorod, ruled by a burgher-aristocracy, and linked by trade with the

[1] In the eighteenth and nineteenth centuries known as Tsaritsyn, in the middle decades of the twentieth century as Stalingrad.

German cities of the Baltic, was another important Russian state from the twelfth to the fifteenth centuries. Novgorod not only escaped the Mongol conquest but extended its rule over vast areas of northern forest. Further east was the smaller patrician city state of Vyatka, similar to Novgorod and founded by exiles from that city. But at the end of the fifteenth century Ivan III of Moscow not only formally rejected the suzerainty of the Tatars but also brought Novgorod directly under his rule. From now on there were only two states with Russian subjects: the principality of Muscovy and the kingdom of Poland-Lithuania.

The growth of the grand duchy of Moscow into the Russian empire is not unlike the process by which land-locked nuclei of territory in western Europe grew into powerful states—for instance the Île-de-France of the Capets or medieval Castile. The subjugation of Ryazan, Tver, and Novgorod is comparable to that of Brittany, Aquitaine, or Burgundy. In one important respect the similarity to the case of Castile is particularly close. Both Kievan Russia and Visigothic Spain were Christian kingdoms destroyed by the infidel. In Spain the first conquerors were Arabs owing allegiance to distant Damascus, followed by various waves of Moors converted to Islam. In Russia the first conquerors were Mongols, owing allegiance to still more distant Karakoram, succeeded by a Turco-Tatar power which accepted Islam. In both cases the reconquest by the Christians was more than a dynastic military enterprise: it had something of the character of a Crusade, its aim not only the recovery of territory but also the restoration of the faith. In both cases the reconquest took centuries, and Moslem rump states survived long after the main Moslem power was broken (the Moors in Granada till 1492, the Tatars in Crimea until 1783).

The difference is that Russia had no Pyrenees. Certainly the Spanish rulers had to take account of France, but the Muscovite princes faced, in Lithuania and then in Poland, a state equally powerful, more consistently hostile to themselves, and separated from them by no major natural barrier. The grand duchy of Lithuania was as much the heir to Kiev Rus, as much a Russian state, as the grand duchy of Muscovy. Of the two Russian states, in fact, it might have been expected that the westernmost would have the greater power of attraction, as the nucleus from which 'the Russian Land' would be liberated. It was free from the humiliating subjection to the Tatars which Muscovy accepted until late in the fifteenth century. Its association with Poland might have been expected to be a source of strength.

That Lithuania did not become the leading Russian state was due in part to the cunning and patient determination of several princes of Muscovy, supported by the metropolitans of Moscow. But it was equally due to the mistakes and arrogance of the kings of Poland and to the ambitions of the Church of Rome. The union between Lithuania and Poland was transformed into a subjection of Lithuania to Poland. The Russo-Lithuanian ruling class became polonized, in speech and manners, and institutions. The Union of Lublin in 1569 formalized the process. At the end of the sixteenth century the Uniate Church was created, as an instrument of Romanization and polonization in the borderlands of White Russia and the Ukraine.[1] Only Muscovy remained as a champion of Russian Orthodoxy, and it was able to exploit Russian sentiment to its advantage. Having at last broken the power of the Tatars, it was able to stand up to Poland as a serious military rival.

In the fifteenth century the Golden Horde broke up into a number of principalities, whose centres were Kazan on the middle Volga, Astrakhan at the mouth of the Volga, and the Crimean Peninsula. The first two were conquered in the mid sixteenth century by Tsar Ivan IV (Kazan in 1552, Astrakhan in 1555). By their acquisition Muscovy obtained a large number of Turkish-speaking Moslem subjects, and Russian supremacy was finally asserted over the Volga river basin. In the south, however, the Tatar khanate of Crimea remained a serious menace to Moscow's security. The Crimean Tatars continued for many years to make raids far into Muscovite territory. In 1478 Crimea became a vassal of the empire of the Ottoman Turks, which since the conquest in 1453 of Constantinople had become the greatest power in the eastern Mediterranean.

In the second half of the sixteenth century Russian expansion spread into Siberia. This was the work not of the Tsar's regular

[1] The Uniate Church was based on the principles of the Union of Florence of 1439 by which the Catholic and Orthodox Churches were to have been reunited. The Union was, however, repudiated by the Russian Orthodox Church (see below, p. 31). The Uniate Church, set up by the Union of Brest of 1596, recognized the authority of the pope, but it differed from the Church of Rome in various respects. Its lower priesthood were married, and its services were conducted in Slav.

forces but of peasants, hunters, adventurers, and persons who had some reason for escaping the direct control of the central government. The Urals, low wooded hills, formed no major physical barrier, and the inhabitants of Siberia were few and primitive. The terrain of Siberia was not unlike that of North America east of the Rockies, even if its climate was more severe, and the disparity in civilization and military ability between the Russians and the Siberian peoples is comparable with that between the English or French and the North American Indians. The Russian conquest was completed during the seventeenth century, and the Russian government concluded in 1689 an agreement with the Chinese government (the Treaty of Nerchinsk), which fixed the frontier between the two empires on the middle course of the river Amur.

In the west, the main direction of Muscovite expansion for more than a century was the Baltic coast. Ivan IV fought bitter wars against Poland for the possession of Livonia, a province inhabited by Latvian peasants but with a German landowning class.[1] The southern coast of the Baltic was also of interest to Sweden, which, in the century which followed its separation from Denmark in 1523, became a major Power and a rival first to Poland and then to Muscovy. In 1561 Sweden annexed the northern part of the lands of the Order of the Sword, the province of Estland. During the internal disorders which ravaged Muscovy after the death of Tsar Boris Godunov—the 'Time of Troubles' from 1605 to 1613—both Polish and Swedish troops occupied Russian territory. The recovery of Muscovy from this disaster was facilitated by the fact that the power of her most dangerous neighbours Poland and Turkey was declining, and that Sweden was occupied in conflicts with Poland. During the seventeenth century in the northern part of the borderland between Muscovy and Poland—the region known as 'White Russia'—the Russo-Polish frontier became fixed as a result of successive wars. By the peace of 1667 the two most important

[1] German traders first appeared in Livonia in the twelfth century. They were followed by Christian missionaries. Germans built cities and acquired land. In 1202 the Order of the Sword was established in the newly founded city of Riga. Its members were both monks and soldiers. During the thirteenth century it conquered most of the territories known in modern times as Latvia and Estonia. In the following centuries political, economic, and ecclesiastical power was in German hands.

cities of the western frontier, Smolensk and Kiev, passed from Polish into Russian hands. Further south, however, the situation remained very confused.

In the seventeenth century the territory now known as the Ukraine, stretching from Galicia to the Don and from the Pripet Marshes to the Black Sea, was a sparsely populated no-man's-land between Russia, Poland, and the Tatar state in the Crimea. The word 'Ukraine' itself means 'border region'. The area west of the Dnieper ('right-bank Ukraine') was part of Poland, but the effectiveness of Polish authority was highly doubtful. Where some sort of order existed, the landowners were Poles, while the peasants were mostly Orthodox and spoke what were considered to be 'Little Russian' dialects. Apart from the peasant serfs, there were Cossacks, a border population of soldiers and brigands, supposedly defending Poland from the raids of the Tatar bands which emerged from their Crimean fastness to plunder, kidnap, and massacre. Among the Cossacks were many fugitive serfs, fleeing from their Polish landlords. In the area around the rapids of the Dnieper a considerable military power was established by the Zaporozhian Sich, a Cossack community with a primitive social and political organization of their own, who recognized no other law, and conducted warfare and diplomatic manœuvres between Poland, Muscovy, and Crimea. Beyond the Dnieper (in 'left-bank Ukraine') conditions were equally unstable, and there was a similar steady flow of fugitive serfs, southwards from Muscovy, especially towards the 'Slobodskaya Ukraina', the area around the modern city of Kharkov. Here too, largely autonomous Cossack bands waged a war of all against all.

At the end of the 1640's there was a major rebellion in the Ukraine against Poland. Bands of Cossacks sacked Polish castles and murdered Polish men, women, and children. Polish forces were equally brutal in return. Under the able military and political leadership of Bogdan Khmelnitsky, the Cossacks held their own against Polish armies. In 1654 Khmelnitsky made an agreement, at Pereyaslavl, with the representatives of Tsar Alexei of Muscovy. This has been variously interpreted, by Russian and Ukrainian nationalist historians, as an alliance between two states, a personal union between two states and nations, or the simple submission of the Orthodox Little Russians to the Orthodox Russian Tsar. In practice, for fifty years after the Pereyaslavl agreement, left-bank Ukraine was only loosely connected with Muscovy. The Cossacks elected their own ruler, the Hetman, who was little less than an independent sovereign.

At this time the people of the border region (*Ukraina*) were known in Russia as Little Russians, and neither then nor later would Russian officials or historians admit that they were a separate nation. On the other hand, modern Ukrainian nationalist historians have insisted, not only that there is in the twentieth century a separate Ukrainian nation, but that it is the true successor to the first Russian state, to Kiev Rus. The Muscovites, they have claimed, are a racial mixture of Finns, Slavs, and Tatars, who usurped the Russian name.

This question cannot be definitely decided either way. The people of the Ukraine in the seventeenth century mostly belonged to the same Church as the Russians, though the Uniate Church claimed the loyalty of a considerable minority. They also called themselves by the same names—*Rus* and *russkii*. Their social institutions were, however, different. They had no village commune like the Russian *obshchina*.[1] Their legal and cultural traditions were Western, with Polish influence predominant. Their language, though related to Russian, was different. It would be more exact to say that they spoke various dialects, all different from the Russian of Moscow. It was not until the nineteenth century that there began to emerge a single literary Ukrainian language.[2] Their outlook too was different from that of the Russian people. They were frontier pioneers, robbers, individualists, not docile serfs with collectivist traditions. In short, all the conditions for a separate nation were there: only the consciousness of being a nation was not yet developed, and has only been retrospectively attributed to them by the Ukrainian nationalists of a later age. But a sense of being different from the Russians of Muscovy (*moskaly* in Ukrainian), and a reluctance to accept orders or institutions from Moscow, they certainly had already in the early eighteenth century.

Peter the Great (1689–1725) sought to extend his territory to the west and the south, at the expense of Sweden, Poland, and Turkey. It was he who assumed the formal title of emperor

[1] See below, pp. 232–3. [2] See below, pp. 271–2.

(*imperator*), and from his time onwards, Muscovy became known as the Russian empire. His greatest successes in foreign policy were achieved in the Baltic region, at the expense of Sweden. In 1700, in alliance with Poland, he invaded Estland, but suffered a crushing defeat from the Swedish army of Charles XII at Narva. In the next years Charles was occupied in Poland, and Peter was able to rebuild his army, occupy Livonia and Ingria, and lay the foundations of his new capital in the swamps of the river Neva, at the head of the Gulf of Finland. In 1708, however, Charles XII invaded the Ukraine, with the support of the Cossack Hetman of left-bank Ukraine, Isaac Mazepa. At the Battle of Poltava, in June 1709, the Swedish army was decisively defeated by the Russians, and both Charles XII and Mazepa fled to Turkey. In 1711 Peter followed up his victory by invading Turkish Moldavia. But this time his good fortune did not hold; he found himself surrounded on the river Prut by superior Turkish forces, and was compelled to make peace, restoring to the Turks the Black Sea coastal fortress of Ochakov which he had conquered in 1696.

The Northern War with Sweden continued until 1721. Peter's armies during 1713–14 occupied all Finland, including the Åland Islands, which cover the entrances to the gulfs of Finland and Bothnia and extend to within seventy miles of Stockholm. He also constructed in the Baltic the first substantial Russian naval force. In 1721 the war was ended by the Treaty of Nystadt, which confirmed Russia in possession of Estland, Livonia, Ingria, and the city and district of Vyborg, but restored the rest of Finland to Sweden.

Russia now possessed a large stretch of Baltic coast. Peter had secured his 'window on Europe', and his new capital, St. Petersburg, grew in the next century into one of the great and beautiful cities of Europe. The central government's control over the Ukraine was also strengthened. After the treason of Mazepa, the Tsar would not again trust to the loyalty of a Hetman elected by the Cossacks. This office came to an end in 1722, and Peter replaced it with a 'Little Russian College' of appointed officials. In Poland it was Peter's ally, King Augustus, who obtained the throne, while the Swedish candidate, Stanisław Leszczyński, went into exile. Poland still retained the right-bank Ukraine, and in the south the Crimean Tatar vassals of the Ottoman Sultan were still powerful. Thus not all 'the Russian Land' was yet united under the Tsar. But that the Russian empire was now one of the Great Powers of Europe there could be no doubt.

Autocracy and Nobility

If there is one single factor which dominates the course of Russian history, at any rate since the Tatar conquest, it is the principle of autocracy. In Kievan Russia there existed representative assemblies which may be regarded as embryonic parliaments. But the Tatar conquest put an end to them. From the time that Russia began to recover from the Tatar yoke, one can say with little exaggeration that every important change was due to monarchical power. In this respect Russian history differs from that of all west European countries, except perhaps Spain. The Western nations were formed in a long struggle between the monarchical power and the social *élite*. This trend has continued right up to the present time, though the *élites* have changed, beginning with feudal barons and continuing through landed gentry, city merchants, and factory owners to trade union leaders. Whatever one may feel of the merits of the contending parties, one cannot deny the existence of the struggle. In different Western countries the results differed. In England the victory was usually on the side of the *élites*, though the monarchs were at times formidable opponents, and each rising *élite* had to fight not only the central power but the established *élites* that had prevailed in earlier struggles. In France the monarch prevailed until the explosion of 1789. In the revolution a new *élite* violently seized power, but was soon replaced by a new monarch, after which the struggles of competing *élites* continued to make strong government difficult. Yet even here it would be wrong to underestimate the part played by the machinery of government inherited from the monarchical past. In Holland the balance of the struggle was, as in England, on the side of the *élites*: in Prussia, as in France, on the side of the monarch. The American republic might be thought to have rid itself of both monarchy and *élite*. But the truth is more complicated. American democracy started on the foundation of English and Scottish history, whose traditions were shaped by this struggle. And even in the history of the United States the struggle has continued.

In Russia after the Tatar conquest it hardly existed. There was, it is true, a period of rivalry between the central Russian principalities, the tributaries of the Golden Horde, which ended in the supremacy of Moscow. Individual magnates, and groups of magnates, quarrelled with each other. Individual grand dukes or Tsars were weak puppets in the hands of powerful counsellors or favourites. Periods of minority, with infants on the throne, were periods of weakness. In the 'Time of Troubles' (*smutnoe vremya*), which followed the death of Tsar Boris Godunov in 1603 and lasted till the establishment on the throne of Tsar Michael Romanov in 1613, rival pretenders, foreign invaders, and selfish boyars reduced Russia to anarchy. But these disorders were concerned with who should be autocrat, and government was weak when the autocrat was weak. There was never any suggestion that government by autocrat should give place to government in which power would be divided between classes and institutions. The only important exception to this statement were the republics of Novgorod and Vyatka, which had their own forms of oligarchical representative government until they were suppressed by Grand Duke Ivan III towards the end of the fifteenth century.

The supremacy of autocracy has been taken for granted by many Russian historians, with the result that it has been underrated by non-Russians. To almost all Russians the admitted horrors of tyranny by the autocrat have appeared less deadly than the imagined horrors of tyranny by an oligarchy. The attainment of privileges by small social *élites* at the expense of the central power has been, in the West, a progressive factor. The history of the origins of European (and ultimately also of American) democracy has been the history of the extension of privileges to ever wider and larger *élites*, until political freedom has become the possession of the whole people. But Russians, including historians and writers of indisputably democratic convictions, have regarded privileges as inherently evil. It is better that all should be equal in their subjection to the autocrat. In the nineteenth century, when Russian political thought became articulate, this attitude was explicable partly in terms of justifiable indignation at the power exercised by landowners over serfs. But it caused a certain blindness with regard to the inherent threats from autocracy.

Many writers, not only Marxist, have pointed out the connexion between modern political democracy and capitalism. It has become a familiar platitude that democracy flourishes where there is a strong business element, and—which is not the same thing—a *bourgeoisie*. It has often been pointed out that there was a connexion between the Reformation and the rise of capitalism. It is in the Protestant countries (with the significant exception of Lutheran north Germany) that the struggle between *élite* and monarch has most strongly inclined in favour of the *élite*. Russia had no Reformation, and can hardly be said to have had a *bourgeoisie*.

But one should go further back than this. Democracy has flourished in countries in which capitalism has a long history. But these are also the countries in which, at an earlier stage, feudalism was strong. A feudal past, no less than a *bourgeois* past, seems to be necessary for a strong habit of resistance to autocracy. In the history of the United States, of course, this feudal stage occurred back in Europe, chiefly in England, before the voyages of discovery. But feudalism, no less than the *bourgeois* stage, is almost absent from Russian history. There was a Russian aristocracy, there were great landowners, and there was serfdom. But feudalism in Europe was more than the existence of a nobility, a landowning class, and serfs. In feudal Europe the landowning nobility had a corporate consciousness and organization, and the rights and obligations of the lords and sovereigns in relation to each other were defined by law. The feudal nobility in western Europe was an autonomous factor in the making of history. This it never was in Russia. No social group held political power, or made policy. This role was reserved to the autocracy, which used nobles as its instruments, rewarding them materially but not compromising in matters of power.

One reason for the prevalence of autocracy in Russian history is military. Russia had no natural boundaries except the Arctic ice and the mountain ranges of Caucasus and Central Asia. It was subject for centuries to invasion from both west and east. Imagine the United States without either the Atlantic or the Pacific, and with several first-rate military powers instead of the

Indians, and there would be some sort of a parallel. The principality of Moscow grew in wars against the Tatars and Poland-Lithuania. For this struggle for existence, military force and military subordination were required. Muscovy was essentially a barracks-state. The danger of invasion was an ever-present justification for monarchical power. The armies of the autocrat made the Russian state, and under autocracy it expanded to the Black Sea and across northern Asia. A partial exception is the colonization of Siberia, in which enterprising individual adventurers played a leading part. In the southern steppes too, fugitive serfs made their mark. But it was not long before the power of the autocrat caught up with all these rugged individualists. The contrast with America provides an admirable example of the danger of applying formulas to history. Both America and Russia had an 'open frontier', but its significance was diametrically opposite in the two cases. In America the open frontier meant opportunity, and so freedom: in Russia it meant insecurity, and so subjection.

A second factor strengthening autocracy was the Church. It may be argued that in the period of the Tatar yoke, it was the Church's interpretation of the Byzantine conception of the emperor (*autokrator*) which shaped the ideas of Russia's rulers. This influence was more important than any direct contacts with Constantinople in the age when Byzantium was great and Kievan Rus free. Certainly the metropolitans of Moscow gave invaluable support to the grand dukes, and were largely responsible for Moscow's triumph over its rivals of Vladimir, Tver, and Novgorod. The identification of Church and State continued in the Muscovite state of the sixteenth and seventeenth centuries. Church and State supported each other from mutual interest. But more than this, the teaching of the Orthodox Church was inherently favourable to autocracy. Its emphasis was on ritual and on the other world, on the individual's improvement of his own soul. It was not felt to be the duty of the Church to interfere in the things of this world. This again is in marked contrast to the Western Churches, both Catholic and Protestant. Both of these have usually taught that if a ruler acts contrary to Christian faith or morality it is the duty of Christians to oppose him. 'Render unto Caesar . . .' applies to secular government but not to matters of morality. But there is a strong trend in

Russian religious thought that the affairs of this world are no concern of the Christian, that a ruler, even if he be Antichrist himself, may dispose of the believer's body in this world, but if the believer leads a Christian life and performs the ritual he will inherit eternal life. The passivity of the Church in political matters benefited the autocracy indirectly, no less than its active support of many rulers helped it directly. Indeed, in the purely political field, religion was much more frequently 'the opium of the people' in Russia than ever in the western countries of which Marx was thinking when he invented the phrase.

Peter the Great drastically reorganized the military and civil organization of the Russian state. He replaced the earlier militia by a standing army. Its most important units were the three Guards regiments—Semyonovsky, Preobrazhensky, and the Bodyguard Regiments (household cavalry). These totalled less than 3,000 men at the end of his reign. The bulk of the regular army was provided by a system of recruitment, by which a quota had to be provided by each community, according to the number of households. The government from time to time assigned quotas to the village communities, and the communities designated individuals from their midst. Recruits were obliged to serve for their whole lifetime if required. Landowners were obliged to ensure that the quota was filled from their serfs. Noblemen were exempt from recruitment in the ranks, but were expected to serve as officers. Peter's army was larger and more efficient than its predecessors, though still a less efficient force than European armies of similar size. Perhaps because Russian society was altogether so militarized, officers as such had relatively less social prestige or political influence than in the West. No general attempted to set himself up as a political figure. The Guards, it is true, played an important part in the palace revolutions of the earlier part of the eighteenth century, but with one exception they made no political claims. They stood neither for direct military rule nor for a constitutional régime, but accepted the supremacy of the sovereign.

Peter laid down that the nobility must serve the state, in the army or in the civil government. In 1722 this principle was systematized by the Table of Ranks, which provided that attainment of certain ranks in the hierarchy should confer noble status. In the army this was achieved by reaching commissioned rank (*oberofitserskii chin*). All officers became hereditary noblemen, their children being like themselves exempt from taxation, recruit duty, and corporal punishment. In the civil service fourteen ranks were laid down, based on German titles. The highest eight conferred hereditary nobility, the next six personal nobility—for the official but not for his children.[1] Thus it became possible for able persons of humble origin to rise into the nobility.

Noble status did not, however, confer political independence. The whole nobility was an instrument of the government. The highest officers of state wielded great power under the emperor, but their power came from their office, and from the emperor's confidence, not from their noble birth. There were some families richer and more distinguished than others—above all the princely families that traced their descent to Rurik, the alleged founder of the dynasty in 862, or Gedymin, the Lithuanian king who was the ancestor of several aristocratic families. Some of the favourites of the Tsars received vast landed estates, especially

[1] The main ranks, still in use in the 19th century, included in the fourteen classes of the Table, were the following:

1st class	chancellor (civil); field-marshal (military); general-admiral (naval)
2nd	Active privy councillor; general of cavalry, or infantry, or artillery; admiral
3rd	privy councillor; lieutenant-general; vice-admiral
4th	active civil councillor, or senior procurator, or master of heralds (civil); major-general; rear-admiral
5th	civil councillor
6th	collegial councillor or military councillor; colonel; captain of 1st rank (naval)
7th	aulic councillor; lieutenant-colonel; captain of 2nd rank (naval)
8th	collegial assessor; captain or rotmistr
9th	titular councillor; staff captain or staff rotmistr
10th	collegial secretary; lieutenant; midshipman
11th	ship's secretary
12th	provincial secretary; sub-lieutenant or cornet
13th	senatorial registrar, synodal registrar or cabinet registrar; ensign
14th	collegial registrar

This list is taken, with the omission of various ranks, mostly with German names, which became obsolete, and with the omission of ranks in the Imperial Court, from the text of the 1722 decree, published in the official collection of laws, *Polnoe sobranie zakonov Rossiiskoy Imperii* (hereafter referred to as PSZ), first series, St. Petersburg, 1830, no. 3890 (in vol. 6, pp. 486–493). The provisions regarding hereditary nobility are in articles 11 and 15.

The place of publication of all works published abroad is stated unless unidentified. SPB is used hereafter for St. Petersburg, for all publications in that city up to 1914.

in the reign of Catherine II. But there were no traditional family properties going back for centuries. There was no long association between certain families and certain provinces, as with the territorial aristocracies of England, France, or Germany.

Peter's successors were weak, and inevitably powerful individuals or cliques competed for the spoils. But of a corporate spirit of the nobility, of a political programme of the landowning class, there is little sign.

Peter abolished by a decree of 5 February 1722 the regular order of succession, leaving it to the emperor himself to appoint his heir.[1] He himself died without doing so, and the Guards proclaimed his widow as Empress Catherine I. During her reign the chief figure was Prince Alexander Menshikov, Peter's favourite and Catherine's former lover. When she died in May 1727 her son became emperor as Peter II at the age of eleven. Menshikov proposed to betrothe him to his own daughter Maria, but he was arrested on 8 September and the Dolgoruky family gained control of the boy Tsar. Peter was betrothed on 13 November 1729 to Princess Catherine Dolgorukaya. But in January 1730 Peter died, and the throne passed to the Duchess of Kurland, Anna Ivanovna, daughter of Peter the Great's elder brother Ivan V. During her ten years' reign the Dolgoruky and Golitsyn families were removed from influence, and power was held by a number of high bureaucrats, mainly Baltic Germans, chief among them being the empress's lover Bühren and the Chancellor Osterman. When she died in October 1740 the throne passed to Ivan VI, the baby son of her niece Princess Anne of Mecklenburg (known as Anna Leopoldovna). In November 1740 a group of Guards officers overthrew Bühren, and made Anna Leopoldovna regent for the infant Tsar. His reign only lasted a year, and on 25 November 1741 the Guards installed Elizabeth, daughter of Peter the Great by his first wife, as empress. She reigned for twenty years. Her heir was the son of her sister Anna, who had married the Duke of Holstein-Gottorp. He ascended the throne as Peter III, but within half

[1] Peter's son by his first marriage, Alexei, had become involved in seditious opposition to him. In 1718 he was persuaded to return to Russia from exile in Vienna, arrested, and tortured to death. By his second marriage Peter had a son who was a child at Peter's death.

a year, on 28 June 1762, he was overthrown by a conspiracy in favour of his wife, who became Empress Catherine II.

Of all these violent changes of rulers, or violent accessions of mostly non-Russian sovereigns, the only one which was accompanied by political demands was that of Anna Ivanovna in 1730. On this occasion the members of the highest organ of government of the time, the Privy Council, led by Prince D. M. Golitsyn, drew up a series of Conditions which they required her to sign. She was to agree not to take any of the following actions without the consent of the Privy Council: to declare war or make peace, impose taxes, confer army or civil ranks above that of colonel, grant estates to nobles or deprive them of estates without trial, confer titles on Russians or foreigners, or make court appointments. It was also specified that 'the Guards and other regiments' were to be under the direct command of the Privy Council. Golitsyn was inspired by the example of Swedish institutions. He wished to introduce an oligarchical aristocratic form of government, but made no provision for specific representation of the interests of the nobility as a class. A delegation visited Anna in Kurland, and she agreed to the Conditions. But on her arrival in St. Petersburg she was advised by rival dignitaries to restore the autocracy. At the same time groups of nobles, who had come to the capital for the previously planned marriage of Peter II and Catherine Dolgorukaya, put forward confused demands, denouncing the rule of favourites, asking for representatives of the nobility to take part in government, and for the reduction of the period of state service. They showed no sympathy for Golitsyn's constitutional projects. Some days after Anna had arrived in the capital, troops of the Guards surrounded the Palace, and their officers clamoured for the restoration of autocracy. To this the empress graciously agreed, and solemnly tore up the Conditions. Thus the nobility themselves, in the person of the Guards officers, repudiated constitutional limitations and upheld autocracy.

Anna Ivanovna took some actions favourable to the nobility. A decree of Peter the Great of 23 March 1714 had instituted entails, intended to safeguard estates of the nobility. An estate-owner might leave his property to any one of his heirs, but must not divide it. This law met with no gratitude from the nobles. The Senate later declared that it had been contrary to the principle of divine justice, which requires that children should share equally in their father's estate. Landowners in practice sought to compensate their other children by giving them livestock and movable property and so ruined the estate which passed to the single heir. In fact, though the law had forbidden sale or mortgage of land, land sales had increased. The law was abolished by Anna in 1730, to the general delight. As Florinsky remarks, 'Entail, basically an aristocratic principle, had no root in the Russian tradition, was ill adapted to the needs of the bureaucratic state, and was discarded after a few years' trial'.[1] Anna's other main act was a decree of 31 December 1736, which limited the period of compulsory state service for nobles to twenty-five years, and provided that in each family with more than one male member, one male should be exempted from service in order to look after the estate.

Peter III went further than this. His manifesto of 18 February 1762 freed the nobility from service except in time of war, allowed those in the army or civil service to resign, and permitted them to travel abroad and even to enter the service of foreign Powers. Catherine II maintained this system on her accession. During these years many of the nobles left the capitals or other cities, and remained on their estates. Catherine hoped that they would interest themselves in economic improvements and in local government, but her hopes were disappointed. Most were content to carry on the part-despotic, part-patriarchal rule over their serfs and to live on their revenues. The most able and ambitious continued to make careers in the government service, and the brilliance of Catherine's court attracted them to the capital. Catherine formulated the rights and status of the nobles more definitely in her Charter (*zhalovannaya gramota*) of 21 April 1785.[2] Their exemption from taxation, recruit duty, and corporal punishment was confirmed, as was their freedom of choice whether to enter state service. The nobles were also allowed to elect assemblies in each province (*guberniya*) and county (*uezd*), and at each level they were to elect an official known as the marshal of the nobility (*predvoditel dvoryanstva*) who was to preside over the corporation of the

[1] M. T. Florinsky, *Russia: A History and an Interpretation* (New York, 1953), pp. 422–3.

[2] The text of the Charter is in PSZ 16187 (vol. 22, pp. 344–358).

nobility in his area. The assemblies were given the right to make representations to governors on the needs and interests of the nobility of the area, and to send deputies with representations or complaints to the Senate or the sovereign. The assembly was responsible for the *rodoslovnaya kniga*, the book in which the names of noble families were registered. They also administered a nobles' treasury, based on voluntary subscription and used for local purposes.

The institutions of central government were considerably changed by Peter the Great. In 1711 he set up the Senate, whose task was to be to administer the country while he was absent with the army. It was to be the supreme court of appeal, and to supervise all branches of the administration. In 1722 he created the office of procurator-general, attached to the Senate. This official became a sort of grand vizier. He had to confirm all the Senate's decrees, to enforce the laws and generally to see to it that the Tsar's will was being carried out. For this purpose he headed a large organization of public prosecutors (*prokurory*) and financial spies (*fiskaly*). The first holder of the office was Paul Yaguzhinsky. Peter also systematized the central government's administrative departments, reducing them to nine 'Colleges': Foreign Affairs, War, Navy, Mining and Manufacture, Revenue (*kammer-kollegiya*), Control (*revizion-kollegiya*), State Expenditure (*shtats-kontora*), Commerce, and Justice. Each college was to have a board of eleven persons and a chairman, and decisions were to be taken by majority vote. In practice this deliberative element in central government did not turn out to be very important.

Under Peter's successors the Senate played a secondary role. It remained the supreme judicial authority, but Russian justice was so obscure, cumbrous, and corrupt that it would be wrong to overestimate this role. Real power was held by small circles of high dignitaries, especially the Supreme Privy Council under Catherine I and Peter II, the Cabinet of Her Imperial Majesty under Anna Ivanovna, the empress's private chancery under Elizabeth, and a State Council of nine members under Catherine II from 1769 onwards. The colleges continued to exist until Catherine II's provincial reforms of 1775, which transferred to provincial governors many of the powers formerly exercised by central departments.

Peter the Great in December 1707 had divided the empire into eight 'governments' (*gubernii*) under a *gubernator*. These were Ingermanland, Moscow, Kiev, Smolensk, Archangel, Kazan, Azov, and Siberia. They were subdivided into 'provinces' (*provintsii*) under a *voevoda*, and these into counties (*uezdy*) under a *komissar*. There was no government unit lower than this: power at the lowest level remained entirely in the hands of serf-owning landowners. Peter also set up a city government, the *magistrat*, the members of which were elected by the two richer categories ('first and second guilds') of townsmen. In the following fifty years the number of *gubernii* increased to fifteen. Catherine II increased them to fifty, each of which was divided into *uezdy*: the intermediate level of *provintsiya* was abolished, and the *guberniya* became in effect a province. Some provinces were headed by a civil governor, others (the capitals, certain frontier regions, some other areas of special character) by a governor-general who had direct access to the sovereign. The statutes of 1775 introduced 'the collegial principle' at the provincial level. The governor was responsible to the central government, but his advisory board (*gubernskoe pravlenie*) was directly responsible to the Senate, and the 'treasury chamber' (*kazennaya palata*) to the financial department of the office of the procurator-general of the Senate. Attached to the governor's office were departments of social welfare (*prikazy obshchestvennogo prizreniya*), which had charge of such schools, orphanages, hospitals, pharmacies, workhouses, and prisons as existed in the province. The chief executive officer at the *uezd* level was the *ispravnik*, who was elected by the nobility, and presided over the local court which was an administrative rather than a judicial body, responsible for the maintenance of public order within the *uezd*.

Catherine also issued a Charter to the cities on the same date as her charter to the nobility, 21 April 1785.[1] These were to be ruled by a council (duma)[2] with an executive board

[1] Text in PSZ, first series, vol. 22. It is the document immediately following the Charter to the nobility, but it is wrongly numbered in the 1830 edition as 16187, it should be 16188.

[2] The word duma originally means 'thought'. It was used to denote a council of advisers. Historically the most important use is the Boyars' Duma which was a consultative council of magnates in pre-Petrine Russia. For later uses of the word to denote various proposed or established institutions, see below pp. 104–5, 158, 189, 190, 385, and part 6, chapters 17 and 18 *passim*.

of six, each member representing one of six classes into which the population was divided: owners of real estate; merchants; artisans; non-resident and foreign merchants; 'distinguished citizens',[1] and unskilled workers or small traders (*possadskie*). The head of police in the city was an appointed official. In practice city self-government was quite ineffective for another hundred years.

The People

The great majority of the people of Russia were peasants, and in the eighteenth century almost all the peasants were either serfs of private landowners or in bondage to the state.

In Kievan Russia, and under the Tatar yoke, most peasants had been freemen, though there were some who were simple slaves (*kholopy*). During the fifteenth century the peasants became increasingly dependent on the nobles as tenants, paying them in money or in kind for the use of their land. The peasants also paid taxes to the state. Increasing numbers of peasants borrowed money from landowners, and agreed to remain on the same land until they could repay their debts. As this was seldom possible, the effect of indebtedness was that a large part of the peasantry remained bound to the soil. The government had an interest in this state of affairs, since it needed the peasants' taxes for its revenue, and thus wished to ensure that its taxpayers should always be available in the same place. During the seventeenth century there was a constant threat of labour shortage in agriculture, damaging the interests both of the landowners and of the state treasury. Both had an interest in depriving the peasants of the right to change their abode or their employer. Though the process of the establishment of serfdom in Russia is obscure, and is still variously interpreted, it can be said that it was brought about by these three factors—peasant indebtedness, the fiscal needs of the government, and the landlords' need for labour. It had become widespread by the end of the sixteenth century, and was finally fixed by the Code of Laws of 1649, instituted by Tsar Alexei. None but noblemen might own estates worked by servile labour. The

[1] This title was applicable to persons of long service in city administration, members of the learned professions, artists, merchants with a capital of more than 50,000 roubles, bankers with a capital of 100,000 to 200,000 roubles, wholesale traders, and ship-owners. Article by S. Latyshev, *Brockhaus Encyclopaedia*, ix. 324.

nobility itself, however, was essentially a class of serving men, holding land under the form of tenure known as *pomestie*, which obliged them to give service to the state, while being supported by the labour of their serfs.

Peter the Great confirmed this system. He imposed on the nobility more precise and more far-reaching duties of service. He also increased the state revenues by introducing in 1718, in place of the tax on households, a poll-tax, to be paid by all classes except the nobility and a few other privileged groups. It was levied on every living male soul including old men and babies. The technical expression used for a male taxpayer was 'revision soul'—derived from the word in use for census of population (*reviziya*). The poll-tax was socially harmful, since it weighed especially heavily on large families. It proved, however, a more efficient device for raising revenue than any yet tried in Russia. In 1724 poll-tax was paid on behalf of 5,570,000 persons. The yield of all earlier direct taxes had been 1,800,000 roubles, whereas the poll-tax produced 4,600,000

The poll-tax also had an important effect in evening out the differences between groups of peasants who were not serfs. All these groups were increasingly reduced to dependence on the state, paying in money or labour dues for the land they tilled. During the eighteenth century there came into use, to describe them, the expression 'state peasants'.[1] They had on the whole better material conditions than the serfs of landowners, but they were no longer, as their fathers had been, free men.

The most numerous of these groups were the peasants of the north Russian provinces and of Siberia. There were also the peasants on former Church lands, secularized by Catherine II in 1764, who were known as 'economic peasants'. Then there were various types of colonists settled on military borderlands in the south and south-east, towards the Turkish frontier. The most important of these were the *odnodvorsty* of the Ukraine, who had formerly provided a regional militia, but ceased to do so when Peter instituted a regular army. A similar group, the *pantsyrnie boyare*, existed in formerly Polish territory, being the descendants of frontier guards of the Lithuanian princes. There

[1] The classic work which describes the origins and status of the various categories of state peasants is V. I. Semevsky, *Krest'yane v tsarstvovanii Imperatritsy Ekateriny II* (SPB, 1901–3), vol. ii.

were also various special categories of Polish and Tatar peasants. Along the Caucasian and Ural borders, facing Persia on the Central Asian steppes, and also in the Far East towards the Chinese frontier, were Cossack communities who combined farming with military service.

The tax censuses of the eighteenth century give the following figures for the relative numbers of male 'revision souls' who were serfs and state peasants:

	Serfs	State peasants
1743–6	3,400,000	3,000,000
1762–6	3,800,000	3,300,000
1781–3	5,100,000	4,500,000
1794–6	5,700,000	5,000,000

Thus throughout this period the serfs represented about 53 per cent. of the peasants and 45 per cent. of the total population of European Russia and Siberia. These figures do not include the Baltic provinces or the territories acquired from Poland. It is interesting to note, for comparison, that in Prussia at this time more than two-thirds of the whole population were serfs.

The proportion of serfs to state peasants varied as between different areas. It was highest in the central provinces, where estates worked by serfs had been established for longest, since it was here that the government had most needed the military support of the nobility in the period after the establishment of the Romanov dynasty, when foreign danger was great. For example, in the 1760's in Smolensk province 77 per cent. of the population were serfs, in Moscow 72 per cent., and in Nizhnii Novgorod 60 per cent. On the other hand, in the less densely populated regions to the south or east, the proportion was lower—in Voronezh 45 per cent., in Kazan 32 per cent. In Siberia there were virtually no serfs.[1]

In 1762, when Peter III abolished compulsory service by the nobility, the whole theory on which serfdom was based broke down, for now the nobles were exploiting the labour of the serfs without discharging a duty to the state for which this could be considered a compensation. Catherine II had three courses of policy open to her. She could emancipate the serfs personally

[1] Details are given in Semevsky, op cit., vol. i, ch. 2.

from the landowners without giving them any land, thus creating a rural proletariat. She could emancipate them from the landowners' personal power but bind them to the soil, thus creating a peasantry without personal liberty but with their livelihood assured from small land-holdings. Or she could bind them to their landowners but not to the land, thus placing their persons at the mercy of their lords, to move and employ as and where they willed. This third course, the most unjust of the three, was the one she adopted. At the beginning of her reign Catherine was fired by reforming zeal. She was aware of the iniquities of serfdom. She summoned in 1767 a Legislative Commission of more than 500 persons elected by all classes of the population except the serfs, to create a new system of laws and reforms. But though the deliberations of the commission informed her of the wishes of her subjects, and may be said to have had some effect on the introduction of the provincial government statute of 1775 and the Charter of 1785,[1] they led to no significant improvements in the status of the peasants.

Eighteenth-century serfdom in Russia was marked by great variety in the nature of the service performed by the serfs. There were two main categories of service—*obrok* (money payment) and *barshchina* (labour service). In the central non-black earth area about 55 per cent. of the serfs paid *obrok* and 45 per cent. performed *barshchina*. Within this area, however, there were exceptions—in Smolensk and Pskov *barshchina* prevailed. In the black-earth area the reverse was the tendency—a predominance of *barshchina*; but here too there were exceptions—in Penza 52 per cent. paid *obrok*, in Voronezh 64 per cent.[2]

In 1777 it is estimated that 84 per cent. of all serf-owning landowners owned less than 100 serfs, and 32 per cent. less than 10. Sixty years later the first figure was still valid. There are no data to make possible an estimate of what proportion of the total number of serfs belonged to which category of serf-owners in the eighteenth century. In 1834, however, 30 per cent. of all serfs belonged to 870 landowners, and 15 per cent. to a further 1450 landowners. These figures are probably not very different from the proportions of the last quarter of the eighteenth century. At the end of the eighteenth century the three richest serf-owners were Prince P. B. Sheremetyev, who had 60,000 souls,

[1] See above pp. 18, 20.

[2] Semevsky, op. cit., i. 20–30, 48.

Count K. G. Razumovsky, who had 45,000, and Count A. S. Stroganov, who had 23,000.[1]

Catherine II made a practice of presenting large areas of government land, inhabited by peasants, to individual noblemen as a reward for services or favours. These peasants became serfs. Catherine is estimated to have so transferred more than 800,000 state peasants, and her successor Emperor Paul a further 600,000.

The amount of *obrok* paid averaged 1–2 roubles a year in the 1760's, 4 in the 1780's and 5 at the end of Catherine's reign. This was a more rapid rise than can be explained by movements of prices. It is estimated that in the 1760's the equivalent of the *obrok* in grain was somewhat more than a quarter of rye, in the 1770's one and a half quarters, in the 1780's and 1790's rather less than one and a half. Additional payments in kind to the landowners by serfs paying *obrok* (supplies of food and miscellaneous services for brief periods) amounted to about half the value of the money payment. The total value of *obrok* paid by serfs in the period 1760–80 was from one and a half to two and a half times as much as that paid by state peasants.

An inquiry by the Free Economic Society of St. Petersburg in 1765 showed that the average labour service performed by peasants giving *barshchina* was three days a week. This could mean that half the members of the household worked for the landowner all the time, or that all the members worked half the time. In many cases, however, more than this was demanded. Demands were especially severe in the busiest seasons of the year, and at this time it often happened that the serfs' own plots of land had to be neglected, to their great economic loss. Count Panin proposed to Catherine II that she should decree a maximum of 4 days a week *barshchina*, but this was never enacted.

It seems likely that serfs who paid *obrok* were in a less arduous situation than those who gave *barshchina*. The historian Semevsky estimates that in the 1760's the value of *barshchina* was three and a half to four times higher than that of *obrok* (7–8 roubles instead of 2), and in the 1790's two to two and a half times higher (14–16 roubles instead of 7).[2]

The landowner had enormous powers over the persons of his

[1] Ibid., i. 32–33.

[2] Ibid., i. 55 ff.

serfs. He could sell them without land to another landowner. He could also sell individual members of a family separately from the others. In the 1780's it was normal to see groups of serfs being sold in a market-place. A decree of 1771 forbade this being done to discharge a landowner's debts, but in 1792 the decree was modified to apply only to cases where the sale was done by auction with a hammer. The landowner could also order or forbid a marriage between his serfs. He was the only judge on his domains except for the gravest criminal offences. For offences within his jurisdiction he could order flogging or imprisonment or, by a decree of 1765, penal labour in Siberia. Landowners had not the right to inflict death sentences, but in fact they could impose torture which ruined the serf's health, or brought about death within a short time. It was not considered that they had killed a serf unless he died during or immediately after the physical punishment ordered by them. They could also send their serfs to Siberia, not as a punishment, but as free colonists. For every serf so sent, they received from the government recognition for having provided a recruit to the army, thus reducing the total number of recruits that they had to give. This provision acted as an incentive to get rid of elderly and physically weak serfs who were not useful to them as part of their labour force. The serfs so selected, and the national army, correspondingly suffered while the landowner profited.

Under the 1649 Statute the serfs had the right to petition the government against their landowner, but only in matters affecting the sovereign's health or high treason. A decree of 1767 specifically forbade petitions on other grounds. Russian historians have argued that this was a false interpretation of the 1649 law, which in the preceding century had certainly at times been interpreted more liberally. The 1767 decree thus represented an appreciable worsening of the peasants' lot.

In 1772–4 a great peasant rising took place in the east, in the area between the Volga and the Urals, where there were fewer serfs than state peasants. Its leader, Emelyan Pugachov, was a Don Cossack. His main armed strength came from the Cossacks of the Ural river. The rebellion was, however, supported by much wider sections of the population, by religious schismatics, by fugitive serfs, and by the local Moslems, especially the Bashkirs, as well as by the serf labourers in the Ural mines.

Pugachov pretended to be the murdered Emperor Peter III, who was popular because of the belief that he was tolerant towards the non-Orthodox. The rebels for a time captured Kazan and Saratov, and in the spring of 1774 it was feared that they would advance on Moscow. They were never able to capture the fortified towns of Ufa or Orenburg. The government's position was weakened by the fact that its main armies were at this time engaged in war with Turkey. General Peter Panin was given the command of such forces as could be spared against Pugachov in 1774, and the conclusion of the war with Turkey in July set more troops free. Horrible atrocities were committed on both sides. By the autumn of 1774 the rebellion was crushed. Pugachov was handed over to the government army by his former supporters, and in January 1775 was publicly beheaded and quartered in Moscow. The Pugachov rebellion struck terror into the landowning class and the empress herself. Thereafter she gave up any idea of radical reforms in the interests of the peasants, believing that it was wiser to leave things as they were than to risk provoking a new explosion.

The urban population of Russia was only a tiny portion of the whole: it was estimated as 328,000 in 1724 and 1,300,000 in 1796. Peter the Great had encouraged industry, as he needed cloth for uniforms and metal for weapons in his wars. Industrial enterprises were owned by the state, by nobles, and by plebeian businessmen, known officially as 'merchants' (*kuptsy*). State mines and factories were worked by state peasants, usually in servile conditions. Nobles employed their own serfs. Merchants were allowed to employ serf labour in the so-called 'possessional' factories. These were created under a decree of 18 January 1721. Under this system the servile labour force was assigned to the factory, not to the individual owner. The state had the right to intervene in their management, but seldom exercised it. In practice it seems, from recent research by Soviet economic historians, that not very much use was made of this system, though it was reinforced by further decrees of 1736 and 1744, and the numbers of the 'possessional' factory labour force somewhat increased in the second half of the century.[1] A large part of the

[1] See the discussion in an interesting article by Roger Portal in *Revue Historique* (July–Sept. 1949), 'Manufactures et classes sociales en Russie au XVIIIe siècle'.

industrial labour force of Russia was not servile, but worked for money wages. These paid workers consisted partly of permanent city residents; partly of state peasants living in cities on passports delivered to them by the local authorities; and partly of serfs who were allowed by their owners to work in cities for wages, and paid their *obrok* to the owners out of their earnings. This last group, most of whom had families living in the countryside, belonged legally to the category of landlords' serfs, but economically they were wage-earning workers. They formed an increasing proportion of the labour force.

The most important industrial centre in Russia in the eighteenth century was the Urals, whose mines produced a substantial proportion of all iron mined in Europe, bringing great wealth to the Demidov family, which rose from humble origins in a few generations into the highest aristocracy, and to the Stroganovs, whose domains in the Urals and the western border of Siberia were somewhat older.[1] Russia exported iron, and also flax and timber, the latter largely to Britain, which needed it for the navy.

The official classification of the urban population of Russia bore little relation to economic realities. The business class was grouped under the name of 'merchants', and was divided into three categories—*gildii*, a word which can be conveniently translated 'guild' but has little to do with guilds as understood in European history. Artisans were a more precise grouping: they were organized in corporations (*tsekhi*) which had their own rules about the training of apprentices. The term *possadskie*, which in the nineteenth century was replaced by *meshchane*—roughly equivalent to 'small burgher'—covered a multitude of persons of whom little could be said except that they were not capitalists and that they were not artisans registered in a corporation. The *meshchane* included the floating population of the growing cities, making a precarious living, nearly all poor, some desperately poor, a few doing well for themselves for irregular periods.

Russia had business people, bureaucrats, and a few intellectuals, the three essential elements of which the middle class, or *bourgeoisie*, of western Europe, as it had arisen since the Reforma-

[1] A full treatment of this industry is Roger Portal, *L'Ourale au XVIIIe siècle*, Paris, 1950.

tion, was composed. But Russia had no *bourgeoisie*. None of these groups had the outlook of Western *bourgeois*. The Western spirit of enterprise and individualism was almost completely lacking in the Russian merchant, accustomed to servility towards authority, and expecting restrictive privileges and favours from the autocrat. The bureaucrats, mostly of noble origin but including some persons who had risen by ability through Peter's Table of Ranks, were servants of the Tsar: considerations of individual rights and liberty, as conceived by the European *bourgeoisie*, were alien to them. The third middle-class element of European society, the secular intellectual *élite*, the forerunner of the 'free professions' of post-industrial society, was only just beginning to appear in Russia as the foundations of a modern system of education were laid. But the merchants, the government servants, and the incipient intellectual *élite* of Russia certainly formed no homogeneous social or cultural group, still less did they possess the *bourgeois* ethos of Europe. The absence of either *bourgeois* or feudal traditions, as these existed in Europe, is fundamental to an understanding of Russia in the nineteenth century.

The Church

In medieval Russia, as in medieval Europe, the centre of cultural as well as spiritual life was the Church. The contacts of the early Kievan state with Christianity were through Byzantium. In 957 Princess Olga, regent of Kiev, became a Christian. Her grandson Vladimir (reigned 978–1015) was converted in 988, and established Orthodox Christianity as the official religion. Pagan beliefs continued to be strong for a long time after this, but the Church, at first largely directed by Greek monks from Constantinople, extended its authority into Russia, reaching up to Novgorod in the north-west. It was during the same period that Catholicism became established in Poland.

Under the Tatar yoke the Church was cut off from Constantinople. But it maintained its loyalty to the eastern branch of Christianity, and its hostility to Catholicism, which, after the conversion of the pagan Baltic peoples and the union of Lithuania with Poland in 1386, reached to the western border of Russia. The Mongol conquerors of the thirteenth century were pagans, but their successors, the Tatar khans of the

Golden Horde, were converted to Islam. Like the Ottoman Sultans in the conquered Balkans a hundred years later, the Tatars guaranteed the freedom of the Christian religion. Indeed the Orthodox Church was in some respects a privileged institution. It became the rallying-point of Russian patriotism and culture. Its important role in the strengthening of the Russian princely house in general, and of the principality of Moscow in particular, has already been mentioned. The metropolitan see of the Church was transferred from Kiev to Moscow in 1326.

During the fifteenth century the great monasteries became a considerable force in Russia. The most prominent ecclesiastical figure of this time was Joseph Sanin (1439–1515), founder and abbot of the monastery of Volokolamsk. He was a firm upholder of autocracy, a rigid conservative in matters of dogma and ritual, and a champion of the right of the Church to own land, the purpose of which, however, was not the personal enrichment of the monks (who in Joseph's monastery led an extremely austere life under strict discipline) but the relief of the poor. His principal opponent was Nil of Sora (1433–1508), who laid greater stress on inner faith than on external ritual observance, opposed the ownership of land by the monasteries, and believed that the Church should renounce worldly interest and keep out of politics, neither supporting nor opposing the secular power. The controversy between the two men was connected with the struggle between the Church hierarchy and a heretical movement known as the 'Judaizers'. As the evidence concerning these heretics can only be derived from the writings of their victorious opponents, it is far from clear what their doctrines were. They appear, however, to have been a rationalistic and puritanical movement, opposed to the adoration of icons, to excessive pomp and ceremony in church services, and to the wealth of the Church. Nil of Sora did not belong to this heresy, but he believed that its followers should be persuaded to see their errors rather than physically persecuted or burnt alive, as Joseph and his school urged.

In this controversy Joseph's views prevailed. Heretics were persecuted, the Church kept its lands, and in return supported the secular power. The victory of Joseph reinforced the tradition of emphasis on ritual which always marked the Russian Orthodox Church. It is remarkable how little interest has been shown by the Russian Church (in contrast not only to the Catholics and Protestants but even to the Greek Orthodox) in theological problems. The duty of the Russian Christian has been rather to observe the ceremonies and to obey the rules, than to think about the doctrines of the faith. It is also important to note that the Russian Church did little to transmit secular learning. Whereas the Catholic Church took over the literature and the worldly knowledge of Rome and Greece, and passed it on to medieval European society, and thus also to its Protestant successors, hardly anything of this reached Russia. Constantinople bequeathed to Kiev little of the wisdom of the ancient world, and most of this little perished under the Tatar yoke.

The links between Russia and Byzantium were still further weakened when the patriarch of Constantinople, desperately needing west European help against the pressure of the Ottoman Turks, agreed to meet the representatives of the Catholic Church at the Council of Florence in 1439. The Russian Church was represented by Isidore, a Greek nominated by Constantinople as metropolitan of Moscow in 1436. The council accepted the reunion of the Churches on the pope's terms. When Isidore returned to Moscow in 1441 to justify this decision, he was arrested. A council of Russian bishops repudiated the decisions of Florence, and Isidore was fortunate in being allowed to leave Russia alive. When Constantinople fell to the Turks in 1453, Russian Christians believed that this was a judgement on its sins in capitulating to the bishop of Rome. The independence of the Russian Church from Constantinople was formally asserted by the creation of the patriarchate of Moscow in 1589.

Russia was now the only sovereign state whose official religion was Orthodoxy, its Tsar the only Orthodox autocrat. In the sixteenth century there was developed in Muscovy the doctrine of 'Moscow, the third Rome'. Rome itself had betrayed the true religion, and the popes were heretics. Constantinople too had betrayed, and had fallen to the Turks. Moscow was now the third Rome, and there would be no fourth. This doctrine was used by Ivan IV (the Terrible) as a justification of his autocracy. Though later Tsars did not pay much attention to the doctrine, something remained of it in the fairly widespread belief that Russia had some special right to Constantinople. This was to play a part in Russo-Turkish relations in later centuries.

During the 'Time of Troubles' the Church was again a rallying-point for Russian patriotism, against invading Poles and Swedes. Under Tsar Michael Romanov (reigned 1613–45) the Church's prestige was increased by the fact that the patriarch, Filaret, was the Tsar's father.[1] However, Filaret was an essentially worldly man, his power essentially that of a secular ruler. A more serious challenge to the monarchy came from Nikon (patriarch from 1652 to 1667), who wished both to assert the independence of the Church in relation to the state and to reform the Church itself. Nikon wished to revise both the ceremonies of the Church and the texts of the sacred books in the light of the knowledge which was now becoming available. The most important centre of learning at this time in a land of Russian population (though not within the Muscovite state) was the Kiev Academy, established by Peter Mogila, who was metropolitan of Kiev under Polish rule from 1633 to 1647. In the Kiev Academy Russian priests studied Greek and Latin sources. Nikon was assisted in his plans of reform by former pupils of the Kiev Academy. His reforms, however, provoked fanatical opposition from priests who combined religious devotion to the existing, historically corrupted, texts with Russian nationalist hatred of Greek influences. Tsar Alexei (reigned 1645–76) supported Nikon in his conflict with the conservative priests, at the cost of provoking a schism in the Church. But Nikon's attempts to assert the equality of the Church with the state, or even the supremacy of the spiritual power, antagonized the Tsar, and led to Nikon's disgrace in 1658 and final removal from his office in 1667.

However, the secular power was energetically used against the conservative priests, who enjoyed much support from the peasants. The arch-priest Avvakum, their outstanding spokesman, whose memoirs are not only an intensely moving human and religious document but also a masterpiece of early Russian literature, was imprisoned and persecuted for many years and burnt alive in 1681. But the schismatics were not destroyed.

[1] Filaret was an exception to the rule that bishops could be chosen only from the celibate monastic ('black') clergy. He led a secular life, as a prominent aristocrat, married and had children, before being forced in 1601, when he was more than forty years old, to enter the Church, by Tsar Boris Godunov, who feared him as a possible rival for the throne. Once a priest, however, he was able to rise in the hierarchy.

Many took refuge in the remote northern and eastern provinces. Some communities removed themselves from the attention of the authorities by mass self-immolation: they would shut themselves up in buildings and set them on fire. But many remained, especially in the Volga valley and Siberia. They were divided into two main categories of 'priestly' and 'priestless'. The former received sacraments according to the old ritual from priests who belonged to the official Church and were either secret schismatics, or accepted bribes to perform schismatic rituals. The latter believed that the whole Church was in the hands of Antichrist, and that the faithful should do without priests altogether. From the priestless schismatics derived a number of extreme sects, such as the Wanderers (*stranniki*) who believed in holy poverty and vagrancy. In the eighteenth century there appeared in the south of Russia sects which rejected sacraments and priests, lived a communal existence with sharing of property, and claimed that they could commune directly with God. The most important of these were the Dukhobors (fighters for the spirit) and the Molokane (from *moloko*—milk—so called because they drank milk during fasts). These names date from the end of the eighteenth century, but the origins of the sects are much older.[1]

The repression of the schism in effect confirmed the subservience of the Church to the state. This became still clearer under Peter the Great, who made no secret of his contempt for priests or his indifference to religion. In 1700, when Patriarch Adrian died, Peter did not replace him. Instead Stefan Yavorsky, a former student of Kiev Academy who had at one time been converted to Catholicism but had later returned to Orthodoxy, was appointed as 'the keeper and administrator of the Patriarchal See'. On his death he was replaced by Theophan Prokopovich, who also had once been a pupil of Kiev Academy and for a time had been a Catholic. Prokopovich was a bitter opponent of the principles of papal rule, feeling strongly that it is the task of the monarch alone to regulate the activities of

[1] The traditional view of Russian scholars is that the southern sects arose as a result of German Protestant influence. This is, however, challenged by F. C. Conybeare, who suggests that their doctrines may be derived from the Bogomils of Bulgaria or the Paulicians of Asia Minor whose teaching may have spread round the north of the Black Sea in the Middle Ages. F. C. Conybeare, *Russian Dissenters* (Harvard, 1921), pp. 263–5.

his subjects and to provide for their welfare and happiness. The Church in fact should keep out of politics. This agreed fully with Peter's views. In 1721 Peter formally abolished the patriarchate, and replaced it with a Holy Synod, composed of the three metropolitans (Moscow, Kiev, and St. Petersburg) and of other bishops appointed by the Tsar for fixed periods.[1] In 1722 Peter created the office of chief procurator of the Holy Synod, a lay official, who had under him a large secular bureaucracy, reaching down to the full-time lay secretaries of the episcopal consistories. The Church was thus subordinated to a government department. In the past the Church had seldom opposed the emperor, but it had an authority and an organization of its own which at least would have enabled it to do so had it wished. After 1722 the authority was taken from it, but the organization was made bigger and more complicated than ever. The bishops became prisoners of a machine, smothered in official paper, unable even if they wished to act as spiritual shepherds of their flocks.

In 1701 Peter handed the administration of Church estates to a secular office, the *Monastyrskii prikaz*, under Ivan Musin-Pushkin. Only part of the revenues were spent on Church needs, the rest being made available to the Tsar, who urgently needed money for his wars. Half a century later, the short-lived Emperor Peter III secularized Church lands by a decree of 17 January 1762, placing them under a new office, the *kollegiya ekonomii*, and paying fixed sums to the monasteries and ecclesiastical authorities. Catherine II reversed this decree on 12 August, but on 26 February 1764 she revived it.

At the end of the eighteenth century the Orthodox Church had no political power and little material wealth. The sharp division between the lower priesthood, or 'white clergy', whose members were obliged to marry, and the monks or 'black clergy', who were celibate and from whose ranks bishops were recruited, was a source of internal division. It is worth noting that, in contrast to the Catholic and Protestant countries of western Europe, in Russia an ecclesiastical career made little appeal to persons of worldly ambition. Even younger sons of poor noble families seldom entered the Church. Recruitment to

[1] When Georgia was annexed to Russia in 1801, the head of the Georgian Church became a fourth member *ex officio* of the synod. The number of other bishops invited to attend the synod's meetings varied.

the Church came in fact very largely from children of priests. This tendency was reinforced by the foundation, under a decree of 1737, of seminaries for training priests. In 1764 there were twenty-six of these, and the intention was to have one in every diocese. Teachers for the seminaries were trained at the ecclesiastical academies of Moscow and Kiev, to which were later added those of St. Petersburg and Kazan. Children of priests were admitted free of charge as pupils of seminaries. This provided some incentive to intellectual effort. But as a secular system of education developed, it drew away a growing proportion of the intellectual *élite* among priests' children (*popovichi*).[1] The tendency for the priesthood to remain a separate hereditary caste persisted, but the intellectual level of the members of the caste tended to fall.

The priesthood, however, still exercised a considerable influence over the Russian people. Politically, this influence normally operated in favour of autocracy, nationalism, and intolerance towards non-Russians. The moral and spiritual influence of the Church over the Russian people is not easy to estimate. Evidence is not plentiful, and judgement has been clouded by both clerical and anti-clerical dogmatism. The spiritual, and still more the intellectual, levels of the average Russian priest were probably not high, but it should not be forgotten that the influence of the Church was the only moral and social discipline of a non-coercive kind that was felt by the Russian peasants. It must not be underrated. Among schismatics and sectarians, persecuted minorities, faith was usually stronger than among the Orthodox. As in other lands and at other periods, persecution caused believers to hold to their faith and to ponder it more deeply. It is worth noting that the Old Believers (or 'priestly' schismatics) developed many of the traditional Protestant virtues—sobriety, cleanliness, hard work, and a talent for capitalist enterprise. Many prominent Muscovite merchant families were schismatic. The same Protestant virtues were also found among the southern sects.

Education, Ideas, and Culture

Public secular education in Russia began with Peter the Great. His main interest was in technical training, to strengthen

[1] From *pop*, a village priest.

both the armed forces and the civil administration. He sent young Russians of noble families abroad to acquire European skills. In Russia he set up mining schools and a Marine Academy. The Academy of Sciences, planned by Peter and set up in St. Petersburg in 1726 after his death, was intended to have a university and a secondary school (*gimnaziya*)[1] attached to it, but this was not achieved for the time being. In 1755 the first Russian university was founded, in Moscow, on the initiative of Count Ivan Shuvalov, with the assistance of the Russian scientist Michael Lomonosov. It had two gimnazii under it, one in Moscow and one in Kazan. These were the first state-controlled secondary schools. Shuvalov was also responsible for the creation of the Academy of Arts in 1757. In 1764 was founded the Society of Noble Girls at the Smolny monastery in St. Petersburg, with places for 200 pupils. In 1760 Ivan Shuvalov made a proposal to set up gimnazii in all large cities, to prepare students for the university and for the cadet corps, which had been founded in 1731 for the professional and general education of future army officers; and 'schools of literacy' in smaller towns to prepare for gimnazii. But the human and financial resources were not available, and there was not sufficient interest in high places.

Catherine II paid greater attention to education. In the deliberations of the commission of 1767 several delegates of the nobility showed an active interest in the subject, and a sub-commission made recommendations on the creation of schools. Under the provincial government statute of 1775 the obligation to administer 'popular schools' was placed on the *Prikazy obshchestvennogo prizreniya*,[2] but still shortage of teachers and money prevented action. In 1780 Catherine met Emperor Joseph II, and was much impressed with the system of schools introduced in Austria by his mother Maria Theresa in 1775. This was based on a triple layer of primary schools (*Trivialschulen*), secondary schools, and normal schools, with an educational commission in each province of the empire. Catherine decided to copy this system in Russia, and asked Joseph to give her an expert adviser. He recommended the Serb Janković-

[1] This word was used in German lands for secondary schools. The word was taken over into the Russian language. To render it in English as 'gymnasium' would be absurd, and 'grammar school' is not an exact equivalent. I am therefore obliged to use the word gimnaziya.

[2] See above p. 20.

de-Mirievo, director of schools for the Banat of Temesvár. In 1782 a commission on schools was set up in St. Petersburg. Its chairman was Count P. V. Zavadovsky, and it was composed of two members of the Academy and Janković, who was the organizing spirit. It was instructed to prepare a general plan of national education, to train teachers and to publish both original and translated textbooks. Its plan was approved by the empress on 21 September 1782 for St. Petersburg province only. It was to set up three levels of schools—primary, middle, and high. There was to be an overlap of two years between the first two and of three years between the second and third. The fourth class of the high school would be a two-year course. Training of teachers was to be concentrated in the St. Petersburg high school. In 1786 the training of teachers was transferred to a special institution in the capital, the Teachers' Seminary. In the same year the plan was extended to twenty-five Russian provinces, with the modification that there were to be only two levels, the primary school in district and provincial centres, the high school only in provincial centres. It is interesting to note that these schools were entirely secular institutions, not because the authorities had any prejudice against the participation of the Church in education but because the Church simply could not produce sufficient priests capable of teaching.

During the period 1782 to 1801 the St. Petersburg teachers' training centre trained 420 teachers. In 1782 there were 8 schools under the commission's authority, with 26 teachers, 474 male and 44 female pupils.[1] In 1801 there were 315 schools with 790 teachers, 18,000 male and 1,800 female pupils. During this period the Polish and the Baltic provinces had their own system of education. There was some talk of replacing this by the new Russian system, but no action was taken.

Eighteenth-century Russia produced some intellectual figures of distinction. First among them was Michael Lomonosov (1711–65), the son of a free fisherman in Archangel province. He became a professor of chemistry in the Academy of Sciences, and showed profound interest in and capacity for scientific thought: had he lived in a country of greater opportunities, he might have made original contributions to science. Lomonosov

[1] *Istoricheskii obzor deyatel'nosti Ministerstva narodnogo prosveshcheniya 1802–1902* (SPB, 1902), pp. 21–23. Cited hereafter as *Istoricheskii obzor deyatel'nosti MNP*.

did much to develop a Russian literary language, and himself wrote poems, including odes in honour of Peter the Great and of the following rulers. He was responsible for a large part of the practical work of founding Moscow University. Alexander Sumarokov was the author of several plays in verse, and was the director of the first theatre opened in the capital. In the second half of the century the most important Russian poet was G. R. Derzhavin (1743–1816), not a great figure yet important in the development of Russian as a language of poetry. His contemporary D. I. Fonvizin (1745–92) was the author of two comedies which have real merit as social satire. In 1783 was founded the Russian Academy, whose purpose was to do for literature and for the purity of the language what Peter's Academy of Sciences was to do for the natural sciences. Its first president, Princess Catherine Dashkova (*née* Vorontsova), at one time an intimate friend of Catherine II, was the author of an interesting volume of memoirs.

The study of social and political ideas at first enjoyed the encouragement of the empress. She herself corresponded with such prominent figures of the European Enlightenment as Grimm and Voltaire, and bought Diderot's library. The reputation for enlightenment which she studiously cultivated was to some extent a matter of propaganda: the dishonesty of some of the claims she made on behalf of her régime, and the eagerness with which Voltaire accepted them, while regarding her treatment of Poland as defence of tolerance against Catholic obscurantism, make distasteful reading. Nevertheless, it is unfair to dismiss her as a hypocrite. She may have played with ideas, but at least she was interested in them. She also encouraged the Free Economic Society, founded in 1765, which conducted serious inquiries into social conditions.

An important intellectual influence on educated Russians was Freemasonry, which was introduced into Russia in the first half of the eighteenth century. The most distinguished Russian Freemason was Nicholas Novikov (1744–1818), who was active as journalist, editor, and publisher in Moscow from 1779 to 1791. Novikov's intellectual interests were in philanthropy, education, and moral philosophy. From the proceeds of his publications he financed two private primary schools and gave scholarships for study abroad. He also organized relief during the famine in 1787. Other wealthy men contributed to his enterprises, and he enjoyed great moral authority.

In the last years of her life, however, Catherine II became obsessed by the example of the French Revolution, and feared the subversive effect of the very ideas to which she had previously expressed devotion. Novikov fell victim to this change in the empress's outlook. His publications were suspended in 1791, and in August 1792 he was imprisoned in the Schlüsselburg Fortress, though no serious evidence of treason or other crimes could be brought against him. Another victim was the writer Alexander Radishchev (1749–1802), author of *A Journey from St. Petersburg to Moscow*, published in 1790. This work described, in the form of a traveller's tale, the injustice and cruelty of serfdom and the malpractices of the bureaucracy. The empress was enraged, and ordered Radishchev's arrest and trial. He was condemned to death, but the sentence was commuted to ten years of exile in Siberia.

During the eighteenth century the European visual arts made an impression in Russia. Russia's own tradition in architecture and painting was almost entirely religious. Russian medieval churches and Russian icons formed a distinct and splendid branch of Byzantine art. Secular architecture was undistinguished until the late fifteenth century, when Italian architects built some magnificent reception rooms in the Kremlin in Moscow. In the eighteenth century there was a new flowering, in which such foreigners as Bartolomeo Rastrelli (1700–71), Charles Cameron (1740–1820), and Giacomo Quarenghi (1744–1817) played a leading part, but two talented Russian architects appeared in V. I. Bazhenov (1737–99) and M. F. Kazakov (1733–1812). The northern climate and the vast size of Russia imposed a Russian idiom on European eighteenth-century architecture. During this period were built the palace of Peterhof, begun by Peter the Great and continued by Elizabeth; Catherine II's two palaces at Tsarskoe Selo; and the Winter Palace in St. Petersburg.[1] In 1780 was completed Falconet's 'Bronze Horseman', the equestrian statue of Peter the Great in

[1] The Great Palace at Tsarskoe Selo was begun under Elizabeth and completed by Catherine II. At the end of her reign she had the Alexander Palace built close to it, as a gift to her grandson, the future Emperor Alexander I. The Winter Palace was completed in 1768, under the direction of Rastrelli.

St. Petersburg inscribed *Petro primo Catharina secunda*. In painting, Russia had nothing to contribute after the tradition of icons fell into decay. But Catherine II busily bought the private collections of European art (among them that of Sir Robert Walpole) which made possible the growth of the Hermitage Gallery, in a wing of the Winter Palace, into one of the world's greatest collections of painting.

When Peter had first forced young Russian noblemen to undergo a modern education, he had met with fierce opposition. But during the first decade of the century the nobility had acquired a taste for foreign ways of life. At first those who acquired European skills were automatically employed in civil or military service. But when Peter III abolished compulsory state service, the nobility continued to seek European education, not so much for the sake of professional advancement as of social and intellectual pleasure. There thus grew up, in the capitals, in the provincial centres, and on landowners' estates, a leisured educated class, familiar with French literature or German philosophy, and to a lesser extent with the economic ideas and agricultural improvements now popular in Britain.[1]

This Russian leisured class certainly had its ridiculous aspects. Frenchmen, even wig-makers or valets, tended to be treated as all-wise oracles by Russians obsessed by a naïve snobbery for 'culture'. The use of the French language by the Russian aristocracy was often pushed to the point of forgetting their own. But the spread of European influence had more lasting and beneficial effects. Genuine intellectual curiosity was aroused, and the scientific, moral, and political ideas of the Age of Enlightenment were beginning to reach at least a small stratum of the Russian people, to bring out their great latent abilities.

[1] A minor but noteworthy contribution to Russian social life was the English Club, founded in 1770 by an English merchant resident in St. Petersburg named Francis Gardner. A branch was founded in Moscow some years later, closed by Emperor Paul, but reopened in 1802. In the reign of Alexander I both branches were socially fashionable. The St. Petersburg English Club's motto was *Concordia et laetitia*. For some curious reason its journal was kept in German until 1817 and thereafter in Russian. Its membership was fixed at 300 in 1780, and only raised to 400 in 1850, by which time there was a waiting-list of 1,000. Among its members in the reign of Alexander I were Karamzin, Speransky, Zhukovsky, Pushkin, the fable writer Krylov, General Miloradovich, Count Kochubey, and Count Paul Stroganov. Honorary membership, for exceptionally distinguished persons, was introduced in 1798. Two who enjoyed this status were Kutuzov (elected 1813) and Paskevich (1828).

II

RUSSIA AS A GREAT POWER

Foreign Policy after Peter

EIGHTEENTH-CENTURY Russia was one of the European Great Powers. Her foreign policy was especially concerned with her neighbours Sweden, Poland, and Turkey, but she also maintained regular relations with more distant France, Austria, Prussia, and Britain.

France was at this time the greatest of the continental Powers. She had risen to her supremacy, in the sixteenth and seventeenth centuries, in conflict with the Habsburgs of Spain and Austria. The most important other enemy of the Habsburgs since the sixteenth century had been Turkey. In 1529, when Turkish power was at its height, the armies of Sultan Suleiman the Magnificent had besieged Vienna. In 1535 Francis I of France had made an alliance with the Sultan. From this time onwards France was first in influence of the European Powers at Istanbul. During the eighteenth century Turkish power declined, chiefly as a result of internal weaknesses, and in the same period a new external danger to Turkey appeared in the growth of the military power of Russia. For Austria, Russia was a welcome ally against Turkey. For France, Russia was a nuisance, as the enemy of her own ally and the friend of her enemy, though there was no major direct cause of conflict between France and Russia. France supported those Powers which were potentially hostile to Austria, and, increasingly, towards Russia. These were Sweden, Poland, and Turkey. French influence had been strong in Sweden since the reign of Gustav Adolf. In Poland too French influence was of old standing, even if Poland had at times inclined towards Austria and against Turkey. Thus the dominant pattern in the first half of the eighteenth century was for Russia to be with Austria and against France, and to find that her three main immediate enemies—Turkey, Poland, and Sweden—enjoyed French support.

Austria concluded an alliance with Russia in 1726, directed mainly against Turkey. In 1733 Austria and Russia were allied against France in the War of the Polish Succession. On the death of the pro-Russian king of Poland, Augustus II, the Polish Parliament had elected as his successor Stanisław Leszczyński, the former ally of Charles XII of Sweden and now the candidate of the French government. The pro-Russian party in Poland set up a counter-parliament, or 'Confederation', and elected the late king's heir to the kingdom of Saxony as Augustus III, king of Poland. They were supported by a Russian invasion. The French armies were fully occupied in war with Austria, Spain, and Sardinia, and Stanisław Leszczyński had to fight Russia alone. He was defeated, and Augustus III was established as king of Poland. This was recognized by the peace signed at Vienna on 3 October 1735 between France and Austria.

In 1735 Russian forces invaded the Crimea, and this led in October 1736 to war with the Ottoman empire. In May 1737 Marshal Münnich forced the isthmus of Perekop, into the Crimean Peninsula, but then retreated. In June the Russians took the fortresses of Kinburn and Azov, repeating Peter the Great's exploit of forty years earlier. Austria was bound by the alliance to come to the aid of Russia against Turkey, but postponed her entry into the war until June 1737, and even then gave little help. In July the Russians took the fortress of Ochakov, which controlled the mouth of the Dnieper. In 1739 the Russian army entered Moldavia, and in September captured its capital, Jaşi. Meanwhile, however, French diplomacy had entered the field, with the aim of securing the most favourable possible terms for France's traditional ally Turkey. The Austrian government had little enthusiasm for the war, had little success, and was quite willing to make peace. Russia, thus diplomatically isolated, was obliged to accept the Treaty of Belgrade of 18 September 1739. The Turks ceded Azov to Russia, but the Russian government undertook to dismantle its fortress, not to fortify the city of Taganrog on the Sea of Azov, and to keep no naval forces in the Black Sea. The Crimea remained in the hands of the Tatars.

Since the mid seventeenth century a new Power had arisen in Germany in the shape of Prussia. Under the Great Elector

Frederick William (1640–88) the Prussian state was internally consolidated, and its territory increased at the expense of Poland. The defeat of Sweden in the Northern War removed a major obstacle to the growth of Prussian power. But though Prussia had to some extent a common interest with Russia, the relations between the two Powers were not at first friendly. The main reason for this was the hostility of Austria to Prussia, which greatly increased when another brilliant and aggressive Prussian ruler, King Frederick II (1740–86) profited from the weakness of Austria on the succession of a woman, Empress Maria Theresa, to the Imperial throne, to seize the Austrian province of Silesia. This led to the War of the Austrian Succession, in which Prussia was allied with France and Austria with Britain.

In Russia too the year 1740 brought a new ruler to the throne, the Empress Elizabeth. Her first foreign minister, Bestuzhev-Ryumin, stood for alliance with Austria, while the heir to the throne, Grand Duke Peter, sympathized with Prussia. Russia remained out of the Austro-Prussian war, but in July 1741 was attacked by Sweden. The Russian army had some successes in Finland, but when peace was made in August 1743 at Åbo, Russia made no significant gains of territory. In 1747 Russia made a treaty with Britain, by which in return for a large financial subsidy she was to send troops to fight against France. In fact the Russian army did not have to take part in the war, as the prospect of its intervention caused France to conclude peace with Britain and Austria.

In the reversal of alliances in the mid 1750's, which led to the Seven Years' War (1756–63) in Europe and overseas, Russia found herself allied not only with Austria but also with France, and not only Prussia but also Britain was her enemy. The Russian army played an important part. From the summer of 1757 to the end of 1761 Russian troops were on Prussian territory, and though Frederick II resisted with great fortitude his country was reduced to desperate conditions. The Russian army won important victories at Grossjägerndorf (19 August 1757) under Count Apraksin, and at Kunersdorf (1 August 1759) under Count Peter Saltykov. Königsberg was occupied in January 1758 and Berlin in September 1760. Frederick was saved by the death of Empress Elizabeth. Her successor, Peter III, was a fervent admirer of Frederick, and at once ordered an armistice with Prussia and the restoration of all occupied Prussian territories. When Catherine II overthrew her husband in June 1762, she did not reverse his policy.

From 1763 to 1780 Catherine's chief adviser in foreign affairs was Count Nikita Panin. His basic aim was an alliance of 'Northern' Powers (Russia, Prussia, Britain, the Scandinavian states and Poland) against Austria and France. This aim was not in fact achieved. But Prussia was substituted for Austria as Russia's main ally, and the main effort of Russian policy was once more directed towards the two traditional objects of Poland and Turkey.

The death of Augustus III in October 1763 provided an opportunity for Catherine II to intervene in Polish affairs, and in this she had the support of Frederick II. Catherine's candidate for the Polish throne was her former lover Stanisław Poniatowski, related by marriage to the powerful Czartoryski family. In April 1764 a Russo-Prussian alliance was signed. Apart from mutual support in war, it provided that both governments should defend the existing constitution of Poland, and that both should intervene when necessary on behalf of the religious minorities ('dissidents'). The Polish constitution, with its unanimity rule in parliament and its system of 'confederations' or counter-parliaments, whose policies could be supported by the armed forces of great territorial magnates in opposition to the will of the sovereign and of the national parliament, doomed Poland to a condition of near-anarchy. As for the 'dissidents', the Protestant Germans and Orthodox White Russians and Ukrainians, they undoubtedly suffered from disabilities, and even persecution, under Catholic Polish rule, but the concern of those two far from devout sovereigns Frederick and Catherine on their behalf was primarily an excuse for unscrupulous intervention in Polish affairs. In the summer of 1764 a Russian army occupied Poland with the consent of the Czartoryskis, and the Russian ambassador Prince Repnin secured the election of Poniatowski by the Parliament on 7 September. Polish subjection to Russia reached a climax with a treaty of 24 February 1768, by which Russia guaranteed 'for all time' the Polish constitution, and a separate act conferred full civil and political rights on the 'dissidents'. But Polish opposition, in which patriotism, chauvinism, and religious intolerance were mingled, was very strong. In March 1768 the anti-Russian party formed its counter-parliament, the Confederation of Bar, which rejected the treaty and was encouraged, though not supported militarily, by Austria and France. There resulted four years of sporadic warfare between Poland and Russia.

Turkey observed with alarm the rise of Russian power at Poland's expense. Violations by Russian Cossacks of the Turkish frontier in the south-west Ukraine led to the arrest of the Russian ambassador in Constantinople, and war began between Russia and Turkey in the autumn of 1768. It was in this war that the Russian government first thought seriously of rousing the Balkan Christians—Greeks, Slavs, and Roumanians—against Turkish rule, and of seizing Constantinople. A Russian fleet was sent from the Baltic round Europe into the Aegean. The British government watched its progress with sympathy, and the British admirals Greig and Elphinstone held commands in it, the supreme commander being Catherine II's lover Alexei Orlov. In June 1770 the Russian fleet won a complete victory over the Turkish at Chesme in the Aegean. It was, however, unable to follow it up by forcing the Dardanelles or liberating peninsular Greece. On the main land front in the Roumanian principalities the Russian army had some important successes. In the summer of 1769, led by Field-Marshal Rumyantsev, it occupied Jaşi and Bucarest. In 1770 Rumyantsev retreated in the early months but recovered Bucarest in November, while the Turkish fortresses in his rear in Moldavia were taken. In the summer of 1772 peace negotiations were opened at Focşani, and in the autumn continued in Bucarest, but without success. Meanwhile Austria was alarmed at Russian successes, and Catherine feared diplomatic or even military intervention by Austria on Turkey's side.

This danger was averted by agreement between Russia, Austria, and Prussia at the expense of Poland. By the First Partition of 1772, which the Polish Parliament was bribed and forced into accepting in September 1773, each of the three Powers took substantial territories. Russia's share was a large portion of White Russia, with a population of nearly two million, mostly Orthodox by religion, and a strip of territory in Livonia. The war with Turkey was resumed in 1773 but without any important further victories. The Russians failed to capture Silistria on the Danube. Eventually Turkey proved to be more exhausted by the strain than Russia, and accepted terms favourable to Russia by the Treaty of Kuchuk Kainardji of 10 July 1774. Crimea became an independent state, no longer subject to the Ottoman empire. Russia acquired the Black Sea coastal fortresses of Kinburn, Kerch, and Yenikale, and the whole territory between the Bug and the Dnieper, as well as substantial gains in the Kuban and North Caucasus area. She also acquired an ill-defined right to protect the Christian subjects of the Sultan.

Russia's close co-operation with Prussia continued during the 1770's. In 1779 by the Treaty of Teschen, which ended the War of the Bavarian Succession, in which Russia had mediated to the advantage of Prussia, Russia obtained a position as a protecting Power in relation to the constitution of the Holy Roman Empire. During the 1780's, however, under the influence of Catherine's new favourite Potyomkin, Russian policy moved away from Prussia towards Austria, whose Emperor Joseph II (who succeeded in 1780) admired Catherine as much as his mother Maria Theresa had disliked her.

Potyomkin was especially interested in a forward policy towards Turkey. He was responsible for the final annexation of the Crimea by Russia, without war, in 1783. In 1787 Catherine made a triumphal progress through the recently acquired southern provinces, accompanied by Potyomkin, and joined by Joseph II and by Poniatowski, king of Poland. This was a demonstration against Turkey, whose government responded to the provocation by declaring war in August 1787. In 1788 Austria in her turn joined the war on Russia's side. Catherine's aims were now more ambitious than in 1768. Encouraged by Potyomkin, she dreamed of completely expelling the Turks from Europe, and of establishing her second grandson Constantine on a Greek throne in Constantinople. Potyomkin himself was to receive a principality of Dacia, to be formed from the Roumanian lands.

The Power which now came forward in opposition to Russian policy was Britain. Anglo-Russian relations had been traditionally friendly. For this there were two main reasons. One was that there was a flourishing trade between the two countries.

Britain was the best single market for Russian exports, and was particularly interested in naval stores, of which the Russian forests were an abundant source. British merchants were established in Moscow and other cities, and the Russia Company, which had been founded in the reign of Mary Tudor, and to which belonged the British merchants engaged in the Russian trade, was influential in London. Anglo-Russian trade was regulated by a commercial treaty of 1734, renewed with some changes in 1766. The second main reason was that both Powers were opposed to France. Britain had offered subsidies to Russia in return for Russian military action against France in 1747, and again in 1755. Though neither of these agreements had led to action, the knowledge of a common interest was a fact. This had been reduced by the Seven Years' War, though no direct clash of British with Russian interests had occurred.

A more serious situation, however, arose during the War of American Independence. The Russian government could not accept the British claims in regard to blockades and the control of neutral vessels. When agreement proved impossible, Catherine II made in 1780 a Declaration of Armed Neutrality, in which she was joined by Sweden, Denmark, and Prussia. The doctrine proclaimed by the declaration—that a neutral flag offered protection to all cargoes carried under it, including not only enemy goods destined to neutral subjects but also any goods destined to enemy subjects—was not accepted by the British government.[1] Trade between Russia and Britain continued during the War of American Independence, but political attitudes on both sides changed. From the British point of view Russia seemed no longer a traditionally friendly state, but one whose policies were potentially hostile. The territorial aggrandizement of this unpredictable Power was thus to be regarded with suspicion.

During her first war with Turkey (1768–74) Catherine II had enjoyed British sympathy, and British assistance had been given to her navy. By contrast, in the second Turkish war (1787–92) British diplomacy organized opposition to Russia in the north. Gustav III of Sweden, who in 1772 had taken power into his

[1] For detailed treatment of this question, see Isabel de Madariaga, *Britain, Russia and the Armed Neutrality of 1780*, London 1962. Another useful study, of broader scope but less depth, is Dietrich Gerhard, *England und der Aufstieg Russlands*, Munich, 1933.

own hands and abolished the constitution which favoured the aristocracy, was looking for an opportunity to restore his country's international position. In 1788 he declared war on Russia. Britain and Prussia jointly forced Denmark, which had been allied to Russia since 1773, to refrain from attacking Sweden. The Russo-Swedish war was, however, inconclusive, and was ended by the Treaty of Verela of 14 August 1790, without territorial changes.

The war with Turkey meanwhile went well. In December 1788 the Russian army captured the fortress of Ochakov, and in August 1789 Rumyantsev took Jaşi. The fall of Ochakov was taken surprisingly seriously by William Pitt, who saw visions of Russian naval power extending through the Black Sea into the Mediterranean. Pitt co-operated closely with Prussia, and intended in the spring of 1791 to present Russia with an ultimatum, demanding the evacuation of Ochakov and the conclusion of peace with Turkey without any new annexations. But opposition in England, organized by the Whigs in co-operation with the Russian ambassador Count Simon Vorontsov, caused him to call off the planned naval demonstration in the Baltic, which would probably have led to war. Catherine stuck to her demands on Turkey, and the Ottoman government finally agreed, by the Treaty of Jaşi of 9 January 1792, to the surrender of Ochakov and all territory between the Bug and the Dniester, and to the final Russian annexation of the Crimea.

The last major event of Russian foreign policy in the reign of Catherine II concerned Poland. Frederick William II of Prussia (who succeeded Frederick II in 1786), partly under British influence, for a time played the part of friend and protector of Polish independence against Russia. In November 1788 he declared himself willing to interpret his obligation to defend the Polish constitution in such a way as to permit the radical reforms which the growing patriotic movement in Poland was demanding. Catherine herself in May 1789 agreed to a Polish request for the withdrawal of Russian troops. On 29 March 1790 Frederick William signed a treaty of alliance with Poland. On 3 May 1791 the Polish Parliament enthusiastically accepted a new constitution. This abolished the unanimity rule and made possible both an efficient central government and the execution of political and social reforms. Meanwhile the accession to the Austrian throne of Leopold II in 1790 had further improved the prospects. The new emperor sought better relations with Prussia, was well disposed to Poland and reserved towards Russia.

The situation was transformed by the death of Leopold II in March 1792 and by the declaration of war by Austria and Prussia on revolutionary France. While the two German monarchs were occupied in the west, Catherine was free to proceed against Poland. She induced the pro-Russian party in Poland to set up the Confederation of Targowice (14 May 1792), and to invite her to intervene on their behalf. She then sent her troops into Poland 'to combat Jacobinism', as represented by the constitution of 3 May 1791, and to 'restore Poland's ancient liberties', the unanimity rule and other old abuses. Prussia now ignored her obligation to defend Poland. Catherine blandly assured Austria and Prussia that it was for them to obtain 'compensations' in the west, that is in Germany, for their efforts against France, while she took her own 'compensation' in Poland in return for her efforts against Polish Jacobinism. But the Austrians and Prussians were losing the war with France, and were clearly not going to obtain any territory in Germany. Frederick William therefore decided to demand his share of Poland, and Catherine decided it was wisest to consent. The Polish parliament was forced by the Russian ambassador, Baron Sievers, to ratify two separate treaties, with Russia and with Prussia. Russia acquired by this Second Partition the provinces of Vilna and Minsk and part of Podolia and Volhynia, with about three million inhabitants, mostly White Russian, Lithuanian, or Ukrainian. Prussia took the western region of Greater Poland, with an ethnically compact Polish population.

Polish opinion could not endure this humiliation. In March 1794 a revolt broke out in the rump territory which the partition had still left, against the occupying Powers. It was led by Tadeusz Kościuszko, a hero of the American War of Independence. The Prussian troops were driven out of Poland, and the Russians suffered several defeats. Fresh Russian forces were, however, sent in, and General Alexander Suvorov occupied Warsaw, with great brutality, in November 1794. It was now decided that Poland should be finally destroyed, and this time Austria again took a share in the spoils. The final convention for the Third Partition was signed on 26 January 1797 between the three Powers. Austria took Western Galicia, Prussia central Poland with Warsaw, and Russia the rest of Podolia, Volhynia, and Lithuania. Russia had already annexed the Baltic principality of Kurland in April 1795.

Thus during the eighteenth century Russia had expanded to the two seas, and now held the coasts of the Baltic from the mouth of the Niemen to the port of Vyborg, and of the Black Sea from the mouth of the Dniester to the Sea of Azov. However, the Russian empire still did not include all lands whose people spoke a 'Little Russian' (Ukrainian) dialect. The most important exception was Eastern Galicia, which under the partitions of Poland went to Austria. Here a substantial proportion of the Ukrainian-speaking people belonged to the Uniate Church. But contrary to the original intentions of its founders, this Church had become a centre not of Polish but of Ukrainian anti-Polish feeling. Eastern Galicia became the birthplace of modern Ukrainian nationalism, directed equally against Poles and Russians. In Bukovina, a province at the north-east corner of the Carpathians, annexed by Austria from Turkey in 1776, there were also people of Ukrainian speech. Finally, one small group should be mentioned, which was closely related to the Ukrainians, but whose national orientation remained very uncertain. This was the people of Ruthenia, on the south side of the Carpathians adjoining Bukovina and Galicia. Ruthenia had been for centuries part of the historic kingdom of Hungary. Its people spoke Russian dialects, but had been exposed neither to Polish nor to Muscovite influences.

An important category among Russia's new subjects were the Jews, who were numerous in the former eastern provinces of Poland. The Russian government introduced special legislation to regulate their situation. Though anti-semitism had never been widespread in Muscovy, the same general hostility to the Jews was found in the Orthodox Church as in the western European Christian churches. This hostility, based on a distrust of Jews as 'the people who crucified Christ' and on the belief that they were a race of usurious money-makers, affected the policies even of so irreligious and allegedly tolerant a sovereign as Catherine II. A decree of 23 December 1791 set up the so-called Pale of Settlement, consisting of the western and south-western provinces, to which the Jews were confined. Residence or travel outside this region was only permitted in exceptional circumstances.[1]

Regions and Peoples of Russia

The Russian empire in Europe, as it was at the end of the eighteenth century, may be divided into a number of fairly distinct regions according to agricultural, historical, or ethnical differences.

Agriculturally, we may mention seven regions. In the extreme north was the Arctic tundra, along the Murman coast and the White Sea. South of this was the forest zone, of firs and birches, stretching through the provinces of Archangel and Vologda south to approximately the latitude of St. Petersburg on the sea and Nizhnii Novgorod on the Volga. In the western part of this area are the great lakes of Ladoga and Onega, besides many smaller lakes and swamps. The soil was of poor quality, mainly the so-called *podzol*, 'a thoroughly washed-out soil of rather coarse granular structure . . . generally whitish-grey in colour',[2] with a very thin admixture of humus. Cultivation of this soil, in the areas cleared of forest, produced meagre crops, but parts of the region were suitable for livestock. The third region was the mixed forest zone, which covered most of central and west-central Russia, extending almost to Kiev in the south-west and including the province of Vladimir in the east. Here the forest was less dense, and included deciduous trees, and the soil was of rather better quality, with admixtures of sand and clay. South-east of this region could be distinguished a narrow zone of transitional quality, where woodlands covered only a small part of the ground, and the soil showed great variety, from *podzol* to black earth. To the south of this zone came the great black-earth region, covering most of the Ukraine and the middle course of the Volga, and including vast areas of some of the richest agricultural soil in the world. In the northern part of the black-earth zone small plantations of trees were still to be seen in the nineteenth century, but the southern part was open

[1] These provinces were: Kovno, Vilna, Grodno, Mogilev, Vitebsk, Minsk, Volhynia, Podolia, Kiev (but excluding the city of Kiev), Ekaterinoslav, Kherson, Crimea, Poltava, and Chernigov. Bessarabia was added after 1812.

[2] G. Pavlovsky, *Agricultural Russia on the Eve of the Revolution* (1930), pp. 13–14.

steppe, rolling plains stretching away to the horizon. In the coastal steppes, along the Black Sea and in the area between the Don and the Caucasus, the black earth was varied with browner soil, and was somewhat less rich. Finally, the lower course of the Volga, and the territory between the Volga Delta and the Caucasus which faces towards the Caspian, had poorer soil, and large areas of salt-marshes.

The climate of European Russia as a whole is continental, with cold winters and hot summers. The severity of the climate increases from west to east, as the moderating influence of Atlantic air currents disappears, and the winters are of course colder in the more northerly latitudes. The Black Sea coastal areas have rather low rainfall, and the Caspian steppes very little indeed.

Historically the areas which have been inhabited for long periods by agricultural populations are those surrounding the cities of Kiev, Novgorod, and Moscow, dependent on the communications of the Dnieper, Dvina, Volkhov, and Volga rivers. Both military and political factors, and the central position between the great waterways, led to the development of the region around Moscow as the centre of industry. The southern regions, as we have seen, were acquired by stages as the Muscovite state expanded—the left bank of the lower Dnieper in the seventeenth century, the right bank from Poland a hundred years later, and the coastal steppes with the conquest of the Crimea about the same time.

The classification of Russian regions normally used in nineteenth-century historical literature is based on a combination of historical and economic factors. We thus have the following regions; northern, Lakes, Baltic, Lithuania, White Russia, central industrial, central black earth, Ukraine, New Russia, Volga, and Urals.[1]

[1] The provinces of European Russia were divided among them as follows: *northern*: Archangel, Vologda; *Lakes*: Olonets, St. Petersburg, Pskov, Novgorod; *Baltic*: Estland, Liefland (Livonia), Kurland; *Lithuania*: Vilna, Kovno, Grodno, Suvalki; *White Russia*: Mogilev, Vitebsk, Minsk, Smolensk; *central industrial*: Moscow, Tver, Kaluga, Yaroslavl, Vladimir, Kostroma; *central black earth*: Kursk, Oryol, Tula, Ryazan, Tambov, Voronezh, Penza; *Ukraine*: Kiev, Volhynia, Podolia, Kharkov, Poltava, Chernigov; *New Russia*: Kherson, Crimea, Ekaterinoslav, Don Cossacks, Stavropol; *Volga*: Nizhnii Novgorod, Kazan, Simbirsk, Samara, Saratov, Astrakhan; *Urals*: Vyatka, Perm, Ufa, Orenburg. In addition to these were Bessarabia, acquired in 1812 and thereafter reckoned as part of New Russia; the

The Russian empire was ethnically diverse, not only at the periphery but even at the centre. In the Volga valley lived a number of small ethnic groups, descendants either of the Finnish tribes with whom the medieval Slav colonists from the south had disputed the forests, or of the more culturally developed peoples who had established states along the Volga before the Mongol invasion. The Chuvash, who lived in the western part of Kazan province, spoke a language related to that of the original Bulgars who had once been a considerable power on the middle Volga. The Cheremyss (or Mari), inhabiting the right bank of the Volga in Simbirsk province, had been tributaries of the Bulgar state. Their language, belonging to the so-called Volga group of Finno-Ugrian languages, was closest to that of the Mordvins, who lived further west, between Ryazan and Simbirsk provinces. Further to the north-east, in the provinces of Vologda and Vyatka, were the Zyryans (or Komi) and Votyaks (or Udmurt), whose languages, closely related to each other, belong to the so-called Perm group of Finno-Ugrian languages.

The Zyryans and Votyaks came under Russian rule in the fourteenth and fifteenth centuries, with the expansion of the territory of Novgorod, and its smaller sister-republic of Vyatka. The Zyryans were converted to Christianity fairly quickly, but there were still some pagans among the Votyaks well into the nineteenth century. The Chuvash, Cheremyss, and Mordvins became Russian subjects after Ivan IV conquered the Tatar khanate of Kazan. Among these three peoples pagan beliefs were still strong in the nineteenth century, but many had also been converted to Christianity or Islam. Russian and Tatar missionaries continued to compete for proselytes.

Along the Volga, right down to the Caspian, were large numbers of Tatars, both in cities and in villages. In the Russian folk-song, the rebel Stenka Razin exclaims: 'Volga, Volga, my own mother, Volga the Russian river!'[1] But the truth is that, for most of known history, the Volga had been a Turkish—or Tatar-Turkic—river. The danger of anachronistic use of the

territories between the Sea of Azov and the Caucasus, which were conquered and reorganized at various times during the century; and Siberia and Central Asia. This classification is not completely satisfactory—for example, Smolensk belongs rather to the Moscow region than to White Russia, but it was not an industrial area. However, this is perhaps as good as can be made. See map no. 1, p. xxi.

[1] *Volga, Volga, mat' rodnaya / Volga, russkaya reka . . . .*

principles of one age in studying another is well illustrated by the cases of the Volga and the Balkans. If in the sixteenth–eighteenth centuries the expansion of states had been determined by Wilsonian principles of self-determination based on linguistic, religious, and cultural affinity, the Ottoman empire would have extended up the Volga beyond Kazan, while the Russian empire would have stretched down the west shore of the Black Sea to Constantinople. Things happened otherwise. A power based on a central position between the great Russian waterways expanded down the Volga to the Caspian and Caucasus, and through the southern steppes to the Black Sea. Having thus ignored the religious and ethnical interests of Tatars and other Moslems, it put forward the claim to defend the religious and ethnical interests of its own fellow Christians in the Balkans. On the other hand the Ottoman empire, involved in the Arab lands and warring with Persia or Venice or Spain, paid no attention to its fellow Moslems north of the Black Sea, and in its period of declining power found itself robbed of European and Arab provinces alike.

On the periphery of the empire the ethnical variety was still greater. In the Baltic provinces the peasants were Estonians or Latvians, and the upper class in town and country were Germans. Estonians, speaking a language closely related to Finnish, formed a majority in the historic province of Estland and in the northern part of the historic province of Livonia (Liefland). Latvians, whose language belongs to the separate Baltic group, were the majority in most of Livonia and in the adjacent province of Kurland. In all three provinces the religion was Protestant, and the political and cultural *élite* were German.

In the northern part of historical Lithuania the peasants were Lithuanians, speaking a Baltic language closely related to Latvian. Their religion, however, as a result of centuries of association with Poland, was Catholic. In the whole of the territory annexed from Poland the upper classes, and a considerable proportion of the peasants, were Poles, while the commercial class consisted primarily of Jews. The majority of the peasants, however, were not Poles. In the north they were Lithuanians; in the central portion White Russians, with a distinct spoken language of their own but as yet without a firm national consciousness; in the south 'Little Russians' or Ukrainians.

Thus, at the end of the eighteenth century Russia was a multinational empire. Non-Russians formed at least two-fifths of the population, and if Little Russians are regarded as a separate Ukrainian nation, then the Russians formed only about half the subjects of the Tsar.

But the appetite of Russian rulers for conquest was not yet satisfied. To the south-west, south-east, and east there were further lands to be won. Moldavia, with its Christian Orthodox Roumanian population, was longing (so they believed in St. Petersburg) to be liberated from the Turkish yoke. Beyond it lay the Danube, Bulgaria, and Constantinople.

To the south-east was the Caucasus range, and beyond it lay Persia. The Caucasus and Transcaucasia will be separately discussed in the following section.

To the east, beyond the Urals, lived nomadic Bashkir tribes. Beyond them, in the steppes reaching to the Aral Sea and to the edge of the Central Asian mountain ranges, were the nomadic Kazakhs.[1] These were Sunni Moslems, but their religion was to some extent mixed with remnants of earlier shamanistic beliefs, and they were governed not by the Moslem religious law (*shariat*), but by customary law (*adat*). They were divided into three main groups, known as the Little, Middle, and Great Hordes. The Little Horde accepted Russian suzerainty in 1731, the Middle Horde in 1734. The Russian authorities in Orenburg made little attempt to interfere in their internal government or social life, but were concerned only with peace and order along the undefined frontier.

In the Far East the Russians established themselves in Kamchatka in the reign of Peter the Great. In 1700 V. Atlasov captured a Japanese clerk from Osaka named Dembei,[2] and sent him back to Europe. He was received at Preobrazhenskoe Selo, near Moscow, by Peter himself, who showed great interest

[1] Kazakh is the name favoured by modern Russian historians, and officially used in the Soviet Union. In the nineteenth century the Kazakhs were usually called 'Kirgiz'. The people known in modern times as Kirgiz, much fewer in numbers and dwelling in the mountains at the south-east corner of the steppes, were distinguished from them in the nineteenth century by the name Kara-Kirgiz, or Black Kirgiz.

[2] There is an interesting account of this episode in G. A. Lensen, *The Russian Push towards Japan*, Princeton, 1959. This excellent book may be strongly recommended for the study of Russian activities in the Pacific up to the late nineteenth century.

in Japan, and gave instructions for future exploration in that direction. In the next years Russians visited some of the Kurile Islands and the coast of the Sea of Okhotsk. In the 1730's the Dane Vitus Behring, a naval captain in Russian service, travelled widely in the northern Pacific, and gave his name to the straits which separate Asia from North America. In 1739 an expedition under his subordinate, Lieutenant-Commander Martin Spanberg, sailed to the coast of Japan, but the Japanese, under the policy of isolation from the outer world pursued by the Tokugawa Shogunate, would not allow them to proceed further. A second expedition in 1742 was no more successful. In October 1792 a Russian expedition, bringing some Japanese subjects who had been shipwrecked in Russian waters, visited the island of Hokkaido. Officials from the Japanese capital Yedo accepted the repatriated Japanese, but told the Russians that no communication with the Japanese government would be permitted except through the small Dutch settlement at Nagasaki.

In the eighteenth century Russian settlements were established on the North American continent. A Siberian merchant named Shelikhov equipped expeditions to the Kuriles in the 1770's and to Unalaska and Kodiak Islands and the mainland of Alaska between 1783 and 1789. In 1788 Shelikhov entrusted the settlement on Kodiak to A. A. Baranov, who spent the next thirty years in the region. In 1797 a United American Company was created, and in 1799 it was renamed Russian-American Company. Under the statute granted by Emperor Paul, it was solely responsible for administering the Russian settlements in North America, north of 55°, and the Aleutian and Kurile Islands. It had a monopoly of the exploitation of resources and trade within this area, and was also given the task of establishing regular relations with Japan. The company was modelled on the great European trading companies of the East, but in practice was controlled to a greater extent than its western prototypes by government officials, if only because the merchant class was so much smaller and weaker in Russia than in England, Holland, or France. The administrative centre of the company was the settlement of Novo-Arkhangelsk on Sitka island off Alaska.

The Caucasus and Transcaucasia

Kievan Russia had some contact with the peoples and principalities of the Caucasus. As the Tatar power receded from south-eastern Russia, Cossacks established themselves in the Kuban steppe and the Russian state was again brought into touch with the Caucasians. But it was not until the eighteenth century that Russian expansion in this region became important, and that Transcaucasia became a major theatre of war with both Turkey and Persia. At this point it is necessary briefly to explain the physical and human geography, and the earlier history, of the Caucasian region.

The main Caucasus range stretches for about 600 miles from north-west to south-east, between the Black Sea and the Caspian, reaching in places higher altitudes than the Alps. There are two natural points of crossing. One is along the Caspian coast, where there is a strip of flat land between the foothills and the sea, only six miles broad at its narrowest point near Derbent. The second is by the Daryal pass in the centre of the range. From the north this route mounts the valley of the Terek to the Daryal gorge, and there crossing the watershed descends the valley of the Aragvi until it joins the Kura. The Black Sea coast is much steeper than the Caspian, and no satisfactory roads were built there until long after the Russian conquest in the nineteenth century.

The peoples of the Caucasus are of various origin, and separated by language barriers. The westernmost of the main groups were the Circassians, or Cherkess, long famous both as slaves and as mercenary soldiers in the kingdoms of the Middle East. Further to the east was the kingdom of Kabarda, of mixed population but ruled by Circassian nobles, with which Russia entered into friendly relations early in the eighteenth century. To its east, inhabiting both sides of the watershed at the Daryal pass, were the Ossetins, a Christian people speaking an Indo-European language who also became friends of Russia at an early stage. To the east of them were the Chechens and Ingush, and beyond them the area known as Daghestan, whose two most important peoples were the Lezghians and the Avars. The Circassians in the west and the Chechens and Daghestanis in the east were fanatical Moslems and bitterly resisted Russian penetration. In their mountain fastnesses they were at this time invincible. But the friendship of Kabardans and Ossetins enabled the Russians to use the Daryal pass.

Beyond the main Caucasus lie two river basins, separated from each other by the lesser but still formidable range of the Little Caucasus, or Suram. The westerly region, the basin of the Rion, faces the Black Sea, the easterly, the basin of the Kura and Araxes, the Caspian. These two basins, and the mountainous area between them, were inhabited for centuries by the various branches of the Georgian people, Christian by religion and speaking closely connected languages.[1] But the lands nearest to the Caspian had, since the Arab invasions of the seventh century, been populated by Moslems. In the eighteenth century their inhabitants spoke a language very close to the Turkish of Anatolia. This region was known as Azerbaidjan, its people as Azeri Turks, or more loosely as Tatars. They belonged to the Shia branch of Islam: thus while their language linked them to the Turks, their religion bound them to Persia. Beyond Georgia and Azerbaidjan were the Ottoman and Persian empires. But in the border regions of both empires a large part of the population were Armenians, a Christian nation with a very ancient history. A few words are necessary at this point on the earlier history of both Georgia and Armenia.

The basin of the Rion was the ancient land of Colchis, the home of the mythical Golden Fleece. Central Georgia was known in Roman times as the kingdom of Iberia, and the Caspian region as the kingdom of Albania. In the centuries of war between Rome and the Parthian or Sassanid rulers of Persia, Colchis was normally a satellite of Rome, while Iberia was an object of rivalry. Both kingdoms became Christian in the fourth century. In the seventh century they were overrun by the Arabs.

As the Abbasid Caliphate of Baghdad declined, Moslem rule in the Caucasus area split up into several small principalities, and though in the eleventh century the Seldjuk Turks for a time

[1] In modern times three branches have been distinguished within the Kartvelian group of related languages: Georgian, Zan (which includes Mingrelian, Chan or Laz dialects), and Svan. For a brief survey see article on Ibero-Caucasian languages in *Bolshaya Sovetskaya Entsiklopediya* (2nd edition, Moscow, 1949–57), xvii, 250–3. For a brief survey by a British scholar see W. K. Matthews, *Languages of the U.S.S.R.* (Cambridge, 1951), pp. 86–101.

imposed a strong united power, the same splitting process set in again. The result was that the Georgians for more than a century freed themselves from foreign domination, and united in a single kingdom. The greatest period of medieval Georgian history was the reign of Queen Tamara (1184–1212) whose realm extended to most of Azerbaidjan. Soon after her death the Mongol invasion brought the disintegration of Georgia into several more or less independent small principalities. The rise of the Ottoman empire in the fifteenth century, and of the Safavid dynasty in Persia in the sixteenth restored Georgia to its traditional situation of buffer state between two Great Powers, one based on Asia Minor and the other on Iran. But now for the first time both these Powers were Moslem.

In the eighteenth century there were three Georgian principalities on the west side of the Suram, all more or less dependent on Turkey, and two on the eastern side, vassals of Persia. The first group were Mingrelia and Guria, both of which had a portion of Black Sea coastline, and Imeretia, which lay inland from them. All three were Christian kingdoms. There were, however, peoples of Georgian language and Moslem faith, Adjars and Lazes, loyal subjects of the Ottoman Sultans, living to the south and west of Guria. The two principalities on the eastern side were Kartli, with its capital at Tiflis, in the centre of the isthmus and in the upper valley of the Kura, and Kakhetiya to the east of it.

Armenia had a still longer history. Based on the eastern part of Asia Minor, it was an ally of Rome in the second century B.C. Under King Tigranes the Great (95–66 B.C.) it extended into Syria and Mesopotamia. Defeated by Pompey, Tigranes became a client of Rome. The Armenians became Christians at the turn of the third and fourth centuries A.D., and later embraced the monophysite heresy. This has been the doctrine of the Armenian Church ever since, but the Georgian Church, which was also monophysite in the sixth century, reverted to orthodoxy in 608. Armenia was for centuries an object of contention between Rome and Persia, and often a field of battle.

Rome was replaced by Byzantium, and Persia by the Arabs and then the Seldjuks, but the Armenians' basic predicament remained. From 809 to 1045 the Bagratid dynasty (which for a time also ruled part of Georgia) obtained wide autonomy for

Armenia, under the nominal suzerainty of Baghdad, but in the wars between Byzantines and Seldjuks in the second half of the eleventh century it broke up. There were Armenian rulers further south, in Cilicia, in the twelfth and thirteenth centuries, in alliance first with the Crusaders and then with the Mongols against the powerful rulers of Egypt. But in the Armenian homeland of eastern Asia Minor there was no more independence.

By the beginning of the sixteenth century all Armenia belonged to the Ottoman empire. The Armenian Church, like other non-Moslem religious organizations, enjoyed its cultural autonomy under the Sultans, but there was no question of political rights. As a result of war between the Ottoman and Safavid empires at the beginning of the seventeenth century, the region of Erivan was annexed to Persia. There were also Armenian trading communities in Tiflis and in many cities of the Middle East and of Europe.

The first major Russian expedition into Transcaucasia was undertaken by Peter the Great. Persia at the beginning of the eighteenth century was torn by internal disorders, and weakened by invasions of tribesmen from Afghanistan. The empire was on the verge of collapse. The Russian governor of Astrakhan stressed in his reports to the emperor the strategic importance of Transcaucasia for future conflicts with Turkey. Once the Great Northern War had been settled by the Peace of Nystad, Peter decided to undertake an invasion of Persia. In the summer of 1722 he led an army along the Caspian coast. Derbent was captured in August, and Baku fell in the summer of 1723. However, the Russian successes alarmed the Turks, who invaded Georgia. The king of Kartli and Kakhetiya, Wakhtang VI, though a vassal of the Shah of Persia, had joined the Russians in the war. Now his kingdom was overrun by the Turks, and Peter gave him no help. A Russo-Turkish peace treaty of July 1724 left Georgia in the hands of the Turks, while the Sultan recognized Russian gains on the eastern side of the Suram watershed, including Derbent and Baku.

This settlement did not last long. In Persia a military adventurer made himself emperor, with the title of Nadir Shah, and embarked on a brilliant career of conquest of India and in the Caucasus, which was Persia's swan song as a Great Power. Peter's successors were not interested in Transcaucasian conquests, and welcomed a strong Persia as a counterbalance to the Ottoman empire. By the Treaty of Gandja, in 1735, Empress Anna restored to Persia Derbent and Baku, and Nadir Shah reconquered Georgia. He was loyally aided in all his campaigns by the Georgian prince Hercules II, whom he installed as king of Kartli and Kakhetiya, and who ruled from 1744 to 1798.

After Nadir Shah was murdered in 1747, Persia was once more torn by internal struggles for forty years. Hercules sought protection against the more serious Turkish danger, and found it in Russia. He was the ally of Catherine II in her war of 1768–74 against Turkey. In 1783 he signed the Treaty of Georgievsk, by which Georgia was placed under Russian protectorate. Georgia was to have no foreign relations except through Russian channels, and there were to be Russian troops in the country. Russia was committed to defend Georgia, and to uphold the authority of the Georgian monarchy.

The desire of the Georgian ruler for Russian help was genuine, and in the circumstances it was the best policy available. As a Christian Orthodox Power, Russia was far more likely to respect Georgian interests than either Turkey or Persia. But Georgia was not of great importance to Russia. In 1795 the founder of a new Persian dynasty, Aga Mohammed Shah, decided to reconquer his predecessors' tributary. His troops captured and sacked Tiflis, and massacred the population, including some Russian subjects. No Russian help was available. In 1796 a Russian army was sent, under the Zubov brothers, to avenge the disaster, but when Catherine II died, the Emperor Paul recalled the expedition before any decisive results had been achieved.

King Hercules did not, however, give up the hope of Russian protection. Aga Mohammed Shah was murdered in 1797, and Persian pressure was relaxed. In 1798 Hercules died. His successor, George XIII, decided that the best solution would be to incorporate Georgia in the Russian empire. He wished, however, to make sure that his son David would succeed him, and that the Russian emperor would guarantee the right of his dynasty to rule the country under his suzerainty. Paul had now changed his mind, and decided to take an interest in Georgia. During 1799 negotiations took place in St. Petersburg. Paul decided that he would simply annex Georgia. The death of

George XIII in December 1800, and the murder of Paul in March 1801, complicated matters. The new emperor, Alexander I, hesitated for six months, but finally issued a manifesto on 12 December 1801, confirming the annexation.

The Reign of Paul I

When Catherine II died in 1796, she was succeeded by her son Paul. He had been born in 1754 but was removed from his mother's care by the reigning Empress Elizabeth. He received a good education under the supervision of Count Nikita Panin. In 1776 he married, as his second wife, Princess Sophie Dorothea of Württemberg (renamed Marya Fyodorovna on her acceptance into the Orthodox Church) and in 1782–3 the grandducal couple made a long tour of Europe. Paul's outlook can perhaps be described as one of enlightened absolute monarchy. He had a high idea of the vocation of the ruler, believed that he should preserve a strict morality, should care for the welfare of his subjects, but should keep the power in his hands. This of course accorded with the traditions of Russia, in which the initiative was expected to come neither from the people nor from a social *élite*, but from the Tsar. Paul detested the French Revolution not because he sympathized with the old régime but because the revolutionaries had laid sacrilegious hands on the monarchy.

Paul was on bad terms with his mother. When he was a child, she feared that he might be used by her enemies to take the throne from her. When he had grown up, she kept him out of affairs of state. He was ignored or humiliated by several of her favourites. His first two sons, the granddukes Alexander and Constantine, were taken away from him by Catherine, as he had been taken from her by Elizabeth. Paul and his wife were only allowed to bring up their younger children—Nicholas (later Emperor Nicholas I), Michael, Catherine, and Anna (later queen of Holland). In the words of Queen Anna, written many years later,

Mon père . . . nous faisait venir chez lui, Nicolas, Michel et moi, pour jouer dans sa chambre pendant qu'on le coiffait, seul moment de loisir qu'il eût. C'était surtout dans le dernier temps de sa vie. Il était tendre et si bon avec nous que nous aimions aller chez lui. Il disait qu'on l'avait éloigné de ses enfants aînés, en les lui enlevant dès qu'ils étaient nés, mais qu'il voulait s'entourer des cadets pour les connaître.

In 1783 he was given the palace and estate of Gatchina, not far from St. Petersburg, where he maintained his own small court, and took an active interest in the management of the land, and especially in the small private army which he clad and drilled according to his tastes. Catherine, however, never overcame her dislike for him. She wished to make his eldest son Alexander her successor, thus bypassing Paul. In the end, however, no definite decision was taken,[1] and Paul became emperor.

His first acts were magnanimous. Catherine's favourites lost influence, but were not punished. Novikov was freed from prison, and Radishchev allowed to live on his estate. Paul released the Poles taken prisoner in 1795, personally received Kościuszko in audience, and allowed him to leave Russia. He permitted himself one macabre gesture at the expense of his mother. Peter III's remains were disinterred, and his coffin was placed beside Catherine's in a joint funeral procession which ended in their burial side by side in the Cathedral of Peter and Paul.

Paul's use of the machinery of government tended in the direction of centralization. He restored some of the central departments abolished by Catherine in 1775—those of mining, industry, trade, and revenue. Though these and the other central departments retained Peter's name of 'colleges', in practice they were bureaucratically subordinate institutions, and the consultative element on which earlier emphasis had been placed was little more than a fiction. The office of procurator remained the most important under the Tsar. The procurator combined the duties of a minister of justice, finance, and public order. For the first two and a half years of the reign this office was held by Prince Alexei Kurakin, but in the last two it was held successively by three persons, none of whom made much mark. The Senate remained the supreme judicial authority, and it was made somewhat more efficient. The number of senators was reduced, while their clerical assistants were increased. Its business was more speedily conducted.[2]

[1] See below p. 70.

[2] In 1797 20,838 decisions were given, in 1800 44,480. M. V. Klochkov, *Ocherki pravitel'stvennoy deyatel'nosti vremeni Imperatora Pavla I* (Petrograd, 1916), p. 219.

Paul to some extent reversed the policy of his mother towards the nobility. He had little sympathy for their privileges or liberties. Though the decree of 1762 was not repealed, he urged provincial governors to press young noblemen into state service. The provincial assemblies of the nobility, established by the 1785 Charter, were abolished, and state officials at the district level were appointed by the government instead of being elected by the nobility. Only the officials of the nobles' own class organization, the provincial and district marshals and the persons charged with keeping the records of families of noble status (*rodoslovnaya kniga*) were now elected by the nobles. Paul also levied a tax on landed estates. Another aspect of Paul's policy which displeased the nobility was his insistence on much tighter discipline in the army, greater devotion to duty and to professional efficiency, and less display of wealth and finery. Paul also sought to diminish the privileged status of the Guards regiments in relation to the rest of the army, while promoting officers who had served in his Gatchina force.

But though Paul was severe to the nobility, it would be too much to represent him as a benefactor of the serfs. He did restore the right of petition to the Tsar, though only for an individual and not for a group of serfs. He also forbade landlords to make serfs work on Sundays. The same manifesto in which this was stated also said that serfs should only work three days in the week for their lords, but it has never been clear whether this was an order or a statement of a pious intention, and it is certain that it was not effectively carried out. A decree of October 1798 prohibited the sale of serfs without land in the Ukraine only.

He introduced some changes affecting the state peasants. A decree of 7 August 1797 introduced, for territories belonging to the state, a new administrative unit, the *volost*, at a level intermediate between the *uezd* and the village. The *volost* mayor and notary were to be elected for two-year periods of office by all the householders of the area. This system was applied in a large part of northern Russia, but did not affect the population of landlords' private estates. Whether the state peasants benefited much from the change is doubtful. Paul also made clear the distinction between state lands and the property of the Imperial family. By a decree of 5 April 1797 the latter were placed under a separate Department of Appanages (*udely*). On the other hand, Paul in effect harmed many state peasants because, following Catherine's example, he made large presents to his friends of state lands inhabited by peasants. More than half a million peasants in this way became serfs of private landowners during the reign.

In foreign policy Paul was at first pacific. He withdrew Russian troops from Persia, thus leaving his ally the king of Georgia to Persian revenge. He also decided not to send the expeditionary force to the Rhine, to join the Austrians against France, which Catherine had been planning. But within two years he was brought into conflict with France by another, inherently rather trivial, affair.

The Maltese Order of Knights had had a priory in Volhynia, which was annexed from Poland to Russia by the partitions. In 1795 an emissary of the Order, Count Litta, came to Russia to obtain recognition of the Order's rights. Catherine was unfriendly, but when Paul became emperor he received Litta well, accepted the Order's claims, and made further endowment of funds to the priory. When in June 1798 Napoleon occupied Malta, the Volhynian priory offered the grand mastership of the whole Order to Paul. Though their constitutional right to make such an offer was dubious, Paul accepted it. When Napoleon ignored his requests to evacuate the island, Paul decided to join the enemies of France.

Napoleon's occupation of Malta was part of the strategy of attacking England in the east, the central feature of which was the invasion of Egypt. But Egypt was legally part of the Ottoman empire. The Sultan, finding himself suddenly attacked by the European Power which was the traditional ally of his country, looked for help to his traditional enemy, Russia. In 1798 Russia and Turkey made a treaty of alliance, and Russian warships passed through the Straits as friends.

By the Peace of Campo Formio of October 1797, which had ended war between France and Austria, the territories of the Venetian republic had been divided between the two Powers. In compensation for the loss of Lombardy to France, Austria received the main Italian territories of Venice, while France acquired the Dalmatian and Ionian islands. Paul decided to attack the French in the Adriatic. In October 1798 a joint

Russian and Turkish fleet attacked the Ionian islands. The population gladly greeted the Russians. The only serious resistance came from the French garrison of Corfu, which held out until March 1790. A Greek administration was set up, and a Russo-Turkish convention approved the establishment of an independent republic of the Seven Islands. The new state's constitution, under which power was held by an aristocratic and patrician oligarchy, was submitted to Alexander I shortly after his accession.

Nelson's victory over Napoleon in August 1798 at Aboukir Bay in Egypt encouraged Austria to return to the struggle, and in 1799 the Second Coalition against France came into being, composed of Britain, Russia, Austria, Turkey, and Naples. An Austro-Russian army under Suvorov invaded Lombardy in April. It was extremely successful. A first victory on the Adda (26–27 April) led to the capture of Milan and Turin. On 17–19 June Suvorov defeated Macdonald on the Trebbia, and on 16–17 August he won his third victory, over Moreau, at Novi. Meanwhile the Kingdom of Naples had been cleared of French troops.

All this time Napoleon himself was cut off in Egypt. But in France new armies were assembled for a counter-offensive against the enemy, and Suvorov was ordered to bring his army into Switzerland to meet them. Relations between Suvorov and the Austrian supreme command (the *Hofkriegsrat* in Vienna) had deteriorated, partly because he had shown some encouragement to Italian nationalism, partly because of a conflict between Paul's policy of restoring the king of Sardinia and Austria's further territorial ambitions in north Italy. At the end of August the Austrian Archduke Charles decided to evacuate Switzerland, leaving the Russian forces to face the French alone.

At the end of September a Russian army under Korsakov was defeated with heavy losses by Marshal Masséna at the Battle of Zürich. About the same time Suvorov crossed the Alps in extremely difficult conditions, fought some successful rearguard actions against the French, and retreated through Bohemia into Russian territory. Austro-Russian relations had now become extremely bitter, and Paul was infuriated when he heard that an Austrian general had insulted the Russian flag at the Italian town of Ancona. At the end of October Paul wrote to Emperor Francis: 'From this moment I abandon your interests.'

Relations with Britain were also deteriorating. At the end of August 1799 some British troops landed in Holland, and were joined two weeks later by two Russian divisions. The joint operations were a failure, and the commander, the Duke of York, asked the French for an armistice and withdrew the allied forces. The occupation of Malta by the British in October 1800, though justifiable in terms of allied Mediterranean strategy, infuriated Paul as grand master of the Order. British treatment of neutral shipping also harmed Russian interests. This caused Paul to return to the earlier policy of Catherine II, of a common front against Britain with Sweden and Denmark. In December 1800 these three Powers and Prussia signed a Treaty of Armed Neutrality, clearly directed against Britain.

Paul also quarrelled with the exiled heir to the French throne, the later Louis XVIII, to whom he had previously granted hospitality, and expelled him and his court from their residence in the Baltic city of Mitau in February 1800. Meanwhile Napoleon, who had got back from Egypt, took command in Italy and defeated the Austrians at the Battle of Marengo on 14 June 1800. He then made overtures to Paul for peace and for an alliance against Britain. Paul did not accept, but by this time he certainly considered Britain rather than France as his main enemy. Meanwhile hostilities between France and Austria were ended in December 1800, and peace was made at Lunéville on 9 February 1801.

In January 1801 Paul ordered 20,000 Cossacks to march from Orenburg to invade British India. This grotesque plan had no military significance, but at least showed its author's state of mind. On 2 April Nelson attacked and destroyed the Danish fleet at Copenhagen. It seemed possible that British warships would enter Russian waters.

The situation of Russia was extraordinary. She was still at war with France, though Napoleon was continuing his efforts to make Russia his ally. With Austria she had no diplomatic relations, and with Britain she was in a state of undeclared war. The only considerable Power with which Russia had relatively good relations at this time was the traditional enemy, the Ottoman empire.

To those closest to him, Paul was an unpredictable master, changing without notice from cordiality to hatred, alternating acts of great generosity with brutal injustices. The contradictions of his foreign policy were bound to alarm Russian patriots. The emperor was believed to be mad, though the evidence is not sufficient to prove this view. Court intrigues and jealousies, the resentment among the Guards and the nobility, and the atmosphere of personal insecurity at the top almost inevitably combined to produce the result so familiar in the political life of eighteenth-century Russia, a conspiracy to dethrone the Tsar. The first eminent plotter was Count Panin, Paul's first foreign minister, who had been replaced by the Anglophobe Count F. V. Rostopchin. His soundings of leading figures, including Grand Duke Alexander, led to nothing. But at the end of 1800 the matter was taken up by a more formidable character, the governor-general of St. Petersburg, Count Peter von Pahlen, who obtained the consent of the grand duke to the deposition and carried it out with the help of a small group of army officers. On 23 March 1801 the conspirators seized the Mikhailovsky Palace, and not only deposed the emperor but strangled him.

PART II

THE ALEXANDRINE AGE

III

REFORM AND RESISTANCE

The Unofficial Committee

THE future Emperor Alexander I was born on 12 December 1777. Without consulting his parents, his grandmother Catherine II entrusted his education to General N. I. Saltykov, a firm believer in the principles of autocracy. Among his tutors were the German geographer Pallas and the writer Michael Muravyov, who later played a leading part in the creation of the Ministry of Education. The most important, however, was the Swiss César Laharpe, who came to Russia in 1783 at the age of twenty-nine, escorting the brother of Catherine's favourite Lanskoy, obtained the post of tutor in French to Alexander, and shortly afterwards became his principal tutor. For ten years, until his departure from Russia on Catherine's orders, he exercised a great influence over the young prince. Laharpe was a radical, and preached the doctrines of the French radical thinkers of his day, tempering these, however, for prudence's sake with recognition of the virtues of enlightened absolutism.

As Alexander grew up, Catherine somewhat relented in her practice of separating him from his father. He was allowed to visit Paul's little court at Gatchina. Here Alexander and his younger brother Constantine rapidly acquired a taste for the drill-ground. Uniforms, parades, and shouting of orders gave him great pleasure, and continued to do so throughout his life. At Gatchina Alexander made friends with one of his father's intimates, Alexei Andreyevich Arakcheyev.

Arakcheyev was born in 1769, the son of a small landowner in Tula province. He became an artillery officer, and in 1792 was brought to the attention of Grand Duke Paul. He became Paul's chief adviser at Gatchina, in command of his private army. Personally unattractive: (a contemporary speaks of his 'small, terribly cold eyes' and his 'thick, very inelegant nose, shaped like a shoe'), he was a fanatical upholder of discipline, but an extremely able and honest organizer. While serving Paul, he also paid close attention to his heir, and won the confidence of Alexander as an adolescent by frequent minor services and attentions. He prided himself on being a blunt speaker, incapable of subtle intrigues or false ingratiating tactics. With his cruelty to subordinates, his prurient interference in people's lives, his belief that anything could be done if orders were sufficiently brutal and repeated, his refusal to make himself popular, and his strong devotion to duty, Arakcheyev was an invaluable servant of his two masters. For Alexander, he operated as a political lightning-conductor, diverting discontent from his master to himself. 'He was the shadow cast over Russia by the imposing figure of Alexander, all shining with glory, surrounded by hymns of delight and praise. But surely the outline of a shadow is determined by the figure which it accompanies?'[1]

During her last years Catherine II seriously considered removing Paul from the succession and making Alexander her heir. At various times in the last three years of her reign she tried to enlist the support of Laharpe, of her daughter-in-law, and of the Council of State. Later still Catherine approached Alexander himself. In a letter of 24 September 1796 he gave his consent, in vague terms.[2] At the same time, however, Alexander stressed his devotion to his father, and wrote to Arakcheyev referring to Paul in anticipation as Imperial Majesty.

The pupil of Laharpe was filled with indignation at the injus-

[1] A. Kizevetter, *Istoricheskie ocherki* (Moscow, 1912), p. 289. He refused all decorations offered to him by Alexander, and appeared at magnificent receptions clad in a dirty service overcoat. His motto was '*Bez lesti predan*' ('devoted without flattery'). It was certainly true that he was unable or unwilling to cultivate charming manners, but not perhaps true that he was incapable of flattery. His enemies adapted his motto to '*Bes, lesti predan*' ('a devil, given up to flattery').

[2] The text of the letter is in N. K. Shilder, *Imperator Aleksandr I, ego zhizn' i tsarstvovanie* (SPB, 1897), i. 279.

tices of Russian political life. In a letter of 10 May 1796 to Count Kochubey, he wrote: 'Nos affaires sont dans un désordre incroyable, on pille de tous les côtés.' To govern Russia, and still more to correct its abuses, was 'impossible non seulement à un homme de capacités ordinaires, comme moi, mais même à un génie'. He therefore intended to give up his rights and 'ayant une fois renoncé à cette place scabreuse', to go and live quietly with his wife beside the Rhine.[1]

A year later, however, he had changed his mind. In a letter sent by safe hand of his friend Novosiltsov to Laharpe in Switzerland, dated 27 September 1797, he asked his former tutor's advice on a matter of the greatest importance, 'celle de faire le bonheur de la Russie en y établissant un [*sic*] constitution libre'. His father's reign had begun well, but had soon gone wrong:

> Tout a été mis sens dessus dessous à la fois, ce qui n'a fait qu'augmenter la confusion déjà trop grande qui régnait déjà dans les affaires. Le militaire perd presque tout son temps et cela en parades. Dans le reste il n'y a aucun plan suivi. On ordonne aujourd'hui ce qu'un mois après on contremande. On ne souffre jamais aucune représentation que quand le mal est déjà fait. Enfin, pour trancher le terme, le bonheur de l'État n'entre pour rien dans le régissement des affaires; il n'y a qu'un pouvoir absolu qui fait tout à tort et à travers.[2]

He himself was forced to spend his time on 'devoirs de bas officiers'. He had wished to give up his rights, but now felt that the best way to remedy these evils was a revolution 'opérée par un pouvoir légal qui cesserait de l'être aussitôt que la constitution serait achevée et que la nation aurait de représentants'. Meanwhile he and his intimate circle were trying to select good books for translation and circulation, in order to educate the people and spread useful knowledge. When 'his turn' came, he would prepare a constitution, and then hand over power to the people.

As we have seen, Alexander gave his consent to the conspiracy against his father. It can, however, be argued that he honestly believed that his father's life would be spared, that the tragedy of his grandfather would not be repeated. Alexander was indeed

[1] Ibid. i. 276–8. [2] Ibid. i. 280–2.

capable of self-persuasion, or self-deception, capable of keeping his ideas at an abstract level, ignoring unpleasant details of reality. The brutal murder of Paul left its traces on him for the rest of his life. Among other things, it partly explains the ascendancy of Arakcheyev over him. Arakcheyev liked to emphasize that he had been personally loyal to both father and son. At his estate at Gruzino, Arakcheyev had a sort of shrine devoted to the memory of Emperor Paul, which he showed to Alexander when he visited him there.

Alexander became emperor at the age of twenty-four. His accession was greeted with enthusiasm at least in the capital, where those threatened by Paul's arbitrary terror could breathe again, and where those who hoped for new things could put their hopes in the young prince. Contemporary accounts agree that he had great charm. His manner was friendly and modest, even ostentatiously so, to the point of deliberately scorning pomp and ceremony. But on the parade ground he showed himself a worthy pupil of Gatchina. He all too readily expressed agreement with those with whom he talked, but when it came to translating his words into action delays and obstacles soon appeared, chief among these his own caution. The need to be all things to all men, and in particular to make a good impression on both his grandmother and his father, had developed in him at an early age great ability as an actor. Those who knew him best insisted on his extreme distrustfulness. It was not so much that he was insincere, or that he changed his opinions—though during twenty-four years of reigning, including many years of war and Napoleon's invasion of Russia, his outlook inevitably evolved. It was rather that he formed his opinions slowly and secretly, trusting no one. He could be extremely tenacious, not to say obstinate, as Napoleon found to his cost. In his political outlook, liberalism and autocracy, the ideas of Laharpe and Arakcheyev, existed side by side. His reforming zeal was genuine, but abstract. It existed in him at a different level from practical political action. Sometimes the two levels intersected, but often they did not.

Alexander began his reign by remedying some of the injustices committed by Paul against individuals. About 12,000 army officers and civil officials whom Paul had disgraced were reinstated in their appointments. Count N. P. Panin was recalled to St. Petersburg and placed in charge of the College of Foreign Affairs, but his tenure was brief. The regicide Count von Pahlen did not enjoy power for long: on 10 June it was announced that he had retired to his estate on grounds of health.

Alexander also showed concern for the liberties of his subjects. He repealed various prohibitions on exports and imports, and granted an amnesty to persons who had fled from Russia. He abolished the Secret Expedition (secret police) and transferred to the Senate all matters that had previously come under the Expedition's jurisdiction. He also instructed two senators to inquire into the condition of the Dukhobor sect, which had been involved in some disorders in Tambov province. As a result of their report, he decided to permit the Dukhobors to move as a community to some land set apart for them near Melitopol in the province of Crimea, and to live there according to their beliefs. This was announced in a decree of 16 December 1804, and the movement to the Crimea was completed in the following years.

Alexander promised to return to the policies of Catherine. He announced on 2 April 1801 that Catherine's Charter to the nobility of 1785 and her regulations for the cities were fully restored. On 5 April he instituted a Permanent Council of the highest dignitaries, corresponding approximately to the council created by Catherine in 1768. It was divided into four sections—foreign and commercial, military and naval, civil and spiritual, and state economy. D. P. Troshchinsky, who had served as procurator-general under Catherine II, was appointed head of its chancery. On 5 June the Tsar declared his intention to restore the ancient authority of the Senate, and set up a commission to establish the laws. All these measures were pleasing to the surviving dignitaries of Catherine's reign. They hoped indeed that, the nightmare of Paul's autocracy over, there would be a return to oligarchy, and that they would manage the young ruler. But they were at least partly disappointed. Alexander was also concerned to introduce major reforms, to transform Russia and bring new forces to power. In this he had the enthusiastic help of four intimate friends of the 1790's—Adam Czartoryski, Paul Stroganov, Victor Kochubey, and Nicholas Novosiltsov.

Prince Adam Czartoryski, born 1770, belonged to the leading aristocratic family of Poland, which in the last decades of that country's independence had been associated with a Russophil policy. Prince Adam was, however, brought up by his mother in a strongly patriotic Polish outlook, and took part in the war against the Russians in 1792. He spent several years in England and France, and acquired liberal sympathies. In May 1795 he and his brother were sent to St. Petersburg to enter Russian government service, this being a condition required by Catherine II for the restoration of the family estates, which had been confiscated after the Third Partition, and for whose restitution the Austrian emperor had interceded. In the spring of 1796, during a walk in the garden of the Taurid Palace, Alexander declared to him his abhorrence of Catherine's treatment of Poland, his love of liberty, and his joy at the establishment of the French republic, despite the excesses of the Revolution.[1] Thereafter Prince Adam saw a great deal of Alexander, and Catherine encouraged the friendship.

Among the houses at which Czartoryski was a frequent visitor was that of Count Alexander Stroganov, a great magnate who owned vast areas of the Urals and Siberia. Though closely acquainted with most leading figures of the time, Stroganov had kept out of politics and devoted himself to the patronage of art and letters. He sent his young son Paul to France with his tutor, a Frenchman named Gilbert Romme, and they were there during the first years of the Revolution. Romme used to take his pupil to meetings of the Jacobin Club, of which he himself was a member. When news of these activities reached Russia, his father decided to bring him home and sent his half-nephew, N. N. Novosiltsov, to fetch him back. Novosiltsov thus acquired great influence in the Stroganov family. He was considerably older than Paul Stroganov and Czartoryski, being born in 1762. He had at this time liberal sympathies. He was, however, much less emotional and warm-hearted than the younger Stroganov. He had few prejudices and few scruples, little book-learning but great administrative ability. It was Czartoryski who introduced Alexander to Novosiltsov and Paul Stroganov, at the time of Paul's coronation in Moscow, when they had a frank and intimate discussion of their political ideas. Alexander thereafter obtained a passport for Novosiltsov to go to England, where he remained until the end of the reign. Czartoryski was sent as

[1] *Mémoires du prince Adam Czartoryski* (Paris, 1887), i. 95–97.

Russian minister to Sardinia in 1798. Paul Stroganov, however, remained in contact with Alexander during the reign of the Emperor Paul.

The fourth member of Alexander's intimate circle, Count Victor Kochubey, was a nephew of Catherine's procurator, Prince Bezborodko. When he was still under thirty years of age, he was appointed Russian ambassador at Constantinople. On his return to St. Petersburg in 1798, the emperor asked him to be an adviser to his son, and they were often in contact. Kochubey also made friends at this time with Paul Stroganov. The influence of his uncle Bezborodko was strongly in favour of autocracy. A statement which he gave to his nephew contained the following passage:

> Russia must be an autocratic state. The least weakening of autocracy would lead to the separation of many provinces, the weakening of the state, and countless disasters to the nation. But an autocratic ruler, if he is endowed with qualities worthy of his rank, must feel that unlimited power has been granted him, not to conduct his affairs according to his whims, but to keep the laws of his ancestors respected and executed, and to have them defined by himself; in a word, declaring his law he is, so to speak, the first person to honour and obey it, that others may not think that they can avoid it or deviate from it.[1]

It is interesting that these views were accepted enthusiastically by Paul Stroganov, to whom Kochubey showed the memorandum. Stroganov was a passionate reformer, but he believed that reforms should be carried out from above, by a strong ruler.

These four men formed Alexander's intimate circle soon after his accession. Czartoryski and Novosiltsov were quickly recalled from abroad. The four men formed an 'unofficial committee', to meet with the emperor frequently in the evenings and discuss general policy. At an early stage they agreed that it would be better not to try to produce a constitution for Russia (which had been Alexander's original plan), but to examine the machinery of government as it existed, and to decide how it could best be reformed. The committee met frequently during 1802 and 1803. It discussed the problem of serfdom, but with virtually no practical results. Its examination of the machinery of government was more fruitful, though the changes made by the Tsar cannot be

[1] Shilder, op. cit. i. 172.

attributed solely to its influence, but rather to a compromise between various political forces.

The members of the committee agreed in condemning serfdom, but the measures which they considered can hardly be regarded as more than palliatives. One was to allow persons who were not nobles to buy land inhabited by serfs. Another was to prohibit the sale of serfs by their masters without land. Novosiltsov was against introducing the two measures together: the second, he thought, should be postponed in case it should cause a dangerous degree of alarm among the nobility, who might believe that the emperor intended suddenly to emancipate all the serfs. He was supported by Laharpe and Admiral Mordvinov,[1] who had been consulted. He was opposed by Kochubey and Czartoryski, who argued that it was better to get the reform through in one piece, and that if concessions were being made, by the first measure, to state peasants and merchants, then something should also be done for serfs. Still stronger opposition came from Stroganov. He argued that there was no need to fear the discontent of the nobility:

> La noblesse chez nous est composée d'une quantité de gens qui ne sont devenus gentilshommes que par le service, qui n'ont reçu aucune éducation et dont toutes les idées ont été portées à ne voir au-dessus du pouvoir de l'Empereur. Ni droit, ni justice, rien ne peut leur faire naître l'idée de la plus petite résistance. C'est la classe la plus ignorante, la plus crapuleuse et dont l'esprit est le plus bouché. . . . Une partie vit dans les campagnes et est de la plus crasse ignorance; l'autre, au service, est animée d'un esprit qui n'est pas dangereuse; les grands propriétaires ne sont pas ceux qui sont à craindre, que reste-t-il donc après cela et où sont les éléments d'un mécontentement dangereux? . . . Dans le règne passé que n'a-t-on pas fait contre la justice, le droit de ces gens, leur sûreté personnelle! S'il y avait une occasion où on aurait dû craindre quelquechose, c'était bien à cette époque. Ont-ils soufflé? Au contraire. Toutes les mesures de répression s'exécutaient avec une ponctualité étonnante et c'était le gentilhomme qui exécutait des mesures inventées contre son confrère et qui étaient contre et les intérêts et l'honneur de son corps.

On the other hand, Stroganov argued, it was more appropriate to fear the discontent of the peasants, more necessary to

[1] Mordvinov, an Anglophil liberal with an English wife, was made minister of the Navy in Sept. 1802, but his main interest was in economic problems, on which he wrote various memoranda in the following decades.

do something to satisfy them. Though there were differences between different parts of Russia, serfdom was the same:

. . . partout ils sentent également le poids de l'esclavage, partout la pensée de n'avoir aucune propriété resserre leurs facultés et fait que l'industrie de ces neuf millions est nulle pour la prosperité nationale. . . . Ils sucent de bonne heure une grande inimitié contre la classe des propriétaires, leurs oppresseurs nés. Il règne entre ces deux classes une haine, on peut dire, qui est très grande; le peuple est toujours porté pour la couronne, parcequ'il croit que l'Empereur est toujours porté à le défendre. Et lorsqu'il sort une mesure oppressive, ce n'est jamais à l'Empereur qu'il l'attribue, mais toujours à des ministres, qui, dit-il, l'abusent, parcequ'étant nobles ils ne sont guidés que par leur intérêt personnel. Si on voulait faire la plus petite atteinte à la prérogative impériale, il serait le premier pour elle, parcequ'il ne verrait là-dedans qu'une augmentation de pouvoir pour ses ennemis naturels. Dans tous les temps, chez nous, c'est la classe des paysans qui a eu part à tous les troubles qui ont eu lieu, ce n'est jamais la noblesse qui a remué, et si le gouvernement a quelque chose à craindre et quelque parti à surveiller, c'est bien la classe des serfs et non pas les autres.[1]

The emperor did not, however, accept Stroganov's arguments. He introduced only the first measure, and the prohibition of individual sales of serfs was postponed indefinitely. In 1803, on the suggestion of Count N. P. Rumyantsev,[2] a minor measure in favour of the serfs was passed. This was the so-called Free Cultivators Law, which permitted the emancipation of serfs by landowners as a purely voluntary act. Only a few thousand serfs benefited from this law during Alexander's reign. Alexander did not even discontinue his grandmother's and father's practice of transferring state peasants into serfdom to private landowners.[3] To sum up, fear of the hostile reaction of the nobility, reinforced by knowledge of the fate of both his father and his

[1] Grand Duke Nikolay Mikhailovich, *Le comte Paul Stroganov* (SPB, 1905), ii. 61–62. Cited hereafter as *Stroganov*.

[2] Born 1764, son of the victorious field-marshal of Catherine II's first Turkish war. In 1802 he was appointed minister of commerce, and from 1807 to 1814 he was minister of foreign affairs.

[3] According to information in the State Archives, quoted by the Soviet historian Druzhinin, in Alexander I's reign 259 gifts of state land amounting to 731,482 *desyatin* were made to private individuals. The number of peasants connected with these lands is not stated. N. M. Druzhinin, *Gosudarstvennye krest'yane i reforma P. D. Kiselyova* (Moscow, 1946), i. 87–88.

grandfather, combined with the necessity of dealing with many other pressing problems of internal and foreign policy, prevented Alexander I from ever seriously facing the problem of serfdom.

In the strictly political field it was clear that the new Tsar repudiated the tyrannical methods of his father, but it was not clear how he himself was to rule. Essentially the alternatives were to go back to the policies of Catherine, or to move forward to more daring reforms. The choice between policies also involved a choice between men, between the dignitaries of Catherine, many of whom were still in their prime, and the small circle of intimate advisers of Alexander's own generation, the Unofficial Committee. The latter maintained good relations with some of the elder statesmen, especially with the brothers Simon and Alexander Vorontsov. But in general it is true that there was a conflict not only of personalities but of policies between the Unofficial Committee and Catherine's notables. The latter hoped for an oligarchic system, with an extension of political liberties to the upper class but without more radical social changes, while the former stood for reform from above, were suspicious of oligarchy, and did not wish to diminish the authority of the emperor. Though the Unofficial Committee did not maintain its influence for long, on this main issue, of the choice between autocratic power and oligarchy, it may be said to have prevailed. This was shown by the treatment of the two main institutional problems of these years, which concerned the functions of the Senate and the ministers.

A commission of the Senate under Count P. V. Zavadovsky, acting on the decree of 5 June 1801, prepared a report with recommendations on the future functions of the Senate. This was discussed by its full assembly during July. The most systematic proposal made in those debates was by G. R. Derzhavin. He distinguished between four powers—the executive, legislative, judiciary, and supervisory. All four should be concentrated in the Senate. Each of the four powers should be entrusted to a minister and to a subordinate assembly.[1]

[1] There is some confusion as to Derzhavin's real views, since his proposals in the Senate debate differ substantially from those given in his memoirs. One of the obscurities concerns the relative status of the ministers and of the procurator-general. The latter at times appears to be the equal of the ministers, at others to be set above them, as was the procurator-general in the eighteenth century.

Derzhavin claimed in his memoirs that Alexander was greatly impressed by his project, and rewarded him for it by conferring the Order of St. Alexander Nevsky. But the Unofficial Committee opposed it. At its meeting of 5 August 1801 Novosiltsov argued that Peter the Great had never intended the Senate to have legislative powers, and that 'par sa composition, il ne peut point mériter la confiance de la nation'. If the Tsar were to give it extensive rights, 'il pourrait bien se lier les bras de manière qu'il ne pourrait plus éxécuter ce qu'il projette en faveur de la nation'.[1] He therefore urged that the Senate be a purely judicial body. On 10 February 1802 the committee discussed whether the Senate should have the right to demand reports from ministers, and whether ministers should be made specifically responsible to the Senate. Alexander was against this.

Derzhavin had also suggested that senators be elected. Assemblies of officials of the first five ranks in the state service, in all government offices in the two capitals, should elect candidates for senators from among officials belonging to the first four ranks only, and the emperor should then select one person in three from these lists. Mordvinov, who may be described as a liberal oligarch, supported election of senators in the Permanent Council on 1 May 1802. 'Political rights', he argued, 'must be based on an aristocratic estate, highly respected, in order that the rights themselves may receive equal respect.' Catherine had granted the nobles the right to elect judges. In her day Russia was perhaps not mature enough for the right to be extended to election for the highest office in the land, but now circumstances were more favourable. Mordvinov proposed that a portion of the senators consist of persons elected by the provincial nobility, two for each province. They would have equal rights in the Senate with those senators directly appointed by the emperor. They would serve for three years. The Unofficial Committee meeting of 6 January 1802 opposed Derzhavin's proposal for election of senators: 'car dans nos provinces ces gens des quatre premières classes ne sont pas assez connus pour pouvoir en espérer un choix éclairé. D'ailleurs dans les élections actuelles, c'est presque toujours la volonté du gouvernment qui dirige le choix, à plus forte raison pour des places aussi importantes que

[1] Minutes of meeting of 5 Aug. 1801. Nikolay Mikhailovich, *Stroganov*, ii. 45.

celles des sénateurs'.[1] Election of senators was not in fact accepted by the Tsar.

When the new system of ministries was introduced on 8 September 1802, it provided that the ministers were to be subject to the surveillance of the Senate, and must submit accounts of their actions to it.[2] But in practice this remained an empty clause. Paragraph 9 of this decree stated that the Senate had the right to draw the Tsar's attention to conflicts between new and existing laws. But this too soon proved valueless. Count Severin Potocki proposed that the Senate should question the action of the minister of war, confirmed by the Tsar on 5 December 1802, establishing a period of twelve years' service for nobles who served in the army but did not reach officer's rank, on the ground that this was incompatible with existing laws. A delegation of senators asked for an audience with the Tsar, who received them coldly and stated that he would issue a decree. This followed on 21 March 1803, and simply declared that the Senate's right, under the September 1802 decree, did not apply to new or recently confirmed legislation.

Thus the desire of the supporters of oligarchy, to concentrate all power in the Senate, to make it a council of elder statesmen placed between the emperor and the administrative apparatus, proved unsuccessful. In practice the Senate remained, as it had been in the previous reigns, a judicial body only.

Instead the government of Russia became more than ever a bureaucratic apparatus, headed by ministers, directly responsible to the emperor. The establishment of ministries in September 1802 was not in fact a radical change. The title had not previously existed, but to some extent the reality had been there. The procurator-general had been a sort of grand vizier—a combined minister of justice, finance, and interior, not merely checking but directing the administration. As for the ministries, they were in effect centralized departments, and the consultative element in their organization was little more than a fiction: in the Russian terminology of the time, the bureaucratic principle prevailed over the collegiate. Paul had reinforced this trend.

[1] Nikolay Mikhailovich, *Stroganov*, ii. 96.

[2] The law on the rights and duties of the Senate is PSZ 20405 (first series, vol. 27, pp. 241–243) and the law on the establishment of ministries is the immediately following document, 20406.

The Unofficial Committee devoted much attention to the planning of a central ministry. One point which they stressed was that the ministry was to be a united team, with similar aims, not a heterogeneous collection of individuals. Of the existing state of affairs, Kochubey wrote to Prince Simon Vorontsov on 12 May 1801: 'Les gens qui occupent les premières places font, si je peux m'exprimer ainsi, autant de puissances séparées. Chacune travaille d'après sa tête et ses vues, et il n'y a aucun ensemble. De là un décousu dans les différentes branches de l'administration; de là beaucoup d'abus continuent de se perpétuer.'[1] At the meeting of the committee of 10 February 1802 Czartoryski put forward a plan for a Council of Ministers. All the members agreed that

> dans le choix de ses ministres, il faudrait absolument se décider à ne mettre que des gens dont la façon de penser serait uniforme, pour qu'il ne forme qu'une unité parfaite, de manière que les sottises de l'un soient reprochables aux autres et qu'en quelque sorte ils soient tous responsables pour la même faute . . . . Tandis qu'à présent Sa Majesté convient elle-même que la désunion des ministres était singulièrement dommageable à l'Empire, puisque l'un tirait d'un côté, l'autre de l'autre, et qu'au milieu c'était l'État qui souffrait.[2]

Alexander agreed, but remarked, 'mais trouvez-moi des gens'.

The persons whom the Tsar nominated to the eight new ministries[3] did not in fact form a team. There was no question of a united Cabinet, with a recognized head, or with any collective responsibility. Instead, each minister was individually responsible to the Tsar. The choice of ministers showed a balance between the young reformers and the conservative oligarchs. Czartoryski, Novosiltsov, and Stroganov obtained the posts of deputy minister in the Ministries of Foreign Affairs, Justice, and the Interior respectively, and Kochubey became minister of the interior. The deputy-minister of education, M. N. Muravyov, was also a strong supporter of reform, and the minister of the navy, Admiral Mordvinov, had liberal sympathies. The outstanding reactionary among the ministers was G. R. Derzhavin,

[1] *Arkhiv knyaz'ya Vorontsova* (Moscow, 1870–95), xviii. 239–41. Cited hereafter as *Vorontsov Archives*.

[2] Nikolay Mikhailovich, *Stroganov*, ii. 103–4.

[3] These were: Foreign Affairs, War, Navy, Finance, Interior, Justice, Commerce and Education. The first three had long existed as 'Colleges', the next three in embryonic form under the procurator-general's authority. Education was essentially a new ministry. Its formation is discussed below pp. 97–101.

the minister of justice. Most of the heads of ministries were conservative and uninspired dignitaries. It is hardly surprising that this team proved a disappointment to the members of the Unofficial Committee. Kochubey wrote to Simon Vorontsov on 20 January 1803: 'Il n'y a aucun ensemble. Les ministres se détestent et se chicanent, et cet accord si nécessaire dans une administration n'a pas existé un seul instant.'[1] Novosiltsov wrote to the same correspondent on the same date: 'Peu d'union, peu d'harmonie; quelques-uns ont trop d'activité, d'autres pas assez; les uns s'isolent et ne pensent qu'à leur patrie, les autres se mêlent de tout et obliquement contrôlent tout.'[2]

The Committe of Ministers, specifically mentioned in point 15 of the manifesto of 8 September 1802, was not a Cabinet, but it nevertheless became an institution of some importance. The Permanent Council, of which the ministers were *ex officio* members, languished in practice, and Troshchinsky exercised very small influence. It was actually the Committe of Ministers which considered current political matters at the highest level. There was no other body of comparable importance. In practice its efficiency was greatly reduced not only by the lack of unity of outlook among its members but also because it was flooded with matters of detail, often of minor importance, which reached it either because an individual concerned in a dispute was connected with some influential person or family, or because a provincial governor did not wish to take responsibility. During four months of 1802 the committee met 23 times, and the emperor presided at 20 of these meetings. In 1803 there were 42 meetings, all attended by the emperor, 31 in 1804, of which he attended 26, 16 in 1805 of which he attended only the first 4.[3] The reason for the Tsar's absence was of course that he went to join the army in its campaign in central Europe against Napoleon, culminating in the disaster of Austerlitz. During his absence the committee conducted the government of Russia. It was given the right to decide matters which there was no time to submit to the Tsar by correspondence. Decisions were taken by majority vote. Members took the chair for four consecutive meetings in turn.

The Unofficial Committee ceased to exist after 1803, and its members lost their influence in the following years. Czartoryski,

[1] *Vorontsov Archives*, xviii. 283. [2] Ibid. xviii. 453.

[3] S. M. Seredonin, *Komitet Ministrov, istoricheskii obzor 1802–1902*, (SPB, 1902), i. 5–8.

bitterly disappointed by the international developments of 1805–6, gave up the Foreign Ministry and devoted himself to his duties as curator of Vilna University. Novosiltsov also concentrated on education, as curator of St. Petersburg. Kochubey resigned the Ministry of the Interior in November 1807, and Stroganov had resigned already earlier to serve in the army. All four had been strong supporters of the British alliance, and were opposed to Alexander's new policy of co-operation with Napoleon after 1807.

Foreign Policy 1801–1807

In foreign policy Alexander's first aim on his accession was to restore peace in order that he should be free to pursue a policy of reform within Russia. He therefore resolved to liquidate the quarrels with both formal enemy and former allies, and if possible help to bring about peace between France and Britain.

After Nelson's victory at Copenhagen the British fleet passed into the Baltic and approached Reval. However, no further hostilities took place, British ships left the Baltic, and negotiations began for an Anglo-Russian settlement. The resulting agreement, which was signed on 17 June, was denounced in some circles in St. Petersburg as a betrayal of the principles of Catherine II, and attributed to the excessive Anglophily of Count Panin and of Count Simon Vorontsov, who now resumed his post as ambassador in London. The convention granted the British claim that regular warships of a belligerent (but not privateers) should be allowed to search ships convoyed by a warship of a neutral Power, and laid down procedure for the search and for the examination of documents. The convoying warship must not under any pretext forcibly oppose the detention of a ship in the convoy, but if the ship were found to be wrongfully detained, compensation would be paid to its owners. On the other hand the British abandoned the notion of a 'paper blockade', agreeing that a port could be considered under blockade only if there were 'a clear danger in entering it'. The notion of contraband was also restricted to a specific list of articles of military and naval equipment.[1] Denmark and Sweden later, though reluctantly, adhered to the convention.

[1] Text in F. M. Martens, *Sobranie traktatov i konventsiy, zaklyuchonnykh Rossiey s inostrannymi derzhavami* (SPB, various dates), xi. 28–49.

In September 1801 Count Razumovsky was appointed as ambassador to Vienna. The Tsar's instructions to him emphasized that Russia must co-operate with Austria in German affairs, while protecting the lesser German states from the ambitions of either Austria or France. The two Powers should also have a common interest in upholding the integrity of the Ottoman empire.

Negotiations also took place between Russia and France, and a peace treaty was signed in Paris on 8 October 1801. Both Powers recognized the independence of the republic of the Ionian Islands, in which no foreign troops would be stationed. Russia was to help in the negotiation of peace between France and Turkey. French troops would be withdrawn from the territory of the Kingdom of Naples as soon as the fate of Egypt had been decided. Both Powers were thereafter to recognize the Kingdom of Naples as neutral, and Russia would endeavour to obtain British and Turkish acceptance of such neutrality. The two governments would co-operate in German affairs, and would endeavour to reach agreement on the problems of Italy, and especially of the Kingdom of Sardinia.[1]

In 1802 Alexander decided, without consulting Czartoryski, to pay an official visit to the king and queen of Prussia at Memel. The visit, which took place on 10 June, was impressively arranged, and Alexander went out of his way to express his friendship for Frederick William and his admiration for Queen Louise. The visit proved to be important, for it created a bond of genuine personal devotion between the Tsar and the Prussian monarch, and established the position of Prussia as the most closely linked to Russia of all her neighbours, as a sort of privileged junior partner. Despite the changes of the following years, something of this special relationship remained.

The year 1802 brought peace between France and Britain, by the Treaty of Amiens of 27 March, and between France and Turkey on 25 June. Russia's relations with France, however, were uneasy. The two governments agreed on a new settlement of German affairs which was accepted reluctantly by Austria and duly approved by the Imperial Diet in Regensburg in February 1803. No less than 112 sovereign principalities disappeared. The simplification of the political structure of Germany

[1] Text in Martens, op. cit. xiii. 263–70.

was in itself desirable, but in practice the survival or abolition of a principality, and the extent of the compensation granted to the ruler, depended not so much on abstract considerations of merit as on whether the ruler possessed personal connexions with the courts of Russia or Austria, or was in a position to buy the gratitude of French agents. The February 1803 settlement did not eliminate disputes, and during the year Russian diplomacy was frequently defending against French the interests of Austria or of Austrian-protected princes. A further cause of Franco-Russian friction was the refusal of Napoleon to pay any attention to the interests of the king of Sardinia, to whom, as a former ally of Russia, Alexander felt moral obligations, although Article 6 of the treaty of October 1801 clearly committed France to consult with Russia on this matter.

Anglo-Russian relations too were not free from friction. The British government disliked Russia's efforts to bring about Franco-Turkish peace. The British proposed that a Russian garrison be sent to Malta, but this was declined on the ground that it was too far from Russia. The Tsar, however, was willing to be protector of the Order of Malta, though rejecting the grand mastership claimed by Paul. When the British government undertook, in the Peace of Amiens with France, to evacuate Malta, Alexander was indignant that no reference had been made to Russia's special status in the island. When the failure to decide the future of Malta led to the renewal of war between Britain and France in May 1803, Alexander considered that the British were largely to blame. With fresh Anglo-French hostilities on the seas, new incidents occurred between British privateers and neutral vessels trading with Russia, causing damage against which Russia was not protected by the convention of June 1801. Napoleon asked Alexander to mediate with Britain, but his proposals, made in July 1803, were not acceptable. Napoleon considered that Russia had favoured the British side, and Franco-Russian relations grew markedly worse. The Russian ambassador in Paris, Count Morkov, was accused of intriguing with French enemies of the first consul, and after Napoleon had publicly insulted him at a diplomatic reception on 25 September, the Tsar decided to recall him. On his return he was ostentatiously awarded a high decoration.

On 14 March 1804 the duc d'Enghien, a member of the

French royal house, was kidnapped from the territory of Baden by French agents, taken to Paris, and a week later executed on the grounds that he had been involved in a royalist conspiracy against Napoleon. The violation of Baden was the more insufferable to Alexander because his wife was a Baden princess. He summoned a meeting of the Permanent Council on 5 April, at which it was agreed, with the one dissenting voice of Count Rumyantsev, that diplomatic relations must be broken with France. A Russian note was sent in protest to the French government and to the Imperial Diet of Regensburg, of which Russia was a member under the Treaty of Teschen of 1779. Napoleon replied with a note which referred insultingly to the failure of Alexander to prosecute the murderers of Tsar Paul. At Regensburg the Russian note was neither accepted nor rejected, being supported by the king of Sweden and by the king of England as Elector of Hanover. On 18 May 1804 Napoleon took the title of emperor, which Russia, Austria, Sweden, and Turkey refused to recognize. The French ambassador left St. Petersburg at the end of May, and the Russian *chargé d'affaires*, Baron d'Oubril, left Paris in September. The main task of Russian diplomacy was now to arrange alliances with Britain, Austria, and Prussia.

The British government was eager for an alliance, and was strongly backed by the Anglophil Russian ambassador, Count Simon Vorontsov. Though well disposed to Vorontsov, Alexander wished to have the negotiations conducted by someone enjoying his intimate confidence, and therefore sent Novosiltsov to London on a special mission. His instructions, dated 11 September 1804, expounded the views on the whole field of European policy held by the Tsar and by Adam Czartoryski, who was now Alexander's chief adviser on foreign affairs, though the title of minister of foreign affairs was held by Count Alexander Vorontsov, brother of the ambassador. The instructions emphasized the need to outbid the French in appealing to the principles of liberty and the welfare of humanity. The allies must on no account appear anxious to restore the régimes of the past. The king of Sardinia must be persuaded to give a constitution to his people once the French were removed, and there must be reforms in liberated Holland and Switzerland. The French people must be assured that the allies were not their enemies, but were fighting only against their government, which was 'as tyrannical for France as for the rest of Europe'. When peace was achieved, a new league must be created to ensure 'a new code of the law of nations'. In future it was desirable that states should have natural frontiers, outlets for the products of their industries, and 'homogeneous peoples who can agree among themselves'. There must also be a natural balance of power between the states. Three specific problems were stressed. It was proposed that a German federation should be set up, from which both Austria and Prussia should be excluded and which would balance them; Britain and Russia should concert their policy towards the Ottoman empire, and consider what should be done with its various territories if it should collapse from within, or if it should ally itself with France; and the British government must be persuaded to make changes in its maritime law.[1]

Pitt expressed general sympathy with the Tsar's more idealistic aims, and agreed with the desirability of constitutions and reforms in the countries to be delivered from Napoleonic rule. He absolutely refused, however, to consider any modification of British maritime law. He also refused to give up Malta, which he now intended to annex to Britain. He was opposed to a federation of Germany without the two German Great Powers: he preferred to induce Prussia to enter the coalition by offering her territory in north-west Germany, thereby reinforcing Holland and setting up a strong barrier against France. He showed no inclination to consider the disruption of the Ottoman empire. Novosiltsov's naive remark, that if Russia acquired Constantinople, surely 'England, our best friend, would not be alarmed, and her trade would be better assured than ever', left him unmoved.[2] However, on the more practical issues in view, a treaty of alliance was concluded, on 11 April 1805. The aim of the alliance was to liberate Germany, Switzerland, Holland, and Italy from the French. Russia and her continental allies were to provide not less than 400,000 men, and Britain was to give a subsidy of £1,250,000 per year for every 100,000 men.[3] Sweden, traditionally the ally of France, was brought into the

[1] The full text of the instructions is in the collection of documents published by the Ministry of Foreign Affairs of the U.S.S.R., *Vneshnyaya politika Rossii XIX i nachala XX veka*, series I., vol. ii (Moscow, 1961), pp. 138–46.

[2] Martens, op. cit. xi. 98–99.

[3] Text ibid. xi. 433–61.

allied camp by King Gustav IV's rage at the murder of the duc d'Enghien. An Anglo-Swedish convention was signed in December 1804, and a Russo-Swedish alliance in January 1805. The ratification of the Anglo-Russian convention was, however, delayed owing to Alexander's anger at British obstinacy on Malta and on maritime rights.

Negotiations with Austria continued during 1804. They were delayed by the decision of Emperor Francis to recognize Napoleon's Imperial title in exchange for the latter's recognition of the new title assumed by Francis of emperor of Austria.[1] There were also disagreements on the number of troops to be put in the field by Russia, and on the extent of British subsidies to be made available to Austria. However, on 6 November 1804 an alliance was signed in St. Petersburg. Austria was to provide 235,000 troops, Russia 115,000 with an additional reserve force to be kept on the Prussian frontier to ensure against a Prussian attack on Austria. The treaty also provided maximum and minimum aims for the restitution and compensation of dispossessed Italian rulers.[2] But the Austrian government at first showed no inclination to make the military preparations to which the treaty committed it. It was not until Napoleon had proclaimed himself king of Italy in March 1805, and had annexed Genoa to his new kingdom in June, that the Austrian emperor decided to commit himself. At last serious military plans were concerted between the Austrian and Russian commands, and on 9 August 1805 Austria formally adhered to the Anglo-Russian alliance, which Alexander had meanwhile ratified.

The attitude of Prussia now became extremely important. Since 1795 Prussia had been at peace, and in the last years there had been a struggle at the Prussian court between French and Russian influences. Alexander was eager to enlist Prussia in the alliance. His friendship for Frederick William and Louise strengthened his desire, on practical grounds, to be able with Prussian consent to send his armies across Prussian territory to link up with the Austrians. Adam Czartoryski did not share the

[1] Additional to the traditional title of Holy Roman Emperor. Francis eventually abandoned the latter title, and the Holy Roman Empire was officially dissolved, in 1806.

[2] Text in Martens, op. cit. ii. 406–20.

Tsar's wishes. He hoped that a victorious war against Napoleon would lead to the restoration of Poland. If Prussia were on the enemy side, then she could be deprived of her Polish territories, which could be added to those already under Russian rule to form a Kingdom of Poland with Alexander as its sovereign. He hoped that the unity of Poland could then be completed by persuading Austria to cede Galicia in return for compensation in Germany. In 1805 this project had considerable support among the Polish nobility. Alexander was believed to be a true champion of liberty and a true friend of Poland. In September, on his way to join his army, Alexander stayed at the Czartoryski estate at Puławy, and was visited by Polish notables who assured him of their loyalty and of their people's enthusiasm.

But Alexander was less committed to the Polish cause than he appeared. Unknown to Czartoryski, he sent his aide-de-camp Prince P. P. Dolgoruky to Berlin to persuade Frederick William to join the allies.[1] What Dolgoruky's arguments could not effect, Napoleon himself achieved. French troops marched across Prussian territory at Ansbach, in their movement against the Austrians. Enraged at this news, Frederick William invited Alexander to Potsdam, where he stayed from 25 October to 5 November. By a treaty of 3 November Prussia undertook to propose to France terms for a general peace which included most of the points concerning Italy, Holland, Switzerland, and Germany embodied in the Anglo-Russo-Austrian treaties. In the expected event of a French refusal, Prussia was to join the allies with an army of 180,000 men. Thus the Prussian alliance seemed to have been won, but Czartoryski's hopes were dashed and Polish enthusiasm for Alexander destroyed.

Meanwhile the allies had fared badly. The Austrian army under General Mack was decisively defeated by Napoleon at the Battle of Ulm on 19 October. The Russian forces under Prince Michael Kutuzov[2] successfully retreated into Moravia, but Napoleon entered Vienna on 13 November. Alexander

[1] Some of Dolgoruky's correspondence from Berlin is in Grand Duke Nikolay Mikhailovich, *Knyaz'ya Dolgorukie, spodvizhniki Imperatora Aleksandra I*, SPB, 1910.

[2] M. I. Kutuzov, born 1745, served with distinction in the Turkish wars of Catherine II, especially at the storming of Izmail in December 1790, and had also performed several diplomatic missions. He was the best-known Russian general at this time, and was exceptionally popular both with his own soldiers and with the civilian public.

went from Potsdam to Olmütz, the Russian military headquarters in Moravia, and insisted, against the advice of Kutuzov, that the army should give battle to the advancing Napoleon. The Battle of Austerlitz, fought on 2 December 1805, was the greatest of Napoleon's victories. The interference of Alexander in military operations, Kutuzov's sulky passivity, and the disagreements between Austrian and Russian general staff officers contributed to the confused leadership on the allied side. As in 1799, common disaster led to recriminations between Austria and Russia. Alexander was unable to provide immediate help, and Francis was not prepared to fight on alone in Hungary. On 26 December Austria accepted Napoleon's conditions in the Peace of Pressburg. Austria ceded Dalmatia and Venetia to Napoleon's Kingdom of Italy, and Tyrol to Bavaria. The surviving forces of Kutuzov's army retreated into Russian territory. The king of Prussia decided that discretion was the better part of valour. Alexander's entreaties, coupled with the offer to place at his disposal the still unused Russian armies commanded by Bennigsen and Tolstoy, had no effect. Frederick William sent Count Haugwitz to Napoleon at Vienna, ostensibly to propose peace on the lines agreed at Potsdam. Instead, Haugwitz signed on 15 December a treaty of alliance with France. In January 1806 Prussian troops occupied Hanover, part of the domains of the British Crown, with the consent of Napoleon, and became engaged with Swedish troops in Pomerania, which had previously been intended by the allies to be a base for a joint Anglo-Russo-Swedish force to act against the French in North Germany. The Franco-Prussian alliance was made still closer, on terms less favourable to Prussia, by a further treaty signed in Paris on 15 February.

A minor theatre of war was the Kingdom of Naples. In September 1805 the Queen Regent Marie Caroline undertook that if the small French garrisons on her territory were reinforced she would admit British and Russian forces to resist them. Shortly afterwards she was forced to sign a treaty with France promising neutrality in case of war, but she secretly informed the Russian government that she considered this obligation invalid as extracted by force. In November a force of 13,500 Russian and 5,500 British troops joined the Neapolitan army of 40,000 in attacking the French. The allies, under the command of the Russian General Lacy, cleared Neapolitan territory and marched northwards, hoping to link up with the Austrians in North Italy. When he learned that the Austrians were evacuating Italy, Lacy retreated to Naples. In January 1806 French forces under Marshal Masséna invaded Neapolitan territory. The allied forces were too weak to resist them. British troops retired to Sicily, taking with them the Neapolitan royal family. Napoleon declared the Neapolitan Bourbons deposed, and installed his brother Joseph as king. The Russian troops were evacuated to the Ionian Islands.

These now became for Russia a position of importance. The alliance with Turkey still made it possible for Russian forces to be brought through the Straits. When the terms of the Peace of Pressburg became known, the Russian government was determined to prevent the port of Cattaro in southern Dalmatia from falling into French hands. The Russian admiral Senyavin persuaded the Austrian authorities to hand over Cattaro to him. His position was reinforced by an alliance, in February 1806, with the independent Slav Christian principality of Montenegro. Commanding the Adriatic with his fleet and supported by the Montenegrins on land, Senyavin was able to isolate the French in Dubrovnik and to capture the islands of Vis and Korčula. Napoleon, who considered possession of the Adriatic an essential step to the fulfilment of the plans which he still cherished for conquest of Turkey and the East, pressed Austria to insist on Russian evacuation. The Austrian government, however, dragged on negotiations with Russia. It was able to avoid being forced into armed conflict with its former ally, but also refused to be drawn back into the struggle against France. Alexander sent Count Pozzo di Borgo[1] to Vienna in November 1806 to try to persuade Austria to re-enter the war, but without success.

In the spring of 1806, with no point of contact between the Russian and French forces except in the Adriatic, and little prospect of striking an effective blow against Napoleon, there seemed much to be said for seeking peace with France. In

[1] Count Charles Pozzo di Borgo, born 1764 in Corsica, and a personal enemy of Napoleon, entered Russian service in 1803. In 1807 he resigned, in opposition to the Treaty of Tilsit, and settled in Vienna. In 1812 Alexander invited him to return to Russian service. After 1815 he was for many years Russian ambassador at the Court of Louis XVIII.

Britain the same view was held after the death of Pitt and the formation of the Grenville ministry, in which Fox was foreign secretary. Paul Stroganov was sent to London to replace Simon Vorontsov. As a strong Anglophil, Stroganov was determined to maintain close friendship between Britain and Russia. But it was agreed that the two governments should negotiate separately with Napoleon, keeping each other informed. On 20 July, however, the Russian emissary, Baron D'Oubril, signed a treaty with France which obtained certain advantages for Russia and for the German Powers, but completely ignored the interests of Britain and her Mediterranean allies. The news of the treaty caused dismay in London, and bitter shame to Stroganov. The Russian government, however, decided not to ratify it, and for the time being Anglo-Russian relations became cordial again.[1]

Meanwhile negotiations were continuing between Russia and Prussia. Frederick William was still torn between the Francophil and Russophil factions, unable as ever to make up his mind. While Haugwitz, as his chief minister, stood for the pro-French policy, and dealt with the Russian ambassador Stackelberg, his predecessor, Prince Hardenberg, who was much more inclined towards Russia, dealt with the former Russian ambassador Alopeus. The king thus maintained two separate and contradictory sets of foreign relations without committing himself to either. He was displeased by the formation, in July 1806, of Napoleon's Confederation of the Rhine, from which Prussia was excluded. The Anglo-Swedish blockade of the north German ports was seriously damaging Prussia's economy. These grievances, the appeals to friendship of Alexander, and the opposition to France of the patriotic party, which enjoyed the sympathy of Queen Louise, decided him to come down on the Russian side. On 13 July a secret Russo-Prussian declaration was signed, which took the form of explaining that the existing Franco-Prussian alliance did not apply to a number of eventualities affecting Russian interests, but in fact amounted to a new Russo-Prussian military alliance. Further points of detail were negotiated during August.

[1] The text of the D'Oubril treaty is in Martens, op. cit. xviii. 332–8. Papers relating to the Stroganov mission are in Nikolay Mikhailovich, *Stroganov*, iii. 1–94. Correspondence relating to the D'Oubril treaty is on pp. 80–93. This is also discussed in correspondence between Stroganov and Czartoryski in ii. 246–53.

On 26 September Frederick William addressed an ultimatum to Napoleon demanding the immediate evacuation of Germany up to the Rhine. War broke out on 7 October, and on 14 October the Prussian armies suffered two crushing defeats at Jena and Auerstedt. On 25 October Napoleon entered Berlin. The French advanced into Prussian Poland, and were received by the Poles as liberators. Polish troops served, under General Dąbrowski, in Napoleon's army from the beginning of the war. The French army captured Warsaw on 28 November. Soon afterwards a Polish provisional government was set up, known as the Governing Commission. It was composed of five Polish directors, of whom Prince Józef Poniatowski was in charge of the department of war. He raised three divisions of Polish troops, amounting to nearly 50,000 men, to fight on the French side.

Very little was now left either of Prussian territory or of Prussian military strength. However, Alexander, whose territory was now accessible to the French armies, and who was directly faced with a very serious political threat in Napoleon's support to the Poles, decided to continue the war. Russian troops were brought into Poland, and on 26 December General L. L. Bennigsen successfully withstood a strong French attack at Pułtusk, near Warsaw. On 8 February 1807 a second battle was fought at Eylau in East Prussia. This was perhaps the fiercest and bloodiest battle that Napoleon had yet fought, and its result was indecisive. Russian casualties amounted to 26,000 and French losses were nearly as numerous. Bennigsen retreated to Königsberg, leaving the field to Napoleon.

At the end of March Alexander left St. Petersburg to join the army. He joined the king and queen of Prussia at Memel, and on 26 April 1807, as a new gesture of Russo-Prussian unity, was signed the Convention of Bartenstein.[1] This undertook to restore Prussia to her strength of 1805, or to provide her with equivalent compensation. It also proposed to set up a German constitutional federation, with a good military frontier and a line of defence parallel to the Rhine. Austria and Prussia should be reconciled, and a way found for these two Powers to share in the direction of the defence of the federation. Austria, Britain, Sweden, and Denmark were to be associated with the agreement.

Meanwhile Russia had been weakened by the action of

[1] Text in Martens, op. cit. vi. 409–18.

Turkey. Ever since the restoration of peace in 1802, the French government had done its best to intrigue against Russia in Constantinople. The Turks had good reason to fear Russian intrigues among their Greek and Slav subjects. The insurrection of 1804, in Serbia, led by Kara Djordje, though not aided by the Russians, was likely to encourage rebellion among the other Orthodox Slav populations. On the other hand the French too had engaged in intrigues with the Greeks, not unknown to the Turks. In 1805 the Turkish government still considered Russia the more formidable Power, and so formally renewed their alliance with her on 11 September 1805. The news of Austerlitz transformed the situation. If the French were capable of smashing Russian armies, they could protect the Turks against their northern neighbour. The presence of Russian troops at Cattaro, in contact with the Montenegrins, who belonged to the same church and spoke the same language as the insurgent Serbs, was further cause for alarm. From April 1806 onwards the Turkish government objected to the passage through the Straits of Russian warships bound for the Adriatic, on the ground that Turkey was not at war with France. On 18 August the Sultan deposed the rulers of the two Roumanian principalities of Moldavia and Wallachia, replacing them by two men of pro-French sympathies. This was not only a provocative gesture towards Russia, but actually violated an agreement of 1802, by which the Turkish government had undertaken to appoint the two Roumanian princes for seven years, to remove them only in the event of definite offences on their part, and in this event to consult the Russian government. The Russian government therefore demanded revocation of the decree of 18 August. The Sultan hesitated, but at last agreed on 17 October to revoke the appointments. It was too late, for on the previous day the Russian army had crossed the Dniester. On 24 December 1806 the Russians were in Bucarest, and three days later Turkey formally declared war on Russia.

In the first half of 1807 Anglo-Russian relations also deteriorated. The Russians were not satisfied with the size of the subsidies received: £500,000 seemed very little in proportion to the sacrifices made by Russia. They were also disappointed by the refusal of the British to make a landing on the Continent. The disputed rights of neutral shipping, and the actions of privateers, continued to cause ill feeling. The British government wished to renew the Anglo-Russian commercial treaty of 1797, and frequently showed concern for the rights and privileges of British merchants in Russia. To the Russians this preoccupation with commercial interests, at a time when Russian soldiers were dying in battle against the common enemy, seemed outrageous. There were also disagreements on European policy. The British government did not like the notion of a German federation, proposed by the Convention of Bartenstein, as they suspected that it would be used by Prussia to maintain its hold over Hanover. They also feared Russian aims in the Balkans. British and Russian naval forces were still co-operating in the Aegean. But when Admiral Duckworth forced the Dardanelles in February 1807, and anchored in the Sea of Marmara opposite Constantinople, the Russian reaction was not one of pleasure. When the Sultan refused to yield, and Duckworth retired into the Aegean, the Russians were less disappointed than might have been expected by the failure of their ally's action against their enemy. The British government favoured the maintenance of the Ottoman empire, and was alarmed both by Russian occupation of Roumania and by Russian designs for the creation of Slav or Greek states.[1]

Alexander increasingly came to feel that he need not take seriously his obligations to an ally that contributed so little to the common cause, and that frustrated his aims in so many directions. In Prussia the war was not going well. There was still some hope that a major battle would bring victory. But when this at last took place, at Friedland on 14 June, it was a decisive though costly victory for Napoleon. The Tsar decided to ask for peace, and Napoleon agreed.

The two emperors met on a raft on the river Niemen at Tilsit on 25 June 1807. There is no documentary record of their talk, but the remark attributed to Alexander that he hated the English as much as did Napoleon, probably reflects his mood at the time. Napoleon showed the greatest courtesy to the Tsar, and made it clear that he wished not only to end the war but to make Russia his ally and Alexander his friend. The Tilsit Treaty thus has two aspects—a settlement of the war and a Franco-Russian alliance.

[1] These problems are discussed in Martens, op. cit. xi. 130–42.

Prussia lost all her territories west of the Elbe, and all the territories that she had acquired from Poland since 1772. The latter were formed into a new state, the grand duchy of Warsaw, whose sovereign was to be the king of Saxony. One section of the formerly Prussian Polish territory, however, the district of Białystok, was handed to Russia: Alexander thus not only agreed to the loss by his Prussian ally of half his territory, but shared in the spoils. Russia abandoned Cattaro and the Ionian Islands to the French. Alexander recognized Napoleon's brothers as kings of Naples and Westphalia. Napoleon promised to help the restoration of peace between Russia and Turkey.

A further separate and secret treaty of alliance between France and Russia had three important provisions. If Britain had not made peace with France by 1 November, Russia would announce that she would go to war with her unless she made peace by 1 December. In this event, Denmark, Sweden, and Portugal would be requested to stop trading with Britain and declare war on her, and if Sweden should refuse Denmark should be asked to declare war on Sweden. Thirdly, if Turkey should not make peace with Russia, despite the efforts of France to mediate between the two Powers, then France would join Russia in war against Turkey, and the two Powers would agree on a plan for the partition of European Turkey.[1]

The Rise and Fall of Speransky

During the years 1803 to 1807 the new system of central government began to take precise shape.

The Ministry of the Interior was responsible for public security, and made serious efforts to increase the numbers and efficiency of the city police forces. These were paid from city funds, but the ministry began to insist on a more standardized system throughout the country.

The wars with France made necessary the revival of a special organization to ensure state security. At the beginning of his reign, Alexander had abolished Catherine's 'Secret Expedition', but in 1805 he found it necessary to order the formation of a special committee, consisting of the ministers of war, the interior, and justice, to deal with affairs of 'higher police'. On

[1] Full texts in Martens, op. cit. xiii. 309–26.

2 January 1807 the Tsar gave instructions for the formation of a permanent committee for the preservation of public security, composed of the Minister of Justice P. V. Lopukhin, Privy Councillor Makarov, and Novosiltsov, to be attended when necessary by the minister of the interior and the military commander of St. Petersburg. It was to watch over suspicious persons and societies, with special attention to Masonic and other secret societies. Any case that came to the notice of a provincial police chief, which looked like espionage or treason, must be reported by him to this committee, which would then give instructions how to handle it.[1]

The Ministry of the Interior was also responsible for public health. In this it was hampered by extreme shortage of medical personnel and of medical stores, both of which were still further reduced by the demands of the army. In 1808 a serious outbreak of plague was halted by severe quarantine measures. The ministry did its best to vaccinate the population against smallpox, despite the hostility of the peasants and the indifference of the educated classes. It was also responsible for organizing food supplies. A rudimentary system of store-houses existed by the beginning of the century, but it was quite inadequate to meet a serious harvest failure, such as occurred in 1808. The ministry was the only central authority in any way concerned with improvements in agriculture.

The Ministry of Finance was only indirectly concerned with factory industry, but was entirely responsible for mining. It was not concerned with farming, but it controlled the state forests, and was responsible for the economic administration of all state properties. Its most important function was to control taxation and the issue of currency. The Ministry of Commerce was concerned with foreign trade and customs.

The Ministry of Education was based on the foundations laid by Catherine's commission on schools, whose first President, Count P. V. Zavadovsky, became the first minister of education. The policy-planning body in the new ministry was the *Glavnoe pravlenie uchilishch* (Directorate of Schools),[2] over which the minister presided. Its first members included Prince Adam

[1] The full texts of the instructions are reproduced in Shilder, op. cit. ii. 362–7.

[2] The Russian word *uchilischche* has a more general meaning than 'school' (which in Russian is *shkola*). A literal translation would be 'place of teaching'.

Czartoryski and the administrator of its office was V. N. Karazin. Later Novosiltsov, Paul Stroganov, and Speransky were members of the *Glavnoe pravlenie*. It began its work in January 1803, and produced a new Statute of Schools in the following year.[1] This provided for four tiers, each designed to lead to the one above, each subordinated to the one above. The empire was divided into educational districts, each of which was to have a university. The head of the district was the curator (*popechitel'*) of the university. He exercised authority over the provincial gimnazii within his district. At the provincial level the senior official was the director of the gimnaziya, who had authority over the *uezd* schools within his province. At the *uezd* level there was to be a supervisor of schools with a general authority over the lowest tier, the parish schools. The creation of the latter was left to the 'enlightened and nobly intentioned tutelage' of landlords, parish clergy, and 'most notable inhabitants'.

Moscow already had a university. In 1803 new universities were established in Vilna and Dorpat, where instruction was respectively in Polish and in German. Kharkov and Kazan received universities in 1804. In St. Petersburg the Teachers' Seminary, which had been closed in 1801, was revived in 1803 and became the nucleus of the university of the capital, which did not, however, receive its formal status as such until 1819.

By 1808 some useful results had been achieved in secondary education.[2] Proportionately to its population, Vilna district was by far the most successful. This was of course due to the great progress that had been made in education during the last decades of Polish independence. Dorpat too had a high proportion, at least in relation to the German-speaking minority of the population.

[1] The statute, dated 5 November 1804, is in PSZ, first series no. 21501 (vol. 28, pp. 626–647).

[2] The following official statistics show the number of gimnazii and uezd schools, and pupils in them, in five educational districts.

District	*Gimnazii*	*Pupils*	*Uezd Schools*	*Pupils*
St. Petersburg	3	294	5	1,066
Moscow	10	447	44	2,356
Vilna	6	1,305	54	7,422
Kharkov	8	477	18	1,747
Kazan	5	315	5	248

Source: *Istoricheskii obzor deyatel'nosti MNP*, p. 71.

The first curators included some distinguished names. In Moscow was M. N. Muravyov, the deputy minister, a man of the eighteenth-century enlightenment, author of a number of minor educational books, formerly one of the tutors of the young Alexander I. In St. Petersburg from 1804 to 1810 was Novosiltsov, in Vilna from 1804 to 1824 Czartoryski.

Another type of institution was also founded in these years, the 'gimnaziya of higher learning' or '*lycée*', with a status intermediate between university and gimnaziya. The first was founded in Yaroslavl, with money provided by P. P. Demidov, a member of the rich family of Ural ironmasters and landowners, and approved in January 1805 by the Tsar. In the same year a similar institution was created at Nezhin in the Ukraine with funds provided by the Bezborodko family. More important was the *lycée* founded in 1810 in Tsarskoe Selo, the small town near St. Petersburg which contained the great palaces built by Catherine II and Alexander I. In 1813 a nobles' boarding-house was added to the *lycée*. The purpose of this *lycée* was defined as 'the education of youth especially predestined for important parts of the state service'. It was especially frequented by the children of the highest aristocracy, and was not amalgamated with the new University of St. Petersburg when the latter was formally opened in 1819.[1] The fourth institution was the *lycée* of the duc de Richelieu, founded in 1817 in Odessa. It included a teachers' training college and schools of law, political economy, and commerce. It formed the nucleus from which emerged fifty years later the University of Odessa.

An example of the practical difficulties in the way of education in Russia is the story of Kharkov University. The initiative came from a young landowner from Kharkov province, V. N. Karazin. A romantic idealist, Karazin had come to the attention of Alexander in the first year of his reign, when he left on

[1] Among its most distinguished pupils was Pushkin, who frequently expressed his devotion to it. His famous poem 'The Nineteenth of October' contains passages that inevitably recall the 'old school' sentimentality of nineteenth-century England, the derision of which has become a literary and journalistic cliché in the English-speaking world. In Russia this sentimentality remains in vogue. A monument can still be seen beside the *lycée*, on which are inscribed the verses:

Kuda by nas ni brosila sud'bina
I schastie kuda b ni povelo
Vsyo te zhe my: nam tsely mir chuzhbina;
Otechestvo nam Tsarskoe Selo.

the emperor's study table an anonymous letter greeting his accession in exalted language and appealing to him to lead Russia into a glorious new age. The identity of the writer was eventually discovered, and the Tsar embraced his admirer.[1] In May 1801, having first obtained the support of some of the local nobility, he put to the Tsar the idea that Kharkov should be the site of the new university which was needed in southern Russia. Alexander welcomed the idea, and Karazin prepared a statute. In August 1802 he went to Kharkov to make his plans known. A private meeting of local landowners agreed to give 100,000 roubles, another to raise a million roubles among the nobility of Slobodskaya Ukraina. Karazin then returned to St. Petersburg and asked for an audience with the Tsar. He was not received, but was told to submit his proposals through the proper channels. The wheels of bureaucracy turned slowly, but Karazin was wildly impatient, and kept urging Kochubey to get action taken. In January 1803 Count Potocki was appointed curator of Kharkov educational district, and sent Karazin back to Kharkov to manage local arrangements. He found that nothing had been done to raise money on the spot, and that a sum which was due from the central government to the Kharkov assembly of the nobility, and which the assembly had promised to the university, was being held back in St. Petersburg. Karazin then mortgaged his own estate with the governor's office and devoted the funds to the preparation of the university. When these ran out, he persuaded Kochubey to obtain an order from the Tsar for the release of the sum due to the nobility. But a further delay occurred when the Ministry of Finance asserted that the emperor's instruction applied only to the following year. Meanwhile Potocki had been unable to employ the foreign professors whom he had recruited on his voyage abroad, as the Russian government refused to pay their travelling expenses to Kharkov. Karazin's status as secretary of the *Glavnoe pravlenie uchilishch* did not help him. His relations with the minister of education, Zavadovsky, were extremely bad, and his former patron Troshchinsky gave him no help. In August 1804 he resigned his post in the ministry, returned home, brought build-

[1] The letter is in Shilder, op. cit. ii. 324–30. Alexander for a time appeared to show great favour to Karazin, who became known—in allusion to Schiller's *Don Carlos*—as the Russian Marquis de Posa.

ing craftsmen from abroad at his own expense, and personally corresponded with foreign professors. This tragi-comic story of over-enthusiasm, vague promises, unrealistic schemes, and bureaucratic obstruction ended in a modest success. The university was opened on 17 January 1805, and by the second quarter of the century it was working tolerably well.[1]

The story of Vilna University is also interesting. Here Czartoryski was concerned not only to develop Polish education but to spread Polish cultural influence in Lithuania and the Ukraine, with the protection of the Russian government. The work was supported partly by the funds of the former Polish Education Commission,[2] partly by religious organizations. A proposal by Zavadovsky to set up a university in Kiev was resisted by Czartoryski's able Polish assistant Tadeusz Czacki, who wished to prevent Russian influence from spreading in the Ukraine. Instead the lycée at Kremenets, which was controlled by Poles, was given in 1805 a semi-university status. In 1801 the Jesuits had been allowed to found a college at Polotsk. Czartoryski was hostile to the Order, but it had an energetic defender at St. Petersburg in the distinguished writer and diplomat Joseph de Maistre, and Zavadovsky was also well disposed. His successor Count A. K. Razumovsky, who became minister in 1810, was still closer to the Jesuits. If Czartoryski was forced to tolerate them within his district, at least he could console himself with the thought that their influence would favour Polish rather than Russian culture.

After peace had been made with Napoleon in 1807, Alexander reverted to his interest in internal reforms. In this new period of his reign his main adviser was Michael Speransky. Born in 1772, the son of a village priest in the district of Vladimir, Speransky was educated in seminaries at Suzdal and St. Petersburg. He was an outstandingly brilliant student, and became a teacher of mathematics in the main church seminary of the capital. On the recommendation of the Metropolitan of St. Petersburg, he was employed by Prince Alexey Kurakin as his private secretary, and when the latter became procurator-

[1] V. V. Abramov, *V. N. Karazin, ego zhizn' i obshchestvennaya deyatel'nost'*, (SPB, 1891), pp. 34–47. For Karazin's later career and personality, *Sochineniya, pis'ma i bumagi V. N. Karazina*, ed. Professor D. I. Bagaleyev, Kharkov, 1910.

[2] Set up in the last years of the Polish state, to develop public education, and taken over by the Russian government after the partitions.

general in 1797 he entered his office with the rank of titular councillor. He survived the changes of Paul's reign, and in March 1801 was appointed assistant to Troshchinsky in the chancery of the Permanent Council. Kochubey obtained his transfer to the Ministry of the Interior in 1802, and he soon became director of one of its departments. Alexander first met him in 1806, when Kochubey sent him to report to the Tsar with some state papers. In 1807 Alexander took him with him on a journey to Vitebsk for army manœuvres, and in 1808 to his meeting with Napoleon at Erfurt. For the next four years he became his principal adviser on most problems of internal administration and reform, more trusted than any of the ministers, a sort of unofficial and irresponsible grand vizier.

Speransky was perhaps the most brilliant bureaucrat that ever served a Tsar. He had an exceptionally clear mind, and a quite unusual capacity for expressing himself in writing, whether in reports and memoranda or in the drafting of laws. He impressed all his contemporaries by his brilliance, but endeared himself to few. The writer Wiegel records that his face had the expression 'd'un veau expirant'. He accused him of indifference, insincerity, and hypocrisy.[1] Many denounced Speransky as an atheist masquerading as a pious believer, but the truth seems to be that he was a convinced Christian. He was a lonely man. He married an English girl, Elizabeth Stevens, daughter of a governess, but she died after less than a year, leaving him a daughter. Except for his child he had no interest in life but his work, into which he plunged up to the limit of his strength. He took little trouble to make himself liked, trusting in his own judgement and the confidence of the emperor. He refused to ingratiate himself with the aristocracy, and did not enjoy the company of men of intelligence. His few intimates were men of mediocre talents, who formed a circle of admirers in whose society he could relax, enjoying their flattery and crude humour.[2]

Speransky was aware of both political and social injustice, of the need both for liberty and for social reform. He was also aware of the difference between the desirable and the possible,

[1] F. F. Vigel (Philippe Wiegel), *Zapiski* (Moscow, 1928), pp. 154–7.

[2] An admirable biography of Speransky, which is also by far the best available single-volume survey of the reign of Alexander I, is Marc Raeff, *Michael Speransky, Statesman of Imperial Russia, 1772–1839,* The Hague, 1961.

and of the various grades of the possible, determined by changing political circumstances. In his cold and practical approach to problems he was most untypical of the Russians of his time or of a later date. His comments on the Russian social system were more profound than those of his contemporaries. The most striking of them are to be found in a memorandum written in 1802, which includes the following passages.[1]

The outward impression is that we have everything, and yet nothing has any real foundation. If monarchical government ought to be something more than a phantom of liberty, then of course we are not yet under a monarchical government. In reality, leaving aside the political uselessness of the various government offices, let us ask what is the nobility itself, when its person, property, honour, indeed everything depends not on the law but on a single autocratic will; does not the law itself, which this will alone creates, depend on this will?

I should like someone to point out the difference between the dependence of the peasants on the landlords and the dependence of the nobles on the sovereign; I should like someone to discover whether in fact the sovereign does not have the same right over the landlords as the landlords have over the peasants. Thus, instead of all the splendid divisions of a free Russian people into the very free classes of nobility, merchants, and the rest, I find in Russia two classes: the slaves of the sovereign and the slaves of the landowners. The first are called free only in relation to the second, but there are no truly free persons in Russia, except beggars and philosophers. What completes the mortification of all energy among the people in Russia, is the relationship in which these two kinds of slave are placed to each other. The interest of the nobility is that the peasants should be in their unlimited power; the interest of the peasants is that the nobility should be in the same degree of dependence on the throne. The nobles, having no sort of political existence, must base the freedom of their life entirely on their incomes, on their land, on the cultivation of the land, and consequently, according to the custom introduced in our country, on the enslavement of the peasants. The peasants, in the condition of slavery which oppresses them, look up to the throne, as the single counterforce, which is able to moderate the power of the landlords.

[1] The best version of this memorandum yet available is published in *M. M. Speransky: proekty i zapiski*, Moscow, Academy of Sciences of the U.S.S.R., 1961. The passages quoted are on pp. 43 and 44. For an account of the history of the manuscript and of the incomplete extracts previously published, see the introduction to the volume by the editor, S. Valk.

But Speransky realized that it was not possible suddenly and radically to transform the system. He saw that the task of statesmanship was to remove the worst injustices. He believed that it would be possible both to improve the lot of the peasants and to establish a less arbitrary form of government. He saw that there was a difference between autocratic government, as it existed in Russia, and the form of government characteristic of eighteenth-century Europe, in which the monarchs exercised supreme political power but were obliged to operate according to known rules and through a regular machinery. Speransky called the European system 'monarchical government'. Something of this sort, based on the traditional division of powers between executive, legislative, and judiciary, was what he hoped to introduce in Russia.

In 1809 he produced, at the request of the Tsar, a draft Statute of State Laws, which included an executive headed by ministers, a legislature consisting of several levels of elected assemblies, and a judiciary headed by the Senate. In addition to these three branches of government there was to be a supreme body, a Council of State of elder statesmen, the closest advisers of the emperor. This rather cumbrous system represented something like a compromise between the oligarchic council desired by the statesmen of Catherine's era and the bureacratic administration preferred by the Unofficial Committee, combined with representative legislative institutions which neither had proposed.

The legislative apparatus was to have four tiers of assemblies, known by the name of duma.[1] The lower dumas would meet only once in three years, and they would elect their own local executive board. The State Duma would meet every year, and the length of its session would depend on the amount of business. It would have no say in the appointment of ministers, which was reserved to the emperor: it could, however, propose from its members three candidates one of whom would be selected by the emperor as its president (Speaker). No new law could come into force unless it had previously been discussed in the Duma.

[1] The *volost* duma would consist of all landowners resident in the *volost*, together with one representative each of every five hundred male state peasants. It would elect representatives to the *uezd* duma, which would elect to the provincial duma, which would elect to the State Duma or Imperial Parliament.

A law rejected by a majority of the Duma would be invalid, and a law passed by the Duma must be confirmed by the emperor. The emperor could dissolve or prorogue the Duma on the advice of the Council of State. Normally business would be introduced by a minister or a member of the Council of State. The Duma might, however, take the initiative in raising matters that affected 'the needs of the state', or question measures contrary to the 'fundamental laws of the state'.[1]

This project was never carried out as a whole, but one part of it was realized. The Council of State was established, and was formally opened by the emperor on 1 January 1810.[2] It could not perform the function intended by Speransky, since the rest of his structure did not exist. It remained, however, an institution of some importance during the nineteenth century, as the supreme advisory body on legislation, composed of a number of appointed elder statesmen, embodying the accumulated wisdom of the most experienced bureaucrats. Most draft laws of importance were discussed by it, though emperors did not necessarily accept the opinions of its majorities. The machinery of the Council of State was operated by the Imperial secretary. The first holder of this office was Speransky himself.

Speransky was also responsible for a reorganization of the ministries. The office of state treasurer, created by Paul but abolished in 1802, was restored, side by side with the Ministry of Finance, and its head held ministerial rank. A new post of equal status was that of state controller, responsible for the public accounts. A third new ministry was the Directorate of Communications, responsible for all transport. It was decided to divide the Ministry of the Interior in two. Public security and public health were transferred to a new Ministry of Police, entrusted to General A. D. Balashov. The residual Ministry of the Interior remained responsible for the encouragement of agriculture and industry, the organization of food supplies, and trade policy. The Ministry of Commerce was abolished, most of its functions being given to the Ministry of the Interior but some to the Ministry of Finance.[3]

[1] The full text of the statute is in *M. M. Speransky: proekty i zapiski*, pp. 143–221.

[2] The law establishing the Council of State is in PSZ, first series no. 24064 (vol. 31, pp. 3–15).

[3] The details of delimitation of the ministries are in PSZ, first series nos. 24307 and 24326, of 25 July and 17 Aug. 1810 respectively (vol. 31, pp. 278–80, 323–8).

Speransky was also much concerned during these years with education, both in the new ministry and in the organization of religious schools which came under the Holy Synod. He was appointed in 1808 secretary of the commission for the codification of laws. Speransky's work in this field was criticized as a mere copy of Napoleonic legislation, far too hastily compiled, though this he hotly denied. The first two parts of his Code were discussed in the Council of State during 1810 but never came into force. Speransky was also responsible for preparing taxes, which during the years of growing danger from Napoleon, heavy defence needs, and economic hardships caused by Russia's participation in the Continental System,[1] were inevitably high, and thus made him unpopular. He angered the aristocracy by a decree of 3 April 1809, which suppressed the practice by which the court titles of *Kammerjunker* and *Kammerherr*, conferred by the monarch on young people of aristocratic families, automatically entitled their holders to enter the state service respectively in the fifth or fourth grade, thus exempting them from many years of work at lower levels. Still greater anger was caused by the decree of 6 August 1809, which prescribed study in a university, or a written entrance examination, as a condition for attaining the higher ranks of state service. Speransky's humble origin, cold personality, and unpopular measures combined to make him enemies, and Alexander was increasingly pressed to dismiss him. The Tsar was the less able to resist, as his own policy of co-operation with Napoleon, which had never been accepted by the upper classes, was clearly failing, and he would need their support more than ever as the international danger increased. Speransky's admiration for French institutions, methods, and style of government further increased his unpopularity.

The military defeats of 1805–7 had only strengthened Russian patriotism. An important factor in the growth of this feeling was the development of the Russian language itself and the appearance of a considerable number of people who were interested in literature, not only in foreign languages, but in their own. In these years a literary debate began in Russia which had wider implications. The question was whether Russian should be based on the old ecclesiastical language or should be made more

[1] See below p. 123.

like modern European languages. The controversy concerned not so much the introduction of foreign words as questions of style and thought. The exponents of the two rival schools were Admiral A. S. Shishkov and N. M. Karamzin. Shishkov, born in 1772, had a rather successful career in the navy but was always interested in literature. In 1803 he published a book entitled *Reflections on the Old and New Formation of the Russian Language*. He maintained that Russian and Church Slavonic were the same language, and that the modern language should be based solely on the old. This literary doctrine was also associated in Shishkov's mind with political views: he was a firm upholder of all traditional institutions as such, and he believed in a common interest binding all Orthodox Slav peoples to Russia. Karamzin, born in 1766, began his literary career under Catherine II, when he published from 1790 to 1792 the *Moscow Journal*, in which appeared his 'Notes of a Russian traveller' describing his impressions of western Europe. In 1792 he won great popularity with a sentimental novel entitled *Poor Liza*. In 1802 he started another periodical, *Vestnik Evropy* (Messenger of Europe) which was to have a long and influential existence. From 1804 he devoted himself chiefly to the study of Russian history, working on the monumental *History of the Russian State*, of which eleven volumes came out before his death in 1826, and the uncompleted twelfth was published posthumously. Karamzin had the eighteenth century's passion for enlightenment and admired Europe, though the admiration was mixed with growing criticism. He believed that the Russian language should be based on contemporary speech rather than on ecclesiastical models, and that new words should be created, based on existing Russian Slav roots, to introduce the new ideas that modern life required. Shiskhov's denunciations of Karamzin's neologisms were supported by a group of his personal and literary friends, including the poet and former minister of justice G. R. Derzhavin, which took the name 'Gatherings of Lovers of the Russian Word'.[1]

The controversy between Shishkov and Karamzin recalls in some ways the controversy that was developing about the same time, among Greek patriots, between the supporters of the

[1] *Besedy lyubiteley russkogo slova*. The group used to meet from about 1807 onwards but took this formal title in 1811.

'pure' and 'popular' language. In the Greek case the purists prevailed, and this had far-reaching effects on Greek public life. It may be argued that the artificial 'purification' of modern Greek acted as a powerful brake not only on literature but on social development. But in Russia the school of Karamzin prevailed, and the following years were the greatest period of Russian literature. It is interesting to note that this great flowering of Russian poetry, first with Zhukovsky and then with Pushkin, should have coincided with the great crisis of Russia's destiny, the threat of Napoleon and the ultimate victory of Russian arms. The simultaneous appearance of three great forces—a mortal danger to the nation, an upsurge of patriotism, and a flowering of the language—can be seen also in the history of other nations, especially perhaps in Elizabethan England and sixteenth-century Spain.[1]

This Russian patriotism operated against Speransky, though he was no less a Russian patriot than were his enemies. His reforms were not only resented in themselves by the extreme conservatives, but damned by an understandable, even though unjust, association with the Napoleonic model. Opposition was largely grouped around the Dowager Empress Maria Fyodorovna and her daughter Grand Duchess Catherine, married since 1809 to the Duke of Oldenburg, who was governor-general of three central provinces with his residence at Tver. One spokesman in this circle of Russian conversatism was Count F. V. Rostopchin, who had been for two years Paul's minister of foreign affairs but had been in retirement since February 1801. During these years he became increasingly obsessed with the danger to Russia from subversive ideas spread by secret agents of Napoleon. He feared a combination of radical doctrinaires and disaffected serfs. He detested Freemasons and feared still more the disciples of the French eighteenth-century writer Saint-Martin. Everywhere among the educated

[1] In the case of Spain it was perhaps not so much a matter of 'mortal danger' as of sudden rise to greatness—from the obscurity of fifteenth-century Castile and Aragon to the glories of Charles V, with the Americas open to Spain. However, it can also be argued that the threat to the Catholic Church from the Reformation, and the threat to Christendom from the Turkey of Suliman the Magnificent—defeated by Spanish arms at Lepanto—were felt by the rulers and politically minded class of Spain as no less a 'mortal danger' than was Napoleon's invasion to Russia or the Spanish Armada to England.

class of the two capitals Rostopchin claimed to detect the evil influence of 'Martinists'. Speransky, he believed, was making use of them for his own purposes. Rostopchin was horrified by the trends of Russian society: 'Notre jeunesse est pire que la française; on n'obéit et on ne craint personne. Il faut convenir que pour être habillés à l'européenne, nous sommes encore bien loin d'être civilisés. Le pire est que nous avons cessé d'être Russes et que nous avons acheté la connaissance des langues étrangères au prix des mœurs de nos ancêtres.'[1] Rostopchin was a passionate character, at times also a witty writer. He was a rebellious individualist, as well as a reactionary. In the words of a later historian, 'he was inspired by the fanatical idea of the independent citizen professing a doctrine of political slavery'. He combined 'the ideology of a slave with the temperament of a mutineer'.[2] Rostopchin was introduced by Grand Duchess Catherine to the Tsar in 1809, and on her recommendation he was appointed governor-general of Moscow in May 1812.

Shishkov naturally supported the extreme conservative viewpoint. But Karamzin himself was moving in the same direction. His historical studies were causing him to admire the Russian past, while the spectacle of contemporary Europe inspired him with growing disgust and alarm. In 1810 he stayed at the house of Grand Duchess Catherine in Tver, and in the following year she introduced him to her brother. It was at the request of the grand duchess that he wrote his reflections on contemporary policies in the light of his view of Russian history, entitled *Memorandum on Ancient and Modern Russia.* In this work he deplored the abandonment of the collegiate principle in government in favour of ministerial subordination. Ministers now had too much power. Deliberations in the Committee of Ministers were no substitute for the discussions of experienced public servants within the old collegiate bodies. Ministers did not and could not know each other's business, and so could not advise each other. Karamzin in fact was pleading for bureaucratic wisdom, for discussion not among the Tsar's closest advisers but at the highest level within departments clearly separated from each other. Karamzin strongly supported the principle of

[1] Letter of Rostopchin to Count Simon Vorontsov of 23 Aug. 1803. *Arkhiv knyaz'ya Vorontsova*, xxix. 307–8.

[2] A. Kizevetter, *Istoricheskie otkliki* (Moscow, 1915), pp. 103, 105.

autocracy, and objected to any constitutional limitations on the sovereignty of the monarch. At the same time, however, he rejected arbitrary rule, which he called 'despotism', and upheld the rights of the nobility, including their complete domination over their serfs. Belief in autocracy and in liberty did not seem to him a contradiction. The notion, upheld by the lessons of centuries of European history, that the liberties of the citizen, including the nobleman, can be guaranteed only by legal privileges and corporate representation, was entirely alien to him, and to almost all Russians of his time. The *Memorandum*, which is a fine piece of writing, and an historically valuable expression of conservative thought, was presented by Catherine to Alexander, but whether he read it is not known.[1]

Another close adviser of the Tsar, whose influence certainly operated in a different direcion from that of Speransky, was Arakcheyev. He returned to the centre of power on 14 May 1803, when Alexander appointed him inspector of the artillery. In this he was extremely successful. The artillery did well in the wars with Napoleon, and Arakcheyev's foundations remained the basis in later years of what continued to be perhaps the best arm of the Russian forces. In 1806 Alexander made Arakcheyev minister of war. In this capacity he took command of the Russian armies which invaded Finland in 1808. In the following year, however, he suffered a set-back, largely brought on by his own arrogance. During the years 1807–9 Alexander had considered Speransky his adviser on internal political affairs and Arakcheyev his adviser on military affairs, but saw no reason to consult either of them on matters concerning the other. In January 1810 when the Council of State was instituted, Arakcheyev was appointed head of its military department. Arakcheyev, however, was furious that he had not been consulted beforehand on the preparation of the Council of State, and resigned his post as minister of war. Alexander's reply was angry. He declared himself unable to take the excuses at their face value. Everyone else had approved of the Council of State.

But you, on whose co-operation I had most counted, you who have

[1] The full text in Russian of the *Memorandum* has recently been published, together with a translation into English, commentary, and an introductory essay, by Richard Pipes—*Karamzin's Memoir on Ancient and Modern Russia*, Harvard University Press, 1959.

so often asserted to me that you are inspired by love for me as well as by devotion to the fatherland, none the less you alone, ignoring the interest of the empire, hasten to throw aside the department administered by you, at a time when your conscience cannot fail to feel how necessary you are to it, how impossible it is to replace you. . . . At a time when I had the right to expect that all persons of honourable thoughts, devoted to the fatherland, would give me their warm and eager co-operation, you alone abandon me, and by preferring your personal ambition, which has been allegedly hurt, to the interests of the empire, you will genuinely harm your reputation.[1]

Arakcheyev allowed himself to be persuaded to accept the chairmanship of the military department of the Council of State, but insisted on giving up the ministry, which was taken over by General Barclay de Tolly. It is possible that this incident created a resentment in Arakcheyev's mind against Speransky. There is, however, little reason to believe that there was any very bitter personal feeling between the two men, or that Arakcheyev was directly involved in Speransky's overthrow.

There were others, however, whose reactionary views were strengthened by strong personal hostility to Speransky. One was a Swedish Count Armfeld, who wanted for himself the curatorship of the Finnish University of Åbo, which Speransky held. Another was Baron Rosenkampf, who was probably the author of a memorandum later published by the poet I. I. Dmitriev, who had been appointed minister of justice in 1811. This accused Speransky of overweening pride, of atheism, and of antagonizing all social classes alike. He had destroyed the valuable collegiate system and replaced it with an administrative machinery so complicated that 'il paralysait le principe de l'unité et du contrôle'. His taxes had ruined the state finances.

Ses principes administratifs prouvent, à peu d'exceptions près, qu'il a eu l'intention de désorganiser l'ordre de choses existant et d'amener un bouleversement général . . . . L'homme qui a pu entreprendre avec sang-froid une pareille tâche, en jouissant de la confiance et des bienfaits de l'empereur Alexandre; qui sait cacher avec un art inoui la vérité et masquer le danger auquel il exposait l'empire; qui en affectant une âme pénétrée de sentiments religieux, ne craignait ni les reproches de sa conscience ni le mécontentement

[1] Grand Duke Nikolay Mikhailovich, *Imperator Aleksandr I.* (SPB, 1912), ii. 571–2.

de son maître, ni les murmures de toute la nation; un tel homme, dis-je, avait pris son parti depuis longtemps et se conduisait d'après un plan mûrement réfléchi.[1]

On 17 March 1812 Speransky was summoned to an audience with the Tsar at eight o'clock. He emerged after two hours, and Prince A. N. Golitsyn, who was in the antechamber, noticed signs that he had been weeping. At his house he found the minister of police, Balashov, who escorted him, as soon as he had packed his things, on the way to Nizhnii Novgorod. Later he was exiled to Perm in the Urals. There is no authentic account of the Tsar's conversation with him. The testimony of persons who spoke with Alexander shortly afterwards is, however, of interest. He told Golitsyn on 18 March: 'Last night they took Speransky away from me, and he had been my right hand.' He told Nesselrode on the 20th: 'only present circumstances could force from me this sacrifice to public opinion'. He told Novosiltsov: 'Speransky was never a traitor.' In St. Petersburg rumours circulated that Speransky was a traitor and a French spy, but not only is there no evidence that this was so, but there is no reason to believe that Alexander took them seriously. He was offended with him for minor personal reasons, he no longer felt it possible to proceed with his reforms, and he knew that the coming conflict with France would force him to placate public feeling, which was hostile to Speransky. So he abandoned him.[2]

This disaster was not the end of Speransky's career of public service. But it was the end of his major reforms. It was the end of one opportunity that was given to a Russian Tsar to modernize and liberalize his country's government. Whether the blame be attributed to Alexander, or to Napoleon, or to forces greater than either, the fact remains that the opportunity was lost.

[1] The full text of the *Memorandum* is reproduced in Baron M. A. Korf, *Zhizn' grafa Speranskogo* (SPB, 1861), ii. 31–40.

[2] Ibid., pp. 24–26. See also I. I. Dmitriev, *Vzglyad na moyu zhizn'*, (Moscow, 1866), pp. 193–9, and a letter from Speransky to Alexander, and a memorandum in justification of his policies, written in Perm, without a date, published in Shilder, op. cit. iii. 515–32. Apart from the factors mentioned above, Alexander objected to Speransky's intervention in foreign affairs, including correspondence with Russian diplomats abroad. This rather complicated matter is discussed in Korf, op. cit.

Alexander and Napoleon, 1807–1812

It seems likely that Alexander at Tilsit was neither the dupe of Napoleon's flattery nor impervious to his charm, neither the willing satellite of France nor the Machiavellian Russian statesman planning far ahead the downfall of the Corsican upstart. These roles, attributed to him in his lifetime and since, are creations of fantasy or prejudice rather than a true likeness, though each of them contains perhaps some elements of the truth. Alexander knew that Russia was weak, believed that co-operation with Napoleon was possible, felt a measure of unwilling admiration for his great antagonist, and hoped that with his consent advantages could be gained for Russia. He was, therefore, determined to try out a Francophil policy, but never intended Russia to be a vassal of France or to renounce the status of a Great Power. His new minister of foreign affairs, Count Nicholas Rumyantsev, who alone at the council meeting of April 1804 had opposed the breach with France, was well suited to carry out the new policy.

The news of Tilsit was received in England with regret but without indignation. Canning admitted that Britain had done so little to help Russia that she had no right to condemn her for ending the struggle. In the Mediterranean the British still held Malta and Sicily, and when the Ionian Islands were handed over by the Russians to the French they were attacked by British naval forces. Only Corfu was able to hold out until 1814. Senyavin's fleet sailed out into the Atlantic, and then took refuge in Lisbon, where in 1808 it surrendered on honourable terms to the British. In the first weeks after Tilsit, Sir Robert Wilson remained in St. Petersburg, and was received in a friendly manner by the Tsar. At the beginning of September, however, in order to forestall a reconstitution of the Armed Neutrality, British sea and land forces suddenly attacked Copenhagen, destroying the Danish fleet and inflicting serious damage on the capital. This aggression enraged Alexander. Shortly afterwards Wilson, who had circulated a pamphlet that contained insulting references to the Tsar, was expelled. On 7 November diplomatic relations were broken. Thus Alexander had fulfilled his Tilsit obligation nearly a month early.

Denmark naturally joined the Franco-Russian front against

Britain. But Sweden refused to do so. Trade with Britain was of the greatest importance to the Swedish economy. King Gustav also remained an implacable enemy of Napoleon. He therefore refused Russian advice. Napoleon, through his ambassador in St. Petersburg, Caulaincourt, urged Alexander to go to war with Sweden, and promised his support for the annexation of Finland to Russia. Such a large gain of territory, which would also protect St. Petersburg against attack from the west, appealed to the Tsar as a means of appeasing Russian patriotic feeling offended by Tilsit. Napoleon also promised to help by a joint attack from the west of Danish forces and of a French army under Bernadotte. The war began in February 1808. The Danes and French did not move, but their presence caused Swedish troops to be kept in the west. In Finland the Russian armies were at first very successful. In three months the whole peninsula was overrun, and the admiral commanding the extremely strong naval fortress of Sveaborg handed it over to the Russians without resistance.

But if the Swedish armies had been defeated, the people of Finland, both its Swedish nobility and its Finnish peasantry, remained hostile. In the summer and autumn guerrilla forces became a serious threat to the Russian armies. An armistice was signed in November, but hostilities were continued at the beginning of 1809. Arakcheyev, as minister of war, himself came to Finland in February. Soon after his arrival a successful attack was made, under General Barclay de Tolly, across the ice of the frozen Gulf of Finland, on the Åland Islands, a strategically important archipelago which controls the entry to the Gulfs of Finland and Bothnia and the approaches to Stockholm. At the same time other Russian forces crossed the Gulf of Bothnia to the Swedish mainland at points further to the north, and the capital itself was in danger. At the beginning of March 1809 King Gustav was overthrown by a conspiracy, and Sweden was ready to make peace.

Meanwhile great efforts had been made to win over the people of Finland. A deputation of Finnish representatives visited St. Petersburg in the autumn of 1808. Alexander declared himself determined to uphold all the existing liberties of the Finnish estates and people. He summoned a Finnish elected Diet in Borgå, and came personally to address it on

27 March 1809. From this time Finland was united with Russia only through the person of the monarch: Alexander was emperor of Russia and grand duke of Finland. Finland kept its own laws and institutions, and for nearly a century the Tsars respected them.

Peace was signed with Sweden at Frederikshamn on 27 September 1809. Sweden renounced all Finland east of the Tornio river, and including the Åland Islands. Sweden also joined Napoleon's continental blockade, and in 1810 declared war on Britain.

At the end of June 1807 hostilities were suspended between the Russians and Turks, and in August an armistice was signed, by which both sides should withdraw their troops from Roumania, and the Russians should restore to the Turks the island of Tenedos in the Aegean and some captured Turkish ships. Further discussions should lead to a treaty of peace. However, Alexander was not eager to give up his hopes of expansion in the Balkans, and for the new foreign minister Rumyantsev this was the supreme object of Russian policy. Alexander was also displeased that Napoleon had not reduced his troops in Prussian territory. He argued that if he evacuated the Roumanian Principalities, Napoleon must evacuate Prussia, and that it was an obligation of honour for him to ensure that his former ally King Frederick William was treated with respect. After some hesitation Napoleon decided that he was not prepared to evacuate Prussian Silesia, and in return agreed to Russian troops remaining in the Roumanian Principalities. This would, however, mean that peace would not be made between Russia and Turkey. In this case the alternative mentioned in the secret treaty of alliance of Tilsit—a partition of Turkey between the two empires—must be examined.

Napoleon decided to go further still. He had never abandoned his hopes of conquest in the East, of a more brilliant repetition and extension of his Egyptian enterprise of 1798. His aim was the conquest of India, both because he believed that this would bring his rival England to her knees and because the role of Oriental conqueror, heir to Alexander the Great, appealed irresistibly to him. He expounded, in a personal letter to Alexander of 2 February 1808, his plan of a joint invasion of India through Turkey and Persia by French and Russian armies. Southern Italy and the Ionian Islands were to be the French base, and steps were at once to be taken to build up the necessary forces there. Having no enemy to face on land, Napoleon could in fact concentrate his forces, recruited from all occupied Europe, on this task. But first France and Russia must agree on the division of the Ottoman empire.

This was the subject of negotiations in St. Petersburg during the spring of 1808. The account given in Caulaincourt's dispatches[1] provides a fascinating picture of cupidity, obstinacy, and ignorance of geography. Caulaincourt found that neither the Tsar nor Rumyantsev were inferior to his own master in their appetite for territory.

The minimum claims of each side could be agreed without difficulty: Russia was to have the Roumanian Principalities and Bulgaria up to the Balkan Mountains, while France was to have Albania, the Peloponnese, and the Greek islands. Austria would have to receive some gains in the area of Bosnia and Serbia. Here there was already some disagreement, because France claimed part of Bosnia, and Rumyantsev would have liked some say in Serbia, though he was prepared to settle for a separate state under an Austrian archduke or other European prince, provided that he were married to a Russian grand duchess.

The serious arguments concerned the southern portion of Turkey in Europe (known by the vague name of 'Roumelia' which from this time figures confusingly in diplomatic literature) and above all the Straits. Rumyantsev insisted that Russia must have the city of Constantinople, the Bosphorus, and the Dardanelles. He proposed that the Russian acquisitions should be separated from the French by an Austrian corridor which should stretch from Serbia through Macedonia to the sea, but excluding Salonica, which should go to France together with all Bosnia, Albania, and peninsular Greece. France should also acquire the Aegean Islands, the Aegean coast of Turkey, Syria, and Egypt. Croatia should belong either to France or to Austria. Caulaincourt objected that Russia should not have Constantinople, but that if she did, then France must have the Dar-

[1] The diplomatic papers of Caulaincourt, describing his conversations with Alexander and with Rumyantsev, are published in Grand Duke Nikolay Mikhailovich, *La France et la Russie*, SPB, 1905, 6 volumes. The discussions on the partition of Turkey are in i. 105–230.

danelles. In this case there would be no Austrian corridor, but the French territory would be bounded by a line from Priština across northern Macedonia, then following the line of the Balkan Mountains and descending through Adrianople to the Sea of Marmara at Rodosto. Alternatively Constantinople might be left with its own independent government, in which case Russia could be compensated by Trebizond in the eastern Black Sea. He also insisted that if France were to acquire Syria and Egypt, Russia must help her conquer them.[1] Alexander, however, declared that though he was willing to join with the French in the conquest of Turkey he was not prepared to fight for Syria and Egypt as well.[2]

The negotiations showed such profound differences that there could be little hope of agreement. However, the Turkish problem did not lead to Franco-Russian conflict, for with the outbreak of revolt in Spain in May 1808 Napoleon was faced with an enemy on land who was to occupy a substantial portion of his armed forces for the next five years. Russia's armies also remained occupied, by the war with Turkey in Roumania, which dragged on inconclusively for four more years. The grand project was therefore tacitly abandoned.

Russia also had military commitments in Transcaucasia. The annexation of Georgia did not proceed smoothly, for there were rival claimants to the throne of George XIII, supported by Turkey or Persia. In 1802 the Russian General Tsitsianov, himself of Georgian origin, was sent to pacify the new territory. He also persuaded the ruler of Mingrelia to accept incorporation in the Russian empire in 1803. In the following year he declared a protectorate over Imeretia. But here he met with fierce resistance, and when Turkey declared war on Russia in 1806 the Imeretians made common cause with the Turks. Tsitsianov also provoked war with Persia in 1804 by attacking Erivan, which he was unable to capture. In 1806 Tsitsianov was treacherously murdered while negotiating with the Persians at Baku.

Fathali Shah of Persia sought French help. In May 1807 his emissary signed a treaty of alliance with Napoleon at Finkelstein in East Prussia, and a strong military mission, under General Gardanne, was sent to train the Persian army. However, even before Gardanne arrived, his master had signed the

[1] Ibid. i. 216–17. [2] Ibid. i. 224.

Peace of Tilsit, and for the time being lost any interest in support to the Persians against Russia. Napoleon's aim was rather to use Persia as an ally in the invasion which he planned, with Russian help, against British India. But the Shah was interested only in the recovery of Azerbaidjan from the Russians: disappointed with the French he turned to the British as military advisers. But here too, through no fault of his own, his timing was unfortunate. As the relations between France and Russia deteriorated, the British sought a reconciliation with Russia. They therefore used their influence in Persia to favour a Russo-Persian settlement, which inevitably meant a surrender of Persian interests to Russian. In 1812 the Persian forces suffered two serious defeats at Russian hands, and the Shah reluctantly accepted British advice. Peace was not in fact secured until after Napoleon had been expelled from Russia. It was confirmed by the Treaty of Gulistan, of 12 October 1813, by which Russia finally acquired the northern part of Azerbaidjan, with the cities of Derbend, Baku, and Gandja.[1]

In European affairs the friendship of Napoleon and Alexander received its most sensational expression at their second meeting in the small central German city of Erfurt from 27 September to 14 October 1808. The pageantry was impressive, and the German princes danced attendance on Napoleon. He and the Tsar effusively proclaimed their friendship for each other. At the same time Alexander showed himself friendly to the emperor of Austria, while Talleyrand did his best to ingratiate himself with Alexander and to urge him to resist Napoleon's ambitions. He is supposed on this occasion to have remarked that France had a civilized people and an uncivilized ruler, Russia a civilized ruler and an uncivilized people, and that Europe thus needed an alliance between the emperor of Russia and the French people. The practical outcome of Erfurt was a new Franco-Russian treaty by which Napoleon recognized Russia's acquisition of Finland, Moldavia, and Wallachia.[2] Napoleon wished for a formal military alliance against Austria,

[1] Persian accounts of these events, based overwhelmingly on French not Persian documents, are Sayid Nefisi, *Tarikh-i ijtama'i va siyasi-ye Iran*, vol. i (Tehran, 1952 (A.H. 1330)), and Ahmed Tajbakhsh, *Ravabat-i Iran va Rusyeh dar nimeh-ye aval-i garn-i nuzdahum* (Tehran, 1959 (A.H. 1337)).

[2] The Treaty of Erfurt is in Martens, op. cit. xiv. 68–73.

but Alexander would do no more than assure him verbally that he would help him in the event of war with Austria.

From the beginning of 1809 such a war grew probable. Napoleon's defeats in Spain seemed to offer an opportunity to Austria, whose army had been greatly reinforced and more efficiently trained and equipped to get her revenge for 1805. The Austrian ambassador in Paris, Count Metternich, strongly favoured war, and was encouraged in this view by Talleyrand, now a fierce though still discreet enemy of Napoleon. In February 1809 Prince Schwarzenberg came to St. Petersburg to try to win Russian support for Austria. Alexander made it clear that he had obligations to France which he would fulfil, but also allowed his visitor to understand that the fulfilment would be neither swift nor efficient. In April 1809 war began. Napoleon won some small successes, the Austrians retreated, and he entered Vienna. But the main Austrian army, under Archduke Charles, remained intact on the northern bank of the Danube facing the capital. On 21–22 May Napoleon fought a bloody and inconclusive battle at Aspern, but failed in his objective of bringing his army across the river. Six weeks later, in the same area, he defeated the archduke in the no less bloody battle of Wagram, 6 July 1809.

Alexander duly declared war, but no action followed. The Russian armies waited on the Galician border until June. When at last they moved, it was not so much to fight the Austrians as to forestall the Poles. The army of the grand duchy of Warsaw, under Prince Józef Poniatowski, had eagerly fought on the French side, hoping to unite Galicia with the grand duchy. This Alexander was anxious to prevent. He had favoured the Poles so long as it was a question of uniting Poland under his crown. But the prospect of a French-protected Polish state being enlarged at the expense of Austria was highly alarming: such a state could only be an enemy of Russia, for its rulers would inevitably seek to recover from Russia the lands taken in the partitions. Therefore, in 1809 the Russian forces in Galicia regarded the Poles, rather than the Austrians, as their enemies. On 14 July the Austrian garrison of Kraków, which had held out against Poniatowski, surrendered to the Russians, who arrived after no fighting, simply in order to deprive the Poles of their victory.

Napoleon bitterly resented the failure of the Russians to give him any effective help. During the critical weeks between Aspern and Wagram he had needed them, and they had failed him. For his part Alexander was now deeply suspicious of Napoleon's Polish policy. Yet the French emperor made great efforts to conciliate the Tsar. The greater part of Galicia was left to Austria, the grand duchy received only a territory with about 1,000,000 inhabitants, and Russia was given a piece of Eastern Galicia with some 400,000 inhabitants, mostly not Poles but Ukrainians. On the other hand Austria was obliged to cede to Napoleon further territories, of Croatian population, in the south. These were combined to form the province of Illyria, annexed directly to France.

Napoleon was still anxious to remove Alexander's fears about Poland, and during the winter of 1809–10 the two governments discussed the wording of a convention to be signed on the Polish question. The French text, which Napoleon ratified in advance on 9 February 1810 as a conciliatory gesture, contained in its first article an undertaking that France would 'give no assistance to any Power aiming at the restoration of Poland, and would give no support or encouragement, direct or indirect, to any insurrection or rising of the inhabitants of the provinces which composed that kingdom'. The second article provided that neither France nor Russia, nor the king of Saxony (the sovereign of the grand duchy) would in future use in any public act 'the words "Poland" or "Poles" to designate any part of the former Kingdom of Poland and its inhabitants'. Rumyantsev was not satisfied with the wording of the first article, and proposed that France should simply undertake 'that the Kingdom of Poland shall never be restored'. He also made a number of lesser amendments to the text. Napoleon refused to accept the change in the first article. Of the proposed statement that Poland shall never be restored, he remarked: 'Divinity alone can speak as Russia proposes, and in the annals of the nations one could not find such a formulation.' France had promised not to restore Poland or to help its restoration, but she was not prepared to promise to use force against the Poles, or third parties assisting the Poles, in defence of Russian interests, just as she had not asked Russia to help her by force to prevent the restoration of any of the European states which had been conquered by France. 'On ne peut donc concevoir le but que peut avoir la Russie en refusant une rédaction qui lui accorde ce qu'elle désire, pour y substituer une rédaction dogmatique inusitée, contraire à la prudence humaine, et telle enfin que l'empereur Napoléon ne peut la souscrire qu'en se déshonorant'.[1]

The curious Russian insistence on useless phrases revealed an ineradicable distrust, and Napoleon's final refusal of the Russian amendments reflected the fact that he no longer placed so much value on his alliance with Russia. Parallel with the negotiations about Poland had gone negotiations for the hand of a Russian grand duchess for the French emperor. Napoleon needed a son, and as it became clear that his Empress Josephine could not give him one, he decided to divorce her. Even at the time of the Erfurt meeting he had been thinking in these terms, and had hoped that he might marry Alexander's favourite sister Catherine. But meanwhile she had been married to Prince George of Oldenburg, and Napoleon therefore asked for the younger sister, Anna, now fifteen years old. Alexander assured Caulaincourt of his sympathy, but said that the decision must be left to his mother, the Dowager Empress Maria Fyodorovna. The empress disliked the prospect, and Alexander temporized. After more than a year of Russian evasion, Napoleon lost patience, and decided to take as his bride the Austrian Archduchess Marie Louise. His decision was announced on 6 February 1810, before Alexander's refusal of Anna, in the form of a proposal to postpone the marriage for two years because of her youth, had reached Paris.

The failure to arrange either the marriage or the convention on Poland meant that in effect the Franco-Russian alliance had ceased to exist. Napoleon no longer counted on Alexander as a partner: it was only a matter of time before he became his declared enemy. Meanwhile a new candidate for the role of junior partner to France appeared in the person of Emperor Francis of Austria, coached for the part by Metternich, who was now his chief adviser on foreign affairs. Formerly the most resolute opponent of France, Metternich had decided, after the defeat of 1809, that there was no alternative to co-operation with the master of Europe. At the same time Metternich distrusted Russian aims in both Poland and the Balkans, both of

[1] Nikolay Mikhailovich, *La France et la Russie*, iv. 407–19.

which threatened Austrian interests. If the Tsar had abandoned his former allies and fellow monarchs to do a deal with the usurper, Metternich would play the same game at his expense.

Alexander decided that he must conciliate both the Poles and the Austrians. For the first purpose he tried to enlist the help of his old friend Adam Czartoryski. In a letter of 6 January 1811 the Tsar asked Prince Adam for his views on the state of opinion in the grand duchy, and whether he thought that the Poles could be induced to support Russia against Napoleon. Czartoryski replied that the Poles had reason to be grateful to Napoleon for creating the grand duchy, and were convinced of his overwhelming strength. They could only be brought on to the side of Russia if the Tsar would promise the restoration of the constitution of May 1791 and the reunification of all Poland under one ruler, as well as assuring outlets for Polish trade. Alexander replied that he did not know the 1791 constitution, but would like to see a copy! He declared himself willing to proclaim the restoration of Poland, but only provided that it were united for ever with Russia, with its emperor as king of Poland. As for reunification, this could only be secured if Austria would agree to part with Galicia. He proposed to offer her compensation in Roumania in return for this. But if Austria refused to part with Galicia, then he would be able to offer the Poles only the formerly Prussian and Russian portions of their divided country. Nothing came of this correspondence. Czartoryski's soundings of his countrymen were not encouraging. In a letter a year later, on the eve of war, Alexander explained his failure to reply because 'your previous letters left me too little hope of success to authorize me to act, which I could not reasonably have done unless I had some probability of success'.[1]

Alexander had, however, tried to persuade Austria to give up Galicia. In a letter of 20 February 1811 to Emperor Francis he had offered all Wallachia, the portion of Moldavia between the Siret and the Wallachian border, and Serbia, in return for the cession to Russia of Galicia. But Metternich would not consider abandoning his new policy. Alexander's proposed exchange never had a chance of success.[2]

[1] This correspondence is in *Mémoires du prince Adam Czartoryski*, ii. 248–84.

[2] On Russo-Austrian relations from 1810 to 1812 see Martens, op. cit. iii. 70–89.

A further cause of Franco-Russian conflict in 1810 was the operation of the continental blockade. Britain had been by far the most important customer for Russian exports, especially for flax, hemp, and various naval stores, and the most important source of supply for Russian imports, especially textiles. The trade with Britain was not in fact completely cut off, as some British goods reached Russian ports in neutral, mainly American, ships. But the volume was enormously reduced. France and her dependencies could not provide a sufficient substitute, though trade with them did substantially increase. Russian textile manufacturers, and many small craftsmen producers, gained from the removal of British competition, but the main trading merchants and the landowners who produced flax and hemp suffered heavy losses. The loss of customs revenue to the government was also a serious factor, and contributed to the steady depreciation of the currency through the issue of paper money. Thus there were strong economic as well as political reasons for Alexander's growing hostility to Napoleon. They were dramatically expressed by a decree of 31 December 1810 which imposed heavy duties on goods imported by land, especially on luxury goods, while treating much more generously imports by sea, provided that they were carried in ships of a nation with which Russia was not at war. Though ostensibly inspired by fiscal motives, this decree was clearly aimed against French interests, for imports from France came by land, and largely consisted of luxuries, while the goods brought by sea largely consisted of re-exports from Britain by way of America. Napoleon was enraged by this action since he had recently been pressing Alexander to close Russian ports to neutral ships on the ground that they were in effect agents of the British. In his determination to tighten the blockade against Britain, he had on 13 December annexed to France the north coast of Germany, including the ancient free cities of Bremen, Hamburg, and Lübeck. On 22 January 1811 he annexed the duchy of Oldenburg, the heir to which, Prince George, was the husband of Alexander's sister Catherine.

During 1811 and the first months of 1812 both sides made military and diplomatic preparations for the war which was now inevitable. Alexander's appeals to the friendship of Frederick William of Prussia were no more successful than his overtures to Austria or his soundings of Polish opinion. On 24 February 1812 Prussia accepted a military alliance with France. On 14 March Austria did the same on more favourable terms. Napoleon was prepared to treat his father-in-law with some respect, and promised that, whatever might be done with Russian Poland after conquest, no more Austrian territory should be given to Poland. Metternich could also hope for gains in the Balkans.

Alexander was, however, able to achieve important successes on his northern and southern flanks, by reaching agreements with both Sweden and Turkey.

When the heir to the Swedish throne was killed in a riding accident, the Swedish Parliament invited Napoleon's marshal, Bernadotte, to succeed him, and formally elected him in July 1810. The news naturally alarmed the Russian government. It soon became clear, however, that Bernadotte had no intention of becoming a tool of Napoleon, with whom his personal relations were already strained. He decided to take his new position seriously, to be a good Swedish patriot. He did not wish to plunge Sweden into an arduous war with Russia to regain Finland: instead he proposed to acquire Norway from Denmark. This ambition Alexander could enthusiastically approve. Franco-Swedish relations were further strained when in January 1812 Napoleon ordered Marshal Davout to occupy Swedish Pomerania.

On 5 April a Russo-Swedish alliance was signed in St. Petersburg. Russia undertook to support the Swedish conquest of Norway, diplomatically and if necessary with military aid. Russia obtained an imprecise promise from Sweden of military aid against Napoleon, but her most important gain was that the right flank of her armies was protected. After war had begun between France and Russia, a formal treaty of peace was signed at Orebrö between Sweden and Britain, and at the same time the British envoy, Sir Edward Thornton, signed a treaty of peace with Russia. In August 1812 Alexander met Bernadotte at Åbo in Finland, and friendly relations and mutual support were reaffirmed, although Napoleon's invasion of Russia was then approaching its climax.

In the Turkish war the Russian armies won some successes after the appointment of the veteran hero Kutuzov as commander-in-chief in 1811. The Turks were feeling the strain, and it was clearly desirable to exploit their desire for peace before the outbreak of war between France and Russia could encourage them to hope that they could defeat their enemy. To this end Russia would have to give up most of her acquisitions in Roumania. Negotiations for a peace treaty began in April 1812. The Turks were in an unfortunate position, as the army commanded by the grand vizier was cut off on the left bank of the Danube and in danger of destruction by the Russians. In Constantinope the Russian cause was assisted by the diplomacy of Stratford Canning, who was in charge of the British Embassy pending the arrival of a new ambassador.[1] French diplomacy did its best, with the support of Francophil members of the Sultan's court, to obstruct the negotiations. Even at this stage Alexander entertained fantastic plans in the Balkans. Admiral Chichagov, whom he appointed in May to succeed Kutuzov in command of the army of the Danube, received instructions to persuade the Turks to make an alliance with Russia and to allow Russian forces not only to march across the Balkans to the Adriatic, but to raise great armies from the Christian Slavs of Serbia, Bosnia, and Croatia to fight against Austria and France. The project is of some historical interest as it foreshadows the Russian appeal to the Austrian Slavs a hundred years later. But at the time it had no basis in reality. When Chichagov reached his post, he found that Kutuzov had signed the armistice.

Russia was obliged to give up all Wallachia, and of Moldavia she kept only the eastern portion, between the rivers Dniester and Prut, which thereafter became known as Bessarabia. The Serbs, whose ability to maintain their newly won independence had been greatly helped by the fact that the Turkish armies had been engaged against Russia, were now in effect abandoned to their fate. There was no question of a Russo-Turkish military alliance. After some hesitation the Sultan finally ratified this Treaty of Bucarest. Though the terms seemed disappointing in St. Petersburg, at least the left flank of Russia's front was protected, and the army of the Danube under Chichagov was available to reinforce the main armies on the western frontier.

The last comprehensive statement of the Russian point of

[1] Diplomatic relations between Britain and Turkey were broken after Duckworth's attack on the Straits but were restored in Jan. 1809.

view was made by the Tsar to the French ambassador, General Lauriston (who had succeeded Caulaincourt in 1811) on 8 April 1812. Alexander was prepared to accept the indemnity offered by Napoleon to the Duke of Oldenburg, and to make some modifications, to the advantage of French goods, in the customs tariff of 1810. But he insisted on his complete freedom to trade with neutrals, and demanded that French troops should evacuate Swedish Pomerania and Prussia. If French troops crossed the Oder, or the advanced posts on the Vistula were reinforced, he would consider this an act of war. In May Alexander joined his army headquarters in Vilna. Napoleon made no reply to the Russian demands, but kept up some diplomatic contact simply to gain time. At the end of May he arrived in Dresden, where he was surrounded by impressive pageantry, and the emperor of Austria, the king of Prussia, and lesser German sovereigns appeared in person. From there he moved eastwards with his armies. On 24 June 1812 the Grand Army crossed the Niemen, and without a formal declaration war had begun.

IV

WAR AND PEACE

The War of 1812

NAPOLEON's invasion army numbered about 368,000 infantry and 80,000 cavalry, and possessed over 1,100 guns. During the campaign he received reinforcements which brought the total to more than 600,000 men, if the allied armies of Austria and Prussia are included. About half came from France or French territories, including the Low Countries, parts of Italy, and Illyria. The number of Frenchmen was probably not above 250,000. There were nearly 200,000 Germans and 100,000 Poles, and the rest was made up of Italians, Spaniards, Portuguese, and Croats. The most valuable troops were the Imperial Guard of 46,000, commanded by Mortier, and the First Corps of 72,000 under Davout.

Alexander was with the army at Vilna when the invasion began. As a last gesture to impress European opinion, but without any hope of success, he sent General Balashov with a letter to Napoleon, promising that if he would take his men back out of Russian territory, he would be willing to negotiate on the basis of his proposals of April. Balashov was kept at Davout's headquarters for some days. On 28 June Napoleon entered Vilna, and on 1 July he received Balashov in the room which the Tsar had occupied a week earlier. According to Balashov's own dubiously reliable account, Napoleon asked him which was the best way to Moscow, to which he answered that he might choose which he wished, but that Charles XII had chosen the road to Poltava. Balashov returned to Russian headquarters without achieving anything. Napoleon himself spent three weeks in Vilna, while his armies advanced eastwards.

The main Russian forces at the beginning of the campaign were the First Army of 90,000 men under Barclay de Tolly, the minister of war, and the Second Army of 60,000 under Prince Bagration, with its headquarters at Volkovysk. In addition there was a Third Army of 45,000, under Tormazov, held in reserve at Luck in Volhynia, and the Moldavian Army of some 35,000 under Admiral Chichagov which until recently had been engaged in war with Turkey. Both Barclay and Bagration began to retreat at the end of June, intending to join forces in the interior.

Barclay detached 25,000 men under Prince Wittgenstein, and sent them to cover the right flank, to hold the line of the river Dvina and protect the approach to St. Petersburg. Napoleon sent 30,000 men under Macdonald in the direction of Riga, and 40,000 under Oudinot to face Wittgenstein. In the south Schwarzenberg's Austrian corps faced Tormazov in Volhynia.

The main field of operations was in central Russia. Davout decided to advance between Barclay and Bagration, cut them off from each other and force Bagration to the south. He quickly occupied Minsk, and Bagration was placed in great danger, being caught between the forces of Davout and of Jerome Bonaparte, king of Westphalia, Napoleon's brother. He was, however, saved by the irresolution of Jerome, who took no notice of several requests from Napoleon himself to join the attack. Napoleon finally informed Jerome on 10 July that he was putting him under Davout's orders. Davout received the same instructions, and immediately issued an order to Jerome. In a personal rage, Jerome abandoned his command to his chief of staff, and no action was taken. Bagration escaped to the south-east. So one of the great opportunities of the campaign was lost. On 4 August the armies of Barclay and Bagration were reunited at Smolensk.

Alexander himself had been persuaded to give up the supreme command in the field. His experience at Austerlitz had not been encouraging, but at this great crisis in his country's history he was bound to feel the responsibility was his. However, on 30 June near Polotsk he was persuaded by Arakcheyev, Shishkov, and Balashov that he was needed in the capital to maintain civilian morale and ensure national unity. The examples of Peter the Great, Frederick the Great, and Napoleon, they argued, were not really relevant. Bravery is fine for personal glory, but 'serves to darken the fame of him who surrenders excessively to it'. It is commendable in a soldier, but sometimes deserves to be condemned in a commander, still more in a sovereign. If the sovereign is in the interior of the country, it can survive a series of defeats. But if he is obliged to flee from the army, or still worse if he is captured, then demoralization follows. Alexander accepted these arguments, and went to Moscow to rally the nation.

While Napoleon was in Vilna he had the opportunity of winning support among the Russian masses by promising the abolition of serfdom. This he did not do. When the French revolutionary armies had first spread into Europe, they had brought with them the idea of political liberty and the abolition of feudal institutions. In Italy and Germany they had found social groups that desired these things, that thought much the same way as the new rulers of France, that welcomed their help. In fact, the reforms which took place were the result not only of French military victory but also of internal social forces. This was true even in such backward countries as Spain and Naples. The social groups that responded to the ideas of the revolution, which were at first maintained by Napoleon himself, may be loosely described as *bourgeois*: they included intellectuals and lawyers as well as merchants and business-men. But in Russia similar forces did not exist. The merchants had no political ideas at all, intellectuals were very few and were loyal to their country. There was nobody in Russia with whom Napoleon could find a common language. The half-savage serfs whom he saw in the Russian villages appeared to him nearer beasts than men. To rouse these creatures against the landowners, the only Russians who possessed anything that could be called a European culture, was repugnant to him. His statement made to the French Senate on 20 December 1812, after the campaign, that peasant deputations had come to him but that he had refused to stir them up against their masters as this would have led to horrible massacres, contains an element of truth.

Another reason for not stirring up serfs against landlords was that in the territories which his armies first occupied, the landlords were Poles, potential or real friends of his enterprise. But Napoleon was not willing to go to extremes even in support of Poles. The Polish Diet in Warsaw on 28 June proclaimed the reunion of historical Lithuania with Poland. But Napoleon would not specifically confirm this, and when a deputation of Poles visited him in Vilna he was vague about his intentions. He contented himself with setting up a Provisional Government of Lithuania, in which several local notables were included, but which was intended to do little more than organize supplies to his armies, guard communications, and raise recruits. Lithuania provided Napoleon with some 15,000 soldiers.[1] In general, the population was friendly to his cause, especially in the western districts where the proportion of Poles, or at least of Catholics, was higher in all classes.[2]

The main reason for Napoleon's hesitation in regard to the two problems of serfdom and of Lithuania was that he hoped, after inflicting a decisive defeat on the Russian armies, to persuade Alexander to make peace, restoring the situation after Tilsit, with the difference that Russia would be more definitely his junior partner than had then been the case, and would be his instrument in his further struggles against Britain in the East. But if he took from Russia all the provinces (largely inhabited by Russians) which she had acquired in the partitions of Poland, Alexander would be irreconcilable. This would have been still more the case had he incited the Russian serfs against their masters.

On 16 August Napoleon was before Smolensk where the main Russian army awaited him. At this time the force under Napoleon's command amounted to about 185,000. When allowance is made for the forces detached to the flanks and to guard communications, there still remains a gap of about 100,000 lost since the beginning of the campaign. Many of these were deserters from non-French units. The largest category of casualties were, however, the sick, and as hospital facilities had not been planned on a sufficient scale, a large number of the sick needlessly died. At Smolensk, Bagration pleaded for a major battle in front of the city, but Barclay was hesitant. On the 17th heavy fighting took place with about 20,000 casualties on each side, but in the evening Barclay decided to retire, after having destroyed a large part of the city. On the following day, as his main army held the Valutina plateau to the east of the city, dominating the Moscow–Smolensk road, he was attacked in

[1] Marian Kukiel, *Wojna 1812 roku* (Kraców, 1937), ii, p. 500.

[2] The *locus classicus* in Polish literature for description of the patriotic enthusiasm of the Lithuanian Poles is Books XI and XII of Mickiewicz's epic poem *Pan Tadeusz*. Though written long after the events and influenced by the romanticism of the 1830's, it is still not only a great and moving work of literature but also a document for the history of ideas.

force by Marshal Ney. If Marshal Junot had at the same time attacked his flank, Barclay would have been in a desperate plight. But Junot did nothing, and Barclay extricated himself. The second great opportunity of a major victory for the French was lost.[1]

The retreat from Smolensk had increased the friction between Bagration and Barclay to an unbearable point. Barclay was in a weak position because he was of foreign origin.[2] There was dangerous discontent among the officers at their commander's repeated avoidance of a decisive battle. In the capital too there was a demand for a new commander-in-chief. The general feeling was that the elderly Kutuzov should be called to service. Alexander had personally disliked the old marshal ever since his bitter experience at Austerlitz. But he left the decision to a committee of six which included Arakcheyev, Balashov, and Kochubey. They unanimously recommended the appointment of Kutuzov, and the new commander reached the army on 29 August. Barclay and Bagration remained army commanders under him.

Meanwhile battles had been fought on the northern and southern flanks. On 17 August Wittgenstein attacked Oudinot, who was wounded in the fighting. Next day St. Cyr, who took over his command, repelled the attack. This first Battle of Polotsk, in which the newly enrolled Russian militia gave a good account of themselves, was claimed by both sides as a victory. In the south Reynier, whom Napoleon had sent to help Schwarzenberg, had a success over Tormazov at Gorodechno on 12 August, but a few days later Tormazov inflicted a serious reverse on Reynier and tied Schwarzenberg down, preventing him from joining Napoleon's main army as he had been told

[1] The famous German military writer, General Carl von Clausewitz, who was serving with the Russian army at the time, believed that Napoleon should have made a large-scale attack on Barclay before he reached Smolensk, in which case he would not only have damaged his opponent but would have taken the city whole. See Clausewitz, *The Campaign of 1812 in Russia* (1843), p. 129.

[2] His ancestor left Scotland in the seventeenth century and settled in Riga, where later generations adopted German speech and habits. He himself was born in 1761 and had an extremely honourable military career. Despite the high positions he held, he never won wide popularity. He died in 1818, and so never saw the poem *Polkovodets* ('The Commander') which Pushkin wrote in his honour, but which may perhaps be considered an *amende honorable* from the Russian people through its greatest poet to an unjustly treated servant.

to do. Napoleon, however, was encouraged by the versions of these engagements which were reported to him, and believed that the main Russian army would at last accept battle. He would have been wiser to spend the winter in Smolensk to organize supplies and reinforcements and to mobilize the human and material resources of Lithuania for a new campaign in the following spring. However, he decided to renounce these advantages and to press on to Moscow. He left Smolensk on 24 August.

On 5 September the two main armies at last came into close range of each other at the village of Borodino. By now Napoleon's army had dwindled to about 125,000 men and 580 guns. The weather was exceptionally hot, and the arrival of supply columns was already becoming difficult. The Russian army numbered about 120,000 men and 640 guns. On 5 September a fierce preliminary battle was fought for control of an artillery redoubt on the hill of Shevardino. This was at last captured by the French, and became Napoleon's post of observation for the main battle which, after a day of rest for both armies, began after dawn on 7 September. The battle was the most costly that Napoleon had yet fought. French casualties were more than 30,000 and Russian nearly 40,000 of whom more than 9,000 were dead. The Russians held a strong position on high ground, with the small river Kolocha covering their right flank. Their right front was commanded by Barclay, their left by Bagration. The main centres of fighting were some heights covering the village of Semyonovskoe, on Bagration's front, and the great Kurgan battery in the centre of Barclay's front. The French ultimately took both positions, after repeated attacks and counter-attacks and extremely heavy artillery fire by both sides. Bagration received wounds from which he died some weeks later. Barclay, embittered by the knowledge of his unpopularity, went out of his way to court death, showing himself in the most exposed positions in his full general's uniform. He was never hit, but he succeeded in putting still greater courage into his men. Though the Russians eventually had to give ground, they did not retreat far, and their discipline was not broken. By about five p.m. the main fighting came to an end. Napoleon held his Guard in reserve to the end. Had he used it, he could probably have destroyed the Russian army. But he reckoned that this price was too high to pay, for it would leave him too weak after the victory. As things were, he believed that if he now entered Moscow, Alexander would make peace. But the Guard, preserved at Borodino, wasted away in the later part of the campaign, and there was no peace.

On 13 September Kutuzov held a council-of-war in Fili, and put to his officers the question: 'The salvation of Russia is in her army. Is it preferable to risk the loss of the army and of Moscow, by accepting battle, or to give up Moscow without a battle?' He listened to the various opinions raised, but his mind was already made up. He gave the order to retreat through the city and to leave it by the Ryazan road. On the same day, 14 September, Napoleon's forces began to enter.

The governor-general of Moscow, Count Rostopchin, had continued to be obsessed by his fear of secret societies working for Napoleon. He was afraid that there might even be revolts of serfs against the nobility, organized by revolutionary Martinist conspirators. But nothing of the sort occurred.

The nobility had responded enthusiastically to the Tsar's manifesto of 6 July 1812, demanding a new recruitment of militia, and they had greeted him loyally when he came to Moscow later in the month. The country was divided, for the purpose of raising militia, into three districts: for the defence of Moscow (provinces of Moscow, Smolensk, Tula, Yaroslavl, Tver, Vladimir, Ryazan, Kaluga); for the defence of St. Petersburg (provinces of St. Petersburg and Novgorod); and for a reserve (provinces of Nizhnii Novgorod, Penza, Kostroma, Simbirsk, Kazan). These three districts produced respectively 125,000, 25,000, and 41,000 men. The Moscow nobility at first proposed to raise four militiamen from every hundred male souls on their lands but then voluntarily increased the proportion to ten per hundred. The merchants competed with each other in offering sums to the Treasury.[1]

The serfs responded loyally to mobilization, except in three towns of Penza province (Insar, Saransk, and Chembar), where there were mutinies in December 1812. In Insar the peasants

[1] The organization of the militia is described in the chapter by A. K. Kabanov, entitled 'Opolchenia', in *Otechestvennaya voyna i russkoe obshchestvo*, ed. A. K. Dzhivelegov, S. P. Melgunov, and V. I. Picheta (Moscow, 1912), v. 43–74.

refused to believe the Tsar's manifesto that was read to them. Some speakers claimed that the emperor's wish was that the nobles should go to the war, but that the nobles were forcing their serfs to serve instead. In this case at least there is clear evidence of class hatred against the nobility. The mutinous peasants arrested three officers and proposed to hang them but postponed the action, and troops arrived in time to save the officers. About 300 men were punished, by beating or passing through the ranks, and sent to penal labour or to service in remote garrisons. These incidents cannot, however, be regarded as typical of the peasants' attitude.[1]

Rostopchin felt it his duty to keep up morale by issuing posters, written in what he believed to be racy, popular Russian, assuring the people that their army was winning victories. When the French advance could no longer be concealed, he claimed that all was going according to plan, and Moscow would certainly be defended. He was understandably bitter when informed at the last moment that the city would be abandoned without a battle, and he never forgave Kutuzov.[2]

There has been controversy ever since 1812 as to who was responsible for the fires in Moscow which broke out soon after Napoleon entered. Russian opinion at the time was convinced that the French in savage hatred had destroyed the holy city. Indignation based on this belief was successfully exploited to arouse Russian patriotic fervour. Deliberate arson by the French can, however, be safely ruled out by the historian. The future of the army largely depended on the supplies which Napoleon confidently expected to find in Moscow, and with which he intended to feed his men for the winter. The fires, which were briefly brought under control on 15 September, but broke out again on a larger scale a day later, destroyed three-quarters of the city. They were a major disaster for the French. It is therefore not surprising that the French were convinced that the Russians had deliberately set fire to their capital. The legend

[1] See chapter entitled 'Volneniya krest'yan' by V. I. Semevsky, *Otechestvennaya voyna . . .*, v. 74–113.

[2] In Apr. 1814, a year after Kutuzov was dead, Rostopchin wrote to Michael Vorontsov: 'La seule chose que je regrette dans les événements passés, c'est le concours de circonstances qui ont placé à la tête des armées ce coquin de Koutouzow et l'ont fait entrer par une fausse porte au temple de l'immortalité.' Rostopchin to Michael Vorontsov, 28 Apr. 1814. *Vorontsov Archives*, xxix. 471.

grew up that Rostopchin had ordered it. He himself found that he had acquired great popularity in Europe through the belief, and so allowed it to circulate. Later, when his supposed exploit had not brought him the public honours for which he had hoped, but had made him unpopular at home, he denied it. His views of the origins of the fire, or the views attributed to him, must thus be treated with reserve, and the whole affair still remains obscure.[1]

Napoleon at first seems to have believed that the destruction of Moscow would make Alexander eager to make peace, and sent two messages to him. On 18 September he saw Major-General Tutolmin, the commandant of the Moscow Orphanage, who wished to send a message to its patron, the Empress Maria Fyodorovna. Napoleon told him to include a message to the effect that he now wished for peace. On 22 September he had a conversation with the landowner I. A. Yakovlev,[2] and gave him a letter to the Tsar. In this he declared that 'a simple note from you' would have caused him to stop hostilities after his last battle. He asked the Tsar to read his letter kindly 'if you preserve even if only in part your previous feelings for me'. Both messages were ignored by the Tsar.

In September the popularity of Alexander had sunk to its lowest point. He shut himself up at Kamennoy Ostrov, went for walks by himself in the garden, left the administration of the

[1] His son relates that as they left Moscow Rostopchin said to him: 'Salue Moscou pour la dernière fois; dans une demi-heure elle sera en flammes.' He himself undoubtedly ordered his own house at Voronovo to be destroyed in order to prevent the French from using it. The incident was personally witnessed by Sir Robert Wilson, who greatly admired him, and made the story widely known. Rostopchin left an inscription: 'Français, j'ai vécu heureux pendant dix ans avec ma famille dans ce château, et j'y ai mis le feu, avec tout ce qu'il contenait, pour qu'il ne serve pas de repaire à une horde de brigands.' The most significant incident in connexion with the fire is that Rostopchin undoubtedly removed the fire-fighting apparatus when he evacuated the city. Writing in 1823, Rostopchin argued that with so many opportunities of plunder and plenty of alcohol to drink, in a wooden city in unusually hot weather, with the regular civil authorities all removed, with nobody caring on the Russian side or taking precautions on the French, the fire broke out almost of its own accord. This, in fact, is probably the nearest possible approach to the truth. A collection of miscellaneous writing by Rostopchin, entitled *Matériaux — grande partie inédits pour la biographie future du comte Théodore Rostaptchine, rassemblés par son fils* (Brussels, 1864), contains 'La vérite sur l'incendie de Moscou', originally published in Paris in 1823. The passage on the pumps is on pp. 247–50.

[2] Whose infant illegitimate son, born the previous year, grew up to be the revolutionary Alexander Herzen.

empire to the Committee of Ministers, the army to Kutuzov, and commended the fate of Russia to the Almighty. It was at this time that his thoughts began to turn to religion, to which as a young man he had been indifferent. His friend Prince A. N. Golitsyn, the procurator of the Holy Synod, claimed that it was he who had advised him to seek consolation in reading the Bible. From this time he acquired the habit, and in the following years became keenly interested in religion, including mystical and sectarian beliefs.

He was naturally unpopular with the conservatives, who had disliked his earlier taste for reforms and had detested his policy of co-operation with Napoleon after Tilsit. His sister Catherine did not spare him reproaches. On 5 August she wrote: 'Il faut sans perdre de temps un chef en qui la troupe ait confiance, et sous ce rapport vous n'en pouvez inspirer aucune.' On 6 September she wrote: 'On vous accuse hautement du malheur de votre Empire, de la ruine générale et particulière, enfin d'avoir perdu l'honneur du pays et le vôtre individuel. Ce n'est pas une classe, c'est toutes qui se réunissent a vous décrier. . . . Je vous laisse à juger de la situation des choses dans un pays dont on méprise le chef.'[1] On 27 September when he appeared on the steps of the Kazan Cathedral for the celebration of his coronation anniversary, he was received by the crowds in silence. But Alexander never faltered in his determination not to negotiate with Napoleon as long as a single invading soldier remained on Russian soil. In this the emperor was more inflexible than his courtiers, his civilian political chiefs, and even his generals. For this implacable attitude he deserves more credit than he has been given by most historians. The liberation of Russia and of Europe were due to him as well as to that more glamorous figure, the aged Kutuzov.

After leaving Moscow by the Ryazan road, Kutuzov made a sudden turn to the south and west, and after several days' rapid marching—during which the French advanced units completely lost trace of him—brought his main army into a position south of Moscow. In his camp at Tarutino he now had direct contact with the main Russian centres of supplies and of arms production, Kaluga and Tula, while cutting off Napoleon

[1] Grand Duke Nikolay Mikhailovich, *Perepiska Imperatora Aleksandra I s sestroy velikoy knyaginey Ekaterinoy Pavlovnoy*, SPB, 1910.

from the undamaged southern provinces and threatening his communications westwards. This brilliant manœuvre contributed largely to the later Russian successes.

Meanwhile Napoleon, having received no reply from St. Petersburg, decided to make a more formal overture. On 5 October he sent General Lauriston, his former ambassador to Russia, to Kutuzov's camp with a request that Kutuzov should meet him outside his lines to discuss peace. Kutuzov was at first willing to do this. But fierce protests by some of his generals, of whom Sir Robert Wilson made himself the spokesman, caused him to change his mind and insist that Lauriston should come to his headquarters. He there accepted a letter from him, and forwarded it to St. Petersburg. The Tsar replied by formally forbidding all contact with the enemy, and rebuking General Bennigsen, who had had a conversation with Murat, King of Naples and one of Napoleon's marshals. The only effect of all these overtures was that Napoleon showed the Russian government how desperate he was, and that he lost time waiting in Moscow for a reply when he would have done better either to retreat to winter quarters in Smolensk, or even to march on St. Petersburg. He had in fact proposed the second course after the Moscow fire but had given it up in the face of strong opposition from his marshals. For the first two weeks of October there were no skirmishes between the outposts of the two armies, and the French appear to have believed that Kutuzov had agreed to an armistice. On 18 October Kutuzov ordered a surprise attack on Murat's forces near Tarutino, and this cost the King of Naples between 3,000 and 4,000 casualties. This battle was a final warning to Napoleon that he had nothing to hope from staying in Moscow. On the following day his army moved out of the city. The rearguard had orders to blow up the Kremlin before leaving. At this time the army numbered about 100,000, having received some 15,000 reinforcements. This figure excludes the forces on the northern and southern flanks, and Marshal Victor's reserve army waiting in Smolensk.

Napoleon at first moved southwards, intending to return through territory which had not been ravaged by war, where it was expected that supplies would be available. But the Russian army barred his advance near the town of Maloyaroslavets. Here there was a fierce battle on 24 October. The town changed hands five times. On the French side the Italian division of General Pino distinguished itself by forcing its way up a steep ravine against superior Russian forces. At nightfall Kutuzov withdrew the remaining Russian outposts in the ruined town. But if the battle was technically a French victory, its heavy cost discouraged Napoleon: he decided not to force his way southwards, but to retreat by the old route to Smolensk. Kutuzov did not pursue him closely, to the annoyance of Wilson, but followed him at a distance on his left flank.[1] On the old route the French army suffered acutely from food shortages and was constantly harried by Cossack raids.

This was the period of most effective activity by guerrilla forces, known as Partisans, of which a vivid picture has been left by one of their commanders, the poet Denis Davydov. His force raided enemy supply columns, made surprise attacks on enemy-held villages, liberated and rearmed Russian prisoners-of-war, and obtained information from the peasants on enemy troop movements. The civil population usually helped the Partisans, though they suffered from their depredations as well as from regular units and deserter bands of the French armies. Davydov and other commanders did their best to stimulate patriotic fervour, and made examples of those who had collaborated with the French. Here even class factors took second place. Davydov on one occasion ordered a noble landowner, who had helped the French and maltreated his serfs, to be flogged in the presence of the peasants.[2] Davydov himself was a chivalrous man and gives examples of generous treatment of French prisoners. He was shocked at the behaviour of another Partisan leader, Figner, who shot his prisoners in cold blood. Horrible atrocities took place on both sides. Napoleon's soldiers robbed and murdered when they could, and Russian peasants rounded up stragglers from the Grand Army, tortured and butchered them, in some cases burying them alive in whole groups.

[1] Wilson recounts a conversation with Kutuzov shortly after Maloyaroslavets, in which the latter stated that 'the total destruction of Emperor Napoleon and his army would not be such a benefit to the world: his succession would not fall to Russia or any other continental Power, but to that which already commands the sea, and whose domination would then be intolerable'. Sir Robert Wilson, *The Invasion of Russia* (1860), pp. 233–5.

[2] *Dnevnik partizanskikh deystviy 1812 goda*, published in the collection entitled Denis Davydov, *Voennye zapiski*, ed. V. Orlov (Moscow, 1940), pp. 253–5.

The invaders now suffered seriously from food shortages. Yet though hungry, they carried vast quantities of loot from Moscow. The horses were unsuitably shod and lacked fodder. Those which could not walk further were eaten by the men. Indeed, horse flesh became one of the main items in their miserable and irregular diet. Yet every horse consumed meant one less beast available to draw the gun-carriages or the vehicles containing ammunition and reserves of food.

After a sharp engagement at Vyazma on 1 November, Napoleon reached Smolensk on the 8th. At this time the army numbered 42,000. More than half those who had set out from Moscow had perished in battle or become prisoners or fallen by the wayside from fatigue. In Smolensk disappointment awaited the survivors. The reserve army under Victor had already consumed a large part of the stores, the distribution of the rest began slowly and incompetently, the men lost patience and started plundering, and in a few days everything was gone. The army had to retreat further. Between 14 and 18 November the Russians made six successful attacks in the neighbourhood of Krasny. The most important were on the 16th, when Miloradovich barred the way to the corps of Eugène Beauharnais, viceroy of Italy, and on the 18th when the rearguard of Marshal Ney also found Miloradovich across his line of retreat. By heroic efforts Ney brought 600 men of his force of 6,000 to join Napoleon at Orsha. The total French casualties from the Krasny battles amounted to about 20,000.

As Napoleon's army, now barely 20,000 fighting men, approached the river Berezina from the east, the two Russian flank armies were converging on it from the north-east and the south-west.

Chichagov had started northwards with his army of Moldavia at the end of August, and in the third week of September had joined up with Tormazov near Lutsk. The united army numbered about 70,000, and was placed under Chichagov. Part of this force was detached, under General Sacken, to cover the Austrian army of Schwarzenberg. The latter made no serious effort to come to the help of Napoleon but retreated in as painless a manner as possible into Poland.

In the extreme north Macdonald's army remained comparatively inactive in the Riga area. On 18 and 19 October

Wittgenstein attacked St. Cyr in the second Battle of Polotsk, and drove him back. St. Cyr was wounded and his command was taken back again by Oudinot. Napoleon sent the reserve army under Victor, previously stationed in Smolensk, to join Oudinot and take over the command of the combined force. On 31 October he attacked Wittgenstein but broke off the fighting without engaging his full strength and retreated to Chereya on 7 November. Wittgenstein sent a corps to storm Vitebsk, capturing large quantities of food and military stores, desperately needed by the French army. Napoleon ordered Victor to attack Wittgenstein again. This he did at Smolyani on 14 November, but again broke off without engaging his full force which was now numerically inferior to its opponent.

Meanwhile Chichagov was moving north-westward. On 16 November his forces took Minsk by surprise, depriving the French of still more valuable stores than at Vitebsk. Four days later he captured Napoleon's bridgehead on the west bank of the Berezina facing Borisov, which was defended by the Polish general Dąbrowski, and then crossed the river and took Borisov itself. The pincers were closing on Napoleon, while Kutuzov's main force was slowly following his retreat. The weather was not yet cold enough for the Berezina to be frozen, and it formed a redoubtable barrier.

At this desperate crisis Napoleon's genius revived. Reunited with Victor and Oudinot, he now had some 30,000 fighting troops. Oudinot recaptured Borisov from Chichagov by a surprise attack, but the bridges had been destroyed. Napoleon chose for the crossing Studyanki, a point some miles north of Borisov. Fortunately for him Chichagov, whether misinformed or guessing, decided that the most likely place for Napoleon to make the attempt was some twenty miles south of Borisov, and moved in that direction with his main force on 25 November. Later the same day the troops which he had left opposite Studyanki were recalled to the Borisov bridgehead, and on 26 November there were only a few hundred men to bar Napoleon's passage. A French vanguard crossed on horseback and on rafts, a bridgehead was secured, the pontoon bridges were completed, and the army began to move over. In the afternoon a second bridge was finished, capable of taking artillery and vehicles. It was not until late on 27 October that Wittgenstein and Chichagov, who had at last understood what was happening, were able to make serious attacks. On the east bank Victor held out against Wittgenstein during the 28th, but his rearguard under General Partouneaux, in Borisov itself, was cut off and almost completely destroyed or captured. On the west bank a fierce battle was fought in the forest of Stakov against the returning forces of Chichagov. On 29 November Victor crossed, and destroyed the bridges. During the last day terrible scenes took place. Thousands of stragglers, including civilians and even women and children, fought to get on to the bridges, many were crushed by gun carriages or baggage vehicles, or forced by their companions into the icy river. About 15,000 persons were left on the east bank, many too tired to move or afraid to leave the warmth of the fires that were still burning. Most of these were massacred by the Cossacks.

The direct military casualties in the rearguard action and in the Stakov battle were heavy, but a hard core of fighting troops, with Napoleon himself at their head, escaped. Napoleon's brilliant feat is not diminished by the fact that his opponents made huge mistakes. Not only had Chichagov miscalculated on 26 November, but his subordinate Chaplitz failed to destroy the wooden causeways over the marshes beyond the Berezina, which would have cut off the French even after they had crossed the river. Moreover, Kutuzov himself had made no serious effort to link up with Wittgenstein and Chichagov. His inertia infuriated Sir Robert Wilson, who was bitterly disappointed that Napoleon himself had not been captured. Kutuzov's defence was that Napoleon was still a formidable enemy, and that it was foolish to risk a defeat for his army when the enemy was bound to succumb to exhaustion, hunger, and cold.

It was in fact only after the Berezina that the cold became exceptionally severe and finished off the hungry, tired, and depleted army. Napoleon himself decided at Smorgoni on 4 December to return to France. He had received news of an attempt to overthrow his government in Paris and was anxious to show himself in Germany and in France, and to raise new armies. His men do not seem to have resented his departure, but when he was gone their morale fell still lower. In Vilna, which they reached on 9 December, the same plundering and rapid exhaustion of stores took place as in Smolensk. The survivors had to go on. In the last days men fell by the roadside and were stripped of their clothing by their freezing comrades even before they were dead. A small hill at Ponari, its surface slippery from ice, proved an insuperable obstacle to the last vehicles, and virtually all the remaining supplies had to be abandoned. On 12 December the remnant reached Kovno, and crossed the Niemen into the less inhospitable Prussia. At the end of the month a substantial portion of the troops of Macdonald, which had retreated from Riga, also escaped, while the Austrians of Schwarzenberg, whose casualties had been lighter than those of any other part of the Grand Army, left Warsaw and re-entered Austrian Poland.

Less than 5,000 men recrossed the Niemen as organized military units. By the beginning of January 1813 some 30,000 had made their way to safety. To these should be added 6,000 from Macdonald's corps, 15,000 from Reynier's, and about 13,000 Polish and Lithuanian troops. A modern authority estimates that if all the stragglers and small groups that eventually returned, together with persons evacuated at some stage of the campaign, were added up, they might total 100,000. At the very least, 400,000 failed to return, probably more than this. Of the Frenchmen taken prisoner by the Russians, only 30,000 returned to France in 1814. Russian losses in the armies of Kutuzov and Wittgenstein were estimated at 210,000. With the casualties in the southern armies added, the total can hardly be less than a quarter of a million.[1]

The Liberation of Europe

The catastrophe of the Grand Army raised the question whether the Russians should pursue Napoleon into Europe, or should remain content with the liberation of their own country. Kutuzov favoured the second course, and it would certainly have been widely popular among a people that had endured terrible hardships. But Alexander was convinced that there could be no lasting peace without the destruction of Napoleon, and in this it must be said that he showed greater wisdom than his more narrowly patriotic advisers. Alexander also believed

[1] Figures of casualties cannot be regarded as more than approximate. For a detailed discussion see the work of the Polish historian, General Marian Kukiel, op. cit., pp. 497–501.

himself to have a mission to save Europe: in this his new religious convictions were doubtless mixed with personal ambition and vanity. He more specifically aimed at the restoration of Poland under his rule, returning to the idea which he had shared with Czartoryski in the first years of his reign. Two foreign advisers had some influence on him, Sir Robert Wilson, who was determined that Russia and Britain should continue together to final victory, and Freiherr Karl vom Stein, the exiled Prussian statesman, who hoped that Russian victory would bring not only the liberation but the unification of Germany. But the decision was the Tsar's, and its historical importance was enormous.

The first country that lay across Russia's forward march was Prussia. On 30 December 1812 the Prussian General Yorck von Wartenburg, whose troops came under the command of Marshal Macdonald, but had been cut off from the retreating French in the Baltic area, made an agreement in the village of Tauroggen with the Russian General Diebitsch of Wittgenstein's army, that his forces should take no further part in military operations but be 'neutral'. Yorck's action was not authorized by the king of Prussia. It was true that his military situation was difficult, and it is doubtful whether he could have fought his way out of Russian encirclement without disastrous losses. But his decision not to try was determined not so much by timidity as by the growing dislike of himself and his men for the French cause.

The Russian forces were greeted in Prussian towns and villages as liberators. Stein, who had organized propaganda among German soldiers of the Grand Army in Russia, and had recruited from them a small German legion to fight on the Russian side, was determined to mobilize the men and resources of Prussia behind the Russian war effort. He was placed by the Tsar in charge of administration in liberated Prussian territory. The situation of Prussian officials was extremely delicate, as their sovereign King Frederick William was still formally allied to Napoleon. But in the conflict between German patriotism and loyalty to the dynasty, it was usually the first that prevailed and consciences could to some extent be satisfied by the argument that the king was not a free agent but would have approved their action if he were.

Meanwhile Frederick William was gradually overcoming his fear of the French, whose forces in Prussia were now extremely small. He moved from Berlin to Breslau and corresponded with Alexander. The Tsar's assurances of friendship and the growing patriotic mood among his subjects at last overcame his inhibitions. On 28 February 1813 a Russo-Prussian alliance was signed at Kalisz, and on 13 March Frederick William declared war on France. Meanwhile large numbers of Prussian subjects had been mobilized, and a strong Prussian force was soon in the field. The Russians had also received large reinforcements. The joint army was commanded by Kutuzov until his death on 27 April, thereafter by Wittgenstein.

Hostilities between Russia and Austria had come to an end, but Austria was still far from joining the allies. One obstacle was the dynastic connexion between the House of Habsburg and Napoleon: Emperor Francis did not wish his son-in-law's destruction, though he was glad to see him lose a campaign. Metternich profoundly distrusted Russian policy. Alexander's Polish plans threatened the Austrian position in Galicia, and though the Peace of Bucarest had given Russia only Bessarabia, it was to be expected that she would renew her pressure on the Balkans to the detriment of Austrian interests. Metternich also profoundly distrusted and feared the policies pursued, with the Tsar's backing, by Stein. To proclaim a *Befreiungskrieg* of the German people against the French was doubly displeasing, both because it gave Prussia greater prestige in Germany than Austria and because it brought the masses into politics. Metternich was utterly opposed to all liberal or democratic ideas, above all to the idea of nationality. Thus, in order to oppose the aggrandizement of Russia and Prussia and the demagogy of Alexander and of Stein, as well as to save his master's son-in-law, the best policy must be a negotiated peace between the four continental Powers.

British policy did not directly threaten Austrian interests, unless the survival of the Bonaparte dynasty be so regarded. But British implacability towards France was a major obstacle to Metternich's plans, the more objectionable because it seemed to him to be based on sordid commercial interests for which he could have neither understanding nor sympathy. British defence of the legitimate dynasties of Spain and Naples barely counted as a virtue for Metternich. By insisting on their interests in the Low Countries and the Iberian peninsula, the British were only making it more difficult for him to settle the affairs of Central Europe.

The British, however, pursued their sordid interests, and these for the time being coincided with the aims of Russia, the generous dreams of Stein, and the personal ambitions of Bernadotte. On 3 March 1813 an Anglo-Swedish alliance, signed in Stockholm, gave the Swedes a subsidy of £1,000,000 and provided for a Swedish army to operate in Germany. Diplomatic relations were restored between Britain and Prussia, and a British embassy reached the allied headquarters at Dresden on 15 April.

At the beginning of 1813 Germany was a power vacuum, lying between France and Russia. The allied forces met with little opposition, overran Saxony and even crossed the Elbe, liberating Hamburg. The pro-French king of Saxony fled to Bohemia. But Napoleon was not idle. He rapidly created new armies in France, and his German subjects in Westphalia and the Rhineland still served as loyal soldiers. In the middle of April he crossed the Rhine and advanced through Weimar into Saxony with forces superior to those of the allies. On 2 May the allies attacked him at Lützen, but lost the initial advantage of surprise by their slow deployment, and were defeated. The allies retreated behind the Elbe, and on 8 May Napoleon entered Dresden. The king of Saxony returned triumphantly to his capital. On 20–21 May a second battle was fought at Bautzen. Reinforced by a new army under Barclay de Tolly, the allies fought bitterly and lost 12,000 men. They yielded the field to Napoleon but retreated in good order. Barclay now replaced Wittgenstein as commander-in-chief. Thus both sides had had heavy losses, but both had good hopes. At this point the Austrian government proposed an armistice and peace discussions. Napoleon and the allies each hoped to gain more from the delay than their enemy, and so the proposal was accepted on 4 June.

Metternich now discussed with the Russian and Prussian monarchs the minimum terms acceptable to them, without taking into consideration the special interests of Britain. The British government signed treaties with Prussia and Russia at Reichenbach on 14 June. They provided for a British subsidy of £2,000,000, of which one-third would go to Prussia and two-thirds to Russia. Britain agreed to the restoration of Prussia to its strength of 1806, while Prussia recognized the integrity of Hanover and ceded to it the district of Hildesheim. Meanwhile Bernadotte had landed an army in Germany, but showed himself much less interested in fighting the French than in forcing Denmark to yield Norway to him. While he hesitated, the French reoccupied Hamburg, and Denmark allied itself to France.

On 24 June at Reichenbach Metternich agreed with the Prussian and Russian monarchs' minimum conditions for peace with France. Metternich personally presented these terms to Napoleon at Dresden. But Napoleon was not prepared to renounce his German and Adriatic conquests and would only consent to hold further discussions at a conference to be held in Prague. The armistice was extended for a further month, to 10 August. Meanwhile the allies were encouraged by the news of Wellington's victory in Spain, the Battle of Vittoria which had taken place on 21 June. At the Prague congress Napoleon would not agree to the allied terms. On 8 August Metternich presented further conditions to Napoleon, in the form of an ultimatum.[1] When these were rejected, Austria joined the allies. Schwarzenberg was made commander-in-chief of the united armies.

At first the war went against the allies. Napoleon won a victory at Dresden on 26–27 August, which was not compensated by successes of the separate armies of Bernadotte and Blücher. On 30 August however Barclay defeated the army of Vandamm at Kulm. During the first weeks of October all the armies of the allies converged on Leipzig, where they were joined by reinforcements from Russia under Bennigsen. Here took place, from 16 to 18 October, the 'Battle of the Nations', which was a decisive defeat for the French. The armies on each side amounted to more than a quarter of a million men, and French losses were estimated at 60,000 and allied at 50,000 (among which 22,000 Russian). Napoleon was obliged to retire into France, having just sufficient strength to inflict a defeat *en route* on the Bavarians who decided at this stage to join the allies.

[1] There is a large literature on the diplomacy of Metternich, and there is thus no need to discuss details here. A recent work is Enno E. Kraehe's *Metternich's German Policy* (Princeton, 1963), vol. i, which has a useful bibliography.

The French domination of Europe was now over, but the allies were far from agreeing as to what should take its place. Alexander was determined to make no peace with Napoleon and to press on to Paris. Metternich still wished for a peace which would leave France strong enough to ensure a European balance against Russia. The British position was between these two. One of Britain's aims, the liberation of Spain, was nearing completion. Another was achieved when the Dutch revolted against the French in mid-November. The British foreign secretary, Viscount Castlereagh, did not wish Napoleon to keep his throne, but in the problem of the European balance of power he inclined to Metternich's view. In November Metternich offered Napoleon peace on the basis of France's 'natural frontiers' which would have included the Low Countries and portions of the Kingdom of Sardinia. These terms were reluctantly accepted by the Russian and British representatives on the spot, Count Nesselrode and the Marquess of Aberdeen, but the French reply was evasive, and nothing came of the proposal.

At the beginning of 1814 the allied armies entered France. Alexander was now more insistent than ever that they must take Paris. However, the restoration of the Bourbons, which was favoured by the British, made little appeal to him. When Castlereagh discussed the matter with him at Langres on 25 January he preferred to talk vaguely of allowing the French to choose their own ruler. Metternich still stood for delay and compromise, and his attitude was reflected by his compatriot the Commander-in-Chief Schwarzenberg who showed the greatest reluctance to move his army if an excuse could be found for inaction.

A peace conference between the allies and the French opened at Châtillon on 7 February 1814. There was now no longer any question of 'natural frontiers': the most that the allies were prepared to concede were the 'former frontiers' of 1792. But Napoleon would still not agree to give up Antwerp or the left bank of the Rhine. After five successful small engagements against Blücher in the first half of February, he ordered Caulaincourt to be more intransigent. Napoleon's attitude caused the allies at last to sign a formal four-power treaty of alliance at Chaumont on 9 March. Napoleon's cause was lost, despite his unfailing military skill. His forces were hopelessly outnumbered, and even his French subjects were at the end of their patience. Talleyrand secretly wrote to Alexander who was able to overcome Schwarzenberg's reluctance to move. On 19 March the negotiations at Châtillon were finally broken off, and on 30 March 1814 Alexander and Frederick William entered Paris.

It had by now been agreed that a restoration of the Bourbons was the only possible solution for France. Metternich consented when he became convinced that nothing could save Napoleon from the results of his obstinacy. Alexander acquiesced less readily. Napoleon abdicated at Fontainebleau on 11 April and was made sovereign of the island of Elba. The terms of the first Treaty of Paris, of 30 May, were generous to France, and for this generosity Alexander took the greatest share of credit. He went out of his way to ingratiate himself with the people and the high society of the French capital.

The Treaty of Paris had settled France's frontiers, but the settlement of the rest of Europe was the task of the Congress of Vienna, to which France was admitted. Before it opened, Alexander paid a state visit to London in June. At this time British public opinion was wildly pro-Russian, and Alexander himself was by far the most popular of the allied sovereigns. Unfortunately, the Tsar's position was made difficult by the fact that his host, the Prince Regent, was extremely unpopular with the London crowds. It was difficult to acknowledge the enthusiasm of the public without slighting the sovereign. Alexander made little attempt to be tactful. He spent much of his time with the political Opposition and with groups in society which were hostile to the regent. He had been preceded by his sister, the Grand Duchess Catherine, who had antagonized many influential people by her arrogant, and sometimes insulting, behaviour.[1] The results of the visit were not unimportant. It created, in the Prince Regent and the government, a dislike of the Russian ruler which reinforced Castlereagh's inclination on more traditional and abstract grounds of foreign policy and pursuit of the balance of power to oppose Russian aims.

[1] The visit is amusingly described in an extract from the memoirs of Princess Lieven, wife of the Russian ambassador in London, published in Nikolay Mikhailovich, *Perepiska Imperatora Aleksandra I s velikoy knyaginey Ekaterinoy Pavlovnoy*, pp. 225–46.

The classical liberal historians have made familiar the contrast in the Europe of 1814 between patriots devoted to liberty and monarchs concerned to restore their despotic rule, between nations seeking unity or independence and dynasties seeking aggrandizement. If Stein stood for liberty and national unity, and Metternich for absolutism and dynastic aggression, Alexander stood somewhere between the two. He was an absolute ruler with territorial and dynastic aims, but he also had some sympathy for the national aims of Germans and Poles and for constitutional government.

Russia as the greatest continental Power took an interest in all European problems, and Alexander, the only monarch who directly controlled and formed his own foreign policy throughout the congress, played his part in all aspects of the settlement. But some problems were of special interest to Russia. Russo-Swedish relations, and the acquisition of Norway by Sweden, had already been agreed, and the affairs of the Ottoman empire were not systematically discussed at Vienna. But Russian interests were above all concerned in the problems of Poland and Saxony.

Alexander was once more on close terms with Czartoryski. He had given clear orders to his armies in 1812 that there were to be no reprisals or persecution of Poles who had shown sympathy for Napoleon, whether in Lithuania or the grand duchy. These orders had not always been carried out. The Poles suffered from the hardships inevitable when a large army passes through a country, and in many cases also from additional humiliations. Nevertheless, Alexander's instructions mitigated their lot and were known and appreciated by the Polish leaders. His attitude was all the more magnanimous because, even at this late stage, a large part of the Polish nation still supported Napoleon. In the campaigns of 1813 about 40,000 Polish soldiers fought on the French side. Both Poniatowski and Dąbrowski held commands, and the former was killed at the Battle of Leipzig. On 14 March 1813 a Temporary Supreme Council was set up with Count Lanskoy as chairman and Novosiltsov as his deputy. It was responsible for the civil government of Poland under Russian military occupation. On 16 September 1814 the Tsar's brother Grand Duke Constantine was placed in charge of a Polish Military Commission in Warsaw. His task was to create a new Polish army for the proposed Kingdom of Poland under Alexander's rule.

One of the main tasks before the Congress of Vienna was to decide the limits of this Kingdom of Poland. The Tsar's aim was to annex the whole grand duchy of Warsaw to Russia, thereby uniting more than two-thirds of the Polish nation in one kingdom, and if possible to persuade Austria to cede Galicia to him, thereby completing Polish unity. Prussia should be compensated by receiving the whole of Saxony, whose ruler, by his continued alliance with Napoleon, had incurred the anger of his fellow sovereigns. If Austria ceded Galicia, she too would obtain compensation.

The Prussian statesmen did not like this proposal, but it was acceptable to Frederick William, and he was in a position to compel their obedience. Metternich, however, was utterly against the plan. In the first place, he would not consider surrendering Galicia, and wished Russia to restore to Austria that portion of East Galicia which she had received in 1809. Secondly, he was against the acquisition by Russia of the grand duchy, as the new Kingdom of Poland under Alexander's rule would undoubtedly exercise an attraction on the Polish subjects of Austria. Thirdly, he objected to the acquisition of Saxony by Prussia as this would unduly strengthen Austria's main German rival in the vicinity of the Austrian frontier. Metternich, therefore, did his best to persuade the Prussian statesmen to oppose the plan and to make possible a common resistance to Russia of the two German Great Powers. When this failed, he strongly opposed Prussian aims.

Alexander's plan was also unacceptable to Castlereagh for two separate reasons. In the first place, he objected to a large territorial gain which would make Russia dominant in Central Europe, and would also strengthen her for future expansion at the expense of the Ottoman empire. Secondly, he wished Prussia to obtain her territorial gains not in the east, where she would be in conflict with Austria, but in the west, in the vicinity of Holland, where she would strengthen the barrier to any future aggression by France. The proposal that if Prussia acquired Saxony, the dispossessed king of Saxony should be given some compensation in western Germany, was particularly objectionable, for a weak prince who had once been a satellite of

Napoleon could in no way reinforce the barrier against France.

Castlereagh, therefore, opposed Alexander's Polish aims. In view of British public sympathy for Polish liberty, he went through the motions of proposing that Poland should be re-united as an independent state. But if independence could not be achieved, he argued, it was better that a balance should be preserved among the three partitioning Powers than that one should gain disproportionately to the other two. Castlereagh made much of the fact that Alexander intended to keep as part of Russia the former Lithuanian provinces of Poland which Catherine II had annexed but proposed to give self-government only to those territories which had been Prussian. It was more reasonable, he argued, that the three Powers should keep their previous gains, but that all should give liberties to their Polish subjects. Castlereagh was in fact demanding a restoration of the old partitions, in the name of the balance of power, and his advocacy of complete Polish independence was no more than a demagogic gesture. As his prime minister, Lord Liverpool, wrote to him on 21 October, 'We must take care so to manage this question as not to get the discredit of resisting the Emperor of Russia's proposition upon a principle of partition'.[1] This was in fact precisely what the British government was doing.

The conflict on the Polish and Saxon questions reached a crisis at the end of December 1814. On 3 January 1815 an alliance was signed between Britain, Austria, and France, and it seemed possible that these Powers might find themselves at war with Russia and Prussia. However, negotiations continued, and in February agreement was reached. Prussia retained of her Polish possessions the province of Poznań and the city of Torun on the Vistula, and she received about two-fifths of Saxony as well as some territorial gains in western Germany. Kraków was made a free city, and Austria received from Russia the Galician area ceded in 1809. Three-fifths of Saxony remained as a sovereign state under its king. The rest of the grand duchy of Warsaw went to Russia. Thus Russia obtained most of her demands, and the fate of the Poles was somewhat better than it would have been if the partitions of 1795 had simply been reaffirmed. All

[1] Quoted in C. K. Webster, *The Foreign Policy of Lord Castlereagh 1812–1815* (1931), p. 351.

three of the continental Powers made territorial gains. Yet these were of somewhat different character. Russia's gain made sense from the point of view of Russian strategic interests, and was at least potentially compatible with the interests of the Polish people. Prussia's gains also made strategic sense, and were in territory inhabited by fellow Germans. But Austria made her strategic position worse by expanding south of the Alps and by maintaining Galicia to the north of the Carpathians. Her new subjects in Venetia and Dalmatia had little in common with the peoples of the traditional Habsburg lands. By insisting on retaining her share of Poland, Austria deprived herself of freedom of action in relation to Prussia and Russia, as the later history of the nineteenth century was to show. Metternich was probably more satisfied with his work than were any of the other statesmen, but a century and a half later it seems rather that he damaged the interests of his country and his dynasty.

Allied solidarity was restored by Napoleon's return to France in March 1815. Napoleon sent to Alexander a copy of the Anglo-French-Austrian treaty of January 1815, which he had found in the archives in Paris. But whatever Alexander may have thought of his allies, he showed no tenderness to Napoleon. The Battle of Waterloo was won on 18 June without the Russians, but Russian troops took their part in the occupation of Paris. The banishment of Napoleon to St. Helena was decided by the British, and the Tsar had to accept it. The second Treaty of Paris, of 20 November 1815, deprived France of some territory in the Saar valley and Savoy, an indemnity of 700,000,000 francs was imposed, and there was to be a five-year military occupation by 150,000 allied troops, of which Russia was to provide 30,000.

V

THE AFTERMATH

The Age of Arakcheyev

It was natural that the great victories of 1812 to 1814, which had brought Russia greater glory and influence in Europe than she had ever known, should arouse among the Russians themselves an expectation of better things. It might have been expected that the peasants, who had fought bravely in the long wars, would be rewarded by emancipation from serfdom, and that the aspiration of the educated minority, that the country whose armies had liberated Europe should itself receive free institutions, might be fulfilled. These hopes were, however, disappointed. Serfdom was re-established, autocracy was reinforced, and the direction of internal policies was largely concentrated in the hands of Count A. A. Arakcheyev. This generally hated favourite of the emperor became the symbol of reactionary repression, and the Russian word derived from his name, *arakcheyevshchina*, has been used by historians to describe the post-war decade.

After their quarrel of 1810 the Tsar and Arakcheyev had been reconciled. In 1812 and in the campaigns in Europe in 1813–14, Arakcheyev was often at his master's side. The Tsar's affection for his old friend was strikingly expressed in a letter written to him from Saint-Leu in France on 22 May 1814. After granting Arakcheyev's request for leave on grounds of ill health, Alexander wrote:

> Accept once again all my gratitude for so many services you have rendered me, the memory of which will always remain in my heart. I am distressed and embittered to an extreme degree: I see myself, after fourteen years of burdensome government, after two years of destructive and most perilous war, deprived of the man in whom my confidence was always unbounded. I can say that I never had such trust in any one, and nobody's departure could be so painful to me as yours.

Arakcheyev replied to this:

> My love and devotion to Your Majesty have surpassed in my feelings everything on earth. My wishes have had no other aim than just to earn your confidence, not to use it for obtaining rewards or revenues for myself but in order to report to you on the misfortunes, burdens and humiliations that are endured in our beloved country.[1]

The Tsar was not deprived of Arakcheyev's services for long. During 1812 the importance of the Committee of Ministers, which had declined in the period of Speransky's greatest influence, once more increased. The new office of president of the committee was created. Its first holder was Count N. I. Saltykov. During the war the committee was in fact responsible for the internal government of the empire. Alexander, who no longer attended its meetings, was fully occupied with foreign relations and military affairs. The committee set up sub-committees on finance, on tariffs, on Siberia, and from time to time on particular provinces or problems that required special attention. The Tsar had complete confidence in Saltykov and urged him to take the necessary decisions. His main criticism of the committee was that it referred too many matters to his decision while he was with the armies in Europe from 1813 to 1815. In particular he complained, in a letter to Saltykov from Warsaw of 15 November 1815, that it did not assume full responsibility for handling supplies to the army.[2] On his return to the capital he appointed Arakcheyev as deputy to Saltykov on 24 December 1815, with the task of general supervision of the committee's activities.

Arakcheyev remained for ten years a sort of viceroy for all internal affairs. The committee's reports reached the Tsar through him. His office was the centre of government. To gain Arakcheyev's favour became the first task of any one who sought advantage, or hoped for redress of a wrong. Arakcheyev undoubtedly enjoyed his authority and was at pains to show all who came to him how powerful he was. He does not, however, appear to have profited materially from his position. Cruelty and lust for power were combined in him with a strong sense of duty, and his arrogance expressed itself in an appearance of modesty, absence of outward pomp, and indifference to reward.

[1] Shilder, op. cit. ii. 601, 664.

[2] S. M. Seredonin (ed.), *Komitet Ministrov, istoricheskii obzor 1802–1902*, i. 19.

The Committee of Ministers was largely concerned in delimiting departmental functions, for example in the distribution of the duties of the Ministry of Commerce—abolished in 1811—among the three Ministries of Police, the Interior, and Finance, and of the responsibility for censorship between the Ministries of Police and Education. It was also constantly involved in disputes between governors-general and ministries. In so far as the former were personally responsible to the emperor, they escaped direct subordination to the central ministries, which made the task of the latter difficult and impeded uniform administration of the empire. For example the governor-general of Riga, Marquess F. O. Paulucci, quarrelled with the Ministry of Finance about customs in Baltic ports, with the Senate about its verdicts in legal disputes, and with the minister of education on the relationship of Dorpat University to his office. In practice both the Tsar and Arakcheyev were inclined to hold a balance between governors-general and ministries rather than always support the latter. There were frequent complaints of abuses of power by local officials, and senators were sent to carry out inspections on the spot. There were also constant complaints of the low pay given to provincial officials, which was a main cause of corruption. In 1817 governors' salaries were graded in three categories, dependent on the cost of goods in an area, its nearness to the capital, and to a frontier. In 1822 and 1823 it was proposed to increase provincial budgets, but on both occasions the minister of finance declared that he had not got the resources. Arakcheyev himself wished to strengthen the powers of the president of the committee. In an undated memorandum to Alexander he urged that there should be a president 'who has seniority over the ministers; decides the matters on the agenda; has authority to publish instructions to ministers; and may appoint special sub-committees to consider special matters'. He should have the casting vote when votes were equally divided.[1] This proposal was never formally put into effect by Alexander, and was rejected as impracticable by the advisers of Nicholas I at the beginning of his reign.

From 1811 to 1819 the reduced Ministry of the Interior was held by O. P. Kozodavlev. Its main task was to encourage

[1] *Sbornik Imperatorskogo russkogo istoricheskogo obshchestva* (hereafter *SIRIO*) (SPB, 1867–1916), vol. 90, pp. 123–5.

industry and agriculture. In 1807 it had been estimated that domestic factories could deliver only 267,000 *arshin* of cloth when the army needed 759,000. The ministry therefore made great efforts in the following years to encourage native manufacturers, offering them money loans, state lands, and the right to buy landowners' estates with serfs if they wished to found cloth factories. During 1812 industrialists were rewarded with medals and titles, and the social prestige of industry appreciably raised. Some results were achieved. On a visit to England in 1818 the Grand Duke Michael was informed by a Leeds manufacturer that wool from Odessa was better than Spanish or Saxon. In 1818 and 1819 the ministry imported high quality livestock from Holland and England to improve Russian animals. Under the reorganization of 1811 responsibility for internal trade was also transferred to the Ministry of the Interior, from the dissolved Ministry of Commerce.

The Ministry of Police took over public security and public health. It had three departments—economic police, executive police, and medical. A new Medical Council was set up, to supervise medical supplies to the army and measures against epidemics, while the existing Medical Council, a purely scientific body, was transferred to the Ministry of Education. The main medical tasks were to combat plague which appeared in the southern provinces in 1812, 1813, and 1814, and was handled by severe quarantine measures; and to carry out vaccination, which between 1806 and 1815 was applied to nearly two million persons. The ministry also had its Special Chancery, which was concerned with movements of foreigners, passports, and the execution of censorship regulations.

In 1819 the Ministries of the Interior and Police were reunited under Prince Kochubey. Security, public health, and supervision of the economy were once more placed under a single authority. In 1822 the medical bodies under the Ministry of Education were transferred to the Ministry of the Interior. In 1819 the supervision of internal trade was transferred to the Ministry of Finance, and in 1821 the treasurer's department was formally reunited with the same ministry. Mining in the Urals came under the authority of a special official, the governor-general of Perm and Vyatka. There was a central office in Perm for the administration of the mines. The tax on alcohol had been collected throughout the eighteenth century by the tax-farming system. Individuals obtained the licence to sell alcohol from the provincial governors' offices and made their profit from the drinking public. The system was confused and inefficient, and tax arrears were heavy. In 1817 it was decided to abolish the farming system and replace it by a government alcohol monopoly, administered through the treasury chambers.

Russian finances suffered heavily from the series of wars. The government was obliged to make frequent issues of paper money. The monetary circulation, which had been somewhat over 200,000,000 roubles in 1801, was nearly 826,000,000 in 1816. In that year the value of the paper rouble was only a quarter of a silver rouble (25 silver kopeks). The finance minister, Count D. A. Guryev, floated four domestic loans between 1817 and 1822 and used them to reduce the monetary circulation to slightly under 600,000,000 roubles, but the improvement in the value of the paper rouble was negligible.

Guryev was somewhat more inclined to liberalize foreign trade than his predecessors. His tariff of 1819 kept import duties high, but removed the previous complete prohibition on the importation of certain goods. This tariff aroused great opposition from Russian landowners and industrialists who not only objected to the competition of foreign goods but complained that other countries were not following Russia's liberal example but were keeping their markets closed to Russian goods. In 1822 a new tariff was introduced, which restored the previous prohibitions and raised the level of duties.[1]

Alexander still toyed with the idea of a constitution for Russia and regarded the constitution which he had given to Poland as an experiment in this direction. In 1818, after he had opened the Sejm in Warsaw,[2] he instructed Novosiltsov to prepare a draft. In the summer of 1819 in St. Petersburg, Alexander told Prince P. A. Vyazemsky that he intended to carry it out in time, but that he was hindered partly by lack of money and partly by prejudices against constitutions held by his advisers who strongly attributed to them the evils of the age.

Novosiltsov's draft was found in Warsaw in 1831 by the Polish rebels and published by them to the great annoyance of

[1] *Ministerstvo finansov 1802–1902* (SPB, 1902), i. 62–70, 142–3.

[2] See below p. 173.

Nicholas I. The empire was to have been divided into lieutenancies, themselves composed of provinces.[1] Each lieutenancy, and each of the two capitals, was to have a duma, with two chambers. The upper chamber of each lieutenancy duma would count as a department of the Senate in each lieutenancy capital, and its members would be appointed by the emperor from persons at least thirty-five years old who had served with distinction in military or civil service and had an income from immovable property of not less than 1,000 silver roubles. The lower chamber, or Chamber of Deputies, would be elected. In each *uezd* of every lieutenancy three deputies would be elected to the lieutenancy duma by the nobility and the city community. The city electorates would comprise house-owners, distinguished citizens, masters of corporations, and merchants of the first two guilds.[2] The lieutenancy dumas would consider measures set before them by the emperor. They would meet once every three years. Their members would elect from their number a list of deputies, of whom half would be appointed by the emperor to form the Chamber of Deputies of the Land, the lower chamber of the Imperial Duma. The upper chamber would consist of the St. Petersburg or Moscow department of the Senate. The Imperial Duma would meet once every five years in St. Petersburg and Moscow alternately. The sessions of the Imperial Duma would last thirty days, and they would examine the business placed before them by the Tsar. There would be complete freedom of discussion, but measures accepted by both chambers would not be valid if disapproved by the Tsar.

This scheme has some points of similarity with Speransky's project of 1809 but of course gives even less power to the Duma,

[1] One version of the division of provinces into lieutenancies is contained in the minutes of the Committee of 6 Dec. 1826. *SIRIO* vol. 90, pp. 212–13. It named twelve: Riga (comprising the provinces of Kurland, Livonia, Estland, and Pskov); Vitebsk (Vitebsk, Smolensk, Mogilev, Kaluga); Kiev (Chernigov, Kiev, Poltava, Kharkov, Kursk): Odessa (Bessarabia, Kherson, Crimea, Ekaterinoslav); Archangel (Archangel, Olonets, Vologda); Tver (Novogorod, Tver, Yaroslavl, Vladimir, Kostroma); Tula (Tula, Oryol, Voronezh, Tambov, Ryazan); Orenburg (Vyatka, Orenburg, Perm); Kazan (Nizhnii Novgorod, Kazan, Simbirsk, Saratov, Penza); Tiflis (Astrakhan, Caucasus, Georgia, Imeretia, Mingrelia); Tomsk (Tomsk, Irkutsk with Kamchatka); and Vilna (Vilna, Grodno, Minsk, Volhynia, Podolia, Białystok). The test of the draft constitution itself is in Shilder, op. cit. iv. 499–526. It is subjected to detailed commentary in G. Vernadsky, *La Charte constitutionelle de Russie*, Paris, 1933.

[2] See above p. 28.

which is a purely consultative, not a legislative body. Historians have noted that the draft has elements of federalism,[1] and it is most likely that Alexander was influenced at this time by the example of the Constitution of the United States. He had had talks with John Quincy Adams when he was in St. Petersburg in 1809–13, and he had corresponded with Jefferson. At the same time it must be stressed that, even if the lieutenancies bear some superficial resemblance to the states of North America, the constitution completely fails to incorporate the federal principle. The essence of federal government is that the central and regional authorities each have powers of their own, that they are co-ordinate with each other, that the latter are not subordinate to the former. Of this there is not a trace in Novosiltsov's draft. It stresses the unity of government and the supremacy of the emperor. At most one can speak of decentralization, devolution of business from the central government to the lieutenancies.

Pursuing the idea of decentralization, Alexander in 1819 appointed the former minister of police, General A. D. Balashov, as governor-general of a large area in central Russia, consisting of the provinces of Tula, Ryazan, Tambov, Oryol, and Voronezh, with his seat in Ryazan. During the next five years Balashov set up some new institutions at the provincial level and at the higher level, but the changes were not far-reaching. Two other governors-general who had authority over large areas were Paulucci in the Baltic provinces to which was added Pskov, and Prince M. A. Vorontsov in Odessa with authority over New Russia, Bessarabia, and the Caucasus.[2]

Still more important was the reappearance of Speransky as a provincial governor. On 30 August 1816 he was made governor of Penza, and on 31 March 1819 he was appointed governor-general of Siberia. At the end of three years he prepared a new draft organization for the government of Siberia which marks a landmark in the history of that vast region. Two governor-

[1] For example, Vernadsky, op. cit., and G. von Rauch, *Rußland: Staatliche Einheit und nationale Vielfalt*, Munich, 1954.

[2] The man mainly responsible for the development of the city of Odessa is Armand-Emmanuel, duc de Richelieu (1766–1822) who entered Russian service as an exile from France and held the post of governor-general of New Russia from 1803 to 1815. His papers relating to this period form vol. 54 of *SIRIO*. After the war Richelieu was twice prime minister of France under Louis XVIII.

generalships were created, for western and eastern Siberia, each with subordinate provinces (in the West Tobolsk and Tomsk provinces and Omsk region, in the East Yenisei and Irkutsk provinces and the Yakut region with the maritime administration of Okhotsk and Kamchatka). A regular hierarchy of subordinate areas was created on the normal Russian pattern, but special native administrations (*inorodcheskie upravleniya*) were established for the non-Russian peoples. During his period of office Speransky tried to combine bureaucratic centralization and discipline with initiative for local authorities, made necessary by the vast distances. He was obliged to rely on the bureaucracy as the only available civilizing force, but he endeavoured both to fight corruption and to encourage local private initiative. In the absence of a landowning nobility, the only social force which could give public leadership were the merchants, on the whole a very conservative group, with narrowly corporative notions and a preference for restrictive privileges and monopolies. Speransky was able to do something to free trade from restrictions and to encourage the bolder spirits to embark on more daring enterprise.[1] The fact that during the nineteenth and early twentieth century Siberian businessmen became the most active exponents of the capitalist virtues may in some measure be attributed to Speransky's reforms. Speransky was thanked by Alexander for his work, but his hope that his former close personal relations with the Tsar might be restored was never realized.

Little was done for the serfs in the second half of Alexander's reign. The 1803 law on free cultivators had small effect. Only 37,000 persons were emancipated under it during the whole reign. More important was the emancipation of serfs without land in the Baltic provinces. This was carried out in Estland in 1811, in Kurland in 1817, and in Livonia in 1819. The peasants gained personal freedom, but the landowners were freed from all obligations towards them, and their economic condition deteriorated. It seems possible that Alexander regarded the Baltic reforms as a pilot project for action in Russia. In February 1818 he asked Arakcheyev to prepare a plan for the emancipation of the serfs. Arakcheyev suggested the creation of a

[1] For an excellent modern study of Speransky's Siberian reforms see Marc Raeff, *Siberia and the Reforms of 1822*, Seattle, 1956.

commission to buy land and serfs from landowners. On the lands so bought, the serfs would become free men. The value of the land would be estimated by local committees of five persons, with county marshals of nobility as chairmen. In the case of serfs who paid *obrok*, this sum would be treated as 5 per cent. interest on the land, and the value thus estimated as twenty times the *obrok*. He suggested that the commission should have a capital to spend of 5,000,000 roubles a year. Nothing ever came of the plan.[1]

The famous military settlements, which were one of Arakcheyev's main tasks in these years, may perhaps in a sense be regarded as an enterprise of social reform. It seems likely that Alexander's first visit in 1810 to Arakcheyev's estate at Gruzino, which was kept with model cleanliness, symmetrical order, and efficient planning, inspired the emperor to try the same thing on a much vaster scale. Troops were to be settled on the land, and combine soldiering with farming, and to some extent with crafts and manufacture. It was hoped that the cost to the state of the upkeep of the army would be reduced, the quality of farming improved, and the welfare and education of the population advanced. The colonies, if successful, could perhaps even provide a model for wider reforms. A few small colonies were actually set up in 1810 in Mogilev province, but it was only after the war with Napoleon that they were instituted on a large scale. The period of most energetic action was from 1816 to 1821. At the time of Alexander's death the military settlements comprised 90 battalions in Novgorod province, 12 in Mogilev and 36 in the Ukraine, and 240 squadrons of cavalry in the southern provinces, totalling 750,000 men, women, and children. No outside persons might live in the area given to military settlements. Landowners who owned property in the area were compensated with estates elsewhere. Merchants or middle-class persons received monetary compensation, usually below the value of the property they were obliged to leave. Thus the whole area of the military colonies was literally a state within the state, responsible through Arakcheyev to the emperor.

[1] For Arakcheyev's plan, and for proposals by Admiral Mordvinov and others, see the communication by N. A. Milyutin, published in a collection of articles by the editor of *Russkii arkhiv*, P. A. Bartenev, entitled *Devyatnadtsaty vek* (Moscow, 1872), vol. ii.

The colonies enjoyed undoubted advantages. Money was lavished on them. They received excellent building materials for their houses, and skilled craftsmen were recruited to serve them. Agricultural techniques were improved, and the yield of cereals substantially increased. The schools were above the general level, and pupils were taught even foreign languages and literature. Hospitals, medical care, and sanitation were good. Foreign visitors usually took away a favourable impression.

They were, however, extremely unpopular. The nobility disliked experiments with peasants, which might put ideas in their heads. Some landowners feared the economic competition of the colonies with their own produce. Some observers feared that the colonies conferred too great power on potential adventurers, who might use them as a praetorian guard. The colonists themselves detested the system. This was largely due to the poor quality of the commanders, brutal and unimaginative men, many of whom had been pressed against their will into an enterprise in which they did not believe. The example of Arakcheyev himself, who believed in mechanical discipline and savage penalties for any shortcomings, communicated itself to his subordinates. Though the discipline and penalties were not worse than in the ordinary army, and though the standard of life of the colonists engaged in agriculture was certainly higher than that of most serfs or state peasants, it was the combination of the two that was resented. The soldiers objected to being made to farm, the peasants objected to having their lives ordered for them on military lines. There was no room for leisure and laziness, the joys which the peasant most treasured after heavy work. It may all have been for the good of their souls and the betterment of their children, but it was not what they wanted. In the words of a modern historian, 'The prospect of working at back-breaking tasks day after day in order to receive in return education or more property, and to feel pride in being a military colonist, or to have English latrines and clean hospitals simply made no sense.'[1] In August 1819 there was a mutiny in the Chuguyev colony in the Ukraine. Arakcheyev suppressed it and executed a number of soldiers by the cruel method of pass-

[1] Richard Pipes, 'The Russian Military Colonies 1810–1831', in *Journal of Modern History*, xxii, no. 3 (Sept. 1950), p. 218.

ing them through the ranks. In a letter to him the Tsar urged severity, and expressed his sympathy for the suffering which the incident must have caused to 'your sensitive soul'.

Alexander's own sensitive soul was hurt by an incident which occurred in the following year. On 16–17 October 1820 there was a mutiny in the Semyonovsky Regiment in St. Petersburg, the unit with which Alexander had been especially linked since March 1801. The reports of the officers who investigated the affair showed that it was due to the harsh treatment of the men by their commander Colonel Schwarz. But this explanation did not satisfy Alexander. 'There is some foreign, non-military inspiration', he wrote to Arakcheyev from Troppau, where he was attending the international diplomatic conference. 'I attribute it to secret societies.'[1] These he believed were trying to disrupt the work he was doing for the benefit of peace, monarchical government, and Christian principles.

The last dramatic episode in the relations of the two men was in the autumn of 1825, when Arakcheyev's serfs murdered his mistress, Anastasiya Milkina, whose cruelty had become intolerable. Arakcheyev wrote to Alexander in Taganrog on 12 September: 'My health and reason have been so ruined that I wish to seek for myself only death, and have not the strength or understanding to concern myself with any work.' Alexander on 22 September expressed his sympathy and invited him to Taganrog. 'You have no friend who loves you more sincerely. ... Conversation with a friend who shares your grief, alleviates it somewhat.' Having had no reply by 3 October, he sent one of his officers to see him, and wrote: 'It is sinful of you to forget a friend who has loved you so sincerely for so long. And still more sinful to doubt his share of your grief. I urgently entreat you, my beloved friend, if you cannot do so yourself, then instruct someone to tell me in detail about yourself. I am extremely anxious.' On the same day he wrote to Archimandrite Fotius,[2] telling him to go and see Arakcheyev in his despair and 'to work upon his spiritual forces'. Thereby he would be rendering a service to the state and to the Tsar, 'for the service of Count Arakcheyev is of great value to the fatherland'. Arakcheyev sent a brief letter of thanks on 1 October,

[1] The Tsar's letter is in Nikolay Mikhailovich, *Imperator Aleksandr I*, ii. 614–15.
[2] See below p. 169.

and others on 14 and 27, saying in the last that he would love to come to Taganrog but that the pain in his chest prevented him.[1] Less than two months later Alexander was dead,[2] and with him Arakcheyev's career too came to an end.

Education and Ideas

The only other man whose influence on the Tsar in this period could be compared with that of Arakcheyev was Prince A. N. Golitsyn, who became minister of education in 1816, and who was also a powerful force for reaction. Slightly older than Alexander, he had been his friend from an early age. In 1802 Alexander made him senior procurator of the Holy Synod. In 1810 Golitsyn took over the newly created Directorate of Spiritual Affairs of Foreign Confessions, whose purpose was to deal with the religious communities in the Russian empire other than Orthodox. During the Napoleonic invasion he was very close to Alexander, and it was apparently he who first urged the emperor to find a consolation from worldly troubles in Holy Writ. Golitsyn became a sort of spiritual adviser to the Tsar.[3]

When Golitsyn became minister of education in 1816, he remained senior procurator. The Holy Synod and the ministry were now combined in a larger ministry known as the Ministry of Spiritual Affairs and Education.[4] Its department of spiritual affairs had four sections—for Orthodox; for Roman Catholic, Uniate, and Armenian; for Protestant: and for Jewish, Moslem, and other faiths. The fact that Orthodoxy was placed on the

[1] Nikolay Mikhailovich, *Imperator Aleksandr I*, ii. 660–1, 712–13.

[2] The belief later became widespread that Alexander I did not die in Taganrog, that the corpse which was buried in the Peter Paul Cathedral in St. Petersburg was not his, and that he survived for nearly forty years more under the disguise of the *starets* Fyodor Kuzmich, who died near Tomsk on 20 Jan. 1864. There is no doubt that Alexander had previously expressed a desire to retire to a life of prayer and meditation, and the official accounts of his illness and of the arrangements for his burial, published in Shilder, op. cit., vol. iv, are unconvincing and contain contradictions. But the Tsar's identity with Fyodor Kuzmich cannot be regarded as established. For an intelligent presentation of the case, based on study of the documents, see Prince Vladimir Baryatinsky, *Le Mystère d'Alexandre Ier*, Paris, 1925.

[3] Such was his authority that he could even permit himself to write to Alexander in 1814, on the occasion of the death of the emperor's illegitimate daughter by Princess Naryshkina, which caused him much grief: 'Dieu vous a arraché miraculeusement au péché.' Nikolay Mikhailovich, *Imperator Aleksandr I*, i. 574.

[4] Text of law in PSZ, first series no. 27106 of 24 October 1817 (vol. 34, pp. 814–34).

same level as other religions caused much discontent in clerical and conservative circles. In general, Golitsyn showed tolerance to all religious groups, including sects of Christianity. His enemies accused him of favouring 'mysticism', a word which they vaguely associated with both Freemasonry and revolutionary political doctrines.

Alexander himself became deeply religious from 1812 onwards and showed special interest in unorthodox doctrines, including those of various Protestant sects that were making themselves known in western Europe. The importance of his contacts with Madame de Krüdener, a Russian subject of Baltic extraction,[1] has been exaggerated. But the emperor was undoubtedly receptive to religious ideas of various origins, and this combination of religious feeling and curiosity was rather typical of the mood of the Russian upper class at the end of the war.

In December 1812 Alexander authorized the foundation of the Russian Bible Society, based on the model of the British and Foreign Bible Society. Its purpose was to spread the Bible in the languages of the Russian empire, and membership was open to persons of any Christian confession. Its first committee, elected in January 1813, included such eminent persons as Kochubey, Razumovsky, and Kozodavlev. Its first president was Golitsyn. In 1814 two Orthodox metropolitans joined the committee. Branches were set up in the capitals and in a number of provincial centres. The society began with translations into several Oriental languages, but in 1816, on the express recommendation of the emperor, the Holy Synod decided to sponsor a translation of the Bible from Church Slavonic into modern Russian. In 1818 a version of the New Testament was completed, with modern and original texts side by side, by the St. Petersburg Spiritual Academy, under the supervision of its rector, the Church's outstanding scholar Archimandrite Filaret. The society founded several schools, based on the model of the schools for the poor by mutual instruction devised by the English

[1] Julie de Vietinghoff, a descendant of the eighteenth-century Marshal Osterman. Some of her letters to the Tsar and to Golitsyn are published in Nikolay Mikhailovich, *Imperator Aleksandr I*, ii. 215–47. Her first meeting with Alexander is described by an eye-witness in *Mémoires de la comtesse Edling* (Moscow, 1888), pp. 231–2. A recent book about her, based partly on unpublished documents, is Francis Ley, *Madame de Krudener et son temps*, Paris, 1961.

Evangelical missionary Joseph Lancaster. It also disseminated religious booklets, some translated from the English and some written in Russian by Princess Meshcherskaya. Several English pastors travelled extensively around Russia and came back impressed by the society's achievements. It is difficult to estimate its effective impact. As long as it was known to enjoy the emperor's favour, the provincial governors gave it their support, and careerists and social climbers flocked into its ranks. When official favour was withdrawn, all this ceased. The residual effect on the Russian people was no doubt smaller than the enthuasiasts had claimed, but it was perhaps not negligible.

One of the most active members of the society was A. F. Labzin, a Freemason, who had published a periodical entitled *Messenger of Zion*, which appeared for some months in 1806, but was suppressed at the end of that year. Golitsyn allowed him to revive it in 1816. He was appointed vice-president by the Academy of Arts in 1818, but soon quarrelled with the members and with Golitsyn, was banished from the capital and died in Simbirsk province in 1823 in great poverty. Labzin was personally domineering, ambitious, and arrogant, and quickly made enemies. His Masonic connexions and unpleasant character gave the enemies of the Bible Society an opportunity to attack it. There were also more exotic religious groups in the capital, tolerated by Golitsyn. One was the sect of eunuchs (*skoptsy*), whose leader Kondraty Selivanov called himself 'Redeemer'. Another was the group of Madame Tatarinova, a colonel's widow, who occupied an apartment in the Mikhailovsky Palace in which meetings were held. Her disciples considered themselves to be loyal Orthodox, and had no subversive dogmas, but believed that they could achieve an inner mystic joy by dancing in circular motion—like Moslem dervishes. In the ecstasy induced by these evolutions, they felt themselves visited by the Holy Spirit, and uttered prophetic sounds. The activities of these groups, much distorted and exaggerated, were held by his enemies to be evidence of Golitsyn's sinister plans to corrupt the souls of the Russian people.[1]

[1] On Labzin see an article by I. A. Chistovich in *Russkaya starina* (hereafter *RS*), June 1894, and a series of articles by Dubrovin, 'Nashi mistiki-sektanty', in *RS*, Sept. 1894 to Nov. 1895. The writer S. T. Aksakov has some interesting reminiscences of Labzin in his own memoirs; see S. T. Aksakov, *Sobranie sochineny* (Moscow, 1955), ii. 222–65. On religious activities under Alexander I, and espe-

But if Golitsyn was unconventional in his religious attitudes, he was certainly no political radical, or even liberal. The Ministry of Education in his period of office was dominated by extreme obscurantists. One of these was A. S. Sturdza, son of a Phanariot Greek landowner who had come from Constantinople to Russia towards the end of the eighteenth century. His sister Roxandra, later married to Count Edling, was for some years lady-in-waiting to the Empress Elizabeth. As a diplomat at the Aachen Conference of 1818, Sturdza wrote a pamphlet attacking German universities, which so enraged the German students that he had to flee for his life. Leaving the diplomatic service, he entered the Ministry of Education. Two other eminent reactionaries in the ministry were M. L. Magnitsky and D. P. Runich, who were made curators respectively of Kazan and St. Petersburg. In the early 1820's the German universities acquired a reputation for extreme radicalism. Alexander himself described them as 'the theatre of all sorts of irregularities, where young people acquire notions that are most opposed to religion and morality'.[1] Magnitsky wrote: 'The professors of the godless universities transmit to the unfortunate youth the fine poison of unbelief and of hatred for the lawful authorities.'[2] The ministry regarded Jena, Heidelberg, and Giessen, and later also Würzburg, as specially harmful. The governor-general of Riga, Marquess Paulucci, was ordered to advise parents in his province who had children studying at these universities to recall them. Dorpat University announced that no person who had studied at any foreign university would be admitted as one of its students.

M. L. Magnitsky was a remarkable figure.[3] As a young man he was a close friend of Speransky. At this time he specialized in expressions of cynicism and unbelief, and in bitter jokes at

cially the Bible Society, see A. N. Pypin, *Religioznye dvizheniya pri Aleksandre I*, Petrograd, 1916.

[1] *Istoricheskii obzor deyatel'nosti MNP*, p. 117. [2] Ibid., p. 116.

[3] His policies are described in the official history of the ministry. Among other sources the following may be mentioned: two official memoranda by Magnitsky himself dated 1823, printed in *Russkii Arkhiv* (hereafter *RA*) (1864), pp. 322–9; a memorandum in self-justification, written in 1829 and printed in the miscellany published in 1872 by *RA*, entitled *Devyatnadtsaty vek*, i. 238–55; an obituary by his friend Sturdza, written in 1844 and published in *RA* (1868), pp. 926–38; and an article by Pavel Morozov entitled 'My acquaintance with Magnitsky', published in *RA* (1875), vol. iii, pp. 240–50.

the expense of government and church. When Speransky was disgraced, Magnitsky too was exiled for five years. In 1816 he was made vice-governor of Voronezh province, in 1817 governor of Simbirsk. When an official in his administration was refused a Chair, for which he had applied, at Kazan University, Magnitsky began a campaign of denunciation of the university. As a result of his agitation, he was instructed to make an official inquiry into its affairs. In a written report to the Ministry of Education in St. Petersburg, he recommended that it should be abolished, in fact that it be 'publicly destroyed'. The Tsar was content drastically to purge and to change the young university. Emphasis was to be placed on theology, 'politically unrealiable' professors were to be dismissed, and a new post was to be created, parallel in authority with that of the rector—a director of economic, police, and moral affairs. In 1820 Magnitsky was appointed curator of Kazan educational district. He himself lived in St. Petersburg, sent directives to Kazan, and reported to the ministry that everything was now going splendidly.

Some points in his régime are worth quoting. The foundation of the teaching of philosophy was to be the Epistles to the Colossians and Timothy. The principles of political science were to be taken from Moses, David, and Solomon, to some extent also from Plato and Aristotle. Hobbes and Machiavelli were to be 'mentioned with loathing'. Professors of physics must stress the 'limitations of our emotions and our instruments for the understanding of the wonders that constantly surround us'. In teaching Arabic and Persian literature (Kazan as the easternmost Russian university was intended to be a centre of Oriental studies) lecturers 'should not enter into the details of the religious beliefs and customs of the Mohammedan peoples'. The director's activities recall the principles of Mr. Squeers of Dotheboys Hall. In 1819 the director reported that the state scholars had been cultivating the university garden during the summer, in allotments exactly divided up according to the number of the students. The director was to concern himself not only with sound hard labour for the students: their political and moral health was also in his charge. He must from time to time examine their lecture notes, to see that 'the spirit of free-thinking should neither openly nor secretly weaken the doctrines of the church in philosophical, historical, or literary teaching'. Professor Solntsev of Kazan was dismissed and forbidden to teach in any establishment in Russia, being accused, on the evidence of his pupils' lecture notes, of having said that natural law expounds the rights and duties of rulers and ruled as deduced from the principles of reason. He had failed to recognize, the university council decided, that 'reason cannot be the guide: it is obliged reverently to take note of, and with fear to bow before, the supreme legislator'.

In St. Petersburg the Pedagogical Institute had been transformed in 1819 into a university, on the advice of the district curator, S. S. Uvarov. In 1821 he was replaced by D. P. Runich, a worthy colleague of Magnitsky. One of his first actions was to dismiss four professors for 'teaching in a spirit contrary to Christianity and subversive to the social order'. Their students' lecture notes were produced as evidence that they had spoken contrary to Holy Writ. They were subjected to a long inquisition, in writing and orally, before the university authorities, who were not agreed in their verdict. The ministry decided they were guilty, and dismissed them, and Golitsyn asked the Committee of Ministers whether they should also be subjected to criminal prosecution. A special commission was set up to consider this, but its proceedings were quashed by the new Emperor Nicholas I in 1827. The university was, however, tamed and purged. In 1825, only six years after its foundation, half of its thirty-four professors had been changed.[1]

Golitsyn himself in 1823 began to lose his influence with Alexander. The campaign against him was led on the one hand by the Orthodox prelates who disliked his religious tolerance, on the other hand by Arakcheyev, who was jealous of the only man who enjoyed an authority with the Tsar comparable with his own. His enemies found a useful mouthpiece in an eloquent young priest of extreme obscurantist outlook, the Archimandrite Fotius, who was protected by the very rich and very pious Countess Orlova-Chesmenskaya.[2] Fotius was secretly brought to an audience with the Tsar, and impressed him with the

[1] M. I. Sukhomlinov, *Izsledovaniya i stati*, vol. i, *Materialy dlya istorii obrazovaniya v Rossii v tsarstvovanie Imperatora Aleksandra I* (SPB, 1889), pp. 264–6.

[2] The memoirs of Fotius were published in successive numbers of *RS* between Mar. 1894 and Aug. 1896—*Avtobiografiya Yuryevskogo arkhimandrita Fotiya.* As a document of the life and outlook of an obscurantist fanatic, filled with hatred and gifted in intrigue, they are of considerable interest.

strength of clerical opposition to Golitsyn, even though he may not have convinced him of the justice of the arguments. Golitsyn naively sought reconciliation with Fotius, and visited him in Countess Orlova's house. The archimandrite refused to make peace, and when Golitsyn left the house he came out after him and publicly pronounced anathema on him from the doorstep. Golitsyn then resigned his post on 15 May 1824.

His successor was Admiral Shishkov, who, as was to be expected, roundly condemned the educational policy of the first part of the reign: 'It seems that all our places of teaching have been transformed into schools of vice.' His aim was to make education nationally Russian in spirit, to free the youth from 'pseudo-clever cerebrations, vaporous dreaming, swollen pride, and sinful self-conceit, which lead a man in his adolescence into the dangerous delusion that he possesses the wisdom of old age, and end by reducing him in his old age to the condition of callow youth'.[1] Under Shishkov the ministry was reduced to its original functions, and the Holy Synod became a separate department of state, with sole authority over Orthodox affairs. The Directorate of Spiritual Affairs of Foreign Confessions was also for a time a separate institution, under D. N. Bludov.

From its foundation the Ministry of Education had been responsible for censorship, which was handled by the offices of the district curators, with a Special Censorship Committee in St. Petersburg at the head of the whole apparatus. In the first years of the reign it was liberally applied. In 1811 the Special Chancery of the Ministry of Police was given powers which overlapped with those of the censorship proper. The police had the right, if they thought that some work which the censors had passed was liable to 'subversive interpretations, contrary to public order and security', to report this to the Tsar. In June 1820 a special committee was set up to draft new censorship rules, among its members being Magnitsky and Runich. Shishkov had long held somewhat exalted views on the moral importance of censorship, and had submitted a proposal to the Council of State in June 1815 for the formation of a corps of censors who were to be 'mature, of good morals, learned, connoisseurs of the language and literature' and were not only to prevent noxious material from publication, but to improve the literary quality

[1] *Istoricheskii obzor deyatel'nosti MNP*, p. 166.

of what was written. Shishkov's curious ideas were embodied in the Censorship Statute which he produced at the beginning of the next reign.

The obscurantist policies of Arakcheyev and Golitsyn did not prevent the post-war years from being a great period in Russian literature. The leading figure at first was V. A. Zhukovsky.[1] Born in 1783, he began to write poetry as a pupil of the Moscow nobles' boarding-house, where his fellow students of literature included S. S. Uvarov, D. A. Bludov, and the Turgenev brothers. In 1812 he won immense popularity with a poem entitled 'The poet in the camp of the Russian soldiers'. In 1817 he was appointed as teacher in Russian to the German wives of the young Grand Dukes Nicholas and Michael,[2] and in 1825 to Nicholas's son Alexander. Zhukovsky was a gifted poet, a large part of whose works were translations. He was a gentle and melancholy person whose life was dominated by his love for a girl whom he was prevented by her parents from marrying. He was generous in his help and advice to others,[3] and was able by his influence in high places both to mitigate the severities of the decades after 1815 and to implant more liberal ideas in the next generation.

Zhukovsky was a leading member of a literary group known as the Arzamas Society. It was so called by Bludov, who had been delighted to discover that there was a group of painters in a small town of this name in central Russia, and greeted it as proof that culture was reaching even the benighted Russian provinces. The society met in St. Petersburg from 1815 to 1818, usually in the house of Uvarov or Bludov. Its members were disciples of Karamzin and Dmitriev, and opponents of the literary school of Shishkov.[4]

[1] He was the illegitimate son of a Russian landowner named Bunin and a captured Turkish girl, and was adopted by a neighbouring landowner whose name he took.

[2] The wife of Grand Duke Michael, Elena Pavlovna, played an important part in Russian public life, creating the first organization of nursing sisters in the Crimean War and actively helping the work of emancipation of the serfs. See below pp. 327, 335.

[3] For example, he was responsible for the emancipation from serfdom of Nikitenko and Shevchenko (see below p. 271) and helped Puskhin in his difficulties with the authorities.

[4] Other members included the partisan leader and poet Denis Davydov, the critic Prince Vyazemsky, the memoirist Wiegel, and the later political conspirators Prince M. F. Orlov and Nicholas Turgenev.

Among the members of Arzamas was Alexander Pushkin, Russia's greatest poet and one of the outstanding figures in the whole of world literature. Born in 1799, he was educated from 1811 to 1817 at the Tsarskoe Selo Lycée. His first poems were published in 1814, and he became widely popular with his *Ruslan and Ludmila* in 1820. Already at this stage he got into trouble with the authorities with some unpublished political epigrams. From 1820 to 1823 he served as an official in Kishinyov in Bessarabia, then from 1823 to 1824 in Odessa. In August 1824 he was dismissed from the service and ordered to live on his mother's property at Mikhailovskoe near Pskov.[1] During these years Pushkin wrote some of his best lyric poems, and the first chapter of *Eugene Onegin.*

The Kingdom of Poland

Alexander set up a constitutional régime in the second country of which he was sovereign, the Kingdom of Poland. This was designed not only to give satisfaction to Polish aspirations but also to serve as an experiment which might provide lessons for later application in Russia.

In 1815 the Polish constitution was prepared, largely by Adam Czartoryski. In the second half of November Alexander came to Warsaw, did his best to charm the Poles, and was everywhere well received. On 27 November he signed the Constitutional Charter. It provided for a Parliament of two chambers. The Senate of 83 persons was composed of Catholic bishops and representatives of aristocratic families. The Chamber of Deputies had 100 representatives from the countryside and 60 from the cities. The electors were the country gentry and the urban property-owners and professional people. The Parliament was to meet for a session of 30 days every second year. It was to examine legislation placed before it, but had no initiative. The main executive body was the Council of State, which was made up of five ministers and a number of other prominent persons nominated by the king. Among these was Czartoryski. Liaison between the Polish and Russian governments was

[1] The official reason given was the expression of atheist views in an intercepted letter. More important was his involvement with Countess Elizabeth Vorontsova, wife of the governor-general of Odessa and New Russia.

maintained by an Imperial commissioner in Warsaw and a Polish minister-secretary of state in St. Petersburg. The first of these posts was entrusted to Novosiltsov.

The Kingdom had its own army, of about 35,000 men, under Grand Duke Constantine. He was also in charge of a separate Lithuanian Corps, created by a decree of 13 July 1817. This arrangement encouraged Polish hopes that the borderlands, taken from Poland in the eighteenth-century partitions, would be reunited with the Kingdom. Alexander himself maintained these hopes by vaguely benevolent assurances in private. In March 1818 he opened the first session of the Sejm in Warsaw. His speech contained the phrase: 'Les résultats de vos travaux dans cette première assemblée m'apprendront ce que la patrie doit attendre à l'avenir de votre dévouement pour elle comme de vos bons sentiments pour moi, et si, fidèle à ma résolution, je puis étendre ce que j'ai fait pour vous.' But these words were not followed by action. Opposition in Russia, both in the bureaucracy and among the educated class as a whole, was too strong.

Polish cultural influence, however, remained extremely strong in the borderlands. Czartoryski, who was now on bad terms with his old friend Novosiltsov, and found himself unable to achieve much in the Council of State, once more devoted his main energies to his job as curator of Vilna educational district. Vilna University remained the most important academic centre, overshadowing the newly created University of Warsaw.

The Polish political class were not reconciled to union with Russia. Social and economic discontents inevitably took nationalist form. Poles refused to abandon the dream of recovering all historical Lithuania. The centres of political radicalism were the army and the students. In 1819 a major named Walerian Łukasiński founded a Freemasons' Lodge in the Polish army. In April 1821 the former Polish general, J. N. Umiński, now a Prussian subject, came from Poznań to Warsaw on behalf of a secret society in Prussian Poland. He met Łukasiński, and on 3 May a secret meeting was held at Potok near Warsaw, at which it was decided to found a Polish Patriotic Society, to have branches not only in the Kingdom but also in Lithuania, Volhynia, Kraków, Poznania, and Lwów, as well as within the army. Already in October 1820 Łukasiński had been denounced to the authorities. At first no action was taken, but when the story came to the notice of Novosiltsov he investigated it thoroughly. The result was that Łukasiński and seven others were arrested in May 1822, and were condemned to prison by a military tribunal in June 1824. In 1823 a conspiracy was discovered among Vilna students. There had been talk of assassinating Grand Duke Constantine, and there were two secret societies among the students. Arrests were made and some students were banished to Russia. This affair caused the dismissal of Czartoryski from his curatorship, and Novosiltsov took over the effective direction of education. The Patriotic Society, however, still existed. It was led by Seweryn Krzyżanowski, who later conducted negotiations with the Russian Decembrists. The arrests of 1826 in Russia, however, led to his arrest and the final suppression of his organization.[1]

There were able Poles who believed in co-operation with Russia. The most important of them was the finance minister, F. K. Drucki-Lubecki, who held this post from 1821 to 1830. He succeeded in restoring Polish finances, by introducing new taxes and insisting on ruthless collection of existing taxes. He encouraged industry and established banks. During his period in office both the textile and metal industries made substantial progress. He was able to obtain a reduction in the Russian tariff for Polish goods. Drucki-Lubecki certainly laid the foundations of modern economy in Poland. But his policies did not benefit the Polish peasants, nor did they persuade the upper class to turn away from political dreams to practical economic construction.

The Concert of Europe

Alexander's conception of the place of Russia in Europe was not confined to the traditional interests in Poland and the Balkans: he expected that Russia should play a leading part in all the affairs of the Continent, and even overseas. But beyond considerations of national interest, he was deeply concerned to establish a new system of international order and peaceful co-operation. This idea had interested him already at the time of the Novosiltsov Mission to London in 1804: it now had an added dimension of religious fervour. This was clearly expressed

[1] See below pp. 281–2.

in the text of the Holy Alliance, which Alexander himself drafted in September 1815. The monarchs were to undertake 'to take for their sole guide the precepts of the Christian religion'. All the rulers except the pope and the Sultan were invited to adhere to the alliance, but in the first instance Alexander secured the signatures of the emperor of Austria and king of Prussia. The alliance did not in fact have practical significance, but because of its origin it became a symbol of the association of the three eastern monarchies, and of the increasingly reactionary internal policies which they pursued.

At a lower level of thought than this, both Alexander and Castlereagh believed that periodical meetings of rulers and foreign ministers, to discuss matters of policy, would serve the peace of Europe. A clause expressing a desire for such meetings had been inserted in the Quadruple Alliance of 1814. Metternich was at first less eager, but soon found that such conferences were to his advantage. The first was held at Aachen from September to November 1818. Its main business was to arrange for the evacuation from France of the allied armies of occupation. From this time France was in fact admitted to the inner council of the European Great Powers—the Concert of Europe—although the Quadruple Alliance still remained in force. At Aachen Alexander proposed the creation of a universal league of sovereigns, who should guarantee not only each other's frontiers but also each other's political systems, which should as far as possible be based on constitutions to be granted by the monarchs. Both Metternich and Castlereagh objected, the former because he was against constitutions and the latter because he did not wish to commit Britain to intervention, or to approval of intervention by other Powers, in the internal affairs of other countries, with the single exception of a Bonapartist revival in France.

The main subjects of discussion between the Powers in the next three years were a series of revolutions. The first was in Spain. Discontent was caused not only by the generally reactionary policies of the restored Bourbon king, Ferdinand VII, but by his determination to send Spanish troops to reimpose his rule on the American colonies which had revolted against him. On 1 January 1820 army units in Cadiz, destined for America, revolted, within a few days the revolution spread to Madrid, and the king was forced to restore the liberal constitution of 1812. In July 1820 there was a revolution in Naples, clearly inspired by the Spanish and led by officers who had been devoted to Murat. The king of Naples too had to accept the Spanish constitution of 1812. In August 1820 there was a military revolt in Portugal, and by October the king had accepted a constitution. On 10 March 1821 came a similar revolution in Piedmont, and in the same month two risings in the Ottoman empire, both in the cause of Greek independence. These events raised the problem of a general revolutionary threat to the established order, but they also specifically affected the interests of Great Powers—of Britain in Portugal, of Britain and France in Spain, of Austria in Naples and Piedmont, and of Russia in Roumania and Greece. They were discussed at the Conferences of Troppau (Opava) from October to December 1820, of Laibach (Ljubljana) in January 1821, and of Verona from September to December 1822.

Alexander was more and more convinced that peace and order were threatened by sinister revolutionary conspiracy, which menaced all governments alike, and should be fought by all together. No ruler could afford not to give help to another ruler thus threatened, for the danger was common to all. Action taken against revolution should be European action, not simply action by the Power most nearly affected. Alexander certainly did not neglect Russian state interests, but he did not confine himself to these. Castlereagh took the opposite view. He was certainly not less hostile to liberalism and to revolution than was Alexander, and he was perfectly willing that Austria, whose Italian interests were endangered by the Neapolitan revolution, should act against it. But he had to deal with the British Parliament, with British public opinion, and with Cabinet colleagues who were less hostile to liberalism and less interested in the solidarity of the European Powers than he was. Certainly he could not obtain British support for a general denunciation of revolution, for the British Constitution owed its origin to a revolution. In his famous State Paper of April 1820 he argued that the suppression of revolution could not be elevated into a generalized principle. 'No country having a representative system of government could act on it. . . . Great Britain is the last government in Europe which can be expected or can venture to commit herself on any question of an abstract character.' Apart from this general objection, Castlereagh was anxious to avoid intervention by other Powers in Spain, whose strategic importance to Britain placed it in a special category. This objection applied still more strongly to any European intervention in Spanish America. In this matter the British view was similar to that of the United States.

At the Conference of Troppau Metternich was mainly concerned to obtain a free hand against the Neapolitan revolutionaries. He had no more desire than Castlereagh to see Russian troops in Italy. But in order to get Alexander's support for Austrian action he was certainly willing to make general statements against revolution, which in any case accorded with his own views. Alexander's offer of an army of 100,000 to act against Naples, he received with outward gratitude, but with the inward resolve to do without it if possible. The news of the Semyonovsky Regiment mutiny reached Alexander at Troppau, increased his anti-revolutionary fervour, and helped Metternich to manœuvre him as he wished. A 'Preliminary Protocol', drafted on behalf of the three eastern monarchs on 19 November 1820, proposed that all the Powers should refuse to recognize a régime brought to power by revolution, and should concert steps against it, including armed force if necessary. British protests caused the proposal to be dropped. But a circular note of 8 December, intended for the three monarchies only, repeated much of the earlier doctrine. It became known to Castlereagh, who replied with a circular of 19 January 1821, which was later published in the press, and clearly dissociated Britain from the policy. Castlereagh, however, agreed to Austrian action in Italy. During April 1821 Austrian troops suppressed the revolutionary government of Naples, and also entered Piedmont with the consent of the new king, who had already crushed the revolution.

The Conference of Verona was concerned mainly with Spain, whose revolutionary government was still in power. Canning, the successor of Castlereagh, was reluctant to involve Britain in European alliances, and disliked the principles of the European rulers. The conference approved armed intervention in Spain, from which the British government formally dissociated itself. Action was, however, entrusted to France, the Power most directly concerned, and Alexander's plan to send a Russian army into Spain was politely overruled. France in 1822 was in the same situation as Austria in 1820. The French rulers were as willing as Metternich had been to denounce the wickedness of revolution, and indeed held this view, but they were keen that the action should be left in their hands and not be entrusted to a crusade in the name of Europe. In April 1823 the invasion took place, and Ferdinand VII celebrated his return to absolute power by imprisoning and executing as many liberals as he could lay hands on. However, the attempt of the Spanish king to enlist European support for the reconquest of America failed, despite Alexander's sympathy.

During Alexander's reign the efforts to establish Russian power on both sides of the northern Pacific continued. Baranov remained in command at Sitka until 1818. In 1812 he established a new Russian settlement at Fort Ross, about a hundred miles north of San Francisco Bay. In the same year he sent a Russian ship to explore the Hawaii islands. From 1815 to 1817 a German doctor in Russian service, Georg Scheffer, was in the islands, and attempted to exploit hostility between the rulers of different islands to make a treaty on behalf of Russia. In 1817 he was expelled by the Hawaiians, and the Russian government disowned his activities.

Further attempts were made to establish relations with Japan by the diplomat Nikolai Rezanov, who was married to Baranov's step-daughter. Rezanov reached Nagasaki in October 1804, but was not allowed to move outside a small compound allotted to his mission on shore, and did not meet the emissaries of the Yedo government until 16 April 1805, when his request for regular diplomatic relations was rejected. Angry at this rebuff, Rezanov arranged for an attack by a Russian naval force on a Japanese post on Etorofu, one of the Kurile islands. When the next Russian ship called at a Japanese port in July 1811, the Japanese took reprisals for the Etorofu raid by capturing Lieutenant-Commander Vasily Golovin, who was kept imprisoned on Hokkaido until October 1813. Russian hopes of contact with Japan, which would have been valuable for supplies to their settlement in North America, were still far from fulfilment. But at least the Japanese were being made aware of the presence of an increasingly formidable northern neighbour.

Alexander I took some interest in American affairs. He corresponded with President Jefferson, and even after 1815 was still attracted by the American Constitution. He was anxious to eliminate friction with the United States on the Pacific coast. By a treaty between the two countries of 17 April 1824, Russian claims in Alaska were reduced to the area north of 54° 40′ latitude, and freedom of navigation in the Pacific was recognized. The status of Fort Ross, close to the ill-defined Spanish or Mexican possessions in California, remained uncertain. In 1825 an Anglo-Russian treaty accepted the same definition of Russian territory in Alaska. At this time the boundary of British Canadian territory in the Oregon area was not clearly established.

The Greek war of independence proved to be a more difficult matter than any of those discussed above, and indeed dominated European policy through the second half of the 1820's. Two distinct areas were involved. One was the Roumanian principalities, traditional area of contention between Russia and Turkey. The other was the southern part of the Greek peninsula, the homeland of the hard core of the Greek nation and a position of strategic importance for naval power in the Mediterranean. A somewhat smaller, but still important part was played by Serbia, whose struggle for independence had broken out again in 1815 under a new leader, Miloš Obrenović.

The Greeks had always played a special part in the Ottoman empire. They had their irreducible homeland in the peninsula, but they were also scattered all over the empire, especially in its trading cities. The commercial, seafaring, and intellectual professions in the Ottoman empire were mainly filled with Greeks. It was inevitably through educated Greeks that western liberal and radical ideas reached the Ottoman population. Greeks provided the trading class in the Roumanian principalities, and for two centuries the rulers of Moldavia and Wallachia had been rich Greeks, who ruled as tax-farmers, paying a large sum to the Sultan and recouping themselves by extracting as much as they could from their subjects.[1] Throughout European Turkey, including the principalities, the upper hierarchy of the Orthodox Church consisted of Greeks.

One of the most important Greek communities outside the

[1] For the Roumanian background at this time, see R. W. Seton-Watson, *A History of the Roumanians*, Cambridge, 1934.

Ottoman empire was in Odessa, which since its foundation in 1794, and under the able direction of the duc de Richelieu, had grown to be Russia's main Black Sea port. Odessa became a centre not only of commerce, carried mainly in Greek ships with Greek crews, but also of Greek political activity. Here was founded in 1814 the *Philike Hetaireia* (Society of Friends), whose aim was the liberation of Greece. On 4 March 1821 Alexander Ypsilanti, a Greek who was an officer in the Russian army, crossed the Moldavian frontier with a small force. At the end of March a rising began in the Peloponnese, and in April there were other risings on the mainland north of the Gulf of Corinth and in some of the islands. The revolt had not been systematically planned by any one. Ypsilanti's action was certainly influenced by the events in Spain and Naples, and each of the local actions in the Greek peninsula provided a stimulus for the next action. Ypsilanti was not authorized by the Tsar, though he believed that he could count on Russian sympathy.[1] When he entered the Moldavian capital Jaşi, he was greeted by the Orthodox metropolitan, who naturally believed that a force coming from Russia, led by a Russian officer, expressed the wish of the Russian Tsar to liberate the Greeks. When the Tsar's disapproval became known at the end of March, the enthusiasm of the Greek communities in Roumania quickly diminished. Ypsilanti, however, reached Bucarest and attracted more soldiers to his cause. Here, however, a tragic conflict developed between Greeks and Roumanians. The Roumanians too had bitter grievances against the Turks, and as a Christian people disliked subjection to a Moslem Power. But at the same time they had good reason to dislike the Greek rulers whom the Sultan had placed over them, and the Roumanian peasant's attitude to the Greek merchant was the usual attitude of the primitive villager to the primitive capitalist. A large section of the Roumanian nobility were

[1] The extent of Russian complicity in the revolt is still not clear. This is an important task for future historical research. In his contribution to the collective work *Istoria Românei*, the distinguished Roumanian historian Professor Oţetea argues that Ypsilanti misunderstood the nature of the Tsar's support. Alexander wished the revolt to take place in order that Russia should have an excuse for invading Ottoman territory 'to restore order'. Ypsilanti, however, announced that the Tsar supported the *aims* of the revolt. This placed Alexander in an impossible position. Unable to appear as a patron of revolution, he had no alternative to formal denunciation.

willing to make common cause with the Greeks, but they had no intention of satisfying the social aspirations of the peasants. In western Wallachia the leader of the revolt was Todor Vladimirescu, a Roumanian who had served in an auxiliary formation of the Russian army in the war of 1812, and was in touch with the *Hetaireia*. Vladimirescu made himself the champion of peasant demands, and inevitably came into conflict with Ypsilanti, who had him murdered. Meanwhile the Turks brought substantial forces into Wallachia, and Ypsilanti's army was crushed.[1]

Though Alexander was not responsible for the action, it was bound to lead to Russo-Turkish tension. On 22 April 1821 the Sultan ordered the oecumenical patriarch Gregorios to be hanged in front of his palace in Constantinople. This inevitably aroused horror in Russia. The presence of large Turkish forces in Roumania was also unacceptable to Russian government.

Another source of alarm was the future of Serbia. Miloš Obrenović, by a combination of military prowess and diplomacy, had established effective autonomy. Turkish garrisons remained in Serbia, but civil government was conducted by Miloš. But the ferocious outburst of Moslem hatred against Christians, provoked by the Greek rebellion, and the presence of Turkish troops in force in Wallachia, promised trouble for the Serbs. The Treaty of Bucarest of 1812 contained a clause promising self-government to Serbia, which the Russians could now invoke on their behalf. The three problems of the persecution of the Orthodox, the occupation of Roumania, and Serbian autonomy, brought Russo-Turkish relations to a critical state, and the Russian ambassador left Constantinople.

Alexander's policy towards the Greek rebellion remained ineffective, as he was torn between sympathy for the Orthodox and hostility to rebellion, between concern for Russian aims in Roumania and Serbia and a desire to support a sovereign menaced by revolutionaries. Metternich had no such problems of conscience or conflicts of interest: he was wholeheartedly in favour of the Sultan. In both Britain and France there were

[1] The Roumanian side of the events is discussed in the recent collective work published by the Roumanian Academy of Sciences, *Istoria Românici*, vol. 3, pp. 850–904. The Academy has also published five volumes of documents *Răscoala din 1821*, Bucarest, 1959–1962.

growing Philhellene movements, affecting the whole educated class, including a part of the high aristocracy. From the point of view of British Mediterranean interests, it was not clear whether a stable Ottoman empire would be preferable to a small but friendly Greece. Canning inclined rather towards the Greeks, while Wellington preferred to back Turkey.

During 1822 and 1823 the Greeks held out in the Peloponnese and some of the islands, and defended the town of Mesolonghi on the north side of the Gulf of Corinth, where Byron died of fever. In March 1823 Canning recognized the Greeks as belligerents. Though sympathetic to their cause, he was not willing to join any European action designed to compel Turkey by force to accept a settlement. In 1824 Alexander proposed that a diplomatic conference be held in St. Petersburg. His circular of January 1824, which proposed the creation of three separate Greek principalities under Turkish suzerainty, was published in the French press soon afterwards. Canning, who objected both to the proposals themselves and to the principle of imposing terms on Turkey, refused to take part in the conference. Alexander reacted by forbidding his diplomats to discuss the Greek question with the British. 'His Imperial Majesty regards all further deliberation between Russia and England on relations with Turkey and on the pacification of Greece as definitely closed.' However, the conference, which took place in the spring of 1825, proved most unsatisfactory to the Tsar. Metternich opposed the creation of three Greek principalities, as he feared that Russia, having obtained her demands in Roumania and Serbia, would dominate the Ottoman government, and would have the main influence in Greece as well as in the northern Balkans. He also lost hope of persuading the Sultan, whom his diplomacy had hitherto been designed to help, to make any significant concessions. He therefore surprised the conference by proposing that a small completely independent Greek state should be created. This was unacceptable to the Tsar. The conference came to an end without any decision. Alexander now reverted to the idea of co-operation with Britain to exclude Austria. He made overtures to the British government through Princess Lieven, giving it to be understood that he would be glad to receive proposals from London.

During the last decade of Alexander's reign Russia was at

peace with Persia. However, almost continuous military operations were necessary against the Caucasian mountaineers. In 1816 the Tsar appointed General Yermolov as commander-in-chief in the Caucasus. Ably assisted by his chief of staff, General Velyaminov, Yermolov conducted numerous punitive expeditions into the mountains, and built several strongly fortified Russian bases. The most important of these was Grozny, founded in 1818. In 1819 the strength of the Russian army in the Caucasus was raised to 50,000 men. Yermolov annexed the territory of Shirvan in August 1820 and Karabagh in 1822. He inflicted several defeats on the warlike Avars and Chechens, and carried out reprisals with great savagery, burning villages, and massacring civilians. These methods did not lead to the subjugation of Daghestan, but they certainly inspired fear and hatred of the Russians. Yermolov was a man of great courage and impressive personality, very popular both with his own men and with the Russian public. Among his admirers was Pushkin. He did not, however, complete the pacification of the Caucasus, and it may be argued that his methods won Russia more bitter enemies than reliable subjects.

The Decembrists

In the 1820's there appeared the first groups in Russian history which formed precise political aims and planned to seize political power.

The impact of Europe, from Poland to France, on the younger officers of the Russian army cannot be exaggerated. During their service abroad, especially after the fighting was over, they came into social contact with Europeans, both allies and Frenchmen, and since many of them were able to speak and read foreign languages, they were subject to the attractions and influences of Europe. They were impressed by the contrast between life in Europe and in Russia, and between the reality of France and the picture that had been given of it in the official patriotic propaganda of 1812–13 by Rostopchin or Shishkov or their disciples. Knowledge of what a civilized society could be did not necessarily imply uncritical desire to imitate it, or shame towards their Russian fatherland. Russians could and did feel proud of their nation's role as the liberator of Europe. Young Russians of the educated class were also becoming more aware of the beauty of their own language and of the possibilities of Russian literature. Admiration for European culture, desire for European liberties, and pride and patriotism on behalf of Russia could be and were combined.

Great wars in modern times have often produced a belief that after it is all over things will be better than they were before. Sustained patriotic effort tends to create a demand for a 'New Deal'. This was true in Russia from 1812 to 1815 and was not confined to the educated class. Yet when the war was over, the old order was upheld and demobilized peasant soldiers were expected to go back to being docile serfs. The political scene was dominated by Arakcheyev, all the more odious to the returning officers because he had not been a fighting general. Those who had absorbed new ideas felt the disillusionment more bitterly, and those who were disillusioned looked more eagerly for new ideas.

An important source of ideas dating back to the previous century was Freemasonry. At the end of her reign Catherine had suppressed the Masons as subversive, but under Alexander I they had been allowed to operate again and had attracted recruits from Russian noble families.[1] The aim of the Masons, including the disciples of Saint Martin, was not so much political change as individual self-perfection. One leading Masonic lodge in Russia, Astrée, laid down that 'a Mason must be an obedient and loyal subject' and 'must not participate in any secret or open societies which would be harmful to his country or sovereign'. However, the emphasis of Masonry on philanthropic activities, on humane treatment of fellow human beings, and on just behaviour was inevitably a challenge to the existing judicial practices and to the institution of serfdom. Many who later became revolutionaries were for a time Masons.[2] One important effect of membership in Masonic lodges was that their secret ceremonies and varying degrees of initiation made attractive the idea of conspiracy.

[1] For details on Freemasonry in Russia the best work is A. N. Pypin, *Russkoe masonstvo, XVIII i pervaya chetvert' XIX veka*, Petrograd, 1916.

[2] For example the following persons involved in the conspiracy of December 1825 (or 'Decembrists'): Pestel from 1812 to 1817, Nikita Muravyov 1817–81, S. P. Trubetskoy, 1816–19, N. I. Turgenev 1814–17, Ryleev 1820–1, M. S. Lunin in 1818, the Küchelbecker brothers 1818–22.

Another important factor was the well-known sympathy of the Tsar himself for liberal ideas, the reputation for which lasted on even after Alexander had modified his views. According to the report on the Decembrists submitted to Nicholas I by the commission of inquiry in 1826,[1] they declared that 'the government fed them with free thought as with milk'. Even Alexander never completely renounced his earlier ideas. On 24 May 1821 Prince I. V. Vasilchikov, governor-general of St. Petersburg, made a report to the Tsar, on his return from Europe, on the activity of secret societies. Alexander replied: 'Vous savez que j'ai partagé et encouragé ces illusions et ces erreurs. Ce n'est pas à moi à sévir.'[2] A year later he wrote the rescript of 1 August 1822 to the minister of the interior, Kochubey, which forbade all secret societies, including Masonic lodges. But members were not persecuted.

The example of European revolutions was also important. The Spanish events of 1820 made a deep impression on radical-minded officers. Riego was their hero. The revolutions in Piedmont and Naples were also followed with attention.[3] The southern group of Decembrists had some contact with Carbonari, the Swiss branch rather than the Italian. Perhaps the event which excited them most of all was the Greek revolution of 1821. Some of the Decembrists personally knew Ypsilanti. The fact that Alexander I did nothing to help the Greeks, but associated himself with the legitimist point of view of Metternich, even to the advantage of the Ottoman Sultan, was one of the things that they held most bitterly against him.

One of the first persons to think of political organization was General Count Michael Orlov.[4] In 1816 he and Count Dmitriev-Mamonov planned to create a secret society called the 'Order of Russian Knights', and consulted another man who was a leading intellectual figure of the later 'Decembrist' group[5] and

[1] See below, p. 196.

[2] See the comments of the governor-general's son, Prince Alexander Vasilchikov, on some letters of Alexander I, published in *RA* (1875), vol. i, pp. 338–359.

[3] Among the conspirators were two brothers of Italian origin, whose part is described in Franco Venturi, *Il moto decabrista e i fratelli Poggioli*, Turin, 1956.

[4] His brother, Count A. F. Orlov, was head of the Third Department of the Imperial Chancery (security police) in the second part of Nicholas I's reign. They were members of the same family as Catherine II's lover, Gregory Orlov.

[5] The name 'Decembrists' (dekabristy) was given to those involved in the conspiracy of 1825, because the final attempt at action in St. Petersburg took place

an official of the Ministry of Finance and expert on taxation and serfdom, N. I. Turgenev. He did not consent to join them, and their plan was not carried out.

In February 1816, however, was formed the first secret society, the Union of Salvation (*Soyuz spaseniya*). Its original founders were Nikita Muravyov, Alexander Muravyov, Prince Sergei Trubetskoy, I. D. Yakushkin, and the brothers Matvei and Sergei Muravyov-Apostol in whose house in St. Petersburg the first meeting was held. All these men were Guards officers and members of distinguished noble families. They recruited other members later, among whom were General Orlov, Michael Fonvizin, and Pavel Pestel. Pestel was the son of the governor-general of Siberia. He was wounded at Borodino at the age of nineteen, was aide-de-camp to General Wittgenstein after the war, and in 1821 was already a colonel in command of a regiment. During his service in Europe he had read widely in political theory, diplomacy, and fine literature. He was the most learned of the conspirators, as well as possessing the strongest will. The general aims of the Union were constitutional government and the abolition of serfdom. Some members stressed 'removal of foreigners from influence in the state'. Among the papers of one of its members, F. N. Glinka, was later found by the police a note, which stated: 'Reject—Arakcheyev and Dolgorukov; military colonies; slavery and beatings; the laziness of the dignitaries; blind devotion to heads of chanceries; the cruelty and negligence of the criminal court; the extreme lack of consideration of the police in preliminary inquiries. Desire—open courts. . . .'[1] There were differences among members, some being more radical in their aims and more revolutionary in the methods they recommended to attain them.

In February 1817 an elaborate constitution of the Union was produced, with different degrees of initiation as in Masonic lodges. Later in the year the whole Imperial Guard accompanied the Imperial court to Moscow for nearly ten months. The conspirators held meetings in Moscow, and the society was reorganized with a new name and a new constitution. It was

on 14 December (see below, pp. 195–6). Henceforth, the name will occasionally be used for convenience to describe members of the conspiracy, even in anticipation of the events of 1825.

[1] *Dekabristy, otryvki iz istochnikov*, ed. Y. G. Oksman (Moscow, 1926), p. 69.

called the Union of Welfare (*Soyuz blagodenstviya*). Its statute, known as the Green Book, was closely copied from that of the Prussian *Tugendbund*. The two main differences from the Prussian model were that the members did not express their loyalty to the monarch and the dynasty, and that there was no specific commitment by each member to liberate his own serfs. The statute set up a Supreme Council (*korennoy soviet*) of six members. There were no elaborate initiation ceremonies. Members were divided into different 'administrations' (*upravy*), each with a chairman who was to make regular reports to the Supreme Council on its activities. New members could be accepted by general agreement of the members of an *uprava*. Members were urged to engage in philanthropic activity, such as organization of hospitals, promotion of prison reform, care of the aged, sick, and orphans. In 1820 a meeting of some leading members of the Union was held in Moscow. Information had been received that the government was aware of the Union's activities, and it was decided formally to dissolve it. Some members, however, decided to keep a smaller secret society in existence in St. Petersburg. Pestel, who was stationed at the army headquarters in Tulchin in Bessarabia, also maintained a secret group after the dissolution.

Thus, after 1820 there were in effect two centres of political conspiracy. The southern society, with its directory headed by Pestel, was based on Tulchin, and had *upravy* also in Kamenets and Vasilkov. The northern group was based on St. Petersburg, with a following also in Moscow and hopes of a following in Smolensk. The two groups did not fully trust each other, but maintained contact and made some effort at co-operation. The two groups were divided not only by personal friction but also by important differences of political doctrine. These can best be seen by a comparison of two documents, the constitution prepared by Nikita Muravyov for the northern group and the *Russkaya pravda* and *Gosudarstvenny zavet* written by Pestel.[1]

Nikita Muravyov's constitution began with the declaration that 'the Russian people, free and independent, is not and

[1] There was more than one version of each of these. In both cases the second version was more radical. For detailed discussion of the differences see M. V. Nechkina, *Dvizhenie dekabristov* (Moscow, 1955), vol. i, ch. x. and vol. ii, ch. xii. The texts of the two versions of *Russkaya pravda* are published in *Dokumenty po istorii vosstaniya dekabristov*, ed. M. V. Nechkina, vol. vii (Moscow, 1958).

cannot be the possession of any person or any family. The source of the supreme power is the people.' Serfdom was to be abolished, the peasants were to be guaranteed ownership of their houses, gardens, instruments, and livestock, but the landlords' ownership of their estates was also to be guaranteed. Classes, titles, and civil service ranks were to be abolished, and guilds were to disappear. Police officials were to be replaced by persons elected by the population. Freedom of speech and religious worship were promised, and freedom of association was assured to any society whose activities were not contrary to law. Military colonies were to be dissolved. The constitution promised trial by jury in all criminal cases and in civil cases involving sums of more than twenty-five roubles. Citizens were divided into those entitled both to vote and to be elected, and those only entitled to vote. The qualifications for being elected were based on property, and the higher the level of the office the greater the property qualification.[1]

The institutions to be set up were closely modelled on the Constitution of the United States. Instead of a President there was to be an emperor, but his functions were very similar to those of the President. He was called 'the supreme official of the Russian government'. He was to retain the title His Imperial Majesty, but all other traditional titles were abolished, and there were to be no privileges for members of the Imperial family. The emperor would have an annual salary of 2,000,000 roubles. Like the President of the United States, he had a veto over legislation, which could be overruled by a two-thirds majority.

The country was to be divided into thirteen states, each with its capital, and two provinces of equal rank.[2] These corresponded to traditional regions, but their traditional names were replaced by names of rivers.[3] The states and provinces were

[1] A candidate for election to the national assembly must have a property of 60,000 silver roubles in money or 30,000 silver roubles in real estate. The qualification for the lowest level of representation was 1,000 roubles in money or 500 in real estate.

[2] The states were to be: Bothnia (capital Helsingfors); Volkhov (St. Petersburg); Baltic (Riga); Western (Vilna); Dnieper (Smolensk); Black Sea (Kiev); Ukraine (Kharkov); Transvolga (Yaroslavl); Kama (Kazan); Delta (Saratov); Obi (Tobolsk); Lena (Irkutsk). The two provinces were Moscow and the Don, the latter's capital Cherkassk.

[3] This change reflected the belief of early nineteenth-century progressives all

divided into 568 *uezd* and these into *volosts* of 500–1,600 inhabitants. The national legislature was to be bicameral. The lower house was to be called the Chamber of National Representatives. The upper chamber, or Supreme Duma, was based on the American Senate. It was to be elected for six years, and one-third of its members were to be re-elected every two years. Each state would have three members, Moscow province two, and the Don province one, in all forty-two members. All members of both chambers would receive a salary and refunding of expenses. Below the national legislature were to be fifteen state or provincial assemblies, also bicameral, and there were also to be unicameral *uezd* and *volost* assemblies.

Pestel's *Russkaya pravda* was more radical, and more concerned with social change. All class institutions must be abolished, and there was a warning that aristocracy of wealth was even worse than feudal aristocracy. All privileges of the nobility were to be abolished, serfdom and immunity from taxation included. There would be no more titles of nobility. But even Pestel laid down that the liberation of the serfs 'must not deprive the nobles of the income received by them from their estates'. At the same time, emancipation must 'afford the peasants a better situation in comparison with the past, and not give them a fictitious freedom'. Household servants were to be freed after a fixed period of service or the payment of a fixed sum of money. Factory serfs were to be given the same status as state peasants, and factory labour would in future be performed partly by wage labourers and partly by sentenced criminals. Pestel wished all land to be divided into two categories. Both were in the last resort the property of the state. The first category was to be reserved to the peasants, or other persons who wished to cultivate land themselves, the poorest being considered first. This land could not be sold, exchanged, or mortgaged by the person who tilled it. This provision would, Pestel believed, eliminate pauperism.

over Europe in the merits of uniform centralism. The *départements* created by the French Revolution had been called by the names of rivers, mountains, or points of the compass, in order to replace traditional names which appealed to local loyalties. In fact, centralization was a principle which the French Revolution had taken over from the absolutist monarchy of Louis XIV. However, centralization was legitimized in the eyes of liberals by the successful struggle of the French Revolution against the local patriotism of the Vendée. The decision to create 13 states was presumably a conscious imitation of the American example.

Everybody would be registered in a *volost*. He might seek to earn a living elsewhere, but in the last resort he could always claim land from the *volost* authorities of his home area.

Every Russian will be completely assured of the necessities of life, and will be certain that in his *volost* he can always find a piece of land, which will assure his nourishment, not from the charity of his neighbours, and not at the cost of becoming dependent on them, but from the labour which he would put into the cultivation of the land which belongs to him, as a member of the *volost* community, equal with its other citizens. Wherever he may wander, wherever he may seek his fortune, he can still keep in mind that if success does not reward his efforts he may always find in his *volost*, that political family of his, a haven and the bread of life.[1]

The second category of land was to provide a surplus in state hands, to be rented to enterprising persons, and used for the development of agriculture by scientific methods. Some of this land could be sold to individuals, and could not then be recovered by the state.[2] Pestel also wished to encourage industry and trade. Every citizen was to be free to engage in the trade of his choice, in any part of the country. All guilds and crafts were to be abolished. As far as possible, all restrictions on trade, including protective tariffs, were to be removed. Individualism and private enterprise were stressed.

The legislative power was assigned to an unicameral Assembly of the People (*Narodnoe veche*). It was to be elected for five years and could not be dissolved. One-fifth of its members were to be elected every year. The executive power was to be held by a State Council (*Derzhavnaya duma*) of five persons, elected for five years, one every year. Each year one candidate would be put forward by each province, and from this list the *Veche* would elect one person. The country would be a republic. The Duma would act as a collective head of state, and would supervise the actions of ministers, who would work under it. There was also to be a 'controlling authority' (*blyustitelnaya vlast*), entrusted to an assembly (*sobor*) of 120 persons, to be known as boyars. Their task was to ensure that the laws conformed with the constitution. They would appoint a procurator-general to each ministry

[1] This passage comes from ch. 4, section 12 of the first version of *Russkaya pravda*. It can be found in *Dokumenty po istorii Vosstaniya dekabristov*, vii. 185.

[2] The principles of the division of the land are laid down in ch. 3, section 8 (ibid. vii. 171) and ch. 4, sections 10–12 (ibid. vii. 183–8).

and a governor-general to each province, to supervise on their behalf. They would also appoint commanders-in-chief of armies on active service. This is a curious combination of Peter's procurator-general and the United States Supreme Court. There are also echoes of the American Senate in the *Veche*.

Pestel was strongly opposed to federalism. He stood for a centralized government and for the definite domination of the Russians over the other nationalities. He had no use for small peoples. They could not, he believed, have independent existence, and they were merely liable to be an object of contention between great states. The best thing that could happen to them was that they should 'completely fuse their nationality with the nationality of the dominant people'. Only those nations that were capable of independence should have the right to nationhood: those incapable of this could have only the right to an orderly and decent existence. As areas whose peoples fell into this second category Pestel mentioned Finland, Estland, Livonia, Kurland, White Russia, Little Russia, New Russia, Bessarabia, Crimea, Georgia, the Caucasus, the lands of the Kirgiz, and all Siberia. The only non-Russians whom Pestel placed in the first category were the Poles, whose long history entitled them to independence. But Pestel insisted on certain conditions for Polish independence. The frontier between Poland and Russia must be decided according to the convenience of Russia; there must be a military alliance between the two countries; and the Polish government must be based on the same principles as the Russian. Pestel also urged that Russia should annex certain neighbouring territories. These were Moldavia, because its people were the same as those of Bessarabia, and because the line from the Danube Delta to the Carpathians was the most defensible southern border of the future Russian republic; the whole Caucasus, whose mountain peoples had not yet been subdued; the Kirgiz steppes up to the Aral Sea; and part of Mongolia.[1]

In 1823 the northern society appointed a triumvirate to manage its affairs—Nikita Muravyov, Prince E. Obolensky, and Prince S. Trubetskoy. During the year Pestel repeatedly sent emissaries to the capital to plead his more revolutionary

[1] The relevant passages are ch. 1, section 2, and ch. 2, sections 4–16 of *Russkaya pravda*, printed in *Dokumenty po istorii vosstaniya dekabristov*, vii. 122–5, 139–50.

policies, but with little success. In March 1824 Pestel himself came to the capital. He argued with individual members separately, and finally put his case to a meeting of the northern council. His political views were most strongly opposed by Nikita Muravyov, who believed that it would be possible to introduce the constitution he had planned without serious upheaval. Muravyov objected to terror and regicide, and rejected Pestel's suggestion of a *garde perdue* of assassins commissioned to rid the country of the Imperial family, if necessary at the cost of their own lives. He was also against Pestel's proposal that there should be a transitional period during which a provisional government would exercise dictatorial powers. Pestel's economic ideas were attacked by Turgenev, especially his ideas about agrarian property. The meeting ended with no real agreement but with verbal compromises on inessentials. During the following year the northern society was somewhat reinvigorated by the growing influence of the poet K. F. Ryleyev. Though his ideas were hazy, he had greater driving force than Muravyov or Trubetskoy, both of whom were for a time obliged to leave the capital.

Meanwhile in the south, Pestel's organization had found two other allies. In 1823 Sergei Muravyov-Apostol and Michael Bestuzhev-Ryumin established contact through Count Chodkiewicz with the Polish Patriotic Society.[1] In the spring of 1824 there was a meeting in Kiev, at the time of the annual fair, between representatives of the two societies. They agreed to give each other armed support, the Poles specifically to detain Grand Duke Constantine and to disarm the Lithuanian Corps when revolution should break out in Russia. The Russians agreed to restore the independence of Poland, but there was no decision on the frontier between them. A map drawn by Pestel, and found later among his papers, showed the provinces of Minsk, Volhynia, Vilna, and Grodno as Polish, but in his testimony to the committee Pestel stated that 'not a word was said about the provinces of Brest, Białystok, Podolia, or Volhynia'. In January 1825 a further conference was held in Kiev, at which it was agreed that the Poles should do to Constantine whatever the Russians did to Alexander. There was no decision between republican and monarchical government for Poland, or on the

[1] See above pp. 173–4.

frontier. The Poles promised to help communication between the Russians and similar secret societies in western Europe.

The other ally was the Society of United Slavs, formed in 1823 by the brothers Andrei and Peter Borisov and Julian Lublinsky. Its members were some thirty-five officers of medium rank, from the poorer levels of the nobility. Their outlook was basically atheist and humanitarian. They committed themselves to fight against all forms of prejudice, class distinctions, luxury, and religious intolerance. Members who owned serfs were to emancipate them: those who did not own serfs should set aside a tenth of their income for a fund designed for the redemption of all serfs. They desired a republican and democratic government, but did not work out their programme in such detail as the northern and southern societies. Their aims went beyond Russia itself, for they aspired to liberate all Slavdom from autocracy and to unite all Slav peoples in a federation. The list of eight Slav peoples intended for liberation is an interesting indication of the disproportion between their enthusiasm and their knowledge. The eight included not only Russians, Poles, Serbs, Bulgarians, Bohemians and Croats, but also Moravians and Hungarians. Their emblem displayed four anchors, indicating the four seas of Slavdom—the White, Black, Baltic, and Mediterranean. The existence of the United Slavs became known to the southern society in 1824, as their centre of Leshchin was close to Vasilkov, where there was a branch of the southern society. One of their members was authorized by Peter Borisov to talk to Muravyov-Apostol. In August 1825 representatives of both societies met to discuss co-operation, and the eloquence of Muravyov-Apostol and Bestuzhev-Ryumin, who wildly exaggerated their strength and their opportunities of revolutionary action, persuaded the United Slavs to fuse the two organizations. They remained, however, disparate bodies. The United Slavs were simpler and also more radical, desiring quite concretely to begin the revolution. They were also somewhat suspicious of the southern society leaders. This to some extent reflected the difference between the two social *milieus*, the distrust of poor gentry for the aims of aristocrats.

The southern leaders made several unsuccessful plans for action. In 1823 there was a plan to kidnap the Tsar during a visit to Bobruysk. In 1824 he was to have been assassinated when attending manœuvres at Belaya Tserkov, and the rebellious army was to have marched on Kiev and thence to Moscow. In 1825 there was talk of a mutiny when the corps gathered for manœuvres in Leshchin. Nothing came of these projects, but there was general though vague agreement that there should be revolution in 1826. Of the northern leaders Ryleyev had at least tacitly approved.

Events anticipated them. On 19 November 1825 Alexander died in Taganrog. Everyone expected that the second Imperial brother, Constantine, would succeed him. But in 1820 Constantine had married the Polish Countess Jeannette Grudzińska, a Catholic, who received the title Princess of Lowicz. This marriage was an obstacle to the succession, and Constantine himself felt increasingly at home in Poland and unwilling to come to St. Petersburg. Meanwhile the third brother, Grand Duke Nicholas, had had a son, duly baptized in Orthodoxy, thus promising a continuation of the dynasty in the main line. Already in June 1819 the Tsar suggested to Nicholas that he might become emperor.[1] In a letter to Alexander on 14 January 1822 Constantine declared his decision to renounce the succession in favour of Nicholas, and Alexander confirmed this in a reply of 2 February. Alexander signed on 16 August 1823 a manifesto written by Filaret, metropolitan of Moscow, which declared Nicholas heir-apparent. The manifesto was not, however, published. Sealed copies were placed in the Moscow Uspenski Cathedral, the Council of State, the Senate, and the Holy Synod, with instructions that in the event of the Tsar's death they should be opened before any other action was taken.

Nicholas knew of his brother's intention, but his own mind was not made up. He was personally unpopular in the army, whereas Constantine was little known owing to his long absence in Poland, and illusions were current which attributed to him a liberal outlook and kindly character that he did not possess. General Miloradovich, governor-general of St. Petersburg, advised against the proclamation of Nicholas's accession, and Nicholas himself took the oath of allegiance to Constantine and ordered that it should be administered throughout the empire. Constantine, however, refused to accept the throne, yet would

[1] The account of this conversation by Nicholas's wife, Grand Duchess Alexandra Fyodorovna, is quoted in Shilder, op. cit. iv. 498.

neither come to the capital nor issue an official statement that would remove all doubts. Meanwhile news was received that there was a conspiracy among officers of the southern army, and Nicholas was informed by an officer in St. Petersburg, Lieutenant Rostovtsev, whom Obolensky had unsuccessfully invited to join the northern society, that there was a conspiracy in the north as well, though Rostovtsev refused to give names of the persons involved. In the light of these alarming reports Nicholas decided to wait no longer, but to have himself proclaimed emperor, and the oath administered, on 14 December.

The leaders of the northern society decided that they must act now, or lose the chance of action for a long time to come. During the days before 14 December they made some ineffective attempts at oral propaganda among the troops, and also tried to win over commanding officers. The commanders of the reformed Semyonovsky Regiment and of the Finland Regiment refused to join. On the fatal day, the only forces of the revolution were a battalion of the Moscow Regiment, incited by Michael and Alexander Bestuzhev, and some of the Grenadier and Marine Guards. These assembled on the Senate Square, and refused to take the oath to Nicholas. Meanwhile Ryleyev wandered around, and Trubetskoy, whom the society had chosen as revolutionary 'dictator', took refuge in the Austrian Embassy. By midday about 3,000 troops had come out for the revolution, while the government could rely on 9,000. But Nicholas, who did not wish to begin his reign with bloodshed, tried to end the affair peacefully. First he sent Miloradovich to persuade the rebels to return to their quarters, but he was shot dead. Metropolitan Serafim then appeared in his episcopal robes, but the rebels told him to go back and pray for their souls. Finally, the Grand Duke Michael appeared, but was told to leave as he was only endangering his life. Eventually the Tsar gave orders to fire on the square with cannon, and the rebels fled in disorder.

Already in November the southern society had been reported to the authorities by several informers. The reports were at first ignored by Alexander, and further delay was caused by the fact that Arakcheyev was fully occupied with punishing the serfs who had murdered his mistress Milkina at Gruzino,[1] and papers

[1] See above pp. 163–4.

accumulated on his desk. But in December the government at last acted, and on the 13th Pestel was arrested. Orders came later to arrest several of the other leaders. But Sergei Muravyov-Apostol escaped, and together with Bestuzhev-Ryumin decided to raise an armed rebellion, since there was now no other hope, and the failure in the north was not yet known. On 29 December the police found Muravyov-Apostol and detained him in a house in the village of Trilesy, but he was freed by four members of the United Slavs who overpowered his guards. For six days he led a force of about 800 men around the neighbourhood, considered attacking Kiev but decided against it, and on 3 January 1826 near Pologi met a force of cavalry and artillery under General Geissmar. He himself was severely wounded in the battle which followed, his brother shot himself, and his men were either killed or captured.

Nicholas set up a special commission of inquiry to collect evidence on the conspiracy. It examined about 600 persons, of whom 121 were put on trial by a specially constituted high court, one of whose members was Speransky. Five persons were condemned to death. These were Pestel, Ryleyev, Sergei Muravyov-Apostol, Bestuzhev-Ryumin, and Kakhovsky (who had killed Miloradovich).[1] There were 31 sentences of exile for life with hard labour in Siberia, and 85 sentences for shorter terms. Some of the condemned men were accompanied to Siberia by their wives.[2]

The Decembrist rebellion is the first chapter in the history of the Russian revolutionary movement. It is true that it was an insurrection of officers, and this has made some historians treat it rather as the last in the series of military *coups d'état* of which there had been so many in the eighteenth century. But it was basically different from them, for it was a movement with definite political aims. It was the first and last political revolt by army officers. Thereafter the army remained loyal to the Tsars. There was in Russia in the following century nothing comparable to the political activity of army officers which

[1] Mickiewicz's comment on the execution of Ryleyev was 'A curse on a people which murders its prophets' (Klątwa ludom, co swoje morduje proroki). From his poem, 'Do przyjaciół Moskali', in *Dziady*, part 3.

[2] At the coronation of Alexander II in 1856 there were still 29 Decembrists living in Siberia, and they were then allowed to return home, provided they did not reside in St. Petersburg or Moscow.

marks the history of Spain, Latin America, Greece, or Serbia. It is also true that the Decembrists were members of the nobility, many of them even of the highest aristocracy. But this is not of primary importance. To explain the movement as one by the nobility as such, defending its interests as a class and failing because it failed to consider the interests of other classes; or to point out that it took insufficient account of the claims of the rising business class, and that there were too few persons connected with this class in its ranks—all this is too doctrinaire, even if there are undoubted elements of truth in such arguments.

Essentially the Decembrists were not so much officers or noblemen as rebellious intellectuals. They were the first active representatives of a new social group that was to play a part of immense importance in Russian history—the modern secular intellectual *élite*, or intelligentsia. In the 1820's this *élite* consisted overwhelmingly of noblemen, since it was only the nobility that had access to higher education. Equally, at this time most able young noblemen were, or had recently been, in the army. The nature and predicament of the intelligentsia will be discussed later.[1] But the essence of the Decembrists is that they were intelligentsia who happened to be of noble birth and who happened to be in uniform.[2]

The basic reason for the failure of the movement was that those who held, or were capable of understanding, modern ideas were only a tiny section of Russian society. The overwhelming majority, not only peasants but even the urban middle classes, thought only in terms of traditional Russian loyalty to the autocracy. The Decembrists could only have succeeded if they had made greater and more systematic use of their only practical asset, their command of their men's loyalty. If they had prepared the rising well beforehand by gaining the definite support of a large part of the army, and had then seized the capitals and some other large cities, something might have been done. In the conditions of the 1820's this was immensely difficult. But perhaps it is unwise to say that anything is ever

[1] See below pp. 225–6.

[2] The category of intelligentsia-in-uniform has also played its part in the history of other countries subjected to rapid modernization, at comparable stages of their development. The Ottoman empire, and its successor states in both the Balkans and the Middle East in the nineteenth and twentieth centuries, provide some good illustrations.

impossible. Certainly, one may regret the failure of the insurrection, which not only caused official policies in the following thirty years to be still more reactionary than they need have been, but deprived Russia of the services of many of her bravest, ablest, and most attractive sons, perhaps the noblest figures in the whole history of Russian revolutionary action. The tragedy of the Decembrists symbolizes, more clearly than anything else, the contrast between the magnificent promise of the Russia of 1812–15 and the reality of stagnation and decline which enveloped the Russia of the mid century.

PART III

THE GENDARME OF EUROPE

IV

GOVERNMENT

The Ruler

NICHOLAS succeeded to the throne at the age of twenty-nine. Born in June 1796, he was nearly twenty years younger than Alexander. He and his younger brother, Michael, had grown up in his parents' house.[1] His nurse was a Scottish girl, Jane Lyon. His chief tutor, General Lamsdorff, was a strict and even brutal disciplinarian. Nicholas learned languages well, but showed little aptitude for the study of literature, law, or history. He was a keen horseman, and enjoyed military drill. Between 1814 and 1817 he visited Prussia, France, England, and Scotland. Though he acquired a liking for both English and French society and culture, he was completely unimpressed by the political institutions of either country. His favourite foreign country was Prussia, and his preference was increased by his marriage in 1817 to Princess Charlotte.

Nicholas took his profession as a soldier seriously. In 1817 he was made inspector-general of the Army Engineering Corps and soon improved its organization and efficiency. He commanded a brigade, and later a division, of the Guards. He was not a popular commanding officer, as he insisted on minute observance of discipline by his subordinates and was over-zealous in his efforts to detect and punish slackness of any kind. However, he felt more at home among soldiers than civilians, and all his life tended to think in terms of military concepts of loyalty, efficiency, and obedience.

[1] See above pp. 62–63.

Brought up in the Orthodox Church, he remained a firm if unimaginative Christian. He had hesitated to accept the throne in December 1825, but once he assumed it, he had no doubt that he had been entrusted by the Almighty with the task of caring for Russia. He was completely devoted to the service of the state and of the principle of autocracy, as he understood it.

It was not his fault that his reign began with armed rebellion, and that he was obliged to execute or imprison the rebels. The sentences imposed on the Decembrists were not severe by comparison with the practice of any European government of the time. Yet inevitably Nicholas appeared to educated Russians, especially to those who were related to a family of which some member had been connected with the conspiracy, as a dark and sinister figure. He for his part profoundly distrusted the social *élite*, and was unwilling to grant them any share in the power which belonged by God's law to the autocrat. To subordinates who served him faithfully he could show warmth and generosity.

Nicholas was distrustful of innovation, but did not reject it in principle. He accepted the results of his brother's policies. In particular, he took the oath to the Polish constitution. He ordered a careful study to be made of such projects for further reform as were still under consideration at the time of Alexander's death. He realized the injustice of serfdom, but did not believe it could be quickly abolished: he preferred a series of gradual reforms, to be prepared through regular bureaucratic channels and put slowly into operation. Such instruction as he had received in jurisprudence had not made much impression on him, and he certainly did not appreciate the significance of an independent judiciary. But he believed himself to be a faithful servant of the law. He told one of his principal assistants in this field: 'I wish to base the whole structure and administration of the state on the full power and vigour of the law.' He also regarded himself as the heir to Peter the Great. He kept a bust of his great predecessor on his working desk, and told the same high official: 'Here is the model which I intend to follow for the whole of my reign.'[1] Indeed, in a sense Nicholas was a scrupulous observer of the law, and in a sense also he continued the

[1] M. A. Balyugansky, assistant to Speransky in the Second Department of His Imperial Majesty's Own Chancery, as reported by his daughter, Baroness M. M. Medem, in *RA* (1885), vol. iii, p. 419.

process of modernization of Russia initiated by Peter. But as the years went by, the Tsar in his lonely eminence came more and more to identify law with his own will, and the interests of Russia with his policies of the moment.

He was capable of choosing for high office persons of great ability, and even of independent mind. Uvarov, for sixteen years (1832–49) minister of education, was a cultured man genuinely anxious to promote learning. Kiselyov, for twenty years (1834–56) in charge of the state peasants, was a liberal reformer. Nicholas was able to make good use of the talents of Speransky, and of such talented lesser figures as Bludov and Perovsky. Sometimes also he gave power to inferior persons. Such were Prince A. S. Menshikov, whose incompetence both as an ambassador and as a commander-in-chief cost Russia heavily, or General Kleinmikhel, who for thirteen years (1842–55) mismanaged Russian communications. Apart from his own family, the two persons closest to him were probably Field-Marshal Paskevich and General A. K. Benckendorff. Nicholas regarded Paskevich, with whom he had served in the army, with great respect and affection, and addressed him in his correspondence as 'Father-Commander'. Benckendorff hardly fitted the conventional stereotype of a chief of security police. He was not only an amiable companion, but a genuinely kind man, and his main characteristic was extreme vagueness. He sometimes could not even remember his own name. Most of the hard work of the police was done by his subordinates. But Nicholas trusted him. He said of him in 1837: 'In eleven years in his post he never involved me in a quarrel with anyone, and he reconciled me with many people.'[1]

Nicholas soon rid himself of several of the most odious figures of the previous reign. Arakcheyev was removed from the Committee of Ministers, Magnitsky and Runich from their curatorships. The Tsar's permission to Pushkin to return to St. Petersburg was a genuine act of generosity, and was accepted as such by the great poet. Reproached by his friends for flattering the Tsar in a poem, Pushkin replied with another in which he repeated his gratitude: 'He honoured my inspiration, he set free my thought. And I, in the delight of my heart, shall I not sing his praise?' Certainly, Nicholas never understood Pushkin,

[1] Baron M. A. Korf, Memoirs, *RS* (1899), vol. 100, pp. 484–90.

and never had much sympathy for men who lived by ideas. But to blame the Tsar for Pushkin's tragedy is unreasonable.

Within a short time of his accession Russia was at war with Persia, and then on a much more serious scale with Turkey. Then came the revolutions in France and Belgium and the war with Poland. These events inevitably increased the fear of revolution which since the Decembrist rebellion had been an important part of Nicholas's mentality, and correspondingly strengthened his unwillingness to risk weakening the machinery of state by radical reforms. Even so, he empowered Kiselyov to reorganize the administration of the state peasants in the 1830's, and during these years a good deal of creative and critical thought got through the censorship. It was not until the second wave of European revolution, in 1848, that the controls became really stifling, and Nicholas fully earned his title of 'Gendarme of Europe'.

Central Government

Nicholas personally studied the statements made by the Decembrists on the causes of conspiracy and the nature of the abuses against which they had revolted. He decided that it would also be useful to examine thoroughly all proposals for reform that remained undecided in his brother's office, and to reconsider the whole structure of government. For this purpose he set up a secret committee, known by the date of its appointment, 6 December 1826. Its chairman was Kochubey. Its members were Prince I. V. Vasilchikov, Prince A. N. Golitsyn, Count P. A. Tolstoy, General Diebitsch and Speransky. The committee, which met at intervals over a period of five years, dealt with three main problems—the relations of the branches of central government to each other, the provincial administration, and the status of the main social classes.[1]

The committee started from the principle that the emperor is an autocrat, and does not entrust the whole of his power to any single authority, but 'makes use of institutions and persons that are individually entrusted with his confidence, for consultation in the preparation of new laws and for the revision of

[1] The minutes of the committee from 1826 to 1832 were published in vol. 74 of *SIRIO*. The most important documents placed before the committee for its consideration were published in vol. 90 of the same series.

previous enactments, or for the appropriate execution of his will as sketched in these laws, and for the supervision of their correct and exact fulfilment'. In the light of this principle, the committee considered it essential to achieve the demarcation of authority which had been the aim of all attempts at reform since 1801.

The Council of State, it believed, should be only an advisory legislative body. It should have no judicial powers. It should examine reports from ministers, but the only action it should take on these was to draw the emperor's attention to omissions, abuses, or other disorders. Equally, ministers should take no part in judicial affairs. The existing Committee of Ministers had best be abolished. Its competence had never been clearly defined, and it had caused great confusion of powers. The executive and judicial powers had become mixed, and it was essential to good government that these should always be separated. The Senate must have the status of a Supreme Court, and should be named 'Judicial Senate'. Its governmental powers, now vested in its first department and its general assembly, should be given to a separate body, to be called the Governing Senate, and to consist of ministers and other persons possessing the monarch's confidence. These would be 'dignitaries, who, being free from the burden of current affairs and not belonging to any particular public department, would be the better able to judge of the general needs and interests of the state'. This was essentially a return to the proposal for an oligarchical council of elder statesmen that had been discussed and rejected in 1802–3. The idea of separating the Senate into two bodies, of course, derives from Speransky's proposal of 1811, which had then passed the Council of State but had not been carried out.

Only a month after making this proposal, however, in January 1827 the committee was suggesting the formation of a special Conference of Ministers, to exist outside the Senate, for 'maintaining some unity in the actions of ministers'. To this the Tsar remarked reasonably enough that this would simply be a recreation of the Committee of Ministers, with all its old defects. The committee also proposed the creation of a separate court of accounts, based on the *Cour des Comptes* in France. Public accounts were at this time the task of the Senate, in which the ministers themselves sat. This proposal was not adopted.

The committee proposed that the task of inspecting the

administration should be given to the Governing Senate, and should be exercised by those of its members who were not ministers. These inspections should be a regular procedure, not an exceptional measure. The committee approved in principle the idea of setting up four regional branches of the Judicial Senate—in St. Petersburg, Moscow, Kazan, and Kiev—but proposed that for the time being, as qualified persons were few, there should be branches only in the two capitals. It also rejected the proposal which had been discussed twenty years before by the Unofficial Committee that senators should include some persons elected by the nobility. The furthest it was willing to go in enlarging the basis of recruitment for senators was to allow some of them to be chosen from members of the fourth rank of the state service. These persons would exercise the same powers as the other members but were not to receive the title of senator: they were to be called only 'participants' (*prisutstvuyushchie*). The emperor suggested that all provincial marshals of the nobility might in turn serve in the Senate, with full voting rights, in order to bring in fresh elements from outside. This suggestion was considered by a sub-commission of the committee, which recommended against it, on the grounds that marshals were not usually persons of sufficient calibre, and that if they were made senators their relations with the provincial governors would become difficult. Nicholas did not insist. The committee considered whether senators should be made irremovable, recognized that this was desirable, but advised against it, again on the ground of low quality of personnel.

The committee devoted some attention to the problem of a Supreme Court of Appeal. A proposal by State Secretary M. A. Balyugansky, based on the experience of the *Cour de Cassation* in France, that the Senate should not itself conduct a re-trial of cases appealed to it, but should confine itself to quashing verdicts where the law had been incorrectly applied, and order a new trial by another court, was rejected by the committee as too daring. It also turned down a proposal for reducing the number of instances, by making a single decision in the Senate sufficient. The committee preferred to maintain the existing procedure, by which cases passed in effect through at least five instances (county, province, Senate section, Senate department, Senate assembly), although well aware that this would perpetuate the bureaucratic formalities and delays which it deplored in the Russian system of justice. The committee also recommended against the abolition of the right of appeal to the emperor himself, thus maintaining a custom which both lowered the authority of the Senate and increased the burdens of the Tsar.

The Committee of Ministers was not in fact abolished. It continued to perform the same functions as under Alexander. It had, however, less real power, and no member of it had an authority comparable with that of Arakcheyev between 1815 and 1825. Kochubey was chairman of the committee from 1827 to 1834, Novosiltov from 1834 to 1838, and Prince I. V. Vasilchikov from 1838 to 1847. It became more important in the Tsar's absence during the Turkish war in 1828, but when he was in the capital, Nicholas kept it closely under his control. He showed extreme punctiliousness for matters of detail, and great impatience at delays. He kept pressing the committee not to accept on its agenda minor matters which could be settled at a lower level, but the practice of Russian bureaucracy made this little more than a pious aspiration. He also sternly insisted on the duty of ministers not to miss meetings of the committee. In December 1830 State Secretary Gezhelinsky was removed from the post of managing secretary of the committee and was placed under arrest, when it was proved that he had repeatedly delayed business, had suppressed notes made by the emperor on reports, and had failed to convey to the emperor decisions of the committee. He was replaced by Baron M. A. Korf, who tried with some success to simplify office procedure. In 1840 the Tsarevich Alexander was made a member of the committee, and during the emperor's absences from the capital in 1841, 1844, and 1849 he was given the power to confirm the decisions of the committee. In practice he preferred when possible to hold over confirmation until his father's return.

Though the Senate was not substantially reorganized, and both the Committee of Ministers and the Council of State survived, these were not the centres of power. One characteristic of Nicholas's reign was his preference for special *ad hoc* secret committees, set up for special purposes. The changes proposed by these committees had to be considered at length by the Council of State, and sometimes by other institutions as well.

As this process was usually protracted, the committees themselves at times exercised executive power. The multiplication of authorities increased the power of the Tsar himself, who was the only co-ordinating authority between them. Ministers were no more than individual servants of the emperor. A united government, operating as a whole though under the sovereign, which had been the aim both of the Unofficial Committee of 1802–3 and of Speransky, and which Alexander had certainly desired to achieve, was further away than ever. In Nicholas's reign the aim was simply abandoned.

Perhaps the most important modification introduced by Nicholas into the machinery of government was the development of His Imperial Majesty's Own Chancery into an important centre of power. The chancery was divided into departments which covered a wide field of public life. The First Department was his own personal secretariat. The Second Department was charged with the codification of laws. This was entrusted to Speransky, who produced in 1833 his 'Complete Collection of Laws of the Russian Empire', containing all enactments from the Code of 1649 up to 1 January 1830, and the Code (*Svod*) of laws still in operation. This was perhaps the most important practical achievement of Speransky's long and controversial public career. The Third Department was responsible for state security. The Fourth Department administered the charitable foundations and girls' schools of the late Empress Maria Fyodorovna. In 1835 a Fifth Department was created for a short time to deal with the affairs of the state peasants.

The Third Department, which was established on 3 July 1826, deserves some attention. Its first head, Count A. K. Benckendorff, was at the same time head of the gendarmerie. A separate Corps of Gendarmes was formally established in 1836, and the offices of the chief of the two bodies were later formally united. Benckendorff was succeeded in 1844 by Prince A. F. Orlov, who held the post until 1856. The powers of the Third Department included the collection of all information relating to 'higher police', political security, religious sects and schismatics, falsification of money and documents. It was responsible for the surveillance, and banishment to remote provinces, of politically suspicious persons, and for the supervision of foreign subjects in Russia. It administered all places where 'state criminals' were imprisoned. It collected statistics, and 'reports on all events without exception'. It was also charged with theatre censorship. Both Benckendorff and Orlov were members of the Committee of Ministers. The gendarmerie was a uniformed and well-armed military force, divided into five districts for the whole empire—increased to eight in 1843. Apart from this force the Third Department also relied on a host of anonymous informers.

Benckendorff, who had submitted to Nicholas in January 1826 a memorandum on whose proposals the whole organization was largely modelled, considered that it was his task not only to spy and repress, but also to study and as far as possible to redress the grievances of the population. The reports made by his assistant von Fock on the state of public opinion in the years 1827 to 1830[1] make interesting reading. They show antipathy to courtiers and to the aristocracy, and a certain sympathy for what the writer called 'the middle classes'. This term covered landowners, merchants, and literary people. Discontent, he claimed, was most widespread among those aged seventeen to twenty-five, enamoured of 'liberty' which 'they do not understand in the least, but suppose to be the absence of subordination'.[2] The 1827 report spoke harshly of officials, the most corrupt element in society. 'Among them honest people are seldom met. Plunder, fraud, perverse interpretation of the laws—these are their trade.'[3] They are politically discontented and call themselves 'Russian patriots', but really they are concerned to protect themselves against higher authority that seeks to interfere with their corrupt practices. The gendarmerie, on the other hand, so the 1829 report argues, are the true protectors of the people. The report quotes 'some influential persons' as saying: 'The gendarmerie has made itself the people's moral physician. Every man runs to it in his need and despair, and if other departments did not harmfully act against it, it would do still more good. Against the gendarmerie are only those guilty of abuse, and the notables. But the guilty must be silent, while the notables have not the least influence on the larger public.'[4] This ideal picture probably had but slight relation to reality,

[1] *Krasny Arkhiv* (Moscow, 1922–41, Tsentralny Arkhiv RSFSR), nos. 37 (1929) and 38 (1930).

[2] Ibid. 37, p. 150.

[3] Ibid. 37, p. 145.

[4] Ibid. 38, p. 132.

but it reveals something of the mentality of high police officers and indeed of Nicholas himself.

The Administration

The creation of the Third Department reduced the importance of the Ministry of the Interior, whose Special Chancery was transferred to it in 1828. The ministry was held by seven persons during the reign, of whom the most important were D. N. Bludov (1832–9) and L. A. Perovsky (1841–52). In 1832 Bludov brought with him to the ministry the Directorate of Spiritual Affairs of Foreign Confessions, of which he had been Head since 1824, and which was from this time fused with the ministry. In 1834 a statistical department was set up.

Repeated attempts were made to simplify office procedure and the volume of paper reaching the ministry's desks. A new system introduced in 1833 was claimed to have reduced business by half as compared with 1827 (17,000 items instead of 35,000). Nevertheless, business did not become any less complicated, or take less time to transact. The sum allocated to the ministry in 1834 was 453,810 roubles, but this was increased in 1839 to 1,091,043. The number of full-time officials (graded from the 14th class upwards) did not grow strikingly. In 1834 there were 239, in 1839 287, in 1854 they were reduced to 270.[1]

The committee of 6 December 1826 had studied carefully the problem of provincial administration. It heard the evidence of Balashov on his experience as the Regent of a group of provinces. He himself was not enthusiastic. He emphasized that the administrative changes he had made were such as could be rapidly undone, and the old system be simply restored. The committee felt that there was no good reason to maintain the office of governor-general, directly responsible to the emperor and placed above the regular provincial governor, as it merely complicated the chain of command and conflicted with the desirable normal subordination of the provinces to central ministries. There were, however, exceptional regions where the institution had to be maintained. Such were the Caucasus,

[1] The number in the department of executive police in these three years was 42, 47, and 49; in the department of religious affairs 25, 27, and 20. *Ministerstvo vnutrennikh del, istoricheskii ocherk 1802–1902* (SPB, 1902), i. 52–56.

which was still only partly conquered, and Siberia, whose immense distance from the centre required far-reaching decisions by someone on the spot vested with high authority, and where conditions were in any case too unlike the normal Russian pattern to impose a uniform system. New Russia, the Baltic provinces, and Orenburg also had many special problems of their own, and there was a strong though different case for having a governor-general in each of the capitals, with direct access to the emperor on police matters.

With these important exceptions, the ideas of the committee of 6 December 1826 were carried out in the decree of 1837 on provincial organization. The decree reinforced the authority of the provincial governor over his offices, while placing him directly under the minister of the interior. The provincial board (*gubernskoe pravlenie*) had previously been a collegiate body, directly responsible to the Senate. Henceforth it was subordinate only to the governor. It was to consist of four councillors, each in charge of one of its four departments, the senior of them to be known as the vice-governor.

One of the troubles of provincial administration in the first decades of the century was that business accumulated in the offices, and no action was taken. From time to time the central government tried to remedy this by increasing the numbers, and even the pay, of provincial officials and sometimes by creating temporary commissions in certain provinces to deal with arrears. In 1820 a special committee had recommended that the funds allotted to provincial officials' salaries (3,000,000 roubles) should be at least trebled, but the Ministry of Finance replied that money was not available. In 1831 the minister of the interior, Zakrevsky, put a strongly worded report before the emperor, describing the large number of idle and wretchedly underpaid officials, whose condition was the main cause of corruption. The Tsar strongly supported the report, but the minister of finance replied that at least an additional 3,000,000 roubles would be needed to implement Zakrevsky's proposals and he could only provide 500,000. Further action was postponed until another committee under Prince Vasilchikov had made recommendations on provincial establishments. This in turn depended on further proposals from the provinces which, when they came in, were so diverse and incompatible that little sense could be made of them. At least in 1835 the Ministry of Finance increased the sum by 2,500,000 roubles. This enabled the Ministry of the Interior not only to raise salaries in provincial governors' offices, but also to make grants to city police authorities. Nevertheless, officials' salaries remained small. Excessive paper work also continued to plague senior bureaucrats. In 1845 the minister of the interior, General Perovsky, obtained the Tsar's approval for a decree which differentiated between merely executive matters, which could be handled by the vice-governor, and matter of policy (*rasporyaditelnye dela*), which required the governor's attention. It was hoped that this distinction would give the governor more free time to think of the needs of his province, and personally to supervise its affairs by travelling around it.

The evils of overcentralization were not remedied. A host of minor problems continued to burden ministers, the Committee of Ministers and the Tsar himself. Towards the end of the reign, Baron Korf reports a conversation with an official who for a short time had been placed in charge of Nicholas's personal secretariat in the First Department of the Chancery. This official told of his astonishment to discover how, 'in the midst of matters of first-rate importance, on which the sovereign's attention should be concentrated, they loaded him with an innumerable multitude of trivial affairs, and yet how simple and convenient it would have been to lighten the emperor's labours at least by half, without doing any harm to the business of government'.[1] P. A. Valuyev, who served as a provincial governor under Nicholas, and as a minister in the following reign, noted in a memorandum of August 1855 that the effect of overcentralization was that, as the highest authorities were simply unable to cope with everything that was submitted to them, many important matters were referred to minor officials in central offices. 'The fate of proposals made by provincial governors or governors-general very often depends not on the ministers but on desk chiefs of this or that ministry.' The same writer emphasized the mental dishonesty, the preference for flattering euphemisms over factual description, that were to be found in so many official reports. 'The variety of administrative forms outweighs the essence of administrative activity, and ensures the prevalence

[1] M. A. Korf, Memoirs, *RS*, vol. 101, p. 272.

of the universal official lie. Glitter at the top, rot at the bottom. In the creations of our official verbosity there is no room for truth. It is hidden between the lines; but who among official readers is always able to pay attention to the space between the lines?'[1]

Laziness and corruption were found at all levels. Count P. A. Tolstoy had a distinguished military career, and was appointed a member of the committee of 6 December 1826 and head of the military department of the Council of State. Baron Korf, who had frequent dealings with him in his capacity of Imperial Secretary to the Council of State, describes him as 'combining an indescribable indifference to all official business with an exemplary, legendary laziness'. Another pathetic figure was Count P. K. Essen, governor-general of St. Petersburg, who simply allowed business to accumulate in his office while his head of chancery took bribes or stole public funds. The abuses came to light in 1843 in a major scandal.[2] In 1853 the manager of a committee handling funds for invalids of the Napoleonic wars, a chamberlain of the court and privy councillor named Politkovsky, died, and it was found that he had embezzled and spent 1,200,000 silver roubles of the funds.[3]

At lower levels, medium-rank officials were able to tyrannize the local population, to extort bribes or gifts. In the local offices of the Ministry of State Properties, whose creation was in itself a major reform intended to benefit the state peasants, many officials extracted, almost as a seigneurial right, tributes in kind or in cash from those whom they were supposed to protect.

Yet it is possible that the picture of bureaucratic vice, derived from the memoirs of contemporaries, the satirical writings of Saltykov-Shchedrin, and the denunciations of exiled revolutionaries, and incorporated in the historical literature of the early twentieth century, is exaggerated. The highest ranks of the bureaucracy included both brilliant and conscientious men. It was largely the bureaucracy which made the drive to abolish serfdom effective. The best Russian officials were not merely obedient to their superiors, but consciously worked for the modernization and strengthening of their country. Such men

[1] Valuyev, 'Duma russkogo,' *RS* (May 1891), pp. 354, 356.
[2] Korf, Memoirs, *RS*, vol. 100, pp. 37–45, 483–4.
[3] The case is described in the diary of A. V. Nikitenko, *RS* (Apr. 1890), p. 29.

should be remembered by the historian, together with the ignorant bullies and the sycophants, the characters in Gogol's *Dead Souls*, the officials of Saltykov's city of Glupov, or the governor of Vyatka under whom Herzen served and suffered.[1] As for corruption at lower levels, though it should not be condoned, it is possible to understand it. The small official was miserably underpaid, and he was expected to administer laws which were cumbrous, unjust, and difficult to apply. He was also obliged to support his family, often including many more or less close relatives. In these conditions, corruption was bound to flourish. Exemption from the rules, and bribes for granting the exemption, were subject to the laws of supply and demand. A market price for illegal actions was determined by economic forces. Any opportunities for placing one's relatives or friends in jobs at suitable levels of the state machine were taken. It may indeed be argued that in a poor and backward country, with very few educated persons, corruption is needed to make the wheels of the state machine turn, and that nepotism is a necessary substitute for the welfare state. This problem is not limited in space to Russia, or in time to the mid-nineteenth century.

The main function of the Ministry of the Interior continued to be the general supervision and development of the economy. The creation of the Ministry of State Properties in 1837 removed a large part of the direction of agriculture from it, while the increasing importance of the Ministry of Finance diminished its influence on industry and trade. One of its major tasks, the assurance of food supplies, continued to prove difficult. Harvests were particularly bad in 1833, 1840, 1845, 1846, 1848 and 1855. The argument between the respective supporters of grain stores and of money funds for buying grain in emergencies was settled in 1834 by compelling all provincial authorities to use both methods. The results were, however, not satisfactory. Much time was to pass before the construction of railways and of better roads solved these problems.

Public health made slow progress. At the end of the 1820's there were still not enough trained persons to fill the very small

[1] See the famous book of M. E. Saltykov-Shchedrin, *Istoriya odnogo goroda.* The portion of Herzen's Memoirs, *Byloe i dumy*, which refers to his service in Vyatka, is in Herzen's Works, *Polnoe sobranie sochineniy i pisem*, ed. M. K. Lemke (Petrograd, 1919–25), xii. 254–93. This work is hereafter cited as Lemke, *Herzen's Works.*

number of established posts in the central and local public health service. Private practices developed fairly well in the two capitals, and to some extent in the western provinces, but elsewhere hardly existed. In 1845 there were 8,078 doctors in Russia. In 1855 there were 533 hospitals with nearly 19,000 beds. The number of pharmacies grew from 414 in 1827 to 749 in 1852, mostly in the capitals and in the western provinces.

During Nicholas's reign Russia suffered terribly from the scourge of cholera.[1] It appeared in a few southern and Caucasian districts in the 1820's. The official belief was that it was not infectious, and no quarantine measures were taken. In 1829 it was brought from Bokhara by merchants to Orenburg, where it caused severe losses. The authorities became convinced that it was infectious, and began to institute a quarantine system, but were ordered by St. Petersburg to stop. In 1830 the disease spread to Central Russia. The Minister of the Interior, General Zakrevsky, headed a special commission, which made its headquarters in Saratov. He was now converted to quarantine, and strongly urged his view on the Tsar. But now it was too late to stop the disease. In October 1830 Nicholas visited Moscow, and personally entered cholera wards in hospitals, showing himself as widely as possible. This courageous action seems to have raised both his popularity and the public morale. Order was maintained in Moscow, but there were riots in Tambov from 18 to 20 November in which more than 200 persons lost their lives. In 1831 the disease spread still further. In the army in Poland, both the Commander-in-Chief Marshal Diebitsch and Grand-Duke Constantine fell victims. In the summer of 1831 there was a cholera epidemic in St. Petersburg. The quarantine regulations were carried out brutally by ignorant policemen, and caused hardship and annoyance, which led to public riots, in one of which a doctor lost his life. On 24 June Nicholas came up from Peterhof to the capital and made a speech in the Haymarket, appealing to the people to obey the regulations which the government had made in order to protect them, to trust the doctors, and to show

[1] There is an interesting discussion of the medical and administrative sides of the cholera epidemic, and also of the wider social implications, in Roderick E. McGrew, *Russia and the Cholera 1823–1832*, University of Wisconsin, 1965. This admirable piece of research only came to my notice after I had completed my text.

'that they are not like Frenchmen or Poles'.[1] In 1831 the total deaths from cholera in the empire were more than 100,000. In 1847 there was another epidemic, spreading up the Volga valley to Moscow and westwards to Vitebsk, with 116,000 deaths. In 1848 the losses were 668,000.

Religious Policy

During the reign of Nicholas I the Church was brought even more thoroughly under the control of the government than had been the case in the past. This was the achievement of Count N. A. Pratasov, a former army officer who was Supreme Procurator of the Holy Synod from 1836 to 1855. His main concern was for formal order, and he made the synod look more and more like a secular government department. He increased the number of lay officials, paid them comparatively well, and gave the synod a fine new building for its headquarters. He neglected the financial needs of parishes and of church schools, and did little to improve either the material lot or the moral authority of the village priest. Theological doctrine interested him not at all, and he felt uneasy in the presence of the few bishops who had convictions and personality of their own, such as Filaret, the former rector of St. Petersburg Spiritual Academy, since 1821 metropolitan of Moscow.

In 1842 Pratasov was able to humiliate Filaret. A group of students at the St. Petersburg Spiritual Academy distributed a lithographed translation into Russian of some books of the Bible of which there was no authorized Russian version. Filaret took the opportunity of this scandal to suggest that a modern commentary, in Russian, on the Slavonic text of the Bible, based on a scholarly study of Biblical sources and Patristic comments, be prepared. This was opposed by the senior metropolitan, Serafim of St. Petersburg, with Pratasov's backing. The Tsar took the same view. It was considered, in fact, to be better that theological students should continue to memorize Church Slavonic texts, much as Moslem students memorize the Koran in classical Arabic, than that they should be helped to think

[1] Shilder, *Imperator Nikolay I, yego zhizn' i tsarstvovanie* (SPB, 1903), ii. 598–601.

about Christian doctrine, which might lead them into dangerous thoughts. After this defeat Filaret asked to be excused attendance at meetings of the synod, and devoted himself solely to his diocesan duties in Moscow.

The affairs of confessions other than the Orthodox Church were managed by the Directorate of Foreign Confessions headed by D. N. Bludov, which operated as a separate government department from 1824 until 1832, when it was transferred to the Ministry of the Interior. It was divided into separate sections to deal with each of the main religions.

There was a Roman Catholic Spiritual College in St. Petersburg, headed by the Metropolitan Archbishop of Mogilev, with jurisdiction over six sees in the former Russo-Polish borderlands. Its authority did not extend to the Kingdom of Poland. The Uniate Church at first came under the same authority, but after the Polish war of 1831 there was strong pressure to place the Uniates under Orthodox authority. The Uniate Church was regarded by the Orthodox hierarchy, and by Russian nationalists, as an instrument of Rome and of Poland for depriving the non-Polish population in historical Lithuania of their true Russian character. There was historical justification for this view. However, the methods used to bring reunion with Orthodoxy included as large an element of pressure by the secular power as had been used in the opposite direction by the Catholics in the sixteenth century. In this action Count Bludov, the head of the department, was supported by Joseph Semashko, bishop of Lithuania from 1833. The process was gradual but methodical. Orthodox books were substituted for Latin in the seminaries, Uniate theological students were forbidden to study in Catholic academies, or to go to Rome, converts from the Uniate to the Roman Church were persecuted, and in 1835 Uniate church schools were placed under the Russian Orthodox commission for church schools. In 1837 the administration of Uniate affairs was handed to the Holy Synod, and Pratasov thus took over the concluding stages from Bludov. In 1839 the Church was forcibly reunited with Orthodoxy, and deprived of any legal existence within the Russian empire.

Protestant affairs were reorganized by Bludov in 1832. An Evangelical-Lutheran General Consistory was set up in St. Petersburg, with a General Synod of deputies from the six provincial and two city consistories.[1] New regulations for the Armenian Church were drafted by priests and laymen in Tiflis, forwarded to Bludov and confirmed by the emperor in 1836. The religious leadership of the Moslems of Russia was vested in the Moslem Spiritual Administration, set up by Catherine II in 1788. Its head was a mufti who resided in Orenburg. It was responsible for the Moslem seminaries (*medrese*) and schools (*mekteb*). In 1841 the seat of the mufti was transferred to Ufa. The Buddhist Kalmyks received a charter for the free exercise of their religion in 1828. From 1836 to 1848 the government recognized a special lamas' spiritual administration. In 1848 the authority was vested in the senior lama.

Schismatics and sectarians of the Christian faith did not enjoy toleration. Secession from Orthodoxy, and proselytism among the Orthodox, were criminal offences. Children of parents married under schismatic ceremonies were treated as illegitimate. A decision of the Committee of Ministers of 1826, that Old Believers might worship in their own way but must not try to convert others, was communicated to provincial governors, but was not published. Thus, the Old Believers did not know that they had this right, and the authorities in practice often ignored it. In 1838 a network of secret committees was set up in the provinces to study schismatic and sectarian affairs, with a central committee in St. Petersburg. The Tsar took a personal interest in their activities, the result of which was generally to tighten up the regulations against these religious groups. They continued to suffer from many civil disabilities. For example, their testimony could not be accepted in a civil law case against an Orthodox, they might only be temporarily admitted to urban guilds, and their children could be admitted to school only if they accepted Orthodoxy. These and other discriminatory measures affected not so much the mass of serfs or state peasants as members of the middle classes, who but for them might have been able to improve their social condition. Such persons often had a little money to spare, and it is not surprising that willingness to overlook some of the regulations became an important source of additional income to officials.

In 1842 Count Pratasov issued a directive in which he distin-

[1] The six provinces were St. Petersburg, Moscow, Livonia, Kurland, Estland, and Esel. The two cities were Riga and Reval.

guished between 'most harmful', 'harmful', and 'less harmful' religious groups. The first included not only Khlysts and Skoptsy[1] but also *Molokane*, Dukhobors, and those priestless schismatics who refused to recognize the sacrament of marriage or to pray for the Tsar. The remaining priestless fell into the second group, while the priestly Old Believers formed the third. The community of Dukhobors in Melitopol *uezd* were tolerated in the first part of the reign, but as the Crimea began to fill up with settlers, and Dukhobor doctrines began to spread, the government became alarmed. The Tsar decided in 1841 to give them the choice of accepting Orthodoxy or moving to Transcaucasia. They chose the latter, and were settled in the Akhalkalaki district near the Turkish frontier, where their hard work and collective discipline soon made them prosperous farmers.

In 1847 Metropolitan Ambrose, a bishop of the Orthodox Church in Bosnia, a province of the Ottoman empire, agreed to consecrate three Russian Old Believer priests as bishops at Bela Krinitsa in Austrian Bukovina. These priests in their turn appointed other bishops. The Old Believers thus had a hierarchy of their own. By 1859 there were ten bishops, and the means of perpetuating the Old Believer church was available.

In 1853 a new special committee was set up, and new regulations issued for dealing with schismatics and sectarians. Existing rules were more strictly applied, interference with places of worship and cemeteries increased, and the authorities were instructed gradually to break up their surviving monasteries or communities.

Persecution did not destroy them: it merely drove them into greater secrecy. Nobody in Russia knew how many schismatics and sectarians existed. The official figure in 1850 was 829,971 persons. The minister of the interior, L. A. Perovsky, did not believe this figure, and set up a commission to inquire in three provinces only. It reported a total more than ten times as large. Basing itself on these figures, the ministry estimated in 1859 that there were 9,300,000 schismatics and sectarians in Russia.[2]

Not all high officials approved of religious persecution. Valuyev wrote in his memorandum of 1855:

[1] For Skoptsy see above p. 166. Khlysts were another extremist sect whose ceremonies, or orgies, included self-flagellation.

[2] J. S. Curtiss, *Church and State in Russia* (New York, 1940), p. 138, quoting the Russian expert on sects, P. I. Melnikov, *Complete Works*, (SPB, 1909), vii. 408.

Are we entitled to regard religious beliefs as a political instrument, and arbitrarily to use or try to use them for political aims? . . . Perhaps if our spiritual leaders would rely a little more on the higher power of the eternal truths which they preach, and would believe a little less in the value of co-operation from the police of this world, their harvest would be more bountiful. . . . Everywhere in our country prevails the effort to sow good by force. Everywhere there is contempt and dislike for any thought which develops without being expressly ordered to do so.[1]

But melancholy reflections of this sort, even though approved by so exalted a person as Grand Duke Constantine Nikolayevich, to whom the memorandum was addressed, had no effect on practical policy.

Education

During the reign of Nicholas I the system of public education in Russia made considerable quantitative progress, though the policies which inspired it can hardly be qualified as 'progressive'.

The main concern of Shishkov, who held the Ministry of Education at the time of Nicholas's accession, was the reorganization of the censorship, which will be discussed later.

Shishkov was replaced as minister in 1828 by Count Lieven, in whose period of office was enacted the Statute of Primary and Secondary Schools, confirmed by the emperor on 8 December 1828.[2] This maintained the existing structure of four levels of education, but its authors laid emphasis on the principle that each level was chiefly designed for one social class. Parish schools were for 'the lowest classes', county schools for giving to 'children of merchants, artisans, and other urban citizens the information most useful for their way of life, needs, and practice', and gimnazii for children of nobles and officials. During the preliminary discussions Count Lambert had proposed that the system should be based on a rigid class distinction and complete separation. Count Lieven, however, opposed this. He argued that, though this might be possible in some Western states with an ancient class structure, it was impossible in Russia, where

[1] P. A. Valuyev, 'Duma russkogo', *RS* (May 1891), p. 357.

[2] Text in PSZ, second series, no. 2502 of 8 December 1828 (vol. 3, pp. 1097–1127).

persons could rise into the nobility by state service, where 'there is no middle class or citizens' class', where peasants can become merchants, and where 'the boundary of the noble estate is so far extended beyond sight that at one end it touches the foot of the throne and at the other it is almost lost in the peasantry'.[1] The result was a compromise. The rescript of 19 August 1827 confined itself to recommending that the type of education should fit the social status and future destination of pupils, and should not encourage excessive efforts to rise above their station. The universities should, however, admit persons from all free classes, including emancipated serfs, while serfs and household servants should be admitted to parish and county schools and to 'various technical and industrial schools'.

Lieven was replaced in 1833 by his deputy, S. S. Uvarov, who remained in charge of Russian education for the next sixteen years and was one of the dominant figures of Nicholas's reign. Born in 1786, he was educated by a French abbé, and served as a diplomat in Vienna and Paris from 1806 to 1810, when he was appointed curator of St. Petersburg, probably owing to his marriage to the daughter of the minister of education, Count A. K. Razumovsky. Uvarov was a man of intellectual ability and of genuine literary tastes. He wrote essays on ancient history, classical literature, and Oriental subjects. As we have seen, he was one of the founders of the 'Arzamas' literary society. In 1818 he was appointed president of the Academy of Sciences, and held this post until his death. In 1819 he was responsible for the formal transformation of the Pedagogical Institute of St. Petersburg into a university. In 1821 he fought bitterly against Runich's victimization of the St. Petersburg professors,[2] resigned from the ministry and was transferred to the Ministry of Finance, where he remained for six years, being made a privy councillor in 1824 and a senator in 1826. In 1828 Lieven brought him into the committee that prepared the School Statute, and in 1832 he became deputy minister of education.

In August 1832 Uvarov was sent to inspect the University and the gimnazii of Moscow, and submitted a long report in Decem-

[1] *Istoricheskii obzor deyatel'nosti MNP*, pp. 197–8.

[2] Uvarov's written statements on this affair, including a letter to Alexander I of Nov. 1821, are published in M. I. Sukhomlinov, *Issledovaniya i stati*, vol. i—*Materialy dlya istorii obrazovaniya v Rossii v tsarstvovanie Imperatora Aleksandra I*, pp. 378–86.

ber through Lieven to the emperor.[1] This report, which clearly reveals both the prejudices of its author and the outlook of the educated upper class of the period, is one of the basic historical documents of the reign of Nicholas I. Uvarov found the spirit of the students satisfactory, though they were exposed to bad influences. The press was among these. 'Corruption of morals is prepared by corruption of taste.' Uvarov wished to see greater emphasis placed on Russian history. This would provide alternative interests, and replace 'excessive impulses towards the abstract, in the misty field of politics and philosophy'. It would also provide a bulwark against the influence of 'so-called European ideas'. Nevertheless, the students were good material. 'They need only a carefully planned leadership, in order that the majority of them may be formed into useful and devoted instruments of the government.' The authorities should not judge too harshly the mistakes of those to whom the education of youth is entrusted. A combination of trustful and tender concern for their moral welfare with strict and penetrating supervision can ensure them a good education: 'a correct, fundamental education, essential in our age, with deep conviction and warm faith in the truly Russian saving principles of Autocracy, Orthodoxy, and the National Principle (*narodnost*) which constitute the sheet-anchor of our salvation and the most faithful pledge of the strength and greatness of our country'.[2]

The report made an excellent impression on Nicholas, and he made Uvarov minister in March 1833. His period of office was a time of reactionary policies, for which Uvarov himself was largely responsible, but this should not conceal the fact that it was precisely in the reign of Nicholas I that the material foundations of a modern system of education in Russia were laid. In his report to the emperor of 1843, on the results of ten years' work, Uvarov gave some interesting statistics. The number of university students in 1832 in the empire (but excluding the Kingdom of Poland and the Grand Duchy of Finland) was 2,153, in 1842 3,488. The number who took a university degree in Russia in 1832 was 477, in 1842 742. The number of school-

[1] The full text is in *Sbornik postanovleniy po Ministerstvu narodnogo prosveshcheniya, tsarstvovanie Imperatora Nikolaya I* (SPB, 1875), no. 209, cols. 502–32.

[2] Ibid., col. 511.

children for the same area was 69,246 in 1832, and 99,755 in 1842. These figures exclude church schools, military colleges, and the girls' schools coming under the foundations of the Empress Maria Fyodorovna. In the same period gimnazii had increased from 64 to 76, county schools from 393 to 445 and parish schools from 552 to 1,067. Private schools (including boarding-schools) had increased from 358 to 531. The number of teaching staff and other officials engaged in education was 4,836 in 1833, and 6,767 in 1842.[1] To set these figures in proportion we may note that at the census of 1851 (the 'ninth revision') the total population of the empire was about 60,000,000, private landowners' serfs 21,700,000 and urban population 3,400,000.[2]

Uvarov took an active interest in one of the measures recommended in 1828, namely to set up special boarding-houses for children of the nobility, to be attached to the gimnazii in provincial capitals. By 1842 there were 47 of these. Both the government and the provincial nobility provided funds to support poor nobles' children. The nobility's contribution was raised by a levy on each individual noble according to his wealth, as determined by each provincial assembly of nobility. Children who had been supported by the state at one of these establishments, or by the provincial nobility both at a school and at a university, were obliged to do at least six years' state service in the same province. In the boarding-houses the pupils were given some instruction in matters considered important for the social position of a nobleman, but they received their formal education in the gimnazii together with non-noble children. Exceptions were the nobles' institutes at Moscow, Nizhnii Novgorod, and Penza, which were complete boarding-schools. In the 1840's a conscious attempt was made to reduce the non-noble element in gimnazii. In 1845 Uvarov raised the fees. In his report of 2 June 1845 to the Tsar he justified this as designed 'to keep the aspiration of youth to be educated within the limits of a certain conformity with the civil status of the various classes'. Nicholas, in a handwritten note on the memorandum, asked Uvarov to examine whether there were not some means

[1] *Desyatiletie MNP 1833–1843* (SPB, 1864), pp. 103–4.

[2] P. I. Lyashchenko, *Istoriya narodnogo khozyaistva SSSR*, vol. i (Moscow, 1952), p. 481.

to make entry into gimnazii more difficult for *raznochintsy*.[1] He was, however, in favour of admitting children of merchants of the first guild.

Uvarov firmly believed in a classical education, and in the curriculum of the gimnazii the main stress was placed on Greek and Latin. In 1851 Greek was taught in 45 out of 74 gimnazii in the empire. Apart from his genuine devotion to the classics, Uvarov believed that they would make for sound moral and political principles in their pupils. This belief, which was widely held in the upper levels of the Russian government, was clearly expressed in a letter from Count Michael Vorontsov, the governor-general of New Russia, to Uvarov of 10 May 1836. Vorontsov, like his father a strong Anglophil, wrote:

> Les études classiques d'Oxford et Cambridge non seulement restent intactes et étrangères à ce qu'il y a de mauvais dans l'esprit du siècle, mais forment un corps de résistance aux mauvais principes d'autant plus admirable que c'est l'élite de la jeunesse du pays qui forme cette phalange conservative, et cela dans le même temps qu'en France et en Allemagne, par l'abandon des études classiques dans les établissements publiques, les jeunes gens sont à la tête d'un mouvement tout à fait contraire: ce sont les apôtres de la sédition, de l'irreligion et de l'immoralité.[2]

At the same time the Ministry of Finance wished to develop economic and technical education, and in 1839 instituted additional scientific courses in the gimnazii at Tula, Vilna, and Kursk and in county schools at Kerch and Riga. Persons of the poll-tax-paying classes who completed a course were entitled to buy exemption from military service and from corporal punishment, by a further payment of 500 roubles. In 1839 a third gimnaziya was opened in Moscow, in which there were parallel classes, classical and 'real'. The Ministry of Justice also instituted special courses in law in gimnazii in Vilna, Minsk, Simbirsk, Voronezh, and Smolensk. The Ministry of State Properties was given authority, by a decree of 13 July 1842, over schools for state peasants. Church schools remained under the authority of the Holy Synod. The only control by the

[1] This word, meaning literally 'persons of other ranks', was at first applied to persons who were not nobles or officials but had some substantial degree of education. Later it came to be used more generally of the lower middle classes and can perhaps be translated as 'plebeian'.

[2] *Vorontsov Archives*, xxxviii. 446.

Ministry of Education was that arch-priests were obliged to make a yearly report on the church schools of their area to the local director of schools, who was an official of the ministry. Private schools continued to play an important part, as they had done since the eighteenth century. They were, however, brought increasingly under the supervision of the ministry. By the regulations of 1834 their teachers were given the same rights and status as teachers in government schools. A decision of the Council of State of 9 January 1845 also substantially raised teachers' salaries and pensions, and their rank in the state service.

Uvarov took a keen interest in the development of Oriental studies, which were centred in the Lazarev Institute in Moscow and the University of Kazan. 'Russia is chosen by fate', he wrote in his 1843 report, 'before all other enlightened nations, for the study of the East, its languages, literatures, monuments, history, and beliefs.' There were Asiatic pupils in the Kazan gimnaziya. 'The half-savage sons of the steppes of Mongolia eagerly accept the fruitful seeds of enlightenment.'[1] There was even one Buryat-Mongol student at Kazan University. Courses were given in Oriental languages at the gimnazii of Astrakhan, Simferopol, Odessa, Tiflis, and Stavropol. The Academy of Sciences was doing pioneer work in Oriental languages, including Tibetan.

Uvarov was less interested in the natural sciences, but these too made progress. Russia's outstanding scientist in these years was the mathematician N. I. Lobachevsky, of Kazan University. It is of interest that this great man's place of activity should have been the university which was so nearly wrecked by Magnitsky. Indeed, the earlier part of his career, when he was dean of the physical-mathematical faculty between 1820 and 1825, was largely spent in defending his colleagues and his institution from Magnitsky's assaults. He then served as rector of the university from 1827 to 1846. These heavy responsibilities did not prevent him from doing pioneering work in the field of non-Euclidean geometry, for which he got no recognition in Russia in his lifetime but which was acclaimed by scientists all over the world after his death.

The universities received a new statute on 26 July 1835. The powers of the curators of districts were strengthened at the

[1] *Desyatiletie MNP 1833–43*, pp. 23, 25.

expense of the university councils. Each curator was to be assisted by a district council, of which the rector of the university, the district inspector of schools, and the directors of gimnazii were members, but it was to be purely advisory. This system was applied in 1835 in the six Russian districts, in 1836 in White Russia, and in 1837 in Dorpat. Uvarov thus described the aims of the new statute:

> Firstly, to raise university teaching to a rational form, and, placing it on a level attainable by long and constant effort, to set up a wise barrier against the premature entry into state service of unprepared youth; secondly, to attract into the universities the children of the highest class in the empire and to put an end to the harmful practice of educating them at home by foreign teachers; to reduce the prevalent passion for foreign education, externally brilliant but lacking in depth and true scientific quality; and finally to implant among young people of the higher classes, and in general among university youth, the desire for a national, independent education.[1]

Entrants to the university must be at least sixteen years old and have a satisfactory report on their performance at school. Uvarov in 1840 consulted the curators on the desirability of keeping non-nobles out, preferring to do this not by outright prohibition but by the indirect method of raising fees. The curators of St. Petersburg, Odessa, Dorpat, and Kharkov agreed with him. The curator of Kazan, Prince Musin-Pushkin, did not think this necessary. He pointed out that the children of non-nobles mostly studied philosophy or medicine, and thereafter found jobs as teachers or doctors, in both of which professions there was a need for people. In the faculty of law, from which one went into government service, noble children already predominated. There was thus no need for change. The curator of Moscow, Count S. G. Stroganov, a cautious but sincere liberal, was the only one to object on principle to raising fees. The Tsar supported Uvarov, and the increase was announced in June 1845 and carried out as from the end of 1848.[2]

The development of the universities depended on a supply of adequate teachers. In the first decades of the century these were mostly foreigners. Parrot, the rector of Dorpat, put forward an elaborate scheme for training of Russians as professors, partly at Dorpat, which in the 1820's was financially and intellectually

[1] *Istoricheskii obzor deyatel'nosti MNP*, pp. 244–5.

[2] Ibid., pp. 254–5.

the most flourishing university of the empire, and then abroad. In a modified form, the scheme was carried out by Lieven. Seven scholars were selected by Moscow, seven by Kazan, but Kharkov failed to produce any candidates. They were sent abroad at state expense, and had to guarantee to serve for not less than twelve years after receiving a professorial chair. Among the first lot were T. N. Granovsky and M. P. Pogodin, eminent figures later in the reign. Uvarov continued the practice of training scholars abroad.

In the thirty years of Nicholas I higher education in Russia undoubtedly advanced, perhaps more in quality than in quantity. Despite restrictive class policies, a considerable number of non-nobles had obtained a complete education. The Russian intellectual *élite* belonged to the contemporary European culture. They were the equals of the graduates of Paris or Oxford. But the bulk of the Russian people remained quite unaffected by European culture. It still lived in the same squalid swamp of poverty and ignorance, inseparable from the institution of serfdom. As the highly educated increased in numbers, and came from poorer and less cushioned homes, whether of the small nobility or of the middle classes, their awareness of the cultural gap between themselves and their own people inevitably grew. A new note of urgency came into the thought of educated Russians. It is true that in an earlier period there had been noblemen, not engaged in government service, who, living a life of leisure, had read foreign literature, had travelled abroad, and had become familiar with, and sympathetic to, radical ideas. An unofficial cultural *élite* had grown up under Catherine II, and in the 1820's revolutionary ideas had penetrated the aristocracy in the generation of the Decembrists. But it is one thing to live by the labour of one's serfs and enjoy ideas, another to have to earn one's living by ideas—as a teacher or a writer. In the 1830's there began to appear a new social group of people who lived by ideas. In the 1860's there came into use a new word to describe them—*intelligentsiya*. The reign of Nicholas was from this point of view a transitional period. Of the radical thinkers of this period, Herzen and Bakunin were rich noblemen as well as men of ideas, while Belinsky was clearly of the new non-noble intellectual *élite*. The fierce urgency, even the note of desperation, in some of his work is a result of the tragic predicament of the intellectual *élite*, uneasily placed between the rulers and the masses, hostile to the first and yet isolated from the second.

A gap between the intellectual *élite* and the masses has existed, of course, to some extent in all societies and at all times. But it is exceptionally painful at a time when a society is embarking on a new process of economic and cultural transformation, whose origin lies not in its own history but in external forces, a process into which it has not grown, as in western Europe since the sixteenth century, but has been impelled by the will of rulers resolved to acquire for their country the advantages and the power of the modern world. This is the problem of the 'under-developed society', so familiar throughout the world in the mid-twentieth century, of which Russia was one of the first examples in history. The gap is bound to be there at the beginning of the process, and it is bound to have painful political and social consequences. Everything depends on whether, and how quickly, the gap is narrowed. This in turn depends on the extent to which, parallel with the more obviously desirable expansion of the higher education needed to train an *élite* in military or technical skills, there is also created an efficient network of primary schools. The sooner the whole nation becomes literate, the healthier the society and the more powerful the state. This is the lesson of the history of Prussia in the first half of the nineteenth century, and still more strikingly of Japan in its last decades. Russia is, however, the classic example of the opposite, an example which later had its parallels in China, Persia, and the Ottoman empire. In Russia the government dreaded the spread of education. It did not wish the people to be taught to read and write, because it feared that this would lead to the spread of the ideas that had infected so large a part of western, southern, and even Central Europe. Russian statesmen admitted that serfdom was an evil thing, but argued that it could not be abolished until the nation was more educated. Yet they hindered mass education. Uvarov deserves credit for enlightening and modernizing the upper stratum of Russian society. He was a civilized man, steeped in European culture. He defended learning against the obscurantists. But by maintaining the vicious circle of sterile thinking on popular education, he did much to prepare the disasters of the following reigns.

VII

SOCIAL DEVELOPMENT

The Problem of Serfdom

THE problem of serfdom, discussed by the Unofficial Committee, driven into the background by the series of wars with Napoleon, forgotten in the glow of victory, and left unchanged by Alexander at his death, confronted Nicholas at the start of his reign. The confessions and memoranda of the interrogated Decembrists did not allow him to forget it. The Third Department was aware of the sullen discontent of many serfs:

> There are more thinking heads in this class than one would expect. They know well that in all Russia it is only the victor-nation, the Russian nation, whose peasants remain in a state of slavery: all the others, Finns, Tatars, Estonians, Latvians, Mordvin, Chuvash, etc., are free. Wandering preachers, dissenters, and travelling petty officials put harmful ideas into their heads. They expect a liberator, whom they call Metelkin. They say: 'Pugachov gave the masters a fright, but Metelkin will sweep them away.[1]

Nicholas himself expressed his views on serfdom in the speech he made at a session of the Council of State on 30 March 1842.

> There is no doubt that serfdom in its present situation in our country is an evil, palpable and obvious for all, but to attack it *now* would be something still more harmful. The late Emperor Alexander, at the beginning of his reign, intended to give the serfs freedom, but later he himself abandoned his thought, as being altogether premature and incapable of execution. I too shall never make up my mind to do this, considering that if the time when it will be possible to undertake such a measure is in general very far away, any thought of it *at present* would be no less than a criminal sacrilege against public security and the welfare of the state . . . . Nevertheless, the

[1] *Krasny Arkhiv*, no. 38, p. 152. The name Metelkin was taken from Ataman Zametayev, a bandit on the Volga in 1774–5. The words quoted from the peasants are a pun on the names of the two rebel leaders and the words for 'frighten' and 'sweep'. In Russian *Pugachov popugal gospod, a Metelkin pometyot ikh.*

present position cannot last for ever. The reasons for this change in ideas and for the disorders which have been repeating themselves more often in recent times, I cannot but attribute above all to two causes: first, to the carelessness of the landowners themselves, who give their serfs a higher education unsuited to their station, and thus, developing in them a new circle of ideas, make their position yet more painful; and secondly, to the fact that some landowners—though thank God the least number of them—forget their honourable duty and misuse their power, and the marshals of the nobility, as many of them have complained to me, find no means in the law, which places hardly any limitation on landowners' power, to put an end to such abuses. . . . The only answer is thus to prepare the way for a gradual transition to a different order, and, not fearing change as such, to examine cold-bloodedly the advantage and the consequences of change.[1]

The emperor's caution was not without justification. The Russian state machine extended from the throne down to the *ispravnik* of each *uezd*. But below that level, all authority was exerted by the landowners. If they were to be deprived of their power over the serfs, some other authority must be put in their place. Junior governmental officials, capable of taking over the landowners' administrative functions, did not exist. To deprive the landowners suddenly of their serfs would not only antagonize a powerful class, but would shake the foundations of the state. Nicholas not only did not challenge the fundamental social interests of the landowners, but even continued, on a smaller scale than his brother, the practice of transferring state lands and peasants to private ownership.[2]

Meanwhile the change of opinion to which Nicholas referred in his speech was undoubtedly taking place. It was to be seen in the educated society of the capitals and to a lesser extent in some of the provincial centres. In the higher ranks of the bureaucracy the belief that serfdom could be maintained was rapidly disappearing. But most of the landowners, actually living on their estates, still wished to preserve it. There were high officials who still defended serfdom. But its opponents were gaining in numbers and influence, and a cleavage of opinion between bureau-

[1] *SIRIO*, vol. 98, pp. 114–15.

[2] According to the same source quoted by Druzhinin, 109 gifts of land amounting to 301,342 *desyatin* were made during the reign of Nicholas I. Druzhinin, op. cit. i. 87–88.

cracy and nobility steadily developed during the 1840's and 1850's.

It has often been argued that serfdom was bound to disappear as a result of economic forces. Serfdom was incompatible with a modern economy. Serf labour was inefficient, and thus, it is said, it was to the advantage of employers, whether landowners or factory-owners, to replace serfs by wage-labourers. In general terms this argument is probably true, but it must be treated with some caution.

In the first place, even if it was true it does not follow that it was recognized as true. Certainly there were members of the Russian upper class who used the argument during the reign of Nicholas I. It does not, however, follow that it expressed their whole view. An opponent in principle of serfdom, who wished to ensure its abolition, naturally used the arguments which he thought were most likely to convince his less enlightened fellow noblemen. An appeal to their self-interest was obviously desirable.[1] The fact that he stressed such arguments does not prove that he was actuated by no more idealistic motives. Neither the climate of opinion under Nicholas I nor the reform of 1861 can be understood if humanitarian principles are left out altogether.

Secondly, it is arguable that in many cases replacement of serfdom by wage labour was not in the interest of landlords. In the central provinces, where craft industries were well developed, and a large part of the peasants' livelihood thus came from money earnings, the right of the landowner to claim a portion of these earnings in the form of the *obrok* which the peasants paid him as his serfs, was a valuable asset. In the words of P. B. Struve, the *obrok* was 'a pleasant privilege in whose abolition landowners were certainly not interested'.[2] In the purely agricultural provinces of the Volga valley and the south, the situation varied. In highly populated areas of fertile soil, the land

[1] For example, Zablotsky-Desyatovsky, who passionately hated serfdom on moral grounds and devoted his whole career in government service to the struggle against it, wrote a memorandum in favour of abolition in 1841, in which the appeal to landowners' interests was stressed. It is printed in its author's life of his chief, Kiselyov: A. P. Zablotsky-Desyatovsky, *Graf P. Kiselyov i ego vremya* (SPB, 1882), iv. 271–345.

[2] P. B. Struve, *Krepostnoe khozyaistvo* (SPB, 1913), p. 140. This short work by one of the most brilliant social thinkers of pre-revolutionary Russia argues strongly against the view that landowners were materially interested in abolition.

was more valuable than the manpower. Here it was burdensome for the landowner to be obliged to support large numbers of serfs. It would be to his advantage to employ a smaller number of paid labourers, whose output per head would be larger than that of serfs, and be rid of all obligations towards the rest of the population on his estate. To such a landowner abolition would bring financial gain. But this was not the case in the more sparsely inhabited areas. Here manpower was of great importance, and if only wage labour were available, the landlord's costs would greatly increase. During the 1840's and 1850's landowners in these areas had been paying more attention to technical improvements, to the study of agronomy, and to the introduction of machinery. But their achievements had been based on serfdom, on the use of *barshchina*, and indeed their demands on their serfs had been growing. They stood to lose by emancipation. It can, of course, be argued that the mobility of labour which would result from the abolition of serfdom would make it possible for the peasants of the over-populated central industrial region to seek employment in the sparsely inhabited east and south, and that the landowners of those areas would, in fact, find an adequate supply of wage labourers at moderate cost. This did, indeed, happen after 1861. But it was not understood in the middle of the century.

The Peasants

During the nineteenth century the proportion of state peasants to the total rural population increased. In 1858 the number of state peasants of both sexes was estimated at 19,379,631 and the number of serfs at 22,563,086.[1] During the same period the number of household servants (*dvorovye lyudi*) also increased, as the landowners removed serfs from agricultural tasks to various forms of personal service. This process was accelerated during the 1850's. The ninth tax census in 1850 showed 422,622 'revision souls' as household servants, the tenth in 1858 724,314. In the latter year household servants of both sexes with their children totalled 1,462,994. The largest proportions were found

[1] N. M. Druzhinin, *Gosudarstvennye krest'yane; reforma P. D. Kiselyova* (Moscow, 1946 and 1958), ii. 297, based on the figures of the Central Statistical Committee from the 10th census in 1858.

in the densely populated black-earth provinces, where the labour force most greatly exceeded the needs of agriculture.[1]

The living conditions of peasants changed little. The normal peasant house in northern and central Russia, the *izba*, was built of wood and consisted of one room linked by an entrance-hall or passage (*senyi*) with a storeroom. In the living-room the stove was usually on one side of the furthest corner from the door and the bed on the other side. On the side of the room opposite the bed was a table, and in the corner opposite the stove was a place for cooking, which was sometimes separated off by a curtain or a wooden partition. There would be benches along part of the inside walls. The floor was either of plain earth or of boards laid on the earth. The roofs of the houses were higher and steeper in the northern provinces. In Central Russia there was often a raised floor, with a low cellar underneath. In the north the cellar was often much deeper. In the Ukraine the house, known as *khata*, was more often of clay, sometimes of stone. Alternatively, it might have a framework of wood or wicker, faced on the outside and inside with clay, and white-washed. The roof was often of thatch in the Ukraine and White Russia. In the great majority of peasant houses the smoke was allowed to escape through a hole in the roof, and the rooms had a stifling atmosphere. Fireplaces and chimneys were rare in the first half of the century.

The Russian peasant wore a smock, which was sometimes embroidered at the ends of the sleeves and on the hem, breeches and puttees or bark shoes. Leather boots were worn only by the prosperous few. The over-garment was a coat of sheepskin of varying length and quality. In the case of rich peasants part of the coat might be of some sort of fur. In the Ukraine men's dress was a shirt worn over baggy trousers, with a loose cloak as over-garment. Women in the north wore a smock, with a sleeveless over-garment (*sarafan*). In the Ukraine the tendency was to a wider skirt, with profusion of petticoats. For festive occasions

[1] These figures come from the report of the Editorial Commissions of the reform of the following reign—*Pervoe izdanie materialov redaktsionnykh komissiy dlya sostavleniya polozheniy o krest'yanakh vykhodyashchikh iz krepostnoy zavisimosti* (SPB, 1859) (cited hereafter as *Editorial Commissions*), vol. iii, Statistical appendix. The provinces with largest numbers of household servants were Kursk (138,130 of both sexes out of a total serf population of 561,616), Kharkov (91,085 out of 379,795), Poltava (85,851 out of 595,760), and Oryol (87,389 out of 620,720).

both men and women had elaborately embroidered smocks and dresses, which they or their relatives had made. These were not confined solely to the rich. There were families, however, which were too poor and too unskilled to have any festive costumes. Food was basically rye bread in the north, and wheat or maize in the south. But in the poorer districts, and even in naturally rich districts in years of bad harvest, the bread was of very poor quality, even mixed with grass or straw.[1] Most Russian and Ukrainian peasants seldom, if ever, ate meat.

The type of village varied between north and south. At the end of the 1850's 22 per cent. of all rural settlements consisted of five or fewer households. These were mostly in the north, but the eastern Ukraine also had a high proportion of small settlements. At the other extreme, settlements of more than a hundred households were only 6 per cent. of all and were most widespread in the Volga valley.[2] More than half the villages of Russia had between 50 and 300 inhabitants. Those which had more than 2,000 were almost all in the southern black-earth area. This can probably be explained historically by the need to concentrate in large units in areas threatened by Tatar raids.

The great majority of peasants in northern and central Russia, whether serfs or state peasants, lived in village communes known by them as *mir*.[3] This institution of peasant life became in the middle of the century the object of a public controversy which was to have important effects on the development of Russian political thought. In 1847 the German traveller, Baron von Haxthausen, published a book about Russia, in which he extolled the *mir* as a social bulwark against the formation of a proletariat, with all the lamentable consequences which had resulted therefrom in Europe. The Slavophils[4] took up his

[1] For example, N. A. Mombelli, a member of the revolutionary group led by Petrashevsky, described at his interrogation in 1849 the appalling food he had seen consumed by peasants in Vitebsk province. *Delo Petrashevtsev* (Academy of Sciences of U.S.S.R., Moscow, 1937), i. 280.

[2] Jerome Blum, *Lord and Peasant in Russia* (Princeton, 1961), pp. 504–7, gives details based on the List of Inhabited Places, published by the Central Statistical Committee and relating to 1859. The provinces which had a high proportion of settlements of less than 5 households were St. Petersburg (38 per cent.) and Vologda (33·6 per cent.) in the north, Chernigov (40 per cent.) and Poltava (34 per cent.) in the Ukraine. Those which had a high proportion of settlements of more than 100 households were Samara (29 per cent.) and Saratov (26 per cent.).

[3] The word *mir* in Russian also means both 'the world' and 'peace'.

[4] See below pp. 256 ff.

ideas, and represented the *mir* as a specifically Russian institution based not on contract but on Christian love. The writer A. S. Khomyakov contrasted it with the English model, of land concentrated in a few wealthy hands, and the French, of subdivision of landed property leading to fragmentation and moral disunity. He hoped that in the future industry too would be based on the institution of the commune. The controversy continued with learned arguments on the commune's historical origin, with one school maintaining that it went back to Varangian times, the other that it was created by the state as a means of collecting taxes, and assumed its current form only in the late eighteenth century.[1] This still remains an unsettled controversy. It is, however, fairly clear that the practice of redistributing land among peasant households, according to the number of mouths to feed and arms to work, dated only from the eighteenth century, when it became important for the landowner to see that each labour team (*tyaglo*)[2] of his serfs had enough land to be able to earn the means of paying his share of poll-tax, which it was the landowner's task to collect and pay to the state. The landowner found it most convenient to leave it to the commune itself to allocate the tax and to allocate land.

The amount of land available to the average peasant household varied considerably among regions of Russia. The most densely populated provinces were in the north-east Ukraine and the central black-earth region—the provinces of Kursk, Kharkov, Chernigov, and Poltava. In the Central Industrial area and the Lakes Region there was more land, but it was of poor quality, and here too the population was beginning to be too large in relation to the available acreage and the output of land with existing methods of production. The areas in which there was land to spare were the lower Volga and New Russia. Both attracted seasonal agricultural labourers from the north and west, and in both permanent settlers were established by government or private landowners.

[1] The principal champions of each school were two professors of Moscow University, B. N. Chicherin (who argued for the fiscal origin) and I. D. Belayev (who argued its antiquity). Chicherin's article, 'Obzor istoricheskogo razvitiya sel′skoy obshchiny v Rossii', appeared in *Russkii vestnik* in 1856, Belyaev's reply in *Russkaya beseda* in the same year.

[2] This consisted usually of a man and his wife, but was sometimes taken to cover a larger number of able-bodied persons.

Some regions specialized in certain crops or offered opportunities of non-agricultural employment. In the neighbourhood of some great cities there was a notable growth of market-gardening. The cucumbers of Moscow province, the cabbages of Kostroma, the apples of Rostov district of Yaroslavl province, the cherries and strawberries of Moscow and Vladimir won a high reputation. In the northern regions flax was the most profitable crop, in Kiev province sugar-beet. The great rivers and lakes offered employment in transportation of various kinds. On the great lakes of the north-west there were large and small boats belonging to families of peasants, while others worked on craft belonging to larger entrepreneurs. On the rivers of Lithuania and White Russia timber-floating employed thousands. A special group were the Volga *burlaki*, teams of workmen who towed boats upstream, walking with ropes tied around their bodies for weeks on end. Fishing was an important occupation on the lower Volga and on the coast of Archangel province. The Archangel fishermen had a hard life, but they had a long tradition of freedom and self-reliance, and many of them grew prosperous, building themselves fine wooden houses of two stories with wooden chimneys to take the smoke out. Industrial crafts were most developed in the central provinces. The proportion of the male state-peasant population working away from their home village on a passport, whether in agriculture or industry, in the mid 1840's was 25 per cent. in the Central Industrial Region and 29 per cent. in the Lakes Region.[1]

The Government and the Peasants

The cholera epidemic of 1830–1 and bad harvests in 1832–4 drew attention to the plight of the peasants, if only because payments of poll-tax and *obrok* had declined. In 1834–5 there was a serious outbreak of peasant rebellion in Perm province in the Urals: troops had to be brought in to suppress it. In 1833 the Council of State considered the prohibition of the sale of serfs without land, but its deliberations led only to a decree of 2 May 1833 forbidding the sale of human beings in the public market-place and the sale of individual members of a family to

[1] Provinces with especially high proportions were Tver (45 per cent.), Pskov (33 per cent.), and Archangel (33 per cent.). Druzhinin, op. cit. ii. 451.

different persons. This was no more than a reassertion of laws dating respectively from 1771 and 1798. In March 1835 Nicholas set up a secret committee to examine the whole question of improvements in the condition of the peasants. Its chairman was Prince I. I. Vasilchikov, and its members included Speransky, Kankrin, and General P. D. Kiselyov. Its general conclusion was that the aim of policy should be to enable peasants to move freely from one estate to another and to undertake work on the basis of contracts, as in the Baltic provinces—in other words, that the serfs be legally emancipated but receive no land. But no action was taken.

This did not correspond to the wishes of Kiselyov, who had introduced a successful reform in the Roumanian principalities of Moldavia and Wallachia, of which he had been military governor after the war of 1828–9.[1] Nicholas was much impressed by a memorandum which Kiselyov submitted. He told Kiselyov that he himself held very much the same views on the peasant problem but could find little sympathy for them among his dignitaries. The emperor decided to take up the problem of the state peasants alone and to entrust it to Kiselyov. A decree of 29 April 1836 set up a Fifth Department of H.I.M. Own Chancery, and appointed Kiselyov as its head. All matters relating to the administration of state peasants and the land they cultivated were placed under his authority.

Kiselyov began by examining the condition of state peasants in four provinces—Pskov, Moscow, Kursk, and Tambov. He concluded that the first need was uniformity in the administration of all state lands: when this had been attained economic improvements would be possible. The Tsar accepted his advice, and on 26 December 1837 instituted a new Ministry of State Properties, of which Kiselyov became minister. Each province was to have a chamber of state properties, headed by a director with two councillors, one in charge of state peasants, their cultivated lands and *obrok*, the other in charge of state forests. The chamber came under the general supervision of the provincial governor, but the regulations laid down which matters could be decided by the director and which must be referred to the governor or the minister. The provinces were divided for the

[1] See below pp. 298–302.

ministry's purposes into regions (*okrug*) whose area might coincide with an *uezd* or contain more than one. The head of each region, who had two assistants, for economic affairs and for state forests, was responsible for the 'tutelage' of the state peasants. The county police were responsible only for general security and for criminal investigations: they had no special protective authority over the peasants. Below the district was the *volost*, an area of up to 6,000 male peasant population. It was ruled by a mayor and a board elected by the peasants themselves for three years. The mayor had two assessors, one for local police and one for economic affairs. There was also a *volost* court for disputes among the peasants. Below the *volost* was the village community (*sel'skoe obshchestvo*) which normally corresponded to the existing *mir*. The state peasants were declared to be 'free inhabitants residing on Crown land' but not serfs. Thus the new ministry, in fact, set up a complete new machinery of local government affecting about a third of the population of the empire. It was an embryonic Ministry of Agriculture. It was also inevitably a rival to the Ministry of the Interior whose general leadership over agriculture now applied only to the half of the peasantry who were landowners' serfs. The ministry was generally responsible for public welfare among the state peasants and for agricultural improvement on the state lands. It set up eight model farms, in which 8,130 peasants were given some training during the years 1844–56, though only about 15 per cent. of them finished the course. It organized agricultural exhibitions with prizes for the best exhibits, and this did encourage some peasants at least to improve their farming. Resettlement of peasant families from densely to sparsely populated areas affected over 160,000 persons between 1838 and 1856. In 1839 responsibility for warehouses for food supplies was transferred to the Ministry of State Properties. It also organized anti-fire precautions and sanitary measures and made some provision for advancing small loans to state peasants. The ministry set up its own primary schools. In 1856 it was claimed that it had 2,536 schools with 112,000 pupils, of whom one-sixth were girls. Medical services improved, though they were still very sparse. In 1856 there were 25 hospitals controlled by the ministry, accommodating 3,600 patients—more than twice as many as in 1845. The number of the ministry's doctors fluctuated yearly but tended to increase—from 90 in 1843 to 151 in 1856.[1]

It did not, however, follow from this that the peasants were grateful for the change, or even that their condition on balance much improved. The elected *volost* and village authorities were of disappointing quality, and power was in fact exercised by a few individuals closely controlled by officials. The usual corruption, illegal exactions, and arbitrary acts of injustice, characteristic of the Russian bureaucracy as a whole, soon made their appearance in the ministry. It proved impossible to carry out the replacement of poll-tax by a land tax, which was Kiselyov's intention. The trend of policy was to replace labour dues by money rents, but this was completely effected only in the western provinces. Measures intended for the peasants' benefit were often so clumsily carried out as to provoke resentment. Such was an order of August 1840 to increase the cultivation of potatoes. The peasants greatly resented the obligation to set aside some land, to be cultivated by communal labour, in order to produce a reserve of food for state granaries. Dislike of innovations sometimes combined with hatred of individual officials to produce large-scale disorders. In 1842 about 130,000 people were involved in resistance to the authorities in Kazan province, troops had to be brought in, and in one village there was hand-to-hand fighting. Public whipping of captured rebels set off another riot, and more peasants were whipped or passed through the ranks or conscripted into the army. In 1843 there were large-scale riots in the Ural provinces of Orenburg and Perm. More than 4,000 persons were arrested, and there were further sentences of whipping or exile. Lesser outbreaks continued in the next two years.[2]

Kiselyov wished to introduce reforms to the benefit of landowners' serfs as well. In 1839 the Tsar set up a new secret committee whose task was deliberately camouflaged even from the senior bureaucracy by calling it a 'committee on obligations on Crown properties in the western provinces'. Its chairman was again Vasilchikov, and its members included Kiselyov, A. F. Orlov, and Bludov. Kiselyov put before it a proposal which he described as designed 'to strengthen the effects of the law (of

[1] Druzhinin, op. cit. ii. 189, 239, 249–50, 264–6.
[2] Ibid. ii, pp. 467–70, 483–8.

1803) on free cultivators'. He proposed that the landowners retain the ownership of their land, their peasants receive personal freedom, the landowners make allotments available for their use without the right to take them back, and that in return for this the peasants be bound to precise obligations towards them. The peasants should also be entitled to make agreements with the landowners for the complete purchase of their allotments. With Nicholas's express permission the project was put to the committee in March 1840. It met with fierce opposition. In February 1841 Nicholas declared that he had no intention to use compulsion and felt that the aim should be a measure complementary to the 1803 law, which should presuppose the landowners' own consent to the emancipation of their peasants. In this watered-down form the measure was accepted in 1842 by the Council of State. In 1858 the total number of 'free cultivators', established under the law of 1803 or the law of 1842, amounted to 151,895 male souls.[1] The law of 1842 was from the beginning weakened by a circular from the minister of the interior, Count L. A. Perovsky, which emphasized the entirely voluntary nature of the transactions. It specifically stated that no one should read into the text of the decree any more than the bare words implied: if the emperor had intended more, he would have said so.[2]

Nicholas also set up a secret committee in 1840 to examine the condition of household servants. It achieved nothing. In 1844 a second committee, with much the same membership, examined the same problem. It produced a decree of 12 June 1844 enabling landowners, if they wished, to liberate household servants without land by bilateral contract. In November 1845 the minister of the interior, Perovsky, submitted a memorandum to the Tsar on the abolition of serfdom. This was studied by a new committee in 1846 (Tsarevich Alexander, Vasilchikov, Orlov, and Perovsky) with no result. More important was the establishment of precise obligations of serfs to their landlords in the south-western provinces of Kiev, Podolia, and Volhynia in the 1840's. The motive behind this action was not so much the

[1] Blum, op. cit., p. 541.

[2] The text of the circular of 1842 is in Zablotsky-Desyatovsky, op. cit. iv. 216–17. The text of the law, as finally approved, is in PSZ, second series, no. 15462 of 2 April 1842 (vol. 16, pp. 261–2).

desire for social justice as the wish to weaken the economic position of a largely Polish landowning class. However, the measures, which included conversion from labour dues to money rent, certainly benefited the peasant. They were the work of Gen. D. G. Bibikov, governor-general of Kiev. An attempt to carry out similar measures in White Russia and Lithuania had to be postponed. The two remaining acts of the reign were the decree of 8 November 1847 which gave serfs the right to buy their freedom if the land on which they worked were sold in the public market-place; and the decree of 3 March 1848 which permitted serfs to own immovable property. In the last years of his reign the Tsar, alarmed by the European revolutions of 1848–9, considered no more measures for peasant reform.

The Nobility

The committee of 6 December 1826 devoted much attention to the status of the nobility. The limitation of its numbers was, of course, much desired by those already securely established in this class, as indeed it had been in other noble classes in history, for example the French nobility in the seventeenth and eighteenth centuries. It was not, however, practicable. Nicholas sympathized to some extent with the exclusive aims of the nobles, and indeed regarded himself as one of their number. But he also needed the best men he could get for government service and could not therefore give up the appeal to the ambition of plebeians offered by the chance of rising into the nobility under Peter the Great's Table of Ranks. All that he would do was to make this rise more difficult. By a manifesto of 11 June 1845 he laid down that in the armed forces, commissioned officer's rank would confer only personal nobility, while hereditary nobility could be won only with the rank of 'first staff officer' (major). In the civil hierarchy, hereditary nobility was reached only at the fifth rank (active civil councillor), personal nobility at the ninth rank (titular councillor).

Another problem was the large number of persons in territories recently acquired by Russia who claimed noble status on the basis of their families' position before annexation. The status of the Georgian nobility was decided by the publication in 1850 of an official list of noble families. The nobility of the Ukraine, which based its claims on Polish law or Cossack practice, was treated more harshly, as a result of the general reaction against things Polish after the war of 1831. In the three south-western provinces of Kiev, Podolia, and Volhynia in the years 1845 to 1850, a special commission examined such claims. It confirmed only 581 persons in noble status, referred 22,000 claims to detailed examination by heraldic experts, and rejected 81,000 out of hand.[1]

In 1858, as a result of these various measures, the number of persons of both sexes who were entitled to noble status in Russia was 604,000. Only 738 families had been noble before 1600.[2]

The committee of 6 December 1826, though jealous for the rights of the nobility, wished to give some encouragement to the urban middle classes. It recognized that the passion of these people to enter the nobility, which it deplored, was largely due to the insecurity of their social status. Persons who attained wealth or distinction were not able to assure the future of their children who, if their success was not as great as their parents', would relapse into *meshchanstvo*. The committee therefore suggested that a more secure social status be devised for such people, which would give incentive to their ambition yet keep them separate from the nobility. This proposal was carried out by the manifesto of 10 February 1832 which introduced the title of 'honoured citizenship' (*pochotnoe grazhdanstvo*), which could be either hereditary or personal. It was granted for state service falling short of the ninth rank, and for merit in the arts, literature, science, trade, or industry. It exempted its possessors from recruit duty, poll-tax, and corporal punishment.

A measure designed to help the landed nobility by protecting their estates was the law of 1845 on entailed properties. Estates of not less than 400 or more than 4,000 'revision souls', bringing in a revenue of not less than 12,000 or more than 200,000 roubles, might be entailed, in which case they could pass only to legitimate offspring within the family, in primogeniture, with preference for male heirs. In practice noble landowners seldom made use of this law in the following decades.

[1] 'Obozrenie Kievskoy, Podolskoy i Volynskoy guberniy s 1838 po 1850 god', article by P. I. Savvaitov in *RA* (1884), no. 5, pp. 13–15.

[2] A. Romanovich-Slavyatinsky, *Dvoryanstvo v Rossii ot nachala XVIII-go veka do otmeny krepostnogo prava* (Kiev, 1912), pp. 24–25.

The system of provincial self-government of the noble class itself was reorganized by a new settlement in December 1831. The rights of individual nobles were differentiated according to their wealth. Every hereditary nobleman had the right to be present at the provincial nobles' assembly, but property and service qualifications were required for a vote in its deliberations, and still higher qualifications for a vote at elections of officials of the nobles' organization. The elected officials included the provincial and county marshals of nobility, the secretary of the assembly, the board of the assembly, and the deputies who prepared the estimates of local taxation and labour dues. The provincial marshal was henceforth to be chosen by the minister of the interior from two names put forward by the nobility, and the choice to be personally confirmed by the emperor. The tendency of the reign was to make the marshal increasingly a state official, spending his time on organizing services for the governor and the central ministries rather than representing the interests of the landowning class in relation to the government. Provincial marshals were placed *ex officio* in the fourth rank of state service, county marshals in the sixth rank. A symbolic detail is that Nicholas ordered that on official occasions the uniform worn by the nobility should be the uniform of the Ministry of Interior officials. The nobility continued to elect the chief county official, the *ispravnik* (this office was in fact sometimes held by county marshals of the nobility), and the assessors of the superior land court. The nobility continued to have the right of petition to the Tsar. An individual nobleman could send a personal letter, and not more than three deputies might be sent by the nobility of a province to make representations at court.

The Urban Classes

In 1833 the population of all towns in the Russian empire (excluding the Kingdom of Poland and Finland) was a little less than 2,000,000. Apart from the two capitals there were nine towns of more than 30,000 (Odessa, Kazan, Riga, Kiev, Vilna, Kishinyov, Saratov, Kharkov, Astrakhan). In 1864 the population of St. Petersburg was 586,000 as compared with 445,000 in 1833. During the same period Moscow had only slightly increased from 333,000 to 378,000. In 1864 Odessa had risen to 118,000, Saratov to 84,000, and Riga to 74,000, and there were twelve towns of more than 50,000 which together totalled nearly 1,700,000 inhabitants. The number of towns of population between 10,000 and 50,000, which in 1833 had been 46, was 144 in 1864. But Russia was still an overwhelmingly rural country.

Russian cities were still for the most part marketing and administrative rather than industrial centres. The Volga cities lived largely by the trade which followed the great waterway, especially in grain and fish. The rapid growth of the Black Sea ports was due to the development of the sea-borne grain trade: although railways did not reach the coast until the third quarter of the century, export trade was already attracting population. Industry was largely concentrated in Moscow and the central provinces, with substantial progress also in St. Petersburg and Kiev. The population of the cities was ethnically more mixed than that of the countryside. The Baltic townspeople were mostly German, while the peasants of the surrounding country were Latvians or Estonians. Kazan had its Russian and its Tatar merchants. In Odessa and Kherson many of the traders were Greeks. In the Lithuanian borderlands and in Bessarabia there was a large proportion of Jews in every town. Such cities as Kishinyov and Berdichev were almost exclusively Jewish.

City amenities were primitive. St. Petersburg had its magnificent public buildings and aristocratic mansions. In Moscow, rebuilt after the fire of 1812, there were many town houses of noble families, well built of stone. Old cities like Smolensk, Kazan, or Ryazan had their kremlins and their churches, giving them character and beauty. But most of the houses of the citizens were not only wooden but fragile. Few streets in any town had any sort of sidewalk elevated above the mud, and street lighting was scarce even in the capitals. Municipal authorities had very small budgets, and what little they had was often ill spent. All that could be said of the hospitals and the county schools was that they were more numerous and better than in rural areas. A shattering picture emerges from figures for orphanages in four cities of Yaroslavl province between 1828 and 1842, where of all children received more than 90 per cent. died.[1]

[1] P. G. Gryndzyunsky, *Gorodskoe grazhdanstvo doreformennoy Rossii* (Moscow, 1958), p. 398.

The Ministry of the Interior sent inspectors to examine urban conditions, and some of these reported abuses courageously. But the usual obstacles, lack of public funds and indifference in high places, inhibited action. Nevertheless, there were men who tried. Nicholas Milyutin, the great reformer of the 1860's, began his career as head of the cities division in the ministry's economic department. He was responsible for a new city statute, issued on 13 February 1846, which gave cities wider powers of self-government. The city assembly was to be elected by five separate estates,[1] and it was hoped that it would not only ensure that the interests of the estates were taken into account, but that they would learn to think and act together on behalf of the city as a whole. It was first introduced in St. Petersburg, and was extended to Moscow in 1862 and Odessa in 1863. In practice the unwieldy size of the assembly (500 to 750 members) made it ineffective, and the estates did not co-operate well.

The old classification of the urban population persisted. In 1854 there were 1,865,000 'revision souls' in the city population of the empire, of whom 180,000 were reckoned as merchants and 1,685,000 as *meshchane* and members of corporations.[2] The latter category included a varied multitude of more or less skilled, more or less regularly employed manual workers.

During the first half of the century there was uneven progress in various branches of industry. The number of workers in cloth factories increased between 1830 and 1860 from 67,000 to 120,000; in the cotton industry from 76,000 to 152,000; and in steel, iron, and pig-iron from 20,000 to 55,000. The sugar refining industry, which barely existed at the beginning of Nicholas I's reign, in 1860 employed 65,000 persons.[3]

The provinces in which the number of workers most strikingly increased were Moscow (from 32,000 in 1815 to 107,000 in 1860), Vladimir (from 28,000 to 87,000), St. Petersburg (from

[1] These were: (*a*) hereditary noblemen owning property in the city; (*b*) personal noblemen, 'honoured citizens', and *raznochintsy* (in this context, intellectuals and artists who did not belong to either of the first two groups); (*c*) merchants of the three guilds; (*d*) *meshchane* not inscribed in a corporation; (*e*) artisans or *meshchane* who were members of a corporation.

[2] These figures therefore exclude not only all females but also the rather small number of city dwellers who were not liable to poll-tax (nobles and 'honoured citizens'). Source: Gryndzyunsky, op. cit., p. 370.

[3] P. A. Khromov, *Ekonomicheskoe razvitie Rossii v XIX i XX vekakh* (Moscow, 1950), p. 31.

5,000 to 33,000), and Kiev (from 1,600 to 32,000).[1] The growth in Vladimir province was due to the development of cotton textiles in the area of Ivanovo-Voznesensk. In Kiev it was due to the creation of a sugar-refining industry based on the specialization of this area in sugar-beet cultivation. The first modern cotton-spinning machine, of 104 spindles, had been introduced in 1793. In 1828 there were nine of these in Russia, in 1843 48, with 350,000 spindles (compared with 3,500,000 in France and 11,000,000 in Great Britain at that time). The first mechanical loom had been set up in Russia in 1808 in the Aleksandrovskaya factory in St. Petersburg. The use of this machine spread very slowly. In 1834 there were 100,000 in operation in Great Britain, while in the Russian Empire there were only 2,000 at the beginning of the 1850's, and this figure includes Finland where there were 300 at Tammerfors. The rapid growth in Ivanovo was partly due to the losses caused in Moscow by the fire of 1812. In the middle of the century the Russian cotton industry largely consisted of house-industry, the peasant producers selling their products to intermediaries who worked for large merchant capitalists.[2]

In the eighteenth century Russia had been one of the leading producers of pig-iron from her Urals industry, but during the nineteenth her importance in this field declined. In 1830 she still produced 12 per cent. of world output, in 1859 only 4 per cent. Her total output in 1828–30 was about 11,000,000 poods. More than 70 per cent. of this came from the Urals, 15 per cent. from central Russia, and 7 per cent. from Poland.[3]

The total number of miners in Russia in 1860 was estimated as 245,000. Of these 62,000 were in state mines and 117,000 in privately owned. Of the rest the largest group consisted of individuals prospecting for gold in Siberia and the Urals.

Between 1824 and 1860 the total number of workers in Russia increased from 201,000 to 565,000. Of these it is estimated that 118,000 were serfs, 17,000 were employed in 'possessionary' factories, and 430,000 were wage-earners. Serfs predominated in the cloth factories (82 per cent. of the labour force) and in steel, pig-iron, and iron (78 per cent.). In the cotton industry,

[1] P. A. Khromov, op. cit., p. 35.

[2] The development of the cotton industry is well summarized ibid., pp. 38–60.

[3] Ibid., p. 61.

however, already in 1825 only 5 per cent. were serfs, and in the following thirty years this proportion did not rise.

In this period, as in corresponding periods in the history of other countries, the phrase 'working class' escapes precise definition. Workers regularly employed in factories, mines, or transportation formed only a part of those who earned their living by non-agricultural manual labour. To this regular labour force should be added a much larger floating population who somehow kept alive without regular employment in the growing cities, and a still larger number employed in house industry, especially in the central provinces. Such were the makers of ropes, buckets, scythes, nails, or clothing, the roof-makers, river pilots, or coachmen. The *burlaki*, or Volga bargemen, may have numbered as many as 300,000 in the first half of the century. They worked in teams, with wages agreed between them according to the skill of each particular job. The journey from Astrakhan to Nizhnii Novgorod, walking along the bank upstream with the tow-rope around them, took fifty to seventy-five days. Wages were sometimes good but liable to great fluctuations. It was important to keep to the agreed date of delivery: thus, if contrary winds held the team up, the journey might end with a terrible spurt, with only three hours' sleep or so in twenty-four for days on end.

Economic Policy

Financial policy under Nicholas I was dominated by Count E. F. Kankrin who was minister of finance from 1823 to 1844. Born in 1774 in Hesse, Kankrin was a German, his original name Krebs. Following his father's example, he joined the Russian state service, in 1797. He served for fourteen years in various posts in the economic administration, and then was transferred to the War Department, after he had attracted the attention of the emperor by two books on supplies to armies in time of war. In 1812 he distinguished himself as the quartermaster (*general-intendant*) of the western army, and in 1813 of the whole Russian army. In 1820 he resigned from the army, in which he had reached the rank of lieutenant-general, in 1821 became a member of the Council of State, and two years later was appointed minister of finance.

Kankrin was a strong believer in protection. He influenced his predecessor Guryev in making his tariff of 1822, and his own tariff of 1826 increased the protectionist trend. One of his aims was to tap the resources of the untaxed noble class. For this very reason the nobility, the main buyer of imported goods, disliked his policy. The Third Department's report to the Tsar on public opinion in 1829 reported the widespread conviction that tariffs only give unfair advantages to home-made products of poor quality.[1] The minister had organized an impressive industrial exhibition of Russian-made goods, but though there were splendid prototypes in the exhibition, there were only shoddy wares in the shops. On the other hand protection was not sufficient for the demands of some of the businessmen who complained that Kankrin was favouring foreigners.[2]

On the whole it may be said that Kankrin proved a good friend of the small but rising business class. He set up official bodies for the purpose of consultation with them. One was the Council of Manufactures, created in 1828 and attached to the manufactures and internal trade department of his ministry. The director of the department was chairman of the council, which included not less than six representatives of industrialists, merchants and nobility, two professors, and one technologist. It had a section in Moscow, and it was decided to appoint further committees in provinces where there were many industrial enterprises, with the provincial governors as chairmen. Another was the Trade Council, which also had sections in Moscow, Riga, Archangel, Odessa, and Taganrog. It was composed of twelve persons, elected by merchants' societies from merchants of the first two guilds and from foreign businessmen, and confirmed by the minister. Kankrin also took an active interest in technical and commercial education. He was mainly responsible for the foundation of the St. Petersburg Technological Institute in 1825. In 1829 he reorganized the St. Petersburg Forestry Institute, opened new schools of forestry, and sent students to study forestry abroad. He reorganized the Corps of Mining Engineers, improved mining schools, and encouraged geological surveys.

During Nicholas's reign exports of grain became steadily more important. In 1802–5 cereals represented 20 per cent. of

[1] *Krasny Arkhiv*, no. 38, p. 117. [2] Ibid., p. 149.

Russian exports, in 1856–60 35 per cent. In the same period exports of flax declined from 28 per cent. to 13 per cent. of the total. The quantity of grain exports from Russia (yearly average for 5-year periods) was 18,000,000 poods in 1831–5, 27,000,000 in 1841–5, and 69,000,000 in 1856–60. There were large fluctuations in the decade 1846 to 1856, as the Repeal of the Corn Laws in Britain brought a striking increase, and the Crimean War a considerable fall. The proportion of Russian grain that was exported also increased: in the 1830's it was about 2 per cent. of domestic production, in 1856–60 about 5 per cent. The value of foreign trade increased from 1826–30 till 1856–60 (yearly averages) about two and a half times, exports from 86,000,000 gold roubles to 226,000,000 and imports from 80,000,000 to 206,000,000. Russia's share of world trade, however, hardly changed: it was 3·7 per cent. in 1800 and 3·6 per cent. in 1850. The main customers of Russian exports at the mid-century were Great Britain, Denmark, France, Germany, and China. The main sources of Russian imports were Great Britain, Germany, France, China, and the Netherlands. It is interesting to note that during the half-century imports of tea from China increased more than ten times from 45,000 poods in 1802 to 461,000 in 1860.

During Nicholas's reign railway construction began in Russia. Curiously, Kankrin was opposed to it. He did not appreciate its value to the economy, and thought it would merely lead to unnecessary travelling. Just under 1,000 versts were in operation by 1855, which was a fifth of the length then working in France and a sixth of that in Germany. The first line opened was for the short distance from St. Petersburg to Tsarskoe Selo in 1837. Work began on the Warsaw–Vienna line in 1839 and on the St. Petersburg–Moscow line in 1842. The first train ran from St. Petersburg to Moscow in 1851. About 8,000 versts of hard-surface roads were built during the reign, mainly centred on Moscow, and mainly for strategic needs. They did not stand up well to the strain put on them by the Crimean War. The Directorate of Communications and Public Buildings was unfortunate both in its chiefs and in its officials. Lt.-General Toll, director from 1833 to 1842, had a brilliant record in the Napoleonic wars, but he knew or cared little about transport. Though personally honest, he was surrounded by men who shamelessly wasted or misappropriated public funds. The same state of affairs continued under General P. A. Kleinmikhel who held this office from 1842–55. A close friend of the Tsar and an agreeable companion, he proved a thoroughly incompetent administrator.

The most important sources of government revenue were the poll-tax and the *obrok* paid by state peasants. In 1827 the state monopoly of the sale of alcoholic drinks was abolished, and the system of farming out to individuals was reintroduced. Nearly 30 per cent. of government revenue came from this source, but the sums received by the drink trade permitted it a large margin of profit. The monopoly should have ensured both a higher revenue to the government and fairer prices to the public, but the costs of administration—including the corruption of the monopoly's employees—had proved too high. The remainder of government revenue, which fluctuated between 2 per cent. and 15 per cent., came from import duties.[1] The frequent deficits had to be made up by numerous loans, both internal and foreign. As the Russian state debt rose, the currency declined.

Kankrin was keen to restore the value of the rouble. The new wars of Nicholas's reign, against Persia, Turkey, and Poland, made his task very difficult. In 1839 he was able to have a manifesto issued which made a silver rouble the basic monetary unit. The paper notes (*assignats*) continued to circulate as legal tender, but were acceptable only at the official parity of 3·5 to 1 silver rouble. In June 1843 Kankrin went a step further, and all *assignats* were compulsorily exchanged for Treasury notes. The volume of currency was thereby reduced from 596,000,000 to 170,000,000. The new currency was backed by a special reserve fund of precious metals of not less than a sixth of the circulation. Kankrin did not create an independent bank of issue, but left control of the new paper currency in the hands of the Treasury. Not surprisingly, in view of the innumerable demands for expenditure, the reserve fund was used for unintended purposes, and the circulation rose to 310,000,000 by 1848. The Crimean War wrecked it again. Convertibility was restricted in 1854 and abolished soon after. In 1858 the circulation was 733,000,000, and the currency problem was no nearer

[1] Khromov, op. cit., p. 117.

solution than before the reform. These disasters cannot, however, be attributed to the minister of finance, and it can be argued on Kankrin's behalf that he at least retarded the process of financial decay.

VIII

IDEAS AND MOVEMENTS

Literature and Censorship

IN the first years of Nicholas I's reign St. Petersburg was an intellectual centre, in the sense that the greatest writers of Russia lived there, but not in the sense that there was much intellectual intercourse, discussion, or exchange of ideas. The Tsar in 1826 responded to Pushkin's request to be released from his provincial banishment, allowed him to reside in the capital and promised him his personal protection, declaring that he himself would act as the poet's censor. Zhukovsky too lived in St. Petersburg, having been appointed in 1825 as tutor to the Tsarevich Alexander. In 1831 Zhukovsky introduced into literary society a young newcomer from the south, Nikolai Gogol, who held a minor government post and for a short time taught history at a girls' school.

Writers and editors had to devote a disproportionate amount of time and ingenuity to the appeasement or circumvention of the censorship. Their task was made more difficult by the new Censorship Statute devised by Admiral Shishkov, which was confirmed by the emperor on 10 June 1826. It set up a Supreme Censorship Committee of the three ministers of education, the interior, and foreign affairs. Beneath this came the Chief Censorship Committee in St. Petersburg, directly responsible to the minister of education, and censorship committees in Moscow, Dorpat, and Vilna, responsible to the curators of these educational districts. The new statute to some extent embodied Shishkov's conception that censorship should be not merely negative but should give a positive lead to literature, both as to form and as to content. Its task was defined as 'to give to publications a direction that was useful or at least harmless for the welfare of the fatherland'. Clause 15 forbade censors to permit any passage with a double meaning if one of these meanings were contrary to the censorship regulations. They were also forbidden to permit passages in which 'the rules and purity of the Russian language are clearly violated, or which are full of grammatical errors'.

This would have set up bureaucrats as arbiters of literary taste. Fortunately, it did not remain in force for long. The admiral's bizarre, if morally elevated, principles proved impossible to apply, and in the following year, on the initiative of the minister of the interior, Lanskoy, a new committee was appointed, which produced a new statute, confirmed by the emperor on 22 April 1828. This laid down that it was not for the censor to pronounce a verdict on the merits of a book but merely to decide whether parts of its text were in conflict with the regulations. Censors were told not to concern themselves with literary style or with double meanings. Their criterion must be 'the clear meaning of the word, not permitting themselves an arbitrary interpretation of it in a bad sense'. Under the new statute the highest authority was to be the Directorate of the Censorship in the Ministry of Education. It was to consist of the presidents of the Academies of Sciences and of Arts, the deputy minister of education, persons representing the Ministries of Foreign and Internal Affairs and the Holy Synod, the head of the Third Department, and the curator of St. Petersburg educational district. There remained a special censorship, for 'spiritual affairs', vested in the Holy Synod.

Under this régime it was possible, if care was taken, to get a good deal published. It is also important to note that many of the censors were liberals who did their best to let things through. Such for example was A. V. Nikitenko, for many years professor of Russian literature, whose diary over a period of forty years is a valuable source on the history of Nicholas's reign.[1] However, the liberalism of censors was but a precarious protection. From time to time some article would offend some dignitary, or even the Tsar himself, and like a thunderbolt from a blue sky, the wrath of authority would descend on editor, writer, and censor alike.

St. Petersburg was too much overshadowed by the central government machine, too closely under the eye of the emperor, for ideas to circulate very freely even in the small educated

[1] Nikitenko (b. 1804, d. 1877) was born a serf, became the secretary of a district branch of the Bible Society, and was helped to buy his freedom in 1824 by Zhukovsky.

class. The aftermath of the Decembrist Rising was marked by an atmosphere of caution and sycophancy. The St. Petersburg press was reasonably well informed and written, but had small place for original or daring ideas. The two most important papers were *Syn otechestva* ('Son of the Fatherland'), founded in 1812, and *Severnaya pchela* ('The Northern Bee'), founded in 1825, both of which were edited by N. Grech and F. Bulgaryn. Both these men, of whom the latter was a renegade Pole, were detested by people of independent views for their subservience to the authorities. Bulgaryn enjoyed the special protection of Benckendorff, and was generally believed to report to the Third Department on the activities and opinions of writers. He was himself a writer of second-rate but not entirely negligible talent. Grech also wrote a novel, and a history of Russian literature which was ahead of anything that had been written up to that time. He too was a servile and unattractive person, but he was never accused of being a police informer. Only a little less unpopular was a third paper, *Biblioteka dlya chteniya* ('The Reading Library'), founded in 1834 and edited by another Pole, Józef Seńkowski, an oriental scholar of some distinction. Seńkowski antagonized the writers by his consistently negative criticism and by his sneering and cynical tone towards all the literature of his time. But he was a man of ability and had an influence, for good or ill, on the whole style of Russian journalism.

Pushkin lived in effect in a gilded cage. He had little taste for the ceremonial pleasures of the court but was obliged to take part in them. Many of his greatest poems were written in this period. *Boris Godunov* was completed in 1825 and *Eugene Onegin*, of which successive chapters were published in the 1820's, received its final form in 1831. In 1836 he attempted to enter journalism, by founding a literary quarterly, *Sovremennik*. In the same year appeared Gogol's satirical play, *Revizor*. Surprisingly, it was much admired by the Tsar. To criticize the bureaucracy, even bitterly, was permissible, provided that the system of autocracy itself was not challenged. Nicholas showed himself more perceptive than the liberal and radical thinkers of the time, who welcomed Gogol as an opponent of the régime. As was to appear later, Gogol was not a radical but an extreme conservative. He did not remain in St. Petersburg to bask in his success, but went abroad to Rome, where he spent most of the rest of his life.

In January 1837 came the tragic death of Pushkin, killed at the age of thirty-eight in a duel with a certain Baron d'Anthès, whose attentions to Pushkin's wife had been made the subject of a malicious campaign against the poet. The tragedy was the subject of a denunciatory poem, *The Death of the Poet*, by Michael Lermontov, which could not be published but was widely circulated in the capital. Lermontov, born fifteen years later than Pushkin, had been in St. Petersburg as a cavalry cadet and then as a Guards officer since 1832. His poem caused him to be expelled from the Guards and transferred to a regiment in the Caucasus. Two years later he returned to the capital for two years but was banished again as a result of a duel, in which neither party was seriously hurt. In 1841, however, in the Caucasian holiday resort of Pyatigorsk, he fought a second duel, in which he was killed at the age of twenty-seven. The recurrence of the duel *motif* in the lives and works of Russia's two greatest poets—the duel scenes in *Eugene Onegin* and *A Hero of Our Time*, and the actual deaths of both men—is a melancholy example of the influence of one of the less admirable social customs of Europe on Russian life. Both men can in a sense be said, like their heroes Onegin and Pechorin, to have been victims of the political and social system—and in particular of the boredom, the sterile way of life, and outmoded standards of behaviour of the upper class. The heroes of the two works won their duels but obtained little satisfaction from their victories: the poets themselves lost their lives.

A freer and intellectually more fertile atmosphere was found in these years in the second, and ancient, capital. The court and the emperor were far away, the bureaucracy was less numerous, there were few prizes to attract ambitious careerists, and there was a considerable society of cultured and leisured noblemen, who in addition to their country estates in the central Russian provinces kept town houses in Moscow. The university had better teachers and students, and a longer tradition, than that of St. Petersburg, and in Count S. G. Stroganov, curator from 1835 to 1847, it possessed a liberal-minded protector. Moscow possessed for a time a serious periodical in the *Moskovskii telegraf*, founded by N. A. Polevoy in 1825. Polevoy was a self-taught man, and an amateur historian, undistinguished as a writer but full of ideas and willing to encourage the ideas of others. Unfortunately, he incurred the hostility of Uvarov, who regarded him as a revolutionary, resolved to make of his paper a centre of subversive activities.[1] In April 1834 Polevoy's paper was suppressed by the censorship for publishing an unfavourable review of a patriotic play. A second monthly, *Teleskop*, founded in 1831 by N. L. Nadezhdin, professor of archaeology at Moscow University from 1832, also contained material of intellectual merit. But it only survived for four years, being suppressed in 1836.[2]

In this freer intellectual atmosphere of Moscow social, philosophical, and political problems were seriously discussed, and men of outstanding quality appeared. Three discussion groups must be mentioned.

The first was centred around A. I. Herzen and N. P. Ogaryov, at the university. Herzen was the illegitimate son of the landowner Yakovlev, whom Napoleon in 1812 had sent from Moscow with a message to Alexander I. As a schoolboy he was profoundly impressed by the Decembrist tragedy, and tells in his memoirs how he and Ogaryov took a vow, standing on the Sparrow Hills overlooking Moscow, that they would complete the martyrs' work. At the university they became interested in the ideas of Saint-Simon and Fourier. Their discussion group of students was denounced to the police, and in 1834 Herzen was banished to the remote province of Vyatka, where he was given an official post in the governor's office. This experience gave him an insight into the works of the Russian bureaucracy, which he brilliantly described years later in his memoirs. In 1840 he was allowed to return to Moscow, where he came in contact with the second of the groups.

This was the Stankevich Circle, whose main intellectual interest in the late 1830's was the philosophy of Hegel. Stankevich himself, who died in 1840 at the age of twenty-seven, survives as an historical figure chiefly through the memory of his friends. He was clearly one of those people who deeply influence the characters and thought of others, who help them to develop their gifts and personality, yet leave no work of their own by which posterity can directly judge them.[3] Something

[1] Nikitenko, *RS*, Aug. 1889.

[2] See below p. 258.

[3] A long essay by his friend Annenkov, entitled *N. V. Stankevich, biograficheskii ocherk*, first published in 1857, is included in P. V. Annenkov, *Literaturnye vospominaniya* (SPB, 1909), pp. 367–469.

of the sort can be said of a second member of the group, T. N. Granovsky, one of the first of those sent abroad by the government to be trained as professors. Having completed his studies at St. Petersburg with great brilliance, he was offered in 1835 by Count Stroganov a chair of general history in Moscow after a period of study abroad. From 1836 to 1839 he was in Germany where he met Stankevich. He began his lectures in Moscow in September 1839, and for the next sixteen years exercised enormous influence on the intellectual youth. His great achievement lay not in any original contribution to historical knowledge, but in his ability to arouse interest in history and in Europe, among his audience, and in the enormous efforts which he expended in doing things for people, in helping his students with their personal problems and their careers, and in supplying information in reply to vast numbers of written and oral inquiries.[1] The third leading member of the group was Michael Bakunin, who had also studied in Germany, and who until his departure from Russia in 1840 was the most effective and enthusiastic exponent of Hegel's doctrines. A man of great intellectual gifts, passionately interested in political ideas, vain and courageous, intolerantly possessive in his relationships with others, and with extraordinary gaps in his moral sense, he was later to make a flamboyant career as a revolutionary and as the founder of anarchism. In the 1830's his most important role was as a popularizer of Hegel, to whose ideas he introduced the fourth important member of the group, Vissarion Belinsky. Born in 1811, the son of a poor navy doctor and the grandson of a priest, Belinsky was the outstanding example of the early plebeian intelligentsia. He was expelled from the university for writing a story attacking serfdom in 1832, and began a career in journalism. He worked for *Teleskop* until its suppression in 1836, then for two years edited with Bakunin *Moskovskii nablyudatel* ('The Moscow Observer') until it closed for financial reasons. In 1839 he was invited to write articles of literary criticism for *Otechestvennye zapiski* ('Notes of the Fatherland'), a previously undistinguished journal which had been acquired in 1838 by the publisher Krayevsky. His articles, apart from

[1] Some letters by Granovsky are contained in F. F. Nelidov, *Zapadniki 40-kh godov*, Moscow, 1910. There is also a biography by A. Stankevich, *T. N. Granovsky, biograficheskii ocherk*, Moscow, 1869.

their merits as criticism, were of enormous importance because they were the first expression, permitted by the censorship, of critical thought on social problems. Belinsky at first, as a disciple of Hegel, held the view that 'the real is rational', and so took a generally conservative attitude.

The third group in Moscow consisted of those who became known as the 'Slavophils'. Its most important members were A. S. Khomyakov, the brothers Ivan and Peter Kireyevsky, and the brothers Konstantin and Ivan Aksakov. These men were practising landowners, living a large part of the time on their estates in close contact with their peasants and genuinely interested in agriculture. In this they differed from the two other groups, the noble or landowning members of which had little experience of Russian rural life. Khomyakov had served as an officer in the war against Turkey in 1828, then settled on his estate and married. He was a talented though not outstanding poet, and was always profoundly interested in theology. Ivan Kireyevsky, born in 1806, two years later than Khomyakov, was at first a Hegelian, but his travels in Germany disillusioned him. In 1832 he founded a journal in Moscow entitled *The European*, but it was suppressed after its first number because of an article, written by Kireyevsky himself, on 'The Nineteenth Century', which criticized narrow Russian nationalism and urged Russians to study Europe. The Aksakov brothers were substantially younger: Konstantin was born in 1817, Ivan in 1823. Their father, S. T. Aksakov (born 1791), published in the 1840's and 1850's his splendid descriptions, based on a slightly fictionalized version of his own life and his family's history, of rural life in eighteenth- and early nineteenth-century Russia.

Westernizers and Slavophils

In the 1840's Russian intellectual life and political thought were divided into the two main schools of 'Westernizers' and 'Slavophils'. The former consisted of the original Herzen and Stankevich circles, and its most effective spokesmen were Belinsky, Herzen, and Granovsky. The second found its main exponents in Khomyakov and Ivan Kireyevsky The controversies between Westernizers and Slavophils have been obscured by certain false stereotypes of traditional Russian historical literature, and must therefore be examined with some caution.

The great debate about the relationship between Russia and Europe was opened by the publication in *Teleskop* in 1836 of a 'Philosophical Letter' by Peter Chaadayev. Chaadayev was an older man than the members of the discussion circles. Born in 1793, he had served through the war of 1812–14 and afterwards in Europe. He had friends among the Decembrists, but was not directly implicated in the conspiracy. Under Nicholas he lived in Moscow, meeting large numbers of people socially but not belonging to any particular group. A leading figure of the English Club in Moscow, he is thought to have provided to some extent the model for Pushkin's Onegin. Embittered by the development of the post-war years and the Decembrist tragedy, and disgusted with the Russian régime as it was, he wrote around 1830, in French, his *Philosophical Letters* on the history and religion of Russia from a point of view that was strongly European and sympathetic to Catholicism. The letter which Nadezhdin published and which is usually known as the 'First Letter,'[1] was the most sensational of them from the political point of view. Russia, he argued, belonged neither to the West nor to the East. It had no part either in European civilization or in the great civilizations of Asia, nor did it represent any civilization of its own.

Situés entre les deux grandes divisions du monde, entre l'Orient et l'Occident, nous appuyant d'un coude sur la Chine et de l'autre sur l'Allemagne, nous devrions réunir en nous les deux grands principes de la nature intelligente, l'imagination et la raison, et joindre dans notre civilisation les histoires du globe entier. Ce n'est point là le rôle que la Providence nous a départi. Loin de là, elle semble ne s'être nullement occupée de notre destinée. Suspendant à notre égard son action bienfaisante sur l'esprit des hommes, elle nous a livrés tout-à-fait à nous-mêmes, elle n'a voulu en rien se mêler de nous, elle n'a voulu rien nous apprendre. L'expérience des temps est nulle pour nous; les âges et les générations se sont écoulés pour nous sans fruit. On dirait, à nous voir, que la loi générale de l'humanité a été révoquée pour nous. Solitaires dans le monde, nous n'avons rien

[1] It was not chronologically the first to be written. For a full discussion of Chaadayev's life and the text of the letters see *Sochineniya i pis'ma P. Ya. Chaadaeva*, edited by M. Gershenzon, Moscow, 1913. A more recent study by a French scholar is Charles Duénet, *Tchaadaev et les Lettres philosophiques*, Paris, 1931. Further unpublished *Philosophical Letters* appeared, not in the French original but in a Russian translation, in the periodical *Literaturnoe nasledstvo* (Moscow, 1935), nos. 22–24.

donné au monde, nous n'avons rien appris au monde; nous n'avons pas versé une seule idée dans la masse des idées humaines; nous n'avons en rien contribué au progrès de l'esprit humain, et tout ce qui nous est revenu de ce progrès, nous l'avons défiguré. Nous avons je ne sais quoi dans le sang qui repousse tout véritable progrès. Enfin nous n'avons vécu, nous ne vivons, que pour servir de quelque grande leçon aux lointaines postérités qui en auront l'intelligence; aujourd'hui, quoique l'on dise, nous faisons lacune dans l'ordre intellectuel.

Appearing in the same year as Gogol's *Revizor*, the Letter was very differently received. This was criticism not of the misdemeanours of bureaucrats but of the whole social and cultural order. The periodical *Teleskop* was closed down by the censorship. Nadezhdin was exiled for a year to Ust-Sysolsk in Vologda province. The Tsar personally ordered that Chaadayev should be considered mad and should be regularly inspected by a doctor.[1] After some months of this humiliating treatment he was left alone and continued to live in Moscow for another twenty years, always taking care not to become involved in any political activity. He did not, however, retract the opinions of the *Letters*. In 1837 he wrote an essay entitled *Apologie d'un fou*. In this he defended his right to criticize his country's past, but insisted that he had always been a patriot. He distinguished between the patriotism of a Samoyed, who loves his country simply because it exists, and the patriotism of an Englishman, who loves in his country a whole humane and brilliant civilization. However, he argued—possibly under the influence of Karamzin's *History*, which he read with special care at this time—the very fact that Russia had no historical culture of her own gave her certain advantages in the modern world. 'Nous arrivons, esprits vierges, en face de chaque idée nouvelle.'

Chaadayev's Letter deserves serious consideration as a comment on Russia's relationship to Europe: it is also important for its effect in setting off the long controversy between Westernizers and Slavophils.

It is wrong to imagine that the Westernizers, in their desire to introduce Western ideas and institutions into Russia, wished to abolish Russian national identity and slavishly to follow

[1] The instruction to this effect from Benckendorff to the governor-general of Moscow, dated 22 Oct. 1836, is published in *RA* (1885), i. 132–3.

European development. It is equally wrong to imagine that the Slavophils, in their determination to defend Russian traditions, and in their conviction of the moral superiority of the Russian people over European peoples, turned their backs on all Western civilization. In fact there was much common ground between them. In the late 1830's they frequented the same houses and engaged in amicable discussions. Granovsky was on friendly terms with Peter Kireyevsky, Belinsky with Konstantin Aksakov, and Herzen with Khomyakov. It was not until the 1840's that their relations became hostile. During these later years the main organ of the Westernizers was *Otechestvennye zapiski*, published by Krayevsky, of the Slavophils *Moskvityanin*, published by Professor M. P. Pogodin.

Both Westernizers and Slavophils disliked the existing social and political system and wished for reform. The Slavophils for the most part desired the emancipation of the serfs. In the political field the Aksakovs wished for at least some form of consultative representative institutions. Both Westernizers and Slavophils also believed that Russia had a mission in the field of social policy, that the Russian people would be able to solve social problems which had proved insoluble in the West. This social messianism is found no less in the writings of Herzen and Bakunin than in those of the Kireyevskys or Aksakovs. The emphasis placed by the Slavophils on the village commune, as the central institution in Russian society, found its echo in the belief of Herzen that the commune could be made the foundation of a Russian socialist society.

The cleavage between Westernizers and Slavophils went deeper than shades of difference on contemporary issues. It was concerned essentially with religion and with history. The Slavophils were devout Christians, the Westernizers for the most part atheists. The different attitudes of the two schools to the history of Russia were largely responsible for their different opinions on government and politics.

Khomyakov was a pious son of the Orthodox Church, while Ivan Kireyevsky came rather later in life to religion, after a period of devotion to German philosophy. Khomyakov was an outstanding exponent of Orthodox theology. It is worth noting that at a time when the general intellectual level of the Orthodox Church was low, when bishops and monks were virtually indifferent to thought, and when the secular intellectual *élite* in Russia, as in western Europe, was drifting away from religion, a layman should have concerned himself seriously with theology. Khomyakov's contribution was to formulate the doctrine of *sobornost*. He was convinced of the spiritual superiority of Orthodoxy to Roman Catholicism and Protestantism. The Catholic Church, he believed, was a captive to human hierarchy. There was no equivalent of the pope in Orthodoxy: the sole head of the Church was Christ himself. The Orthodox Church was based on the teaching of the œcumenical councils (*sobory*), which expressed the wisdom of the whole Church, the whole body of Christians united in the Holy Spirit. The Catholic and Protestant Churches, in Khomyakov's view, were too much dominated by cold rationalism. In Western thinking the rational and emotional faculties of the mind had become too much differentiated from each other. According to Ivan Kireyevsky, Orthodox thinkers stressed 'an inner unity of the mind, a focus of mental forces, where all separate activities of the soul are fused into a complete living unity'. Kireyevsky claimed that in the writings of the patristic fathers of the Church were to be found not only theological truth but all the wisdom needed to guide man in the modern world.

However, though the depth of the Slavophils' faith cannot be questioned, it was curiously intertwined with essentially secular doctrines derived from European, and especially German, romanticism. Indeed, they became exponents in Russia of romanticism at a time when western Europe was turning away from it: this in part accounts for their hostility to the West. In the words of a modern historian, 'the Slavophils had to condemn the contemporary West in the name of romanticism itself, and they formed a haven for their romantic beliefs in their idealistic conception of old Russia'.[1] They tended to exaggerate the peculiar virtues of the Russian people and to identify the Church, and true religion itself, with the people. Only Russians, they claimed, could understand Russia, and only Russians were a people devoted to Christ. At a less exalted level, another grotesque distortion of the facts of history, dear to the Slavophil school of thought, was the assertion that the Russians, unlike

[1] N. V. Riasanovsky, *Russia and the West in the Teaching of the Slavophils* (Harvard, 1952), p. 172.

the chief European nations, were not conquerors or oppressors of other nations. A generation later the Russian religious philosopher Vladimir Solovyov reproached the Slavophils for basing themselves not on universally applicable Christian principles but on a subjective concept of the Russian spirit:

If we believed the Slavophils, and took their words about the Russian people as an expression of what the Russians really thought themselves to be, then we should have to regard this people as some sort of Pharisee, righteous in its own eyes, extolling its own virtues in the name of humility, despising and condemning neighbour peoples in the name of brotherly love, and ready to wipe them off the face of the earth to ensure the complete triumph of its own gentle and pacific nature.[1]

These, however, were not the considerations that mattered most to the Westernizers. With the exception of Granovsky, who kept some sort of deist faith to the end of his life, the Westernizers were atheists, the most militant of them being Belinsky. To them, as to the radicals of the French eighteenth century, religion could only be superstition, and all churches reactionary and baleful institutions. The classical exposition of the Westernizers' attitude to religion was Belinsky's *Letter to Gogol*, written from Salzbrunn in Germany in 1847 only a few months before his death. Belinsky had been an enthusiastic admirer of Gogol's works of the 1830's, culminating in the first part of *Dead Souls*, published in Moscow in 1842.[2] The great writer's satires on Russian social life and human types had fitted well with the political radicalism of the Westernizers. They had thought of him as one of their own kind. But Gogol had never really been a radical. In 1847 he published a work entitled *Selected Passages from Correspondence with Friends*. In this he expressed his devotion to autocracy and the Orthodox Church, extolled the piety of the Russian people, and justified existing institutions, including serfdom and corporal punishment. The book was written from

[1] V. S. Solovyov, *Slavyanofilstvo i ego vyrozhdenie*, first published in *Vestnik Evropy* (1889), nos. 11 and 12. This work is reproduced in *Sobranie sochineniy Vladimira Sergeevicha Solovyova*, ed. S. M. Solovyov and E. L. Radlov (SPB, n.d.), v. 181–252. The quoted passage is on pp. 242–3. My attention was drawn to this important work of Solovyov by the excellent study by N. V. Riasanovsky, *Russia and the West in the Teaching of the Slavophils*.

[2] Gogol wrote a second part of his novel, but destroyed nearly all of it shortly before his death.

an other-worldly religious standpoint and was certainly sincere. But it had little literary merit, and bitterly offended all liberal-minded people, the Slavophils no less than the Westernizers. Belinsky was appalled by it. He regarded it as treason by a man whom he had regarded as a democrat like himself. As for Gogol's proclaimed religious convictions, and the piety of the Russian people, Belinsky regarded them as mere nonsense. Belinsky expressed his indignation in the *Letter*, which could not be published until many years later, but which soon circulated among intellectuals in Russia, and has been ever since the classical expression of Russian atheist radicalism.[1]

The Orthodox Church, Belinsky wrote, 'has always been the bulwark of the whip and the handmaid of despotism'. 'Our priesthood is the object of universal contempt by Russian society and the Russian people.' 'Look a little closer, and you will see that this is by its nature a profoundly atheistic people.' Christianity in Russia is mere superstition, not genuine religious belief. As civilization spreads, the superstition will disappear. Belinsky admitted that there were nations among whom religious belief was strong, and which retained their beliefs after civilization had triumphed over primitive material conditions: the French were an example. The Russian people, however, was not like this. In Russia only the sectarians had deep religious convictions, and they were numerically insignificant compared to the masses of the people.

This tirade has for long been treated as the last word on religion in Russia. Taken out of its context and petrified, it has been uncritically accepted by generations of Russian historians, and has indirectly influenced Western historical writing on Russia, at least far more than any other pronouncement on the subject. Yet it is only a part of the truth. Certainly, village priests were the object of contempt and mockery, both by educated Russians and by peasants: but in what Christian society have anti-clerical jokes not been popular? Certainly, the level of education and

[1] The circumstances in which Belinsky wrote and dispatched the *Letter* are described in the reminiscences of Annenkov, *Zamechatel'noe desyatiletie*, first published in 1880 and included in *Literaturnye vospominaniya* (SPB, 1909), pp. 170–366. Annenkov remonstrated with him on the sharpness of tone of the *Letter*, to which Belinsky replied: 'We must use every means to save people from a madman, even if he were Homer himself. As for insults to Gogol, I could never insult him as much as he has insulted me in my intimate thoughts and in my faith in him' (p. 356).'

the quality of theological thought in the Russian Church were low: but this must be seen against the background of a whole society that was culturally backward. Certainly, the Church was subservient to the civil power, and appeals to piety and submission were made by both ecclesiastical and secular leaders, not so much for their own religious merit as in order to ensure submission to landowners, governors, or the Tsar. But abuse of Church authority for secular purposes was not a phenomenon peculiar to Russia. Belinsky's outburst against Gogol is indeed understandable. When he said, in the *Letter*, that in Russia those who proclaim their devotion to the Church 'immediately burn incense rather to an earthly god than to God in Heaven', he was scoring a point. Much the same was written a few years later by the conservative governor of Riga, P. A. Valuyev.[1] Belinsky had every reason to be disgusted by the servile tone of Gogol's book. Yet it is rash to dismiss, as he does, the influence of the Church in Russia. Belinsky's *Letter* well describes what the radical intelligentsia hoped was the attitude of the masses to the Church. In fact, the Russian peasant's mind was largely moulded by Orthodoxy, whether or not he respected the particular individual who was the priest of his village. To attempt to separate from each other the performance of ritual and the inner spiritual feeling of the worshipper, his submission to the serf-owner and his submission to God, is a virtually impossible task, and certainly not one for which the radical journalists of the two capitals were qualified. Orthodoxy, with its good and bad features, was the largest single factor in the mental and spiritual lives of most Russians. Second in importance only to Orthodoxy was the influence of the schismatics and sectarians whose conviction Belinsky admitted, but whose numbers he vastly underestimated.

Belinsky's *Letter* is important from another point of view. He not only attacked Gogol's religious convictions, he also attacked Gogol for betraying the high vocation of a writer.

> Only in literature, despite the Tatar censorship, is there still life, and forward movement. . . . The title of poet, the calling of literary writer in our country have already dulled the tinsel of the epaulettes and the many-coloured uniforms. That is why among us a so-called liberal tendency is especially rewarded with universal and respectful

[1] See above p. 218.

attention, even when it lacks literary talent, and why there is such a quick decline in the popularity of great poets who sincerely or insincerely give themselves up to the service of Orthodoxy, Autocracy, and the National Principle.

Belinsky was a gifted literary critic by any standard. He showed profound insight into the greatness of Pushkin and did more than anyone to make him understood by his countrymen.[1] But his obsession with social and political issues led him to the position, clearly stated in the passage quoted above, that a work of literature should be judged by whether it serves the cause of social and political progress. In the 1840's this was a healthy phenomenon, a much-needed reaction against the stifling régime, and an intelligent use of one of the few loopholes still left by the censorship. But in the hands of Belinsky's less talented successors, who had less enthusiasm and far less understanding than he for literature, Belinsky's doctrine became a dogma of revolutionary utilitarianism which inhibited literary appreciation among educated Russians. Later still, it became petrified into an obscurantism which operated parallel with the official obscurantism.

It is wrong to imagine that the Westernizers as such had a better understanding of Europe and its history than the Slavophils. Chaadayev knew intimately the culture of contemporary Europe. So did Granovsky, who was genuinely interested in the European Middle Ages, and succeeded in communicating his passion to his students. Herzen was well read, spoke the main Western languages, and spent nearly half of his life abroad. Yet how much he understood of the past or present society and culture of the West remains a matter for argument. Belinsky knew and understood less. For these two men, and for the next generation of radicals, Europe was of interest because it had produced modern radical political ideas which could be used to bring about revolution in Russia: the historical development from which these ideas had emerged was of secondary importance to them. Much as the Africans of the twentieth century

[1] The long essay by Annenkov, referred to in n. 1 on p. 262, gives a sympathetic and moving portrait of Belinsky. Annenkov's title has also been taken for four brilliant lectures by Isaiah Berlin, 'The Marvellous Decade', published in *Encounter*, 1953–1954, surveying the intellectual life of Russia in these years (1838–48), but with special attention to Belinsky.

were interested in Europe and America for their scientific discoveries, the Russian radicals of the mid-nineteenth century were interested in Europe because it had produced radical ideas: neither were concerned to go much deeper. The Slavophils were more genuinely interested in history. They appreciated tradition, in other countries as well as in their own. Khomyakov was favourably impressed by the respect of the English for tradition, by their tendency to graft reforms on the existing structure rather than to destroy the old and to build anew according to a rational plan. This was how he wished Russia to develop. Serfdom must be abolished, the bureaucracy must have less power, the people must be consulted by the ruler, but the basic structure of autocracy and Orthodoxy must not be shaken.

Yet though in general the Slavophils had perhaps a greater capacity for historical understanding and imagination than the Westernizers, they were also guilty of historical distortion, of the use of history as a weapon in political polemics. They idealized pre-Petrine Muscovite society. They attributed most of the oppressive features of contemporary Russia to the bureaucracy created by Peter the Great and, in their opinion, excessively staffed by Germans. In pre-Petrine Russia, they believed, a natural harmony had prevailed between autocrat and people. This should be restored by reducing to an absolute minimum the bureaucratic element which had been interposed between the monarch and his subjects and frustrated the will of both. This idea was later expressed by Konstantin Aksakov in a memorandum to Alexander II of 1855: 'To the government unlimited authority over the state; to the people full moral liberty, liberty of life and spirit. To the government, the right to action, and consequently to law; to the people the right to opinion, and consequently to speech.'[1]

The Slavophils had little conception of the meaning of law. They thought they saw, in the whole structure of law in the West as derived from ancient Rome and from the medieval Church, mere dry inhuman formalism, endless litigations about phrases, and a whole profession composed of persons materially dependent on such mean activity. In Russia they believed that

[1] The full text of K. Aksakov's memorandum, presented to the Tsar in 1855, is printed in *Rannye slavyanofily*, a collection of Slavophil writings edited by N. L. Brodsky (Moscow, 1910), pp. 69–102. The passage quoted above is on pp. 98–99.

the people could settle its problems by discussion and by kindness, ending in unanimity. Khomyakov admired the English jury system because it insisted on unanimity. It did not seem to occur to him that if all were made dependent on human kindness and discussion, the results would be unpredictable, and the way opened for tyranny, distortion of justice, and exploitation. The establishment of clearly defined standards, against which actions could be measured, never seems to have appeared important to the Slavophils. Though hostile to the European system of justice, they were well aware that the existing machinery of courts and judges in Russia was monstrously inefficient and corrupt, and therefore favoured judicial reform. But the main enemy was bureaucracy which weighed heavily on the state and on society. As Khomyakov expressed it in a letter to Countess Bludova in 1848, 'in our country government is autocratic which is excellent; but society is despotic which is thoroughly bad'. In another letter he commented on life in St. Petersburg, the bureaucrats' capital, which he considered so inferior to his own dear Moscow:

> I think, I am even convinced, that there is no society anywhere that is more cultivated than that of St. Petersburg. But it is a culture of its own special kind. Everything is limited to understanding: they understand everything and have sympathy for nothing. Such a culture is worse than an absence of culture. The administration goes its way, half-autocratic half-bureaucratic; commerce goes its way; science (in the narrowest sense of the study of foreign knowledge and thought) goes its way; and society does not go at all.

The Slavophils recognized that Peter the Great was an outstanding ruler, but they believed that he had led Russia on to the wrong path. Here they differed from Karamzin, and from the official view, no less than from the Westernizers. It was not only that they were horrified by the inhuman ruthlessness of Peter, by the contrast between his great victories and the sufferings of the common man whom he exploited to win them—a theme whose greatest literary treatment is Pushkin's *Bronze Horseman*. Peter's greatest fault, in their view, was that he had aped Europe too much, and had brought in hosts of German bureaucrats to implement his plans. The Westernizers admired Peter, while regretting his cruelty. But the spokesmen of official *narodnost*, including Uvarov and the Tsar himself, also admired

Peter. They considered themselves his heirs, carrying on his task of making Russia a Great Power in the modern world, which of course implied modernization of Russia itself. In this sense Uvarov and Nicholas were Westernizers. They objected only to the modern political ideas of Europe, which were precisely what formed the attraction of Europe to the Westernizers. These ideas were, of course, repressed by the Russian censorship, but not very effectively. On the other hand the censorship looked with no less suspicion on the Slavophils with their disrespect for Peter and their ideas about social or political reforms. Yet at the same time there was common ground between the Slavophils and the exponents of official *narodnost*, who shared a certain Russian nationalism, hostility to the non-Russian nations of the empire (or at least to the more culturally advanced and articulate of them), and sympathy for the Slav peoples ruled by Russia's traditional enemy Turkey or her uncertain ally Austria.

Russian Nationalism and Pan-slavism

The attitude of the Russian government to nationalism, and the relationship of the non-Russian peoples to the Russians, involve several distinct, though overlapping, issues—the claims of the dynasty, centralization, frontier security, religious diversity, and Russian nationalism.

Loyalty to the dynasty was binding on all subjects of the empire, whether Russian or not. It was perhaps to be expected that Russians would be more enthusiastically loyal than others, but from the Tsar's point of view a Baltic German, a Pole, or a Tatar who served him loyally was not less acceptable or praiseworthy a subject than a Russian.

The tendency to centralize government, and to make the administration uniform in all regions, can be found in seventeenth- and eighteenth-century Europe, and was increasingly adopted in Russia from the time of Peter the Great. Local autonomies and provincial patriotisms were repressed by both Louis XIV and the Jacobins. Both despots and liberals in nineteenth-century Europe favoured centralism: in this Nicholas I agreed with Pestel. But the abolition of local autonomies is not necessarily inspired by hostility or contempt towards the language or culture of the local population.

Measures designed to guarantee the frontiers, where these were inhabited by people of a different nationality, and especially when the latter were akin to the people living immediately beyond the frontier, can be regarded as repression of national minorities, but are not necessarily acts of nationalism. Examples are the establishment of Russian colonists along the Caucasian borders, in the Ural steppes, and to some extent in the Baltic provinces.

Religious intolerance, and more or less forcible conversion of members of other religions, tend to be more closely associated with nationalism, though they are still not quite the same thing. The major religions have tended to be associated with a particular language (Catholicism with Latin, Lutheranism with German, Islam with Arabic). In Russia, the efforts of the Orthodox Church to convert Baltic Protestants, Moslem Tatars, or Lithuanian Jews, and still more the attempts to remove White Russian and Ukrainian peasants from Catholic influence, amounted to something very like turning non-Russians into Russians.

Yet nationalism is something different from this. It is essentially a product of the eighteenth-century Enlightenment. Nationalism cannot be separated from the notion of popular sovereignty. From the point of view of the rulers of mid-nineteenth-century Europe, nationalism was a subversive doctrine, for it introduced a new principle as the basis of the legitimacy of government. It substituted for the old legitimacy, based on monarchy by divine right, a new legitimacy based on the nation. Applied to the Russian empire, this would mean that the Russian nation (the Orthodox whose language was Russian) must have the first place in the Russian empire. From this it was the next step to argue that only Russians would be truly loyal subjects, and that therefore those who were not Russians must be turned into Russians, and until they became Russians must be regarded as second-class citizens.

These principles were not clearly formulated in Russia at the beginning of the nineteenth century. But there was a rising Russian nationalism, stimulated by the war of 1812, and strengthened by the legitimate and growing pride of educated Russians in the beauty of their language as reflected in its new literature. Nicholas I distrusted this nationalism. He shared the widespread anti-semitic prejudices of the Russian upper class, based in part on a certain medieval Christian tradition and in part on ignorance and distrust of the commercial occupations in which Jews were engaged. He therefore gave his support to anti-Jewish legislation. He also objected strongly to any sort of rebellion. For this reason he felt that the Poles must be punished, and Polish influence in the borderlands be drastically reduced. His anti-Polish policies were strengthened by a traditionally Russian hostility to Catholicism. He supported the forcible dissolution of the Uniate Church in 1839. But those of his non-Russian subjects who served him loyally must suffer no disabilities simply because they were not Russian. In particular, he objected to any measures against the Baltic Germans, who had provided so many distinguished soldiers and officials to the empire. Nicholas's family connexion with Prussia, and his liking for German culture, probably increased his good will towards the Baltic Germans.

A more nationalistic note can, however, be detected in the writings of Uvarov. In his 1843 report to the Tsar on the activities of the Ministry of Education over the preceding ten years he remarked that 'Your Imperial Majesty has deigned to recognize that for the advantage of future generations the intellectual fusion of the Polish and Russian cultural principles, with the proper primacy of the Russian, must be considered the only road to the aim so assiduously pursued'. He spoke also of 'the great idea of developing Russian nationality on its true principles, and thus making it the centre of the life of the state and of moral culture'. After the war of 1831 the University of Vilna was closed. In 1836 Russian gimnazii were opened in Grodno and Vilna, and a nobles' boarding-house was attached to the latter. Russian teachers were put in place of Polish in the gimnazii of the Belorussian and Kiev educational districts. In 1836 teaching of the Polish language was stopped. In 1838 after careful examination of the situation in the Vilna, Grodno, and Białystok areas Uvarov felt able to report to the Tsar that 'the establishment of Russian education in the Lithuanian provinces may be considered definitely completed'. The centre of cultural Russification in the borderlands was the new St. Vladimir University of Kiev, opened on 8 November 1833. Uvarov considered that the aim of the new university was 'to smooth away those sharp characteristic traits by which Polish youth is distinguished from Russian, and especially to suppress in Polish youth the thought of its own nationality, to bring it ever nearer to Russian notions and morals, to transfer to it the general spirit of the Russian people'.[1] Of the three principles proclaimed in Uvarov's 1832 report on education—Orthodoxy, Autocracy, and the National Principle (*narodnost*)—the third was gaining ground over the first two. Uvarov was unconsciously appealing rather to the legitimacy of the nation than to the legitimacy of autocracy.

When he came to speak of the Baltic provinces, Uvarov sounded a more cautious note. Nevertheless, an underlying Russian nationalism is unmistakable in the 1843 report. The German population, Uvarov believed, was loyal to the empire but distrustful of Russia and inclined to cling to traditional cultural links with Germany. Germans were unwilling to learn Russian. They did not understand that Russia had grown up, that it was no longer the Russia of Empress Anna or of Catherine. 'They have the cold petty spirit of Protestantism in relation to affairs of state.' They cannot be aroused to enthusiam. 'It is impossible to catch the Germans at one bound; one must, so to speak, conduct a siege. They will surrender, but not at once.'[2] The Orthodox Church, however, was less patient. In 1836 an Orthodox bishopric was established in Riga. During the next decade the Church energetically pursued the conversion of the Baltic peoples, combining administrative pressure with the exploitation of anti-German feeling among the Balts. The governor-general from 1845 to 1848, General Y. A. Golovin, supported these efforts. During the years 1845–7 about 74,000 Latvians and Estonians joined the Orthodox Church. The conversions aroused resentment among the Baltic Germans, and this in turn annoyed nationalist Russians. One of the younger Slavophils, Yuri Samarin, who served for a time in Riga under the next governor-general, Prince Suvorov, circulated in 1849 among his friends in Russia a series of *Letters from Riga* with a strongly anti-German tone. The Tsar ordered him to be shut up in a fortress for ten days, and then brought directly into his presence. Nicholas, who knew his father, received him kindly, but remarked that part of his *Letters* might have produced 'another 14th December'. When Samarin expressed his consternation,

[1] *Desyatiletie MNP 1833–1843*, p. 39. [2] Ibid., pp. 51–52.

the Tsar explained: 'You circulated among the people the dangerous thought that the Russian emperors from the time of Peter the Great have been acting only at the inspiration and under the influence of Germans. If this thought gets round among the people, it will produce appalling disaster.'[1]

In 1847 the Third Department arrested a group of persons in Kiev connected with a secret Society of St. Cyril and St. Methodius. They were Ukrainian nationalists with radical social ideas and a programme of a confederation of all Slav peoples. The outstanding member of the group was Taras Shevchenko. Born a serf in 1814, Shevchenko had acquired a passionate interest in painting and after many sufferings and disappointments had been able to study with a leading St. Petersburg painter. He was able to buy his freedom by the sale of a portrait which he painted of Zhukovsky who took a keen interest in his case. His greatest achievement, however, was not in painting but in poetry. His poems, the first of which were published in a volume entitled *Kobzar* in 1840, were not only great literature but formed a landmark in the creation of a literary Ukrainian language, the one essential element still lacking in order to fuse together all the various feelings of difference which separated Ukrainians from Russians and make of them a sense of Ukrainian national identity.[2] The whole subsequent development of Ukrainian nationalism derives from Shevchenko's poetry. Between 1843 and 1846 Shevchenko travelled in the Ukraine as a member of the Archaeographical Commission whose task was to collect local inscriptions. In 1846 in Kiev he met the historian Kostomarov and others who had formed the Society of St. Cyril and St. Methodius. The group were denounced to the police by an informer. As the result of some unexpected help from one of the gendarmes who interrogated them, they were able to convince the police that their society had been an entirely harmless group of Pan-Slavs, devoted to the Tsar. In fact, according to the autobiography of Kostomarov published forty years later, though they were indeed quite harmless and had no plans for violent action, their ideas were definitely radical. They 'planned to abolish' serfdom, all class privileges, and all corporal and capital punishment, and 'favoured' complete religious equality and compulsory universal

[1] Nikitenko, *RS* (Feb. 1890), p. 403. [2] See above pp. 7–8.

education. Their Slavonic confederation was to have been a republic. Both the election of the president and the division of the Slav world into a number of states were modelled on the American Constitution.[1]

The members of the society received comparatively mild sentences of imprisonment and exile, with the exception of Shevchenko. The great poet was sent to Orenburg as a private soldier, and the Tsar personally ordered that he should be forbidden to write or draw. He spent the next ten years in great hardship, returning to St. Petersburg in 1858 for the last three years of his life. Kostomarov was more fortunate. He spent nine years in Saratov, during which he made the acquaintance of the young Chernyshevsky.[2] He was then allowed to travel abroad, and in 1859 was appointed to a chair of history at St. Petersburg University.

The suppression of the Society of St. Cyril and St. Methodius was not the end but the beginning of Ukrainian nationalism. This was something which Russians were unable to tolerate or even to understand. Not only was the Ukraine of enormous strategic and economic importance to Russia, but its people were regarded as Little Russians, a branch of the Russian nation which happened to speak an odd provincial dialect of their own. Belinsky showed none of his customary generosity or insight in reviewing the poems of Shevchenko: it seemed to him frankly absurd that poetry should be written in this *patois*. The Slavophil Samarin was more magnanimous. He wrote in his diary in Kiev in 1850:

> By all means let the people of the Ukraine keep its language, customs, songs, and traditions, by all means let the institutions created for it be adapted even more closely to its local needs. But at the same time let it remember that its historical role is within the boundaries of Russia and not outside, in the general framework of the Muscovite State, to create and enlarge which the Great Russian people toiled so long and so stubbornly, for which it endured so many bloody sacrifices and sufferings, unknown to the Ukrainians.[3]

[1] The official report by Prince A. F. Orlov is published under the title 'Ob ukraino-slavyanskom obshchestve', *RA* (1892), no. 7, pp. 334–59. Kostomarov's autobiography appeared in incomplete form in *Russkaya mysl'* (1885), nos. 5 and 6. Further details from it are to be found in an article by V. I. Semevsky in *RS*, Jan. 1886.

[2] See below pp. 362–4.

[3] *RA* (1877), no. 6, pp. 229–32.

Another people who suffered heavily during Nicholas's reign were the Jews. Crowded into the villages and small towns of the Pale, earning their living as hotel-keepers, moneylenders, or sellers of alcohol, they were disliked by both landowners and peasants, and were a natural scapegoat when times were hard. The peasant saw his few coins of spare cash go into the Jew's pocket and believed that the Jew grew fat by sucking up the earnings of his own bitter labour. He did not know or care that the Jew was in most cases as poor, as hard pressed by life, as he himself. It became the habit of Russian officials, from the village notary to the provincial governor, to attribute the evils of rural poverty and drunkenness to the Jews. It was argued that the Jews must be forced out of their exclusiveness and made to conform with Russian habits. Nicholas believed that this could best be done through the army. Hitherto Jews had not served in the armed forces but had paid a tax instead. By a decree of 26 August 1827 Jews were made liable to military service, and could be called up at any age between 12 and 25. Every year the Jewish communities had to find 10 recruits per 1,000 population: among non-Jews the proportion of recruits was 7 per 1,000. Recruits aged between 12 and 18 were to be placed in establishments for military training, but these 6 years were not to count as part of their normal 25 years of service. The application of this decree led to great abuses and cruelties. The Jewish municipal organization (*kahal*) in each city was instructed to elect 3 to 6 persons who were to be responsible for selecting the recruits. Their agents raided houses and kidnapped children, sometimes only 9 or 10 years of age. The children were often callously or brutally treated, and subjected to pressure to abandon their religion for Orthodoxy.

During the first years of the reign Jews were expelled from villages in the province of Grodno and from the cities of Kiev, Kherson, and Sevastopol. In 1835 a new statute for the Jews was published. The Pale of Settlement was redefined—fifteen provinces in the west and south, with a number of districts excepted. Only temporary permits were to be given to go to other parts of Russia. Only merchants of the first and second guilds might visit the capitals, the seaports, or the fairs of Nizhnii Novgorod and Kharkov. Jews were forbidden to employ Christians as servants. In public business they might use the Russian,

Polish, or German languages but 'under no circumstances the Hebrew language'. Education was the subject of a decree of 13 November 1844, which set up Jewish schools of a new type, corresponding to the parish and *uezd* schools existing for Russians. A further decree of 19 December 1844 abolished the *kahal* and brought Jews under the same system of city government as other citizens. The revenue from the 'basket tax' on kosher meat, which had been at the disposal of the *kahal*, was now transferred to the provincial authorities but was supposed to be spent for the advantage of the Jewish population.

It would be wrong to accuse Nicholas I's government of antisemitism in the twentieth-century sense: rather it was inspired by a bureaucratic desire for uniformity and an intolerance of anything which it could not understand. But it was carried out by officials who were hostile to the Jews, who were themselves intensely distrustful of Gentile policies. At the end of the reign the situation of Russian Jews was worse than at the beginning.

The Last Years

The outbreak of revolutions in France, Prussia, Austria, Hungary, and Roumania in 1848 profoundly alarmed Nicholas. He personally drafted a manifesto, issued on 14 March, in which he declared Russia's firm resolve to resist the forces of revolution.

There was little active sympathy for the revolutions among politically conscious Russians. Belinsky had returned to Russia at the end of the previous year, but his health was ruined, and he died on 26 May 1848. Herzen had left Russia in January 1847. For some time he had been out of sympathy not only with the régime but with moderate liberals. The gap between his socialism and Granovsky's liberalism was too wide. The death of his father gave him the funds necessary to travel, and he was able to get permission to leave Russia. For the next years his life belongs rather to European revolutionary history than to that of Russia. In Russia in 1848 even liberals like Granovsky were distressed by the anti-Russian attitudes of the European left, and thus torn between their patriotism and their dislike of the old régime in Europe. Prince Vyazemsky expressed widespread emotions in a patriotic poem entitled 'Holy Russia'. A more defiantly conservative statement appeared later in the article 'La Russie et la révolution', published by the poet Tyutchev in the *Revue des Deux Mondes* in June 1850. This bombastically asserted that there were only two forces in Europe—Russia and Revolution. Russia was the only state which was Christian in its very essence. This claim was combined with the more mundane argument that Russia had a duty to protect Slav peoples from Western revolutionary threats.

But though there was no sign of disloyalty or subversion among his subjects the Tsar determined to take strong preventive measures. A special committee was set up on 2 April 1848 to watch over all publications and to ensure the strictest possible censorship. Its chairman, Count D. P. Buturlin, was an extreme reactionary. P. A. Valuyev, then a high official in the office of the governor-general of Riga, visiting St. Petersburg in March 1848, noted that it was being suggested that all universities and gimnazii should be closed down.[1] Some months later Nikitenko commented that the Buturlin committee 'is acting in such a way that it is becoming impossible to write anything in the press at all'.[2] The public mood was further depressed in the summer of 1848 by the ravages of a new cholera epidemic.

The formation of the Buturlin committee was a victory for the enemies of Uvarov, who included such comparatively enlightened high officials as Baron Korf and Count S. G. Stroganov. The latter was bent on revenge for his dismissal from the curatorship of Moscow by an intrigue of Uvarov's. The opportunity came early in 1849. Uvarov encouraged a leading Moscow professor, I. I. Davydov, to write an article in *Sovremennik* in defence of the universities which were being denounced by reactionary gossip as hotbeds of sedition. Buturlin wrote an official letter to Uvarov on 17 March about the article, claiming that though at first sight it appeared harmless, yet 'if one penetrates into its inner meaning', it is revealed as 'an intervention into government affairs most inappropriate for a private person'. Nicholas agreed with this, and wished to be informed 'how this could have been let through the censorship'. Uvarov accepted

[1] P. A. Valuyev, *Dnevnik 1847–1860*, in *RS* (Apr. 1891), p. 172.
[2] A. I. Nikitenko, Diary, in *RS* (Feb. 1890), p. 386.

responsibility for the article, and claimed, in a letter to Nicholas of 22 March, that it was needed in order to restore the morale of university teachers and students, alarmed by the talk of closing the universities, which had become so widespread, and penetrated to such important levels of society, that it had to be taken seriously. Nicholas was unimpressed. He replied that the article was 'inappropriate since either praise or abuse of our governmental measures, merely for the sake of a reply to empty gossip, is incompatible with the order which happily exists in our country'.[1] Uvarov had no alternative but to resign his ministry.

A month later a genuine piece of subversive activity came to light. On the night of 21–22 April 1849 the gendarmerie arrested forty persons connected with a group of socialist intellectuals whose leader was M. V. Petrashevsky, a junior official of the Foreign Ministry. He was one of the authors of a *Pocket Dictionary of Foreign Words*, published in 1845–6, in which radical and socialist ideas were explained. He held gatherings on Friday evenings at which there was free, and at times daring, talk on literary, political, and social themes. Those who attended were younger than Herzen and had never been in contact with him. Petrashevsky was an admirer of Fourier, and made a speech in his honour at a banquet of his friends a few days before his arrest. He was interested in the possibility of transforming the village commune on the lines of Fourier's *phalanstères*. The group disagreed on methods of action. One of them, N. A. Speshnev, spoke of three possible methods—the Jesuitical (or conspiratorial), propaganda, or insurrection. Speshnev wished to organize a centralized conspiracy, with a central committee, and prepare a peasant insurrection, but his friends did not agree, and no action was taken. Another member of the group, R. A. Chernosvitov, who had been a prospector in eastern Siberia, spoke of rebellion in that distant land, and of its separation from Russia. Essentially, the Petrashevsky circle was a discussion group, which had begun a little propaganda and intended to do more. But because there had been loose talk of violence at its meetings, and because the government was terrified of revolution in Europe, they were treated with great severity. Fifteen were sentenced to death, taken to the place of execution and

[1] The texts of these letters are given in N. Barsukov, *Zhizn' i trudy M. P. Pogodina* (SPB, 1888–1910), ix. 524–38.

then dramatically informed that their sentences had been commuted to forced labour in Siberia.[1]

One of those involved in the Petrashevsky group was F. M. Dostoyevsky, who at the age of twenty-eight had already won a reputation as a writer. One of the charges against him was that he had 'distributed a letter of the littérateur Belinsky, full of impudent expressions against the Orthodox Church and the government'. Dostoyevsky spent six years in prison in Siberia, as a result of which he wrote one of his greatest masterpieces *Notes from the House of the Dead.*

The new minister of education, Prince P. Shirinsky-Shikhmatov, prided himself that 'I have no thought, no will of my own —I am only a blind instrument of the will of the sovereign'.[2] Government control over the universities was increased. Rectors and deans could now be appointed or removed by the minister, regardless of the wishes of their councils. In 1850 lectures on philosophy and on the constitutional law of European states were discontinued, and logic and psychology were to be taught only by professors of theology. Count Bludov pleaded that at least the history of philosophy should be retained in university programmes, but this was refused. Shirinsky-Shikhmatov summed up the problem to his own satisfaction in a remark to a philosophy professor: 'The value of philosophy is unproven, but harmful effects from it are possible.'[3] The emphasis on classical education, favoured by Uvarov, came under attack, as putting undesirable ideas into young people's heads. Far from being a bulwark of conservatism, they argued, the classics acquainted young people with the lives and ideas of subversive republicans. Another familiar argument against the classics was used by the governor-general of Kiev, General D. G. Bibikov, who in 1850 suggested that instruction in gimnazii should be on 'more practical lines'. On 16 May 1852 school fees were raised once more, and it was stated precisely that persons from the poll-tax-paying classes could under no circumstances be exempted. Nicholas ordered that not more than 300 paying students should be accepted at each university, in addition to

[1] Full documentation is available in the three volumes of *Delo Petrashevtsev*, published by the Academy of Sciences of the U.S.S.R., the first volume of which appeared in Moscow in 1937.

[2] Nikitenko, Diary, in *RS* (May 1890), p. 286.

[3] Ibid. (March 1890), p. 631.

those studying on government scholarships, and that these 300 should be chosen from those 'outstanding in moral formation'.

In 1854 there were 3,600 university students in Russia, 1,000 less than in 1848. The number of gimnaziya pupils reached 18,000 in 1857. In the same year in county schools there were 32,000 children, and in elementary schools of the Ministry of Education there were 105,000. According to the statistics of the Holy Synod, its parish primary schools in 1853 had 38,000 children of whom 10,000 were girls.

The intellectual atmosphere remained oppressive until the end of the reign. Censorship authorities multiplied: in 1850 Nikitenko reckoned that there were twelve.[1] In April 1852 the novelist Turgenev was kept under house arrest for a month because he had published in a Moscow paper an obituary of Gogol (who died at the end of March) which had previously been refused by the St. Petersburg censorship for publication in a St. Petersburg paper. In 1852 the Slavophils too got into trouble. A miscellany of articles entitled *Moskovskii sbornik* appeared in April 1852. It incurred the displeasure of the minister of education by referring to Gogol as 'great'. The Committee of 2 April also objected to an historical article by I. A. Aksakov on two grounds: first, that historical truths suitable to an expert audience should not be placed before a wider public since the latter might include frivolous or malevolent persons who might put the worst interpretation on them; secondly, that even an article on the medieval Slavs should have ended with an explanation and commendation of the system of unlimited autocracy as developed by Peter the Great. On these remarkable grounds the committee not only refused to allow a second volume of *Moskovskii sbornik* to appear but forbade I. A. Aksakov ever to edit any publication at all. The committee wished to forbid the Aksakov brothers, Khomyakov, Ivan Kireyevsky, and Prince Cherkassky ever to submit any writings

[1] *RS* (March 1890), p. 632. In addition to the Directorate of Censorship in St. Petersburg, the general censorship in the Ministry of Education and the Committee of 2 Apr. 1848 (headed by Gen. Annenkov after Buturlin's death), there were separate censorships dealing with foreign affairs, church affairs, military affairs, and judicial publications, a censorship of theatres attached to the Ministry of the Imperial Court, a censorship of newspapers at the Post Office, a separate censorship section in the Third Department, and special censorship authorities for books used in teaching and for all imported foreign books.

for publication, but it was overruled by the head of the gendarmes, Prince A. F. Orlov, who found this severity excessive.

In 1854 Granovsky wrote a sad letter to Herzen, who had made some unfavourable references to Peter the Great.

> To you, who are cut off from Russia, Peter cannot be so close or so understandable [as to us]. Looking at the sins of the West, you incline towards the Slavs and are ready to offer them your hand. If you lived here, you would speak differently. One has to bear a great deal of faith and love in one's heart in order to keep any hope at all for the future of the most powerful of the Slav tribes. Our sailors and soldiers are dying gloriously in the Crimea; but how to live is something that nobody here knows.[1]

In January 1855 Moscow University celebrated its centenary, and despite the gloomy events of the time the participants derived some satisfaction from it. Granovsky took a liking to the new minister of education, A. S. Norov, who was to some extent influenced in a liberal direction by Nikitenko. Two other figures were prominent at the celebrations who were to play great parts in the reforms of the following reign—General Y. I. Rostovtsev and General D. A. Milyutin.

A month later Nicholas I was dead. Nikitenko noted his amazement in his diary: he had believed 'that Emperor Nicholas would survive us and our children and even our grandchildren. . . . A long and, one must admit, a joyless page in the history of the Russian empire has been written out to the last word.'

[1] Barsukov, op. cit. xiii. 354.

XI

FOREIGN RELATIONS

RUSSIA in the reign of Nicholas I was generally regarded as the greatest of the European land Powers. The failure of the revolutionary movements of 1848–9, the role played by Nicholas in their defeat, and the absence of revolutionary action within Russia itself during those years, all contributed raise still further the estimate by friends and foes of Russian to power. The reign ended, however, in the disenchantment of the Crimean War.

The areas with which Russian foreign policy was mainly concerned were the same as in the eighteenth century—Poland and the Ottoman empire. This period was also marked by expansion on a vast scale in Asia. It involved some contact, peaceful or warlike, with established foreign governments (Persia and China) and with such amorphous structures as the khanates of Khiva and Kokand. The European Great Powers, however, paid little attention to these activities, which raised problems of repression of disorder and administrative consolidation rather than of diplomacy or formal warfare. They occupy, in fact, an intermediate zone between internal and foreign policy, but it is more convenient to treat them under the general heading of foreign relations.

Russian foreign policy was based on the alliance with Austria and Prussia. All three governments sought to uphold monarchical absolutism, and all three were concerned at least after 1830 to prevent the independence of any part of Poland. Nevertheless, Russian and Austrian interests conflicted in the Balkans. Metternich refused to be associated with the Greek policy which was ultimately agreed by Russia, Britain, and France. Russian domination of Roumania, which seemed likely between 1829 and 1834, and again in 1849, was viewed with hostility in Vienna. The Crimean War offered an opportunity for Austria to take Russia's place without having to fight a war, but this too was prevented, essentially by French objection. This balance between Russia and Austria enabled the Roumanians to achieve a precarious independence.

Of the Western Powers Nicholas viewed France with hostility from 1830 onwards: Louis-Philippe, the monarch who got his throne by revolution, was no partner in diplomacy for a Russian autocrat. With Britain his relations were more complex. In the Greek crisis the two Powers were able to co-operate. In the mid 1830's, under the influence of Ponsonby, the Turcophil ambassador at Constantinople, Britain co-operated with France against Russia. The British government placed the most sinister interpretation on every Russian action. At the end of the 1830's the alignments changed. Palmerston was not only alarmed by French influence in Egypt but made no attempt to replace it with his own. Co-operation with Egypt was not seriously considered. Support of the Turkish Sultan became the first aim of policy, and this now required co-operation with Russia against France. This proved advantageous to Russia, as it brought about a settlement for the Black Sea Straits which increased Russia's security. Yet Anglo-Russian co-operation was not lasting. It was followed by misunderstandings and miscalculations on both sides, ending in the Crimean tragedy.

The main events and tendencies in these fields will be described in the following pages. Disregarding the precise chronological order, we shall begin with Poland, then discuss expansion in Asia, and then examine the Eastern Question, from Greek independence and the Russo-Turkish War through the two Egyptian crises to the Crimean War, breaking the sequence only to look briefly at the role of Russia during the revolutionary years 1848–9.

The War with Poland

Nicholas I disliked the constitutional system established by his brother in Poland, but he accepted it. The Poles soon placed a heavy strain on his good will by their treatment of their compatriots who had been involved in the Decembrist conspiracy. The contact between the Decembrists and the Polish Patriotic Society was revealed by a Polish renegade, and Krzyżanowski was arrested. The Polish leaders, however, argued that he could not be accused of treason because Poland was a separate state from Russia, and his offence had been committed in Russia.

They secured the transfer of his trial to a special court of the Diet which convicted him only of the much less serious offence of conspiracy. In spite of this rebuff, Nicholas fulfilled his obligations towards the Poles. He was favourably impressed by Drucki-Lubecki's policies, and Constantine spoke well to him of the Polish army. In 1829 he came to Warsaw for his coronation, and in May and June 1830 was present at the Diet.

Meanwhile a new conspiratorial group was being organized. In December 1828 a junior officer named Piotr Wysocki formed a society among cadets of the officers' training school in Warsaw. He was in contact with radical literary groups, but had virtually no support in the Diet or the civil government machine. Wysocki and his friends began to talk of conspiracy in 1829 and the first months of 1830 but talk was still far from being translated into action. The mood of the people of Warsaw was, however, changed by the revolutions in France and Belgium. With Europe once more in a state of flux, Polish romantic imaginations were soon at work. In the autumn of 1830, following denunciations to the police, Grand Duke Constantine began a slow investigation which was bound ultimately to expose Wysocki's conspiracy. At the same time the Tsar was mobilizing part of his army in Russia, in case he should feel the need for military intervention in western Europe, and Russian troops in the Kingdom, which formed a large part of the empire's western border, were clearly going to increase. It seemed that now was the time to act, before the conspirators were arrested and before Poland was overflowing with Russian soldiers.

On 29 November, when public buildings in Warsaw were being guarded by the 4th Infantry Regiment, in which a large number of the conspirators were serving, they seized the Belvedere Palace. They were unable to enlist the support of any senior officers. But in the confusion some workmen broke into the arsenal and began to distribute rifles to civilians, and the sight of armed civilians roaming the streets and breaking into shops seems to have infected private soldiers in the Warsaw garrison. Officers lost their hold over their men, and by the end of the day Warsaw was largely in the hands of the crowds.

Grand Duke Constantine was not caught in the Palace by the conspirators. He left the city, but decided not to use troops to recapture it. While he waited for the government to act, the government waited for him. Meanwhile no revolutionary leadership had emerged. Czartoryski and Drucki-Lubecki called a special meeting of the Administrative Council, and decided to co-opt some persons likely to be popular with the crowds, among them General Józef Chłopicki.[1] The council issued a proclamation appealing to Poles not to fight each other, and appointed Chłopicki commander-in-chief. Polish troops outside the city received contradictory orders from Constantine and from the council. On 1 December the troops were addressed by a party of revolutionaries from Warsaw, and decided to join the revolution. Their commander, General Szembek, accepted this decision, and the army entered Warsaw not to restore order but to defend the revolution. Meanwhile, yielding to pressure from a group of members of the Diet, the council agreed that Drucki-Lubecki should resign, and that three radicals, including the historian Lelewel, should join it. The radicals set themselves up under the old name of Patriotic Society, and called for war against Russia and for an appeal to the Poles of Lithuania to rebel. On 3 December the council dissolved itself and was reconstituted as the Provisional Government of the Kingdom of Poland. An attempt to overthrow it by the Patriotic Society was defeated, and Chłopicki proclaimed himself dictator.[2]

Nicholas I received the news of the revolution on 7 December, and two days later came the first letters from Constantine, pleading for moderation. The Tsar sent instructions to Warsaw[3] that all civil authorities in the Kingdom should obey Constantine, to whom extraordinary powers had been given. He also ordered General Rosen, commanding the Lithuanian Corps of the Russian army, to enter the Kingdom and accept the submission of the Polish army. Chłopicki was able to postpone the movement of these troops by writing to Rosen, who referred the matter back to St. Petersburg. Meanwhile on 10 December he had sent Drucki-Lubecki and Count Jan Jezierski to St. Petersburg

[1] Czartoryski had remained a member of the council despite his fall from favour in 1824, but had not attended its meetings for some years. Chłopicki, who had served in Napoleon's armies, was admitted to the Polish army after 1815, but in 1818 quarrelled with Grand Duke Constantine, and in 1820 resigned from the army.

[2] My account of the main events of 1830 is drawn chiefly from the excellent work by R. F. Leslie, *Polish Politics and the Revolution of 1830* (1956).

[3] They were addressed to the president of the Admininistrative Council as it had existed before 25 November.

to report on the situation to Nicholas. Constantine recommended them to his brother in a letter of 13 December, as 'tous les deux animés du meilleur esprit'.[1] But before they arrived the Tsar issued a manifesto on 17 December in which he condemned the revolution and ordered the Polish corps commanders to concentrate their forces at Płock. Pardon was promised to those who would submit, but if there were bloodshed it would be the fault of the Poles. The emperor clearly had no thought of compromise.

On 18 December the Diet met in Warsaw. This was an occasion for revolutionary rhetoric. There were cries of 'Long live a free and independent Poland'. The Speaker, Count Władysław Ostrowski, used in his opening speech the words: 'May the composition of the Chamber be augmented by our brother representatives from those Polish provinces which remain under foreign tyranny.' Chłopicki, knowing that attitudes of this sort were bound to lead to war, and that Poland could not face war with Russia, resigned his office. He was persuaded to continue by assurances that he should have complete power, but these promises were not carried out. The government now took another name, Supreme National Council, and its members included Czartoryski and Ostrowski.

At the end of December the Tsar received Drucki-Lubecki and Jezierski and a further emissary from Chłopicki, Tadeusz Wyleżiński. He was unbending but showed willingness to treat the Poles with respect once they had returned to their allegiance. To Jezierski he said: 'Show me a means of settling the affair which would be worthy of a King of Poland who is at the same time the Emperor of Russia! I do not ask for more. My one desire is to get round the difficulties of the present situation through the Poles themselves and in conjunction with them alone.'[2] He also pointed out that he had accepted the constitution of the Kingdom as bequeathed to him by Alexander I. Essentially, the message which Wyleżiński and Jezierski brought to Chłopicki on their return, and which Drucki-Lubecki sent by letter, was that Poland must submit to the terms of the Tsar's manifesto of 17 December.

[1] *SIRIO*, vol. 131, p. 68.

[2] Quoted from the record of the proceedings of the Diet by R. F. Leslie, op. cit., p. 144.

The public mood in Warsaw, however, made this inconceivable. Already on 3 January the manifesto which the Diet had asked Lelewel to draft was published. It demanded the reunion of the eastern lands with Poland and claimed that the Poles were defending the liberties of all Europe. The Supreme National Council heard the report of the messengers from St. Petersburg. Chłopicki saw that war would be disastrous. But none of his colleagues, including Czartoryski, was willing to incur the odium of saying so. On 17 January 1831 Chłopicki resigned.

The radicals now re-established the Patriotic Society, and their influence on public opinion increased. On 25 January the Diet met. Speakers competed in the violence of their invective against Russia. The climax came when Count Jan Ledóchowski shouted out: 'Let us then cry "Down with Nicholas".' The Diet then insisted that an act of deposition be signed by all present. On 30 January a National Government was elected. Its president was Adam Czartoryski, and its four other members included Lelewel.

Poland was now in a state of war with Russia. This had come about by drift rather than planning, without any clear political leadership, and indeed against the wishes of most of those who went through the motions of leadership. The original conspirators had been neither more numerous nor more efficient than the conspirators in St. Petersburg on 14 December 1825. They had found themselves in a vacuum of power because a crowd of workers had seized some rifles, and because some soldiers had followed their example. This had been enough to set alight the smouldering embers of Polish national discontent, and none of the elder statesmen had then dared, or known how, to put out the fire. In St. Petersburg in 1825 the workers had been passive, the soldiers had obeyed their officers, and most of the commanders of troops in the capital had obeyed the emperor. The urban population of Warsaw, at all levels, was more politically minded than that of the Russian capital. Above all, the national factor, which was decisive in Poland, had no relevance in Russia when the Decembrists made their attempt.

The result of the Polish-Russian war could hardly be in doubt, though events moved rather slowly. The first considerable battle was fought at Grochów, east of the Vistula, on 23–25 February.

It was inconclusive but was claimed by the Poles as a victory. On 1 April the Poles won a success by capturing the town of Mińsk Mazowiecki, and the Russians retreated towards Siedlce. Meanwhile attempts were made to cut the communications of the Russian army by insurrection in the south-east and in Lithuania. The force sent to raise support in the south-east, under Józef Dwernicki, met with no response from the population. On 27 April they crossed the Austrian frontier and were interned. In Podolia and in Kiev province about 1,500 men were raised in mid May, but they were quickly scattered by the Russians, and their remnants also crossed the Austrian border. There was more widespread support for the Polish cause in Lithuania. Here the armed forces raised by the gentry amounted by mid April to about 3,500, mostly badly armed. They were too weak to give any hope of capturing Vilna, which had been the original intention. At the end of April larger Russian forces were brought into Samogitia, the region in which the Lithuanian rising was most successful, and by mid May it had been broken.

The revolutionary leaders in Warsaw understood that the support of the peasants was essential, but the landowners who provided most of the Polish political *élite* were slow to take any action about land reform. The Supreme National Council in January 1831 rejected a plea from the Ministry of the Interior for a promise to 'consider means of assuring, gradually at least, property rights to the peasants'.[1] After the Battle of Grochów the problem was regarded as rather more urgent. The minister of finance prepared a bill applicable only to Crown properties. These amounted only to about 15 per cent. of the landed estates in the Kingdom. As finally agreed by the Small Quorum[2] of the Diet at the end of March, it would have permitted peasants to acquire freeholds within 28 years by yearly payments of 6¼ per cent. of the total estimated value of their holdings. On 18 April the two chambers of the Diet met jointly, but decided that each should consider the bill separately. On the following day the Chamber of Deputies simply removed the bill from its agenda.

[1] Leslie, op. cit., p. 183.

[2] The Small Quorum was a minimum of 33 members from both chambers. This minimum had been fixed on 26 February 1831, after the Battle of Grochów, when many members of the Diet had left Warsaw, to join the army or for other purposes.

Land reform was not reconsidered during the remaining months of the rebellion.

In mid May General Skrzynecki won some successes to the north-east of Warsaw, but on 26 May he met Diebitsch's main army at Ostrołęka. Both sides had around 6,000 casualties, but the Poles had the worst of the battle, and streamed back towards Warsaw in disorder. The Russian advance was held up by the death of Diebitsch, a victim of the cholera epidemic, on 10 June. Grand Duke Constantine also died of cholera on 27 June. The new Russian commander-in-chief was Paskevich, the victor of Erivan.[1] He arrived through Prussian territory to take up his command on 25 June, and took his time to prepare the final stages of the reconquest. Meanwhile in Warsaw factions quarrelled with each other, and the political and military commands were changed several times. Savage riots on 15 August were followed by the appointment of General Jan Krukowiecki as head of the government. On 6 September Paskevich reached the outskirts of Warsaw, and two days later the city was surrendered. There was no more effective resistance after this, and on 4 October the last remnants of the Polish army under General Maciej Rybiński crossed the Prussian frontier.

The Polish rebellion had aroused sympathy in Europe, most vocal in France and Britain. But there had never been any question of armed assistance to the Poles by any European Power. It is arguable that the rebellion helped France and Belgium. Nicholas could not attack them while his armies were engaged in Poland. But it is doubtful whether he would in any case have tried to intervene in the West.

After 1831 there was a Polish political emigration, whose numbers were estimated by contemporary Polish writers between 5,000 and 7,000, mostly in France. Prince Czartoryski maintained at the Hôtel Lambert in Paris a sort of exiled court, seeking to preserve a minimum political unity among the exiles and continuing to hope that the Powers would one day act on Poland's behalf. The radicals created in 1832 the Polish Democratic Society. Lelewel founded in 1834 a Young Poland movement modelled on Mazzini's Young Italy.

In the eastern provinces Russian repression was severe.

[1] See below p. 290.

Persons who had taken part in the rebellion were guilty of treason, since they had unquestionably been Russian subjects. There was a campaign against Polish influences in education and cultural life. Many Polish families were deported to other parts of the empire. In the Kingdom policies were milder. On 26 February 1832 the Tsar signed an Organic Statute which bore some resemblance to the constitution of 1815. The Council of State and the Administrative Council remained, with three commissions in place of five. These three were finance, justice, and the interior: the latter covered police, religious affairs, and education. The statute provided for elected assemblies of the nobility at district and provincial level, but these were never created. The middle and lower ranks of the civil government machine were staffed by Poles. The Polish army, however, ceased to exist. Paskevich, rewarded with the title of Prince of Warsaw, became viceroy of Poland. His rule was strict but in some ways benevolent, and his exceptionally close friendship with the emperor was possibly of advantage to his Polish subjects.

The Polish rebellion had been regarded by politically minded Russians with almost unanimous hostility. The demand of the Poles for the eastern provinces, which Russians regarded as part of 'the Russian land', was especially resented, but there was not even much trace of sympathy for the Poles' wish for national independence as such. Pushkin, a generous man and a believer in liberty, wrote two fierce poems, 'To the Slanderers of Russia' and 'The Anniversary of Borodino', in protest against foreign concern for the Poles. The rebellion, he declared in the first of these poems, was 'a dispute of Slavs among themselves, a domestic ancient quarrel, already weighed by destiny, a question which will not be solved by you'. Each side in turn had won and lost. 'Who will prevail in the unequal struggle, the haughty Pole or the loyal Russian? Will the Slav streams flow together in the Russian sea? Or will that sea dry up? That is the question.' Foreigners had nothing to do with this matter. Their comments could be inspired by no emotion higher than envious hatred of Russia, and a bad conscience because they had not played so heroic a role as Russia in resisting Napoleon. But if they followed up their words with action, then 'from Perm to the Crimea, from Finland's cold cliffs to torrid Colchis, from the shaken Kremlin to the walls of unmoving China, with bristles of steel the Russian land will rise up'.[1]

Expansion in Asia

Russian territorial expansion in Asia, in the thirty years of Nicholas I's reign, followed three directions—the Caucasus, Central Asia, and the north-east Pacific. These must be considered in turn.

Russo-Persian hostility in the Caucasus was not ended by the Treaty of Gulistan. The Russians in 1825 claimed the wider region of Gokcha. This was refused by the Shah, who still cherished the hope of recovering Georgia and Azerbaidjan. In June 1826 Persian troops crossed the frontier, and at first met with success. Yermolov reacted slowly, the Russians lost Gandja and were only just able to save Tiflis. In the autumn, however, Russian forces under General I. F. Paskevich made a counter-

[1] Pushkin was no enemy of the Poles. He had both admiration and affection for the great Polish poet Mickiewicz. In 1834 he wrote a poem about him regretting that he had become an enemy of Russia and recalling the day when he had spoken of 'future times when the nations, forgetting their discord, will unite in one great family'. Despite a certain Russian patriotic condescension this poem is clearly written in a tone of friendship. ('On mezhdu nami zhil', published in Pushkin, *Polnoe sobranie sochineniy*, edition of the Academy of Sciences of the Soviet Union (Moscow, 1948), iii. 331). Mickiewicz was less generous. In 1831 he wrote: 'Perhaps one of you, dishonoured by office and by decorations, has for ever abandoned the freedom of his soul to the favour of the Tsar . . . glorifies his triumph with venal tongue, and comforts himself with the martyrdom of his friends.' ('Do przyjaciół Moskali', lines 13–20 from the 'Diversion' in part iii of the epic *Dziady*.) It must be admitted that Mickiewicz had a lot to forgive the Russians. However, when Pushkin was killed, he wrote a warm appreciation of his literary achievement in the Paris periodical *Le Globe* in 1837 (a translation into Polish of the article is in Adam Mickiewicz, *Dzieła wszystkie* (Warsaw, 1936), vii. 53–62). See also the essay by Wacław Lednicki 'Puszkin–Mickiewicz (Mickiewiczowy nekrolog Puszkina)' in his volume of essays *Przyjaciele Moskale* (Cracow, 1935), pp. 147–93. Even in 1831 there were some Russians who disapproved of Russia's treatment of the Poles. Pushkin's close friend, the poet and critic Prince P. A. Vyazemsky, was one: he was moved to indignation by Pushkin's 'Borodino' and 'Slanderers' poems. On the other hand, Chaadayev wrote to Pushkin expressing his admiration for them. Among Pushkin's friends was a Polonophil, to whom he wrote an incomplete poem, found among his papers ('Ty prosveshcheniem svoy razum osvetil', published in Pushkin, 1948 edition, iii. 444). Of the grief of the unknown Polonophil at the fall of Warsaw, Pushkin wrote: 'You sobbed bitterly, as the Jew sobbed over Jerusalem.' For a discussion of the possible identity of the Polonophil, and indeed a most sensitive essay on the attitude of educated Russians to Poland in the age of Pushkin, see Wacław Lednicki, *Russia, Poland and the West: Essays in Literary and Cultural History* (1954), pp. 21–105.

offensive, and in 1827 Paskevich was appointed commander-in-chief. The war was now carried into Persian territory. On 13 October 1827 the Russians captured Erivan, and a few weeks later Tabriz was occupied without resistance. Peace was made by the Treaty of Turkmanchay, signed on 22 February 1828.

By this treaty Russia acquired Erivan and Nakhichevan, that is to say, Persian Armenia, the territory which Persia had acquired from Turkey in the seventeenth century. Thus the easternmost portion of the Armenian homeland came under Russian rule. This was an undoubted gain for the Armenians, who now had a Christian ruler to whom they showed themselves extremely loyal, vainly hoping that he would in time deliver the majority of their compatriots who remained subjects of the Ottoman empire. The border of Russia was fixed on the Araxes river, with a small deviation to the south of its mouth to include the district of Lenkoran. Tabriz was restored to Persia. Thus the Azerbaidjani Tatars, like the Armenians, remained divided: the minority remaining under the Persians, who shared their Shia Moslem faith but not their tongue, while the majority were incorporated in the Russian empire.

The main Caucasus massif, lying between Russia and the Transcaucasian lands of Georgia and Armenia, still remained to be conquered. Two separate centres of resistance existed, in Circassia in the West and in Daghestan in the East.

Paskevich was planning operations against the Circassians when he was taken away from the Caucasus in 1831 to succeed Diebitsch in command of the Russian army in Poland. In the early 1830's the fortified base at Novorossiisk, in the Bay of Sudjuk, was strengthened, and a beginning was made with a plan to build a line of forts from Gelendjik across the mountains to the Kuban valley, and another line from Gelendjik down the coast to Sukhum. These plans had to be postponed for some years as a result of troubles in Daghestan. But in 1837 a force of 3,000 Russian troops was landed at Adler, at the mouth of the river Mzymta, and other Russian troops moved south from Gelendjik. In April and May 1838 there were landings at Sochi and Tuapse, and forts were built. In 1840 there was a large-scale insurrection of the Circassians. Raiding forces, in some cases numbering more than 10,000 men, attacked Russian forts. Several were captured, and their defenders massacred. The crucial siege of the fort of Abinsk ended with the repulse of the attackers, who lost more than 600 dead. The coastal forts were reinforced from the sea, and the Circassian attacks became fewer and less formidable. However, the western part of the Caucasian mountain massif was still out of Russian control, and the line of forts across it was in permanent danger. The Russian government could not spare forces to subdue it, owing to the much more serious dangers which threatened it in Daghestan.

At the end of the 1820's there appeared in Daghestan a religious movement which became known to the Russians as Muridism. The word *murid* means a disciple in a mystical sect. Sects, led by a holy man who could initiate his disciples into the Path (*tarikat*) to the true wisdom, had played an important part for centuries in the history of Islam, and the mountainous borderlands between Persia and Turkey had produced as many of them as any part of the Moslem world. What was new was that a young *murshid* (head of a sect, master of *murids*) named Kazi Mulla, who began to preach in Gimri in Daghestan in 1827, proclaimed a holy war (*ghazavat*) against foreigners and received enthusiastic support. Certainly, the movement had an aspect of social discontent. The people of Daghestan had grievances against the secular rulers and landowners. They were also harmed by the Russian policy of confiscating land and giving it to Russian Cossacks.[1] Social discontent, hatred of the foreigner, and religious puritanism were combined in the movement, and it is virtually impossible for an historian to disentangle them.[2]

[1] N. A. Smirnov, *Myuridizm na Kavkaze* (Moscow, 1963), pp. 222–3, quotes a report from the commander-in-chief in the Caucasus in 1863–5 to the effect that at that time there were 7 Cossacks per square verst of land and 12·6 mountaineers—in fact 600,000 Cossacks had nearly twice as much land per head as 948,000 mountaineers. In 1830 of course this process was at an earlier stage.

[2] The interpretation of this movement has been a subject of controversy for some time in Soviet historical literature. In the first years after 1917 the struggle of the mountain peoples of the Caucasus against the armies of the Tsar was regarded with sympathy. After the Second World War, however, the preoccupation of the Soviet government with the struggle against '*bourgeois* nationalism' brought a change. M. D. Bagirov for many years the leader of the Communist Party of Azerbaidjan, declared that the movement was an instrument of Turkish and British imperialism, and that the Imam Shamil was an agent of these Powers. Soviet historians supported this view. In 1956 and 1957, however, the subject was reconsidered. In articles in *Voprosy istorii* and at meetings of historians in Makhachkala (Derbent) and Moscow it was now admitted that the movement was not created by foreign Powers, and that the mountain peoples had good reason to resist Imperial Russian policies. But whereas some historians (especially A. M. Pikman, in an article in *Voprosy istorii*,

In the minds of those who fought, religious fanaticism was the essential factor. The movement became dangerous to Russian rule because it was led by men who not only were brave but brilliantly understood the tactics of mountain and forest warfare.

Kazi Mulla quickly won support from Avar and Chechen tribesmen who had bitter memories of Yermolov's campaigns. Under his leadership they made raids into Kakhetia and the Terek valley, and threatened the administrative centres of Kizlyar, Derbent, and Vladikavkaz. In October 1832 General Velyaminov invaded Kazi Mulla's territory with 10,000 Russian troops and captured the mountain strongholds of Dargo and Gimri. Kazi Mulla himself was killed. His successor as Imam of the sect was murdered two years later in an act of personal revenge. He was, however, succeeded by Shamil, a man of burning conviction, powerful personality, and brilliant military ability. By 1836 his raiders were again terrorizing the plains and threatening the Russian position in the Caucasus. In 1837 the Tsar himself visited the Caucasus and invited Shamil to meet

no. 3, 1956, and M. N. Osmanov, M. A. Mamakayev, and R. M. Magomedov at the Moscow meeting, reported in *Voprosy istorii*, no. 12, 1956) defended the movement as a fight for liberty, others (especially N. A. Smirnov, A. V. Fadeyev, Kh. G. Adzhemyan, and S. K. Bushuyev) insisted on the fundamentally 'reactionary' nature of the religious ideology of 'Muridism'. In his book *Myuridizm na Kavkaze*, published in 1963, N. A. Smirnov, who bitterly resents the assertions of American historians that Soviet historians are told what to write by the Communist Party (p. 39), yet himself admits that he was previously 'influenced' by the Bagirov doctrine (p. 28, footnote), energetically reasserts the 'reactionary' nature of 'Muridism'. 'It is true', he writes, 'that the Imamat was of great importance for the political consolidation of mountaineer society, without which . . . it would have been unthinkable to carry on any struggle at all, but it was unable to promote its social-economic development. The Imamat rather hindered the formation of social forces which could have curbed or weakened the forces of religious reaction. It hindered the penetration into mountaineer society of the elements of capitalism, whereas at this time the progressive development of Russia was advancing rapidly along this road, insistently demanding the repeal of serfdom.' According to Smirnov religious beliefs were an obstacle to progress. 'Religious morality shackled the mountaineers hand and foot and prevented them from recognizing their own interests, still less fighting for them. . . . Transfer to Imperial Russia did not free the mountaineers from social or colonial oppression. But feudalism in Russia was in its last years, and the development of capitalism was inevitably bound, in spite of a number of barriers, to roll onwards to the Caucasus and take possession of it, thus creating the conditions for the development of the productive forces, and consequently for the fusion of the national peasant actions in the borderlands with the proletarian movement of Russia.' (Ibid., pp. 230–1.) There is an interesting discussion of the controversy among Soviet historians in 1956 and 1957 in an article by Paul B. Henze, 'The Shamil Problem' in *The Middle East in Transition*, ed. Walter Z. Laqueur, 1958.

him. After some thought the Imam refused. In the spring of 1838 General von Grabbe led an expedition into Chechnia, and after a long siege captured the Imam's stronghold of Ahulgo. Shamil himself, however, escaped, and there were 3,000 Russian casualties. The campaigns of 1840–2 cost the Russians another 8,000 casualties (including 1,800 killed). In 1843 Shamil won thousands of new recruits in Daghestan, and his raids brought still more victims. In 1844 Nicholas appointed Count Michael Vorontsov as viceroy of the Caucasus. Vorontsov proposed to proceed slowly, clearing the forest back from the lines of communication and building a series of forts. But the emperor pressed him to achieve quick results. Against his better judgement, in May 1845 he led a force of 18,000 men into Chechnia. The mountaineers retreated without a major battle. Vorontsov then took 10,000 men deep into the forests of Ichkeria. They captured Dargo, but they had still not defeated Shamil's forces. There was nothing to be done except retire again, and as they went the Russians were attacked by Chechen sharpshooters firing from behind the beech-trees. Vorontsov eventually reached Grozny, but he had nearly 4,000 casualties, including 3 generals. In 1846 Shamil raided Kabarda, and there was for a time a danger that he would link up with the Circassians in the west and threaten the Georgian Military Highway. General Freitag, commanding along the line of the Sundja river, was able to prevent this. But Chechnia and Daghestan remained in enemy hands up to the Crimean War.

During the 1830's and 1840's, though Russia was at peace, her regular army was constantly engaged in fighting in the Caucasus. It was here that tens of thousands of officers and men got their military training. The role of the Caucasus for nineteenth-century Russia is thus not unlike that of the Indian Frontier for the British army. The Caucasus also inspired some of Russia's greatest writers. In this respect, it must be admitted, the impact of the Caucasus was greater than that of India. Pushkin's *Captive of the Caucasus*, Lermontov's *Hero of Our Time* and Tolstoy's *Hadji Murat* invite comparison with the works of Kipling.

During the middle years of the century the Russian hold over the Kazakh steppes was strengthened. Around 1840 each of the three Kazakh Hordes[1] numbered about half a million persons. They remained overwhelmingly pastoral and nomadic, but already some of the tribal chiefs were trying to convert tribal lands into personal property and to make peasants into their tenants. Russian traders were also making themselves felt, selling their own goods at high prices and buying Kazakh produce cheap, or lending money at exorbitant interest rates. Some Kazakhs were employed in gold mines or in other manual work by the Orenburg Cossacks. Social and national discontents arising from these causes account for the revolts of Isatay Taymanov from 1836 to 1838 and of Kenesary Kazymov from 1837 to 1847. The first was primarily a social movement against the demands of Kazakh rulers for taxes and tribute, but Russian troops were used to suppress it. The second was primarily anti-Russian. Kenesary, the grandson of a former khan of the Middle Horde, hoped to restore the old system and to make his territory independent of Russia.[2]

[1] See above p. 55.

[2] Recent Soviet historians concede that there were 'progressive elements' in Isatay's revolt but deny this merit to Kenesary's. To oppose Russian domination in the interest of an earlier tradition is 'reactionary'. 'Russia, in spite of the reactionary régime of Nicholas I, was at the same time the Russia of Belinsky, Herzen, Dobrolyubov, Chernyshevsky, the Russia of revolutionary democrats. Kenesary's movement occurred at the time when in Russia the peasantry was fighting with all its strength against the system of autocracy and serfdom. Could the feudal-monarchical movement of Kenesary have helped this struggle of the Russian peasantry? Of course it could not.' (E. B. Bekmakhanov, *Prisoedinenie Kazakhstana k Rossii*, Moscow, 1957, p. 115.) Kenesary, the same writer claims, was willing to accept the sovereignty of the khan of Khiva, who was an instrument of British policy. 'Capitalist England, pursuing its policy of colonization, was aiming at the conquest of the people of Central Asia and Kazakhstan and the establishment of its own colonial power. From the point of view of the general historical perspective of the development of the Kazakh people, the incorporation of Kazakhstan in the sphere of influence of England would have been the greatest disaster for its peoples.' (Ibid., p. 139.) It might perhaps be suggested that if Russia was the land of Belinsky and Herzen as well as of Nicholas I, England was the land of the Chartists and of Dickens as well as of Palmerston. The Soviet author anticipates this point by quoting a letter from Engels to Marx in 1863 [*sic*] to the effect that the English working class was under the influence of the *bourgeoisie*, as a result of the dominant position of England in world markets, and therefore was not a force of progress. Quite apart from the questionable judgements on both Russian and English history, this interpretation is remarkable for the fact that its criterion as to whether an Asian people should be entitled to its independence is not the wish of the people itself, but a subjective judgement by a later generation of the conquering people as to whether, at the time of the conquest, the conquering nation possessed more 'revolutionary democratic' thinkers or a more 'progressive' working class than another nation which might otherwise have conquered the country.

Beyond the Kazakh steppes lay Turkestan, a region of settled agricultural economy and ancient civilization. In the fifteenth century most of this region had been conquered by the Uzbeks, a Turkic people. The original population was mainly Iranian, its culture Persian. The Turkic language of the conquerors had been accepted by the people, but Persian remained beside it as the language of literature and polite society. In the nineteenth century the name 'Uzbek' was used primarily for the people of the countryside, while the town-dwellers were known as 'Sarts'—people of Turkic speech but Persian origin. The settled area of Turkestan was divided at this time among three sovereign khanates. From east to west, from the Chinese border to the Aral Sea, these were the khanates of Kokand, Bukhara, and Khiva. To the south-west of the Aral Sea, between it and the eastern shore of the Caspian, lived the Turcomans.

Russia was inevitably brought into contact with these states and peoples as her authority over the Kazakhs was strengthened. Disputes arose concerning Russian subjects (more often of Tatar than of Russian origin) maltreated by the subjects of the khans, or raids by the forces of Khiva or its neighbours on Russian-protected Kazakhs. There was some pressure on the Russian authorities from trading interests who sought secure access to Central Asian markets. Probably more important was Russian suspicion of the intentions of the British in India, whose influence extended, even if insecurely and irregularly, through Afghanistan to Bukhara and Khiva, and of Persia, which claimed some authority over the Turcomans, and was itself the object of rival Russian and British policies. The suspicions were, of course, reciprocated by the British and by the Persians.

Persian rulers were still concerned with the loss of two territories which they continued to feel were rightly theirs—Transcaucasia and Afghanistan. The first could be recovered only by British help against Russia, the second by Russian support against Britain. The British government in India preferred to maintain the existing Afghan state provided that it did not threaten British interests to the south, and thus showed no sympathy for Persian aspirations to recover the city and province of Herat. As the British were unwilling to help Persia in Transcaucasia and opposed Persian aims in Herat, the Persian government in the 1830's inclined rather to Russia than to

Britain. The British and Russian governments agreed to support Muhammad Mirza as successor to Fathali Shah, and when Fathali died in 1834, British troops helped Muhammad to assert his authority against a rival claimant. The new Shah was, however, determined to recover Herat, and in 1837 led an army against it in spite of strong British opposition but with encouragement from Russia. In the following year British forces occupied the island of Khar in the Persian Gulf, and the British minister left Tehran. The Russian government was not prepared to back Persia up to the point of hostilities with Britain. Nicholas I decided to accept the British view about Herat, and in December 1838 the Persian army abandoned the siege. When Britain was involved in war with Afghanistan in 1839, the Russian government made no attempt to embarrass British interests in Persia.

Consolidation of Russian positions in Central Asia, however, continued. In 1839 the governor of Orenburg, V. A. Perovsky, led an expedition against Khiva. This was a failure, not so much through Khivan resistance as because of the difficulty of the desert terrain and inadequate preparation of supplies and transport. Perovsky left Orenburg in 1842, but in the following years Russian advanced military bases were set up in the steppes—Turgai and Irgiz in 1845 and Raimsk on the Aral Sea in 1847. In 1851 Perovsky returned to Orenburg as governor-general, and in 1853 led an expedition 450 miles up the Syr Darya river from the Aral Sea to capture the fortress of Ak-Mechet in Kokand territory. This was renamed Perovsk and became the principal Russian base in the Aral Sea region. In 1854 a Russian column advanced south-west from Semipalatinsk and established a new fortified outpost at Vernoye which became the eastern base for the later movement into Turkestan.

In the 1840's new efforts were made to strengthen the Russian position in the Pacific. In 1841 the settlement at Fort Ross was abandoned, and the buildings and installations sold to Captain John Sutter for $30,000. But the Alaskan position was maintained. In 1843 Rear-Admiral E. V. Putyatin proposed to the Tsar that advantage should be taken of China's defeat by the Western Powers in the Opium War of 1839–42, and a new expedition sent to explore the mouth of the Amur river and to define Russia's frontier with China on the Pacific. Nicholas was sympathetic, but several years passed before anything was done. In 1847 N. N. Muravyov was appointed governor-general of eastern Siberia, and at once strongly supported exploration of the lower Amur. A special committee was set up by the Tsar in February 1849, and it authorized Captain G. I. Nevelskoy, who already had some experience of navigation in the area, to explore further. In July 1849 his ship entered the mouth of the Amur and found it navigable, and on 3 August he sailed through the straits between Sakhalin and the mainland, thus finally settling the question which had long puzzled geographers, as to whether Sakhalin was an island or a peninsula of Asia.

Nevelskoy was determined to establish the Russian flag at the river mouth, but Foreign Minister Nesselrode, anxious not to antagonize China or the European Powers, discouraged him. Nevelskoy took matters into his own hands, and on 13 August 1850 set up the settlement of Nikolayevskii Post at the river mouth. The Tsar then gave his consent on the ground that 'where once the Russian flag has flown, it must not be lowered again'. In April 1853 the Russian-American Company was instructed to administer Sakhalin and to appoint its own governor, who would be subject to the authority of the governor-general of eastern Siberia. Russian forces were landed at the south of the island in October 1853 but were withdrawn in June 1854. Muravyov succeeded in maintaining some interest in St. Petersburg for the Amur during the Crimean War. The river route was used to reinforce Kamchatka, whose garrison successfully resisted the attack of an Anglo-French naval squadron.

In August 1853 a Russian naval squadron under Admiral Putyatin visited Nagasaki. Following Admiral Perry's expedition, the Russian government was determined to secure for Russia rights equal to any granted to the United States or to any European Power. The Japanese were polite but vague, and in July 1854 Putyatin returned to Russian waters without any result.

The War with Turkey and Greek Independence

When Nicholas first turned his attention to Balkan affairs after his accession to the throne, he was primarily interested in the regions nearest to the Russian border. He told the Duke of Wellington, who attended the coronation ceremonies in St. Petersburg, that he had no sympathy for the Greek rebels and was little interested in the Greek problem. In March 1826, without informing Wellington, he sent an ultimatum to the Sultan, demanding the withdrawal of Turkish troops from Roumania and confirmation of the autonomy of Serbia. At the end of the month, however, the Tsar consented to discuss Greek affairs, and on 6 April the Anglo-Russian Protocol of St. Petersburg was signed. The two Powers agreed to mediate between the Sultan and the Greeks. They were to propose that Greece should have complete internal self-government, but should recognize Turkish suzerainty and pay a tribute to the Sultan. Metternich definitely refused to be associated with the protocol, but France adhered to it. It proved extremely useful to Russia since the fact that the three Powers were agreed on Greek affairs was an impressive warning to the Sultan not to oppose the specifically Russian demands of the March ultimatum. In May the Ottoman government accepted the Russian claims, and negotiations followed which led to the Convention of Akkerman, signed on 7 October 1826. This ensured far-reaching autonomy for the princes of Serbia, Moldavia, and Wallachia under Turkish suzerainty, and granted Russian ships the right to sail in Turkish waters and to pass the Straits.

During 1826 the situation in Greece itself was transformed by the arrival of Egyptian troops commanded by Ibrahim Pasha, son of the Sultan's vassal Mohammed Ali. These were the best soldiers in the Ottoman empire, and by the end of the year the Greek forces were in danger of destruction. In June 1826 Sultan Mahmud had also strengthened his position by exterminating the Janissaries, which for many years had been nothing but an unruly Pretorian Guard, of no use against the Sultan's enemies but a serious menace to his person. Faced with a truculent Sultan, a formidable Egyptian army, and a desperate Greece, the Russian, British, and French governments signed the Treaty of London on 6 July 1827. They thereby agreed to propose an armistice between the Turks and Greeks, which should give Greece complete self-government under Turkish suzerainty. The treaty contained a secret article to the effect that if the Turkish government should not accept an armistice within one month, the three Powers would appoint their own consular agents to the Greek authorities and would interpose their own forces between the belligerents. A tripartite naval force was sent to Greek waters. Its commander, Admiral Codrington, began negotiations with Ibrahim but reached no agreement. On 20 October, without specific authorization from the allied governments, Codrington opened fire on Egyptian ships in Navarino Bay, and the whole Egyptian fleet was destroyed. The danger to the Greeks was now much smaller, for although Ibrahim's army was still in the field, the allied navy cut him off from all supplies and reinforcements.

The news of Navarino, however, strengthened the Sultan's determination not to yield. He called the Moslem faithful to a Holy War, and formally repudiated the Akkerman Convention with Russia. Meanwhile Wellington, who had become premier in England, showed great reluctance to support the Greek cause or to weaken the Turks, though he could not repudiate the Treaty of London. The result was that action was left to Russia. Nicholas waited until the conclusion of war with Persia had permitted him to regroup his forces in the Caucasus and on 26 April 1828 he declared war on Turkey.

There were two distinct theatres of war, in the Balkans and in Transcaucasia. Considerably larger forces were used in the first, under Wittgenstein, than in the second, where Paskevich was in command.

In the first weeks the Russian armies quickly occupied all Moldavia and eastern Wallachia, and at the end of May they crossed the Danube. The fortress of Braila, on the west bank of the river, fell on 19 June, and by mid July the Russians had occupied the Dobrudja, the province lying between the Black Sea and the last north-eastern bend which the Danube makes before entering the sea. Advancing beyond the Dobrudja they found themselves obstructed by the two Turkish fortresses of Varna, on the coast, and Shumen, some fifty miles inland to the west, while Silistria, on the Danube some sixty miles north of Shumen, still held out. The siege of these three places occupied the Russian forces during the next months. Operations were not helped by the presence of the Tsar himself, who did not hesitate to interfere with contradictory and impracticable orders. On 12 October Varna fell, but Shumen and Silistria continued to resist.

In November the main Russian forces were withdrawn north of the Danube, leaving garrisons in Varna and in the Dobrudja.

Meanwhile in Transcaucasia Paskevich had been more successful. On 24 June the Black Sea port of Anapa surrendered after a combined land and sea attack by Russian forces. This freed Paskevich from the fear of operations by Circassians in his rear. He himself advanced on the Turkish fortress of Kars, controlling the main route from Transcaucasia into Asia Minor, and captured it on 5 July. He then turned north and stormed Akhalkalaki on 7 August. Turning westward he inflicted a serious defeat on the Turks near Akhaltzikhe, the principal remaining fortress threatening Transcaucasia, and stormed the city on 28 August. The main army then withdrew to winter quarters in Georgia, leaving garrisons in Akhaltzikhe and Kars.

In February 1829 Wittgenstein was replaced in command of the European theatre by General Diebitsch, who received large reinforcements. The first major Russian success of the year's campaigning was the capture of Silistria on 30 June. Diebitsch's main attention was, however, concentrated on the coastal sector. Between 17 and 19 July the Russians crossed the river Kamchyk, south of Varna, surprising and routing the Turkish forces, and within a week had passed the eastern end of the Balkan Mountains and captured the port of Burgas. The army's advance along the coast was supported by naval forces under Admiral Greig. Diebitsch's position was extremely exposed, for large Turkish forces remained in his rear at Shumen. He strengthened it by turning westward to defeat the Turks again at Sliven, before marching south to Adrianople. Greatly overestimating the Russian forces, and impressed by Diebitsch's rapid movements, the governor surrendered the city on 20 August. Peace negotiations began in Adrianople and were successfully concluded on 14 September.

Meanwhile, in the eastern theatre Paskevich resumed his offensive. Between 25 June and 2 July he crossed the difficult Soganli mountains, outmanœuvring his opponent and defeating numerically superior Turkish forces. On 9 July the important city of Erzurum surrendered. During July and August the Russians won some further successes in the area to the north, between Erzurum and the Black Sea. Still more victories were prevented by the conclusion of peace.

By the Treaty of Adrianople, Russia extended her European frontier with Turkey to include the southernmost branch of the Danube Delta, but otherwise restored to the Turks all territories that had been conquered in Europe. In Asia the districts of Akhalkalaki and Akhalkhitze were annexed, but all other territory was restored, to the great disappointment of the Armenian population, which was to suffer from its Turkish masters for the pro-Russian attitude it had shown during the war. The treaty confirmed the autonomy, under Ottoman suzerainty, of Serbia and of the Roumanian principalities. Russian troops were to be withdrawn from Roumania only when the Turks had paid an indemnity of 10,000,000 ducats. Navigation on the Danube was to be free, and Russia was to be able to trade freely in the territory of the Ottoman empire, the Black Sea, and the Straits. The Straits were to be open to the ships of all Powers that were at peace with Turkey.

In the summer of 1828 a French expeditionary force landed in Greece, unopposed by Ibrahim's army, which embarked for Egypt in October. The presence of French troops in Greece aroused much enthusiasm in France, both because it expressed the widespread Philhellene sentiments and because it was a symbol of the return of France to full stature as a Great Power. Russian influence in Greece was, however, symbolized by the election of Count John Capodistrias, once the intimate adviser of Alexander I,[1] as president by the Greek assembly. During the winter of 1828–9 the ambassadors of the three Powers in Constantinople discussed the boundaries of the future Greek state. Finally, the London Protocol of 3 February 1830 declared Greece an independent state, jointly guaranteed by Britain, France, and Russia. In October 1831 Capodistrias was murdered by a personal enemy, and the search for a suitable European prince as king of Greece was resumed. It was not until 1833 that the Bavarian Prince Otto came to Athens as the first king of modern Greece.

The Russians had made the greatest military contribution to

[1] Capodistrias, a native of the Ionian Islands, had entered Russian service in 1809, was a Russian delegate at the Congress of Vienna, and from 1816 to 1822 shared the duties of minister of foreign affairs with Nesselrode. His own account of his career in Russian service is in a memoir written by him in 1828, and published in *SIRIO*, vol. 3.

the liberation of Greece, but it was the two maritime, trading, and constitutional Powers—Britain and France—which acquired the greatest influence in the new state. Russia's main advantage from the war appeared to be her predominant position in Roumania and Serbia. Russian troops remained for the time being in Moldavia and Wallachia, but no attempt was made to incorporate either of the principalities in the Russian empire. In Serbia, Russian prestige was high, but geographical facts still made it necessary for Russia to reckon with Austrian influence.

Egypt, Turkey, and the Straits

A new phase opened in the Eastern Question—the complex of problems arising out of the rivalry of the Powers in relation to the Ottoman empire—at the end of 1832. Mohammed Ali, ruler of Egypt, considered that he had not been sufficiently rewarded for the help he had given the Sultan in the Greek war, and was determined to bring all Syria under his authority. By the end of July 1832 Egyptian forces, commanded by Ibrahim, had achieved this objective. The Sultan, however, refused to recognize the new situation, and Ibrahim decided to advance into Asia Minor. On 21 December he routed the Sultan's army at Konya, in the centre of Anatolia. There was now nothing to prevent the Egyptians from marching on Constantinople. The Sultan desperately sought the help of any foreign Power willing to defend him against his rebellious vassal.

The Power most friendly to Egypt was France, which since Napoleon's invasion of 1798 had established substantial economic and cultural influences, and had close relations with Mohammed Ali's régime. The British government, to which the Sultan first appealed for help, did not respond: the crisis of the Reform Bill was not long over, and Palmerston was preoccupied with Belgium and Portugal. A French proposal for joint Anglo-French intervention at Constantinople and Alexandria was declined. The Austrian government remained equally inactive. The Sultan was therefore forced to ask for Russian aid. This was quickly granted. On 20 February 1833 Russian ships arrived off the Turkish capital.

The Russian action was approved by the Austrian and Prussian governments, but alarmed both the French and the British. The French ambassador protested to the Turkish government against its dependence on Russia, and at the same time offered to obtain from the Egyptians terms which would be compatible with the Sultan's interests. However, the promise soon proved worthless, as Ibrahim was quite unwilling to make any concessions, and threatened to march on Constantinople. The Sultan therefore appealed to Russia for more help, and Russian troops were sent to reinforce the fleet. On 5 May Count A. F. Orlov arrived to negotiate a treaty with the Turkish government. Meanwhile Mohammed Ali, realizing that he could not fight the Sultan if he had Russian forces at his disposal, accepted, by the Peace of Kutahiya signed on 6 May 1833, extremely favourable terms. Mohammed Ali remained nominally the Sultan's vassal but now had authority over all Egypt and Syria, while the district of Adana was to be ruled by Ibrahim. In July the Russian forces were withdrawn from Turkish waters, and on 8 July a Russo-Turkish treaty was signed.

This treaty, known by the name of Unkiar Skelessi, was a treaty of alliance between the two Powers. If requested by the Turks, Russia would give armed assistance. Turkey, for her part, if requested by the Russian government, was committed to close the Straits to all foreign warships. The terms of the treaty soon became known to the other Powers. It was received with great indignation by the British ambassador, Lord Ponsonby, who had taken up his post in May. When he arrived he was already hostile to Russia: he soon also became a devoted champion of the Turks. In fact, however, the treaty was from the Russian point of view essentially defensive. The Russian government was not at this time interested in sending its warships out of the Black Sea into the Mediterranean: it wished only to prevent the naval Powers of the Mediterranean, Britain and France, from threatening Russia's vulnerable southern coast. The specific provisions about the Straits were defensive. But of course if Turkey became completely dependent on Russia, then a more dangerous situation could arise. If Russia could use Turkey as a satellite, to further Russian aims from Mesopotamia to the Aegean, British and French interests would be seriously threatened.

The two German Powers had no objection to Unkiar Skelessi.

In September 1833 Nicholas I, Francis I, and Crown Prince William of Prussia met at Münchengrätz. A secret convention was signed by Austria and Russia. Both agreed to support the integrity of the Ottoman empire and the existing dynasty, and to prevent Mohammed Ali from obtaining direct or indirect authority over any part of European Turkey. Should the Ottoman empire break up, the two governments would co-operate in establishing a new order such as would guard their own security and the balance of power in Europe. No precise plans for such an event were mentioned.

On 20 January 1834 the Russian and Turkish governments concluded a convention in St. Petersburg which provided for the evacuation of the Roumanian principalities by the Russian troops which remained there from the war of 1828–9. It also reduced substantially the sum of the indemnity which Turkey was still to pay to Russia. However, the terms of the convention alarmed Ponsonby in Constantinople, chiefly because it allowed Russian troops to be kept in Silistria for another eight years and because it involved a small frontier rectification in the Caucasus which brought Russia closer to Kars and to a caravan route between Persia and the Black Sea coast. Meanwhile, Palmerston had arranged with Ponsonby and with the British commander-in-chief in the Mediterranean that the British fleet could be summoned to the Sea of Marmora by the ambassador if he thought this necessary in order to defend Turkey against an imminent Russian danger. This power was actually used in May 1834.

During the next years Ponsonby succeeded in counterbalancing Russian influence in Constantinople. The Sultan was freed from sole dependence on Russia, and was able to manœuvre between Russia and Britain. It must be admitted, however, that Ponsonby's alarmist views of Russian aims were far in excess of the facts, and that Nicholas I at this time pursued a moderate policy. The same can hardly be said of Ponsonby, or of his friend the free-lance journalist and temporary diplomatic agent David Urquhart, who conducted a rather successful campaign in Britain on behalf of Turkey. His pamphlet *England, France, Russia and Turkey*, published in 1834, denounced Russian aims. His weekly paper *Portfolio*, which first appeared on 28 November 1835, argued the advantages of more extensive trade with

Turkey.[1] Another favourite theme of Urquhart's writings was the struggle of the Circassians against Russia. In the summer of 1834 he secretly landed near Anapa and met a number of Circassian chiefs. He later published in *Portfolio* a Circassian declaration of independence, which he had helped to draft. Early in 1836 he returned to Constantinople from London, and with the approval of Ponsonby persuaded a British shipping company, George Bell & Co., to send one of its schooners, *Vixen*, to trade on the Circassian coast at Sudjuk Kale. At this time the Russian government claimed that the Circassian coast was its territory, but the British government had not recognized the claim, while the Turkish government also claimed that the Sultan had some authority over the Circassians. Ponsonby and Urquhart reckoned that if the Russians seized *Vixen* this would cause a major conflict between Britain and Russia, which they desired, whereas if they took no action this could be used as an argument to show that Russia did not control the Circassian coast. *Vixen* was detained and confiscated by the Russians. Palmerston, however, did not wish a conflict with Russia. On 19 April he stated that, though Britain did not accept that the whole coast was under Russian authority, she did admit the right of the Russian government to make quarantine and customs regulations in regard to the port of Sudjuk Kale. It followed from this that the Russians had the right to confiscate *Vixen*, and Palmerston made no claim for compensation to the vessel's owners.

The Peace of Kutahiya did not restore friendly relations between Sultan Mahmud II and Mohammed Ali. The Egyptian ruler wished to make all his possessions hereditary, and even toyed with the idea of a new Arab empire under his dynasty. The Sultan was determined to reassert his authority, and reconquer at least Syria. The French government sympathized with the Egyptians. In these years British foreign policy as a whole was based on co-operation with the French. Palmerston, however, was not prepared to support Egypt.

[1] In the years 1832–6 the British balance of trade with Russia was unfavourable, with Turkey favourable (yearly average exports to Russia £2,300,000 and imports from Russia £4,000,000; exports to Turkey £2,700,000 and imports from Turkey £800,000). See article by G. H. Bolsover, 'David Urquhart and the Eastern Question 1833–37: a study in publicity and diplomacy', in *Journal of Modern History*, viii. no. 4 (Dec. 1936), pp. 444–67.

Mohammed Ali's case was put to him by the British representative in Alexandria, Colonel Campbell, but Ponsonby's passionate contrary opinion prevailed. Russia supported the Sultan, both because Russian influence was well established at Constantinople and because Nicholas I was bound to object to the policies of the revolutionary king, Louis-Philippe, and his protégé the rebellious Pasha. The Austrian government supported the Russian. At a meeting between the Russian and Austrian emperors at Teplitz in July 1838, both governments reasserted their opposition to Egyptian designs and their determination that if necessary the Treaty of Unkiar Skelessi should be carried out.

The Teplitz declaration displeased the British government which was at this time on bad terms with Russia as a result of the Persian-Afghan war for Herat.[1] In the summer Palmerston twice proposed that an international conference be held in London to examine the Turkish-Egyptian conflict. The Russian government refused on the ground that the Teplitz declaration had made its view absolutely clear already. In August 1838 the French government made some cautious overtures towards the Russians. It was clear that in a conflict between Britain and Russia, the French would take the British side. Yet, though favouring the Egyptians rather than the Turks, they were less hostile to Russian interests than were the British.[2] The Tsar made no response to these soundings. His distrust of Louis-Philippe was too profound.

During 1838 the Sultan tried to enlist British help. He needed naval support for his plans against Egypt, and only Britain could offer this. He also wished to reduce his dependence on Russia. On 16 August an Anglo-Turkish commercial treaty was signed. This promised the abolition of Ottoman monopolies, which were damaging to British business interests. As Mohammed Ali upheld the monopolies in his part of the Ottoman empire, the treaty gave Britain a certain interest in his downfall. Joint naval manœuvres were held by the British and Turkish fleets in the Mediterranean in the autumn. The Sultan also leased the port of Aden on the Red Sea to Britain, as a base for action against

[1] See above pp. 295–6.

[2] See Philip E. Moseley, *Russian Diplomacy and the Opening of the Eastern Question in 1838–1839* (Harvard, 1934), pp. 47–66.

Egypt. Reshid Pasha was sent to London to negotiate a treaty of alliance. However, the basic aims of the two governments were too different. The British government was not interested in supporting Turkish action against Egypt, and the Turkish government was unwilling to be pushed by the British into a definitely hostile attitude towards Russia. No treaty of alliance was made. Mahmud went ahead with his plans, and in April 1839 his forces invaded Syria. The Egyptians proved more than a match for them. On 24 June 1839 they routed the Turkish army at the Battle of Nezib.

Again some action had to be taken to prevent the destruction of the Ottoman empire by the Egyptians, and to prevent the development of a fatal cleavage between the Great Powers. In 1833 Britain and France had been aligned against Russia backed by Austria. In 1839 a different alignment occurred. This was due in part to growing disagreement between the British and French about Egypt and in part to the diplomatic efforts of the Russians. The Tsar seems to have come to the conclusion that, as neither Russia nor Britain had proved able entirely to dominate Turkey, it was better that they should co-operate with each other.[1] In September 1839 Nicholas sent Baron Brunnov to London on a special mission. He proposed that all the Powers should agree that the Straits be normally closed in peacetime against all foreign warships. If it were necessary for Russian forces to enter the Bosphorus in order to help the Sultan against Mohammed Ali, this would be a purely temporary action. Palmerston argued that if it were necessary for Russians temporarily to pass the Bosphorus, then British forces should also be allowed temporarily to pass the Dardanelles. Brunnov returned to St. Petersburg, and in December was back again in London, bringing the Tsar's consent to this suggestion. The discussions of the first half of 1840 were mainly concerned with the concessions which they were to offer to Mohammed Ali in return for his submission to the Sultan. He demanded the whole of Syria, and so did the Sultan. The most that the British and Russians were prepared to offer was less than the least that the French claimed on behalf of the Egyptians. In June the pro-Russian grand vizier, Husrev Pasha, was overthrown in Constantinople, and it seemed possible that French influence would

[1] This is convincingly argued by Moseley, op. cit., pp. 134–8.

prevail, and the Egyptians get better terms. At this point Palmerston proposed that the four Powers—Britain, Russia, Austria, and Prussia—should go ahead with their plans without consulting France.

A Four Power agreement was signed in London on 15 July 1840. The Powers were to offer terms to Mohammed Ali. If he rejected them, they would act against him 'according to the means of action of which each disposed'. British and Austrian naval forces would operate against the coasts of Egypt and Syria. If Constantinople were threatened by land, the Powers would unite to protect both the Bosphorus and the Dardanelles. This, however, would be a temporary and exceptional situation, and in the future the closure of the Straits against foreign warships would be upheld by the Sultan. As for the terms, Mohammed Ali was to be offered hereditary rule of Egypt, and rule over southern Syria including Acre for his lifetime only. If he had not accepted this offer within ten days, he would not be given southern Syria, and if he had not within a further ten days accepted the offer of Egypt alone, then the Sultan should consider himself released from it too.

Mohammed Ali did not accept these terms, and events took their course. There was a revolt against the Egyptians in Syria, and British and Austrian forces were landed in the Lebanon. After months of negotiation the Sultan was persuaded to recognize Mohammed Ali as ruler of Egypt by a *firman* of 22 May 1841. All his Syrian lands, and his hopes of an Arab empire, were lost. His defeat was also a defeat for France, which, diplomatically isolated and militarily outnumbered, had not dared to face war with the Powers.

Once the Egyptian crisis was over, the intention of the Powers to settle the Straits problem was carried out. This was a matter of general European interest, and the French government was therefore invited to participate and did so. The Straits Convention of 13 July 1841 was an agreement between the five European Powers and the Sultan. The first article stated:

> His Highness the Sultan on the one hand declares that he is firmly resolved to maintain the principle unchangingly established as an ancient rule of his empire, in virtue of which it has at all times been forbidden to warships of foreign Powers to enter the Straits of the Dardanelles and the Bosphorus, and that as long as the Porte is

at peace His Highness will admit no foreign warship to the said straits. And Their Majesties on the other hand undertake to respect this determination of the Sultan and to conform to the principle stated above.

The convention gave Russia security, and fulfilled the defensive function of the Treaty of Unkiar Skelessi, which now lapsed. It was not objectionable to the other Powers, as that treaty had been, because there was no question of Turkey being placed in a satellite relationship to Russia. Of course Russian security was not complete, since the convention did not cover a situation in which Turkey was at war. But states at war act as their interests dictate, and there would have been no point in trying to commit Turkey to renounce measures of self-preservation in wartime. If Turkey were at war with Russia in future, she would take her own decision as to whether to invite foreign warships into the Black Sea to help her. Thus it was still necessary for Russia to maintain a Black Sea fleet capable of defending her southern coast against naval forces stronger than those of Turkey alone. And the greater the superiority of the Russian over the Turkish fleet within the Black Sea, the greater the danger that Turkey might feel the need to ally herself with a Power hostile to Russia.

Nicholas I was well aware that the affairs of Turkey were not finally solved. There would be further troubles among both the Christian and the Moslem subjects of the Ottoman empire, and these would be likely to cause conflicts among the Great Powers. Knowing this, the Tsar made several attempts to reach agreements with the Powers most concerned, in order to plan common action beforehand. His distrust of France remained insuperable, but he consulted both the Austrian and the British governments. In September 1843 he had four conversations in Warsaw with Count Ficquelmont, a former Austrian ambassador to St. Petersburg.[1] In the event of a collapse of the Ottoman empire, all that he would wish to take was the Roumanian principalities. He would not tolerate any attempt to restore a Byzantine empire, nor could he accept any occupation or domination of

[1] He had had a similar conversation with Ficquelmont when the latter was serving as ambassador, in February 1833. For an account of these various conversations, see G. H. Bolsover, 'Nicholas I and the Partition of Turkey', in *The Slavonic and East European Review*, xxvii, no. 68 (1948), pp. 115–45.

Constantinople by the French or the British. But he did not wish himself to take Constantinople. He would prefer that Austria should have it. 'I shall never cross the Danube, and everything between this river and the Adriatic ought to be yours.'[1] In the second conversation he added that Austria should also have a bridgehead on the Asian side of the Straits. If the English took Egypt and divided the Greek islands between themselves and the French, he would have no objection. The Tsar also expressed the wish that these problems might be discussed at a meeting of the three eastern monarchs. Metternich's reaction was negative. He did not believe that the collapse of the Ottoman empire was imminent, and he did not favour an early meeting of the three monarchs. In March 1844 the Tsar sent Count A. F. Orlov to Vienna, and Turkish affairs were among the matters he was to discuss. This mission brought no results, and no meeting of the monarchs was held at this time.[2]

The negative response of the Austrian government probably contributed to Nicholas's decision to visit Britain in June 1844. On this occasion the British ministers agreed with the Tsar that the Ottoman empire should be upheld as long as possible, and that if it were on the point of collapse, the British and Russian governments should consult each other. Baron Brunnov, now Russian ambassador in London, drew up a memorandum summarizing the content of the conversations, and Lord Aberdeen, British foreign secretary, later wrote to Nesselrode confirming 'the accuracy of the statement'. It also appears that in conversation with the Tsar the prime minister, Sir Robert Peel, stressed Britain's interest in Egypt, and stated that 'too powerful a government there . . . could not be agreeable to England'.[3] These talks unfortunately did more harm than good, as the Tsar became convinced, not only that Peel and Aberdeen were willing to discuss Turkish affairs with him, but that their views, expressed in the memorandum and confirmed by the exchange

[1] Bolsover, loc. cit., p. 127. Full text of the document ibid., pp. 278–80.

[2] Metternich's views, expressed in a letter to his ambassador in Berlin of 23 Nov. 1843, are printed ibid., pp. 280–2. No account of Orlov's conversations in Vienna is available.

[3] The source for the conversations are the *Memoirs of Baron Stockmar* (London, 1872), ii. 107–9. The distinguished Soviet historian E. V. Tarle in his *Krymskaya voyna* (E. V. Tarle, *Sochineniya*, Moscow, 1959, viii. 103) sees fit to interpret it as a statement by Peel that he wished to annex Egypt. He also comments that British historians 'very carefully neglect Peel's words' (ibid., p. 106).

of letters, were constitutionally binding on the governments that would succeed them.

The European Revolutions

The next major European crisis occurred not in the Ottoman empire but in the West. On 24 February 1848 Louis-Philippe was overthrown by revolution in Paris. Nicholas I viewed this event with mixed feelings: he disliked revolution, but he was happy to see the end of the reign of Louis-Philippe, whom he had always regarded as a traitor to the monarchical cause. But worse was to follow. On 13 March revolution began in Vienna, and Metternich fell. On 15 March the Hungarian Diet in Pozsony[1] voted the 'March laws' which reduced Hungary's links with Austria to no more than personal union through the Habsburg dynasty. On 18 March there were riots in Berlin, and Frederick William IV promised concessions. At the end of March there were revolutions in Venice and Milan.

The danger which most alarmed the Tsar was that the new liberties granted in Austria and Prussia would permit the Poles to resume revolutionary action, and that this would affect the Polish subjects of the Russian empire. The centre of Polish revolutionary planning from the early 1830's had been the Polish Democratic Society in Paris. In February 1846 its emissary Mierosławski had gone to Prussian Poland to raise rebellion, but had been arrested. In Russian Poland there had been a minor outbreak at Siedlce, suppressed by the Polish peasants themselves. In Galicia there was a more serious attempt at a rising, led by the local gentry. However, it had been opposed by the greater part of the Polish peasants, and had turned into a bitter civil war, in which Polish peasants had killed Polish landlords and their agents and plundered Polish manors, while the Austrian authorities looked on. Kraków, a free city since 1815, became the scene of a struggle between rival Polish revolutionary factions between 18 and 25 February. This ended with the occupation of the city by Russian troops. On 11 November 1846 the Austrian government announced its annexation of Kraków.

[1] This is the Hungarian name. The old German name is Pressburg, and the modern Slovak name is Bratislava.

These events in 1846 had been disastrous for the Poles, but they had at least shown that revolutionary ideas could enlist support. The Polish cause had the support of the liberal intellectuals in both France and Germany, and in March 1848 these people seemed to be triumphing everywhere. To Nicholas I the talk of German-Polish friendship in Berlin, and of a war of liberation against Russia, was especially alarming. Mierosławski was released from his Berlin prison, and began to raise a Polish force in Poznania. For a moment a Franco-Prusso-Polish alliance, a new 1812, seemed a possibility. But the danger soon proved unreal. The new French government made no official statement about Poland, and in April the Prussian government declared all Polish institutions dissolved. There was a little fighting between Polish and Prussian troops, and on 9 May the Poles capitulated. In Galicia Polish action was even less impressive. The Austrian governor of Lwów, Franz von Stadion, made a gesture to the Polish peasants by abolishing labour services on his own initiative, and encouraged the Ukrainians to send a petition to the emperor stating their own national demands: both were shrewd moves to isolate the politically active Polish gentry. Disorders in Kraków were suppressed on 26 April by a brief bombardment. Much later in the year, workers set up barricades in Lwów, but were dispersed on 2 November by a bombardment which killed fifty-five persons. Throughout these months the Polish subjects of the Russian empire remained quiet.[1]

The rising tide of German nationalism, with which the king of Prussia was at least half-heartedly co-operating, threatened not only the Poles but the Danes. The inhabitants of the two duchies of Schleswig and Holstein, which formed part of the kingdom of Denmark, were Germans. In March 1848 they set up a Provisional Government in Kiel, which on 24 March declared that it would 'join in the movement for German unity and freedom'. The Danish authorities attempted to suppress the movement, and on 10 April Prussian troops entered Holstein. On 2 May they advanced into unquestionably Danish territory, the province of Jutland. Nicholas I protested strongly

[1] For good brief accounts of the Polish events of 1848 see Sir Lewis Namier, *1848: the Revolution of the Intellectuals* (1946) and R. F. Leslie, *Reform and Insurrection in Russian Poland* (1963), pp. 1–43.

to Frederick William IV, and Palmerston attempted to mediate between Danes and Germans. The Prussians evacuated Jutland in June, and an armistice was signed at Malmö on 26 August. The future of the two duchies was still undecided.

At the end of June a revolution took place in the Roumanian principality of Wallachia. On 23 June the prince appointed a revolutionary Provisional Government and then left the country. The Russian government was implacably opposed to the new régime. Russian troops occupied Moldavia in July. The Turkish government at first negotiated with the Wallachian leaders, but in September, urged on by the Russians, it sent an army under Fuad Pasha, in the face of which the rebel forces disintegrated. Russian troops also entered Wallachia. A new political settlement for the two principalities was fixed by a Russo-Turkish Convention signed at Balta Liman on 1 May 1849. The powers of the representative assemblies were reduced, and the principalities were to be jointly occupied by Russian and Turkish troops until the two governments were satisfied that they were 'pacified'. The two princes were to be assisted by a Russian and a Turkish commissar, attached to their respective courts. The result was that the unsuccessful revolution had, in fact, led to yet another Russian occupation of Roumania.[1]

Thus in 1849 Russian troops were on the southern as well as the eastern border of Hungary. The Turkish government wished to adopt a neutral attitude to events in the Habsburg Monarchy. The Russian commander, however, disregarded Turkish neutrality, and in February 1849 marched into the two Transylvanian cities of Sibiu (Hermannstadt) and Brașov (Kronstadt), allegedly at the request of their inhabitants, German communities established in this area since the thirteenth century, who felt their interests threatened by the Hungarian revolutionaries. The Russian forces were withdrawn within a month, but Nicholas I continued to regard Hungarian events with alarm.

The personal union between Hungary and Austria, embodied

[1] For a brief discussion of the events in Roumania see Radu, R. N. Florescu, *The Struggle against Russia in the Roumanian Principalities 1821–1854*, published by Societas Academica Dacoromana, Munich, 1962, pp. 179–248. They are treated in greater detail in *Istoria Romȃniei*, vol. 4.

in the March Laws of the Pozsony Diet, had been rejected both by the emperor and by the Constituent Assembly which met in Vienna in July 1848. Meanwhile the Hungarian government was in conflict with its Croatian, Serbian, Roumanian and Slovak subjects. The most dangerous of these was the governor of Croatia, Baron Jelačić, who was able to raise an efficient army and led it across the Drava into Hungary proper on 7 September. A revolution by the left in Vienna in favour of the Hungarians on 6 October brought only a short respite. The emperor fled to Olmütz in Moravia, the Constituent Assembly to Kremsier, but by the end of October Vienna had been recaptured. On 21 November Prince Felix Schwarzenberg became prime minister, and on 2 December the young Archduke Franz Joseph became emperor in place of his uncle. During the winter the Hungarians held out against their enemies, but the struggle brought increasing bitterness and radicalism. On 14 April 1849 the National Assembly, sitting in Debrecen, declared the Habsburg dynasty deposed, and elected the nationalist leader Louis Kossuth as Ruler of Hungary.[1]

Both the ideas and the actions of the Hungarians were thoroughly objectionable to Nicholas I. He was impressed by the fact that the Hungarian armies had among their commanders Polish revolutionaries. It was not so much that he feared disorders, either in Galicia or in Russian Poland, as that he considered the presence of the Poles as evidence of an international conspiracy against Russia. The physical centre of the European revolutionary movement at this time appeared to be Hungary, a country which bordered on his own lands, and to whose sovereign he had ties of traditional friendship. As he wrote to Paskevich on 25 April 1849, he was moved not only by a wish to help Austria but also by 'the duty to defend the security of the boundaries of the Russia entrusted to me by God . . . for in the Hungarian rebellion are clearly visible the efforts of a general plot against all that is sacred, and especially against Russia, for at the head of the rebellion, and acting as the main instruments of it, are our eternal enemies, the Poles'.[2]

[1] The Hungarian word used—*kormányzó*—is sometimes translated as governor, sometimes as regent. Neither word seems suitable to me, as each has a distinct meaning, inappropriate to this situation.

[2] Prince Shcherbatov, *General fel'dmarshal knyaz' Paskevich, ego zhizn' i deyatel'nost'* (SPB, 1888–9), vi. 281.

Nicholas would not act until he received a direct request from the Austrian government. The young emperor, advised by Schwarzenberg, was reluctant to invoke foreign aid. But his own forces were clearly failing to crush the Hungarians, and he saw no other way. On 1 May he wrote personally to the Tsar asking for Russian military aid. At this time he had not yet received the news of the deposition of his dynasty by the Debrecen Assembly.[1] At the end of May a convention was signed which provided for the co-operation of the Austrian civil authorities with the Russian army. In June the Russians entered Hungary, and on 1 August the main Hungarian army under Görgey surrendered to them. It was not a difficult war. The Russians lost only about 1,000 dead in fighting, though disease killed more than ten times as many. There were no diplomatic complications: the European governments were glad to see the Hungarians defeated, and by this time European democracy was powerless. Nicholas treated the surrendering Hungarians honourably, and was disgusted by the savage reprisals of the Habsburg General Haynau.[2] However, he did not wish those Poles who were Russian subjects to escape, and therefore demanded that those who had taken refuge in Turkey should be extradited. The Austrian government also demanded the extradition of about 4,000 Hungarians. The Sultan refused, and the two Powers broke off diplomatic relations. The Turks appealed for help to the British ambassador, Stratford Canning, and Palmerston sent a British naval squadron to Besika Bay. Meanwhile the Sultan had sent Fuad Pasha to St. Petersburg. Whether he was influenced by the personal letter from the Sultan which Fuad brought, or had simply decided that it was not worth making a major European crisis over a matter in which European opinion as a whole was against him, Nicholas decided to withdraw his demand for extradition, and the crisis came to an end.

[1] The letter is reproduced in a collection of documents edited, with a long introductory essay, by Erzsébet Andics, entitled *A Habsburgok és románok szövetsége*, Budapest, 1961. It is on pp. 373–4, Nicholas's reply on pp. 388–9. The editor gives her views on the Tsar's motives on pp. 168–74.

[2] When Paskevich complained about the Austrians, the Tsar replied: 'I completely share your opinion of the behaviour of the Austrian Government: its dishonesty is being ever more clearly revealed.' (Letter of 3 Nov. 1849, printed in Shcherbatov, op. cit. vi. 344.)

The Sick Man of Europe

The failure of the European revolutions increased Russian prestige, and strengthened Nicholas's self-confidence. Russia and Britain were the only countries in which revolution had not for a time triumphed. Russia had stood alone on the Continent against the flood, had prevailed, and had saved Europe. To men of liberal or radical views Russia was the supreme enemy. They hated her, but they respected her, and recognized that she was indeed the greatest European Power. Yet both the Tsar and his enemies overrated Russia's strength. Her economy was still backward, her communications still wretched, and her people still serfs. Within a few years the illusions were exposed.

Meanwhile, the Tsar made himself felt. He objected strongly to the resumption of hostilities by Prussia against Denmark in April 1849. On 10 July Prussia had to make an armistice with the Danes, and peace was signed on 2 July 1850. The Russian government also supported the reassertion of Danish authority over the two duchies, which was confirmed by the Treaty of London of 8 May 1852.

In the political conflict between Austria and Prussia for the leadership of Germany, which continued through 1849 and 1850, Nicholas supported Austria. He disliked the tendency of the king of Prussia to flirt with the nationalists and democrats and preferred the resolutely conservative attitude of Franz Joseph and Felix Schwarzenberg. In November 1850, when the conflict was at its height, the Russian government placed four army corps in Poland on a war footing. Russian diplomatic intervention brought about the meeting of Schwarzenberg and Manteuffel in Olmütz, which ended in the political capitulation of the Prussians, and in effect a restoration of the system of 1815.[1]

His increased self-confidence made Nicholas eager to advance Russian interests in the Ottoman empire.

Both the Austrian and the French government obtained concessions from the Turks at the beginning of the 1850's. The

[1] The best documentary source for Russian policy in the German problem in 1848–50 is *Peter von Meyendorff, ein russischer Diplomat an den Höfen von Berlin und Wien —politischer und privater Briefwechsel* (ed. O. Hoetzsch, Leipzig, 1923), vol. ii. For a recent discussion see W. E. Mosse, *The European Powers and the German Question 1848–1871* (1958), ch. 1. A. J. P. Taylor, *The Struggle for Mastery in Europe 1848–1918* (1954), pp. 36–45, covers the same ground.

Austrians were alarmed by the brutal repression of an insurrection in Bosnia by Ömer Pasha in 1850 and by a Turkish invasion of Montenegro in 1852. Count Leiningen was sent to Constantinople in February 1853 to insist on the evacuation of Montenegro and the dismissal of Ömer. He obtained satisfaction within a few days. The Austrian demands had had Russian support.

The French demand, by contrast, was in conflict with Russian interests. Louis Napoleon, in search of prestige for France and popularity for himself, sought from the Sultan privileges for the Catholics at the Holy Places in Jerusalem, which could only be granted at the expense of the Orthodox. The intrigues of the priests in the Levant became a matter for a prestige conflict between France and Russia. By the end of 1852 the French were doing better than their rivals. Relations between the two Powers were not improved when, after Louis Napoleon had proclaimed himself Emperor Napoleon III in December 1852, the Tsar refused to address him as 'brother', though the other monarchs of Europe were willing to do so.

Nicholas wished to have the consent of Britain to his own aims. Aberdeen was now prime minister, and the Tsar believed that he was bound by the conversations of 1844. In January 1853 he spoke to the British ambassador, Sir Hamilton Seymour, of his desire to reach agreement with the British government on the disposal of the Turkish empire before this event occurred. He referred to Turkey as 'a sick man', and on another occasion said that 'the bear is dying'. Seymour had four conversations with the Tsar between January and April. In one of them, Nicholas made specific suggestions. He did not wish to take Constantinople, but would not consent to its being taken by any other Great Power or by an enlarged Greek state. Serbia and Bulgaria might be given the same status as the Roumanian principalities, which were 'in fact an independent state under my protection'. Egypt, and perhaps also Crete, might go to Britain. Seymour reported these talks to London, but the British government would not be drawn. Clarendon, the foreign secretary, told Seymour that Britain desired no gains of territory, and he expressed no opinions as to the likelihood of the 'sick man's' demise. On the other hand he expressed on behalf of the government the wish that Britain and Russia should co-operate in upholding the independence and integrity of Turkey.

Certainly Nicholas was not given the impression that Britain was hostile to him.

In February 1853 Prince A. S. Menshikov, one of the Tsar's closest circle, arrived in Constantinople on a special mission. Essentially, his task was to reassert Russian predominance at the expense of French. He was to obtain the repeal of the privileges granted to the Latins at the Holy Places and to claim for Russia a protectorate over the Orthodox subjects of the Sultan. This claim was based on a questionable interpretation of the Treaty of Kutchuk Kainardji of 1774. Menshikov scored a first success at the expense of the grand vizier, Fuad Pasha, who had granted the privileges to the Latins: by publicly insulting him, he forced him to resign. On 5 April Stratford Canning (now Viscount Stratford de Redcliffe) returned to Constantinople.[1] He used his influence to bring about an agreement on the Holy Places. This was achieved by a protocol of 4 May, signed by Menshikov and the French ambassador. Menshikov, however, made the further demand of a new treaty between Russia and Turkey, which should guarantee the right of the Russian government to protect the Orthodox subjects of the Ottoman empire. This the Turks refused as a dangerous infringement of their sovereignty. In their refusal they were supported by Stratford, but they would have refused even without him.[2] Menshikov was unable to get his way, and after several delays he left Constantinople on 21 May. Diplomatic relations between Russia and Turkey were broken. On Menshikov's return Nicholas decided to

[1] He had left in June 1852, after the failure of his attempts to get the Sultan to carry out a programme of reforms.

[2] The role of Stratford is still a subject of keen controversy. It is not possible in a general survey to discuss the details of this very complicated question. The most thorough treatment by an English historian is H. V. Temperley, *England and the Near East: the Crimea* (1936). The distinguished Soviet historian, the late Professor E. V. Tarle, in his *Krymskaya voyna*, takes a diametrically opposite view. He asserts that Stratford came back with the intention to arrange war with Russia, and that he advised the Turks to yield in the Holy Places conflict merely in order to make the other demands of Menshikov appear by contrast more aggressive. Tarle sees fit to describe Temperley's version as 'an impudent lie' (op. cit., p. 183). He also asserts that Stratford was sent by Palmerston, then home secretary in Aberdeen's Cabinet, who 'was managing all foreign affairs. Clarendon was simply a pawn in his hands.' In Tarle's view Temperley deliberately ignores the 'double book-keeping' of Palmerston and Aberdeen (op. cit., p. 185). Aberdeen's pacific and Palmerston's belligerent attitude were an elaborate pretence. The two men played their roles in agreement with the aim of deceiving the Tsar and trapping him in a disastrous war.

occupy the Roumanian principalities. On 2 July 1853 Russian troops crossed the Prut.

The Crimean War

The demands of Menshikov had alarmed both the British and the French governments. On 2 June the British fleet was brought to Besika Bay, and a French fleet arrived some days later. But neither Aberdeen nor Napoleon wished to plunge into action. An attempt was made to solve the crisis by diplomacy. On 1 August the British, French, Austrian, and Prussian governments agreed to proposals, drafted by the Austrian foreign minister, Count Buol, and known as the Vienna Note. They were accepted by the Russian government, but rejected by the Turks, who considered that they would create a Franco-Russian protectorate over the Christian subjects of their empire. They proposed amendments, which were rejected by the Russians. On 7 September Nesselrode made a statement which showed that he interpreted the original terms of the Vienna Note to confirm a Russian protectorate over the Orthodox. Turkey must, in Nesselrode's view, 'take account of Russia's active solicitude for her co-religionists in Turkey'. This was described by Clarendon as a 'violent interpretation' of the Vienna Note. The British and French governments decided to bring their fleets through the Dardanelles.

This action was, however, postponed while Nicholas I and Franz Joseph met at Olmütz on 26 September. The Tsar displayed great moderation and willingness to consider the interests of Turkey and of all the other Powers. As a result of the meeting Buol prepared yet another version of the Vienna Note. Napoleon's reaction was favourable. But the British government feared that there was a plan for the partition of Turkey between Russia and Austria, and that a reconstituted Holy Alliance would act against British interests in the Near East. The British government rejected Buol's proposals and ordered the fleet to pass the Dardanelles. Napoleon followed the British lead. The Turkish government declared war on Russia on 8 October. On 23 October Ömer Pasha sent troops across the Danube at Tutrakhan, and the first fighting between Russians and Turks began.

During 1853 the main theatre of war was the Danube, and there was a second front on land in the Caucasus. In the Black Sea the Russian fleet was stronger than the Turkish. The only considerable battle in the Danube theatre during these months was at Cetate near Craiova on 25 December. A force of 7,000 Russians were engaged by much larger Turkish forces, and had heavy casualties, but the result of the battle was inconclusive.[1] On the Caucasus front on 26 November Prince Andronikov successfully resisted an attack on Akhaltsikhe by a much larger Turkish army commanded by Ali Pasha. On 30 November General Bebutov defeated the army of the Turkish commander-in-chief in Anatolia, Ahmed Pasha, at Başgedikler. But the most important act of war in this period was the naval battle of Sinope on 30 November. The Russian Admiral P. S. Nakhimov surprised the Turkish fleet in the harbour and destroyed it. This was a perfectly legitimate naval operation, and revealed the skill of Nakhimov and the incompetence of the Turkish naval command. But it was denounced in Britain as a 'massacre' and led to increased pressure of public opinion for war. Apart from any real or imaginary cause for moral indignation, the establishment of complete Russian mastery of the Black Sea was alarming to Britain and France. On 12 January 1854 the British and French governments officially informed Nesselrode that their fleets had passed the Bosphorus and were operating in the Black Sea. Nicholas still hoped for the benevolent neutrality of Austria, and sent Count Orlov to Vienna in January. The mission failed. On 27 February the two Western Powers gave the Tsar an ultimatum: he was to evacuate the principalities within two months. He ignored the demand, and war was formally declared before the time was up, on 28 March 1854.

The Crimean War was the result of miscalculations and muddle rather than of deliberate aggression by any party. Napoleon's need for prestige, to strengthen his internal position in France, was an important factor. Because the prestige was sought at the expense of Russia, the Tsar determined to reassert himself at the expense of France. The hesitations of Aberdeen misled Nicholas: if the Tsar had understood British institutions better, or if the tougher Palmerston had been in charge of British foreign policy in 1853, things might conceivably have

[1] Tarle, op. cit., pp. 273–9.

been different. Nevertheless, real issues were involved. Though Nicholas did not intend to destroy Turkey immediately, the Menshikov demands indicated a policy of much more extensive Russian intervention in Turkish affairs. This had to be taken seriously in London: if Turkey were to be turned into a Russian satellite, Russia would before long emerge as a dangerous naval Power in the eastern Mediterranean. In both Britain and France a large section of public opinion was bitterly hostile to Russia. The reason for this was essentially ideological. Nicholas was hated as the 'gendarme of Europe', the commander-in-chief of all the reactionary forces which in 1849 had prevailed against the forces of liberty. Any action by the Tsar was sure to be regarded with greater suspicion than any action by another government. This ideological factor contributed to the making of the war, and it remained important during the fighting. Finally, even those who had no sympathy for any sort of liberalism were impressed by the apparent might of Russia. The failure of revolution in 1849 had caused the Tsar to overrate his strength and to act more boldly in Europe: it had also caused the European governments to overrate him. Since 1849 the balance of power had appeared to be upset. Russia appeared to dominate the Continent, a state of affairs to which even conservative British politicians traditionally objected. It can be argued that the Western Powers entered the war to raise Napoleon's prestige, to protect Turkey, to fight tyranny, or to restore the balance of power. Of these four reasons the last was the most important.

The strategic situation for Russia was now quite different. The land fronts on the Danube and in the Caucasus remained. The uncertain attitude of Austria, and even of Prussia, which kept close to Austria, made it necessary to maintain large forces on the western borders of the empire. Command of the Black Sea vanished as soon as the Western fleets came through the Bosphorus. More than that, all the coasts of Russia were vulnerable to enemy sea-power. This was true of such remote regions as the Arctic and the north Pacific. Much more important was the Baltic: large armies had to be kept to guard the approaches to St. Petersburg. The possibility of a Swedish attack on Finland also had to be borne in mind. Russia had a huge population, but her internal communications were extremely poor. Though the allies were operating a long way from home, their sea communications gave them good mobility.

In January 1854 Nicholas appointed the veteran Paskevich as commander-in-chief of all Russian forces in the west. He advised the Tsar to evacuate the principalities, on the grounds that there was nothing to be done there, no significant help could be expected from the Bulgarian population beyond the Danube, and the attitude of Austria was uncertain. The Tsar, however, decided to continue. At the end of April the Russian army began the siege of Silistria. On 28 May a major assault was repelled by the Turks, with heavy casualties for the Russians. Prince Michael Gorchakov, in command of the army of the Danube, planned a final assault for 21 June. But in the night orders arrived from the Tsar to raise the siege, and the army retired across the Danube.

The political class in both Austria and Prussia was divided between supporters and opponents of Russia. The king of Prussia talked of his solidarity with Russia against revolution. Franz Joseph too was afraid of revolution, especially in his Italian dominions. However, Austria had aims in the Balkans, and these conflicted with Russian aims. Besides, as long as Napoleon was occupied in war with Russia, he could not give Austria any trouble in Italy. Austria and Prussia remained neutral, and signed an alliance with each other on 20 April 1854. However, this neutrality proved more damaging to Russia than to the Western Powers. On 3 June the Austrian government formally requested that Russian troops be evacuated from the principalities. While the Tsar hesitated, the Austrians concluded a convention with the Turkish government on 14 June, by which Wallachia was to be occupied jointly by Austrians and Turks, and Moldavia by Austrians alone. To Nicholas the Austrian demand seemed a monstrous act of ingratitude by the monarch whom he had saved in 1849.

It is of course arguable that the Austrian presence in the principalities benefited the Russians: if it prevented them from marching into European Turkey, it also protected the Ukraine from a joint counter-offensive by the Western and Turkish armies. However, it seemed highly possible that the Austrians intended to remain in Moldavia and Wallachia. The principalities were at least potentially a centre for agitation among the Roumanian subjects of the Habsburgs across the Carpathians, and this seemed a good chance for the Vienna government to put an end to the risk. Moreover, if the Roumanian population within the monarchy were increased, this would provide, from the Vienna government's point of view, a useful counterweight to the basically unreliable and turbulent Hungarians. But from the Russian point of view, it was intolerable that the Austrians should acquire lands which, at least since 1810, had been regarded as part of the Russian share in any conceivable partition of Turkey.

Nevertheless, for the present the Tsar was not prepared to go to war with Austria in addition to his existing enemies. On 8 August the Russian ambassador in Vienna, Prince Alexander Gorchakov, formally announced Russia's withdrawal from the principalities. Austrian troops entered Wallachia soon afterwards. Meanwhile the French and Austrian governments had been discussing a programme which could be put to Russia as conditions of peace. These were reduced to Four Points, accepted on 8 August by the French, Austrian, and British governments. The status of Moldavia, Wallachia, and Serbia was to be regulated by a general European guarantee, in place of a Russian protectorate. There was to be freedom of navigation on the Danube. The Russian government was to abandon the claim to a protectorate over the Orthodox subjects of the Sultan, and their rights were to be guaranteed by the Turkish government. The Straits Convention was to be revised 'in the interests of the balance of power in Europe'. Only the last of these raised difficulties. On 26 August the Russian government rejected the Points.

The first warlike contact between the Western and Russian forces was in the Baltic. Admiral Napier reconnoitred Hangö in the Gulf of Finland in April, and returned to bombard it briefly on 20 May. On 13 June he was joined by a French squadron under Admiral Parseval, and they cruised around Kronstadt at the end of the month, deciding that its defences were too strong for an attack. The Swedish government could not be persuaded to join the allies. It would only consider attacking Finland if Austria should go to war with Russia and engage the Russian armies on land. All that the allied fleet could find to do was to attack a Russian garrison in the Åland Islands. The fortress of Bomarsund was taken by greatly superior French forces on 16 August. This success did not cause the Swedes to change their minds. At the end of September the Anglo-French fleet left the Baltic. Nevertheless, their efforts had not been entirely wasted, for the danger of attack in the north kept about 200,000 Russian troops immobilized in the Baltic area.

On 23 August British ships attacked and destroyed the settlement of Kola on the Arctic coast. A few days later, half way across the world, an Anglo-French squadron attacked the Russian garrison at Petropavlovsk in Kamchatka. There was fierce fighting from 1 to 8 September, but the Russians held out and the allied squadron sailed away.

In the summer of 1854 there was more activity on the Caucasus front. On 15 July Andronikov drove the Turks out of a fortified position on the Cholok river and forced them back to Batum. At the other end of the front General Vrangel, advancing from Erivan, captured Bayazit on 31 July. The most important battle of the year on the Caucasus front was at Kurudere, on the road between Alexandropol and Kars. Here on 5 August General Bebutov defeated the main Turkish army of the Caucasian theatre, commanded by Mustafa Zarif Pasha. The Turks lost 8,000 dead and wounded and 2,000 prisoners, the Russians 3,000 casualties. Mustafa Zarif retired to Kars, but Bebutov's forces were too small to pursue him, and retired to their base at Alexandropol. The Russian victory induced the Persian government to conclude a convention with Russia promising neutrality.

In June the forces of the Western allies began to land on the Bulgarian coast. Varna became the headquarters of the French and British commanders-in-chief, Marshal St. Arnaud and Lord Raglan. In July there were about 20,000 British and 40,000 French troops. The question was, how best to use the command of the sea and the available forces. At the end of June a delegation from the Imam Shamil visited St. Arnaud and proposed a joint attack on Anapa. Possibly a combination of landings on the Circassian coast, risings in the Caucasus, and a Turkish offensive on land might have achieved some results. The alternative was to attack the Crimea. This was not to the liking of the naval chiefs. However, to the governments in both London and Paris a blow at the centre of Russian naval power,

Sevastopol, seemed from both the strategic and political points of view the best answer, and the definite decision was taken at the end of June. No major action was to be taken in Circassia.

The landing began near Eupatoria on 14 September. The total allied army was about 60,000 men, of whom 25,000 were French, 27,000 British and the rest Turks. The Russian forces available in the Crimea were between 50,000 and 60,000. They were commanded by Prince Menshikov. The allies quickly began their advance southward along the coast. On 20 September they met Menshikov's army in a strong position on the heights behind the Alma river. In the Battle of the Alma about 35,000 Russians and 57,000 British and French were engaged. After very heavy fighting the allies drove the Russians from their positions. The allied casualties were more than 3,000, the Russian nearly 6,000.

After the Battle of the Alma the whole Russian position was in danger. The main Russian army had been defeated, and the fortifications of Sevastopol were weak. If the allies had advanced rapidly the city could hardly have resisted. Fortunately for the Russians, the allied command did not know how weak its enemy was. The troops rested for two days, and when the advance was resumed it was decided not to attack the north side of Sevastopol but to make a flank march to the east, cross to the south coast of the peninsula, take the small harbour of Balaklava, in which it would be possible to receive supplies, and then attack Sevastopol from the south. The march was successfully concluded by 26 September. Meanwhile Menshikov had left Sevastopol and taken up his position on the Belbek river to the north-east.

The Russians lost no time in fortifying Sevastopol. This task was directed by General Totleben, a military engineer of exceptional brilliance. He made excellent use of the terrain, and constructed a series of forts and bastions linked by ramparts. The strongest position in the whole system was the famous Malakhov fort. The city was defended by both army and naval units. On 17 and 18 October the allies conducted a heavy bombardment. The Russians guns continued to reply, and the allies did not follow up the bombardment with an attack. The effective command of the city's defences for the next eight months was held by Admiral Nakhimov, the outstanding figure in the whole siege, a man who apart from his high professional ability also commanded to an extraordinary degree the devotion of his men.

The first major attack on the allied forces by the Russian land army came on 25 October. General P. P. Liprandi captured some positions held by Turkish troops and advanced towards Balaklava. The situation was saved by a counter-attack led by General Scarlett. At this point the incompetence and personal jealousies in the British command led not only to the loss of the opportunity to pursue and defeat the enemy but also to the disastrous 'Charge of the Light Brigade'.

The second and more important Russian attack came ten days later. By this time Menshikov had received reinforcements which brought up his strength to more than 100,000 and gave him a superiority of about three to two over the allies. On the morning of 5 November a Russian attack, under cover of mist, surprised the British position on the Inkerman heights to the east of the city. The British held out for four hours, by which time their effective strength had been reduced by about a half. The arrival of French forces under General Bosquet relieved the situation, but these were in turn surprised by another Russian attack. At this point the Russian commanders, General P. A. Dannenberg and Prince P. D. Gorchakov, held huge forces in reserve. If they had used them, the allies would have suffered a disaster. As it was, the allies recovered the lost ground, and the Russians were ordered to retreat. The Battle of Inkerman, a series of extremely confused and largely disconnected engagements, thus ended as a clear allied victory. Russian casualties were nearly 11,000 and allied about 4,000 of which two-thirds were British.

After the Battle of Inkerman both sides settled down to a long siege. The conditions in the allied camp were extremely painful. The troops suffered from food shortages, and disease claimed many victims. The achievement of Florence Nightingale and its long-term effects on both military and civil hospitals in England are well known. But the Russians had similar problems, and the siege of Sevastopol was a landmark in the history of Russian medical organization. Two individuals were mainly responsible for improving the hospitals and the care of the wounded. One was the great surgeon N. I. Pirogov, who was in charge of the hospitals in Sevastopol right through the siege. The other was

Grand Duchess Elena Pavlovna, widow of Grand Duke Michael and sister-in-law to the Tsar, who founded and organized the Community of the Elevation of the Cross, the first Russian nursing sisters to serve in the war zone. There were 250 Russian nurses serving in Sevastopol under Pirogov, among them Elena Pavlovna's lady-in-waiting Baroness Raden.

Meanwhile diplomatic negotiations continued. On 29 November the Russian government accepted the Four Points. On 2 December 1854 Austria signed an alliance with the Western Powers which contained the rather vague provision that if peace were not made by the end of the year on the basis of the Four Points the three governments would deliberate as to 'the best means of securing the object of their alliance'. The allies could not agree on the interpretation of the third of the Points, concerning the Straits. The British wished to demolish Russian fortresses on the Black Sea coast and to limit Russia's Black Sea fleet drastically. The Austrians were content with the vague aim that 'Russian predominance in the Black Sea should be brought to an end'. On 7 January 1855 the Russian ambassador in Vienna, Prince A. M. Gorchakov, accepted the Austrian interpretation.

Before the diplomatic conference met in Vienna, Aberdeen's government had fallen, Palmerston had become premier on 6 February, and Nicholas I had died on 2 March. Shortly before his death the Tsar had received the news of the failure of a land attack on Eupatoria. The port was held by Turkish troops, but they held out, with support from allied naval guns. Nicholas's reign ended in unrelieved gloom: all that he had thought he had achieved in thirty years seemed on the point of collapse. It has been suggested that he committed suicide.[1] Perhaps it would be more correct to say that he had lost the will to live, so that his powerful frame was destroyed by a minor illness.

The conference opened in Vienna on 15 March and dragged on, with periodic adjournments, until 4 June, when Gorchakov finally broke off the negotiations. Essentially, the allies demanded the destruction of Russian naval power, and as long as Sevastopol held out the Russians refused to accept this.

In March 1855 allied naval forces, acting in conjunction with Circassians on the mainland, captured the small port of

[1] This is discussed at some length in Tarle, *Sochineniya*, ix. 316–26.

Novorossiisk. A Circassian chief named Sefer Bey, who had come from Constantinople with them, established himself with a small force on the Taman Peninsula but was unable to achieve anything more.

In the main theatre of war the first important action in the summer was the capture by the allies from the sea of the port of Kerch. On 7 June the French captured two important forts in the Sevastopol defences after heavy fighting. On 18 June, the fortieth anniversary of the Battle of Waterloo, chosen as a demonstration of Anglo-French solidarity, the allies launched a general assault on Sevastopol. It was badly co-ordinated. One of the French generals mistook an explosion for the signal to begin the attack and started before the others were ready. The French entered the Malakhov Redoubt, but the other positions were not taken, and a general retreat was ordered. Casualties on both sides were very high. Two weeks later the Russians suffered an irreparable loss: Admiral Nakhimov was killed when he exposed himself to enemy fire while inspecting one of the forts.

General M. D. Gorchakov, who had replaced Menshikov as commander-in-chief in February, considered the position was now hopeless. He was, however, persuaded by the Tsar to make a last effort to relieve Sevastopol. On 16 August he attacked the allies in the Battle of the Chornaya Rechka and was defeated. Russian casualties were probably nearly 10,000 and Allied less than 2,000.[1] The final assault on Sevastopol came on 8 September. The French under General MacMahon captured the Malakhov Redoubt and beat back Russian counter-attacks. Towards sunset Gorchakov ordered his troops to cross on to the northern side of the harbour, first destroying all depots of ammunition and stores. Sevastopol burnt for two days, and the allies did not enter it until 10 September. The last assault cost the Russians nearly 13,000 casualties and the Allies nearly 11,000.[2]

In the Baltic a British squadron under Admiral Dundas bombarded Sveaborg on 9 and 10 August, without any useful result, and followed this by bombardments of positions in the Åland Islands on 11 and 12 August.

[1] Tarle, *Sochineniya*, ix. 442.
[2] Ibid. ix, pp. 466–7.

On the Caucasus front the viceroy, General N. N. Muravyov,[1] took command of the operations against Kars at the end of June. The city had a strong natural position and had been powerfully fortified under the direction of the Welsh Colonel Williams. It had a garrison of 20,000 men. On 29 September Muravyov launched a general assault, but it was beaten off at the cost of more than 7,000 Russian casualties. After this Muravyov decided not to make another assault, but to trust to blockade. He did not allow himself to be diverted from his purpose by the fact that Ömer Pasha had landed with 8,000 men at Batum in September and invaded Abkhazia and Mingrelia. Muravyov was justified by the result. On 26 November 1855 Kars surrendered. This last success strengthened the public morale in Russia and helped the Russian cause at the peace negotiations.

The allies were far from agreed, and Austrian policy was beset by hopeless contradictions.[2] But with the fall of Sevastopol the immediate allied aim had been achieved, and from the Russian point of view it was less necessary to take a strong stand about the rights of the Russian navy when it had almost ceased to exist. The crisis came with an Austrian ultimatum on 15 December 1855. The Russian government finally decided, after a council held by the Tsar on 15 January 1856, that Russia could not afford to go to war with Austria in addition to the Western Powers. It therefore accepted the Austrian demand that two further Points be added to the original Four Points. Southern Bessarabia was to be ceded by Russia, which would thus be excluded from the mouth of the Danube, and the allies were to have the right to submit further Points to the peace conference when it met.

The conference was held in Paris from 25 February to 16 April. The terms of the peace treaty were unpleasant for the Russians but not disastrous. The naval problem was solved by the formula that the Black Sea should be neutralized. Neither Russia nor Turkey was to have naval forces there. This was of course a limitation from which only Russia suffered. The Turks could have as large a navy as they liked in the Aegean, and

[1] He should not be confused with the other N. N. Muravyov, known as Amursky, the governor-general of Eastern Siberia and founder of Vladivostok (see pp. 297, 333, and 439).

[2] For the complications of Allied and Austrian policy, largely connected with the Italian problem, see A. J. P. Taylor, op. cit., pp. 68–90.

bring it into the Black Sea when they needed it. But Russia could not bring warships in from outside. This effective disarmament was bitterly resented by Alexander II. But it was a comparatively small price to pay for defeat in a war with two Great Powers. Apart from this the most important result of the Paris treaty was the creation of independent Danubian principalities, soon to be united in a single Roumanian state. The period of Russian domination of Roumania was thus ended for nearly a century. Moldavia received back from Russia Southern Bessarabia—that is, a part of its eastern portion which had been taken by Russia in 1812. A separate convention provided for the demilitarization of the Åland Islands.

The Crimean War was fought on a limited scale. It was confined to comparatively small areas, and the forces engaged were small in relation to the available manpower of the belligerents. The political aims and methods of the governments were also limited. When the Russian army was on the Danube, no serious attempt was made to raise rebellion in Bulgaria against the Turks. When the Austrians occupied the principalities and took an increasingly hostile attitude towards Russia, no attempt was made to incite the peoples of the monarchy against their rulers. Admittedly, the Hungarians had little cause to love the Russians (though they might hate Vienna still more), and the Roumanians tended to place their hopes in France, disliking Russia and Austria about equally. But at least from the Slav peoples something might have been hoped. Slavophils wished the government to appeal to the Austrian Slavs. Pogodin in June 1854 wrote to the Tsar, urging him to work for the disruption of Austria. But Nicholas was not willing to encourage revolutionary nationalism.[1] Nor did the allies exploit nationalism against Russia. The hopes of the Polish exiles were disappointed. Czartoryski was kept waiting for three hours by the French foreign minister, Drouyn de Lhuys, in June 1854, and received no satisfaction when he did see him.[2] Napoleon III would have liked to help the Poles, and toyed with the idea in 1855. But the British government did not wish to launch revolution anywhere, and Napoleon realized that if he fought for the liberation of Poland, this would arouse Russian patriotism to a long and

[1] N. Barsukov, *Zhizn' i trudy M. P. Pogodina*, xiii. 118.

[2] Tarle, *Sochineniya*, ix. 19–20.

bitter struggle, and he would have to postpone his Italian plans to an indefinite future.

Russia therefore never faced destruction as a Great Power, as in 1812 or 1914. The limited defeat at Sevastopol, partly redeemed by the victory at Kars, did not threaten the collapse of the régime. The government, it is true, was seriously discredited. Its transport system had been shown to be grossly inadequate. The political and economic structure were deeply infected with corruption, ranging from paymasters who pocketed a percentage of every unit's payroll to contractors who made huge profits from selling shoddy materials or rotted food to the armed forces. At the root of all the weaknesses and abuses was the supreme evil of serfdom. Once the war was over huge tasks of reform and reconstruction lay ahead. But the war was not long or disastrous enough to break the hold of the ruling bureaucracy on power.

Nevertheless, Russia's position in Europe was changed for nearly a hundred years. In 1815 Russia appeared the strongest single power on the Continent, followed fairly closely by Austria. After 1848 she seemed far to have outdistanced the other land Powers: Russian primacy had turned into Russian domination. The Crimean War reduced Russia to one among several Great Powers. For the next years France, and even Austria, were her equals: after 1870 the new German empire was her superior. As long as a Tsar ruled in St. Petersburg, Russia never regained the eminence of 1815.

When he heard the news of the fall of Sevastopol, Nikitenko wrote in his diary: 'Our war is not just two years old—we have been at war for thirty years, maintaining an army a million strong and unceasingly threatening Europe. What was all this for? What advantage and what glory did Russia get from it?'[1]

[1] *RS* (June 1890), p. 627.

PART IV

THE TSAR LIBERATOR

X

THE GREAT REFORMS

The Emperor

ALEXANDER II came to the throne at the age of thirty-seven. His father had ensured that his upbringing would be happier than his own had been. The poet Zhukovsky was placed in charge of his studies, and the tutor most closely attached to his person, from 1824 to 1834, was General K. K. Merder. Both were humane and sensitive, averse to harsh discipline, concerned to develop their pupil's abilities and character by winning his confidence and arousing his interest. Alexander was completely devoted to Merder, whose noble qualities as a man and as a teacher are attested by Zhukovsky.[1] From these men he received not only a good training in the civil and military duties of a ruler, and the knowledge of foreign languages and literature considered necessary to a prince, but also a humane and understanding outlook on life.

In 1837 Alexander made a long journey through Russia, including Siberia, which he was the first member of the Imperial family to visit. Next year he visited Europe, and became betrothed to a princess of Hesse-Darmstadt. The marriage took place in 1842 and the new grand duchess was rechristened in Orthodoxy as Maria Alexandrovna. In the next eighteen years there were six sons and two daughters of this marriage.

In 1841 Nicholas made his heir a member of the Council of State, and in the next years his duties included membership of

[1] A long passage from Zhukovsky about Merder is quoted in the article by S. S. Tatishchev on Alexander II in the first volume of *Russkii biograficheskiy slovar'*, published by the Imperial Russian Historical Society (SPB, 1896), p. 415.

the Committee of Ministers, the Caucasus Committee, and the secret committees of 1846 and 1848 on serfdom. He was also chairman of the committee responsible for constructing the St. Petersburg–Moscow railway. From 1842 onwards, whenever the emperor left the capital for long journeys, he left Alexander in charge of general government affairs and showed increasing confidence in his judgement. In 1849 Alexander became commander of the Corps of Guards and of all military colleges and schools. In the second capacity, he became closely associated with General Y. I. Rostovtsev. In 1850 he visited the Caucasus for two months, and on one occasion became involved in a minor battle with Chechen raiders. In 1851 he played an important part in obtaining the emperor's approval of the establishment by Governor-General Muravyov of the Russian post on the Pacific coast at the mouth of the Amur.

Alexander was less a soldier than his father, though he performed his military duties conscientiously. He had, however, far more experience and understanding of a wide range of problems of civil government than Nicholas had possessed on his accession. His ideas were conservative. He held the traditional view of his obligation to uphold the principle of autocracy. He thought of himself as 'the first nobleman' of the empire. He had no trace of sympathy for radical ideas. At the same time he believed it was his duty to improve the structure of the state when necessary. He was more profoundly and more urgently convinced of the wickedness of serfdom than his father had been: here one notes the effect not only of a difference in generations but of the influence of his tutors.

As a ruler he was milder, less imperious, than his father, but he kept the decisions in his own hands. In his choice of advisers he was fairly fortunate. One striking success was the appointment of Rostovtsev to head the Editorial Commissions.[1] Though he had no special qualification for the task, he performed it brilliantly. The choice of Count Peter Shuvalov in 1866 as head of the Third Department is an example of poor judgement. He usually gave loyal support to the men he had chosen even if they were under attack from powerful persons: the outstanding case is his retention of General Dmitrii Milyutin for twenty years as minister of war.

[1] See below pp. 338–44.

The Decision to Abolish Serfdom

The climate of opinion on serfdom had been developing slowly towards emancipation. The stifling atmosphere of the last years of Nicholas's reign had prevented open discussion, but the war had stimulated serious thinking. The majority of landowners were still opposed to change, but for the most part ineffective in the expression of their views. It was the reforming minority of landowners that were most articulate, and it is their opinions which are most accessible to historians. Among them humanitarian considerations were certainly important. An eminent example is the Slavophil landowner A. I. Koshelyov. A memorandum written by him for the Tsar early in 1858, while using arguments of economic self-interest, also claimed that the landowners themselves were ceasing to believe that they had a moral right to own other human beings like chattels. Koshelyov's last argument, to which he gave the greatest emphasis, was that serfdom demoralizes the landowners themselves: 'This measure', he wrote, 'is more necessary for the welfare of our class itself even than for the serfs. The abolition of the right to dispose of people like objects or like cattle is as much our liberation as theirs: for at present we are under the yoke of a law that destroys still more in us than in the serfs any human quality.'[1]

During the last years the conscious desire of the serfs themselves for liberation had grown stronger. They themselves talked more freely of it, more clearly expected it. The beginning of a new reign was, as in the past, regarded as the opening of a new era. The number of local riots had notably increased since the 1840's. Their importance can be exaggerated: it is too much to speak of a revolutionary peasant movement in these years. The riots were not big enough to threaten the fabric of the state. Nevertheless, they worried the provincial governors and gendarmes, they frightened the landowners, and the reports which reached St. Petersburg were taken seriously in the ministries. They were also used as arguments for reform by independent persons like Koshelyov, Samarin, or the historian K. D. Kavelin.

The riots were taken more seriously because they coincided with the lost war. The war showed the appalling backwardness

[1] *Zapiski A. I. Koshelyova* (Berlin, 1884), 5th appendix, p. 32.

of Russia, and its dependence on the loyalty of the peasant soldier. This loyalty would not last for ever if nothing were done for the serfs. It was believed in St. Petersburg that the commander-in-chief in the Crimea, Prince Michael Gorchakov, had urged the Tsar that peace provided the chance to deal with internal problems, and that 'the first thing is that we must emancipate the serfs, because this is the knot which binds together all the things that are evil in Russia'.[1]

The war also showed the desperate state of Russian communications. The economic as well as the strategical need for railways was more fully understood. The striking fluctuations of grain prices in recent years had caused hardship to both landowners and serfs. Better communications would make it possible for Russian cereals to enter the world market and bring more regular income to the agricultural population. But the railway age, and the penetration of the money economy into the Russian village, were not compatible with the survival of serfdom.

Alexander was subject to liberal influence in his closest circle. His brother Constantine had become an ardent supporter of emancipation. Possibly even more effective was his aunt, the Grand Duchess Elena Pavlovna. Always a liberal, she had yet enjoyed the affection of Emperor Nicholas. Her magnificent work for the wounded during the war had increased her standing in Russian public life. Her palace was a centre of liberal ideas, and she herself gave her protection to liberal officials such as N. A. Milyutin. The influence of these two members of the Imperial family is not so well documented as that of the officials who carried out the reform, but it cannot be doubted that it was very great. The experts prepared the legislation, but it was largely due to the advice of Constantine and Elena that the Tsar was induced to force it through.

The first indication of the Tsar's intentions was a speech to the nobility of Moscow on 30 March 1856, in which occurred the striking phrase: 'It is better to abolish serfdom from above than to wait until the serfs begin to liberate themselves from below.' Alexander appointed a secret committee to examine the problem. Its chairman was Prince A. F. Orlov, the former head of the Third Department under Nicholas I and now president

[1] Letter from Kavelin to Pogodin, 30 Jan. 1856. Barsukov, op. cit. xiv. 208.

of the Council of State. Though responsible for the repressions of the preceding reign, he was less unpopular than his predecessor Benckendorff, perhaps because he was of purely Russian origin and descended from Catherine's favourite. He possessed 'that half-European half-Asiatic lordly arrogance which had so recently produced among us a kind of powerful magic charm'.[1] He was strongly conservative. The two most active reactionaries were Count Panin, who joined the committee some months later, and M. N. Muravyov, Kiselyov's successor as minister of state properties. Muravyov was involved with his brother and cousin in the Decembrist conspiracy but had escaped punishment and made a good career. Already in 1830 he is said to have made the remark that he was 'not one of the Muravyovs who get hanged, but one of those who do the hanging'.[2] This he certainly proved in Lithuania in 1863.[3] Meanwhile he used his great abilities and energy to impede emancipation. The committee also included General Y. I. Rostovtsev. He too was regarded as a reactionary, and was distrusted by liberals because as a young man he had denounced the Decembrist conspiracy to the authorities,[4] but he now proved to be a reformer. The most liberal members of the committee were Count Bludov, former minister of the interior and now head of the Second Department of the Imperial Chancery, General Chevkin, the minister of communications, and Count Lanskoy, the new minister of the interior. The latter was seventy-six years old. As a young man he had been a member of the Union of Virtue, but had not been involved in the Decembrist conspiracy. He genuinely worked for emancipation, and stood up for his subordinates in the ministry who were mainly responsible for the reform.

The Tsar himself opened the first meeting on 3 January 1857. The main questions put to the committee were: whether landowners should retain ownership of the whole of their land; whether the emancipated serfs should be protected in their right to use part of the land; and whether the landowners should receive compensation only for such land as they granted to the peasants, or also for the sacrifice of their rights over the persons of their serfs. The third question was quickly decided in prin-

[1] Memoirs of Y. A. Solovyov, *RS*, vol. 33, p. 230.
[2] Ibid., p. 232.
[3] See below pp. 375–6.
[4] See above p. 195.

ciple: there was to be no compensation for the loss of the person of a serf. The committee was also presented with papers prepared in the previous reign and with certain memoranda from individual landowners, including Yuri Samarin, Kavelin, and Koshelyov. The work went very slowly. In August the Tsar made his brother a member in order to speed things up. It was then decided to entrust to the Ministry of the Interior the task of collecting all necessary information and drafting proposals. The fact was that though the majority of the dignitaries in the committee were against reform, they were too uninformed and too lazy to be effective. The efficient officials of the ministry proved more than a match for them in the next years.

The Machinery of the Reform

In November the governor-general of Vilna, General V. I. Nazimov, arrived in St. Petersburg with some proposals from the Vilna nobility for emancipation of their serfs, on unfavourable terms, without granting them any land. But the Tsar, who attached importance to the co-operation of the nobility in his plans, and had been disappointed that his Moscow speech had so far failed to provoke any initiative from the landowners, seized on these proposals as a means of carrying the work an important stage further. He instructed Lanskoy to draft a rescript for Nazimov, directing the nobility to set up provincial committees in Lithuania to prepare precise proposals. These were to include the following principles. The landlords were to remain owners of the land, but the peasants were to acquire ownership, by purchase over a definite period of time, of their house and the surrounding land (*usadebnaya osedlost'*), and were also to be assured the use of further land, sufficient for their needs, in return for *obrok* or labour services. The peasants were to be allotted to village communities (*sel'skie obshchestva*), but the landlords were to retain police powers and there were to be arrangements to ensure the payment of taxes and the discharge of local services. Two days later, on 22 November, the Tsar asked the governor of Voronezh to persuade his nobility to put forward proposals, and early in December another rescript, somewhat more cautiously phrased, was addressed to the governor-general of St. Petersburg. A few days after this it was decided to release the texts of both rescripts for general publication.

Publication compelled the provincial nobility to face the problem. During 1858 committees were set up in most provinces of Russia. They were composed of two persons elected by the nobility in each *uezd* of the province, together with two further persons chosen by the provincial governor from among the local landowners. Since the governors understood that official policy now favoured reform, they usually appointed persons of markedly more reforming outlook than those elected by the nobility. Meanwhile the existence of the secret committee was revealed to the public under the name of Chief Committee on Peasant Affairs. Its members continued to disagree. In the Ministry of the Interior a special land department was set up under Y. A. Solovyov. Its draft programme of action was rejected by the committee. Instead Rostovtsev, advised by M. P. Pozen, a conservative landowner with some expert knowledge, produced a new plan, more complicated in its procedure and designed to increase the police powers of the landowners over the emancipated peasants and to minimize the amount of land to be placed a their disposal.

In June 1858 Rostovtsev took four months' leave abroad, in order to study the material at leisure. In his absence the reactionaries proposed that special temporary governors-general should be created for the execution of the reform, on the grounds that there would be serious danger of disorders by the peasants. This was an attempt to take control of the reform out of the hands of the Ministry of Interior, of which the reactionaries were understandably suspicious. The Tsar at first approved the idea, which was vigorously opposed by Lanskoy. Alexander expressed his displeasure at the minister's objections, which he claimed to believe had been prepared 'not by you but by someone or other from among your heads of department or chancery', jealous for their own petty authority. This rebuke nearly led to the resignation of Lanskoy. But the Tsar soon afterwards made it clear that he had full confidence in him, and in fact the plan to create temporary governors-general was never carried out.

The publication of the rescript led to animated discussion in the press. Even the extreme left were for a time enthusiastic.

Herzen wrote in his paper *Kolokol*, published in London: 'Thou hast triumphed, O Galilean!' The landowners, he argued, would be helpless when they had united against them 'authority and freedom, the educated minority and the whole nation, the Tsar's will and public opinion'. Chernyshevsky in *Sovremennik* compared Alexander's action with that of Peter the Great, and stated: 'The blessing, promised to the peace-makers and the meek, crowns Alexander II with a happiness with which as yet none of the sovereigns of Europe has been crowned—the happiness of alone beginning and completing the liberation of his subjects.'[1] *Russkii vestnik*, edited by M. N. Katkov, expressed the views of the reformers in the central industrial provinces, such as Unkovsky, the Tver marshal of the nobility, while liberal landowners from black-earth provinces, including Samarin, Prince Cherkassky, and Koshelyov, were grouped around *Russkaya beseda*. Press discussion was, however, limited by the censorship in April 1858, as a result of the publication in *Sovremennik* of an earlier memorandum by Kavelin. This had proposed not only that the peasants be completely emancipated from all authority of their landowners, but that they be enabled to become owners of all the land at present in their use. These radical proposals caused the Tsar to decide not to employ Kavelin as tutor for the Tsarevich, as had been intended, and to instruct the minister of education to order censors to confine press discussion of the problem to 'learned, theoretical, and statistical articles', and to forbid any works that stirred up classes against each other.

During August the Tsar made a tour of a number of provinces, addressing the nobility in Tver, Kostroma, Nizhnii Novgorod, Vladimir, and Moscow. In Moscow he went out of his way to refute the restrictive interpretation placed by the conservatives on the meaning of the phrase *usadebnaya osedlost'*, used in the rescript. He emphasized that this meant not only the house a peasant lived in but also the land immediately surrounding it. In September he also spoke in Smolensk and in Vilna. During the summer too Rostovtsev had begun to change

[1] Herzen, *Works*, ed. Lemke, ix. 128; Chernyshevsky, *Izbrannye ekonomicheskie proizvedeniya*, ed. I. D. Udaltsov (Moscow, 1948–9), i. 423. The passage comes from a long article entitled 'The New Conditions of Village Life' ('O novykh usloviyakh sel'skogo byta'), ibid. i. 417–74.

his ideas as he studied the facts. He became convinced that it was necessary to enable the peasants to buy more than just the plot around their homes. He wrote several letters to Alexander from Germany, and on his return to the capital found himself in close agreement with the emperor.[1] From then onwards he was Alexander's most trusted adviser, and his influence was definitely liberal.

A mass of material was now coming in from the provincial committees. Many committees could not agree and sent two reports—a majority view and a minority view. The main committee had in June set up a commission of four of its members—Lanskoy, Panin, Muravyov, and Rostovtsev. These were now equally divided into two factions, and in any case had not the resources to digest all the material. Rostovtsev therefore proposed that much larger sub-committees of experts be set up to examine all the papers. These were to be called the Editorial Commissions, sub-divided into administrative, juridical, and financial but in fact sitting as one body. The commissions were composed of officials and of non-official experts invited by the government. Reformers were predominant.

The most important individual member was N. A. Milyutin. A nephew of Count P. D. Kiselyov's and much influenced by him, he had served in the ministry since 1835. He had been responsible for the reorganization of St. Petersburg municipal government in the late 1840's and had then acquired a reputation for radicalism. Alexander II at first distrusted him. When Lanskoy introduced him to the Tsar in July 1858, the latter coldly remarked: 'Il paraît que vous possédez la confiance de votre ministre; j'espère que vous saurez la justifier.' Milyutin, however, was highly regarded by the Grand Duchess Elena who probably spoke to the Tsar in his favour. In the autumn he was made deputy minister of the interior but only provisionally, and only after Prince Obolensky, to whom the post was offered, had insisted that it was Milyutin's due. In the spring of 1859, when he was received in audience by the Tsar, he was told that the appointment was 'a chance for him to rehabilitate himself'.

[1] Extracts from these letters are published under the title *Izvlecheniya iz vsepodanneyskikh pisem Gen. Ad. Rostovtseva*, in an appendix to the first volume of the Editorial Commissions' reports.

The most influential of the non-official experts were the Slavophil landowners Samarin and Prince Cherkassky. Milyutin wrote to Samarin on 3 March urging him strongly to accept:

> Je peux vous assurer que les bases du travail sont larges et raisonnées. Elles peuvent être acceptées en toute conscience par ceux qui cherchent une régulière et pacifique solution du problème du servage. Rejetez toute méfiance à ce sujet et arrivez hardiment. Sans doute nous ne serons pas sur des roses; nous serons vraisemblablement en butte à la haine, à la calomnie, à des intrigues de toute genre; mais pour cela précisément, il nous est impossible de reculer devant la lutte sans trahir toute notre vie passée.[1]

Both Samarin and Cherkassky accepted. Koshelyov had hoped to be invited but was not called upon.

The Emancipation

The Editorial Commissions began work in the spring of 1859. The two main problems before them were, first, how much land was to be given to the peasants and on what terms, and secondly, what kind of administrative authority was to take the place of the powers of the serf-owning landlord.

On the first problem there were several possibilities. One was to give the peasant full personal freedom but no land. This had been done by the German landowners in the Baltic provinces under Alexander I. The result had been to create a rural landless proletariat. Such a prospect was not displeasing to some black-earth landowners in well-populated regions. But it was anathema to the Russian authorities who were obsessed with the dangers of creating a proletariat. A second possibility was to let the peasants have the use of part or all of the land they now cultivated, while leaving the property rights over it to the landowner. This is what had been done in the Baltic provinces in the 1840's, when the evil results of the earlier reform had been mitigated by instituting what was called *Bauernland*, a portion of the estates which remained the property of the landowners but was guaranteed in use to the peasants. One suggestion was that such land should be made available to the Russian peasants only for a limited period (twelve years) and then revert unconditionally to the landowners. Another was that it should pass permanently into peasant use, but in a quantity considerably

[1] A. Leroy-Beaulieu, *Un homme d'état russe* (Paris, 1884), p. 47.

smaller than that at present cultivated by the serfs. A third was that it should pass permanently into peasant use in the existing quantity. Samarin suggested that the present allotments should be a minimum, and that in regions of dense population they should where possible be increased. In sparsely populated areas, however, there might be a case for reducing the allotments to a maximum size per peasant family, the landowner to have unconditional ownership of the excess. The problem also arose whether the peasants should have the right to buy, over a period of time, the land that was ensured for their use, and if so on what terms. As we have seen, Rostovtsev had moved from the original idea of a small *usadebnaya osedlost'* (never very clearly defined) to that of agricultural allotments sufficient to support a whole family. It still, however, had to be decided what rent or labour services would be paid for such land, and at what point (after how many years of 'temporary obligation') purchase should begin.

On the second problem the first question was, would the peasants become genuinely free citizens, or merely have their servitude to the landlord replaced by subjection to another bureaucratic authority. Connected with this was the question, to what extent would the landlord, no longer a serf-owner, reappear in a new guise as head of the local police authority. Inevitably, the administrative system instituted by Kiselyov for the state peasants became a model. Some of the leading non-official experts (for instance Samarin, Cherkassky, and Koshelyov) were influenced by Slavophil romanticism about the peasant commune.[1] Self-governing communes, they felt, should be the main organ of government. Moreover, these communes should be responsible not only for taxation and public works but also for the whole process of transfer of land to the peasants and for the organization of agriculture. These men were strongly opposed to basing agriculture on individual small farmers. Not the individual but the commune ought to be both the social and the economic unit of Russian society. The landowners were keen to assert their authority and wished that the *sel'skoe obshchestvo*, the lowest level of administration, should be based not on the village commune but on the boundaries of the landowner's estate. There might thus be more than one *sel'skoe*

[1] See above pp. 232–3.

obshchestvo affecting the inhabitants of one village, and one *sel'skoe obshchestvo* might contain persons from several villages.

The conflict of views between landowners and bureaucrats was not a simple clash between reactionary serf-owners anxious to retain privileges and a progressive government trying to help its subjects. This clash of course existed. But there was also another conflict: between reforming landowners who wished the new régime to allow elected self-government, and ultimately a liberalization of the whole political system, and reforming bureaucrats who were convinced that only a benevolent autocracy could do good. It was the familiar argument between the social *élite* and the central power, which had been so prominent in Russian political thinking since the beginning of the nineteenth century. It came to the surface during the discussions between the Editorial Commissions and the deputies of the provincial committees of the nobility, who came to St. Petersburg in two groups in August 1859 and January 1860.

Milyutin had no sympathy for the aspirations of constitutionally minded landowners. A memorandum of Lanskoy to the Tsar of August 1859, inspired by Milyutin, claimed that the government's main care must be to prevent 'the opinions expressed in a scattered fashion in the various committees from fusing together into like-thinking parties of various hues, which have not yet formed, and which would be harmful both for the government and for the people'. It must be made clear to the deputies that they were being invited to clear up points of detail concerning the special circumstances of their regions, not to discuss the basic principles of the reform, or the application of those principles 'which is the prerogative of the government itself'. The nobility had, however, expected that the deputies of provincial committees would be allowed to do more than this: such had been their impression of the Tsar's own intentions, as expressed in his speeches in the summer of 1858. The first group met in the house of Count Peter Shuvalov in St. Petersburg, and drew up a letter to Rostovtsev, for transmission to the emperor, signed by twenty-eight persons. The reply was that the emperor agreed to the deputies meeting to discuss their common problems, but that such meetings could have no official character. They must confine themselves to discussing the application to their particular conditions of the general principles that had been already accepted and not discuss the principles themselves. They were assured that all their replies would be put before the Chief Committee as well as the Editorial Commission. On 4 September the Tsar met the deputies at Tsarskoe Selo and made them a short speech in which he declared: 'I considered myself the first nobleman when I was heir to the throne, I took pride in this, I take pride in it now, and do not cease to consider myself as belonging to your estate.' The deputies were not, however, satisfied by this compliment. Eighteen of them signed an address to the Tsar, which was a modified version of a draft prepared by Koshelyov. In it they asserted that the proposals of the Editorial Commissions did not correspond to general needs and did not embody the general principles which the nobility had accepted. They asked for permission to submit their views on the final work of the Editorial Commissions before the latter went before the Chief Committee. Another address, signed by five persons,[1] put forward a whole democratic political programme. The serfs were to receive full liberty and full ownership of their land by purchase 'at a price and in conditions not ruinous for the landowners'. A system of economic and executive administratration, equal for all classes, was to be set up on the elective principle. There was to be an independent judiciary, with trial by jury, separation of judicial and administrative power, publicity of court procedure, and responsibility of officials to the courts. Finally, the public was to have the opportunity through the press to bring to the notice of the supreme power 'deficiencies and abuses of local administration'.[2] These addresses infuriated Alexander, who objected to any sort of criticism, and to any participation by non-official representative bodies in the reform. Though some of the demands of the address of five were later granted, the Tsar refused to discuss them at this stage. The signatories of both addresses received official rebukes.

The work of reform suffered a serious blow when Rostovtsev died in February 1860. Alexander appointed Panin in his place. Though himself an undoubted reactionary, Panin did not much influence the further course of the work, and he accepted

[1] D. Khrushchov (Kharkov), A. Shchreter (Kharkov), A. Unkovsky (Tver), D. Vasilyev (Yaroslavl) and P. Dubrovin (Yaroslavl).

[2] A. I. Koshelyov, *Zapiski*, 6th appendix, pp. 171–206.

Milyutin and the liberals loyally as his collaborators. The second group of provincial deputies came mostly from black-earth regions. They did not, like the first group, make demands of a political nature, but they were hostile to the commissions, which they regarded as far too favourable to the serfs. The commissions' chief expert for the south-western area, Samarin, was under heavy attack but stood up for himself vigorously. He wrote at this time to Koshelyov: 'Their remarks were full of accusations (against us) of communism, and of a concealed desire, by annoying the nobility, to deprive the throne of its foundation.'[1]

There was undoubtedly bitter hostility between landowners and bureaucrats, and the bureaucracy was itself divided between reformers and reactionaries. The Ministry of the Interior was the stronghold of the liberals. Harried by the intrigues and calumnies of the reactionaries, the liberals increasingly treated the landowning class with contempt, though they themselves derived from it. The moderate reformer A. I. Levshin believed that they had become determined to crush and humiliate the landowners, and that this harmed their cause.[2] The bitterness of the reactionary party was vividly expressed in a memorandum by N. A. Bezobrazov, addressed to the Tsar in 1853. The author argued that 'around the throne the bureaucracy is on guard, in complicity (consciously or unconsciously) with the so-called Reds'. The revolutionaries had learnt from their previous mistakes, and were now busily penetrating the government machine. 'Secretly promoting each other, they have got control of some branches of the administration, they have first seized certain posts which are not obvious to outside view but are absolutely essential, they have moved up higher still, and now they are using the force of the government to do what their predecessors wished but were unable to achieve.'[3] This memorandum was treated with contempt by the Tsar. Another example was Count D. N. Tolstoy, a landowner and former provincial governor and high official of the Ministry of the Interior. In his memoirs many years later he wrote that there

[1] Baron B. E. Nolde, *Yurii Samarin i ego vremya* (Paris, 1926), p. 130.

[2] A. I. Levshin, 'Dostopamyatnye minuty v moey zhizni', *RA* (1885), vol. ii, pp. 545–55.

[3] *RA* (1888), vol. iii, p. 614.

were at this time two parties in Russia. One consisted of sincere supporters of reform who desired a peaceful settlement of the serf problem in the interests of Russia's national greatness. 'The majority of this party consisted of noble landowners, and in the conditions of St. Petersburg public life there was practically no trace of their influence in the capital. The other party was numerous, powerful, and invincible in St. Petersburg, and had its sympathizers in the provinces too. It consisted exclusively of officials, writers, and journalists. I shall not be far wrong if I call it the Red Party.'[1]

The commissions' work was concluded in October 1860. The Tsar then appointed Grand Duke Constantine as chairman of the Chief Committee, which was responsible for preparing the final proposals. The experts in practice remained as an unofficial advisory group consulted by the grand duke and by the liberal members of the Chief Committee. Alexander himself pressed the committee to act quickly. In January 1861 its proposals were rapidly discussed in the Council of State, and on 19 February the statutes were signed, introduced by a rhetorical manifesto drafted by Metropolitan Filaret of Moscow.[2]

The serfs were emancipated from the personal power of the landowners and were to receive land. Inventories were to be prepared, on all estates, of the existing use of the land, and proposals made as to the obligations which the peasants were to assume. These inventories (*ustavnye gramoty*) were to be submitted to the judgment of specially appointed 'arbitrators of the peace' (*mirovye posredniki*). When the terms had been agreed, within two years, the peasants were to be described as 'temporarily bound' (*vremenno-obyazannye*), and were to pay *obrok* or labour services. At a later stage, to depend on mutual agreement, they were to begin annual payments which were ultimately to give them ownership of the land. Administration of the emancipated serfs was to be based on the rural unit of the *volost*, below which were to be the village communities (*sel'skie obshchestva*). The affairs of the village were to be conducted by the commune (*obshchina*), which was to assume collective responsi-

[1] 'Zapiski grafa D. N. Tolstogo', *RA* (1885), vol. ii, p. 35. The author should not be confused with Count D. A. Tolstoy, the later minister of education.

[2] The Manifesto is in PSZ, second series, no. 36650. It is followed by the detailed legislation, nos. 36652 to 36675 (vol. 36, pp. 128–403).

bility (*krugovaya poruka*) for payment of taxes, and in due course of the annual payments or 'redemption dues', by which the peasants were to become owners of land.

The operation of this settlement will be discussed later. The introduction of the new régime was accompanied by a definite reversion towards more reactionary policies and personalities, caused in part by the government's anger at the rather unfavourable public reaction to the conditions of the settlement and at the continued demands for political reforms that were still being made by some assemblies of the nobility. These will also be discussed later. A symptom of the reaction against liberalism was the resignation of Lanskoy and the removal of Milyutin, who was sent on leave abroad. Though he himself desired a rest after his labours and the intrigues against him, he understood perfectly well that this was a mark of Imperial disfavour to himself, and augured ill for the future. He wrote on 4 May to Prince Cherkassky:

> On m'a donné congé pour une année entière, ou pour mieux dire, on m'a mis de côté en me faisant sénateur et en me conservant mon traitement. . . . Afin de ne pas donner prise à l'accusation d'indifférence pour les affaires publiques, je n'avais demandé d'abord qu'un congé de quatre mois, mais la réaction est venue à mon secours. Lanskoi et moi nous avons été éloignés du ministère (sans aucune demande de notre part) pour complaire à la noblesse. . . . La vraie lutte et le vrai travail ne sont plus maintenant ici à Saint-Pétersburg mais en province, dans les campagnes. Je souhaite de toute mon âme que la portion libérale de la noblesse et les gens dévoués à notre cause ne s'en écartent point; en ce cas, toutes les chicanes des gens de cour et des bureaux ministériels seront impuissantes, comme a été impuissante jusqu'à présent l'opposition des fonctionnaires-propriétaires.

Of the Tsar himself, he wrote to Samarin on 7 May: 'En cédant à la réaction, il espère la vaincre. Le vent qui souffle en ce moment n'est pas favorable aux personalités tranchées.'[1]

The 1861 settlement was no solution to the peasant question: it created more problems than it solved, and difficulties piled up in the following years. However, it is worth noting that serfdom was peacefully abolished in the same year in which failure to abolish slavery in another great country was a principal

[1] Leroy-Beaulieu, op. cit., pp. 75–76, 80.

cause of one of the most bloody wars of the nineteenth century. The proclamation of the emancipation in Russia preceded by a few weeks the firing at Fort Sumter. It is also worth noting that land was made available to the emancipated peasants by government action, even if on too small a scale and on too onerous terms, whereas the systematic endowment of emancipated negroes with land was not undertaken after the American Civil War. This is the more surprising when one considers that the white landowning class of the South were absolutely at the mercy of the federal government in 1865, whereas the landowning nobility in Russia remained powerful after 1861. Two points are perhaps relevant in any search for an explanation—though a detailed comparison of the two situations has yet to be made, and would be well worth undertaking. One is that the authority of the government over all classes was far stronger in Russia than in the United States, even if Abraham Lincoln personally possessed greater moral authority than Alexander II. The second is that the sanctity of private property was greater—for better or worse—in America than in Russia, and that this was further strengthened by the Civil War itself, in so far as the victory of the North was a victory for industrial capitalism over agrarian society. Northern politicians might be glad to humiliate and coerce defeated rebels, but to take away their material (as opposed to human) property did not seem right. In Russia the landowners certainly fought for their material interests, but idolization of private property did not form part of the traditional outlook of Tsars, bureaucrats, or noblemen.

Regional Self-Government

The public discussions aroused by the preparation of the peasant reform did not die down with the promulgation of the emancipation in February 1861. It was inevitable that the major reform should bring great changes in administration, army and judiciary. The government, however, increasingly resented suggestions from the public as to the course that these reforms should take. Already in 1859 Alexander had instructed Lanskoy to issue a circular forbidding assemblies of the nobility to discuss the peasant question. This had been disobeyed by the assemblies of Tver and Vladimir. The latter was careful enough to keep just within the letter of the regulation, but Tver was less cautious. As a punishment, the Tsar ordered the banishment to Vyatka province of the marshal of nobility of Tver, A. M. Unkovsky, one of the leaders of the liberal group among the provincial deputies.

The liberal section of the nobility continued to be interested in the idea of a central representative assembly, thinking on the whole more of the *zemskii sobor* of the sixteenth and seventeenth centuries, as idealized by Slavophil writers, than of a parliament of the Western type. The assembly of the nobility of Tver on 3 February 1862 voted an address to the emperor which argued that 'the convocation of persons elected by the whole Russian land represents the only means to the satisfactory solution of the questions that were raised but not settled by the Act of 19 February'. The address also renounced on behalf of the Tver nobility the 'shameful' privilege of nobles' immunity from taxation, or any exclusive right of the nobility to provide the persons that were to rule the nation. This right should be extended to persons of all classes. Similar ideas were discussed, but not formally adopted, at the same time in the Moscow assembly. In Novgorod, Smolensk, Tula, and St. Petersburg demands were made for a central assembly, but one in which only the nobility should be represented. After the Tver assembly had concluded its meeting, a group of thirteen 'arbitrators of the peace' from Tver province held a meeting of their own under the chairmanship of Alexei Bakunin. They criticized various features of the Act of 19 February, called for a national assembly elected without difference of class, and declared all action contrary to these principles to be 'hostile to society'. These men were arrested by order of the minister of the interior, and imprisoned in the Peter-Paul Fortress in St. Petersburg. They were sentenced to two years' imprisonment, but were set free before the full term had expired. P. A. Valuyev, who had succeeded Lanskoy as minister of the interior, issued in March 1862 a circular to all marshals of nobility to the effect that assemblies of nobility had no right to put forward petitions or representations referring to anything other than the local needs of their area.

Meanwhile the government was itself preparing a reform of local government. A committee on this subject had already been set up in 1860 under the chairmanship of N. A. Milyutin.

When Valuyev became minister, he took over the chairmanship himself. Valuyev was at this time something of a cynic, but he had few illusions about the government machine. In 1855, when he had been governor of Kurland, he had written in the memorandum already quoted:[1]

All levels of government are now more concerned with each other than with the essential objects of their departments. The higher authorities barely manage to ensure the formal correctness of the activity of their lower authorities. The lower levels are almost exclusively concerned with satisfying the formal demands of the higher. The autonomy of local authority is extremely limited, and it seems that the higher officers forget that to show confidence in their subordinates, and consideration for their views of an affair, is also a form of reward, even if these are not the subject of periodical reports to the Committee of Ministers.

The first achievement of the committee was a reorganization of the police at county level. City and county police were united under the command of a single *ispravnik*, appointed by the minister. The former system, by which the *uezd* nobility elected the *zemskii ispravnik*, came to an end. This was an important strengthening of the bureaucracy at the expense of the non-official element. It was, however, an obvious consequence of the abolition of landowners' police powers over serfs.

The committee proposed to introduce elected local assemblies in which all classes should have some say. The preparation of this reform proceeded slowly. On 1 November 1863 the Tsar insisted that an Act should be ready by 1 January 1864. During December 1863 it was discussed in the Council of State. Two points were debated. One was whether the election of members of the assemblies should be on one single roll, or separately by estates. Baron Korf argued that election by classes would be harmful, as it would make each member feel that he represented only the interests of his class, instead of representing interests 'common to the whole locality'. The majority rejected this argument. They felt that election on a single roll would be 'mechanical', and would place the peasant members 'in relationships unsuitable to their notions and habits, and would provoke antagonism between the estates'. The second question was whether the president of the assemblies should be a person

[1] 'Duma russkogo', *RS* (May 1891), p. 355.

elected by the assembly, or should be *ex officio* the marshal of nobility. Opinions were equally divided, but the emperor decided in favour of marshals. The proposal of E. P. Kovalesky, that the assemblies' powers should include the encouragement of education, though not in the committee's original proposals, was accepted. The proposals of Prince Shcherbatov, that as the assemblies would have to carry out various tasks on behalf of the central government, they should be allowed to take part in preparing the estimates of government expenditure, was rejected.

The reform of 1864 instituted an assembly (known as *zemstvo*) at two levels, *uezd* and province. The *uezd* assemblies were elected in three separate electoral colleges—for nobles, townsmen and peasants. The election of peasant deputies was indirect: householders' meetings in the communes elected 'elders', these elected from their number 'electors', and these finally elected the persons who sat in the assemblies. The provincial assemblies were composed of persons elected from their own membership by the *uezd* assemblies. Both *uezd* and provincial assemblies elected from their midst an executive board (*uprava*). The president of the assembly was the *uezd* or provincial marshal of the nobility.

During the first years of zemstvo institutions (1865–7), the proportion of seats in *uezd* assemblies held by nobles was 42 per cent., by peasants 38 per cent., by merchants 10·5 per cent. and by members of priestly families 6·5 per cent. In provincial assemblies the corresponding proportions were 74 per cent., 10·5 per cent., 11 per cent., and 4 per cent. Among voters to *uezd* assemblies in 16 provinces in 1865–6 the proportion of nobles varied from 27 per cent. in Samara to 59 per cent. in Kherson, but in most cases was close to the general average of 41 per cent.

The desire for a national assembly died hard. In January 1865 the assembly of the nobility of Moscow province voted, by 270 to 36, an address which asked the Tsar 'to complete the structure of the state by convoking a general assembly of elected persons of the Russian land for the consideration of needs common to the whole state', and with this aim in view to instruct his loyal nobility 'to choose from their midst the best people'. The Tsar gave an impatient and angry reply, in the form of a rescript to the minister of the interior. The task of reform was his alone. No class was entitled to speak on behalf of others, or to anticipate the reforms decided by the government. 'Such deviations from the order of things established by the laws in force, can only make it more difficult for me to fulfil my plans; in no case can they assist the achievement of the purpose to which they may be directed.'[1] In 1865 also the St. Petersburg zemstvo voted a resolution in favour of 'crowning the structure' by summoning 'a central assembly of the land', but prudently decided not to put forward a formal request to this effect to the emperor.[2]

Alexander never intended to introduce a national assembly. As the régime became more stable, the Crimean War receded into the past, and the emancipation was carried out in an increasingly orderly manner, the pressure for such a reform dwindled. There were in fact two different grounds for opposition. On the one hand the reactionaries were hostile, the great landowners because their social privileges might be threatened, the high officials because their power and prestige would suffer. On the other hand it was opposed by many progressive persons, both within and outside the government machine. They feared that any national assembly would be dominated by the landowning interest, and would hinder social progress. To them, the best agency for reform was the autocracy: all limitations on its power would principally benefit a privileged *élite*, which would replace the rule of the Tsar by the rule of an oligarchy. The intense distrust of all *élites*, which we have already noticed as a continuous element in Russian political thought, was as strong as ever. Two striking examples are N. A. Milyutin and Yurii Samarin, the second of whom voted for the minority in the Moscow assembly. Both men believed that there should be no central representative body in Russia until the whole nation was advanced and educated enough to take a part in its affairs, so that it could be a truly popular assembly.

The decision against a national assembly in the early 1860's was a turning-point in Russia's history. It is of course obvious

[1] Text of the Tsar's reply is in S. S. Tatishchev, *Imperator Aleksandr II, ego zhizn' i tsarstvovanie* (SPB, 1903), i. 525–6.

[2] These actions, and the attitude of the administrative authorities to them, are discussed in B. Veselovsky, *Istoriya zemstva zasorok let* (SPB, 1909–11), vol. 3, ch. 4.

that there could have been no parliamentary government based on universal suffrage at this time. Any maximalist historical interpretation, which judges events against the abstraction of a full democracy that could not have existed in those conditions, is unreal. But the belief that if you cannot have a fully representative parliament, you can and should have no assembly at all, is difficult for an Anglo-Saxon mind to understand. The point is of course that the history of the English-speaking nations—largely also of the Dutch and Scandinavians—has consisted of movements forward from one provisional situation, based on privileges for the *élite* of the time, to the next situation, when a new *élite* obtains its demands. To extend privileges to steadily broadening new *élites* has been a progressive process. Each new stage brought the whole people further forward, up to the modern democratic era. And the process is certainly not over yet. But the dominant Russian view has been that if all cannot have the same rights, none should have any, except the autocrat and his principal servants.

Yet a national assembly, with consultative powers and recruited only from a minority of the Russian people, could have been created in the 1860's, and could have played a useful part. There was a body of opinion, small if compared to the whole population of the empire, yet not insignificant in number, which was accessible to enlightened ideas derived from the European conservative and liberal traditions. Within a parliament based on a restricted franchise, reactionaries and progressives, Slavophils and Westernizers could have argued out their views, and their deliberations would have benefited Russia. The gentry and the rising business and professional classes could have won political experience. The increase of the middle classes and the growing prosperity of at least a section of the peasantry would in course of time have made possible an extension of the franchise. By about 1900 Russia would have reached a stage where a bolder advance towards democracy—universal suffrage and all—could have been achieved by peaceful means. That this is not fanciful is shown by the experience of other countries, for example by Prussia in the first half of the nineteenth century, and by Japan in the decades that followed the Meiji Restoration of 1868.

The dogma of autocracy, the dead weight of bureaucracy, and

the influence of the most reactionary section of the landowning class sufficed to prevent this development. Liberal persons continued to exist, both within the bureaucracy and among private landowners, especially among those who worked in the zemstvos. But their influence was much smaller than it should have been. Without effective pressure from below, or from outside the state machine, the reactionary or unimaginative majority among the bureaucrats could carry on in the old set ways. They had little need to justify themselves, either in practice or in theory.

One important result of the *gran rifiuto* was that conservative ideas were discredited as such with the next generations of the educated. The intellectual heritage of the Slavophils, so promising in the 1840's for all its absurdities, was wasted. Their successors were little more than chauvinists and imperialists. The attitude of mind of reforming conservatism, which they had so well expressed, almost disappeared. Maximalist utopian ideas drove all others out of the field. When one remembers the part played by conservative and traditional ideas in the development of democratic thought and democratic practice in western Europe, one can see how much Russia missed. One might perhaps quote Chaadayev for the view that Russia had no culture of her own, no political traditions of her own, and hence was incapable of producing a conservative tradition. But even a myth is better than nothing, and the mythical picture of the Russian past painted by the earlier Slavophils was something on which to build. The authorities thought otherwise. The contempt shown to the generation of Koshelyov and Samarin had fatal results later.

Judicial Reform

The necessity to reform the system of justice had been a commonplace in Nicholas I's reign. Speransky's codification of the laws had been a great step forward, but the machinery itself had not been touched. There was a multiplicity of courts, with appeals referred from one to the other and taking years to settle. Procedure was extremely slow, and this slowness gave endless opportunities for corruption. The abolition of serfdom made it essential to introduce a better and simpler system. In 1861 Alexander instructed the Imperial secretary, Butkov, to prepare a report on judicial reform, and this task was carried out by a commission of officials from the Ministry of Justice and the Second Department of H.I.M. Own Chancery, headed by the veteran statesman Count Bludov. The leading figure in this commission was M. I. Zarudny, who made a careful study of European systems of justice. It produced its Basic Principles in 1862, and these were discussed in the Council of State and approved by the Tsar in September. In 1863 detailed statutes were prepared in accordance with the principles, and these were thoroughly discussed by senators and the Council of State during the following year. They were finally approved in November 1864, introduced in the capitals in 1865, and then gradually applied in the rest of the country.

Russia now received a modern European system of justice. The basic institution was the regional court (*okruzhny sud*), of which there was to be one in each province, for civil and criminal cases. Above it was the Chamber of Justice (*sudebnaya palata*), of which there were ten in Russia. The final court of appeal was one of the two cassation departments, criminal or civil, of the Senate, or the joint general assembly of the cassation departments. Special procedure was established for dealing with crimes of high officials, which went to the criminal cassation department as a court of first instance, and crimes against the state, which under a regulation of 1872 went to a special bench of the Senate as court of first instance. The final appeal for both these types of case was the joint general assembly of the cassation departments.

An important reservation, in the Note to Article 1 of the Code of Criminal Procedure, declared: 'The administrative power takes measures, in the form prescribed by law, in order to prevent and limit the commitment of felonies and misdemeanours.' Under this provision, the Ministry of the Interior was able to banish to other parts of the country persons whom it regarded as politically suspicious or dangerous. These powers of 'administrative arrest' were at times widely abused. Another limitation was the provision that officials could not be indicted for offences committed in their official capacity unless the consent of their superior were given.

Certain special courts remained outside the general system of justice. Ecclesiastical courts and courts martial dealt with clerical and military offences. More important were the special *volost* courts, created for state peasants by Kiselyov's reforms[1] and extended to former serfs by the Emancipation Statute, which dealt only with cases between peasants. As the years passed, these became an increasingly serious defect in the system, as they kept the peasantry largely outside the Russian judicial system, and perpetuated in a different form the old differences between serfs and free men. There was, however, one most valuable new judicial institution, which had jurisdiction over peasants as well as over the rest of the population in rural and urban areas. This was the court of the justices of the peace, which dealt with offences punishable by a rebuke or reprimand, a fine of not more than 300 roubles, or a prison term of three months to one year. The justices were elected for three years by *uezd* zemstvos and operated at *uezd* level. Appeal could be made from their court to a conference of justices of the peace at provincial level.

Judges were appointed by the Ministry of Justice, but must have clearly defined juridical qualifications. They were paid good salaries, and were irremovable. Criminal cases, in the Chambers of Justice, were tried by juries. There was a slight property qualification for jury service. Juries decided by majority votes, but the Code recommended that they should attempt to reach unanimous decision. Court proceedings were public. A new profession, the Bar, appeared. Russian lawyers, who combined the functions of solicitor and barrister, were subject to professional organization and discipline, and soon attained very high standards. Indeed for a long time the court-room was the one place in Russia where real freedom of speech prevailed, and its main champion was the lawyer.

Despite certain gaps, and despite the inroads which were made into it during the government's later struggles with the revolutionary movement, the system of justice was good, and did as much as any institution to modernize Russia and to raise general moral and even political standards. It was an achievement of which its authors could be proud. This does not mean that it received the recognition that it deserved. The conception of the rule of law, the notion that there must be clearly defined laws and rules, binding on all alike, against which the actions of all citizens must be measured, was never accepted, or even

[1] See above pp. 235–7.

understood, by more than a minority, even if that minority steadily grew in the following fifty years. Tsars, ministers, and reactionary writers like Katkov considered themselves entitled to ignore the law when that suited them, and poured forth their rage when they came up against the resistance of judges or lawyers. Revolutionaries were equally contemptuous. Finding undoubted cases where justice had been warped by class interest, they concluded not that the laws must be more honestly obeyed and the quality of judges improved, but that the conception of an impartial law was a *bourgeois* lie. The baby must be thrown out with the bath water.

Education

The milder tendencies at the Ministry of Education, which had been apparent since Norov succeeded Shirinsky-Shikhmatov, were increased in the new reign. The Tsar on 23 November 1855 repealed the limitations on the number of university admissions, but lectures on European government were not restored until 1857, and on philosophy till 1860. The new regulations on entrance examinations and university fees were unpopular with the students, and still more anger was aroused by the refusal of the government to permit the formation of independent student corporations within the universities. Discontent on these issues was mixed to some extent with political feeling. Kazan University students were involved in the demonstrative requiem for the Bezdna peasants,[1] at which the university lecturer Shchapov declared: 'You have fallen victims, through your innocent ignorance, because we, who serve Enlightenment, did not enlighten you, misguided sons of our fatherland. Forgive us.' In October 1861 there were riots at Kazan University, caused by hostility to one of the professors and a government inspector.[2] At the same time there were larger disorders at St. Petersburg and Moscow universities. These, too, were due more to professional than to political problems. But as they coincided not only with the difficult business of carrying out the emancipation but

[1] See below p. 366.

[2] N. A. Firsov, 'Studencheskie istorii v Kazan'skom universitete', in *RS*, March–Aug. 1890. A different view is expressed by a former student signing himself M. M. S.-n, under the title 'Vospominaniya starogo kazan'skogo studenta' in the same journal for May 1892, pp. 271–91.

also with the first signs of revolutionary activity, and with mysterious outbreaks of fire, it was not surprising that the authorities should be alarmed. Admiral E. V. Putyatin, who had had a distinguished career as a sailor and as a negotiator in the Far East,[1] was appointed minister of education in June 1861, and recommended severe disciplinary action. His policies led to the resignation of several prominent St. Petersburg professors, including the historians Kavelin and A. N. Pypin. Putyatin's proposals were not in the end accepted by the emperor. Instead, a professor of liberal outlook, A. V. Golovnin, was appointed minister. He was responsible for the new University Statute, of 18 June 1863, which gave the universities greater autonomy than they had yet possessed.[2] The governing bodies of the universities were to be the councils of professors, which were to elect the rectors and were to choose new professors as appointments became vacant. The Ministry of Education still retained the right to confirm the councils' choices, but in practice for the next years this right remained a formality. The powers of the university inspectors were reduced, and the curators of educational districts made sparing use of their authority in the universities.

Attempts were made to reorganize the censorship, but despite some simplification it remained complex and burdensome. In 1860 censorship was removed from the Ministry of Education, and a Directorate of Censorship was set up. This was abolished in March 1862, and the main authority in censorship affairs passed to the Ministry of the Interior. There still remained separate ecclesiastical and military censorships, and publishers of books or newspapers were still in some doubt as to where real authority lay, and how much liberty they could claim. It can, however, be said that the tendency was towards milder methods. The oppressive preventive censorship was in practice replaced by the more tolerable punitive censorship, and the authorities tended to let through everything that did not seem dangerous, rather than refuse to let through anything that did not seem positively useful to the government.

[1] See below pp. 438–9.

[2] The situation at St. Petersburg University at this time is well described in the relevant sections of Nikitenko's Diary (*RS*, Jan., Feb. and March 1891). Nikitenko was a member of the commission appointed to re-examine the University Statute.

Golovnin introduced a new statute for secondary education, which was confirmed by the emperor on 19 November 1864. Under this system, gimnazii might have a classical or a modern curriculum. A new category was authorized—the *pro-gimnazii*, or incomplete secondary schools, with only four classes, which might also have either a classical or a modern curriculum. There was a moderate movement back towards the classicism of the Uvarov era. Latin was to be taught in all classical schools, and Greek was to be gradually introduced into some. All secondary schools were to devote considerable periods to divinity, history, geography, Russian language and literature, and mathematics. But apart from these subjects, the classical schools were to concentrate on classics and on modern European languages, the modern studies schools on natural sciences and drawing. The statute expressly repudiated class discrimination: 'In the gimnazii and pro-gimnazii children of all estates are taught, without distinction of profession or religious belief (of their parents).'[1] It was also intended at this time to abolish the intermediate level of *uezd* schools, of which there were 416, with 23,952 pupils, on 1 January 1865. They were in an unsatisfactory condition, and it was thought desirable to convert some into pro-gimnazii and others into two-class parish elementary schools.

Elementary education was regulated by the Statute of 14 July 1864. It covered all schools maintained by any department of government, unofficial society, or private individual. Elementary schools were declared open to all classes and intended 'to strengthen religious and moral notions and to spread basic useful knowledge'. Divinity was to be taught by the local priest or by a special teacher authorized by the Church. Other subjects might be taught by a priest or by a secular teacher approved by the schools council of the *uezd*. This was to consist of representatives of the Ministries of Education and the Interior, the Holy Synod, and other government department maintaining a school in the area, and two members of the *uezd* zemstvo assembly. The council was to elect its own chairman, to be approved by the provincial schools council. This was to consist of the provincial governor, the bishop of the diocese, the provincial director of education, and two members of the provincial zemstvo assembly. The duties of the *uezd* schools council included

[1] *Istoricheskii obzor deyatel'nosti MNP*, p. 439.

authorization of the opening of new schools, investigation of the closure of schools, and the appointment, rewarding, and dismissal of teachers.

These years were the period of activity of two outstanding Russian educational theorists. The first was the surgeon Pirogov, who had done such magnificent work for the wounded in Sevastopol. In 1856 he published in *Morskoy vestnik*, the official publication of the navy, an article on education entitled 'Problems of Life'. His main arguments were that education should not be restricted by class considerations, and that it should be designed not only to give specialized knowledge (the necessity for which he fully recognized) but also to provide a wide culture, and in particular to bring out the talents of the pupil. Teachers should be encouraged to pay at least as much attention to the pupils' personality as to filling their minds with facts. In the same year Pirogov was appointed curator of the educational district of New Russia. Here he played an active part in preparing the transformation of the Richelieu *lycée* into the University of Odessa, a process which was not completed until May 1865. His liberal ideas, however, met with opposition, and he was transferred to the curatorship of Kiev educational district in 1858. Here too his reforming influence made powerful enemies. In March 1861 he was dismissed, and the most important part of his public career was ended.[1]

The other outstanding figure was K. D. Ushinsky, born 1824, who had experience as a school-teacher, a journalist, and an official of the Ministry of Education. In 1860 he became editor of the official journal of the ministry, which he made into an interesting and influential review, with scholarly articles and serious discussion of ideas. Ushinsky also studied foreign systems of education on an official mission abroad in 1862–6. His main concern was to make education available to the whole people now that it was emancipated from serfdom. The former serfs must be made into citizens. To this end he edited two publications designed for popular readers, *Detskii mir* and *Rodnoe slovo*. His principal work was a large-scale study of education, entitled

[1] Pirogov in 1862 was appointed to lead a group of young Russians who were to study abroad in preparation for university teaching in Russia. But he was dismissed from this post in 1866. Thereafter he lived on his country estate but continued his medical work. He died, amidst universal admiration, in 1881.

Man as the Subject of Education, of which two volumes appeared in 1868 and 1869, but which was not completed at the time of his death in 1870.

Pirogov and Ushinsky formulated precisely, and expressed with distinction, ideas which were gaining ground among educated Russians. Unfortunately they were not shared by the government, which regarded with fear the prospect of an educated nation. Both Pirogov and Ushinsky favoured the development of the natural sciences, but both believed that all school-children should also get a grounding in the humanities. The difference between them was that Pirogov believed that this humane element could best be provided by study of the classical languages, while Ushinsky maintained that the valuable intellectual training provided by thorough knowledge of a language could best be obtained by the study of the Russian language itself.

Political Movements

The general expectation of reform, and the milder operation of the censorship, which marked the first years of the reign, stimulated not only the expression but the formation of radical political ideas.

The most influential Russian political thinker in 1855 was Herzen. After the bitter disappointments of the revolutionary years 1848 and 1849, Herzen had wandered around western Europe, and had settled in 1852 in London, where he set up in the following year his Free Russian Press. He had not ceased to be a socialist or a revolutionary, but experience had made him more sceptical about the prospects of revolution, and his observations of the weaknesses and failures of west Europeans had made him somewhat more tolerant of the weaknesses of Russians. The main task in Russia now seemed to him to be the promotion of liberty and social change rather than the assertion of virtuous principles. He was strengthened in this mood by visits or letters from such liberals as Kavelin, Chicherin, and the novelist Turgenev. He tended increasingly to appeal to all persons of good will, including even high officials and the Tsar himself, and to urge the intelligentsia to work for such reforms as were practically possible. From July 1857 he published regularly a periodical entitled *Kolokol* ('The Bell'), which was widely read inside Russia, not least in government offices. It published numerous reports and letters from Russia, denounced abuses and injustices, was well informed even of matters of detail from many parts of the country, and stood for concrete reform rather than empty declamation.

These were the years of Herzen's greatest influence in his country, to which, however, he never returned. He aroused opposition as well as admiration. His attitude was too radical for the moderate Chicherin, who definitely broke with him in 1858.[1] More serious was the opposition of the extreme radicals. These were grouped around the review *Sovremennik*, originally founded by Pushkin, which had languished without influence under Nicholas I, but had been bought by the poet N. A. Nekrasov in 1846. Nekrasov was one of the greatest of all Russian writers, but his poetic inspiration came rather from personal emotion and imagination than from general political ideas. He was also a very successful publisher. His business abilities, his disengagement from politics, and his irregular private life made him unpopular with the elder generation of the intelligentsia. But by opening the columns of his review to the younger and more radical writers, he won the lasting affection of the next generation.

Outstanding among these were N. G. Chernyshevsky (1828–89) and N. A. Dobrolyubov (1836–61). Both were children of Orthodox priests.

The remarkably large proportion, among the revolutionary intelligentsia of the next decades, of priests' children (*popovichi*) deserves emphasis. It can be largely explained by the simple fact that children of priests, being entitled to a free education in religious seminaries, stood a little higher on the ladder of educational opportunity than any other non-noble groups except the children of the few rich business men. Priests' children who showed aptitude for secular education could, though with difficulty, and often did, pass from religious seminaries to the universities to study secular subjects. As the plebeian element in the educated *élite* of Russia grew in relation to the noble

[1] A letter from Chicherin, and Herzen's comments, both published in *Kolokol*, are in Herzen's *Works*, ed. Lemke, ix. 409–15.

element, it was not surprising that the proportion of *popovichi* in its ranks was very much higher than the proportion of *popovichi* among the Russian middle classes as a whole. But this predominance of priests' children left its mark on the outlook of the Russian intelligentsia. To it must be attributed in considerable measure the preoccupation of the intelligentsia with moral issues, the contempt for worldly success and pleasures, the introduction into political issues of notions of absolute right and wrong. It has often been pointed out that when young Russians lost their religious faith, they seldom became rationalist sceptics, as was usual among their contemporaries in north-western Europe,[1] but carried into their atheist beliefs and their doctrines of social revolution a religious fervour, and in many cases a personal saintliness, which recall to Western minds the age of medieval heresies or the religious wars.

Chernyshevsky and Dobrolyubov both possessed these qualities, and revealed them in their writings and in their personal lives.[2] Chernyshevsky was born in Saratov, educated at a seminary, and then came to St. Petersburg University. He was tremendously excited by the events of 1848 in Europe. In 1849 he read Feuerbach's *Das Wesen des Christentums* and lost his faith. He was influenced by the Ukrainian historian Kostomarov, whom he met during the latter's period of exile in Saratov, and by A. V. Khanykov, a former member of the Petrashevsky Circle, whom he knew in St. Petersburg. Chernyshevsky's first writings were literary criticism, and tended towards the rehabilitation of Belinsky's criteria of social utilitarianism. From 1855 he became a regular contributor to *Sovremennik*. His main interest was now in economics, both in general theory and in its application to the special problems of Russia. At first he greeted with enthusiasm the Tsar's announced intention to deal with serfdom. But as the process of reform was dragged out, and as the authorities increasingly interfered with public discussion of the issues, his attitude changed. He opposed not only the government but the moderate liberals. His relations with Turgenev were strained. The exiled Herzen took a strong dislike to his

[1] But not necessarily in southern Europe. For Spaniards and Neapolitans the loss of religious faith tended also to lead not to scepticism but to revolutionary fanaticism of a quasi-religious character.

[2] A recent work, E. Lambert, *Sons against Fathers* (1964), gives an excellent summary of the lives and ideas of Chernyshevsky, Dobrolyubov, and Pisarev.

writings. His irritation culminated in an article in *Kolokol* in June 1859, entitled (in English) 'Very Dangerous'. This not only denounced the attitude of 'the bilious ones', but implied that it was encouraged by the censorship and police as advantageous to them. Chernyshevsky, alarmed by the effect which this article produced in Russia, personally went to London to see Herzen. No account of their interview has survived. Herzen was convinced of Chernyshevsky's political sincerity, and withdrew his insinuation against the motives of 'the bilious' in a later number of *Kolokol*. But the two men were not reconciled. Chernyshevsky wrote to Dobrolyubov that he had been dreadfully bored by Herzen. 'He is a Kavelin squared: that is all.' With these words Chernyshevsky was dismissing the generation that had suffered under Nicholas I, was writing off the age of Russian liberalism, and speaking in the name of the new age of organized doctrinaire politics, an age whose threshold he himself would be unable to cross.[1]

Chernyshevsky's close friend Dobrolyubov, who died at the age of twenty-five, made his mark in literary criticism. He took up the message of Belinsky, but made it narrower and more rigid. He had less insight into literature as such than had Belinsky, and indeed was not much interested in purely literary values. Literary criticism was to him a means, permitted by the censorship, of expressing radical social and political ideas, and the merit of a literary work depended on its utility to the cause of political progress. Dobrolyubov's long articles on Turgenev's *On the Eve* and Goncharov's *Oblomov* are important documents in the history of Russian political thought, rather than literary essays. His writings had a great influence on his generation, and his short life was unselfishly devoted to the service of his political ideas. The price of his achievement was that he did more than any man to shackle upon Russian literature the dogma of revolutionary utilitarianism, which in later years became a heavy burden.

Another remarkable figure of these years was D. I. Pisarev (1840–68), who was not a member of the *Sovremennik* circle but

[1] 'Very Dangerous' is in Herzen, *Works*, ix. 419. Chernyshevsky's comment is in the complete edition of his works, *Polnoe sobranie sochineniy*, ed. V. Y. Kirpotin and others (Moscow, 1939–51), xiv. 379. The letter to Dobrolyubov is from the end of June 1859.

contributed to its rival *Russkoe slovo*. Most of his work was written while he was in prison for political propaganda between 1862 and 1866. His main concern was the need for radical intellectuals to train themselves for the role of a revolutionary *élite* in the future. Mass revolution was not for the moment possible. What was needed was an *élite* of 'thinking realists' who must prepare themselves for action when the opportunity should arise later. Meanwhile they must rid themselves of all prejudices and traditions, and accept nothing from their elders without careful examination. This must apply not only to political and social ideas but to the whole field of morality and to the arts. Pisarev's attitude to literature and art was not very different from that of Dobrolyubov. Education must be based on the natural sciences. History had some utility in relation to the political struggle, but for the most part the humanities were a waste of time. The product of art was 'socially negligible', and talented persons should not waste their time on it. Rather, they should place themselves at the service of the people. 'The final aim of all our thinking and of all the activity of every decent man amounts to this—to solve for ever the unavoidable question of hungry and naked people; apart from this question there is definitely nothing which it would be worth worrying, thinking and fussing about.'[1] Pisarev accepted with pride the name 'Nihilist', invented by Turgenev in his novel *Fathers and Sons*, which appeared in 1861. Liberal and radical opinion had given an unfavourable reception to this work, claiming that it was an unfair caricature. But Pisarev accepted it as a true picture, of which he was proud. The chief character in the novel, Bazarov, appeared to him an excellent model for imitation in real life. Pisarev had a great influence on his readers, but he did not live to play an active part in revolutionary leadership. Two years after his release from prison, he lost his life in a drowning accident in 1868.[2]

In the five years immediately following the emancipation of

[1] From his article 'The Realists', published in *Russkoe slovo* (1864), nos. 9, 10, and 11. The passage quoted is in D. I. Pisarev, *Sochineniya* (Moscow, 1955–6), iii. 105.

[2] The best modern edition of his works is D. I. Pisarev, *Sochineniya*, 4 vols., Moscow, 1955–6. Essays of particular interest are 'Bazarov' (ii. 7–50), 'Realisty' (iii. 7–138), 'Razrushenie estetiki' (iii. 418–35), and 'Myslyashchii proletariat' (iv. 7–48). A valuable modern study of his life and works is Armand Coquart, *Dmitri Pisarev (1840–68) et l'idéologie du nihilisme russe*, Paris, 1946.

the serfs the first small revolutionary groups appeared in Russia. Most of their members were of the intelligentsia. Not content merely to discuss political and social ideas, they discussed methods of action, and made practical efforts to spread propaganda among the people. Shchapov's speech at the service for the peasants killed at Bezdna, attended by Kazan University students, was a political action. The student riots of the autumn of 1861, in which specific professional grievances mingled with wider political discontent, caused a deepening and a diffusion of political unrest. In July 1861 appeared in St. Petersburg a printed leaflet entitled *Velikoruss*. Its authorship has never been established, though it shows some influence of the ideas of Chernyshevsky. It was directed to the educated class, and argued that the policies of the existing government would lead to another Pugachov rebellion unless it was replaced by enlightened people. Two more numbers of the same title appeared in September, and urged that the Tsar be asked to summon a Constituent Assembly.

Also in the summer of 1861 appeared a leaflet entitled *To the Young Generation*, the work of two friends, N. V. Shelgunov and the poet M. Mikhailov. This had a much more extreme revolutionary quality, and combined social radicalism with a sense of the special mission of Russia. The hereditary Tsar should be replaced by 'a simple mortal, a man of the soil who understands the life of the people and is chosen by the people'. Russia had no need of the doctrines or examples of the West. 'We are a backward people, and therein lies our salvation. We must thank destiny that we have not lived the life of Europe. Its misfortune, its present position from which there is no way out, are a lesson for us. We do not want its proletariat, its aristocratic system, its principles of state, its imperial power. . . . We believe in the strength of Russia because we believe that we are called to bring into history a new principle, to say our own word, and not to repeat the stale old lessons of Europe.' Mikhailov was denounced by an informer and arrested. He took full responsibility for the leaflet, and was condemned to exile in Siberia, where he died in 1865.[1]

A still more violent appeal was contained in a leaflet *Young*

[1] The full text of *To the Young Generation* is printed in M. Lemke, *Politicheskie protsessy v Rossii 1860-kh godov* (Moscow, 1923), pp. 62–80.

Russia, which was distributed in May 1862. This was the work of a nineteen-year-old Moscow University student named P. G. Zaichnevsky, who organized a group of some twenty students and distributed lithographed political literature. The group was broken up by arrests in the summer of 1861, and it was while in prison that Zaichnevsky wrote *Young Russia*, smuggling it out to friends who had it printed and distributed. It proposed a republic based on central and regional assemblies, the latter based on village communes. There were to be 'social factories', whose directors would be elected by the workers. Poland and Lithuania were to be given complete independence. The hope was expressed that, when the day of revolution came, only a handful of people would defend the hated Imperial régime. But if serious resistance were offered, then, 'with full faith in ourselves and our strength, in the people's sympathy with us, in the glorious future of Russia, to whose lot it has fallen to be the first country to achieve the glorious work of socialism, we will utter a single cry: "To the axe!", and then, then strike the Imperial party without restraint, just as it does not spare its blows against us. Strike in the city squares—if this riffraff dares present itself there—strike in the houses, in the narrow streets of the cities, in the broad avenues of the capital, in the villages and in the small towns.'[1]

A more moderate, but potentially more effective, group was founded by N. A. Serno-Solovevich. At the age of twenty-four, in 1858, when he was a junior official, he handed the Tsar a memorandum urging reforms, as he was walking in Tsarskoe gardens, and later received a friendly reply. But next year, disillusioned with official policies, he left the state service and went abroad. He met Herzen in London, studied economic problems, and returned to Russia at the end of 1861 to set up a secret group entitled Land and Liberty (*Zemlya i volya*). He ran a lending-library in the capital, which specialized in political literature, and edited a newspaper which passed the censorship. He was arrested in July 1862 after some correspondence between him and Herzen had been intercepted. He was sentenced to deportation to Siberia, and in 1866 was killed there in obscure circumstances. Groups of like mind survived his arrest, not only in the capital but in some of the Volga cities and in Perm in the Urals. In itself his society achieved nothing, but

[1] The full text of *Young Russia* is printed ibid., pp. 508–18.

it has its importance as a link between the two stages of ideas and action.[1]

In the early summer of 1862 a number of mysterious fires broke out in St. Petersburg, and serious damage was done. Popular rumour attributed them to the revolutionaries, but there is no evidence of any connexion. The rumours, however, contributed to the decision of the government to take firm steps against all political offenders. Among the victims of a new wave of arrests was Chernyshevsky himself. The evidence on which he was convicted, at his trial in May 1864, was largely false, but it is not clear to what extent he was involved in the revolutionary activity of these years. Modern Soviet historians are inclined to stress his role as an active revolutionary. He was sentenced to be deported to Siberia, and remained there until 1883. In 1889 he was at last allowed to return to his home town of Saratov, and died a few months later.

The Polish Rebellion of 1863 aroused comparatively little sympathy in Russia: nationalism proved stronger than social radicalism. A conspiracy in Kazan involved some army officers of Polish origin and some Russian civilians connected with *Zemlya i volya*. In exile, Herzen came out boldly on behalf of the Poles. In this he was supported by his old friend Michael Bakunin. Arrested in Dresden during a revolutionary action in 1849, Bakunin had been deported to Russia, spent seven years in prison, and been deported to Siberia. In 1861 he escaped by sea to Japan and thence to Europe, joining Herzen in London at the end of December. The attempts of Herzen and Bakunin to organize material help for the Poles failed, and they lost influence among Russian democrats by their pro-Polish posture. The rebellion provoked a wave of Russian chauvinism, and caused many liberals to rally behind the Tsar. Outstanding among these was the journalist M. N. Katkov, whose literary talents were thenceforth used to defend first the external and then the internal policies of the extreme reactionaries.

[1] An authentic but only partly informed source for *Zemlya i volya* is the memoirs of L. F. Panteleyev, *Iz vospominaniy proshlogo*, ed. S. S. Reiser (Moscow, 1934). The author took an active part in the organization in St. Petersburg, and visited Vologda on its behalf. A more important figure was A. A. Sleptsov, with whom Panteleyev later polemized. Sleptsov did not publish full-scale memoirs, but his version of the organization's history is told by Lemke in a long note in his edition of Herzen's *Works*, xvi. 69–102.

Revolutionary activity, however, still continued to exist. The most important remaining group was the 'Organization' created by N. A. Ishutin, who as a student at Moscow University in 1863 had been in touch with *Zemlya i volya.* The 'Organization' was created in 1865, and set itself the task of propaganda for a general insurrection. Ishutin had a romantic conception of the status and mission of the revolutionary, and intended his 'Organization' to have an inner circle, which was given the melodramatic name of 'Hell' (*Ad*). It is doubtful whether this inner circle had much reality. But a young man on the fringe of the group, D. V. Karakozov, a former student of Kazan University, announced his intention of assassinating the Tsar. Though Ishutin tried to dissuade him, he made his attempt on 4 April 1866. The Tsar was not hit. Karakozov was arrested, and was executed on 4 October. Ishutin too was condemned to death, but the sentence was commuted to deportation to Siberia.

Karakozov's attempt provoked a widespread reaction against the intelligentsia, even among the city workers. Popular feeling thus supported the government's intention to pursue a more repressive and conservative policy. A commission was set up to investigate the assassination, and its chairman was M. N. Muravyov, the butcher of Lithuania.[1] Golovnin was replaced as minister of education by Count Dmitri Tolstoy. Nekrasov did not hesitate to humiliate himself in order to save *Sovremennik*: he wrote a poem in honour of Muravyov. But he could not save his review. It was suppressed in the summer of 1866. Nekrasov was, however, able in 1868 to take over *Otechestvennye zapiski*, in which he had the assistance of the satirist M. E. Saltykov-Shchedrin.

Ever since the emancipation, government policy had been moving to the right, and liberty had been under growing pressure. It is wrong to think of the first ten years of the reign as an age of progress, and the last fifteen as one of black reaction. Nevertheless, the Karakozov attempt may be regarded as a significant landmark. It introduced a new period, in which the change in policies was not so important as the change in the men in power.

[1] See below p. 376.

The Polish Rebellion

The death of both Nicholas I and Paskevich marked the end of an epoch in Russian rule in Poland. The new viceroy, appointed in April 1856, was the former commander-in-chief at Sevastopol, Prince Michael Gorchakov. The Tsar himself came to Warsaw in May 1856 and made a speech to marshals of the nobility. Its general spirit was conciliatory, though he warned his listeners against political illusions ('point de rêveries, messieurs!'). Gorchakov began his rule with important concessions. A new Archbishop of Warsaw was appointed in November 1856. A Medical School of university status was set up in the capital in June 1857. In November 1857 the government agreed to the foundation of the Agricultural Society. This was indeed largely concerned with the technical and economic problems of agriculture, but it also provided an institution in which members of the Polish landowning class could meet and discuss wider problems of a social or political nature.

According to the census of 1859, Poland had a population of 4,764,000 of whom slightly more than three-quarters were Poles. The rest consisted of 600,000 Jews and about a quarter of a million each of Germans and Lithuanians. The number of Catholics was somewhat larger than the number of Poles, since nearly all Lithuanians and a few Germans belonged to the Roman Church. Less than a quarter of the population was literate. The urban population amounted to 1,164,000 of whom 653,000 were Christians and 511,000 Jews.[1] The Polish attitude to the Jews varied from mild distrust to active hostility, and this attitude corresponded in practice to that of the Catholic Church. The steady, if not sensational, growth of industry and of the urban population was bound to make the Jewish problem more acute.

Still more serious was the peasant problem, which the Polish landowners could not hope to avoid at a time when in Russia itself it was under examination. The future of the peasants was also bound up with the development of education, in which the Catholic Church was directly interested. Behind these great social and cultural problems lay the wider political aspirations of the Poles as a nation, and these included the question of

[1] R. F. Leslie, *Reform and Insurrection in Poland 1856–1865*, p. 50. For my general account of these events I am largely indebted to this excellent recent work.

historical Lithuania, on which agreement was no more possible between a patriotic Pole and a patriotic Russian than it had been in the age of Napoleon.

Two alternative policies were being canvassed for a solution to the land question. One was that all existing labour services should be converted to money rents. The second was that the peasants should be enabled to acquire freeholds of the land they cultivated, by paying the landowners the price of the land over a period of years. The landowners preferred the first. The most eminent spokesman of the landowners and the leading figure in the Agricultural Society, Count Andrew Zamoyski, had carried out the conversion to rents on his own estates, on terms comparatively favourable to the peasants. If a policy of conversion to freeholds were adopted, it was to be expected that the landowners would insist on the stiffest terms of payment they could get. Under the *Code Napoléon*, which had been in force in Poland since 1809, landowners were entitled to evict tenants. In June 1846 Paskevich had issued a decree granting fixity of tenure to all tenants of more than three acres, provided that they fulfilled their obligations to their landlords. But this decree had been largely evaded owing to the landlords' control of the local courts and administration. In 1859 there were 324,809 peasant farms in Poland of which 64 per cent. were on private estates and 36 per cent. on state lands. Of the farms on private estates, 52,506 were held on a basis of money rents, 32,636 on a mixture of money rents with services and payments in kind, and 124,840 on a basis of labour services.[1]

The Polish political *élite* fell into two main groups. The moderates were concentrated in the Agricultural Society, and their effective leader was Zamoyski. His policy was to co-operate with the Russian government, to obtain social and economic reforms, and to keep nationalist demands back for the time being. The radicals, whose main strength was to be found in the towns, especially in Warsaw, were not content to wait. They too wanted social and economic reforms, more radical than those desired by Zamoyski. But they were above all Polish nationalists, and would be content with nothing less than the recognition by Russia of Polish nationhood. In 1859 there were a number of radical groups, whose main strength was among

[1] Ibid., pp. 69–70.

the intelligentsia, including university students and young army officers. These groups were in touch with each other, and by the beginning of 1860 there was an embryonic radical leadership, whose main aim was to prevent a reconciliation between the Russian government and the Polish moderates, and to compromise the official reform programme by instigating public disorders. The radicals had some support within the Agricultural Society.

In February 1861 there were two demonstrations in Warsaw, the first in commemoration of the Battle of Grochów of 1831, and the second in memory of two Polish revolutionaries executed in 1833 and 1839. On the second occasion five persons were killed. Public indignation forced the Agricultural Society to sponsor an address to the Tsar, containing political demands, which was handed to Gorchakov on 28 February by Zamoyski and the Archbishop of Warsaw. The Tsar rejected the address, but let it be known that he was considering a programme of reforms. These were revealed a month later when Marquess Alexander Wielopolski was appointed to a newly created post of head of a commission of religion and education.

Wielopolski believed that it was useless to struggle for Polish independence, and had no use for empty patriotic gestures. He accepted the fact of Russian rule, but aimed at making it more tolerable. His policy was to set up Polish governmental institutions, somewhat similar to those of the former Organic Statute of 1832, to ensure the full legal equality of Jews with Christians and to adopt a land policy of conversion to money rents. In this he had the support of Gorchakov and of Alexander II. But the Polish landowning class refused him their co-operation. His policy would have suited their class interests. But the most devoted patriots among them objected to any co-operation with the Russians, at least unless Lithuania were brought under the same system as the Kingdom, while the moderates, whatever their real beliefs as to what was politically possible, were too frightened of the indignation of the radicals to commit themselves. Zamoyski himself was the outstanding case. He was against nationalist agitation, but he was also unwilling to besmirch his reputation as a Polish patriot by helping Wielopolski. His passive attitude contributed largely to the tragedy which followed.

Wielopolski's land policy was conversion to money rents. The Agricultural Society, under pressure from the radicals, had now committed itself, if with little enthusiasm, to conversion to freeholds. Wielopolski therefore decided to dissolve the society, on 6 April 1861. On the following two days the radicals organized large street demonstrations in Warsaw, ostensibly to honour Zamoyski and the society. On the second day the crowds misunderstood or ignored the instructions to disperse, and the Russian troops fired. The number of dead, officially reported as 10, was estimated by some observers as nearly 200.

Wielopolski pressed ahead with his programme. A decree of 4 May 1861 provided for conversion to money rents, at rates which his advisory committee of landlords considered too advantageous to the peasants. Its implementation was left to rural district councils which were to be elected on a property franchise. In practice, in a total rural population of about 3,500,000, the electorate amounted to a little less than 25,000. Elections were held in September. The radicals urged voters to boycott, but Zamoyski came out in favour of voting. About four-fifths of those qualified used their vote. Out of a total of 615 rural district seats, 457 went to landlords and only 7 to peasants.

Wielopolski also set up new political institutions. There was to be a system of self-government, at rural, city, and provincial level. A central Council of State was to be the highest authority under the viceroy. It consisted of the members of the Administrative Council, together with other persons nominated by the viceroy, the bishops, the provincial councils, and the Land Credit Society.

Gorchakov died in May, and was replaced after an interval by Count Charles Lambert. On 5 October the Catholic Archbishop of Warsaw died, and his funeral was made the occasion for a demonstration. This was followed five days later by a provocative demonstration in favour of the reunion of Lithuania with Poland, and on 15 October there was yet another demonstration, this time in commemoration of the death of Kościuszko. On this occasion church services were turned into something like sit-in strikes, with congregations singing Polish patriotic hymns and refusing to leave the buildings. Eventually Russian troops forcibly cleared the churches and a state of siege was declared in Warsaw. The administrator of the diocese of

Warsaw then declared that all churches would remain closed until the government gave satisfaction for its sacrilegious action. Thus not only the radicals but the Catholic Church were in direct conflict with Wielopolski. He was recalled to St. Petersburg for consultations, and meanwhile General Sukhozanet ruled Poland by martial law.

During the following months the Polish moderates established a political organization, with a Directory of six persons. They became known as the 'Whites'. Their most efficient member was the business man Leopold Kronenberg, a convert from the Jewish to the Catholic faith, who could at least place funds at their disposal. At the same time the radicals set up a central command known as the City Committee (*Komitet Miejski*). Their effective leader at this time was Jarosław Dąbrowski, an officer trained and serving in the Russian army, who was posted to Warsaw in February 1862.

After months of indecision, the Tsar decided to make another attempt at winning Polish support for reform, and agreed on 19 May 1862 to a new programme proposed by Wielopolski. It was strongly supported by the Tsar's liberal-minded brother, Grand Duke Constantine, who was appointed viceroy. The extremists were determined to prevent any reforms, and any Russo-Polish reconciliation. On 3 June a workman named Jaroszyński made an unsuccessful attempt on the grand duke at the theatre, and on 7 and 15 August further attempts, also unsuccessful, were made on Wielopolski. Constantine declared that the reforms would go ahead unchanged, and made a rather good impression on the public. But Wielopolski, believing that severity was essential, insisted that the would-be assassins should be executed. This caused popular indignation, which was exploited by the radicals. For his part Zamoyski remained studiously aloof, refusing to give any public encouragement to the government. Wielopolski's main reforms, a law on public education which provided a more extensive system of Polish schools and a university (*Szkoła Główna*) in Warsaw, and a law on the emancipation of Jews, made no impression on his opponents. Intending to force the moderates into co-operation with him, he banished Zamoyski abroad. Intending to deprive the radicals of young men, he declared his intention to conscript young Poles into the army.

The conscription decree brought the Polish crisis to its climax. In the autumn months large numbers of young men, knowing that they would soon be called up, went into hiding. The radicals, now usually known as the Reds, set up provincial commands for armed rebellion, and the town committee turned itself into a central committee to plan the insurrection. It suffered a severe loss when Dąbrowski was arrested, at the end of August 1862, but it went ahead with its plans. At the beginning of January 1863 a definite decision to rebel was taken. The date was pushed forward by the government's decision to speed up its conscription measures. The rebellion broke out on 22 January 1863.

The rebellion lasted more than a year. But in contrast to the war of 1831, no large-scale battles between armies took place, and the Poles held no large cities. In various parts of the country insurgent bands were active. The landowners usually supported them, from a mixture of patriotic enthusiasm and fear of being thought unpatriotic. The peasants' reaction was variable. The land reform proposals of the leaders of the rebellion, which involved substantial compensation to landowners for land converted into peasant freeholds, made little impression on them. In some places peasants gave active support to the insurgents, in others they helped the Russians against them. There were cases of terrorization, even of executions, of peasants by insurgent commanders.

Outside the Kingdom of Poland, the rebellion received some support in Lithuania, but virtually none in the Kiev region. The Polish provinces of Austria and Prussia remained quiet, however great the sympathy for the Polish cause may have been. The sympathy expressed in France and England probably on balance damaged the Poles, for it allowed the Polish exiles to hope that the Western Powers would go to war against Russia on their behalf. Optimistic messages from the exiles probably caused the rebellion to last longer than it need, and so increased the total amount of suffering.[1]

The political leadership of the rebellion was not impressive. It must be remembered that the conditions of the struggle were difficult, and that the maintenance of communication between conspiratorial groups is never a simple task. Even so, the

[1] For the diplomatic aspects of the rebellion see below pp. 434–5.

rivalries and intrigues between Whites and Reds, and within each of these groups, form an unedifying story.[1] It is redeemed by the courage of countless individuals, including the last leader of the rebellion, Romuald Traugutt, who was executed on 5 August 1864.

The rebellion was repressed with special severity in Lithuania. Here the legal position was of course different from that in the Kingdom. As Lithuania was an integral part of the Russian empire, any of its inhabitants who rose against the government were guilty of treason. In May 1863 Count M. N. Muravyov was appointed governor-general of Lithuania, and did his best to justify his boast that he was 'one of the Muravyovs who do the hanging, not one of those who get hanged'. Grand Duke Constantine continued to plead for leniency in the Kingdom. The Tsar inclined the other way, and the grand duke, whose health was poor, retired from Polish affairs. The new commander-in-chief in Warsaw, General Fyodor (or Theodor) Berg, began moderately, but after an unsuccessful attempt on his life on 19 September 1863 he was more severe. There were executions and confiscations of property.

The Russian government was not, however, content to repress. It was decided also to introduce reforms. On 31 August 1863 Nicholas Milyutin was appointed head of a commission to carry out a land reform in the Kingdom. He took with him his old friends from the emancipation period, Yurii Samarin and Prince Cherkassky. The result of their labours was the agrarian settlement introduced in March 1864. About 700,000 families of Polish peasants obtained freeholds, while maintaining their rights to the use of forests and pasture lands. They paid no redemption dues. The government paid compensation to the landowners, on much less favourable terms than Russian landowners had received in 1861, and the cost was recovered through a land tax levied on all owners of land. About 130,000 holdings were also created out of state lands for landless peasants. The reorganization of local administration, which followed from the land reform, differed from that of the 1861 system in Russia. The unit of government, the rural commune or *gmina*, included all inhabitants, landowners as well as

[1] For details see Leslie, op. cit., ch. 8.

peasants. There was no legal separation of the peasants from the other inhabitants as under the Russian *volost* system.

The Russian government's aim was of course to separate the peasants politically from the ruling class, to wean the peasants away from Polish nationalism and make them good Russian subjects. It was an attempt to apply the belief, held by some Russian Slavophils, that Poles were really good Slav peasants, unfortunately corrupted by centuries of Catholicism and landlordism, who, given a chance, would revert to their primeval Slav loyalties.

It is true that as a result of the suppression of the rebellion the Polish peasants got better terms than they would have got if there had been no rebellion, and if Wielopolski's reforms had been carried out. It is even arguable that the terms of March 1864 were better than those promised by the leaders of the rebellion in their 'land decree' of 1 March 1863. But the reform of 1864 did not of course win the Polish peasants to Russian rule. On the contrary, now that the Polish land was theirs, Poland was their country in a much more real sense than it had ever been. Though class differences remained in Poland, as in other societies, yet peasants and landowners and middle classes were able, more than in the past, to merge into one nation. All alike now faced a single common enemy, the Russian state. This point has been well made by a recent historian of the rebellion:

> The victory of 1864 was in the long run empty of advantage for the Russian government. It destroyed the one justification which might have been advanced, that the Russian bureaucracy protected the Polish peasants from the manor. In future the peasants would seek relief from the pressure of Russian officialdom. . . . The inevitable consequence was that the only way by which a Russian government could transform a Pole into a loyal citizen was to convert him into a Russian. From 1864 the process of russification began.[1]

[1] Leslie, op. cit., p. 249. Note that these remarks apply to the Kingdom. Russification had been going on for thirty years, at the expense of the Poles, in Lithuania and the Ukraine, but it was only after 1863 that the Russian authorities tried to russify the Kingdom.

XI

FROM DISENCHANTMENT TO ASSASSINATION

Government and Administration

THE attempt on the Tsar's life by Karakozov immediately strengthened the tendency towards a reaction away from reform in government policy which had already been apparent since 1861, and especially since the Polish Rebellion.

In the following years new men came to the top. The first was Count Peter Shuvalov, a descendant of the eminent statesman of Catherine II's reign. Born in 1827, he entered the army, and distinguished himself in the last stages of the defence of Sevastopol. In 1857 he was appointed chief of police in St. Petersburg, and in 1860 transferred to the Ministry of the Interior, in which he became known as an opponent of the emancipation of the serfs. After two years as acting governor-general of the Baltic provinces, he was appointed in 1866 head of the Third Department and chief of gendarmes. For seven years he held this post, and used his influence to prevent new reforms, to retard the execution of existing reforms, and to appoint persons of reactionary views to important positions. A man of great ability and charm, much trusted by the emperor, he exercised a strong and pernicious influence on internal policy. His appointment as ambassador to London in 1874 was doubly fortunate, since it not only ended his reactionary intrigues at home but also gave scope to his remarkable diplomatic talents in a place where Russia needed them.

A second figure who now became important was Michael Katkov. Born in 1818 in Moscow, the son of a provincial official, he was a brilliant student of Moscow University, and in 1837 became a member of the Stankevich circle and a friend of Belinsky. After some years of study abroad, and literary journalism, living at times in great poverty, he was appointed assistant professor of philosophy in Moscow in 1845. Here he formed a lifelong friendship with P. M. Leontyev, professor of Latin literature, and became an enthusiastic supporter of classical education. In 1850 Katkov lost his job when teaching of philosophy was stopped by Shirinsky-Shikhmatov. In 1851 he became editor of the newspaper *Moskovskie vedomosti*, and in 1856 also of *Russkii vestnik*. For the remaining thirty-six years of his life he was above all a journalist, perhaps the most eminent in Russia. In the new reign Katkov, whose interests had been literary and philosophical, became increasingly preoccupied with politics. He was from the beginning a fervent Russian patriot, convinced of Russia's duty to pursue an active foreign policy as a Great Power. At the same time he was a liberal, and actively supported the emancipation, zemstvo, and judicial reforms. His ideal was constitutional monarchy of the English type. His reforming zeal even involved him in trouble with the censorship on several occasions. Even at this time, however, Katkov disliked radicalism, and polemized with the writers of *Sovremennik* and with the exiled Herzen. The turning-point in Katkov's political development was the Polish Rebellion. From the beginning he denounced the Poles. He became the most effective mouthpiece of Russian nationalism, and rallied many moderate liberals to his cause, isolating the minority of radicals who presumed to believe that Poles as well as Russians have a right to liberty. Katkov's evolution is not unlike that of the Prussian liberals with whom Bismarck dealt: when a conflict arose between liberalism and nationalism, the second prevailed. But having become an enemy of Polish liberties, Katkov began to have doubts of Russian liberties too. As the years passed, he began to criticize the institutions created by the reforms, especially the independent courts. In the 1870's Katkov became the most talented spokesman of all reactionary policies, and his earlier liberal patriotism changed into a sour and aggressive Russian imperialism. In the second half of Alexander II's reign, and still more in the first years of his successor's Katkov did more than anyone to form such unofficial public opinion as was taken into account by the Russian government.

The third important new figure was Count Dmitri Tolstoy, who was appointed minister of education in April 1866. Born in 1823 into one of the leading aristocratic families, a graduate of

Tsarskoe Selo *lycée* in 1843, he became chief procurator of the Holy Synod in 1856.

Tolstoy has become known in Russian historical literature as one of the most bigoted and most influential reactionaries of the nineteenth century. He was uniformly hated by educated Russians of liberal or radical outlook. The rather conservative Chicherin wrote in his memoirs: 'One can name but few people who did more harm to Russia. In this respect Count Tolstoy can rank with Chernyshevsky and Katkov.'[1] According to Chicherin, Tolstoy plagiarized other people's work in his own writings, got his house in St. Petersburg by a dishonest business deal, cheated his peasants at the emancipation, and owed his position to the support of Katkov and to base flattery of Alexander II's mistress, Princess Catherine Dolgorukaya. On the other hand, P. D. Shestakov, who was curator of Kazan educational district from 1864 to 1883 and thus worked closely with Tolstoy for fourteen years, insists in his memoirs that Tolstoy was devoted to his work and thought deeply about it. He stresses his 'direct, cheerful, and frank nature, which exercised a magical, infectious power'.[2] Tolstoy made a point of visiting one educational district of the empire every year, and travelling around it for anything up to two months, although his health was poor and these journeys in rough conditions placed a serious strain on it. Shestakov insists also that Tolstoy scrupulously observed the University Statute of 1863 during his period of office as minister of education, even against the attacks of his friend Katkov. When unjust accusations were made against Kazan University students or professors in connexion with the Karakozov affair, Tolstoy personally supported them.[3]

The main feature of Tolstoy's educational policy was the restoration of the emphasis on classics. In this respect he went far beyond the practice of the Uvarov period. Tolstoy was much influenced by Katkov and Leontyev. Not having himself had a classical education, he was inclined to listen uncritically to

[1] B. N. Chicherin, *Vospominaniya: Moskovskii universitet* (Moscow, 1929–34), iii. 192.

[2] *RS* (Feb. 1891), pp. 396–7.

[3] Same author, *RS* (Apr. 1891), pp. 185, 191–2, 194–5. It is worth noting that the abolition of the 1863 University Statute took place in 1884, when Tolstoy was minister of the interior, but after the revolutionary activities of 1878–81 and the assassination of Alexander II. The validity of Shestakov's evidence on Tolstoy as minister of education is not necessarily affected by Tolstoy's later record as minister of the interior.

those who had. The curriculum of the gimnazii was now so overloaded with classics that the teaching of Russian language and history were seriously impaired, and it became impossible for a gimnaziya pupil to study two modern languages. The argument of the classicists was that a good knowledge of Greek and Latin would not only train the young mind, but make it less vulnerable to subversive ideas. This was of course the opposite of the arguments used by Uvarov's critics twenty years earlier, that an acquaintance with such radicals as Thucydides or Tacitus would put dangerous thoughts into young heads. There is no doubt that Tolstoy's classicist programme went too far, and was adopted too fast, despite a serious shortage of qualified teachers. One of the complaints made against him was that he invited too many Czechs to teach classics in Russian schools. In most gimnazii the teaching of classics, whether by foreigners or by Russians, was pedantic and boring, and far from developing a love of the classics, caused many young Russians to regard them as a form of mental torture.[1]

Arguments about Tolstoy's classicism have, however, been more often political than educational. Tolstoy's encouragement of the classics coincided with the diffusion of the idea that progressive education ought to be based mainly on the natural sciences. Here the diverse influences of German materialist philosophy, Pisarev's thinking realism, and Chernyshevsky's socialism came together in a common dislike of religion and tradition, and a common enthusiasm for the liberating agency of science on the human mind. Tolstoy's policy provoked a reaction whose vehemence can only partly be explained in terms of the merits or defects of classical education. It remains a fact that his policy, by arousing antagonism to the classics, reinforced the worship of science and contempt for the humanities among a large part of the Russian educated class, and so strengthened the doctrine of revolutionary utilitarianism which, first formulated by Belinsky in relation to literature, and further developed in their different ways by Dobrolyubov and Pisarev, extended in the last decades of the century to almost all branches of the arts and learning.

[1] It is only fair to add that Russia was not the only country of which this was true. In fact, this state of affairs was not unknown north of the English Channel well into the twentieth century.

By a law of 30 July 1871, the hours devoted to classical languages, and especially Greek, were greatly increased, and local educational authorities were ordered to apply strictly the curricula laid down by the central ministry. In 1871 a clear separation was made between classical schools, for which the name gimnaziya was exclusively reserved, and modern studies schools, which were now named 'real schools'.[1] The former provided the only access to universities, while the latter could train their pupils for various higher technical institutions. The curriculum of the real schools was regulated by a law of 15 May 1872. It reduced the hours of natural science and increased the hours of mathematics. A new law on the *uezd* schools was introduced in May 1872. It had been Tolstoy's intention to give these a curriculum which would enable children to pass from them to a gimnaziya and thus to a university. In the process of legislation this was modified, so as to allow only the movement from *uezd* school to real school, and hence to a technological institution of non-university status. On this occasion it was Tolstoy who stood for a liberal policy, and the dignitaries of the Council of State who acted on behalf of class privilege and segregation. In May 1871 Tolstoy introduced a statute for teachers' training colleges, and increased the number both of colleges and of teacher trainees. Tolstoy was personally opposed to higher education for women, but unable entirely to prevent it. In 1872 Moscow University organized lecture courses of university standard specially for women. Thanks to the support of the liberal minister of war, D. A. Milyutin, the Military Medical Academy of St. Petersburg admitted women to its courses. In 1876 an official Statute for Women's Higher Courses was issued, under which women were able to study at the universities of the two capitals, Odessa, Kiev, and Kazan. By 1881 there were about 2,000.

During Tolstoy's period of office, the number of institutions and pupils increased substantially. In 1863 there had been 94 gimnazii for boys with 31,132 pupils: in 1876 there were 131 gimnazii and 72 pro-gimnazii with 52,455 pupils between them. In 1881 there were 92 gimnazii and 178 pro-gimnazii for

[1] The Russian title *real'noe uchilishche* is a translation of the German *Realschule*. As there is no exact English equivalent, we shall have to use hereafter the clumsy expression 'real school'.

girls with probably less than 50,000 pupils. In 1873, 23 real schools were opened: in 1882 there were 79 with 17,484 pupils.

During these years provincial self-government achieved some results, in spite of the unsympathetic attitude which now prevailed at the centre of government. Zemstvo institutions were introduced at once in twenty-seven provinces and soon afterwards in a further seven. Within two years restrictive measures were enacted. A law of 21 November 1866 limited the right of zemstvos to tax industrial and commercial enterprises. This could be regarded as a measure protecting the rising business class against the landowning interests, but it was also a reflection of government distrust of local initiatives. A further restrictive law followed on 13 June 1867. It gave greater disciplinary powers to chairmen of assemblies over members who 'deviate from respect for the law'. It forbade zemstvos of different provinces to consult each other on matters of common interest which concerned general government policy, or to discuss the limits imposed by law on the competence of zemstvos. It also empowered provincial governors to censor minutes of zemstvo meetings or any other zemstvo reports intended for publication.[1] In a deliberate attempt to make it difficult for a wider public to be informed about local government activities, orders were given that no more copies of such documents might be published than there were members in the respective assembly.

In 1870 a circular from the Ministry of the Interior to zemstvos asked their opinion on the replacement of the poll-tax by an income-tax to be levied on all classes. The response was generally favourable. This may be partly explained by the fact that landowners believed that the income-tax would fall more heavily on business men than on themselves. It was due also to a fairly widespread belief in the abolition of privileges and equal treatment of all classes before the law. The change was of course opposed by reactionaries. There was also in some cases opposition from liberals. A case in point is Chicherin, who objected to the taxation of the nobility unless it was accompanied by political reforms. He wished to link the surrender by the nobility of their privilege of immunity from taxation, formally enacted in the Charter of 1785, with the demand for

[1] The laws of 21 Nov. 1866 and 13 June 1867 are discussed in Veselovsky, op. cit. iii. 121–6.

constitutional rights. He argued that society should be levelled upwards, not levelled down. At an unofficial meeting of thirty zemstvo dignitaries in Moscow, presided over by Samarin, the majority were in favour of the change. 'They could see no higher', Chicherin commented, 'than democratic absolutism, that is, the worst form of government that there is on earth.' Asked whether he was in favour of abolishing the distinction between taxed and untaxed, black and white, Chicherin replied that he was, provided that the black became white, not that the white became black. To which Koshelyov replied: 'As we can't all be quite white (*belenkimi*), let us all be a little bit black (*chernenkimi*).'[1] Despite the generally favourable response, the reform was not in fact carried out.

The total expenditure of zemstvos was 5,600,000 roubles in 1865, 24,000,000 in 1870, and 33,000,000 in 1880. The zemstvos were compelled to spend money and manpower on carrying out in their regions various tasks required by the central government. These obligations accounted for 51 per cent. of their total expenditures in 1870. Expenditure by zemstvos on public health was 1,300,000 roubles in 1868 and nearly 4,000,000 in 1875. In the same period expenditure on schools rose from 700,000 to 3,300,000. The zemstvos' legal powers in education were small, for the schools councils, though partly financed by the zemstvos, were directed by bureaucrats, and the zemstvo representatives on them were in a minority. Nevertheless, through the zemstvos enlightened public opinion made itself felt. Outstanding among those who campaigned for more modern schools of better quality was Baron N. A. Korf, who was strongly supported by the ageing but still energetic Koshelyov. An example of reactionary opposition to zemstvo education was Prince Meshchersky, who submitted a memorandum to the school council of Moscow province, in which appeared the sentence: 'The teaching of the law of the Christian faith is becoming ever more unsatisfactory, and forms the weakest side of the whole system and way of life of our schools, yielding its place to morally destructive reasoning.' Zemstvo schools, in his opinion, were producing only good-for-nothings.

There were, however, still two important series of reforms carried out in the second part of the reign.

[1] B. N. Chicherin, *Vospominaniya*, iv. 40.

The first was the reorganization of city government, which followed naturally from the reorganization of provincial government in the zemstvo reform. In March 1862 the Tsar instructed the minister of the interior to prepare measures to this effect. In the following years detailed studies were made of existing practices both in Russia and in European countries, and proposals were put before the Council of State in 1866. The bureaucratic processes went ahead at their customary solemn pace, and the new system did not become law until 16 June 1870. It was put into effect in the following years in several stages, region by region. The eight largest cities of the empire were given status equal to that of a province, and their commandant (*gradonachal'nik*) had the rank of a provincial governor. All other cities had the status of an *uezd*, and came under the authority of the governor in the same way as a territorial *uezd*. Every city was to have a municipal council (*gorodskaya duma*).

The councils were large bodies, and they elected from their number an executive board (*uprava*) and a mayor (*gorodskaya golova*). The franchise for elections to the councils was based on a property census. Those who neither owned a house nor paid trade tax had no vote. This excluded not only most workers but many professional people. The election of mayors had to be confirmed by the minister of the interior. In the case of the two capitals, the council put forward two names, one of which was chosen by the emperor personally. Councils did not control their police forces: these were commanded by a *Polizeimeister* who was appointed by the minister of the interior. The councils were responsible for the usual amenities of cities—lighting, sanitation, transportation, and the like. They also had a share in the direction of the schools in their cities, comparable to that of the zemstvos in the territorial *uezd*. The councils were entitled to levy municipal taxes on house property, inns, drink and food shops, cabs, private carriages and horses, and stamp duties on legal and business documents. Gradually in the next decades the external appearance of Russian cities improved. In the central business districts firm pavements offered protection from muddy street surfaces, a few streets at least were lit at night, tram services were started, and drainage and refuse disposal improved.

The last important reforms of the reign were in the army.

They were the work of the minister of war, D. A. Milyutin, brother of N. A. Milyutin and like him a liberal. Unlike his brother, he held high office for a long time, from 1861 to 1881. After his resignation, he lived on to 1912, dying at the age of ninety-six.

Milyutin began by reorganizing the central and regional commands of the army. The number of departments in the Ministry of War was reduced and their functions more clearly defined. The separation of the artillery and the engineers from the other branches, with their own supply services and with direct access to the emperor by-passing the minister, usually through their being placed under a grand duke, was ended. The military training establishments were placed under the ministry. These changes were effected in 1867. Apart from increasing efficiency, they reduced the staff of the central ministry by nearly 1,000 persons, and its volume of correspondence by 45 per cent. In August 1864 Milyutin also introduced a new system of regional commands, dividing the empire into 15 military districts and clearly defining the relations of the regional commander to his branches of service and to the ministry.

Another important task was to organize an efficient reserve. In 1862 the regular army numbered nearly 800,000 and the reserve to be mobilized in wartime a further 600,000. But in fact the available reserve was only 210,000. Whereas the French army could double its effectives in wartime, the Austrians slightly more than double, and the Prussians increase by nearly three and a half times, the Russian army could be increased only by 25 per cent.[1] By a series of measures Milyutin succeeded in increasing the effective reserve to 553,000 by 1870. He also reorganized the system of military schools and colleges, reducing the element of class privilege and improving the purely military side of the training. As a result of his reforms the military colleges (*voennye uchilishcha*) turned out 600 officers a year, while a new type of establishment which he created, cadet colleges (*yunkerskie uchilishcha*) turned out about 1,500 yearly. The old cadet corps were abolished, and transformed into

[1] France from 400,000 to 800,000; Austria from 280,000 to 625,000; Prussia from 200,000 to 695,000. Report to Tsar of 15 Jan. 1862, quoted in the official history of the War Ministry, *Stoletie Voennogo Ministerstva* (SPB, 1902), i. 75.

military colleges. The only exception was the Corps of Pages, which remained an aristocratic institution.

After 1866 Milyutin's position in the government was under attack, but he held his own. Shuvalov disliked Milyutin as a liberal, and as a man who cared little for established privileges when it came to building up Russia's armed strength. The impact of the Franco-Prussian War was not lost on Milyutin. He realized that Russia was still far behind in the competition of the Powers, and he felt that the time had come radically to reorganize the whole system of recruitment, to create for the first time a system of universal military service, to place the Russian army on the same footing as the German and the French. In this he had the backing of Valuyev, and the Tsar himself agreed. But the preparation of the reform was difficult. Inevitably, he had to abolish the privilege granted to the nobility of exemption from compulsory recruitment. Even so liberal a man as Chicherin resented this as 'a violation of the Charter granted to the nobility by Catherine'. Shuvalov and his friends exploited their opportunity. Prince Baryatinsky and Count Berg, two former field-marshals, accused the Ministry of War of extravagance, and the Tsar decided to appoint a special commission in March 1872 to recommend economies in the ministry, with Baryatinsky as its chairman. Nevertheless, Milyutin continued with his plans, and on 13 January 1874 the new system came into effect.

Milyutin's bitterness is shown in a long entry in his diary on 31 December 1873, surveying the previous year:

> For me 1873 passed like a dark cloud; only sad impressions are left of it. In no preceding year did I endure so much unpleasantness, annoyance, and failure. The intrigue begun long ago against me grew to full maturity and unfolded in all its ugliness. . . . Everything is done under the exclusive influence of Count Shuvalov, who has terrified the emperor with his daily reports about frightful dangers, to which allegedly the state and the sovereign himself are exposed. All Shuvalov's strength is based upon this bogey. Under the pretext of protection of the emperor's person and of the monarchy, Shuvalov interferes in everything, and all matters are decided in accordance with his whisperings. He has surrounded the emperor with his people; all new appointments are made at his instructions. . . . Such is the milieu in which I am condemned to operate. Is it possible for one man to fight against a whole powerful gang? What a devastating

and disgusting contrast with the atmosphere in which I entered the government thirteen years ago! Then everything was striving forwards; now everything is pulling backwards. Then the emperor sympathized with progress, himself was moving forward; now he has lost confidence in everything he created, in everything that surrounds him, even in himself.[1]

However, his fortunes took a turn for the better. Shuvalov was appointed ambassador in London in April 1874. In his absence Dmitri Tolstoy was a less formidable opponent. The long struggle between him and Milyutin, as to which ministry was to control the Military Medical Academy, was decided in 1875 by the Tsar in favour of Milyutin. When the war with Turkey came in 1877, the army that Milyutin had reformed gave a good account of itself.

Under the 1874 law, all male Russians aged twenty years and medically fit were liable to military service. Exemption was granted to only sons or only grandsons supporting parents or grandparents, to persons who supported a brother or sister who was a minor, and to those who had a brother serving in the army at the time. The normal period of service was now to be six years, followed by nine in the reserve and five in the militia. Educational qualifications reduced the term—primary to four years, partial secondary to three, completed secondary to two and university to six months.

Russia in 1875 was very different from Russia in 1855. Radical changes had been made in political and social institutions. Yet the dogma of autocracy remained unshaken, and the outlook of the all-powerful bureaucracy remained hostile to public opinion and suspicious of public initiative. The general mood was unhappy. The last years of the reign brought revolutionary activity, a victorious war, a lost peace, and the assassination of the Tsar Liberator, leading to a long period of reactionary government.

The impression of tragic failure in Alexander II's Russia is strengthened if one looks for comparison to another country, which at almost exactly the same time embarked on a process of rapid and deliberate modernization, Japan. It may be that the human material or the economic conditions of Japan were more favourable. The security of the island empire may be compared

[1] *Dnevnik D. A. Milyutina*, ed. P. A. Zayonchkovsky (Moscow, 1947–50), i. 119.

with the strategic insecurity of Russia, great empire though it was. The decisive difference, however, is probably the fact that, whereas in Japan there was a political revolution, and new men took over power by violent action, in Russia the same men stayed in office and the impulse for reform slowed down as it met with the force of inert opposition. It may be argued that Russia needed not so much a vast social upheaval as a political revolution, which might have given power to men of the stamp of Nicholas Milyutin, who belonged no less to the Russian upper class than Ito and Yamagata belonged to the upper class of Japan, yet would have been, like them, ruthless in their will to sweep away rotten fabric and to build new foundations.

Russian writers have given much attention to the question, how near Russia was to revolution at the time when the great reforms were being prepared. The consensus of recent Soviet historical writing is that there was a 'revolutionary situation' in the years 1859–61.[1] There is of course plenty of evidence of discontent among the peasantry, of fear among the ruling class and of revolutionary feeling among the intelligentsia. Moreover, peasant discontent was increasingly expressed in action, in the form of riots and disorders of all sorts in many parts of the country; and the revolutionary sympathies of some members of the intelligentsia were also being transformed into the beginning of revolutionary action.

There were thus undoubtedly revolutionary forces at work in these years. But if the words 'revolutionary situation' are intended to mean that the régime was on the edge of collapse, or that a revolutionary seizure of power was a practical possibility, this seems an exaggeration, even if individual members of the ruling class at the time thought that this was so. The essential point is that the loyalty of the bureaucracy, police, and army was never in doubt. The later revolutions, of 1905 and 1917, became possible because the armed forces had ceased to obey the government (in the first case partially and on the periphery of the empire, in the second case completely and in the capital itself). In both cases the collapse of discipline was due

[1] See in particular two collections of articles, under the chief editorship of Academician M. V. Nechkina, entitled *Revolyutsionnaya situatsiya v Rossii v 1859–1861 gg.*, Moscow, 1960 and 1963. See also the three collections of documents on peasant disorders: *Krest'yanskoe dvizhenie v Rossii*, covering the years 1850–6 (Moscow, 1962), 1857–May 1861 (1963), and 1861–9 (1964).

to humiliating and repeated defeats in war. In 1856 this was not the case. Russia had sustained defeat at Sevastopol, but there had been no humiliation. On the contrary, Russian resistance was felt, both by the Russians and by their enemies, to have been a heroic feat of arms, of which the nation could be proud. The morale of the army remained excellent. Had the war continued after Sevastopol, things might indeed have been different. A series of defeats on land at the hand of the allied armies, including the Austrians, the occupation of Russian territories in the south-west, and perhaps a revolt in Poland might have led to a demoralization of the armed forces, and the fusion of civilian and military disaffection might have led to a collapse of the whole régime. But the enemies of Russia decided not to continue the war, the armed forces remained obedient, and the discontent of peasants and intellectuals sufficed only to force the government to undertake reforms. The régime made concessions, but there was no revolution. Russia was spared a violent upheaval, but in the long run this proved to be a misfortune.

Culture

Though hopes of political progress were disappointed, the reign of Alexander II was a period of intellectual achievement.

The great figure of Ivan Turgenev had become widely known already in the reign of Nicholas I. In 1852, when he was thirty-four years old, his *Sportsman's Sketches* appeared in book form. The 1850's were his most productive period, and his work reached its climax with *Fathers and Sons*, published in 1862. Turgenev was a regular contributor to *Sovremennik*, and was an oustanding representative of moderate liberalism. His novels were largely concerned with social themes,[1] but the quality of his best work transcends the limitations of his country and age, and places him among the greatest writers of world literature. Two other writers of the same period belong in the same class, within which they even surpass him.

Leo Tolstoy, born in 1828, began his literary career with his childhood memories, published in 1851. In 1855 his *Sevastopol*

[1] On Turgenev's involvement in political events and controversies see above pp. 278, 361. During the last twenty years of his life, which were spent abroad, he produced comparatively little. He died in 1883.

Stories appeared in *Sovremennik* while he himself was serving as an officer in the besieged army. After some years in the capital, Tolstoy married in 1862, retired to his country estate and devoted himself to family life and writing. The result of his efforts, *War and Peace*, was published in 1869. Tolstoy's second great novel, *Anna Karenina*, appeared in 1877.

Fyodor Dostoyevsky was released from Omsk prison[1] in 1854, spent five more years in Siberia first as a private soldier and then as an officer, and was allowed to return to St. Petersburg in 1859. During his exile in Siberia he underwent the religious conversion which so profoundly affected his life and writings. In 1861 and 1862 he wrote *Notes from the House of the Dead*, which he published in instalments in a review which he edited together with his brother. In the following years he suffered from repeated financial and personal troubles but between 1867 and 1871, while living abroad, he produced *Crime and Punishment*, *The Idiot*, and *The Possessed*. In the late 1870's Dostoyevsky was much concerned with politics, and shared the Pan-Slav enthusiasm during the war with Turkey. In 1880 *The Brothers Karamazov* appeared. This was only part of what he hoped would be his greatest work, but he never finished it as he died in January 1881.

It is worth noting that neither Tolstoy nor Dostoyevsky conformed to the criteria of social utilitarianism laid down by the school of literary criticism of Dobrolyubov. Nor did a lesser but still brilliant writer, Nicholas Leskov, most of whose works were produced in these years—for instance, *Lady Macbeth of Mtsensk* in 1865, *Cathedral Folk* in 1872, and *The Enchanted Wanderer* in 1874. This is not to say that these three were not aware of social issues, still less that their works do not reflect social reality, only that they were great writers, each with his own individual genius which defies any attempt to classify and label it.

These years also saw progress in Russian learning. In natural sciences the outstanding figure was D. I. Mendeleyev, the great chemist, who achieved international fame in 1869 by his periodic table of chemical elements based on atomic weights.

Three historians must also be mentioned. S. M. Solovyov, born in 1820, became a professor at Moscow University in 1850. He published the first volume of his history of Russia in 1851,

[1] See above p. 277.

and thereafter one volume every year until his death in 1879. A man of immense erudition and moderate Slavophil outlook, he was one of the founders of Russian historical scholarship, with less literary distinction but more exact methods than Karamzin. K. D. Kavelin (1818–85) was the outstanding representative of the 'legalist' school of historical writing, stressing rather the role of political institutions and rulers than of social organisms such as the commune. He was an admirer of Peter the Great, and essentially a Westernizer. Kavelin spent most of his life as a government official, and was involved, as we have seen, in the politics of the reform years. His only academic posts were as assistant professor of history in Moscow from 1844 to 1848 and as professor of civil law and philosophy of law in St. Petersburg from 1857 to 1861. But his literary output placed him in the front rank. The third historian of distinction in this period is A. P. Shchapov (1830–76), whose writings were mainly concerned with the religious sects and with the importance of the regional factor in Russian history. He himself was a Siberian. His speech at the Kazan memorial service to the Bezdna peasants in 1861, and correspondence with Herzen in 1863, involved him in trouble with the police. He was exiled to Siberia, and ill health and financial troubles shortened his life. Even so, he made a lasting contribution to the study of Russian, and especially of Siberian, history.

The third quarter of the century was a great period in the history of Russian music. The Russian Music Society, founded in 1859, organized the St. Petersburg and Moscow *Conservatoires*, and schools of music in several other cities. In the 1860's there also appeared the 'neo-Russian school' of composers, who reacted against the classicism of the Music Society and of its leading personalities, the great pianist brothers Anton and Nicholas Rubinstein, and set up their own Free School of Music in St. Petersburg in 1862. The outstanding figures of this group were M. A. Balakirev, C. A. Kui,[1] M. P. Moussorgsky, A. P. Borodin, and N. A. Rimsky-Korsakov. Their main contention was that Russian composers should make use of Russian popular melodies in their work. Not all of them did so to the same extent. But the last three especially have attained fame

[1] This is a russification of the French name Queuille. The composer's family was of French origin.

and popularity wherever music is loved, no less outside than within Russia. A few years later a still greater composer appeared, P. I. Chaikovsky, who studied at the St. Petersburg *Conservatoire* from 1862 to 1865, and was later a teacher at the Moscow *Conservatoire*. His best-known opera, *Eugene Onegin*, based on Pushkin's poem, was first produced in 1877. Of all Russian music his symphonies are perhaps the works best loved outside Russia. In the words of a modern historian, 'The great tradition established by these masters . . . has added far more to the prestige and lustre of the Russian name than have costly and uncertain victories on distant battlefields.'[1]

Rural Society after Emancipation

The first stage in carrying out the peasant reform of 1861 was the establishment by the arbitrators of the peace of the amounts of land to be made available to the peasants on each estate. During the period of transition the arbitrators, who were appointed by the Senate, held wide executive powers in the countryside. The arbitrators were members of the landowning class, and this fact has sufficed, for some historians, as proof that they were prejudiced against the peasants. In practice, however, conditions varied, and some of the arbitrators behaved with great fairness, justifying the hopes placed in them by Milyutin and Samarin. These conscientious officials had great difficulty both in overcoming peasant prejudice and in resisting the blandishments, threats, and intrigues of landowners who expected them to take their side. They should have been supported by the provincial governors, as representatives of the central government, but many governors proved unable or unwilling to stand up to pressure from the landowners.[2] In practice the first group of arbitrators, appointed for three years in 1861, was purged of its best and most independent men in

[1] Florinsky, *Russia: A History and an Interpretation*, ii. 1052.

[2] The following is an instance of the mentality the arbitrators had to cope with. An arbitrator in Kharkov province was asked by a landowner, whom he knew to be a highly educated and cultured man, to agree to his flogging fifteen peasant women who had been rude to his housekeeper. The arbitrator said that this was forbidden by law, to which the landlord replied: 'Who will know that the women were birched?' N. K. Ponomarev, 'Vospominaniya mirovogo posrednika pervogo prizyva 1861–1863' in *RS* (Feb. 1891), p. 320.

1864. This was done by reducing the number and increasing the size of arbitrators' districts, and simply not reappointing those men who had aroused hostility by their independent behaviour.

The plot of land surrounding the peasants' houses (*usadebnaya osedlost'*) in all cases became the property of the peasant, and the consent of the landowner was not required. The object of the agreements made by the arbitrators of the peace was the remaining land, cultivated by the peasants under serfdom. The transfer of part or all of this land from the landowner to the peasant was to be arranged by a formal agreement (*vykupnaya sdelka*) between landlord and peasant, and was to be financed by a government loan. If the agreement was accepted by both parties, the landowner received 80 per cent. of the agreed price from the government in the form of bonds. The remaining 20 per cent. had to be paid by the peasant to the landowner. In some cases, landowners voluntarily remitted part or all of this 20 per cent. If the landowner wished to part with the land, but the peasant did not wish to accept the agreement, the landowner had the right to insist on the sale, but in this case he forfeited 20 per cent. of the price, receiving only the 80 per cent. in government bonds. If neither landlord nor peasant wished the transfer of property to take place, then the peasant became a 'temporarily obligated' tenant, owning only his house and surrounding plot. Finally, a special provision had been introduced into the Act of 1861, during the last discussions of the Chief Committee, by which a landowner could, if he wished, transfer to a peasant, free of all payment, an amount equal to one quarter of the maximum allotment established for his area, thereby ending all obligations towards the peasant or of the peasant towards him. These transactions became known as 'beggarly allotments'.

The settlement of 1861 consisted of separate statutes for four areas—Great Russia (the greater part of European Russia), the South-West, the North-West, and White Russia. Detailed regulations laid down the size of the allotments (*nadely*) to be eligible for peasant purchase. Here there were three main divisions, according to the nature of the soil—non-black-earth, black-earth, and steppe. In the first two areas, maximum and minimum sizes of allotment were laid down, the minimum being one-third of the maximum. In the steppe area there was only a single size. Each of the three areas was divided up into sub-areas. Thus in each district the arbitrator of peace had fixed limits within which to negotiate, but the limits varied according to geographical and agricultural conditions.

The first reaction of the peasants was unfavourable. The settlement of 1861 clearly contradicted the widespread belief of the former serfs, in regard to their masters and their land: 'We are yours, but the land is ours.' They objected to being made to pay for what they regarded as theirs by right. There were many minor disorders in different parts of the country. Most were appeased without bloodshed. But a major disaster occurred in the village of Bezdna, in Kazan province, where a peasant named Anton Petrov persuaded his fellows that they had been given complete liberty in 1858, and had no further duties or payments towards the landowners. The authorities were frightened of a new Pugachov rising, and brought in troops, commanded by Count A. S. Apraksin. The peasants resisted, and on 12 April 1861 there was a fight in which 102 peasants were killed.[1]

The peasants were reluctant to sign the documents, and nearly half were completed only in the last months of the two-year transitional period. By January 1864 79,468 documents affecting 5,659,680 male souls had established 'temporary obligated' tenancy, while 29,219 affecting 4,026,387 male souls provided for purchase. The latter figure included 'beggarly allotments'. Of the 4,000,000 souls who had made agreements for purchase, 2,716,529 were in the western provinces, the Polish borderlands, where conditions exceptionally favourable to the peasants had been introduced as part of the government's policy for weakening the Polish landowning class after the rebellion of 1863.[2] Thus, of the total who accepted purchase from the beginning, only one-third were in European Russia, and these formed only 19 per cent. of Russian former serf households.[3]

[1] For an account of peaceful settlement of disorders in Yaroslavl province by Lt.-Gen. Dubelt, see *RS* (Feb. 1891), pp. 468–74. The Bezdna tragedy is described by an eye-witness, N. A. Krylov, in 'Vospominaniya mirovogo posrednika', in *RS* (June 1892), pp. 615–36. Official documents relating to the affair are published in *Krest'yanskoe dvizhenie v Rossii v 1857—maye 1861 gg.*, ed S. V. Okun (Moscow, 1963), pp. 350–68. See also above p. 336.

[2] See above p. 376.

[3] P. A. Zayonchkovsky, *Otmena krepostnogo prava* (Moscow, 1954), pp. 179–80.

The transition from 'temporary obligation' to ownership proceeded slowly during the rest of Alexander II's reign. By 1877 in the 39 provinces affected by the Great Russian Statute 61,784 contracts for purchase had been made, of which 35 per cent. were by mutual agreement and 65 per cent. at the request of the landowner alone.[1] In January 1881 the proportion of peasants who were still 'temporarily obligated' in 37 European Russian provinces was 15 per cent., but in some of these it was much higher (44 per cent. in Kursk, 35 per cent. in Nizhnii Novgorod and Vologda).

Appanage peasants,[2] who numbered 850,000 on the eve of reform and of whom two-fifths were in the two provinces of Simbirsk and Samara, were covered by a law of 26 June 1863. This made purchase compulsory, after a transitional period of two years. The yearly sum which they had to pay was the same as that which they had paid as *obrok*. They were thus much more favourably treated than the former landowners' serfs. State peasants formed the subject of a law of 18 January 1866. This allowed them to choose between remaining tenants, on their existing allotments at the existing *obrok*, or becoming owners by paying on similar terms to the former landowners' serfs.

The sum to be paid by the former landowners' serfs was assessed on a capitalization of the existing *obrok* at 6 per cent. This is to say, the total amount to be paid was rather more than sixteen times the existing *obrok*. Four-fifths of this amount had to be paid by the peasants to the government in annual instalments over a period of forty-nine years. One-fifth they were to pay directly to the landowners in a lump sum if the contract had been agreed, but if it had been unilaterally requested by the landowner they were exempted from this portion of the sum altogether.

The basic capital sum on which the annuities were calculated was based on estimates of the value of the land that were excessively favourable to the landowners and unfavourable to the peasants. This is shown by an estimate made in 1906 (which can only be regarded as approximate) of the total amount fixed as payment, compared with the value of the land trans-

[1] Article 'Vykupnaya operatsiya' in *Brockhaus Encyclopaedia*, vii. 513–17.

[2] See above pp. 64–65.

ferred, judged by average prices of land for the years 1863–72.[1] The estimate is related to three distinct regions. In the non-black-earth area 340,000,000 roubles was the sum fixed, while average land prices would have given a total of 180,000,000. For the black-earth area the respective figures are 341,000,000 and 284,000,000. For the western provinces they are 183,000,000 and 184,000,000. The reason for the great disparity in the non-black-earth area is that the main financial loss to the landowners in this part of Russia came from their loss of their share of the serfs' industrial earnings, paid in the form of an *obrok*. It had been formally laid down that there was to be no ransom for the personal freedom of the emancipated serfs, but in practice a ransom was given in the form of excessively high land valuation. The low price required in the western provinces is of course explained by the fact that the landowners were Poles and the serfs Russians, Ukrainians, or White Russians.

The peasants in the black-earth areas did not have to pay such exorbitant prices, but they received less land than those in central and northern Russia. In the black-earth provinces the landowners' chief asset before 1861 had been not the labour of their serfs but the good land. Thus, instead of exacting a concealed ransom for the persons of their serfs, they did their best to reduce the amount of land purchased by the peasants to considerably less than the peasants had had for their use under serfdom. In this they were fairly successful. It is estimated that in 43 provinces of European Russia the total area cultivated by landowners' serfs for their own use was 35,000,000 *desyatin* before the Reform, and 33,750,000 for the same families in 1877. But in black-earth areas the disproportion was much greater than this. It averaged about 25 per cent. less than under serfdom. The provinces in which the reduction of area was greatest were Samara (42 per cent.), Saratov (38 per cent.), and Poltava (37 per cent.). In the western provinces, however, in accordance with the official policy of discrimination against Polish landowners, the land purchased was considerably larger than the allotments under serfdom. The excess of the new over the old allotments was greatest in the provinces of Podolia (90 per cent.), Grodno (54 per cent.), Kovno (45 per cent.), and

[1] Lositsky, *Vykupnaya operatsiya* (SPB, 1906), quoted by G. T. Robinson, *Rural Russia under the Old Régime* (1929), p. 88. The book by Lositsky has not been available to me.

Vilna (42 per cent.). It is possible that these figures are misleading, as the amount actually used by the peasants under serfdom may have been larger than was stated, in which case the discrepancy would be still greater in the Russian black-earth area but smaller in the west.[1]

There was perhaps a case for excessively high payments or excessively low allotments in the first years of transition, in order to enable the landowners to adjust themselves to the new conditions. But the unfavourable terms were not limited to the period of 'temporary obligation': they were maintained for the period of purchase. Thus the burden of the process of emancipation was passed by the landowners and the government on to the peasants.

The administrative system, set up to replace the authority of landowners over serfs, was based on the *volost* and the *sel'skoe obshchestvo*. The latter was to be composed of 'the peasants settled upon the estate of a single landlord'. If an estate were populated by not more than twenty male souls, then these should be joined with others in the neighbourhood to make up a sufficient community. This definition of a community had the advantage of simplifying the transfer of power, since the authorities could deal directly with the landowners. But it led later to great confusion. Peasants became associated for different purposes with different groups of other peasants. A village might consist of peasants belonging to more than one estate. The peasants of one estate might live in several different villages. The peasants of one estate might share a pasture, or the rights of cutting timber in a forest, with different groups of peasants from different estates. No account was taken of these variations in the settlement. The most serious difficulties concerned the demarcation of authority between a new *sel'skoe obshchestvo* and an old-established village commune (*obshchina*[2]). In practice, the old communes usually survived. Subsequent decisions by the Senate, and documents of the Council of State, gave contradictory rulings on the role of *obshchestvo* and *obshchina*, and the confusion was never cleared.

The organization of the village community was similar to that

[1] Zayonchkovsky, op. cit., p. 208.

[2] For practical purposes, this word, which will be used henceforth, may be regarded as the equivalent of *mir* (see above pp. 232–3).

instituted for state peasants by Kiselyov twenty years earlier. There was an assembly of householders, and an elected foreman, at both village and *volost* level. The most important local official was the *volost* notary (*pisar*), who was appointed from above. The *volost* court applied peasant custom in settling disputes between peasants. It had power to inflict small fines, a few days' detention, and flogging with the rod up to twenty strokes.

The village community as a whole was responsible for the payment of poll-tax and redemption dues by all its members. This collective responsibility was known as *krugovaya poruka*. The community also had the right to grant or to withhold passports to any member who wished to leave the village for temporary or more lasting employment elsewhere.

There were two types of land tenure in the villages of European Russia. One was hereditary (*podvornoe*), under which a peasant's land could be transmitted to his heir without any external interference. The other was communal (*obshchinnoe*), under which land was subject to periodical redistribution. In both systems the house and garden plots belonged to the individual families, and the meadows, pastures, and forests belonged to the whole commune. The difference between the two types concerned only the cultivated fields. Under hereditary tenure, these were the possession of the households, under communal tenure of the commune. In the latter case, if the numbers of a household increased, it would become entitled to more land, while if they diminished it would be expected to give up some land to another household suffering from land shortage. The decision was taken by the commune assembly. Redistributions occurred at irregular intervals, often not for many years at a time.

Under both types of tenure, the assembly determined the rotation of crops, which was binding on all members. In order to avoid unjust distribution of land, it was often necessary, in repartitional communes, to give households several small portions of land, where the quality of the soil varied appreciably. When grown-up children set up their own households, they too had to have plots of different qualities. The same phenomenon also occurred under hereditary tenure, since a father would normally feel obliged to give each of his heirs a piece of each quality of land. In this way, holdings became more and more divided into small strips, often separated by fairly large distances. In the interests of efficient agriculture, it was desirable that this fragmentation (*cherespolositsa*) should be ended, and holdings consolidated in compact areas. Such holdings could be independent of the village crop cycle. But the obstacles to consolidation under both types of tenure were almost insuperable. In a village with hereditary tenure, a peasant could only consolidate his land if he obtained the consent of every householder whose land would thereby be displaced. In a repartitional commune, a householder who paid up the full sum of his redemption debt could compel the commune to give him, in exchange for his scattered strips, a holding of similar size and quality consolidated 'as far as possible' in one place, or to pay him an indemnity. This provision was contained in Article 165 of the Emancipation Statute, and had been inserted deliberately in order to make possible the creation of individual farms if there were a demand for it. The reformers of 1861 had been divided between supporters and opponents of communal tenure, and had not wished to impose one form or the other. However, the provisions about collective responsibility for taxes, designed primarily to ensure the financial interests of the state during the period of redemption, had the effect of greatly strengthening the communal system. Few peasants were in any case financially able to make use of Article 165. Up to 1882 it had been used in the case of only 47,735 allotments amounting to an area of 178,000 *desyatin*.

It was also very difficult for peasants to withdraw personally from the commune. In a hereditary tenure village, in the period of 'temporary obligation', a householder could withdraw only if he surrendered his land holding altogether. Once the process of redemption had begun, he could do so only if he had transferred his allotment to someone else willing to assume the redemption debt on it, or had himself paid off the whole debt. As the debt was in most cases larger than the value of the land, it was likely to be hard to find any one willing to assume it. In a repartitional commune, a householder could withdraw, once redemption had begun, only if he would himself pay half the outstanding redemption debt on his allotment, and could persuade the commune to accept the other half of the debt. This the commune was entitled to refuse.

It was possible for a repartitional commune to decide, by a two-thirds majority vote in its assembly, to adopt hereditary tenure. It could also vote by two-thirds majority in favour of a general consolidation of holdings. Such votes were, however, virtually unknown.

It will be seen from the above that, though the peasants were freed from the power of the landlords over their persons, families, and households, they were in fact much less than free citizens. They were partially excluded from the new system of justice, and their freedom of movement and choice of an occupation were tightly restricted by the commune.

The merits and defects of the communal system were the object of much public controversy throughout the last decades of the nineteenth century. Its critics argued that it was an obstacle to economic progress. The prospect of redistribution, they claimed, deprived the peasants of any incentive to improve their holdings. The system perpetuated fragmentation. The crudest type of crop rotation was imposed on all alike. The Valuyev commission on agriculture of 1872 reported unfavourably on the commune. The alternative was to encourage private ownership, initiative, and the spirit of enterprise among the peasants, even at the cost of hardship for the less successful and the poorer. This was the view of some liberals, such as Chicherin, and generally of those who expected and wished Russia to follow a capitalist development.

The prevalent articulate opinion was, however, on the other side. Conservatives believed that peasants could not be left to themselves. There must be some tutelage to replace the serf-owner, and this could best be exercised by the commune. Only the commune could ensure the fulfilment of the essential obligations towards the state. Liberal Slavophils attached importance to the commune as an original Russian institution, rooted in Russian history, and as a protection to the peasants against proletarization, the worst evil that could befall them. Radicals and even the first socialists, such as Chernyshevsky, believed that the commune could form a basis for the future development of socialism in Russia, for a new social order that would avoid the horrors of capitalism, as the latter had grown in the West, and would even make Russia an example for other countries to follow.

The essence of the argument was the balance between the social advantages and the economic defects. Koshelyov, in a short work published in Berlin in 1875,[1] denied that communal ownership was a cause of any economic failures that were not also found where there was private ownership: *cherespolositsa* was common to both. The bad effects of redistribution were exaggerated. This actually did not take place often, and it was desirable that it should be even less frequent; special legislation would not, however, be useful, as it could not take sufficient account of varying local conditions. The main causes of economic backwardness were the poll-tax, which should be replaced by a general income-tax binding on all classes, and the inordinately high rates of redemption payments, which should be reduced, the government to make up the difference to the landowners. The great merit of communal tenure was that it assured the peasants 'an inviolable land fund, guaranteeing for ever a shelter and piece of bread'.[2] The real strength of Russia lay not in its nobility, its merchants, its cities, or its sea-ports, but in 'the spirit of the people, which is strong and deeply rooted only in the peasantry', and this because the peasantry is assured the use of land. The supreme disaster would be that a large part of the peasantry should lose its land, and become a vagabond race, 'moving from place to place in the measureless spaces of Russia, not knowing where it will have to live and die, transformed against all habits and convictions into some sort of homeless gypsies'. As for the alleged despotic power of the commune over its members, 'the despotism of the commune is only a weak reflection of the general despotism that prevails in our country'. The remedy is greater political liberty for all Russians.

The liberal Professor Kavelin, in a rather longer work written in 1881–2, reached somewhat similar conclusions. He too argued that economic progress is possible within a communal system as well as within a system of private ownership. He too insisted on the need to replace poll-tax and to reduce redemption payments. He insisted especially on the failure of the

[1] A. I. Koshelyov, *Ob obshchinnom zemlevladenii v Rossii*, Berlin, 1875.

[2] Observe the similarity to the ideas of Pestel half a century earlier. See above pp. 183–190. It is curious also to note that among other arguments in favour of the commune Koshelyov also quoted remarks made personally to him by Cavour, in which that statesman expressed his admiration for the institution.

government to do anything to instruct the peasants in methods of cultivation. If they stuck to antiquated systems of crop rotation, this was only because they had no reason to believe that better systems existed. It was all very well to have a few model farms with the very best modern machinery and methods to stress the possibilities of the latest agricultural science. But these machines and this knowledge were quite inaccessible to the peasants. The authorities would do better to spend money and effort on teaching the peasants the many cheap and practical improvements they could introduce, on providing them with greatly superior yet not very complicated instruments, on studying the particular needs of different localities, on producing small handbooks of useful knowledge, which could be read out by the literate minority to the illiterate majority, and above all on increasing elementary education.

These arguments of Kavelin are all the more convincing in the light of the experience of another country that at this time embarked on modernization, Japan. The Japanese reformers did precisely what Kavelin had recommended. They took heavy taxes from the peasants, but they put a large part of their revenue back into agriculture, and in a few decades doubled the output per acre. The peasants were encouraged to devise practical tools and labour-saving devices of their own, suited to their needs. Above all the Japanese government introduced within a few decades a system of compulsory elementary education for both sexes. In Russia, however, an attitude of distrustful, if occasionally benevolent, paternalism prevailed. The peasants must indeed be protected from the horrors of proletarization. But it was unwise to impose on them any modern education, which would give them dangerous ideas. The new ideas and new techniques were for the upper classes only. The peasants' task was to pay for industrialization, by taxes both direct and indirect. The commune was an admirable instrument of political power. As for economic improvements in agriculture, they were excellent where a great landowner had the wealth and the enterprise to experiment, but as far as the peasant masses were concerned they had not a high priority. This mentality persisted for fifty years, and helped to destroy Imperial Russia.

In 1877 (when perhaps four-fifths of the peasant allotments

were already in process of redemption), the main categories in the ownership of land were as follows. Peasant allotment land amounted to 111,629,000 *desyatin*, and peasant communes held a further 765,000. The lands of the state, the Imperial family, churches, and monasteries (which consisted overwhelmingly of non-arable land) amounted to 159,952,000. The lands privately owned by noble landowners totalled 73,077,000, by townsmen 11,699,000, by the clergy 186,000, and by individual peasants or peasant collectives 5,788,000. Various other categories (including municipalities, miscellaneous collectives, and the reserve lands of the Cossack Armies) amounted to over 16,000,000 *desyatin*, Thus, peasants held altogether at least 118 million *desyatin*, nobles 73 million, townsmen nearly 11 million and the state nearly 160 million.[1]

Industry, Trade, and Finance

During the decade 1863–72 it is estimated that landowners received in compensation paid by the government 607,000,000 roubles, and in sales of land a further 165,000,000. At the time of the reform, debts on mortgaged estates, which numbered 44,166, amounted to 425,500,000 roubles.[2] The debts were deducted from the compensation payments by the government, and thus account for more than two-thirds of the amount paid out in the first ten years. However, a large sum was left. Some of it was undoubtedly spent on luxurious living. But certainly a considerable portion of the landowners' receipts went directly, and much larger sums indirectly through the repaid creditors, into the industrial boom which occurred in the early 1870's.

With the emancipation began a process which gathered momentum with each decade. This was the increasing separation of the landed nobility from the land. Some landowners, it is true, especially in the Ukraine, retained great estates and made a profitable business of them, developing large-scale agriculture on capitalist principles and concentrating on the growing export trade in grain. But most landowners were not

[1] Figures quoted from Robinson, op. cit., p. 268. They are taken from official sources which were not available to me directly. For certain discrepancies and ambiguities, see the explanations given by Robinson, loc. cit.

[2] *Krest'yanskoe delo v tsarstvovanie Imperatora Aleksandra II*, ed. Alexander Skrebitsky (Bonn, 1862), vol. ii, part 1, pp. 1245–7.

prosperous. The estate would usually not support all the grown-up children, and in many cases not even one owner. As estates were sold, and other sources of income became ever more necessary, young nobles poured into the towns and flocked to the capitals. The needed outlets were found in the army, in the new professions, and above all in the expanding bureaucracy. The word *dvoryanstvo* began to change its meaning. The old regulations on entry into and membership of it remained; one was, or was not, a noble, there was no vagueness on this score. But to be a nobleman no longer necessarily meant to be a landowner, even if one still had relatives who owned land, and one's parents or uncle had done so or still did so. A large part of the *dvoryanstvo*, at any rate in the younger generation, consisted of persons of very moderate income, employed in professional or administrative posts in a town. They were in fact, in economic terms, a middle class. They were not, however, a bourgeoisie. Their ethos was that of a military landowning class, not of a civilian middle class, such as had grown up in the West since the Reformation. There was no such bourgeoisie in Russia: even the merchants had little of the outlook of Western business men. They thought far too much in terms of exclusive guild privileges and favours from the government, to which they were prepared to give unreserved political obedience.

The nobility then were economically a middle class, but in their function they were primarily a bureaucracy. It was less and less true that the landowners ruled Russia. They were able to place a veto on sectors of economic policy, to ensure their own supremacy in agriculture. Their vested interests could not be overridden. But the business of ruling Russia was done not by them but by the bureaucracy. To say that the *dvoryanstvo* were the ruling class is merely to say that those who ruled, ruled. More significant is that the bureaucracy was growing into a large body, a distinct social group, whose interests and prejudices dominated Russian policy. These were no longer the same as the interests and prejudices of the landowners of the 1850's.

The post-emancipation years saw great industrial activity. The most important development was railway-building. In 1857 there were 1,000 versts of rail in Russia, in 1876 17,600. In the 1860's 698,000,000 roubles of private capital were invested in railways, while government loans to railways between 1860 and 1876 totalled 1,833,000,000. The freight carried by the railways increased from 377,000,000 poods as a yearly average for 1865–9 to 1,698,000,000 poods for 1875–9.[1] The freight per kilometre only increased in these years by 15 per cent. The government in the 1860's preferred that railways should be built and owned by private companies rather than by the state, and sold some state-owned lines. However, private companies found it difficult to raise funds in Russia. New regulations introduced in 1865 attracted foreign capital, especially small investors in Prussia. In the late 1860's zemstvos began to raise funds for railway building, especially in the provinces south-east of Moscow.

The main aim of railway-building was strategic. But it also had major economic consequences. In particular it enormously stimulated the grain trade. Railway tariffs were relatively low on long distances. This benefited producers in the more distant provinces, whose soil was better than that of Central Russia, but which had suffered from the heavy cost of transport. During the 1870's the price of rye in St. Petersburg (which had previously of course been much higher than in the provinces) rose by 30 per cent., while in Oryol the rise was 66 per cent., in Kharkov 85 per cent., and in Saratov 100 per cent. Producers could now count on a decent price much nearer home, and this was an incentive to produce more. The growth of steam water transport, on the Volga and other rivers, also contributed to increase trade. The export trade in grain increased both absolutely and relatively. In 1861–5 the average yearly export by weight was 86,000,000 poods, in 1866–70 136,000,000, in 1876–80 286,500,000. The proportion of grain exports to all Russia's exports was 31 per cent. in 1861–5 and 47 per cent. in 1891–5.

The emancipation adversely affected those branches of industry which had used servile labour. The main loser was the government-owned metallurgical industry of the Urals. Iron production in the Urals fell between 1860 and 1862 from 14,500,000 poods to 10,400,000, and by 1867 had recovered only to 12,400,000. The reason was simply that a large part of the labour force left the mines and plants once it was free. The

[1] P. I. Lyashchenko, *Istoriya narodnogo khozyaistva SSSR* (Moscow, 1948), ii. 113–15, 138.

same phenomenon occurred with formerly serf-employing cloth factories in the provinces of Simbirsk, Voronezh, Kazan, Oryol, and Smolensk. In contrast, industries which had previously employed wage labour now prospered, though interruption of cotton imports during the American Civil War was a temporary set-back. The main cotton textile centres were Moscow and Vladimir provinces and the Łódź region of Russian Poland. Some indication of the growth of the textile industry can be given by figures for imports of raw cotton into the Russian empire (including Poland). These were 1,100,000 poods in 1863, 5,200,000 in 1877, 9,700,000 in 1881.

The total number of workers in manufacturing, mining, and metallurgy in 50 provinces of European Russia is estimated as an annual average of 798,000 in the 1860's, 946,000 in the 1870's, and 1,160,000 in the 1880's. The railway-building boom created a demand for steel, and this ought to have provided an incentive to the development of a metallurgical industry in Russia. The coal of the Donetz Basin and the iron ore of Krivoy Rog offered a potential base for this in the south, but in the 1870's only the foundations were laid. In 1869 the Welshman John Hughes obtained a concession for an enterprise to be called the New Russia Company, for the production of coal, iron, and rails. He gave his name to the mining settlement of Yuzovka, which in the twentieth century became one of the greatest metallurgical cities in the world.[1] Output of pig-iron in Russia more than doubled between 1862 and 1886, but in the latter year it was only 32,000,000 poods. An important reason for the slow development of these natural resources was that government contracts for rails were at first given to factories in north and central Russia (Putilov in St. Petersburg, or Bryansk[2] south-west of Moscow) for whom it was cheaper to import ore and fuel from abroad. Thus Russian mining and metallurgy got little encouragement.

In this period also the exploitation of oil in the Baku region began. In 1875 5,000,000 poods were produced, in 1885 116,000,000—still a small amount.

[1] In the 1930's it was named Stalino, thirty years later changed to Donetsk. Population in 1962 was 760,000.

[2] The Bryansk factory was founded in 1874 by V. F. Golubev and P. I. Gubdonin. It was located at the confluence of the Dnieper and Desna rivers, near the town of Bryansk.

It is estimated that between 1861 and 1873 357 joint stock companies were formed in Russia, with a capital of 1,116,000,000 roubles. Before 1861 there had been only 78 with 72,000,000. Of the 357 new companies, 73 were private banks, with 227,000,000; 53 were railways, with 698,500,000; and 163 were industrial, with 129,000,000 roubles capital. Total current and deposit accounts in banks increased between 1861 and 1873 from about 1,350,000,000 roubles to 2,753,000,000 (of which last figure the State Bank held about 1,500,000,000). During this period foreign capital increased rapidly, but was still not very large. In the 1850's foreign investments in Russia were somewhat less than 10,000,000 roubles, in the 1870's nearly 100,000,000. The minister of finance from 1862 to 1878, Count Michael Reutern, systematically encouraged the development of private credit institutions. Important steps in this direction were the regulations for the formation of municipal banks in 1862 and for savings banks in 1869.

Already before the appointment of Reutern as minister an important step had been taken with the creation in 1860 of the State Bank, which replaced the previously existing state-owned banks which had been liquidated after a serious financial crisis in 1857–9, following the strains of the Crimean War. The State Bank was, however, not made the official bank of issue. Reutern tried in May 1862 to make the rouble convertible, but was obliged to abandon the attempt in August 1863. He made valiant efforts to control the circulation and to keep the exchange rate steady, but the Russo-Turkish War of 1877–8 finally doomed him to failure, and caused him to offer his resignation. With difficulty he was persuaded to stay at his post until the end of the war.

Reutern maintained the poll-tax, after an ineffectual attempt to abolish it in 1870. He replaced the farming system of taxing spirits by an excise in 1863. This continued to provide a large share of government revenue (31·5 per cent. in 1869, 34·5 per cent. in 1879). An important reform by Reutern was the introduction from 1862 onwards of a unified state budget, with the accounts of all departments centralized in the Treasury. The amounts of the budget were published from 1863 onwards, and the reports of the state comptroller from 1866. Reutern stood for a liberal foreign trade policy. In 1863 almost all existing export duties were abolished, at a cost to the Treasury of more than a million roubles. Already before his appointment, the Tariff Act of 1857 had lowered import duties on a number of goods, especially on machinery and on industrial raw materials. The Act of 1868 went still further. It was not until after the Russo-Turkish War that Russia reverted to protectionism.

The Nationalities

After the defeat of the rebellion of 1863 the policy of russification, which had been in force in Lithuania since the time of Uvarov,[1] was applied also to the former Kingdom of Poland. Its exponents were the governors-general of Warsaw, Count F. Berg (1864–74) and Count Kotsebue (1874–80). The policy affected the Church, the administration, and the educational system.

In 1864 all properties of the Catholic Church were confiscated, and almost all monasteries closed. In 1865 a new régime for the Catholic Church in the former Kingdom was instituted. There were seven bishoprics, reduced two years later to six. Priests were to receive salaries from the state. The Church administration was placed under the Directorate of Foreign Confessions of the Ministry of the Interior. In 1875 the Uniate Church was abolished in the former Kingdom, and a new Orthodox bishopric was created in Kholm. The Council of State and the Administrative Council were abolished in 1867, and the special governmental commissions in 1868, and all matters previously handled by them were simply referred to the appropriate branches of the central government of the empire. The former Kingdom was divided into ten provinces and eighty-four *uezd*. In 1876 the ninth and tenth departments of the Senate in Warsaw and the Commission of Justice were abolished, and the judicial system of the Russian empire, based on the judicial reform of 1864, came into force in the former Kingdom, with the important exception that the institution of the jury was not introduced. The regulations for secondary education, introduced by Count Dmitri Tolstoy in the empire as a whole, were applied with only minor exceptions to Poland in 1872. In 1867 a Warsaw educational district was instituted,

[1] See above pp. 269–70.

and in June 1869 a new Warsaw University Statute was published. This was based on the Russian University Statute of 1863, but without the provisions for internal autonomy enjoyed by Russian universities. The language of instruction in the new university was to be Russian: teachers of the former Polish university were allowed a period of two years in which to learn to lecture in Russian, and three years in which to obtain a doctor's degree of a Russian university, if they wished to pursue their profession. When the university opened in October 1869, it had 1,031 students.

The Polish Rebellion also made the Russian government especially sensitive to any indications of 'separatism' in the Ukraine. During the decades which followed the suppression of the Cyril and Methodius Society, the gradual process, by which mere awareness of difference from Muscovy became transformed into Ukrainian national consciousness, had not ceased to operate, though few persons as yet were affected by it. The main centre of Ukrainian cultural activity was the south-western section of the Russian Geographical Society, located in Kiev, whose members devoted themselves to the study of language, folklore, popular songs, poetry, and historical monuments. At an archaeological congress in Kiev in 1874, the Ukrainian nationalist trend was clearly visible. There was also a political group called *Hromada*, with mildly socialist and autonomist aspirations, which was in touch with Russian revolutionary groups. The outstanding figure in these various activities was Mykhaylo Drahomaniv, who was appointed a lecturer in history at the University of Kiev in 1870, but was dismissed from his post in 1875. In 1876 he emigrated to Vienna. In the same year an official commission was set up to investigate separatist activities in the Ukraine. It recommended the closure of the south-western section of the Geographical Society, and the prohibition of all publications, other than the texts of historical documents, as well as of theatrical performances and song recitals, in Ukrainian dialect. These recommendations were carried out by the government.

Russian policy in both Poland and the Ukraine was directly affected by the policy of the Austrian government in the neighbouring province of Galicia, whose population was about equally divided between Poles and Ukrainians. From 1867 onwards the Poles of Galicia enjoyed self-government, with a Diet in Lwów, elected by a restricted franchise. The existence of free institutions for the Austrian Poles was a source of constant embarrassment to the Russian authorities in Warsaw. The only feature of Austrian rule in Galicia which was unwelcome to the Poles was that the Galician Ukrainians also were able to benefit from self-government. Being for the most part poorer and less educated than the Poles, they were at a certain disadvantage. Nevertheless, they were able to use their language in public, to publish works in it, and to form social or political organizations. In 1868 a society called *Prosvita* (Enlightenment) was founded in Lwów, which established reading-rooms and organized lectures in small towns. In 1873 was founded the Shevchenko Society, which acquired a solid reputation as a centre of Ukrainian culture. Drahomaniv had visited Galicia when he was still a lecturer in Kiev, and had written about its problems for the public of the Russian Ukraine. After he left Russia, he spent much of his time in Lwów, and played a large part in the development of Ukrainian political activity in Galicia. In this he was successful. Ukrainian national consciousness became deeply rooted in the peasant masses, and Galicia became a sort of Ukrainian Piedmont. For the Galician Ukrainians the main enemy, with whom they were in daily conflict, were the Poles rather than the Russians. But the existence of this Ukrainian movement on the frontier was even more objectionable to the Russian authorities than the existence of a Polish provincial assembly in Lwów.

Drahomaniv himself was no extreme nationalist. He thought not of an independent Ukrainian state but of a democratic and decentralized form of government for the Russian empire. He even made himself unpopular with his compatriots by praising Russian literature and by criticizing the chauvinist attacks made by some Galician politicans against Russians, Poles, or Jews. Within the Russian borders, Ukrainian nationalism was still not strong, but it was felt to some extent by many of those who opposed the régime. For example, the revolutionary A. I. Zhelyabov[1] was in touch with Drahomaniv. At one time he had been drawn towards Ukrainian nationalism, but thought it was too weak, and believed that more could be achieved within an

[1] See below pp. 427–8.

all-Russian revolutionary movement. 'Where are our Fenians? Where is our Parnell?' he wrote to the indignant Drahomaniv.[1] Russian repression of Ukrainian national feeling, contrasted with Austrian tolerance, produced in the following decades, if not Ukrainian Parnells, at least increasingly bitter Ukrainian nationalism.

Alexander II maintained his father's benevolent attitude towards the Baltic Germans. The situation in the Baltic provinces was, however, complicated by the growth of educated middle classes among both Latvians and Estonians, who began to show pride in their own languages and to claim equal status with the Germans. Russian nationalists took an interest. On 9 March 1864, Bishop Walter, of the Livonian Protestant Church, made a sermon before the Landtag, in which he urged the germanization of the Estonians and the Latvians in their own interest, as they were 'fragments of tribes that were disappearing from history'.[2] This provoked fierce replies from Katkov and from Ivan Aksakov denouncing the presumption of the Germans in trying to impose their culture on other subjects of the Russian empire.

Samarin now returned to the field from which he had been so firmly ejected by Nicholas I. His views at this time are freely expressed in his correspondence with Baroness Edith von Raden the chief lady-in-waiting of Grand Duchess Elena Pavlovna, and herself a Baltic German of liberal outlook. Samarin especially denounced the narrow, feudal mentality of the Baltic aristocracy. The preservation of this mentality seemed to him insufferable at a time when in Russia such modern and progressive changes as the introduction of zemstvos and the judicial reform were taking place. The Baltic Germans' privileges, he claimed, were more antiquated than any in Europe. Baroness von Raden replied that this pride in tradition was harmless, and that the Baltic Germans were loyal to Russia and formed no threat to her.

N'est-il pas plus conforme à la sagesse d'une vraie politique

[1] Quoted in article by I. L. Rudnytsky, 'Drahomanov as a Political Theorist' in *Mykhaylo Drahomanov: a Symposium and Selected Writings* (New York, 1952), pp. 113–14.

[2] 'Bruchteile aus der Geschichte verschwindender Volksstämme.' For a modern account sympathetic to the German point of view, see R. Wittram, *Baltische Geschichte* (Munich, 1954), p. 149.

gouvernementale, là où aucun danger ne presse, là où les bons services rendus sont tacites, de laisser se dérouler les événements conformément au caractère et aux habitudes des parties intéressées, sans trancher le nœud gordien pour le plaisir d'en avoir fini plus vite? Jamais vous ne pourrez communiquer à une population allemande l'insouciance proverbiale, la puissance irréfléchie de sacrifice, l'indifférence pour le droit traditionnel, la largeur de vues, la bonhomie tolérante innées au peuple russe.[1]

But Samarin had no use for cultural variety within the empire. The different world of the Baltic Germans could not be tolerated side by side with the Russian world: '. . . c'est le fil d'un rasoir passé entre le cœur et la tête de la nation, c'est un poison injecté dans les fibres les plus sensibles du corps social, un dissolvant bien autrement dangereux que la propagande de Herzen, peut-être le seul dissolvant que nous ayons à redouter'.[2] He rejected the idea that the Tsar should be regarded as the father of many different peoples inhabiting his empire. 'C'est ce qu'on pourrait appeler la polygamie élevée à la hauteur d'un devoir et érigée en système politique.' Samarin insisted that the Tsar was a Russian ruler, and that Russians must have the first place within his empire. 'Nous autres russes, nous prétendons être en Russie ce que sont les français en France et les anglais sur tout le territoire des possessions britanniques.'

In 1867 the first two volumes of Samarin's *Borderlands of Russia* appeared abroad. In November 1868 he was summoned to the governor-general of Moscow, who transmitted to him a formal rebuke from the Tsar for the attacks against the Baltic Germans in this work. Alexander II maintained the tolerant tradition of Nicholas I. This did not restrain Samarin from publishing four more volumes abroad between 1871 and 1876 and engaging in a bitter polemic with the Protestant Pastor Schirren.[3]

[1] *Correspondance de G. Samarine avec la baronne de Raden*, ed. D. Samarin (Moscow, 1894), pp. 23–24.

[2] Ibid., p. 29.

[3] Schirren was professor of history at Dorpat University. His *Livländische Antwort*, in reply to Samarin's book, was a passionate and moving defence of traditional institutions as such, completely oblivious to modern political trends, contemptuous of Russian culture and ignoring the existence of the Baltic peoples. It was published in Leipzig in 1868. Schirren was dismissed from the university and spent the rest of his life in Germany.

The only step taken by the Russian government in this period against German supremacy was the rather reasonable provision that the Russian language should be used in the offices of the higher provincial administration. This was decreed in 1867 and carried out in 1870.

Meanwhile, however, the challenge from the Baltic peoples was growing.

Estonian national consciousness was being rapidly developed with the publication of literature in the Estonian language. Landmarks were the appearance of the epic poem *Kalevipoeg* by F. R. Kreutzwald in 1857, and the newspaper founded in the same year by J. W. Jannsen for peasant readers.[1] It was not concerned with politics but aimed at arousing interest in literature and giving useful information on agriculture and farm economics. The Estonian Student Association, founded in 1870, was more interested in wider problems. Estonian political activity really began with the newspaper *Sakala*, published by K. R. Jakobson from 1878 to 1882. Jakobson attacked the German upper class and directly demanded legal and economic equality for the Estonians. He took care to stress his loyalty to the Tsar, and hoped for Russian support against the Germans.

Among the Latvians too literary movements appeared with nationalist undertones. In 1868 the Latvian Association (*Latveishu Biedriba*) was founded in Riga, and in 1878 appeared in the same city the first daily newspaper in the Latvian language, *Balss* ('The Voice'). The Latvian equivalent to Jakobson was Christian Valdemars, a bitter enemy of the Germans and an advocate of friendship with Russia. He enjoyed the sympathy of the Grand Duke Constantine. The idea that the people of the two provinces of Livonia and Kurland should form a single Latvian nation and should no longer submit to the rule of a German minority, began to gain ground.

The Estonians and Latvians were overwhelmingly rural peoples, but they were beginning to make their way to the cities. This is clearly shown by the population figures for the two capital cities of Riga and Tallinn in these years. Riga in 1867 had 43,980 Germans, 25,772 Russians, and 24,199 Latvians: in 1881 it had 52,232 Germans, 49,974 Latvians, and

[1] Entitled *Pärnu Postimees* from 1857 to 1864, and thereafter *Eesti Postimees.* See E. Uustalu, *The History of the Estonian people* (1952), pp. 121 ff.

31,976 Russians. Tallinn in 1871 had 15,097 Estonians, 10,020 Germans, and 3,300 Russians: in 1881 it had 26,324 Estonians, 12,737 Germans, and 5,111 Russians.[1] These new Latvian and Estonian urban populations consisted almost exclusively of workers or small shopkeepers. The more prosperous middle-class occupations were almost wholly in German hands, while the Russian element consisted primarily of officials and minor state employees.

Finland had given no trouble to Russia during the Crimean War, despite the Anglo-French naval attack on the Åland Islands and the bombardment of Sveaborg. Some exiles in Sweden had made anti-Russian propaganda, but the failure of Sweden to take part in the war had made anti-Russian action in Finland impossible. Alexander II had thus no reason for resentment against Finland, but had perhaps some reason to favour the Finnish majority against the Swedish minority, which, like the German minority in the Baltic provinces, comprised the whole landowning and upper business class, as well as a share of the lower social classes. In 1863 he summoned the Diet in Helsingfors for the first time in fifty-four years. The Diet passed legislation on currency, railway building, and education. Its most important act was the Language Ordinance of 1 August 1863. This laid down that within twenty years the Finnish language must be introduced into all public business on a level of equality with Swedish. A further law of 1865 stated that all employees of the Survey and Forests Office, the Post Office, State Bank, and Customs must serve the public in Finnish whenever requested.

During the following decades the language laws were not fully implemented. The ruling Swedish minority tried to slow down the process, and the spokesmen of the Finnish majority were on the watch for failures, and ready with complaints. However, the progress of the Finnish population could not be stopped. The law of 1866 on elementary education was put into effect within a few years. In 1874–5 there were 15,000 pupils in elementary schools, and the number increased to over 125,000 by the end of the century. In 1873 the first secondary school with instruction in Finnish was founded in Helsingfors. In 1880 there were 3,500 children in *lycées*, of whom 1,300 were Finnish

[1] R. Wittram, op. cit., p. 188.

speaking.[1] A few Finnish-speaking students were reaching the university.

During the reign of Alexander II a few practical measures were taken to improve the lot of the Jews. On 26 August 1856 the discriminatory system of mobilizing Jewish children was abolished, and the recruitment of Jews to the armed forces was placed on the same basis as for the other subjects of the empire. In the next years selected categories of Jews were permitted to reside with their families outside the Pale of Settlement. This right was given on 16 March 1859 to Jewish merchants of the first guild of two years' standing; on 27 November 1861 to Jews holding medical degrees and higher university degrees (but not to ordinary graduates); and on 28 June 1865 to various categories of artisans and mechanics. This more liberal trend aroused some response from a section of the Jewish population. There was a movement towards assimilation with Russian society. Nevertheless, the basic problems of Russian Jewry were unaffected. On the one hand, the distorted social structure of the Jewish community, with its excess of small traders and intellectual occupations, its lack of a peasantry and the exclusion of Jews from government employment, remained a fact. On the other hand, the lower ranks of the Russian bureaucracy continued to treat Jews with contempt and brutality, and in this they usually reflected the prejudices of the local population, especially of the Ukraine and Lithuania.

The end of the Crimean War made it possible for the Russian forces in the Caucasus to break the power of Shamil in Daghestan. In 1857 General Yevdokimov forced his way into the Argun valley, systematically clearing forests, destroying villages, and building fortifications. The Russians now held mountain ridges not far from Shamil's fortress of Vedeno. In 1858 Yevdokimov pushed forward again, and took the fortified village of Shatoy, while another Russian column penetrated into Daghestan from the Lezgian line. The Chechens themselves were becoming exhausted, and numerous villages deserted Shamil and sought Russian protection. In April 1859 Vedeno was stormed. Shamil and his faithful followers retreated to a last stronghold on Mount Gunib. Meanwhile the Chechens and the tribes of Daghestan surrendered one by one to the Russians.

[1] J. H. Wuorinen, *Nationalism in Modern Finland* (New York, 1931), p. 159.

Shamil at first defended himself with about 400 loyal supporters, but realizing that he was completely encircled he surrendered on 25 August 1859. The viceroy of the Caucasus, Prince A. I. Baryatinsky, received him courteously and sent him to St. Petersburg, where he was taken before the Tsar. He was given a residence in Kaluga until 1870, then brought to Kiev, and allowed to go to Mecca, where he died in 1871.

The defeat of Shamil made it possible finally to clean up the territory of the Circassians, on the Russian right flank along the Black Sea coast. General Yevdokimov began his campaign in February 1862, cleared a large area and resettled its population on the plains. In 1863 the attack was continued from two sides, from the Belaya River and the Adagum line. In October 1863, the leaders of the Abadzekh tribe made the best terms they could with Yevdokimov. Those who wished to remain Russian subjects must move to new territories assigned to them by 1 February 1864. Those who preferred exile could have two and a half months to emigrate to Turkey. About 400,000 persons in fact emigrated, more than half the Circassian population. There was still a little more fighting on the southern slopes of the mountains, but by May 1864 all was over.

From this time the whole Caucasus area and Transcaucasia were firmly in Russian hands. The two Christian nations of Transcaucasia gave no trouble at this time. Both were basically loyal to the empire, seeing in the Russians their protectors against Turks or Persians. In Georgia there was social injustice and growing discontent as a result of the especially harsh terms of the 1861 settlement.[1] The Georgian intelligentsia was thus very accessible to revolutionary ideas. There were several Georgians among the revolutionaries of the 1870's, but they acted within the Russian movement, with no significant Georgian nationalist demands. The Armenians were still more devoted to Russia, but they too, as a disproportionately urban and comparatively well-educated group, were sympathetic to revolutionary ideas.

[1] The landlords kept a much larger proportion of the land in their possession than did the landlords in European Russia. In Tiflis the peasants disposed of 34 per cent. less land than they had had as serfs. Provisions for the acquisition of land by the peasants were completely ineffective. The condition of 'temporary obligation' was preserved almost up to the First World War. See below p. 670. For further details and sources see P. A. Zayonchkovsky, op. cit., p. 241.

During the reign of Alexander II, the struggle between Orthodox missionaries and Tatar Moslems in the Volga valley became fiercer than it had been since the reign of Catherine II. The outstanding figure on the Russian side was N. I. Ilyminsky, born in 1821, the son of a priest in Penza, a graduate of Kazan Spiritual Academy, and a distinguished Oriental scholar. Ilyminsky studied for two years in Cairo, travelled in the Ottoman empire and took part in an official commission for the demarcation of the frontier in the Kazakh steppes. In the 1860's he held chairs of Arabic and Turkish in both the University and the Spiritual Academy of Kazan, but resigned in 1870 in order to become director of the Kazan Teachers' Training College. In this post his aim was to train teachers from the Christian minority of Tatars to spread Christianity among the Moslem majority, and also to train teachers from the small Volga peoples whose conversion was the subject of rivalry between Christians and Moslems. Ilyminsky published religious books in a modern colloquial Tatar dialect, purged of literary Arabic phrases and printed in the Cyrillic script, and also in the Finno-Ugrian languages spoken by the small Volga peoples. His activities roused opposition from some conservative Russian officials and priests. But their purpose, as became clear in the following reign, was not to strengthen local nationalism but to spread Orthodoxy and russification.

The Revolutionary Movement

The more effective repression carried out by the police after the Karakozov attempt led to a lull in conspiratorial activity for some years. The main revolutionary figures at this time were the exiles.

The most glamorous of these was Bakunin. His long career as a revolutionary, his sufferings and his sensational escape, his impressive appearance, and his gift for inflammatory rhetoric made him a great romantic figure. But in the last years of his life he had little direct contact with Russia. His main activity was connected with the First International, in which he conflicted with Karl Marx, and with the foundation of an international anarchist movement whose main support was found in Spain and Italy. His very existence, however, offered a model to revolutionary youth in Russia, and his periodical expressions of his belief in a peasant insurrection in Russia found ready admirers.

Bakunin's last important link with Russia was through Sergei Nechayev. Born in 1847 in Ivanovo, the son of a workman, Nechayev became a school-teacher in St. Petersburg in 1866, and in 1868 attended lectures at the university and met students of revolutionary views. In 1869 he made his way to Geneva. He was received with enthusiasm by Bakunin, and was joint author with him of a work entitled *Revolutionary Catechism*, which set out in romantic terms the duties and vocation of a professional revolutionary. At the end of the year he returned to Moscow to found a revolutionary organization entitled *Narodnaya rasprava* (The People's Reckoning). He gathered a few followers, whom he persuaded that he represented a much larger organization. The most important action of the group was the murder of one of its members, Ivan Ivanov, who was accused of betraying it. Whether Nechayev genuinely suspected Ivanov, whether Ivanov was really a spy, or whether Nechayev had him murdered as a diabolical manœuvre in order inextricably to involve his companions in guilt and so bind them to his conspiracy, is obscure, and the truth may never be known. The whole affair has been hopelessly confused by the fact that Dostoyevsky based the character of Peter Verkhovensky in his *Possessed* on Nechayev. Dostoyevsky was a great writer, but his novel cannot be regarded as historical evidence. In December 1869 Nechayev fled abroad again and spent nearly three years in western Europe. In August 1872 he was denounced to the Swiss police in Zürich, and was extradited to Russia. He showed great courage at his trial, and was condemned to twenty years of forced labour, to be followed by deportation to Siberia for life. He survived in Peter Paul Fortress in St. Petersburg until 1882. He was able to communicate with the revolutionaries outside prison in 1879, and they even considered a plan for his escape. This mysterious and ruthless man was greatly admired by other conspirators, and his story or his myth became an important part of the revolutionary tradition.

One of those who had known Nechayev in 1869 was Peter Tkachov. Born of a family of small nobility in the district of Velikie Luki in north-western Russia, he became a student at Moscow University in 1861, and was several times arrested in the following years when taking part in student riots or the distribution of propaganda leaflets. In 1869 he was implicated in the Nechayev affair, but was let off with a period of exile in his home district. In 1873 he escaped abroad. In Geneva he established a paper, *Nabat* ('The Tocsin'), which he edited from 1875 to 1881. In this paper he expressed a doctrine of revolutionary *élitism* in its purest form. Revolutionary leadership, he argued, must come from the intelligentsia. The fact that the masses were backward need not matter. The absence of an urban proletariat on the side of the revolution was more than compensated by the absence of a bourgeoisie on the enemy side.

For the time being the strongest and most powerful enemy with which we have to fight is our government, with its armed forces and its vast material resources. Between it and the people there is as yet no intermediate force, which could for long hold up and restrain the popular movement, once it began. Our class of landowners, taken by itself, is disparate, weak, and both in numbers and economic strength quite negligible. Our *tiers état* consists more than half of proletarians, poor people, and only from a minority of it are real *bourgeois*, in the West European sense of this word, beginning to form. . . .

However, economic development is a fact, and it is bound to produce more powerful social forces opposing revolution:

The landowners *volens-nolens* are forced to introduce improvements into the system of agricultural economy. And the progress of agriculture usually goes hand in hand with the development of a native factory industry, with the development of urban life. Thus, in our country at present all the conditions are present for the formation, on the one hand of a very strong conservative class of peasant-owners and farmers, on the other hand of a moneyed, trading, industrial capitalist *bourgeoisie*. And as these classes are formed and grow stronger, the situation of the people will inevitably deteriorate, and the chances for success of a violent seizure of power will become more and more problematical. That is why we cannot wait. That is why we assert that in Russia revolution is urgently necessary, and necessary precisely now. We do not admit any postponement, any delay. *Now*, or not for a very long time, perhaps never. Now circumstances operate in our favour, in ten or twenty years they will be against us.[1]

[1] P. N. Tkachov, *Izbrannye sochineniya na sotsialno-politicheskie temy*, ed. B. P. Kozmin (Moscow, 1933), iii, pp. 69–70. The passage comes from a long and brilliant

The revolutionaries must seize power, and then use the state machine, which had been an instrument of their enemies, as an instrument of their own power, for the realization of their own social ideals.

Another exile who had a great influence was P. L. Lavrov. Born in 1823, he made a career in the army, reached the rank of colonel, and taught mathematics in the Artillery Academy in St. Petersburg. He published some minor philosophical works in 1859, and in 1862 became a member of Serno-Solovevich's *Zemlya i volya.* For this he was arrested, and banished from 1866 to 1870 to Vologda province. In 1870 he escaped to Switzerland. During his banishment he had published some essays entitled *Historical Letters*, which were first passed by the censorship and later suppressed. In them he argued that the educated classes owed a debt to the people, whose toil had made their education possible, and that they must repay the debt by establishing a new social order. The first necessity, however, was to produce an *élite* of 'critically thinking persons' capable of leadership in the struggle for social justice. Though neither original in thought nor distinguished in style, the Letters made a great impact on Russian youth, whose mood they well expressed. After he left Russia, Lavrov became associated with socialist circles in western Europe, and from 1873 he published, first in Zürich and then in London, a paper entitled *Vperyod* ('Forward'). Lavrov was opposed to the *élitism* of Tkachov and to the insurrectionary anarchism of Bakunin. He believed that the liberation of the people should be the work not of a vanguard of professional revolutionaries but of the people itself. Before this could happen, the people must be politically educated. Thus the main task of the present generation must be political propaganda. The educated *élite* must devote itself to peaceful preaching of democratic and socialist ideas among the Russian people.

When political activity began to revive among the Russian intellectual youth at the beginning of the 1870's, there were

polemical letter addressed by Tkachov to Lavrov's *Vperyod*, and published in 1874 in London as a pamphlet under the title 'The Tasks of Revolutionary Propaganda in Russia'. For an excellent discussion of Tkachov's ideas and his place in the history of the revolutionary movement, see Franco Venturi, *Il popolismo russo* (Turin, 1952), vol. ii, ch. 16, pp. 635–98 (English edition entitled *Roots of Revolution, 1960*).

thus two trends, the 'Bakuninists' or 'insurgents' and the 'Lavrovists' or 'propagandists'. At first the second were the more important. The most active Lavrovist group was the 'Chaikovsky Circle', whose members included N. V. Chaikovsky, the couple Mark and Olga Natanson, and Sofya Perovskaya, a member of the well-known military family of Nicholas I's reign. The group managed a bookshop which sold political works at cheap prices. Though the books chosen were permitted by the censor, the police regarded this activity as suspicious and suppressed the bookshop. The group then distributed literature secretly, including works forbidden by the censorship. They also organized discussion groups for workers. In 1873 these minor activities were replaced by a mass movement, known as 'going to the people'.

This expression was derived from an earlier appeal to Russian youth by Herzen. 'To the people!' (*v narod*) he had written. This slogan also gave a name to the whole revolutionary movement which developed in the 1870's. Its members became known as *narodniki*, or Populists. In 1873, and still more in the summer of 1874, hundreds of young people, girls as well as men, went into the villages and preached revolutionary ideas to the peasants. No immediate results were achieved. Some peasants listened with sympathy, many were hostile, and most understood hardly anything of what they heard. The preachers were extremely conspicuous, and soon they were being rounded up by the police. Between 1873 and 1877 the police arrested 1,611 propagandists, of whom 15 per cent. were women. The investigation proceeded slowly. It was not until 1877 that two major trials of young revolutionaries were held. In February and March 50 persons belonging to a Moscow group were tried, and from October 1877 to January 1878 was held a monster trial of 193 persons, many of whom had been in prison since 1873. Both trials were public, and were reported in the press. They gave the accused an admirable opportunity to publicize their opinions, and the speeches of their defending lawyers were also politically effective. A minority of the accused received prison sentences, but many of those who were acquitted were afterwards deported by the police to remote provinces of European Russia or Siberia under their powers of 'administrative exile'.

Police statistics give an interesting picture of the social composition of the revolutionaries. Of all persons condemned to prison or administratively exiled between 1873 and 1877, 279 were children of noble parents, 117 of non-noble officials, 197 of priests, 33 of merchants, 68 of Jews, 92 of *meshchane*, and 138 of peasants. The last two categories refer to the legal status rather than the actual occupation, and it may be assumed that these were in fact children of city workers. The large number of children of priests is particularly striking.[1]

On 24 January 1878, the day after the conclusion of the trial of the 193, a young woman named Vera Zasulich entered the office of the police chief of St. Petersburg, General Trepov, who had ordered an imprisoned student to be flogged, and shot him. He recovered from the wound, but when Zasulich was brought to trial she was acquitted by the jury. The police intended to rearrest her as soon as she left the court, but the crowd enabled her to escape, and her friends smuggled her abroad. After this incident all matters of 'resistance to the authorities, rebellion, assassination or attempts on the lives of officials' were removed from the jurisdiction of juries and entrusted to military tribunals.

Meanwhile some of those who had escaped arrest in 1874, and others who had got away from their place of administrative banishment and were living illegally in big cities, were keeping the revolutionary movement alive. It became clear to them that they must have a disciplined conspiratorial organization if they were to fight with any hope of success against the Russian state machine. From their efforts emerged what may be called the first revolutionary party[2] in Russia, which took the same name, *Zemlya i volya*, as Serno-Solovevich's earlier group but became a much more effective organization. Its leaders came from St. Petersburg and from the southern cities of Kiev and Odessa. The most important in the north were Mark and Olga Natanson, former members of the Chaikovsky Circle, and A. D. Mikhailov, who became the party's chief expert on techniques of conspiracy and security. In the south the leaders included V. K. Debagorii-Mokrevich, L. V. Deutsch and

[1] Statistics of the Third Department, from an article by N. P. Sidorov in *Katorga i ssylka* (1928, no. 1) quoted by Venturi, op. cit. ii. 966.

[2] As opposed to a conspiratorial group with political aims, of which the first example were of course the Decembrists.

Y. V. Stefanovich. The party was to have a central command, known as the 'basic circle' (*osnovnoy kruzhok*), to which the organizers of local groups, in various cities and provinces, were responsible. The basic circle was divided into five sections. First was the administrative, which dealt with general matters of policy, and was also responsible for providing false papers for persons living illegally. The second, third, and fourth sections dealt with activities respectively among the intelligentsia, urban workers, and peasants. The fifth was known as the 'disorganizing section', and was concerned with the rescue from prison of arrested comrades, assassinations of government officials as reprisals for maltreatment of revolutionaries, and the detection and punishment of traitors or police spies.

The first years of the party's existence coincided with the crisis in the Balkans, which led to the Russo-Turkish War of 1877. The atmosphere was at first rather unfavourable. Many young Russians, of combative temperament and radical ideas, especially in the south of Russia, sympathized with the struggle of the Bosnians, Bulgarians, and Serbs for liberty. Some of them went as volunteers to fight, or to serve as nurses, in the Balkans. When Russia declared war, young men were liable for military service. All this somewhat deflected energies from the internal revolutionary struggle. However, the mismanagement of the war in the winter of 1877–8, and the disappointments of the peace settlement, revived general discontent, and by the middle of 1878 the climate of opinion among the intellectual youth was once more favourable for the revolutionaries.

The aim of *Zemlya i volya* was insurrection by the peasantry, and the first need remained, as always, propaganda among the people. The first 'going to the people' had been crushed: it was therefore necessary to approach the task with more careful planning. In 1876 revolutionaries went in small groups, and sought to gain influence over the people by living among them, learning their mentality, and practising a useful trade, as craftsmen or as employees of the zemstvo medical or social services. They included women. They paid special attention to those parts of the Volga valley where religious schismatics or sectarians were numerous. A. D. Mikhailov made a special study of sectarian beliefs, and even engaged in public arguments with Orthodox priests sent to convert schismatics back to the official

Church. Hopes of enlisting religious dissidents for the revolutionary cause on a mass scale were not realised. However, the leaders of *Zemlya i volya* were right in believing that persecuted religious groups were more accessible than most Russians to revolutionary propaganda. In the following decades the revolutionary parties certainly won an unusually large amount of support in areas where the schism and sects were strong.

Stefanovich and Deutsch succeeded in organizing peasants for insurrection in the Chigirin district of Kiev province in the summer of 1877. It was, however, necessary to persuade the peasants that the Tsar wished them to rise against the nobles. Stefanovich showed them a false imperial decree to this effect. The old tactic of Pugachov, repeated by Anton Petrov in 1861 at Bezdna, was once more effective. Over 900 peasants took an oath to serve, and were organized and drilled in groups of 25. The authorities learned of the plans from a drunken peasant, and in August 1877 the leaders and many peasants were arrested. In May 1878 Stefanovich and Deutsch were rescued from Kiev prison by the 'disorganizing section'.

Though the revolutionaries did win some support among peasants, they were still far from their goal of a mass rising. The truth was that the population of scattered villages could not be welded into any sort of force. Much more promising were the poor of the cities, sons of peasants herded together in the factories of the new industrial quarters, or persons living the still more precarious and painful existence of unskilled labourers in the older towns. Already in May 1870 a textile strike in St. Petersburg had revealed the growth of discontent. In 1875 in Odessa a former St. Petersburg student of noble origin, E. O. Zaslavsky, organized a Union of Workers of Southern Russia, essentially a propaganda group but genuinely concerned with the workers' material interests. Before it had made much headway among real workers it was destroyed by the police and its leaders arrested. More successful was the attempt to create a workers' organization in St. Petersburg. On 6 December 1876 *Zemlya i volya* organized a demonstration of more than 200 workers outside the Kazan Cathedral in the capital, and one of their members, the former student of the Mining Institute, G. V. Plekhanov, made a speech to them. This symbolic action was followed by practical organizing work. By the end of 1878 the Northern Union of Russian Workers had been created by Viktor Obnorsky, the son of an army sergeant in Vologda, who had been in touch with Zaslavsky's group in Odessa in 1875, and Stepan Khalturin, the son of a peasant in Vyatka province. The Northern Union had supporters in many St. Petersburg factories, and was able both to spread socialist ideas among factory workers and to recruit workers to activity within *Zemlya i volya.*

Vera Zasulich's attempt on Trepov marked the beginning of a series of assassinations. The revolutionaries became increasingly concerned with acts of terror, which they felt were their only means of self-defence against the increasing brutality of the authorities, who now frequently resorted to executions, even of persons who had not taken any part in acts of violence. At the same time the revolutionaries began to abandon their earlier belief that political reforms were unimportant. Their aim of course remained social revolution. But their cause could make little progress as long as the police state prevented them from making propaganda to the Russian people. Therefore the replacement of the autocractic régime by a constitutional system with civil liberties, which they had once despised as fit only for liberal landowners and *bourgeois*, became a matter of real importance to the revolutionary cause.

On 4 August 1878 the disorganizing section killed an eminent victim, the head of the Third Department, General Mezentsev. On 20 August the government issued an appeal to the public to help it in the repression of revolutionary terror. The zemstvos showed little enthusiasm. Their more radical members felt it was up to the government to give political rights to the people before it could expect help. Some of the southern leaders of *Zemlya i volya* met two members of Chernigov zemstvo, I. I. Petrunkevich and A. F. Lindfors, in Kiev in December 1878. Petrunkevich asked if the revolutionaries would stop their terrorism if the zemstvos would mobilize the public in a movement to demand constitutional liberties. No agreement was reached. *Zemlya i volya* were quite right not to commit themselves, for the zemstvo liberals were not in fact capable of achieving political reforms. Petrunkevich and his friends made an honourable attempt at political protest in Chernigov, and there were faint echoes in the zemstvos of Kharkov, Poltava, and Tver. But the government ignored their views, and they could do nothing.[1]

The question the revolutionaries had to ask themselves was, if the liberals are unable to obtain political liberties, should we take on the job, and if so, what should be our method? A section of *Zemlya i volya* answered this question in the affirmative, and believed that the result could be achieved by forcing the government to surrender by assassinating its members, and in particular the Tsar himself. In June 1879 the party held a secret congress in Voronezh to discuss its policies. A few days beforehand, those members who favoured political action and terrorism met separately at the neighbouring small town of Lipetsk. The leading spokesmen of this view were A. D. Mikhailov and a southerner, a serf's son and former student in Odessa, A. I. Zhelyabov. Their views prevailed at Voronezh. There was no formal split, but Plekhanov walked out of the meeting in protest. A month later a formal breach occurred. Plekhanov and P. B. Akselrod formed a separate group entitled Black Partition (*Chorny peredyel*), which reasserted their primary concern with the peasants rather than the workers, and rejected terrorism and the struggle for mere political reform. The politically minded terrorists took the name People's Will (*Narodnaya volya*),[2] and made the assassination of the Tsar their main aim.

During the next two years a small number of heroic conspirators, men and women, defied the might of the vast Russian state and its ancient police system, and after a number of failures and heavy casualties in their own ranks they got their man. The first attempt on the Tsar's life was by A. K. Solovyov on 2 April 1879. The assassin missed his victim and was arrested. Next year a more careful plan was made by Khalturin, the founder of the Northern Russian Workers' Union. In 1879 the union had been betrayed to the police by a spy within its ranks, who was later exposed by a counter-spy whom A. D. Mikhailov had placed in the Third Department and duly killed. Khalturin escaped arrest during the round-up of members of the union,

[1] Petrunkevich's account is in his memoirs *Iz zapisok obshchestvennogo deyatelya*, forming vol. xxi of the periodical *Arkhiv russkoy revolyutsii* (Berlin, 1934), pp. 98–109.

[2] The Russian word *volya* has the double meaning of 'will' and 'liberty'.

and obtained employment as a workman in the Winter Palace. He kept his dynamite under his pillow every night in the workmen's quarters, and duly laid it in a room in which the Tsar was to receive the visiting prince of Bulgaria. On 5 February 1880 the explosion took place, but the emperor was not in the room at the time. The organization suffered a severe blow in November 1879, when Mikhailov was arrested as a result of an indiscretion remarkable in so cautious and ingenious a conspirator.[1] During 1880 the plans were directed by Zhelyabov and Sofya Perovskaya, a former member of the Chaikovsky Circle. Mines were laid under railway tracks in order to blow up the Imperial train, but these failed. Zhelyabov was arrested in February 1881, but Perovskaya carried on with her dwindling team. On 1 March 1881 a bomb was thrown at the Tsar's carriage as he returned from a military parade. Unhurt, he got out and was standing in the street making inquiries when a second bomb was thrown and mortally wounded him.

During the last year Alexander II had made sweeping changes in his government, intended both to strengthen the action against the terrorists and to win moderate public opinion by reforms. Dmitri Tolstoy was replaced as minister of education by the liberal A. A. Saburov, and another liberal-minded man, A. A. Abaza, became minister of finance. The main change was the creation of a Supreme Commission, under General M. T. Loris-Melikov, an Armenian and a hero of the Turkish war of 1877–8. The commission was given authority over the whole government machine for the repression of the revolutionaries and for the examination of the causes of the revolutionary movement. The Tsar's private life also changed at this time. In May 1880 the empress died, and two months later Alexander married his mistress, Princess Catherine Dolgorukaya, who received the title of Princess Yuryevskaya.

Loris-Melikov abolished the Third Department of the chancery, and transferred its functions to the police department of the Ministry of the Interior. He himself became minister of the interior after six months, and the commission was abolished.

[1] Khalturin escaped and continued his revolutionary activities for two years more. He was arrested in 1882 and executed in connexion with the assassination of the military prosecutor of Odessa, Strelnikov. Mikhailov died in prison in 1883. The authorities did not connect him with the assassination of the Tsar.

Loris-Melikov was known to be a man of liberal outlook, and his appointment aroused expectations of reform among some zemstvo people. He prepared a scheme for an extremely limited participation of elected persons in legislation. His plan provided for two commissions of appointed experts—an administrative and a financial—which would meet together with local experts, elected by zemstvo assemblies and city councils, in an enlarged General Commission. Proposals made by this body would then go before the Council of State, to which fifteen persons elected by the public would be added.[1] This was very much less than a proposal for a 'constitution', which it has often been called. Nevertheless, it was a step in the direction of representative institutions. A special conference of eight leading dignitaries appointed by the Tsar examined the proposals on 9 and 14 February. They approved, with some modifications, the proposal for the commissions, but did not take a decision about the plan to bring elected persons into the Council of State. The Tsar confirmed the special conference's recommendations on 17 February. On the morning of his assassination he was discussing with Valuyev the procedure for the publication of the government's plans.[2]

[1] Two persons were to be elected to the General Commission by each provincial zemstvo assembly, and by a number of the larger cities. Persons who were not themselves members of zemstvo assemblies or city councils were to be eligible for election. In provinces which did not possess zemstvo institutions, two local persons were to be appointed by the local authorities. The procedure for the selection of the fifteen additional persons attending the Council of State is not clear. Loris-Melikov's proposals are discussed at some length in P. A. Zayonchkovsky, *Krizis samoderzhaviya na rubezhe 1870–1880 godov*, Moscow, 1964. This recent work by a leading Soviet historian, based on archive materials and on some earlier published works that have not been available to me, is a valuable survey of government policies at the end of the reign of Alexander II and the beginning of that of Alexander III.

[2] Ibid., pp. 293–5. The members of the special conference were the Tsarevich, Grand Duke Konstantin Nikolayevich, Count Adlerberg, Prince Urusov, Loris-Melikov, Abaza, Valuyev, and the Minister of Justice Nabokov.

XII

FOREIGN POLICY

Russia and the Powers, 1856–1870

For the first seven years after the Crimean War Russian policy in Europe was based on co-operation with France. This had definite limits. Russian's main aim was of course to divide her victors and to revise the Treaty of Paris. But this Napoleon III was not prepared to do if the price was to quarrel with Britain. The naval disarmament of Russia in the Black Sea was something on which the British government continued to insist. Even a Russian attempt to modify the territorial cessions in southern Bessarabia, by claiming the region of Bolgrad, was unsuccessful. Napoleon would have been willing to agree, but when the British refused to yield, he would not support the Russian claim. In order to preserve his good relations with France, Gorchakov was obliged to give up the claim.[1]

If Napoleon was unwilling to sacrifice his friendship with Britain for the sake of Russia, it was quite otherwise with his relations with Austria. One of Napoleon's main reasons for bringing the Crimean War to a close without a humiliating defeat of Russia was that he was in a hurry to pursue his Italian plans against Austria. For their part, the Russian leaders were far more indignant with Austria than with Britain. The ingratitude for the help given in 1849 still rankled. Thus common hostility to Austria provided a sound basis for Franco-Russian co-operation.

This was first achieved in Roumania. Austria was opposed to a union of Moldavia and Wallachia, because a single Roumanian state would exercise far more attraction over the Roumanians of Transylvania and Bukovina than two rival

[1] Prince A. M. Gorchakov (1798–1883), a cousin of the general of the Crimean War, who served most of his diplomatic career in Germany, was ambassador in Vienna and Russian delegate at the Paris peace conference, and succeeded Nesselrode as foreign minister at the end of 1856. For a brilliant discussion of his personality and of the organization of the Russian Ministry of Foreign Affairs in his time, see B. H. Sumner, *Russia and the Balkans 1820–1880* (1937), pp. 18–35.

principalities. Napoleon was in favour of union, because of his sympathy for nationalist movements in general and for the 'Latin sister' on the Danube in particular. From the Russian point of view the choice was not clear in principle, but in practice whatever displeased Austria would please Russia. The British government's attitude vacillated: the foreign secretary, Lord Clarendon, was prepared to accept union, but Stratford de Redcliffe was against, partly because the Turks preferred two weak principalities to one larger state on their borders, but mainly because any plan supported by the Russians provoked his hostility. In July 1857 an election was held in Moldavia, with methods of intimidation and falsification which the authorites did not even try to conceal. The French ambassador in Constantinople demanded that they be cancelled, and when this was refused broke off diplomatic relations with Turkey. The French action was supported by Russia, Sardinia, and Prussia. Palmerston supported the Turks. However, the British government, preoccupied with the Indian Mutiny, was in no position to take action. On 6 August Napoleon arrived at Osborne for a four-day visit to Queen Victoria. At this meeting a compromise was made. The British government agreed to support the demand to the Turks for the cancellation of the election. Napoleon agreed that the two principalities should remain separate, but should obtain 'similar organic institutions' and 'a common system in all things civil and military'. A diplomatic conference met in Paris from 22 May to 19 August 1858. The Russian representative was Count P. D. Kiselyov, who had begun his long career as a reformer in the Roumanian prinicipalities almost thirty years earlier. The conference laid down the constitution of what were called the United Principalities of Moldavia and Wallachia. At the beginning of 1859 the assemblies of the two principalities elected the same man as prince. Alexander Cuza, chosen by the Moldavians on 22 January and by the Wallachians on 5 February, became the ruler of a state whose division in two was a fiction.[1]

In December 1858 Prince Alexander Karadjordjević of Serbia was forced to abdicate, and Miloš Obrenović was restored. This was a defeat for Austria, and a victory for

[1] For these events see R. W. Seton-Watson, *A History of the Roumanians*, pp. 246–68.

Russian influence. The French too supported the new régime. In the same year there was an armed rising among the Serbs of Hercegovina, and this led to war between Montenegro and the Turks. The Montenegrins defeated a Turkish force at Grahovo in May, and when peace was made Montenegro gained some territory, with the diplomatic support of Russia and France.

In Italian affairs Alexander II sympathized with the established order, and so protested against the breach of diplomatic relations, and threat of a naval demonstration, by Britain and France against Naples in the autumn of 1856. But when it was a matter of French action against Austrian positions in Italy, his attitude was different. A solemn meeting between Napoleon III and Alexander II at Stuttgart in September 1857 had no precise diplomatic results, but it was a demonstration to Europe and a warning to Austria. Napoleon's brother, Prince Jerome, saw Alexander in Warsaw in September 1858, and proposed that Russia should agree to attack Prussia if Prussia helped Austria in the event of a Franco-Austrian war. Further suggestions from the French side involved a full Franco-Russian alliance and a major territorial reorganization in Central Europe after the defeat of Austria, as well as the revision of the Black Sea neutralization clause. These ideas did not attract the Russian government, which did not desire such changes in Central Europe.[1] In January 1859 the French foreign minister, Count Walewski, took over from Jerome, and these wild schemes were replaced by cautious diplomacy. Walewski was no more willing to break with England in order to satisfy Russia in the Black Sea than the Russians were willing to let revolution loose in the Danubian Basin. The eventual result was a Franco-Russian secret treaty of 3 March 1859. This promised the benevolent neutrality of Russia towards France in the forthcoming conflict with Austria. Though it brought no concrete gain to Russia, it was certainly useful to Napoleon, enabling him to go to war with Austria in Italy. The annexation of Nice and Savoy by France in March 1860 was not to the liking of the Russian government: still less were the

[1] For the general European diplomacy of the 1860's see Taylor, op. cit., chapters vi to ix (pp. 99–200). The best detailed secondary work devoted primarily to this period is W. E. Mosse, *The European Powers and the German Question 1848–1871*, 1958.

action of Garibaldi in Sicily and Naples. However, a meeting of Alexander II with Franz Joseph and William I of Prussia in Warsaw from 25 to 27 October 1860 brought no satisfaction to the Austrians. Russia was not willing actively to oppose French policies in Italy, and Austria was not willing to offer the only price which might have made Russia change its attitude—support for the revision of the Black Sea clause.

Franco-Russian co-operation was not so good after the unification of Italy, but relations still remained reasonably cordial for three years more. Massacres of Christian Lebanese by Druses, with the connivance of the Turkish troops, in May 1860 were followed by a massacre of Christians by Moslems in Damascus from 9 to 11 July. Russia supported the proposal, agreed by the Powers in August, that a French expeditionary force be sent to the Lebanon, and joined in imposing on the Sultan in June 1861 a statute for the Lebanon, ensuring the rights of the Christian population.

In October 1862 a revolution in Greece overthrew King Otto. Britain, France, and Russia as the guarantor Powers agreed in recommending Prince William of Denmark as his successor. He was duly elected by the Greek National Assembly on 30 March 1863 under the title of King George I.

Franco-Russian co-operation was ended by the Polish Rebellion of January 1863. The traditional sympathy of both French and British public opinion for Poland expressed itself with great fervour and with complete ineffectiveness. Neither government was in a position to go to war with Russia on behalf of Poland, and nothing short of this could make the Russians yield. Britain was fully occupied with the problems arising out of the American Civil War and the possible need to defend Canada. France was at least partly committed to its intervention in Mexico on behalf of the Habsburg Archduke Maximilian. But Poland was an issue on which Left and Right in France agreed: to the former the Poles were a nation of revolutionary patriots, to the latter they were martyrs for the Catholic faith. Napoleon III had to pay attention to this feeling, apart from any sympathies which he himself, as the champion of the principle of nationality, may have had for the Poles. Yet if he had really wished to help Poland, he would have done better to carry on the war in 1856, seriously to destroy Russian power and to postpone achievement of his Italian plans until he had new allies in Poland and perhaps in Hungary. In 1863 he could only threaten and insult the Russians, and this was not enough. The same applies still more strongly to Austria, which as a Power possessing a large piece of Poland had no interest in defending the Polish cause. Yet Austria joined with Britain and France in their ineffectual protests. If Austria had wished to destroy Russia, even at the cost of strengthening Polish nationalism within her own borders, then 1856 was the time to do it. The revived 'Crimean coalition' of 1863 was bound to be a failure. Of the three Powers, the British lost least. Russia in any case regarded Britain as her enemy, and Britain did not need Russian friendship. But with the future of Germany uncertain, France had need of Russian co-operation, and it was vital for Austria that Russia should not be pushed into the arms of her Prussian rival.

The Polish Rebellion was first made an international issue by the Russo-Prussian convention, signed by General Alvensleben in St. Petersburg on 8 February. This provided for common action against the Poles by the Russian and Prussian forces in the frontier region, and permitted Russian officials to search for Polish revolutionaries on Prussian soil. This agreement was made on the initiative of the Prussian premier, Count Otto Bismarck, and was not very welcome to the Russians. Its immediate effect was to create anger in France against Prussia. This alarmed the British government, which had no wish to see France invade the Rhineland, and therefore insisted that protests about Poland should be directed at the Russians. A breach with Russia made the French government seek alliance with Austria. The Austrians, who still held Venetia in Italy, and thus still had grounds to fear a renewal of Napoleon's support for the Italian national cause, thought it better to co-operate with Napoleon than to antagonize him.

Napoleon in a personal letter to the Tsar in February asked him to restore Polish self-government: the request was refused. On 2 March Earl Russell formally requested Gorchakov to restore the situation of 1815 and to grant an amnesty. The Russian government was prepared only to promise, on 1 April, an amnesty to all Poles who laid down their arms by 1 May. The British, French, and Austrian governments addressed separate but similar notes to the Russian government on 10, 11, and 12 April asking for the creation of a self-governing Polish territory to include the Kingdom, Lithuania, and Ruthenia. Gorchakov's reply stated that the 1815 régime had been freely granted to the Poles by the emperor and had been withdrawn after the 1830 rebellion. It also argued that the current rebellion was the work of intriguers from abroad, supported by some of the gentry, priesthood, and city artisans but rejected by the mass of the Polish peasant population. On 11 June the three Powers jointly demanded a general amnesty, a national assembly, an autonomous Polish administration, freedom for the Catholic Church, the use of the Polish language in public affairs and in the schools, and a regular system of army recruitment. The Russian reply was that there could be no concessions until the rebellion had been suppressed. Further British and French notes of protest in August met with the same reply.

Diplomatic protests by the Powers did the Poles no good. By encouraging vain hopes, they caused them to fight longer and to incur harsher repression. Defeat of the rebellion increased Russian prestige in Europe: the Russians were not more loved than they had been, but they were more respected. However, the suppression of the Poles had required a substantial military and economic effort. Further demands were placed on Russia's resources by the campaigns in Central Asia from 1864 onwards.[1] The result was that for the next years Russian diplomacy was not effective in Europe. These were the years in which Prussia transformed the balance of power by her wars against Austria and France. The results were disquieting for Russia, as for the other Powers. But Prussia alone of the Powers had been on Russia's side in the Polish crisis, and Prussia had repeatedly expressed sympathy with Russia's aim to repeal the Black Sea clauses of the 1856 settlement. This was, from 1856 to 1870, the most important single objective of Russian policy.

In the Schleswig-Holstein crisis of 1864, which led to war by Prussia and Austria against Denmark, Russia was passive. Though Russia had a traditional connexion with Denmark, and did not wish to see Prussia increase her territory in the Baltic, the prospect of a British-led Scandinavian bloc was even more unattractive. The British were not prepared to buy

[1] See below pp. 441–4.

Russian support by a repeal of the Black Sea clauses. The French were not willing to fight both German powers for the sake of the Danes.

In the complex negotiations between Austria, Prussia, France and Italy which filled the next three years, it was at one time proposed by both the French and the Italians that, in return for ceding Venetia to Italy, Austria should acquire Roumania. This would of course have been a provocation to Russia, and the Austrian government was not prepared to face war with Russia in order to get French and Italian friendship. However, it did not at once refuse, and the fact that negotiations had taken place on these lines was revealed to the Russian government by Bismarck. In February 1866 Prince Cuza was overthrown, and the Roumanian leaders decided, contrary to the convention of 1858, to seek a foreign prince as their ruler. They chose Prince Charles of Hohenzollern-Siegmaringen, and in April he was elected by a huge majority in a national plebiscite. This choice was not welcome to the Russian government, but was disliked still more by the Austrian. Britain, France, and Prussia, however, supported it, and in October 1866 the Turkish government agreed.

The Russian government was not sorry to see the Austrians defeated by the Prussians in the war of June–July 1867. The subsequent reorganization of Germany was more alarming. However, General Edwin von Manteuffel, who was sent on a special mission to St. Petersburg in August 1867, was able to reassure the Tsar. He made it clear again that Prussia sympathized with the Russian view on the Black Sea clauses.

The situation in the Balkans remained unstable. Prince Michael Obrenović of Serbia worked steadily for an alliance of the Balkan states against Turkey. In 1866 a revolt broke out in Crete. The Russian government proposed an inquiry into Cretan affairs by the European Powers. This was weakly supported by the French and opposed by the British. In June 1867 the Turkish government rejected the proposal. A visit by Alexander II to Paris in the same month did not lead to any more effective co-operation. The only result was that in September 1867 the Russians proposed that the Powers should address to the Turks a statement that they disclaimed responsibility for further events in Crete. Gorchakov presumably expected that this would help the rebellion in Crete, and perhaps encourage other rebellions in other parts of the Balkans. The French, expecting that the Cretan rebellion would collapse and they themselves be relieved from an embarrassing situation, agreed. The Prussians and Italians joined in the declaration without enthusiasm, but the British and Austrians abstained. The declaration did no harm to the Turks. By the end of 1869 they had suppressed the rebellion, and Russia's Balkan plans were no nearer success.

During the Franco-Prussian War of 1870 the Russian press was mainly pro-French. The Russian government, however, favoured Prussia. Russia's benevolent neutrality was valuable to Bismarck, not only because his eastern frontier was secure but also because Austria was held back from helping France by the fear that if she did Russia might attack her.

The defeat of France enabled Gorchakov to achieve his aim of repealing the Black Sea clauses. He issued a circular note to the Powers, and had it published in the official *Journal de St. Pétersbourg* on 15 November 1870. The British government objected, with some lukewarm support from the Austrian. An international conference was opened in London on 17 January 1871. It was clear to all that Russia could not be kept disarmed in the Black Sea fifteen years after the Crimean War, in a Europe which had undergone so many great changes. At the same time there was reluctance, most strongly expressed by the British, to see a treaty set aside by unilateral repudiation. The London conference therefore issued a declaration that 'it is an essential principle of the law of nations that no Power can liberate itself from the engagements of a treaty, nor modify the stipulations thereof, unless with the consent of the contracting Powers, by means of an amicable arrangement'. The conference then agreed that both Russia and Turkey should have the right to maintain naval forces in the Black Sea. It also laid down that the Sultan might open the Straits in peacetime to warships of friendly and allied Powers if he 'should judge it necessary in order to secure the execution of the stipulations of the Treaty of Paris of 30 March 1856'. Thus the security of Russia in the Black Sea was restored, at the price of somewhat reducing the security of the Straits.

In the new Europe the strongest single continental Power was now the new German empire. Its leader, Bismarck, attached the greatest importance to friendly relations with Russia, but he had also taken care not unduly to antagonize Austria since the war of 1867. In May 1873 William I visited St. Petersburg, and in June Alexander II visited Vienna. From these visits emerged the League of Three Emperors, which was in fact no more than an assertion of an intention of the three governments to return to the relationship which had existed between them for most of the period between the Napoleonic and Crimean wars.

This friendship was not very solid, and was weakened by a certain personal jealousy of Gorchakov towards Bismarck. In the spring of 1875 there was talk of a German intention to attack France, and the French government did its best to alarm the other Powers. Both the British and the Russian governments took the alarm seriously, and protested to Bismarck. Gorchakov gave himself the pleasure of doing this personally, in a visit to Berlin on 10 May. This minor humiliation was no doubt unpleasant for Bismarck. The crisis was largely artificial, but it revealed the fact that, as Germany was now the strongest Power, and had achieved this strength through a Prussian policy which had twice resorted to war, Germany was likely in future to be suspected of aggressive intentions.

Expansion in Asia

Russian policy in the Pacific was not deflected from its course by the Crimean War. Japan had concluded treaties with the United States on 31 March 1854 and with Britain on 14 October 1854, and Russia was not to be ignored. At the end of 1854 Putyatin returned to Japan, and began formal negotiations in Shimoda on 22 December. These resulted in the conclusion of a treaty on 7 February 1855. The two governments declared their intention to maintain peaceful relations and to protect each other's subjects. The Kurile Islands were recognized as Japanese from Etorofu southwards, and Russian from Uruppu northwards. Sakhalin was declared to be a common possession: no attempt was made to define its status more precisely. The ports of Shimoda, Hakodate, and Nagasaki were to be open to Russian ships, Russian merchants were to trade in Shimoda and Hakodate, and there was to be a Russian consul in one or other of the latter ports. In 1857 a further treaty dealt in more detail with Russo-Japanese trade. Finally Putyatin returned in 1858, was admitted to Yedo on 12 August, and signed a third treaty on 19 August. This provided for an exchange of permanent resident diplomatic missions between the two countries, and for the development of trade by the nationals of each country in the other's territory without government interference.[1]

The establishment of Russians at the mouth of the Amur had never been recognized by the Chinese government, and it now became the task of Russian diplomacy to secure this. In 1856 China was again at war with the Western Powers, and the Russian government had an opportunity to extort concessions. Putyatin went to China at the time of the conclusion of peace between China and her Western enemies. The Treaty of Tientsin, which he signed in June 1858 before proceeding to Japan, guaranteed the right of Russian subjects to trade with China by sea and by land, but left the delimitation of the Russo-Chinese frontier to negotiations on the spot. This task was handled by Muravyov, who set off down the Amur in April 1858 and met the Chinese representatives at Aigun. His arguments about the need for a Russian presence on the Amur to deter the aggressive British made no impression, and he brought up some artillery to lend support to his verbal persuasion. In the end the Chinese agreed that the left bank of the Amur should be Russian from its junction with the Argun until the sea, and that the right bank should be Chinese until the junction of the Amur and the Ussuri. The future of the territory between the Ussuri, the Amur, and the Pacific was left to further negotiations.

Meanwhile hostilities broke out again between the Chinese and the Western Powers, and British and French forces prepared to attack Peking. In June 1859 Count N. P. Ignatyev arrived in Peking to continue the negotiations. Muravyov did not wait for formal agreement. He made his fourth journey down the Amur, explored the coast to the south of the delta, and chose the site of a suitable Russian port far down the coast, on which Vladivostok ('Ruler of the East') was later to be built. Ignatyev in Peking negotiated with great ability, but could not at first persuade the Chinese to accept the frontier indicated on

[1] The texts of the treaties of 1855, 1857, and 1858 are reproduced in Lensen, *The Russian Push towards Japan*, pp. 475–94.

his map, which gave Russia all the territory between the Ussuri and the Pacific ocean. He left Peking in June 1860 for Shanghai and Japan, and returned to Tientsin in August with the allied expeditionary forces. During the next months Ignatyev alternately urged the British forces to attack the Chinese and represented himself to the Chinese as a friend who would save them from the wrath of the European invaders. On 16 October he obtained admission to the walled city of Peking, now under allied siege, and persuaded the Chinese to surrender, on his assurance that the city would not be sacked. This assurance was respected, and the Chinese were grateful to Ignatyev. Negotiations about the Russo-Chinese frontier continued in a more friendly spirit, and on 14 November the Chinese government ratified the Treaty of Peking, by which Russia received substantially all the territory she had claimed between the Ussuri and the Pacific. The building of Vladivostok could now go ahead, and Russia's position as a Great Power in the Northern Pacific was assured.

The problem of Sakhalin had still to be settled with Japan. For fifteen years the island remained a no-man's-land, with both Russians and Japanese present. A Japanese mission to Europe in 1862, led by Takenouchi, discussed the question in St. Petersburg. The Japanese claimed the 50th parallel as a frontier through the island; the Russian plenipotentiary—Ignatyev, now head of the Asiatic department of the Ministry of Foreign Affairs—insisted that the whole island must be Russian. No agreement was reached. Another Japanese mission to Russia in 1867 was no more successful, nor did Japanese attempts to use United States mediation in 1870 bring any results. On the Japanese side, the governor of the northern territories was pressing the Tokyo government to conclude an agreement in order to ensure the security of Hokkaido. Agreement was reached at last after the arrival of a new Japanese minister, Enomoto Takeaki, in August 1874. By the Treaty of St. Petersburg, signed on 7 May 1875, Japan recognized the whole of Sakhalin as Russian, while Russia agreed to Japanese rule over the whole chain of the Kurile Islands. This was essentially a strategic compromise: each Power retained possessions from which it could threaten the other if it wished. Apart from this, Japanese were to be free to trade in the ports of the Sea of Okhotsk and in two ports in Kamchatka and to fish in these waters. Japanese vessels and Japanese merchants in Russia were to receive most-favoured-nation treatment. The result of the treaty was essentially to consolidate the good relations between Russia and Japan which had grown up in the preceding decade and a half: they were to remain good for the next twenty years.[1]

In Central Asia Russian expansion was resumed soon after the Crimean War. It was here that N. P. Ignatyev had had the first big success in his career. As military attaché in London after the Crimean War, he had been impressed by the reports of the Indian Mutiny of 1857, and urged a forward policy in Central Asia, where he believed that hostility to Britain could be exploited by Russia. In 1858 he was placed in command of a mission to Khiva and Bukhara. The Khivans refused to allow Russian ships up the Amu Darya river from the Aral Sea, and though the khan received Ignatyev politely he did not grant any of the Russian demands. At the end of September Ignatyev reached Bukhara, and in October its khan agreed to Ignatyev's proposals for the development of trade and the release of imprisoned Russian subjects. The mission had not achieved much, but it was a useful reconnaissance.

In the 1860's the Russian textile industry was becoming more interested in Turkestan as a source of supply of raw cotton. The difficulties caused to Russian imports by the American Civil War increased this interest. The local factors making for a forward policy—border clashes and raids, and suspicion of British designs—remained effective. The political victory of Russia in the Polish crisis of 1863 encouraged a bolder attitude in St. Petersburg. Ignatyev at the Asiatic department of the Foreign Ministry urged an active policy, and he enjoyed the support of D. A. Milyutin at the War Ministry. In the summer of 1864 the advance began, with small forces and limited objectives, but with unexpectedly good results. In June Colonel M. G. Chernyayev set out from Vernoye and took Aulie Ata with very small losses, while Colonel Verevkin starting from Perovsk took the city of Turkestan. The two forces united, and in September captured Chimkent, but failed to take Tashkent. A counter-attack by the forces of the khan of Kokand on the city of Turkestan was repelled in December.

[1] The text of the 1875 treaty is in Lensen, op. cit., pp. 501–4.

In defence of these operations, Gorchakov issued a circular note to the Powers on 21 November 1864. He argued that as a civilizing Power comes into contact with one barbarous tribe and is forced to subdue it in the interests of order, it is brought into conflict with the tribe dwelling beyond it, and so the boundary of civilization is inevitably extended. This had happened with the expansion of the North American settlers westwards, and with the British empire in India, and it was now inevitably happening with Russia in Central Asia. Russia had no aggressive designs, but had the duty to uphold order and civilization. This was an argument which the British could hardly have rejected on principle. It agreed with the general attitude of the European upper classes of the time, and no objection was made at this moment to Russian action.

In 1865 the expansion was renewed. A Bukharan force invaded Kokand territory, and Chernyayev defeated the Kokand forces at Fort Niaz-Bek at the end of April. Some days later he won a second victory before the walls of Tashkent. The Russian government sent him instructions not to attack Tashkent itself, but before these arrived he had stormed the city, which fell on 17 June. In 1866 Chernyayev fought an unsuccessful campaign in Bukharan territory, and was relieved of his command. His successor captured Khodjent. This caused the khan of Kokand to accept Russian peace terms, which included loss of territory, an indemnity, and permission for Russian merchants to trade in his territories. In the late summer of 1866 the governor-general of Orenburg, General N. A. Kryzhanovsky, occupied some Bukharan territory.

In 1867 an important decision was made. A governor-generalship of Turkestan was set up, as part of the Russian empire. Its capital was Tashkent, which thereafter became the centre of Russian power in Central Asia. The first governor-general was General K. P. Kaufman, an administrator of the greatest ability, who for nearly two decades exercised vice-regal authority in this enormous territory. Among his achievements was a land reform, based on the experience of the reform introduced in Poland after 1863.[1]

Kaufman's first task was to round off the conquest of Central

[1] Kaufman served in the military administration of Poland before coming to Turkestan.

Asia. In April 1868 he invaded Bukharan territory, and on 2 May captured Samarkand. The Russian garrison was, however, soon in danger from a Bukharan counter-attack. On 2 June Kaufman defeated the main Bukharan army on the Zerbulak heights near Katta-Kurgan, and a few days later relieved Samarkand. On 18 June the khan of Bukhara made his peace with Russia, accepting loss of territory, an indemnity, and rights for Russian trade. The khan of Khiva, however, still rejected all Russian proposals. The Russian government decided to authorize Kaufman to undertake an expedition against Khiva in 1873. First Gorchakov dispatched Count Peter Shuvalov to London with the assurance that the aim of the expedition was simply to teach the khan a much-needed lesson, that there would be no annexations and no long occupation of Khivan territory. Kaufman planned the operation carefully, and this time Russian supplies were well organized for desert conditions. Four columns set out from Tashkent, Orenburg, Mangyshlak, and Krasnovodsk on the eastern shore of the Caspian. They met at the end of May before Khiva, and on 10 June the city surrendered. A treaty was signed on 12 August. All territory north of the Amu Darya, and the delta of the river, were surrendered to Russia, and the khan accepted an indemnity of 2,200,000 roubles, besides guaranteeing freedom of trade to Russian subjects. Most important of all, the khan agreed to conduct his relations with the outside world solely through St. Petersburg. Khiva had thus become a Russian protectorate. By a treaty of 16 September 1873 the khan of Bukhara also agreed to protectorate status, but did not have to cede any more territory or pay another indemnity. In 1875 a rebellion broke out in the remaining khanate, Kokand, and spread to Russian territory. Kaufman pursued the rebels into Kokand territory. In January 1876 his subordinate, General M. D. Skobelev, captured Andizhan. The whole of Kokand was now under Russian occupation, and the Russian government decided simply to annex it. The decision was announced on 19 February 1876.

There remained an undefined region, inhabited by Turcomans, between the Aral Sea, the Caspian Sea, and the Persian province of Khorasan. The first major Russian move in this direction was the establishment in 1869 of a Russian post on the eastern Caspian coast at Krasnovodsk, where for a time there had been a Russian fortress in the eighteenth century. In 1873 a column moved east from Krasnovodsk as part of the expedition against Khiva. It was not until 1878 that a serious attempt was made to pacify the Turcomans. The operations of that year were inconclusive. In September 1879 the Turcomans of Gök-Tepe inflicted a defeat on the Russian forces commanded by General N. P. Lomakin at Dengil-Tepe. In 1880 General Skobelev was brought from Turkestan and placed in command of operations against the Turcomans. In January 1881 he captured the fortress and ordered a massacre of the male population within the fortress and in flight. On 6 May a new Transcaspian province of the Russian empire was instituted. It was not under Tashkent but under the governor-general of the Caucasus.

Russia made one more conquest in Central Asia in these years which was not retained. In 1867 a former Kokandian general named Yakub Beg raised a rebellion in Chinese Turkestan. Another rebellion had been in progress since 1864 in Dzhungaria, Chinese territory close to the Russian border. Yakub Beg was on good terms with the British, and Kaufman feared that if he spread his power into Dzhungaria this might bring British influence dangerously close to Russian territory. He therefore ordered the governor of Semirechie province, General A. I. Kolpakovsky, to march into the Chinese province of Ili, which was occupied by Russian forces for the next years. In 1877, however, Yakub Beg was killed in battle with Chinese troops, and his régime collapsed. As Chinese authority was now effectively restored, Russia had no further excuse for retaining Ili. In 1883 it was restored to China.

Russia abandoned one piece of territory in the Far East which at that time appeared to possess small importance. Alaska was not bringing in any significant revenue. The massacre of the sea-otters of the north-eastern Pacific had reduced the fur trade to an enterprise of little value. In 1857 the Russian ambassador in Washington was instructed to discuss its sale. In 1862 the Russian-American Company's third charter expired, and was not renewed. The American Civil War postponed the issue. The Russian government was markedly friendly to the North. When the war was over, negotiations were renewed. Secretary of State William Seward wished to acquire Alaska, for strategic rather than economic reasons, and the Russian government, which since the dissolution of the company had been directly responsible for Alaska, was keen to rid itself of a burden. The only difficulty concerned the purchase price. The two governments eventually agreed on $7,000,000 plus acceptance of the outstanding debts of the former company. A treaty was signed on 30 March 1867, and the transfer of authority in Sitka took place on 18 October. There was strong opposition to the price in Congress, and the Russian government had to spend some money on influencing newspapers and congressmen before the treaty was ratified. Almost a century later, it appeared that the United States got a pretty good bargain.

Pan-Slavism and the Balkans, 1875–1878

The restoration of Russian naval power in the Black Sea in 1870 had been achieved by conventional diplomatic methods. Its motives were also conventional—considerations of national prestige and strategic security, made the more urgent by the growing importance of Russian exports of grain through the Straits. But though they had played no part in the success of 1870, the ideological and sentimental aspects of the Straits and Balkan problems remained important for a large section of Russian public opinion. Constantinople remained, for pious members of the Orthodox Church, the holy city of their faith, and the belief in a common destiny of the Slav peoples, led by Russia, was still widespread.

Pogodin's *Moskvityanin* ceased to appear after 1856, for lack of public support. It had an influential successor in *Russkaya beseda* ('Russian Conversation') which lasted until the end of 1859. It was founded by Khomyakov and Koshelyov, and edited in 1858 and 1859 by Ivan Aksakov. From 1861 to 1865 Ivan Aksakov published a new periodical, *Den'* ('The Day'). Both of these maintained a high intellectual level, but they attracted only a small following. Various other attempts at periodicals specializing in Slav problems were even less successful. These problems did, however, receive attention in Katkov's publications, *Russkii vestnik* ('The Russian Messenger') and *Moskovskie vedomosti* ('The Moscow Gazette').[1]

[1] *Moskvityanin* had a circulation of only a few hundreds. *Den'* had some 3,000 subscribers in 1861 and 2,500 for the next three years. For details on other journalistic ventures concerned with Slav affairs in these years, see Michael B. Petrovich, *The Emergence of Russian Panslavism 1856–1870* (New York, 1956), pp. 107–22.

In January 1858 was founded, with official approval, the Moscow Slavonic Benevolent Committee. Its purpose was to support cultural and religious activities of the Slavs under Ottoman rule and to educate students from Slav lands in Moscow. It received funds both from private benefactors and from the Ministry of Education, in addition to its small revenue from members' subscriptions. It was in fact a hybrid organization, in which ideological enthusiasts and officials, Slavophils, and Russian nationalists were uneasily associated. Among its founders were the veterans Khomyakov, Samarin, Koshelyov, and Konstantin Aksakov. Ivan Aksakov became an active member in 1861. Pogodin was the committee's first president, and Katkov was a prominent member.

Slavophil idealism of the old school was a diminishing factor. Its last important expression was the *Epistle to the Serbs*, written in 1860 by Khomyakov and signed by eleven persons including Samarin, both Aksakovs, Koshelyov, and Pogodin. Intended as good advice to the small Serbian nation, which had achieved a precarious independence, it was largely concerned with the spiritual dangers into which they could be led by imitation of the sinful West. Denouncing intellectual and spiritual pride, advocating humility, and deploring the Westernizing policies of past Russian governments, it made an overall impression of Russian national arrogance. The tone was that of a petulant elderly schoolmaster, out of touch with the real world. It made few converts among the Serbs or other Slavs.[1]

In 1867 an Ethnographic Exhibition was held in Moscow, and a Slav section was organized within it, to which a number of distinguished scholars and public figures from the western and southern Slav lands were invited. No Poles came, but there were Czechs, Slovaks, Ukrainians, Slovenes, Serbs, Croats, and a Bulgar.[2] A number of receptions and banquets were held for them, and public speeches were made. These were not entirely satisfactory to the Russian organizers, as the leading Czech statesmen Palacký and Rieger pleaded for a reconciliation between the Russians and the Poles, making it clear that conces-

[1] The *Epistle* is in vol. i of Khomyakov's collected works. It is also in a selection of his work, *Izbrannye sochineniya*, published in New York in 1955.

[2] There were also representatives of two small Slav groups from Germany, the Kashubs of Prussia and the Lusatians of Saxony.

sions must come from the Russian as well as from the Polish side. For their part, the Slav guests were not pleased by the emphasis placed by some Russian speakers on the primacy of the Orthodox Church and the Russian language.

The exhibition stimulated further activity in Russia. In 1868 a St. Petersburg section of the Moscow Slavonic Benevolent Committee was founded.[1] Its members included a considerable number of army officers and central government officials. Among the latter was Count N. P. Ignatyev. The Asiatic department of the Ministry of Foreign Affairs, of which he became director on his return from Peking, dealt with the Ottoman empire as well as with lands further to the east. In 1864 he became Russian ambassador in Constantinople. Ignatyev was both an outstanding diplomat and a genuine enthusiast for the Slav cause. Two other Slavonic Benevolent Committees were founded, in Kiev in December 1869 and in Odessa in April 1870. The practical achievements of the four committees were modest. A rather small number of Slav students, chiefly Bulgarians, were educated in Russia, who nevertheless formed a significant fraction of the politically conscious Bulgarian intelligentsia, which played a leading role both in the liberation of their country and, later, in the government of the young Bulgarian state. Though the funds which paid for the education of these young people came from persons or institutions devoted to the principles of autocracy, the ideas which they acquired in their studies in Russia were those of the radicals and revolutionaries. Chernyshevsky rather than Pogodin was their inspiration. The committees also sent small sums of money to schools and churches in the Slav provinces of Turkey, in independent Serbia and Montenegro, and to a much smaller extent in the Slav lands of the Habsburg monarchy.[2] Probably the most important function of the committees was to provide a nucleus for Russians interested in the Slav world.

Slavophil ideas gave place to Pan-Slavism, and this in turn became ever less distinguishable from Russian nationalism and from the expansionist aims of the Russian state. Some of the original Slavophils were dead, others were involved in the peasant reforms in Russia or Poland, others had retired

[1] In 1877 it became a separate society, independent of the Moscow committee.
[2] For details see Petrovich, op. cit., pp. 146–9.

disillusioned into private life. The main reform urged by the Slavophils, emancipation of the serfs, had been accomplished. The other main object of the more liberal Slavophils, the introduction of central representative institutions, had, as we have seen, been rejected, with dire results. As a party of reform, the Slavophils had ceased to exist. But part of their ideas was taken over by a new generation, whose main concern was with the relations between Russia and the Slav lands, and the opportunities for Russian expansion which these provided.

Pan-Slavism was essentially a creation of the intelligentsias of the small Slav peoples in the first half of the nineteenth century. Russia was a great empire, which could stand on its own feet, but the small peoples needed the feeling that they belonged to a great and powerful family of nations, in order to sustain them in the struggle against more powerful opponents. From the point of view of the small nations, Pan-Slavism was a programme based on the brotherhood of equal Slav nations, including Catholics and Protestants as well as Orthodox. The Russian Pan-Slavs saw things differently. They believed that the smaller Slav peoples should accept the Russians as leaders, and doubted the loyalty of those who were not Orthodox. Of the Catholic Slavs, the Poles were regarded as enemies, and the Czechs were distrusted as being too Germanized and Westernized, even if it was admitted that individual Czech scholars or statesmen were good Slavs.

There is a certain parallel between the Russian version of Pan-Slavism and the Little German idea in mid-nineteenth century Germany. The Little Germans stressed the Hohenzollern dynasty, the Prussian state, and the Protestant religion: the Russian Pan-Slavs the Romanov dynasty, the Russian state, and the Orthodox religion. The parallel is especially striking in Bohemia. Here there was in the last decades of the century a movement among a part of the German minority to break away from the Catholic Church (*los von Rom*) and become Protestant, in order to be acceptable to Bismarck, who was then engaged in his *Kulturkampf* against the Catholic Church, and so be allowed to secede from Austria and join the German empire. At the same time the Czechs were being urged by the Russian Pan-Slavs to abandon the Catholic Church for Orthodoxy, in order to be acceptable to the Tsar and people of Russia as true

Slavs. A few Czechs responded to these appeals. Neither movement in fact achieved much, but they are symptomatic of the internal contradictions of Pan-Germanism and Pan-Slavism.

Russian Pan-Slavism, as an ideology of extreme nationalism, found its prophets in N. Y. Danilevsky, whose work *Russia and Europe* was first published in 1869, and General R. A. Fadeyev, whose *Opinion on the Eastern Question* appeared in 1870. Fadeyev believed that Russia and the Slav nations were indissolubly linked by common interests and sentiments, that Europe was basically hostile to them, and that the Slav cause could be promoted in the last resort only by military force. Russia, he argued, must either advance to the Adriatic or retire behind the Dnieper: the alternative was 'Slavdom or Asia'. Danilevsky, by training a natural scientist, propounded an ambitious theory of 'cultural-historical types' which had succeeded each other in the course of human history. The age in which the Slav cultural-historical type would prevail, definitely replacing the Germanic and Roman types, was about to begin.[1]

Pan-Slavism and Russian nationalism were the ideologies of unofficial though influential groups. The foreign policy of the Russian empire was more conventional and more cautious. Gorchakov had little sympathy for these enthusiams. Nevertheless, he was quite willing to exploit them, and their champions, if these could be useful for achieving Russian aims in the Straits. As ambassador in Constantinople from 1864 onwards, Ignatyev did his best to promote Bulgarian nationalism and opposition to the Ottoman régime.

In April 1875 a visit by Emperor Franz Joseph to Dalmatia, and a meeting between him and Prince Nicholas of Montenegro, raised hopes of Austrian assistance among the Serbian population of neighbouring Hercegovina, whose treatment at the hands of the ruling Moslem minority had recently deteriorated. In June 1875 an armed revolt broke out. It was followed in August by a revolt in Bosnia, in which a secret organization, the United Serbian Youth (*Omladina*) played a leading part. The society had previously received help from the government of independent Serbia, and public opinion in Serbia strongly sympathized with the Bosnian Serbs. Prince Milan of Serbia resisted pressure to go to war with Turkey, and the governments

[1] See also below p. 487.

of the Great Powers tried to find a formula acceptable to the Sultan and the rebels.

The first proposal by the Powers, the Andrássy Note of December 1875, was accepted by the Sultan but rejected by the rebels. In May 1876 the foreign ministers of Austria, Russia, and Germany agreed on a different plan for internal reforms in the disaffected provinces. Their proposals were much more favourable to the rebels than the Andrássy Note. The British government refused to be associated with their plan, which became known as the Berlin Memorandum, and the Sultan rejected it. Public agitation for war in Serbia increased. Prince Milan received contradictory advice from Russian representatives. The Foreign Ministry in St. Petersburg advised against war, but the Russian consul in Belgrade, a keen Pan-Slav, allowed Milan to think that the real wish of Russia was war. Meanwhile the Pan-Slavs in Russia organized a campaign of propaganda in favour of the rebels and in favour of Serbia. Russian volunteers arrived in Belgrade eager to fight the Turks. Milan yielded to public opinion, and on 30 June 1876 Serbia declared war on Turkey.

Already in April 1876 an armed rising had broken out in the Sredna Gora mountains in central Bulgaria. At the end of May a band of Bulgarian revolutionaries crossed the Danube from Roumania. They were quickly dispersed and killed by the Turks, and by the end of June the Bulgarian rising was suppressed and the Bulgarian people subjected to bloodthirsty reprisals by the Turks. Yet the Bulgarians, though defeated, had given proof of their existence as a nation and of their desire for independence. This was noted in Europe, including both Russia and Britain.

In the summer of 1876 the Pan-Slav campaign in Russia was in full swing. On 13 July the metropolitan of Moscow held a special service on behalf of the Serbian and Montenegrin cause. Money was collected all over the country, and volunteers left to join the Serbian army. The Russian government permitted professional officers of the Russian army to enlist as volunteers. The war, however, went badly. The Serbian army was defeated by the Turks; Russian and Serbian officers did not co-operate well, and each blamed the other for the army's failures. Enthusiasm for the Serbian cause waned in Russia. The Pan-

Slavs turned their attention to the Bulgars, who, if only because they had been much more quickly crushed by the Turks than the Serbs, had had no opportunity to show themselves ungrateful to Russia. Bulgaria was also more interesting to the Russian government than Serbia, since it lay closer both to Russia and to the Straits.

The tasks of European diplomacy were to save Serbia from Turkish vengeance by an armistice, and to secure a new status for Bulgaria which would satisfy Russia.[1] On 8 July 1876 Gorchakov and Andrássy, meeting at Reichstadt in Bohemia, agreed that in the event of war between Russia and Turkey and the defeat of the latter, Russia should take southern Bessarabia, which she had surrendered in 1856. They also agreed that Bosnia and Hercegovina should be divided among Austria, Serbia, and Montenegro, and the province (*sandjak*) of Novi Bazar between Serbia and Montenegro. However, the Austrian and Russian texts of the agreement disagreed as to the respective shares of each.[2]

Opposition to Russian aims at this stage came from Disraeli, who believed that a weakening of the Ottoman empire must damage British interests, and feared any expansion of Russian power in the Straits area. On 9 November he made a belligerent speech at the Guildhall. On 11 November Alexander II made a speech to the nobility and civil authorities in Moscow. He praised the Montenegrins, spoke slightingly of the Serbs, and referred to 'our volunteers, many of whom have paid with their blood for the cause of Slavdom'. If Russia's 'just demands' were not fulfilled by the Turks, then 'I firmly intend to act independently'.[3]

[1] For a modern account of the diplomacy of 1876–8, and for bibliographical references, see A. J. P. Taylor, op. cit., ch. xi. The best account of Russian policy is B. H. Sumner, *Russia and the Balkans 1870–1880* (1937). Tatishchev's life of Alexander II gives an official view, and a Soviet interpretation from the Stalin period is V. P. Potyomkin, *Istoriya diplomatii*, ii. 22–50. Anglo-Russian relations are discussed, partly on the basis of Russian diplomatic documents first made available to the author, in R. W. Seton-Watson, *Disraeli, Gladstone and the Eastern Question* (1935). Some Serbian official sources were used by M. Stojanović in his *The Great Powers and the Balkans* (1939). Austro-Russian relations are thoroughly discussed in G. H. Rupp, *A Wavering Friendship: Russia and Austria 1876–78* (1941). The last stages of the crisis are covered in W. N. Medlicott, *The Congress of Berlin and after* (2nd ed. 1963).

[2] Austrian text printed in Sumner, op. cit., pp. 584–5, Russian text ibid., pp. 586–7.

[3] Text of speech in Tatishchev, op. cit. ii. 337–8.

On 23 December 1876 a conference of ambassadors of the six Powers met at Constantinople. They were able to agree on proposals for internal reform in European Turkey and small territorial cessions by Turkey to Serbia and Montenegro. Meanwhile the Sultan had granted a constitution to his subjects and claimed that, as all Ottoman subjects now enjoyed full liberties, no further reforms dictated from abroad were necessary. On 18 January 1877 the Powers' proposals were formally rejected.

On 15 January 1877 Russia and Austria signed a military convention at Budapest, which went further than the Reichstadt agreement. In the event of war and the collapse of Turkey, Russia was to invade Bulgaria, and Austria to take Bosnia. It was also agreed that 'l'établissement d'un grand état compact slave ou autre est exclu'.[1] Russo-Roumanian military conversations also took place in December 1876, and a formal convention was signed on 16 April 1877. These provided that the Russian army should be allowed to pass through Roumania, and committed the Tsar to 'maintain and defend the existing integrity of Roumania'. This last undertaking was in flagrant contradiction with the intention to annex southern Bessarabia, which had been clearly stated in the Reichstadt agreement and accepted by Austria.

Peace was signed between Turkey and Serbia on 28 February 1877, but Russian demands in relation to the Christian provinces of the Ottoman empire had still to be met. On 31 March proposals known as the London Protocol, prepared by Lord Derby, the British foreign secretary, and Count Peter Shuvalov, the Russian ambassador, and approved by the other Powers, were put to the Turkish government. On 9 April it rejected the protocol, and protested against any foreign tutelage over internal reforms in the Ottoman empire. The last attempts of European diplomacy had thus failed, and on 24 April 1877 Russia declared war on Turkey.

The main theatre of war was Bulgaria, while the Caucasus was an important secondary theatre. Considerable Russian forces were reserved for the defence of the Black Sea coast. In the Black Sea the Turkish navy was stronger than the Russian.

[1] Article III of the additional convention to the Budapest agreement, printed in Sumner, op. cit., p. 601.

During May the main Russian armies moved into Roumania. The Roumanian government wished to take part in the war, but the Russian government did not wish it to do so. The official answer given to Prince Carol of Roumania was that if his army took part, it must be placed under Russian supreme command. This demand was, as it had been intended to be, unacceptable to the prince.

The supreme command of the army of the Danube was given to the Tsar's brother, Grand Duke Nicholas, who took as his chief of staff General A. A. Nepokoichitsky.[1] An advance down the Black Sea coast, without command of the sea, was too dangerous. The Russian command therefore decided to make no serious attack on the Dobrudja, the north-eastern corner of European Turkey, defended by the fortresses of Silistria, Ruschuk, Shumla, and Varna. Only a small force crossed into the northern Dobrudja at Galaţi, while larger forces were kept, under the command of the Tsarevich Alexander, in south-east Roumania to prevent a Turkish counter-attack. But the main army was brought to Zimnitsa, to the south-west of Bucarest, and crossed the Danube to Sistovo from 27 June onwards.

The first Russian operations south of the Danube were highly successful. On 16 July Nikopolis surrendered, and on 19 July an advance column under General Y. V. Gurko captured the Shipka Pass in the Balkan mountains, the great range which runs from west to east to divide Bulgaria in two, and took the town of Kazanlik south of the mountains. But the Turks, who had had quite inadequate troops in Bulgaria at the outbreak of war, at last brought up substantial forces. Osman Pasha moved his army east from his seat of command at Vidin, and established himself in mid July at the town of Plevna[2] some forty miles south of the Danube. The army of Suleiman Pasha was

[1] The war minister, D. A. Milyutin, had recommended for this post General N. N. Obruchev, director of the military-scientific committee of the general staff, who had done most of the planning for the campaign, but the Grand Duke refused. According to a modern study, published by the Soviet Ministry of Defence, N. I. Belyaev, *Russko-tyuretskaya voyna 1877–1878 gg.* (Moscow, 1956), pp. 86–87, the reason was that Obruchev was known to have radical political sympathies. He had in fact been a member of the first *Zemlya i volya* in 1862 (Panteleyev, op. cit., p. 291). Obruchev, nevertheless, made a successful career later, and was chief of general staff in the early 1890's.

[2] This is the internationally known, though incorrect, name of the Bulgarian town of Pleven.

brought by sea from distant Montenegro to Enos on the Aegean and thence to Trnovo in central Bulgaria. On 20 July the Russians made their first major assault on Plevna, and were repulsed. A second attack on 30 July was equally unsuccessful. Meanwhile Gurko had been obliged to give up Kazanlik, and to retire to a strong position on the Shipka Pass. Here from 16 to 21 August he was attacked by numerically superior Turkish forces of Suleiman Pasha's army, but the Russians held the Shipka.

On the Caucasus front too the war had begun with Russian successes, followed by serious reverses. Here the commander-in-chief was another brother of the Tsar, Grand Duke Michael. The main army was under General M. T. Loris-Melikov and its effective strength was about 60,000. A much smaller force under General Oklobzhio was kept for action against the port of Batum, and substantial reserves were kept north of the frontier in case of internal rebellion. The Turkish commander in the field, Ahmet Muhtar Pasha, had about 90,000 men available. On 17 May the Russians captured Ardahan, and moved on to besiege Kars. On 12 May, however, the Turks made a landing on the Black Sea coast. They brought with them some Abkhazians who had left their homeland in 1864, and sufficient weapons to arm a local rebellion. On 15 May the Russian commander of Sukhum evacuated the city and retired into the interior. Some Abkhazians rebelled and joined the Turks. Meanwhile another minor rebellion broke out in Chechnia, and later spread to Daghestan. All these activities were on a small scale, but they greatly alarmed the Russian authorities who could spare no more troops for the main front. It was not until the end of August that the Abkhazian rebellion was quelled and the Turks evacuated Sukhum. The Russians had needed 17,000 men to achieve this. The rebellion in Daghestan simmered on until October. In the south, Oklobzhio made no appreciable progress against Batum during the summer. Meanwhile Muhtar Pasha won a victory over Loris-Melikov on the heights of Zivin, south-west of Kars, on 25 June. The Russians were obliged to raise the siege of Kars, and the Turks isolated the Russian garrison of Bayazit, which was relieved with great difficulty on 10 July.

After two defeats before Plevna, the Russian command took a different view of Roumanian help. On 29 August Prince Carol visited the Tsar, who had set up his headquarters beside the army command, and an agreement was made. Prince Carol would take command of the western sector, with two Russian army corps and a Roumanian force of about 30,000. His chief of staff was to be the Russian General Zotov. On 11 September the third attack on Plevna took place, on a far larger scale than the first two. It was a still more disastrous failure. The allied troops fought with great courage, but they were completely unsuccessful. The attack cost 15,000 Russian and 3,000 Roumanian casualties. Among the causes of failure were extremely inadequate reconnaissance of the enemy positions, lack of co-ordination between the units, and confusion in the high command. On 13 September the emperor held a council of war. The Grand Duke Nicholas, depressed by the defeat, wished to retreat north of the Danube. Milyutin strongly opposed this suggestion, and the Tsar upheld him. It was decided to organize a systematic blockade of Plevna, and for this purpose the hero of Sevastopol, General Totleben, was brought from St. Petersburg. General Gurko, with a force of two infantry and one cavalry divisions, was given the task of cutting off all communications from Plevna to the south and south-west. This was achieved by the capture of the Turkish positions of Gorni Dubnyak and Dolni Dubnyak on 24 October and 1 November. Plevna was now completely isolated. It would have been wiser for Osman Pasha to abandon the city, and preserve his army for use in the later stage of the war. He had, however, explicit orders from the Sultan to hold out. This became a hopeless task. On 9 December Osman made a last attempt to break through the Russian lines, but was defeated, and on the following day he surrendered the city. The Russians thereby took prisoner 2,000 officers and 44,000 men.

The next month brought victory to the Russian army in the European theatre. Gurko with about 65,000 infantry and 6,000 cavalry crossed the Balkan range to the south-west and took Sofia on 3 January 1878. Thence he proceeded south-east, and in a battle at Plovdiv from 15 to 17 January decisively defeated Suleiman Pasha's army. On 5 January General Kartsov forced the Troyan Pass, south of Plevna. Further east, General Radetsky had about 50,000 men to destroy the Turkish army entrenched on the southern side of the Shipka Pass. Two columns, commanded respectively by Skobelev and Svyatopolk-Mirsky, crossed the mountains to west and east of the Turkish position and attacked from the south, while Radetsky himself faced the Turks from the north. After three days' fighting, from 7 to 9 January, the Turkish commander Vessel Pasha surrendered with 765 officers and about 22,000 men.

After the battles of Plovdiv and Shipka Turkish resistance in Europe came to an end. The Russians entered Adrianople without resistance on 20 January. On 31 January an armistice was signed.

Meanwhile the Russian army in the Caucasus had done well. The main fighting was in the mountains to the east of Kars. On 25 August Muhtar Pasha won a success at Kizil Tepe. From 2 to 4 October a fierce battle was fought on the Little Yahni and Great Yahni positions. The Russians made some gains but were not able to hold them. After this battle it was decided to send a column under General Lazarev to outflank the Turks on the east and to attack them from the rear while the main army under General Heyman attacked from the north. These operations, which lasted from 12 to 15 October, and are known as the Battle of Aladja Dag, were highly successful. On 15 October Hadji Reshit Pasha surrendered with 12,000 men, and Turkish casualties amounted to 6,000. On 4 November Heyman won a further battle on the Deve Boyun ('camel's neck') plateau east of Erzurum, but failed to capture Erzurum itself in an attack on 8 and 9 November. Shortly afterwards, however, General Lazarev captured Kars. In extremely heavy fighting on 17 November the Russians stormed the forts on the eastern side and entered the town itself. The southern and western forts held out, but on 18 November the Turkish commander decided to evacuate the whole area. Retreating Turkish troops were pursued by Cossacks, and almost all were captured or killed. The Turkish losses were estimated at 2,500 dead, 4,000 wounded and sick, and 17,000 prisoners. Russian casualties amounted to 2,000, of whom a high proportion were officers. All attempts to take Batum had been defeated. It was only after the signature of the armistice at Adrianople that the Turks handed over Batum and Erzurum to the Russians.

Though the British government, as a party to the London Protocol whose rejection by the Turks had brought about the war, could not object to Russia's action in declaring war, it watched with alarm the progress of the Russian armies. Osman Pasha's defence of Plevna caused a revival of pro-Turkish feeling, which the Bulgarian atrocities of 1876 had previously diminished. The British fleet was ordered to Besika Bay already on 30 June 1877. In January 1878, when it looked as if the Russians might enter Constantinople, alarm grew in London. The armistice relieved them, but reports that the Russians were not observing the terms caused an order to be sent to the fleet to enter the Sea of Marmara, and this was done on 13 February. On 3 March a Russo-Turkish peace treaty was signed at San Stefano. Largely the work of Ignatyev, it created a large Bulgarian state, which was to include all Macedonia except Salonica and to have access to the Aegean in western Thrace. This was clearly contrary to the clause in the Budapest Convention of January 1877 precluding a 'large compact state' in the Balkans. Moreover, the treaty left Bosnia and Hercegovina in the Ottoman empire, subject to the institution of reforms, and made no reference to Austrian claims in this area.

Both Britain and Austria objected to the San Stefano Treaty, though they were unable effectively to co-ordinate their policies.[1] Russia was obliged to accept the demand of all the other Powers that there should be an international conference. Bismarck agreed that this should be held in Berlin, and the date of its opening was fixed for 13 June. Meanwhile the Russian government tried to reach agreement with the interested Powers. Ignatyev visited Vienna without result. Shuvalov in London was more successful. Russia agreed to give up the large Bulgarian state: Macedonia was to be left under Turkish rule, and the rest of the country was to be divided along the line of the Balkan range, the northern part being an autonomous principality of Bulgaria, the southern part a Turkish province, with a measure of self-government and a Christian governor, to be named Eastern Roumelia. In return for this Britain agreed to Russian annexations in the Caucasus. These points were embodied in an Anglo-Russian agreement signed in London on 30 May. Disraeli also made an agreement with the Turks on

[1] This is well discussed by Taylor, op. cit., pp. 247–50.

4 June. Britain was to guarantee the Asiatic territories of Turkey against any attack, but Turkey was to allow the British to administer Cyprus under Turkish sovereignty. Hence began the British rule in Cyprus, whose value as a base for Britain or her various allies has always been small. An Anglo-Austrian agreement of 6 June assured British support for the Austrian claim to Bosnia and Hercegovina.

By the Treaty of Berlin Russia obtained her own minimum territorial aims. She recovered the mouth of the Danube by taking southern Bessarabia from her loyal ally Roumania, which received compensation in northern Dobrudja. In the Caucasus she annexed Kars and Batum. As the Black Sea terminus of a railway across the Caucasus isthmus from Baku, Batum acquired enormous importance when the oil industry of Baku was developed in the following decades. The creation of even a small Bulgaria was, from the Russian point of view, an apparent gain. However, the predominant feeling in Russia was anger. The settlement was compared not with the situation before the war, but with the terms of the San Stefano Treaty, and with the great sacrifices made by Russia in lives and in wealth. It was felt that Russia had been cheated of her due, and the blame for this was put not so much on Britain and Austria, whose hostility had been expected, as on Germany. Bismarck had talked of being the 'honest broker', and he had been considered a friend of Russia. Yet at a conference in his capital, at which he had presided, Russia had been cheated. Frustrated Russian nationalists and Pan-Slavs loudly expressed their indignation.

Bismarck, however, had done his best to apply to the situation the diplomatic conventional wisdom of the age. He had tried to divide the Balkans into a western and an eastern sphere. The former, consisting of Bosnia, Hercegovina, and Novi Bazar (placed under Austrian administration, but with the nominal preservation of Ottoman sovereignty), and Serbia (inevitably reduced to a condition of vassalage), formed the share of the Habsburg monarchy: the latter, consisting of Bulgaria, and possibly also Roumania, was assigned to Russia. The Serbs of course were bitterly indignant, and the Serbian population of Bosnia even offered armed resistance to Austrian troops. But nobody bothered much about them: they were a small nation, and their military failures in 1876 had lost them such European sympathy as they had had.

Russian hostility, expressed in the press in 1878, was one factor which induced Bismarck to make the Austro-German Alliance of October 1879: the other was his desire to keep Austria from association with France, or the restoration of the 'Crimean combination'. In 1882 Italy was brought in, and the Triple Alliance was formed. But Bismarck did not wish to tie himself to Austria, or to make Russia an enemy. During 1880 the Russian ambassador in Berlin, Saburov, discussed with Bismarck the restoration of the Three Emperors' League, and negotiations went on between Berlin and Vienna. In March 1881 the Austrian government consented, but the assassination of Alexander II caused the agreement to be further delayed. Signed at last on 18 June 1881, it provided for neutrality in case one of the signatories were involved in war with a fourth Power, with a reservation that if the fourth Power were Turkey the commitment would apply only if there had been a further agreement between the signatories before war began. The treaty asserted the principle of closure of the Straits, and bound the signatories to see to it that the Turkish government should enforce it. Austria agreed not to oppose an eventual union of Bulgaria and Eastern Roumelia. Russia recognized the right of Austria to annex Bosnia and Hercegovina if she should wish to do so later.

Twenty-five years after the defeat in the Crimea, Russia had clearly resumed her place as one of the Great Powers, but she was no longer the first Power on the European mainland. It seemed as if the old co-operation of the three eastern monarchies had been restored, but this was an illusion. On the one hand Russia was not prepared to accept Germany as a senior partner, on the other hand the conflict of interests between Russia and Austria was becoming steadily more unmanageable. The growth of small nationalisms in the Balkans and within the Habsburg monarchy, and of Great Power chauvinism among the Russian and German-speaking nations, sharpened the conflict.

PART V

THE AGE OF COUNTER-REFORM

XIII

GOVERNMENT

Men and Measures

ALEXANDER III was born in 1845, the second son of his father. It was not until 1865 that he became heir to the throne on the death of his elder brother Nicholas. In 1866 he married Princess Dagmar of Denmark, who had been intended for his brother, and who assumed on conversion to Orthodoxy the name of Maria Fyodorovna. During the last fifteen years of his father's reign, he took on a number of military and civil duties, including the command of the Ruschuk detachment in the war with Turkey in 1877. He was a direct, honest, and unimaginative man who usually treated well the ministers whom he had himself chosen, backed them up when they needed it, and was liked and respected by those around him. He did his best to manage the increasingly complex business of government, of which, in the absence of a united ministry or any equivalent to the office of prime minister, the emperor was the only co-ordinator. His best was not good enough, but this did not become clear until after his death, for his reign of thirteen years was marked by peace and outward stability.

Alexander was more sympathetic than any of his predecessors to Russian nationalism and to Pan-Slavism. He reacted against the German orientation of his father and grandfather. The disappointments of the Congress of Berlin reinforced his dislike of the German Powers. Among his advisers was Katkov who may be regarded as one of those who prepared the ground for the Franco-Russian Alliance, though he himself died in 1887 before it was effected. Wishing to strengthen Russia as a Great Power, Alexander III favoured industrial development, in this respect showing himself a man of the modern age. He was strongly opposed to representative or parliamentary institutions, but he liked to think of himself as closely bound to the simple Russian peasant masses who, he believed, had no more use for European legalistic inventions than he had. There was thus an element of populism in his conservatism. There is some truth in the tendentious comparison made between him and Alexander I in a speech in his memory, made at a meeting of the Imperial Russian Historical Society on 6 April 1895.[1] Alexander I, the speaker argued, for all his great merits, did not know the Russians: he dismissed them as 'base people' (*podlye lyudi*), and his own ideal was outside Russia. Alexander III, however, was a true Russian. He knew his people. He would not sacrifice the truly Russian principle of autocracy, or subordinate the interests of Russia to those of Poland or of any other people of the borderlands.

These words were spoken by the man who had the greatest political influence on the emperor, and who inspired him with his mixture of populism, nationalism, and religious piety, Konstantin Petrovich Pobedonostsev. A man of erudition and great intelligence, Pobedonostsev began his career as a professor of law. He gave tuition in legal matters to both Alexander and his elder brother. He was a member of the commission which prepared the judicial reform of 1863. In 1866 he was appointed procurator of the Holy Synod in succession to Dmitri Tolstoy. From this time his views set in a rigid mould. He upheld at every point the claims of the Orthodox Church against other denominations, and his published correspondence shows his contempt for other branches of Christianity and for persons belonging to other religions. He was especially zealous in repression of sects of Orthodoxy. His Russian patriotism admitted of no trace of generosity towards other nations within the empire. He was fanatically devoted to autocracy and regarded parliamentary government as 'the great lie of our time'. He felt himself to be the mouthpiece of true Russians and seems genuinely to have believed that the policies he recommended to

[1] Text in *RA* (1906), no. 1, pp. 618–24.

the Tsar were popular with all but a handful of misguided persons who had nothing in common with the Russian people.[1] Though he had helped to enact the judicial reform in the 1860's, twenty years later he showed in his writings a complete contempt for due process of law, and indeed an apparent inability to understand the nature of law. In a memorandum to the Tsar, written in 1885, he rejected the irremovability of judges, publicity of court proceedings, and the very principle of the separation of the executive and judicial functions, called for severe control by the courts over barristers, and urged the abolition of the jury. Of the latter he wrote: 'It is essential to get rid of this institution, in order to restore the significance of the court in Russia.'[2] Pobedonostsev was more than an ideological mentor of the Tsar, for he interfered constantly in government business, including matters far removed from the the competence of the Holy Synod, and frequently recommended or denounced persons considered for official appointments.

The first year of the new reign was a period of transition. The Tsar had to make up his mind about the projects for reform proposed by Loris-Melikov, which had had the approval of Alexander II. A conference of ministers was held on 8 March 1881 in the presence of the Tsar and three grand-dukes. D. A. Milyutin and Abaza strongly supported the proposals. Milyutin argued that they would 'complete the great reforms of the late emperor which remained unfinished'.[3] As opinions were divided, the Tsar referred the proposals to detailed study. On 21 April there was another full meeting, at which a similar division of opinion appeared. At this meeting there was also talk of a unified Council of Ministers to improve the direction of policy. The reforming ministers believed that the Tsar was on their side. But Pobedonostsev was more than a match for them. In a letter to the Tsar on 23 April he reported that they planned a state of affairs in which 'the government will be concentrated in the Council of Ministers, which will decide questions by

[1] Pobedonostsev's own formal expression of his general views is his *Moskovskii sbornik*, Moscow, 1901. An English translation, entitled *Reflections of a Russian Statesman*, was published in London in 1898.

[2] *K. P. Pobedonostsev i ego korrespondenty* (Moscow, 1923), ii. 508–14. The memorandum is undated but appears to date from Oct. 1885.

[3] *Dnevnik D. A. Milyutina*, iv. 32–37.

majority vote and will report the majority decision to Your Majesty'.[1] Three days later he sent the Tsar the draft of a proclamation, intended as a suitable statement of the principles which would guide him in his reign. This contained the words: 'The voice of God orders us to stand boldly by the task of governing, relying on Divine Providence, with faith in the strength and truth of autocratic power, which we have been called to confirm and protect for the good of the people, against all encroachments.'[2] Without informing his ministers, the Tsar ordered this proclamation to be printed. On 28 April there was another full meeting, at which the Tsar was replaced by his brother Grand Duke Vladimir. When the meeting broke up, after serious discussion of the proposed reforms, at one o'clock in the morning, the minister of justice produced the text of the proclamation, which was being distributed during the night. This resounding proof of lack of the Tsar's confidence left Loris-Melikov no alternative but to resign. Milyutin followed him two weeks later.[3]

As a successor to Loris-Melikov, Pobedonostsev recommended to the Tsar Count N. P. Ignatyev, who had rendered such outstanding services in Central Asia, the Far East, and Constantinople. 'He still has healthy instincts and a Russian soul, and his name has a good repute among the healthy part of the Russian population—that is, the simple people'.[4] Alexander accepted the advice. Ignatyev was a strong nationalist and conservative, but he was not averse to reform. A law of 28 December 1881 put an end to the state of 'temporary obligation' in the thirty-seven 'internal provinces' of European Russia, in which about 15 per cent. of the former serfs were still in this condition.[5] Purchase of the allotment land was now made compulsory. At the same time the amount of the redemption payments was reduced. These measures had, it is true, been prepared under Loris-Melikov, but Ignatyev carried them through. He was also responsible for setting up a committee, under the deputy minister of the interior, Senator M. S. Kakhanov, to consider the reform of the administration at the *volost* and village levels. On

[1] K. P. Pobedonostsev, *Pis'ma k Aleksandru III* (Moscow, 1925–6), i. 330.
[2] *K. P. Pobedonostsev i ego korrespondenty*, i. 52.
[3] *Dnevnik D. A. Milyutina*, iv. 62, 70.
[4] K. P. Pobedonostsev, *Pis'ma k Aleksandru III*, i. 317.
[5] P. A. Zayonchkovsky, *Otmena krepostnogo prava*, p. 200.

the other hand he was the author of a law of 14 August 1881 providing for emergency powers in any part of the empire where public order was in danger. This distinguished between 'strengthened powers of defence' (*usilennaya okhrana*) and 'exceptional powers of defence' (*chrezvychaynaya okhrana*). The first could be introduced by a governor-general or by the minister of the interior and gave far-reaching powers to interfere with civil liberties. The second, which was supposed to be used only when violations of public order had created 'a condition of alarm' among the population, required the authorization of the Committee of Ministers and the approval of the Tsar himself. It provided for the appointment of a 'commander-in-chief' in the affected area. This officer would then have power to set up military police commands, to transfer whole categories of offences to military tribunals, to confiscate property, to arrest, imprison, or fine persons for actions which he might declare exempt from the jurisdiction of the courts. He could remove appointed or elected officials from their posts, suppress publications, and close institutions of teaching.[1] This law was often used in the following thirty years with varying degrees of justification in different parts of the country.

During Ignatyev's period of office there appeared a curious organization known as the 'Holy Host' (*Svyashchonnaya druzhina*).[2] Conceived by several leading aristocrats, it was intended to protect members of the Imperial family, to track down the terrorists, and to organize counter-revolutionary propaganda such as would undermine and divide the revolutionaries. In pursuit of the last aim its leaders showed some ingenuity. They controlled two exiled newspapers in which they put forward fake revolutionary ideas in order to confuse real revolutionaries. It is questionable whether they had much influence on anyone, and they dissolved themselves in November 1882.[3] Rumours about the existence of this organization were widespread, though its members were supposed to preserve strict secrecy. The name became a byword for extreme reaction among liberal Russians.

[1] See article 'Okhrana' by M. L. Trivus in *Brockhaus Encyclopaedia*, xxii. 508–9.

[2] These words are hard to translate. For this version I am indebted to Professor M. T. Florinsky's *History*. It seems to me that he has found just the ideal combination of solemnity and irony to convey the original.

[3] See *Krasny Arkhiv*, no. 21 (1927), pp. 200–17.

It may have been involved in the pogroms of Jews which occurred in 1882. The Holy Host is said to have had about 700 members. Its importance should not be exaggerated. It is, however, interesting for its combination of extreme reactionary outlook with quasi-revolutionary demagogy, anti-semitism, and conspiratorial romanticism, a combination which was to appear again later.

Ignatyev was brought to his fall by romantic Slavophil dreams. Probably influenced by Ivan Aksakov, he planned to revive the *zemskii sobor* of the seventeenth century, which the early Slavophils had idealized as the expression of the union of the Tsars with their people. In May 1882 he submitted his plan to the emperor. He proposed that on Easter Day 1883 an assembly should be convoked in Moscow. It should include all members of the Holy Synod, the Council of State, the Senate, all bishops and ministers, marshals of nobility of all provinces, mayors of both capitals, of the first city of every province and of some *uezd*, and specially elected representatives of landowners, merchants and peasants from each province. Further instructions would be given later as to the representation of the Cossack Armies, Siberia, Turkestan, the Caucasus, the Baltic and Polish provinces, and Finland. Just as the earlier *zemskii sobor* had met not only to crown the Tsar but also 'for the proclamation by the sovereign himself of his sovereign will to the whole land represented by its elected best children, and for the sovereign to hear directly from the elected persons about the needs of their homelands, and in general for the sovereign to consult with the whole land, so let it be from now'.[1] This rather harmless but impracticable scheme, which would have meant a pageant of more than two thousand people, filled Pobedonostsev with horror. As he saw it, the scheme could be interpreted as a 'constitution'. Any move in that direction would be fatal. 'If the will and decision pass from the government to any sort of national assembly whatsoever, that will be revolution, the ruin of the government and the ruin of Russia.'[2] The Tsar seems to have agreed. In any case, on 30 May 1882 Ignatyev was replaced as minister of the interior by Count Dmitri Tolstoy.

With this appointment the course of the new reign was set.

[1] The text is in *K. P. Pobedonostsev i ego korrespondenty*, i. 261–3.
[2] K. P. Pobedonostsev, *Pis'ma k Aleksandru III*, i. 381.

In the strictly political field the most influential persons were Pobedonostsev, Tolstoy, and Katkov. Education since October 1881 had been in the hands of Tolstoy's former subordinate I. V. Delyanov. The only important minister who still stood for reforms was N. K. Bunge, the minister of finance.

The main characteristics of the last two decades of the century, extending into the next reign and indeed up to the war with Japan in 1904, are stagnation in agriculture, progress in industry, retrogression in education, russification of the non-Russian half of the empire's population, and an overall attitude of nostalgic, obscurantist, and narrowly bureaucratic paternalism. Economic development, education, and russification will be discussed separately. It remains here to consider the general principles and practice of government and administration.

The Kakhanov Commission presented its report in the autumn of 1884. Its most important recommendation was that the *volost* should be made an 'all-class' institution, that is to say that it should have authority not only over peasants but over all persons living within its boundaries. Already in 1883 Pobedonostsev had expressed contempt for the commission's labours. Its projects, he wrote to Tolstoy, seem designed 'to break up all power in Russia, to split it up into myriads of grains of sand with nothing to link them together'.[1] Tolstoy asked for various opinions on the 1884 report, and decided to take no action on it. The commission was dismissed in April 1885.

The new expert adviser on reorganization of the administration was an *uezd* marshal of nobility named A. D. Pazukhin, whose main idea was to restore the authority of the nobility, reduced since the emancipation of 1861. Pobedonostsev and Tolstoy both professed admiration for the nobility and the desire to strengthen its social and political position. The centenary of Catherine II's Charter, 21 April 1885, was made the occasion for a manifesto, drafted for the emperor by Pobedonostsev. This declared that, in accepting the 1861 statute, with consequent loss of its privileges, the Russian nobility had shown 'an example of generosity rare in the history of all countries and peoples'. It declared that the nobility must, as in the past, take the first place in military and civil leadership and local adminis-

[1] *K. P. Pobedonostsev i ego korrespondenty*, i. 315–17. Letter to D. A. Tolstoy of 11 Sept. 1883.

tration, and 'in disinterested care for the needs of the local population, and in the diffusion by its own example and leadership of the rules of faith and loyalty, correct principles of public education, good customs and good economy'. The manifesto also announced the foundation of the Nobles' Land Bank, which proved in the following years of some economic advantage to noble landowners. But the truth was that, for all these fine words from high places, the nobility was a declining force. The concern of Tolstoy and his colleagues was not so much to help loyal noblemen as to strengthen the government machine. The social group that benefited from the policies of these years was much less the landowners than the bureaucrats.

This was the effect of the administrative reorganization, prepared by Pazukhin and other officials under Tolstoy's direction, which came into force just after the latter's death. Its essential purpose was to place the peasants firmly under the authority of the Ministry of the Interior and to eliminate the influence on them of the zemstvos elected by the whole population. The most important office which had been a link between the elected bodies and the peasants—in those provinces in which zemstvos existed—was that of justice of the peace. By two Acts confirmed by the Tsar on 12 July 1889,[1] this institution was abolished in the greater part of Russia. In those provinces where there were no zemstvos, and where justices of the peace since 1864 had been appointed officials, no change was made. Elected justices of the peace were retained in the two capitals and six other large cities,[2] together with a few rural districts close to them. Elsewhere the office was abolished. In towns, the judicial functions formerly exercised by justices of the peace were transferred to city judges, appointed by the Ministry of Justice. In rural areas they were shared between the *uezd* member of the provincial district court and a newly created official, the land commandant (*zemskii nachal'nik*). The land commandant must be a member of the hereditary nobility of the district and must have a varying combination of qualifications relating to property, length of residence or state service, and degree of education. Lists of suitable persons were prepared

[1] *Polozhenie o zemskikh uchastkovykh nachal'nikakh* and *Pravila ob ustroistve sudebnoy chasti* (*Sobranie uzakoneniy 1889 goda*, no. 691).

[2] Odessa, Kazan, Kishinyov, Nizhnii Novgorod, Saratov, and Kharkov.

by *uezd* marshals of nobility, and the posts were filled from these lists by the governor. The minister of the interior could reject the governor's choice and could appoint other persons at his own discretion. The commandant's district (*uchastok*) might consist of one or more *volost*. Within this district he had both administrative and judicial powers. The next level above the commandant was the *uezd* conference, divided into an administrative and a judicial branch. The first consisted of all commandants in the *uezd*, the *ispravnik* and the chairman of the *uezd* zemstvo *uprava*. The second consisted of the commandants, city judges, *uezd* member of district court, and honorary justices of the peace (where these existed). The *uezd* marshal of nobility presided over both departments. The third level, above the *uezd* conference, was the provincial office (*gubernskoe prisutstvie*), in which the governor himself was chairman, and which included the chairman of the provincial zemstvo *uprava*, various senior administrative and judicial officials and two further 'permanent members', recruited from local members of the nobility with experience in government service. By 1893 there were 1920 commandants and 443 city judges in office in 32 provinces. Figures taken from about one third of the area covered, for the same year, showed that 42 per cent. of those appointed commandants from provincial governors' lists were civil officials, 40 per cent. were military or naval officers and 18 per cent. were noblemen without official posts.[1]

The land commandant had wide powers over the peasant authorities in the *volost* and the village. He could cancel decisions of assemblies, add items of his own choice to the agenda of their meetings, and remove 'unreliable' *volost* or village notaries from their posts. He could also suspend verdicts of the *volost* courts, but must refer his action to the *uezd* conference for confirmation.[2] Many land commandants were just

[1] These figures apply to the ten provinces of Ekaterinoslav, Kursk, Nizhnii Novgorod, Novgorod, Poltava, Pskov, Simbirsk, Smolensk, Tula, and Kharkov. They refer to 442 Commandants out of 558 for this area. The remaining posts were filled by appointment from the Ministry of the Interior. Among these appointed commandants the proportion of army and navy officers was higher (50 per cent.) and of civil officials lower (31 per cent.). A. Yanovsky, 'Zemskie uchastkovye nachal'niki', in *Brockhaus*, xiia. 513–14.

[2] Articles 25, 29, 30 of the *Polozhenie o zemskikh uchastkovykh nachal'nikakh* and articles 30 and 31 of the Provisional Rules on the *volost* court refer to these points. The full texts are in *Sbornik uzakoneniy o krest'yanskikh i sudebnykh uchrezhdeniyakh*,

and benevolent men, but the institution itself was created as part of a deliberately reactionary policy, designed to maintain the peasants in a condition of tutelage, and to make it more difficult for them to acquire the practice in self-government so necessary to the process of transforming former serfs into citizens of a modern state.

Distrust of the representative principle even in local government inspired two further laws, carried out by Tolstoy's successor at the Ministry of the Interior, I. N. Durnovo. The law of 12 June 1890 reduced the representation of peasants in zemstvo assemblies, and made the peasant franchise for *uezd* assemblies indirect instead of direct. Each *volost* assembly in an *uezd* elected a representative, but the number of peasant seats in the *uezd* assembly was less than the number of *volosti*, and the provincial governor filled them at his own discretion from the *volost* lists. At the same time it was laid down that appointments by zemstvos of salaried officials required the governor's confirmation, and the disciplinary powers of the Ministry of the Interior over chairmen and members of the zemstvo *uprava* were made stricter. The law of 11 June 1892 correspondingly restricted the electorate in the cities. The property qualification of the franchise was raised for owners of house property, apart from whom only members of the first guild in the capitals or of the first or second guild in other cities were entitled to vote. The result was a substantial reduction of the already small electorates. The number of votes in St. Petersburg was reduced, as a result of the law, from 21,176 to 7,152.[1]

The government never quite dared to abolish local self-government, but it was able, by constant obstruction, to make the work of local authorities extremely difficult. It was not only that the authorities objected to the public expression of liberal political opinions: this was only to be expected in an autocracy. The bureaucrats went further than this. They objected in practice to any local initiative. Even proposals of a completely non-political character, designed to improve the material welfare of the local population, met with objections in St.

published by the land department of the Ministry of the Interior (SPB, 1901), i. 30–87 and 383–6.

[1] *Ocherki istorii Leningrada*, published by the Academy of Sciences of the Soviet Union (Moscow, 1956), iii. 889.

Petersburg. The improvement of the people's welfare in Russia was, it was felt, the task of the central government. If the central government's officials were too busy with other tasks, or were simply too lazy, then improvements must be postponed. Better that nothing be done than that something good be done by the wrong persons.

Given this general atmosphere, the surprising thing is that the zemstvos achieved so much. Economically they were helped by a reduction, in 1895 and 1901, of their obligations to carry out at their own expense duties on behalf of the central administration. In 1903 such duties only took up 8 per cent. of zemstvo expenditure. The main sources of revenue were taxes on land and on non-agricultural immovable property. A regulation of 1900 forbade an increase of more than 3 per cent. per year in zemstvo revenues. This increase in fact corresponded approximately to the rate of increase of all zemstvos over the preceding decades, but there were of course large discrepancies between individual areas. Those zemstvos, mostly in economically backward areas, which had in the past levied very low taxes, were now prevented from catching up with their needs. The harmfulness of the measure lay not so much in the injustice of the figure of 3 per cent. as the imposition of any rigid figure at all.[1]

The zemstvos devoted themselves to improving local services, such as roads, fire-fighting, and other material improvements. They shared with the officials of the Ministry of Education the task of developing primary and secondary schools. In 1903 education received an average of 20 per cent. of the expenditure of *uezd* zemstvos and anything between 5 and 15 per cent. of the expenditure of provincial zemstvos. The share of medical services was higher—25 to 30 per cent. at both *uezd* and provincial levels.[2]

The situation of the municipalities was in some respects more favourable. As they were the seats of power of high officials, their natural desire for civic improvement met with some sympathy in powerful quarters, whereas the desire of zemstvos to do good in the rural wilderness provoked indifference or irritation. Moreover, the franchise to city councils was so restricted that they were not thought likely to produce seditious

[1] The law is discussed in Veselovsky, *Istoriya zemstva*, i. 138–52.

[2] Ibid. 257, 259.

leaders, and their mayors in fact were often extremely conservative. Even so, civic progress was hardly startling. By 1900 111 cities had some system of water piping, but this was accessible to only a small part of the population in the central districts. Modern drainage hardly existed. There were 27 electric power-stations in cities, again supplying only small sectors.[1] Street lighting was scanty in the centres and non existent at the periphery. The central streets of the main cities were paved, but suburban streets were largely left to the mercies of nature, being reduced to a sea of mud at the time of the spring thaw.

Both zemstvos and cities employed growing numbers of trained experts. The most important categories were doctors, statisticians, teachers, and engineers. These became known at the end of the century as 'the third element'.[2] They became an extremely important factor in both economic and political life. They were mostly rather young and poorly paid. If they had wanted to make a prosperous career for themselves in their professions, they would have done much better to go into private practice. If they chose zemstvo employment, it was largely from idealism, from the desire directly to know and to help the people. These zemstvo experts formed in the 1880's and 1890's a hard core of politically minded reformers, usually of radical or socialist rather than of liberal views, who did their best, and not without effect, not only to arouse political consciousness among the people, but also to push the regular zemstvo authorities into stronger action on behalf of political reform. They included many of the most able and energetic persons in their professions, and also exercised influence on the attitudes of their professions as a whole. In the 1880's all-Russian professional organizations grew up, such as the Pirogov Medical Society, founded in 1881, the year of the great surgeon's death. The Moscow Law Society, founded as early as 1863, became in the 1880's and 1890's a centre for the discussion of political and social ideas. The same was true of the St. Petersburg and Moscow Committees for the Advancement of Literacy, which combined educational activity with a spirit of political

[1] *Bolshaya Sovetskaya Entsiklopediya*, 2nd ed. (1952), xii. 199–201.

[2] This phrase was used in 1899 by the vice-governor of Samara, Kondoidi, who distinguished three elements in provincial government—the elected zemstvo assembly members, the appointed government officials, and the expert employees. The phrase caught the public imagination and passed into general use.

enlightenment and crusading zeal. In all these activities the zemstvo 'third element' made itself felt. It is also fair to point out that those members of the professions who pursued their careers with success, as highly paid doctors in private practice, or leading barristers, or university professors, usually also supported such activities, and gave to them their time, money, and experience in generous measure.

It is not always easy to distinguish between professional and official occupations. The medical profession is an example. In 1889 there were 12,521 doctors in Russia, of whom 2,629 were in the armed services, 3,465 in the service of central government, zemstvos or municipalities, 1,552 in hospitals or teaching, and 3,289 in private practice.[1] About one-fifth of the total worked in St. Petersburg or Moscow. Most government doctors, while knowing themselves to be on the government payroll, would not consider themselves to be government officials. Rather they would feel themselves part of the intelligentsia. But both in function and in mentality, there was a blurred zone between officialdom and intelligentsia.[2]

At the end of the century zemstvos were confined to European Russia and the greater part of the Ukraine. There were none in the six provinces of Lithuania and White Russia or in the three provinces of the south-western Ukraine, or in Siberia. They were also absent from the completely non-Russian regions of the Baltic provinces, the Kingdom of Poland, the Caucasus, and Central Asia.

The Cossack territories[3] remained administratively apart. Far the most important was the Don Army, with its capital at Novocherkassk and a population, in majority civilian, of over 2,000,000 people, which included from 1887 the two large industrial cities of Rostov and Taganrog. The other ten Cossack armies were the Kuban, Terek, and Astrakhan armies in the south; the Orenburg and Ural to the north of the Caspian; the Siberian and Semirechie in the centre of Asiatic Russia; and the Transbaikal, Amur, and Ussuri in the Far East. Each army was ruled by an *ataman*, whose rank and functions approximated to those of a civil provincial governor. The head of the Don Army

[1] Article on 'Medical Personnel and Medical Aid to the Population' by G. M. Gertsenstein, in *Brockhaus*, xviii. 894–5.

[2] See below pp. 538–40.

[3] See above pp. 7, 23, 57.

had the title of *voyskovy nakazny ataman*, and rank equivalent to a governor-general. The supreme authority for Cossack affairs was the Ministry of War, which contained a Directorate of Cossack Armies and a Committee of Cossack Armies, on which the atamans had their representatives. The armies were divided into *stanitsy*, each of which had an assembly (*stanichny sbor*) composed of elected representatives of Cossack households and of civilians, who could vote only in matters affecting the civilian population. In 1893 the total population of the Cossack areas was 5,443,938, of which Cossacks proper with their families numbered 2,648,049.[1]

During Pobedonostsev's tenure of the supreme procuratorship the schismatics and sectarians continued to suffer hardships. A law of 1883 placed all sects on the same legal basis, with the sole exception of the eunuch *Skoptsy*. This represented some gain for some of the smaller sects which had been treated with special severity in the past, but no progress for the bulk of the Old Believers. Sectarians were freed from some civil disabilities which had affected them, and they were allowed to hold services in houses of prayer of their own, provided that there were no public processions, and that no vestments were used. In practice it was extremely difficult to obtain permission to open new houses of prayer, and official interpretation of the regularity of Old Believer marriages led to much injustice. Conversion of Orthodox to schismatic or sectarian beliefs remained illegal, and the Orthodox Church subjected sectarians to severe pressure to abjure their beliefs. In this they were often helped by local secular officials.

Pobedonostsev was especially hostile to a sect which became known as Stundists. Their doctrines were derived from German Baptists. They were mainly found in the southern Ukraine. They did not formally break away from the Orthodox Church until 1870. Their high personal standards of morality won them great moral authority, and they made many converts among the peasants. They believed in the sharing of property and were opposed to military service. In 1894 Pobedonostsev was able to get the minister of the interior to issue a circular to the effect that the Stundists were an 'especially dangerous' sect and should be prevented from holding prayer meetings.

[1] *Brockhaus*, xiii. 884.

In 1893 the Dukhobor community in the Caucasus split into two groups. The more extreme refused military service and taxes. Many of them were deported and resettled in smaller groups. Some were sent to Siberia for long terms. In 1898 and 1899 most of the Russian Dukhobors were allowed to emigrate: they went first to Cyprus and then to Canada.

Revolutionary activity within Russia in the 1880's was only on a small scale. The remnants of *Narodnaya volya*, led by the intrepid Vera Figner, continued for a year after the assassination of Alexander II, until the police, aided by informers within their ranks, rounded them up.[1] In 1886 some students made a demonstration in commemoration of the fiftieth anniversary of the birth of Dobrolyubov. One of them, named Alexander Ulyanov, was inspired by his disgust at the brutality with which this small effort was repressed to plan the assassination of Alexander III. He and his colleagues obtained explosives and manufactured some bombs, but the plot was discovered and they were arrested. Fifteen persons, who owed their allegiance to *Narodnaya volya*, were tried by the Senate, and five of them, including Ulyanov, were condemned to death. They were executed on 8 May 1887. It is recorded that Ulyanov's younger brother Vladimir swore to avenge him. More than thirty years later, under the name of Lenin, he paid this debt with interest.

Education and Culture

Of the three men who held the post of minister of education for long periods during the nineteenth century—Uvarov (1832–49), Tolstoy (1866–80), and Delyanov (1882–98)—it was the last who had the most disastrous effects. Uvarov had sought to place education on a class basis. Tolstoy had introduced oppressively boring curricula and had tightened discipline in schools and in universities. Yet both men had permitted some progress, and both had believed in the value of education. Delyanov combined harsh treatment of students with social exclusiveness, and the general impression given during his period in office was of obstruction by government to any educational progress. This was the more harmful because the

[1] These events are told in Figner's later volume of revolutionary memoirs *Zapechatlyonny trud*, Moscow, 1920.

economic development both of Russia and of the rest of the world made rapid expansion in education not only more necessary than ever but practically possible. Delyanov was not faced by the same tremendous obstacles, of lack of human and financial resources for teaching, as Uvarov had experienced. Admittedly, it needed an effort both to train more teachers and to get money out of the Treasury, but Delyanov hardly tried to do either.

The students gave the new minister trouble at once. In the autumn of 1882 there were riots at the universities of St. Petersburg and Kazan. In the capital the students demanded the right to form elective corporations to take care of their professional needs and represent them with the authorities. In Kazan a medical student assaulted a professor of history as he was about to begin his lecture. When this man was expelled, large crowds of students invaded the university buildings and demonstrated in the streets. These events strengthened the determination of Tolstoy and Delyanov to abolish the 1863 University Statute and place both professors and students directly under government control. Already in 1875 Tolstoy had set up a commission, under Delyanov who was then a high official of the ministry, to draft a new statute. This had been set aside in 1880 when Tolstoy was replaced by Saburov. Now the earlier draft was brought out again. It was rejected by a majority in the Council of State, but the Tsar upheld the minority, and the new statute became law on 13 August 1884. It increased the powers of the inspectors, who were responsible directly to the curators. Rectors, deans, and professors of the universities were henceforth to be appointed by the minister, not chosen by the academic university councils. University fees were also increased in June 1887.

For some years the university students paid much less attention to politics. But this apathy did not mean conscious support for the government: rather it was due to a sense of the ineffectiveness of political action as shown by the defeat of the revolutionary movement of the 1870's. After five years the mood began to change. In November 1887 a law student at St. Petersburg slapped an inspector in the face at a concert, and incidents or riots occurred at the universities of Kharkov, Odessa, and Kazan. The students began again to demand the right to form corporations, but the government persisted in its refusal. In practice there existed unrecognized organizations, known as *zemlyachestva*, to which students from the same part of the country belonged. These regional societies had their representatives in a combined central committee, known as the Union Council (*soyuzny sovet*). From the end of the 1880's this was controlled by persons active in illegal political movements, and the council was increasingly used to mobilize student discontent, basically caused by professional and material grievances, for political ends.

Delyanov was determined to keep persons of humble origin out of the universities. To this end, he sought to make their entry into secondary schools more difficult. Fees in gimnazii and incomplete gimnazii were substantially raised in June 1887. Apart from this, in a circular of 18 June 1887 Delyanov specially instructed the officials of the ministry in the provinces to admit only children whose home circumstances seemed suitable to them. The circular stated that this should rid the secondary schools of 'children of coachmen, servants, cooks, washerwomen, small shopkeepers, and persons of a similar type, whose children, perhaps with the exception of those gifted with unusual abilities, should certainly not be brought out of the social environment to which they belong'.[1] This mentality was shared by Pobedonostsev, who bitterly denounced the faults of the existing educational system in a letter to the Tsar at this time. The secondary schools, he claimed, do not train children for real life. Instead, they turn them out 'with an unlimited and perverted self-love, which demands everything from life, but does not itself contribute anything to it'.[2]

The result of Delyanov's efforts was that between 1882 and 1895 the number of pupils in gimnazii and incomplete gimnazii diminished, from 65,751 to 63,863. During the same period the proportion of children of nobles and officials in these schools increased from 47 per cent. to 56 per cent. In the real schools there was some modest progress: their pupils increased from 17,500 to 26,000, and the proportion of children of the urban non-noble classes increased from 40 per cent. to 44 per cent.[3]

[1] *Istoricheskii obzor deyatel'nosti MNP*, p. 641.

[2] Letter to Alexander III of 4 March 1887, *K. P. Pobedonostsev i ego korrespondenty*, ii. 652.

[3] *Istoricheskii obzor deyatel'nosti MNP*, pp. 643, 646.

Pobedonostsev did not object to elementary education for the lower classes, but he believed that it should be controlled by the Church. In this he was supported by Dmitri Tolstoy, Delyanov, and the Tsar himself. During the reign of Alexander III the number of church parish schools increased from 4,064 with 105,317 pupils, to 31,835 with 981,076 pupils. The number of girls in these schools increased during the same period from 13,211 to 173,075. However, the standard of instruction left a good deal to be desired. Only 225 of these schools had two classes. The subjects taught in the schools were scripture, church singing, reading of Church Slavonic religious texts, Russian language, writing, and arithmetic. In some schools agricultural or artisan skills were also taught. At the head of the system was the educational council in the Holy Synod, instituted in 1885. In 1894 there were 63 diocesan educational councils in the empire, with subordinate departments in the *uezd*, and an inspector in each parish in which there was a school.[1]

By 1904 there were 3,360,167 children at elementary schools managed by the Ministry of Education and 1,909,496 children in schools managed by the Church. This represented 27 per cent. of the children of school age in the empire at this time (38 per cent. of the boys and 15 per cent. of the girls). There were wide regional variations. The proportion was highest in the three Baltic provinces, Moscow, and St. Petersburg, in all of which the overall figure was above 40 per cent. It was rather high in Saratov (32 per cent.), rather low in Kiev (22 per cent.), and below 20 per cent. in the Asiatic provinces.[2]

At the time of the census of 1897 only 21 per cent. of the population of the empire could read and write. Literacy was highest in the age-group 10–19 (33 per cent.) and diminished with each ten-year age group above, being 19 per cent. for those between 50 and 60 years old. There were more than twice as many literate males as females (18,310,000 to 8,250,000).

In the Russian empire in 1897 there were 104,321 persons who had studied in a university or higher institution of learning, and only 6,360 of these were women. Of this total of present and

[1] *Obzor deyatel'nosti vedomstva pravoslavnogo ispovedaniya za vremya tsarstvovaniya Imperatora Aleksandra III* (SPB, 1901), pp. 711–16.

[2] *Materialy po shkolnomu obrazovaniyu v Rossii,* Central Statistical Committee, Ministry of the Interior, SPB, 1906.

past students, 73 per cent. were children of nobles or non-noble officials, 5 per cent. of priests, 20 per cent. of urban classes and 2 per cent. of peasants. The total number who had studied in the secondary schools of the general type (gimnazii, incomplete gimnazii, and real schools) was 1,072,977. Only slightly less than half of these were women. Among these school graduates children of nobles and non-noble officials formed 40 per cent., of priests 20 per cent., of urban classes 34 per cent., and of peasants 6 per cent. If the rather small number of those who had studied in various specialized secondary or higher institutions is added, the picture is not significantly modified.[1]

Two hundred years after Peter the Great had given the initial impetus to forced modernization, and a century after Alexander I had planned a coherent and logical system of schools and universities, the spectacle of Russian education was depressing. The failure is the more striking if the Russian achievement is compared with that of another country which had embarked much more recently on a policy of modernization, Japan.

At the time of the Meiji Restoration of 1868 Japan had a rather well-developed system of schools, and it seems possible that about half the male population were literate.[2] However, the traditional system of education was quite unsuited to train young people to face the modern world into which Japan had recently been forced to enter. In this respect, Japan was hardly much better situated than Russia on the accession of Peter the Great. But already in the 1870's the Japanese reformers not only accepted universal elementary education in principle but began vigorously to put it into practice. In 1880 the period of compulsory school was three years, and at the end of the century it was six. In 1903 no less than 93 per cent. of all boys and girls of school age were attending school. One should also not forget that the attainment of literacy in the ideographic Japanese language is a much more difficult task than in the alphabetic Russian language. During the nineteenth century

[1] *Obshchii svod po Imperii rezultatov razrabotki dannykh pervoy vseobshchey perepisi naseleniya*, ed. N. A. Troynitsky (SPB, 1905), i. 188–95. This is cited hereafter as *Obshchii svod perepisi*.

[2] See the excellent study by R. P. Dore, *Education in Tokugawa Japan*, 1965. The evidence on literacy and school attendance is discussed in Appendix I (pp. 317–22).

Russia had achieved much at the highest level of the educational pyramid: her universities were as good as those of Europe. But at the lowest level the achievement was wretched. Essentially the Russian governments believed that education was a dangerous thing, which should be withheld from the masses. At most, the peasants should be given a certain amount of religious and moral instruction, but when it came to spending public funds even this enjoyed a low priority. In Japan, by contrast, it was held that a nation can be strong only if it is well educated. This was the lesson which the Japanese observers drew from the experience of Germany. The cliché that 'the Battle of Sedan was won by the Prussian village schoolmaster' was not lost on them. It is true that the purpose of Japanese educational progress was not disinterested philanthropy, but Imperial greatness. The Meiji Era statesmen intended to build a powerful military empire, and they believed that their soldiers and sailors would fight better if they went to school and learned to read and write. The school was for them a political instrument. The famous Imperial Rescript of 1890 was made the basis of a whole system of patriotic indoctrination, which must be distasteful to any Western liberal democrat. It would not, however, necessarily have been distasteful to Uvarov, who in his report of 1832 had stated as an aim of education 'to form . . . useful and devoted instruments of the government'.[1] But Uvarov had been thinking only of the upper classes, and his successors, even in the age of mass armies and mass societies, had not extended his idea to the rest of the nation.

Any society embarking on the process of modernization, not slowly and spontaneously like the maritime nations of northern Europe, but rapidly and by the conscious will of its rulers, has to begin by training a small *élite* in modern skills and in modern ways of thought. At the beginning of this process, this *élite* is bound to be cut off from the bulk of the nation, not only from the masses but even from the traditionally minded majority of the upper class. But as the process of modernization extends in breadth and depth, the gap can be gradually narrowed, and the nation can become one again—or at least as nearly one as any nation divided by normal class differences can hope to be. The speed with which the gap can be narrowed depends on

[1] See above p. 220.

various factors—the growth of industry, urbanization, and the establishment of a nation-wide system of popular education. All three are necessary, and possibly the last is the most important of the three. In Japan all three were pursued. The Japanese certainly did not neglect higher and secondary education, but they also devoted great efforts to elementary. Imperial Russia made great progress in industry and in urbanization, but it neglected popular education. Thus the cultural gap between *élite* and masses was kept wide for an artificially long period, with all the consequences in political frustration of the intelligentsia. In Imperial Japan, whatever other social tensions, political conflicts, and errors there may have been, the gap was quickly narrowed, and the dangerous consequences to society of the alienation of the intellectual *élite* were reduced.

During the 1880's censorship in Russia became more rigorous. Under new rules of 27 August 1882, any newspaper which had been three times 'warned' by the censor would be thenceforth obliged to submit the text of every issue to preliminary censorship on the day before publication. This for a daily newspaper amounted to the threat of suppression if it three times displeased the censor. Special regulations were issued about public libraries and reading-rooms, with special severity towards those to which access was free, and which might therefore be used by people of the poorer classes. A Special Conference, composed of the ministers of justice, education, and the interior, and the supreme procurator of the Holy Synod, was empowered to suppress a periodical and to forbid its publisher or editors to edit or publish any other paper in future.

An early victim of this procedure was *Otechestvennye zapiski*, whose honourable career as Russia's outstanding liberal paper was brought to an end in 1884. This was a terrible blow to its most distinguished contributor, the veteran satirist Saltykov-Shchedrin, who died in the following year. Other members of the team were able to carry on. The most notable of these was the Populist socialist writer N. K. Mikhailovsky. A mysterious and contradictory character, Mikhailovsky was a passionate champion of individual liberty and the individual personality, yet with equal fervour upheld the absolute priority of the individual's duty to serve society. In the last year of Alexander

II's reign he had been associated with People's Will and had spoken with contempt of the very idea of a liberal constitution. In the 1880's he showed both skill and courage in keeping Populist ideas alive while keeping within the letter of the law. He did not always succeed in escaping administrative reprisals, but he was never banned from publishing under the 1882 law. His cautious tactics were appreciated by the liberal and radical public, and he enjoyed tremendous popularity with the young. Though he never held a teaching-post, he had plenty of personal contact with students, and attended and spoke at evening discussion meetings in the university. From 1891 onwards he wrote regularly in the periodical *Russkoe bogatstvo* ('Russia's Wealth') which became the effective mouthpiece of Populist ideology. Mikhailovsky won the reluctant respect of the authorities. It is said that the police chief, later minister of the interior, V. K. Pleve, once said to him: 'Why do you want freedom of the press when even without it you are such a master of saying between the lines all that you wish to say'?[1]

Mikhailovsky was the most eminent exponent of the doctrine of social utility as the criterion of literary criticism, and in the 1880's and 1890's this was largely accepted by the educated class. On the whole the writers of this period conformed to it. Dostoyevsky had died in 1881. In the previous year Tolstoy had experienced his religious conversion, so brilliantly and movingly described in his *Confession*, published in 1882. He continued to write for nearly thirty years more, and he always remained a great writer, but after 1882 his influence in Russia was religious, and even political, rather than literary. Leskov was active until his death in 1895, but as he was not much concerned with social themes his work was underrated by contemporary critics. The most eminent of the socially minded writers was V. G. Korolenko, who apart from his stories was also a collaborator

[1] The reason given for the suppression of *Otechestvennye zapiski* was that members of its staff and contributors had been engaged in illegal political activities. Mikhailovsky's best-known expression of individualism was an article entitled 'What is Progress?' in *Otechestvennye zapiski* in 1869. In December 1878 he said to the radical zemstvo leader I. I. Petrunkevich: 'The people will spit at your landowner-type constitution.' (*Arkhiv russkoy revolyutsii*, xxi. 105). In 1881 Mikhailovsky wrote the famous Letter of the central committee of *Narodnaya volya* to Alexander III. The story of the conversation with Pleve is in Y. Gardenin (pseudonym for V. M. Chernov) *K pamyati N. K. Mikhailovskogo* (?Geneva, 1904), p. 49. A good modern study of Mikhailovsky is J. H. Billington, *Mikhailovsky and Russian Populism*, 1958.

of Mikhailovsky in *Russkoe bogatstvo*. At the end of the 1880's a major new literary figure appeared in Anton Chekhov whose first volume of stories was published in 1886. In the same year he secured a permanent livelihood as a regular contributor to *Novoe vremya* ('New Times'), the daily paper with the largest circulation in Russia, directed by the conservative A. S. Suvorin. This enabled Chekhov to devote himself to writing. His short stories and plays, which include some of the greatest works in Russian literature, were written in the next eighteen years and the combination of Chekhov's plays with the new style and skills of the Moscow Art Theatre, founded in 1897 by K. S. Stanislavsky and V. I. Nemirovich-Danchenko, introduced the most glorious period in the history of Russian dramatic art. *Uncle Vanya* was produced in 1900, *The Three Sisters* in 1901, and *The Cherry Orchard* in January 1904. Chekhov died in June 1904 at the age of forty-four.

Chekhov did not belong to the social utilitarian school of thought. But the melancholy atmosphere of his stories, the dreary drab picture of Russian life, the impression that the existing social system was incurable, and that it was impossible even for people to communicate with each other, fitted well with the mood of the radical intelligentsia. Apart from this, Chekhov in his later years became associated to some extent with the cause of the left. In 1897 he broke with Suvorin in connexion with the Dreyfus affair, and in 1902 he resigned from the Academy, together with Korolenko, as a protest against the annulment by the government of the election to that body of Maxim Gorky.

Gorky was the second great new literary figure of this period. His real name was Alexei Peshkov, and he was the son of a workman who rose in the social scale to become a shipping agent in Astrakhan. He had to earn his living as a child, first as a bootmaker's assistant and then as a pantry-boy on a Volga steamer, where he was taught to read and write by the ship's cook, and then in a series of manual or clerical jobs up and down the country. He began to write stories in 1892, had one published in *Russkoe bogatstvo* in 1895, and had two volumes of collected stories published in 1898. With this publication, 'from a promising provincial journalist, Gorky became the most famous writer of his country. From this date to the First Revolution,

Gorky was, next to Tolstoy, the figure in Russia that aroused the greatest public interest'.[1] Gorky not only wrote about the life of the common people but was definitely interested in putting across a social and political message. He became active in the social democratic movement and it was this which led the government to make the ponderous intervention of 1902, demanding that one who was 'under police supervision' should not be elected an Academician.

Irrespective of their political and social attitudes and of the public reaction to them, Gorky and Chekhov were great writers, and lend distinction to this period in the history of Russian literature, even if it is not so brilliant as either of the preceding quarter-centuries. There are three other writers, all outside the field of imaginative literature, who must at least be mentioned. The first is the Christian philosopher Vladimir Solovyov (1853–1900), the son of the historian S. M. Solovyov. He was a mystic, who at one time came very close to the Catholic Church but never actually joined it. He was a poet as well as a prose writer. His most provocative work, published in the year of his death, and later translated into western languages, was *Three Conversations on War, Progress, and the End of Human History*, written in the form of a discussion between five persons and followed by a *History of Antichrist*. Read half a century later, the arguments and the fable retain their freshness, and even a certain prophetic quality. The second is K. N. Leontyev (1831–91), who was trained as a doctor, served for ten years in the consular service and ended his life as a monk. He was a critic of literature and art and a historian of religious and political ideas, with a special interest in Byzantine civilization. He was much interested in politics and held extreme conservative and nationalist views. Where Solovyov sought in religion mystic truth, Leontyev sought order and submission. 'He was', writes Mirsky, 'a rare instance in modern times (the thing was a rule in the Middle Ages) of an essentially unreligious man submitting consciously and obediently to the hard rule of dogmatic and exclusive religion.'[2] The third writer is the great historian V. O.

[1] D. S. Mirsky, *A History of Russian Literature*, 1949 edition, p. 377. By 'First Revolution' Mirsky, of course, means the February Revolution of 1917, not the Revolution of 1905.

[2] Ibid., p. 331.

Klyuchevsky (1841–1911), the son of a village priest from Penza province, who was educated in a seminary, and only after a long struggle with the hierarchy of the Church obtained permission to go to Moscow University as a student. In 1879 he began to give lectures, and from 1882 to 1909 a yearly general course on the history of Russia. This course, improved from year to year, was published after his death by his former pupils and remains the best single work (in five volumes) that has been written on Russian history. His influence on the intellectual development of thousands of Russian students over a period of some thirty years is incalculable but enormous.

This was also a good period in the natural sciences. Among the eminent Russian scientists of the time three at least must be mentioned. First is D. I. Mendeleyev, whose most productive years in chemical research were the 1880's. In 1890 he was forced to give up his chair in St. Petersburg because he had incurred the displeasure of Delyanov by passing to him a petition from the students. He had already been refused membership of the Academy of Sciences because of the hostility of the government to his materialist outlook.[1] In 1892 the finance minister, S. Y. Witte, took advantage of the heavy-handed action of his colleague to recruit Mendeleyev to the service of his department by appointing him head of the Bureau of Weights and Measures. In 1899 he made an official report on the industry of the Urals and later published other works surveying the Russian economy. These were useful activities, but they did not compensate for the removal from his natural sphere of a man who had not only made great contributions to chemical science but by building up a group of first-class scientists around him had made St. Petersburg one of the leading centres of chemical research in the world. The second great figure is A. S. Popov, son of a priest in Penza province, who began his education in a church seminary, studied mathematics at St. Petersburg University and became a specialist in electro-technology. For nearly twenty years Popov did teaching and research at the naval School of Mines in Kronstadt. He was one of the great pioneers of wireless telegraphy. In 1896 he gave a demonstration and published an article on his dis-

[1] He was elected a Fellow of the Royal Society, and received honorary degrees in Oxford, Cambridge, Paris, and Berlin.

coveries which coincided with, and perhaps preceded, Marconi's independent discoveries in this field. The third great scientist is I. P. Pavlov (1849–1936), like Popov a son of a priest and like him a pupil in a church seminary (in this case in Ryazan) who then studied science in St. Petersburg University. Pavlov followed his university course by studying medicine at the Medical-Surgical Academy, and from 1879 to 1889 did research in the physiological laboratory of the great St. Petersburg doctor S. P. Botkin. In 1891 Pavlov became director of the physiological department of the Institute of Experimental Medicine and held this post for forty-five years. Concurrently from 1895 to 1925 he was professor of physiology at the Medical Academy.[1] Pavlov's career stretches far beyond the revolution, well into the Soviet period of Russian history. His epoch-making work on conditioned reflexes was done in the first years of the twentieth century. Whatever may be thought of some of the later applications of his discoveries, or of some of the claims made on their behalf for non-scientific motives, Pavlov's place as one of the great men in the history of human science is sure.

Russification

It was in the reign of Alexander III that russification became an official policy. Those who believed that the Russian people and the Russian language should have the first place in the empire, and that the other peoples should be made into Russians in the interest of the empire and in their own interest, were becoming more numerous and more influential in government circles than those who asked only that all the Tsar's subjects, whatever their language or nationality, should serve him loyally. A new basis of legitimacy was being claimed for government in addition to the old: loyalty was claimed in the name of the Russian nation as well as in the name of the autocrat appointed by God. A secular ideology of state, Great Russian nationalism, existed side by side with the ancient doctrine of the divine right of monarchy. Of Uvarov's three principles, 'national-mindedness' was slowly gaining more weight than autocracy or Orthodoxy.

[1] In 1881 the Military-Surgical Academy was reorganized and renamed Military-Medical Academy.

The bearers of the new ideology were the bureaucrats, mostly derived from noble landowning families but no longer living the life of country landowners nor retaining the easy-going outlook of noble society in the middle decades of the century. Formally better educated than their parents' generation, honourable members of a disciplined hierarchy based on the more illiberal features of Prussian government, they aimed at order and uniformity and could not tolerate diverse traditions or regional variety. They were supported by soldiers who insisted that special precautions must be taken to strengthen Russian security in border regions like the Baltic coastline, Bessarabia, or Transcaucasia, and by Orthodox prelates anxious to convert the Catholics or the Moslems. The latter could count on the powerful advocacy of Pobedonostsev. Modern political ideas were of small interest to most of these men, but in so far as they had any, they were an amalgam of distorted Slavophily with the kind of aggressive nationalism that was spreading through Europe in the age of the new imperialism. Since the death in 1876 of Samarin and in 1886 of Ivan Aksakov, both of whom, for all their Russian nationalism, had had enough insight and generosity to understand and respect other views, little trace had remained of the liberal outlook of the original Slavophils.

Writing in 1889, Vladimir Solovyov noted the development of nationalism since the time of the Slavophils but held them partly responsible for the views of their successors.

> Adoration of one's own people as the chief bearer of universal truth; then adoration of the people as an elemental force, without regard to universal truth; finally adoration of the national one-sidedness and historical anomalies which cut off the people from educated humanity, that is to say, adoration of one's people with a direct negation of the very idea of universal truth—these are the three gradual stages of our nationalism, represented in succession by the Slavophils, by Katkov, and by the latest obscurantists. The first of these taught pure fantasies; the second was a realist, with imagination; the last are realists without any imagination but also without any shame.[1]

But it would not be fair to treat the new narrow outlook as a specifically Russian phenomenon. This was the age of Kipling, Barrès, and Crispi. It may be noted that Charles Maurras's famous statement that France is more important than justice

[1] V. S. Solovyov, *Sobranie sochineniy*, v. 228.

because there can be no justice without France, was made later than Danilevsky's claim that 'the idea of Slavdom should constitute an exalted ideal above freedom, above science, above learning, above all earthly riches, for not one of these will be attained without the realization of a spiritually, nationally, and politically autochthonous independent Slavdom'.[1] In this case Russian nationalists can claim a melancholy precedence over French in time, if hardly in literary style. But in fact ideas of this sort became generally current in the 1880's and 1890's. No doubt Pobedonostsev well understood the mental processes which caused President McKinley to decide that 'there was nothing left for us to do but take them all, and to educate the Filipinos and uplift and Christianise them'.[2]

The victims of russification were all the non-Russian peoples of the empire, but especially those who had hitherto served it with unquestioning loyalty and were now rewarded with persecution. The Poles had long behaved, and had learned to be treated, as enemies. The Ukrainian nationalist intelligentsia knew that its claim to Ukrainian national identity and autonomy would be rejected. The Jews were accustomed to discrimination. The Moslem Tatars, even in the periods of comparative toleration, regarded Christian Russians with a suspicion which was reciprocated. But the Baltic Germans and the Finns in the north, the Armenians in the south, had shown exemplary loyalty and had counted on the Tsar and his high officials to protect them from their enemies, including Russian extremists. Their situation was now to change.

The result of the policy of russification was to strengthen the determination of the nationalist intelligentsia and to awaken national consciousness in the more numerous classes, in which it had previously been dormant if indeed it had existed at all. Growing minorities, and in some cases majorities, of the

[1] N. Y. Danilevsky, *Rossiya i Evropa: vzglyad na kul'turnye i politicheskie otnosheniya slavyanskogo mira k germano-romanskomu* (SPB, 1886), p. 133. For modern discussions of Danilevsky's ideas, see Petrovich, *The Emergence of Russian Panslavism 1856–1870*, New York, 1956, and E. C. Thaden, *Conservative Nationalism in 19th Century Russia*, Seattle, 1964.

[2] This remark was made in connexion with the annexation of the Philippines after the Spanish-American War of 1898. Quoted by S. E. Morison and H. S. Commager, *The Growth of the American Republic*, ii. 337. Quite apart from the morality revealed in his words, McKinley apparently did not even know that there had been a Christian university in Manila since the seventeenth century.

peasantry were drawn into the nationalist movements. We shall here briefly survey the practice of russification and the nationalist movements which it provoked, in each of the main regions of the empire.

In Poland russification was intensified under General Gurko, who was governor-general from 1883 to 1894, and Alexander Apukhtin, who was curator of Warsaw educational district from 1883 to 1897. The University of Warsaw was now no less Russian, and on the whole less attractive for Polish students, than any of the universities of Russia proper. A law of 1885 provided that even in primary schools in Poland the only subjects which might be taught in Polish should be the study of the Polish language and Catholic religion: in all other subjects the language of instruction for Polish children must be Russian. In these circumstances it is not surprising that the Polish provinces, whose level of education, though not very high, had been in advance of Russia during the nineteenth century, now began to fall behind the Russian.

Poles remained Poles wherever they dwelt. But the failures of 1831 and 1863 had taught them that direct conflict with their foreign rulers would not help them. The new attitude was known as 'realism' or 'triple loyalty'—acceptance of obedience to the three empires which ruled Poland. In these years industry made great progress in Poland, especially in the Russian portion, whose main centres were Łódź for textiles, the Dąbrova Basin for mining, and Warsaw for various manufactures. The social structure of the Polish nation was changing. Even more than in Russia, the children of the landowning class had to look for other occupations. Few young upper-class Poles went into business. The bureaucracy was closed to Poles, at least at the higher levels, within Poland, though careers could be made in other parts of the empire, and in fact a certain number of Poles did make use of such opportunities. But the bulk of those Poles, born of landowning families, who could no longer make a living as landowners, went into the intellectual professions. Even more than the Russians, though less than the Jews or the Armenians, the Poles had a disproportionately numerous intelligentsia. At the base of the social pyramid, however, industrialization offered growing opportunities, as peasants came to the towns and became transformed into miners or factory workers. In the Kingdom of Poland at the turn of the century, the landowners, fewer and poorer than in 1850, were Poles; the bureaucrats Russians; the businessmen Jews or foreigners; the professional classes Poles; the great majority of the population Polish peasants or workers. In the Lithuanian and Ukrainian borderlands, the same divisions existed, and indeed were still more rigid, at the upper levels of the social pyramid, but at the base there were more White Russians, Lithuanians, and Ukrainians than Poles among the peasants. In the borderlands there was still very little industry: the incipient working class of the main city, Vilna, was a mixture of Jews, Poles, White Russians, and Lithuanians.

The first political movement to appear in Russian Poland in these years was a socialist conspiratorial group, internationalist rather than nationalist, and influenced by the Russian *Narodnaya volya.* This was the *Proletariat* group founded by Ludwik Waryński. It was discovered by the police in 1885, four of its members were executed, and Waryński was imprisoned in the Schlüsselburg, where he died. Among Polish socialists arrested in these years was a student of Kharkov University, Józef Piłsudski, who was exiled to Siberia in 1887. Socialism continued to develop among both intelligentsia and workers in all three Polish territories. Polish socialists in Germany and Austria enjoyed a freedom of press and meeting denied to their Russian comrades, but it was in the Russian part of Poland that the potential mass base of socialism was strongest. In 1892 at a meeting in Paris was founded the Polish Socialist Party (PPS), which was intended to be a single party for all Poland, but inevitably had to be organized differently in each of the three empires. In practice Polish socialism was not and could not be united. On the one hand Polish socialists were pulled in different directions by their ties with the powerful social democratic movements of the German empire or the Habsburg monarchy. On the other hand there was disagreement between patriots and internationalists, as to whether socialism or Polish independence should be placed first. The extreme internationalist position was taken by Rosa Luxemburg, who maintained that the partition of Poland was to the advantage of the Polish workers, and that their future lay in three great socialist republics of Germany, Austria, and Russia, each based on great industrial economies and great geographical markets which would make old national boundaries and loyalties obsolete. The followers of Luxemburg broke away from PPS and formed in 1900 a separate party, the Social Democracy of the Kingdom of Poland and Lithuania (SDKPL). But even within the majority party the division remained between those who were essentially the heirs to the radical Polish insurrectionary tradition of the nineteenth century and those who looked to the international, or central European, social democratic movement. Another latent source of disunity was distrust by many Polish workers of the rather large number of Jews in the party.

During the 1880's non-socialist Polish radicalism also developed, though rather more slowly. The first important organization was the National League (*Liga Narodowa*), founded in Switzerland in 1887 by a survivor from 1863, Zygmunt Miłkowski. From 1895 the main exponent of Polish radical nationalist views was the review *Przegląd Wszechpolski*, published in Lwów. The most important of its directors was Roman Dmowski, a citizen of the Russian empire who spent several years in Austrian territory and became the leader of the National Democratic Party, which was derived from the *Liga Narodowa*, and became the main rival for the next half-century of PPS.

Polish politics were inextricably involved in international politics. The revival of political ideas among Poles was in fact largely due to the evidence, provided by the Eastern crisis of 1875–8 and the Bulgarian crisis of 1885–7, that the friendship between the three partition Powers was far from solid. Of these three Powers the strongest was Germany, which also had the most developed economy and the most advanced culture. It was, however, difficult for any Pole to put his faith in the state which was the heir to the Teutonic Knights. Moreover, Bismarck introduced in Prussia in the late 1870's a strongly anti-Polish policy, directed against the Catholic Church and designed also to subsidize the purchase by Germans of Polish landed property. This policy, which amounted to an attempt to Germanize the Polish population of Prussia, was relaxed at the beginning of the reign of William II by Chancellor von Caprivi (1890–4), but this proved a mere interlude, after which the old policy was renewed with greater energy. Austria was the most liberal of the three Powers. Poles enjoyed civil liberties, and the Polish aristocracy had influence at the court of Vienna. On the other hand Galicia was economically backward, rural over-population was reducing the peasants to dire poverty, and the tolerance extended by the Vienna government to the Ukrainians of Eastern Galicia caused extreme annoyance to Poles. Moreover, Austria was the weakest of the three Powers, and since the Austro-German Alliance of 1879 she had become ever more dependent on her northern neighbour. No effective support could be expected from Vienna against Berlin. As for Russia, her policy was undoubtedly the most oppressive of the three. On the other hand Russia was developing industrially, and there were great chances for Polish industry and trade within this great market. The Poles, with their more European outlook and comparatively high level of education and skill, could contribute greatly to their own country and to the Russian empire if only the Russian government would grant them civil liberties and reasonable national rights. These problems were of special interest to Roman Dmowski, who, writing in Austria because Russia denied him freedom of press, advised his fellow Poles to seek co-operation with the Russian people on the grounds that the main danger to the national existence of the Poles came from Germany, that Austria was too weak to help them, and that Poles need not in the long run fear russification since they possessed a higher culture and greater intelligence than Russians.[1]

Repression of Ukrainian nationalism in the Russian Ukraine continued. The social structure of the Ukrainian people hampered its political development. The landowners in the Ukraine were either Russians or Poles, the bureaucrats Russians, the incipient business class Jewish. The rapid growth of industry in the Ukraine in the 1890's brought an influx of workers from Russia, and even some Tatars, Armenians, and members of other nationalities. In Odessa and Kharkov the population was extremely mixed, and even in Kiev and Ekaterinoslav there was a large non-Ukrainian element. Thus the elements which remained definitely Ukrainian, and on which a Ukrainian

[1] Some of Dmowski's writings on these themes were collected together in a book entitled *Myśli nowoczesnego Polaka* ('Thoughts of a Modern Pole'), published in Lwów in 1904.

nationalist movement must be based, were only the peasantry and the intelligentsia. In both these strata the movement did make progress, but it is probably true that in 1900 Ukrainian national consciousness, though widely diffused, was still rather weak, and that active Ukrainian nationalism was only a minority point of view among the people of the Russian Ukraine. The political development in the Ukraine has some general resemblance to that in Russian Poland. Socialism, both Populist and Marxist, was a growing force, but Ukrainian socialists, like Polish socialists, were divided essentially into three groups—those who put Ukrainian autonomy before socialism, those who put socialism before autonomy, and those who denied any need for autonomy at all. There were socialists and non-socialists in the first illegal Ukrainian political party, the Revolutionary Ukrainian Party (RUP), founded in 1901, but this very soon split up into a number of groups.

The existence of free speech and organization in the Austrian Ukraine was essential for the development of Ukrainian nationalism in Russia. The bitter struggle with the Poles in Galicia made Ukrainian nationalism more radical and more intolerant. The influence of Drahomaniv declined because of his internationalist outlook, and in 1889 he accepted a chair at the University of Sofia in Bulgaria, which he held until his death in 1895, only visiting Galicia occasionally and sending articles for the Galician press. His successor, as the most influential Ukrainian political thinker, was Michael Hrushevsky, also Russian-born and also a historian. In 1894 a chair of Ukrainian history was founded at the University of Lwów and was given to Hrushevsky, who spent his next years in exile, bitterly attacking Russia. Hrushevsky was largely responsible for the foundation in Galicia in 1899 of the Ukrainian National Democratic Party, which was non-socialist and generally resembled its political enemy, Polish National Democracy.

The Ukrainians, like the Poles, were involved in international politics. A minority of the Ukrainians in Galicia considered themselves 'Little Russians', and hoped to be liberated by Russia from what they considered the Polish yoke. There were extreme nationalists in Russia who wished to annex Eastern Galicia, part of which had been Russian from 1809 to 1815, but this view was not accepted by the St. Petersburg government. The majority of the Ukrainians in Galicia regarded the Austrian government as their friend, though they would have liked it to support them more strongly against the Galician Poles. Some Ukrainians looked further to Berlin, hoping that the stronger German Power would one day help them to achieve independence from Russia for the whole Ukraine. At this time no German government could take such ideas seriously, but the Austrian government regarded the Ukrainians as a useful instrument against Russia. Co-operation between Ukrainians and Poles was difficult, though not completely unknown. It was most likely on a basis of socialism. Piłsudski, who had genuine sympathy for Ukrainian aspirations, had some influence in this direction when he became one of the outstanding leaders of PPS at the end of the century. The trouble was that not only were there direct conflicts of interest between Ukrainians and Poles in Galicia, but the positions of the two nations in international politics were different. Poles and Ukrainians could unite in common hostility to Russia, but Ukrainians had no desire to be drawn into an anti-German orientation, which for Poles was unavoidable.

The situation of the Jews of Russia deteriorated strikingly in the reign of Alexander III. It is possible to distinguish between two types of anti-semitism. The one was found in government circles. It came naturally to dignitaries of the Orthodox Church, accustomed to speak of the Jews as the killers of Christ. This point of view, which was widespread in western Europe until the end of the eighteenth century and survived much later in some places, was encouraged by Pobedonostsev. It was shared to some extent by both Alexander III and Nicholas II. Anti-semitism was also to be found among many, though by no means all, Russian nationalists of more secular outlook: here too there is a parallel with western Europe, not of the medieval Church but of the age of Maurras. The other type of anti-semitism was to be found in the illiterate masses, among the peasants and small officials of the regions with large Jewish populations. It was based on a crude kind of class hatred, a resentment against the minority which busied itself with money, and into whose pockets the small cash expenditures of the peasants disappeared. This kind of anti-semitism was, in the felicitous phrase of August Bebel, 'the socialism of the imbecile'.

It should be noted that this type of mass anti-semitism was strong among Ukrainians but was not characteristic of the Russian people as a whole. This is not evidence of a less brutal disposition on the part of Russians: it is merely a result of the fact that the large Jewish populations lived among Ukrainians, and that there were no such concentrations in Russia proper. Other nations of the empire, less numerous than Ukrainians but equally addicted to mass anti-semitism, were the Lithuanians, White Russians, and Bessarabian Roumanians.

The assassination of Alexander II was attributed by anti-semitic demagogues in these areas to 'the Jews'. In May 1881 there were pogroms—destruction of Jewish property, assaults on Jews, and some fatal casualties—in Elizavetgrad, Kiev, and Odessa, followed by further outbreaks in the summer, and others in Warsaw in December 1881 and in Balta in Podolia in March 1882. The authorities, to say the least, showed little sense of urgency in stopping the outrages. This attitude, however, changed when Tolstoy replaced Ignatyev as minister of the interior. Tolstoy was no more friendly to the Jews than his predecessor, but he would not tolerate disorder. Tolstoy carried out the 'Temporary Rules' which had been prepared by Ignatyev on the basis of the recommendations of commissions of provincial notables set up in August 1881 in the fifteen provinces of the Pale and in Kharkov province, to investigate 'the injurious influence of the economic activity' of the Jews, and to propose measures to 'protect the Christian population' from them. These rules forbade Jews to live, or to acquire property, outside towns or large villages, thus cooping up their growing numbers into a small area and forcing them into those same professions which they were denounced for monopolizing. In 1882 also the minister of war laid down that not more than 5 per cent. of army medical personnel might be Jews, and saw fit to assert that he had taken this action because Jewish doctors showed 'deficient conscientiousness in discharging their duties and an unfavourable influence on the sanitary service in the army'. In 1887 an upper limit was officially set to the number of Jews to be admitted to secondary schools or universities: 10 per cent. within the Pale, 3 per cent. in the two capitals, and 5 per cent. in the rest of the empire. A decree of 1889 laid down that Jews might henceforth be admitted to the Bar only by specific permission of the minister of justice: in the following decade this permission was not in practice granted. The zemstvo franchise law of 1890 denied Jews a vote in *uezd* zemstvo assembly elections, though they were obliged to pay the same zemstvo taxes as other inhabitants. In 1886 large numbers of Jewish residents were expelled from Kiev, in 1891 from Moscow, in both cases in harsh conditions. In 1894, after the establishment of the state monopoly of the sale of spirits, Jews were refused licences to sell spirits, which removed one of the most important of the few means of earning a living that were left to Jews.

The one serious attempt by the government to examine the situation of the Jews in Russia was the commission set up under Count K. I. Pahlen in February 1883, for 'the revision of current laws concerning the Jews'. The commission made its report in 1888. Its members, conservative but honest officials, reached the conclusion that it was not so much Russian society that was harmed by the Jews as the Jews who 'have a right to complain about their situation'. The report observed that

> the whole five million Jewish population of Russia, unattractive though it may appear to certain groups and individuals, is yet an integral part of Russia . . . . We are not dealing with foreigners, whose admission to Russian citizenship might be conditioned by their usefulness or uselessness to Russia. The Jews of Russia are not foreigners. For more than one hundred years they have formed a part of that same Russian Empire which has incorporated scores of other tribes, many of which count by the millions.

The only solution was to bring Jews and Russians closer together by enabling Jews to live and feel as Russians. 'The system of repressive and discriminating measures must give way to a graduated system of emancipatory and equalising laws.'[1] But the commission's views were not implemented.

It was inevitable that the Jews, subjected to discrimination in addition to the poverty and the denial of liberty which they shared with all Russian subjects, should have been politically discontented; and that, having, as a result of the artificial social structure within which they were confined, a disproportionately swollen intelligentsia—including not only an educated *élite* but

[1] Quoted in S. M. Dubnow, *History of the Jews in Russia and Poland* (Philadelphia, 1916), pp. 367–8.

also far more numerous half-educated aspirants to a culture which was denied them—they should be especially susceptible to revolutionary ideas. There were many Jews in the Populist movement of the 1870's. In the late 1880's and 1890's Marxist socialism became influential among the Jews of the Vilna area. In 1897 was formed the Jewish social democratic organization, usually known as the *Bund*[1] which played an important part in the development of the Russian social democratic movement.

The alternative to revolutionary socialism for the discontented and deprived Russian Jews was nationalism, the determination to assert their national as well as their religious identity as Jews. From this determination came Zionism. The first landmark in this direction was the publication in 1882, in Berlin, of the pamphlet *Auto-Emancipation*, written by the Odessa Jew, Dr. Leon Pinsker. This urged the establishment of a Jewish national territory, in Palestine or in America, by the financial contributions and labour of the world Jewish community. Other groups in Russia developed these ideas. Zionism attracted world-wide attention with the publication in 1896 of *Der Judenstaat* by the Viennese Friedrich Herzl, and the first Zionist Congress in Basel in 1897.

Russification of the Baltic provinces began in earnest with the appointment of M. N. Kapustin to the curatorship of Dorpat educational district in 1883. In 1885 all primary schools in the Baltic provinces were brought under the Ministry of Education in St. Petersburg. By decree of 17 May 1887 Russian was made the language of instruction for all subjects except in the lowest classes of primary schools. In May 1889 this was made applicable also to privately owned secondary schools, in 1890 to girls' schools. In 1893 the German University of Dorpat was closed and was soon afterwards reopened with the Russian name of Yuryev University, with a largely Russian student body. In 1889 not only was the Russian judicial system introduced in the Baltic provinces, but Russian was made the language of the courts. The result was that for some years judicial business had to be conducted mainly through official interpreters. These measures naturally embittered the Germans. The blows of Russian policy were somewhat softened by the devoted labours of those members of the Baltic aristocracy who

[1] Officially, 'General Union of Jewish Workers in Russia and Poland'.

still had good connexions in high places in St. Petersburg, and used them on behalf of their compatriots. Outstanding among these was Baron Friedrich Meyendorff, marshal of nobility of Livonia from 1884 to 1908.

If the new policies hit the Germans, they can hardly be said to have benefited the Latvians and Estonians. The replacement of one foreign language by another was in itself no improvement. The efforts of the Orthodox Church to make converts affected them no less than the Germans. From 1885 onward no new Protestant church could be built without permission from the Holy Synod, which, however, placed at the disposal of Russian governors special funds for building Orthodox churches. In Riga itself a huge Orthodox cathedral was erected. All these measures had the enthusiastic support of Pobedonostsev. In general it may be said that the Russian government lost the opportunity of winning the Latvians and Estonians. It is true that the rising nationalist movements of both nations were primarily anti-German, both because the Germans had been their rulers for centuries and because the peasant majority wanted the land which belonged to German landowners. But the Russian government had no intention of giving German land to Baltic peasants. Soon the Baltic peoples began to see in the Russians an enemy no less dangerous than the Germans had been. At the turn of the century a liberal nationalism was emerging among both Latvians and Estonians, which aimed not at independent states but at guarantees of individual and national rights in the face of both Germans and Russians. The mouthpiece of such ideas in Estonia was the newspaper *Postimees*, directed by Jaan Tonisson. Socialism was also gaining ground, especially in the growing port and industrial centre of Riga. A Latvian Social Democratic Party was founded in 1904.

The Lithuanians, the southern neighbours of the Latvians, were close to them in language, but were bound by their religion to the Poles. The first signs of nationalism came with the development of the written language. The pioneer in this field was Dr. Jonas Basanovicius, who edited, in Tilsit across the Prussian border, a newspaper entitled *Aushra* ('Dawn'). At the end of the century there were about two million Lithuanians in the Russian empire, comprising a majority of the population in the provinces of Kovno and Suvalki and substantial minorities in the provinces of Vilna and Kurland. There were also 200,000 Lithuanians in Prussia, most of whom were Protestants. Lithuanian national consciousness was most advanced in Suvalki province. It was also influenced by Lithuanian emigrants in the United States, of whom there may have been as many as a million. Some Lithuanian priests had Lithuanian nationalist sympathies, others had Polish, but the Catholic Church as such in Lithuania was not committed either way. The Russian authorities made little effort to support Lithuanian aspirations against the Poles.

In Finland the situation of the Swedish minority among the Finnish majority superficially resembled that of the German minority among the Latvian and Estonian majorities. The Finns were, however, better educated and more politically awake than the Baltic peoples, and the Swedes were more willing to retreat before their demands. During the 1880's and 1890's Finland developed a modern industry, especially timber and textiles. Some Russian industrialists were alarmed by the competition of Finnish goods, and caused the Russo-Finnish tariff to be revised in 1885 and in 1897 to protect Russian industry. Commercial hostility was an important factor in the adoption of a policy of russification in Finland, the intolerant passion of St. Petersburg bureaucrats for uniformity was another. The first sign of a new course in St. Petersburg was a manifesto of 1890 placing the Finnish post under the Imperial postal system. No further moves were made for some years. In 1898 General N. I. Bobrikov was appointed governor-general. His first major blow to Finnish interests was the introduction of five years' military service for Finns, who might be drafted to Russian units, while Russian officers might be placed in command of Finnish units. From the Russian point of view it appeared reasonable that Finns, who enjoyed the protection of the Russian empire, should contribute to its defence. Hitherto they had had extremely light military duties—a total obligation of ninety days' service spread over three years—and the whole Finnish army amounted to only 5,600 men. Now they were being asked to do no more than was required of every Russian subject. But the Finnish point of view was that Finland was not part of the Russian empire, and that Alexander I had recognized its separate status. Finland, as a separate state linked with

Russia only by the fact that its grand duke was also Russian emperor, should not be forced to adopt Russian institutions. But this was precisely what the Russian nationalists in St. Petersburg wanted.

The crisis went one stage further with the proclamation in February 1899 of another manifesto which declared that laws of the Russian empire would have precedence in Finland over laws of the Finnish Diet. This was essentially a claim that the Diet was a mere provincial assembly, and Finland a province of Russia. Opposition was universal. Finns and Swedes united in passive resistance. Pastors refused to proclaim the law in their churches, judges refused to carry it out, conscripts refused to obey the call to service. Bobrikov brought in Russian officials to carry out his orders and directly took over the higher levels of the government service, the post, and railways. The Russian language was introduced into the administration. In April 1903 he suspended the constitution. A few leaders of the Old Finnish Party, the extreme right wing in Finnish politics, supported him, since at least they could expect that he would destroy the last remnants of Swedish influence, against which they had long fought. But the main moderate party, the Young Finns, combined with the Swedish Party in opposition to him, while the growing Social Democratic Party was equally hostile. Another group, the Party of Active Resistance, urged armed struggle and assassination. One of its followers, Eugen Schaumann, shot Bobrikov in June 1904. Finland was virtually in a state of war with Russia.

Not content with making enemies of the loyal Germans and Finns and the previously passive Latvians and Estonians, the Russian government proceeded also to antagonize its most enthusiastic friends in the south, the Armenians. Once the Caucasus had been pacified, Armenian help was no longer so useful, and Armenian desires to liberate their kinsmen under Ottoman rule were an embarrassment now that the Russian government, preoccupied by Far Eastern affairs, wished to establish peaceful relations with the Ottoman empire. Prince A. M. Dondukov-Korsakov, who became governor-general of the Caucasus in 1882, decided to close about 500 parish schools maintained by the Armenian Church in 1885, but repealed this decision the following year.

Meanwhile the situation of the Armenians in Turkey grew rapidly worse. In the eastern provinces of the Ottoman empire Kurdish irregular cavalry and Armenian armed bands fought, tortured, and massacred each other. The Armenians fared worst, as the Kurds were supported by the Sultan's government. An Armenian revolutionary party, *Dashnaktsutyun*, conducted the struggle and caused an international scandal in 1896 by the seizure of the Ottoman Bank's head office in Constantinople. This did not, as its organizers had hoped, lead to effective pressure by the Great Powers for reforms in Turkey. Diplomatic consultations and manœuvres occurred, but the Armenians derived no advantage from them. The massacres continued on a larger scale. The *Dashnaktsutyun* leadership was moved to Russian Armenia. Disliking revolutionary activity of any sort, the Russian government saw no reason to make an exception for Armenian revolutionaries simply because they professed devotion to Russia. Determined to avoid complications with Turkey, they began to treat the indigenous Armenian population as 'separatist' and 'unreliable'.

Armenian social and cultural life under Russia was centred on the Gregorian Church, which maintained a network of schools supported by the contributions of the faithful and jointly directed by parish priests and elected laymen. In January 1896 the curator of the Caucasus educational district, K. P. Yanovsky, decided to close these schools and to replace them by Russian schools under the Ministry of Education. The cost of the new schools was to be met by the confiscation of that part of the funds of the Gregorian Church which had previously been used for education. Next year the commander-in-chief, Prince Gregory Golitsyn, decided to go one better and to confiscate the whole fund of the Church. This measure was postponed owing to hesitation in St. Petersburg. At last, however, it was approved and a decree to that effect was issued on 12 June 1903. The Armenians reacted by a passive resistance not unlike that of the Finns. Schools, law-courts, and public administration were boycotted by the population, and unofficial organizations were created to perform these functions. Unable to break this resistance, the Russian authorities resorted to a new type of pogrom. The Armenians' enemies, the Moslem Tatars of Azerbaidjan, were encouraged to attack Armenian fellow citizens and sack their property. This was most successful in cities where the Armenians formed the bulk of the shopkeepers and artisans, occupying much the same status and arousing much the same sort of social envy, as the Jews in the towns of the Pale. The pogrom of February 1905 in Baku caused loss of life and property on a large scale. In rural areas fighting between Tatars and Armenians took the form of guerrilla warfare.

In the Volga valley missionary rivalry between Russian Orthodox and Tatar Moslems for the conversion or reconversion of the smaller peoples of the area was intensified in the 1880's. The efforts of Ilyminsky had the strong support of Pobedonostsev. By the time of his death in 1891 his Converted Tatars' School had founded 128 schools in Kazan province for missionary education among non-Russian peoples, the Central Chuvash School in Simbirsk had founded more than 100 Chuvash schools, and a Central Votyak School had just been set up in Urzhum *uezd* of Vyatka province.[1] At the turn of the century there were estimated to be about 110,000 Christian Tatars and a further 40,000 who had once been converted to Christianity but had reverted to Islam.

In Kazan province alone the 1897 census showed 675,419 Tatars out of a total of 3,737,627 Tatars in the whole empire. The small peoples of the Volga and Vyatka Basins amounted to nearly 3,000,000 persons (1,023,841 Mordvins, 843,755 Chuvash, 420,970 Votyaks, 375,439 Cheremyss, and 258,309 Zyryans).[2] The Votyaks were overwhelmingly Christian, but Moslem missionaries were making converts among them. The Christian missionaries were pleased with their results among the Chuvash. The Cheremyss were at the turn of the century about one-third Christian, one-third Moslem, and one-third pagan.

The ambivalent attitude of Ilyminsky, who regarded himself as a protector of the small peoples, yet also stood for russification, can be seen from two quotations from 1891, the last year of his life.

For a long time past the education of non-Russians has aroused hatred and insults of various kinds from various directions, and the

[1] S. V. Chicherina, *O privolzhskikh inorodtsakh i sovremennom znachenii sistemy N. I. Il'minskogo* (SPB, 1906), pp. 28–29.

[2] Ibid., p. 3. Census figures in *Obshchii svod perepisi*, ii. 10, 11, 12, 30.

longer it has continued the more they have grown. There are people who are almost waiting for my death in the belief that I am the only bulwark and defence of the non-Russians.[1]

In a letter of 27 June to Pobedonostsev he wrote:

This is the dilemma: If, from fear of the separate nationalities, we do not allow the non-Russians to use their language in schools and churches, on a sufficient scale to ensure a solid, complete, convinced adoption of the Christian faith, then all the non-Russians will be fused into a single race by language and by faith—the Tatar and Mohammedan. But if we allow the non-Russian languages, then, even if their individual nationalities are thus maintained, these will be diverse, small, ill disposed to the Tatars and united with the Russian people by the unity of their faith. Choose! But I believe that such diverse nationalities cannot have any solid existence, and in the end the very historical movement of life will cause them to fuse with the Russian people.[2]

The Tatars of course greatly resented Russian missionary activities both among their own people and among the neighbouring small peoples, which they considered should be subject to their Moslem culture rather than to the Russian. The Moslem missionaries held their own in the struggle. At the same time the social structure and mental attitudes of the Tatars themselves were changing. In Kazan were growing both a prosperous merchant class, enriched by trade with Central Asia, and a modern intelligentsia, attracted by secular culture and European ideas. The Tatar merchant and school-teacher formed the nucleus of Moslem nationalism in the Russian empire, which from the 1880's became a serious force.

The single most important figure in this movement, however, was a Crimean Tatar, Ismail Bey Gaspirali. Born in 1851, educated in a school in Moscow, he travelled in France and Turkey, became a schoolmaster in 1875, and was elected mayor of the ancient Tatar capital of Bakhche Saray. In 1881 he published a book in Russian, entitled 'The Moslems of Russia' (*Russkoe musulmanstvo*). In it he proclaimed a programme of modernization for Russian Moslems, including the emancipation of women, a national press in a single Turkic language,

[1] Quoted in Chicherina, op. cit., p. 18.

[2] Quoted in A. A. Vozkresensky, *O sisteme prosveshcheniya inorodtsev* (Kazan, 1913), pp. 38–40.

and the creation of a national Turkic intelligentsia. This was a programme not of Pan-Islamism (though Gaspirali was a pious Moslem), but of Pan-Turkism. The secular category of language was being stressed, together with religion, as a factor determining national identity and national consciousness. Gaspirali believed that a single language could be developed for all Turkic peoples. The word 'Turk', which in the Ottoman empire still had a plebeian and derogatory quality, was being proudly claimed as the name of a nation. Gaspirali proclaimed the principle of 'Turkdom' (*tçürkülük*). One of his slogans was 'Unity in language, thought and work' (*Dilde, fikirde, işte birlik*). In April 1883 he published the first number of a bilingual newspaper, entitled 'The Interpreter' (*Tercümen* in Turkish, *Perevodchik* in Russian), which became widely read in the Russian and Ottoman empire by the small but growing intelligentsia. Still more important, Gaspirali founded a model school on modern principles, with a mainly secular curriculum in place of the traditional Moslem religious curriculum. Gaspirali's 'new method' was quickly copied, and by 1914 it was in force in about 5,000 Moslem schools in the empire.[1]

Gaspirali's Crimean compatriots responded favourably to his ideas, but there were too few of them to make much impression. The total Tatar population in the peninsula was less than 200,000 and formed a majority in only one *uezd*, Yalta. It was in the Volga valley that the modern democratic secular nationalism which he preached made real progress, and Kazan was its centre. He also had some success in Azerbaidjan, and individual disciples even in Central Asia. His attempt to forge a single Turkic literary language proved unsuccessful, but his newspaper played an important part in informing Russian and Ottoman Moslems of each other's affairs, and in spreading the idea that there was a common Turkic cause, from Bakhche Saray to Samarkand and from Kazan to the Aegean.

By contrast, Central Asia remained a colonial territory with no political life, but the changes in social life brought about by the Russian conquest made possible the later development of

[1] S. A. Zenkorsly, *Pan-Turkism and Islam in Russia* (Harvard, 1960), p. 35. This figure is based on Ministry of Education Statistics and on the Moslem press. It must be treated with caution. The units described as 'school' for this purpose varied greatly in number of pupils and quality of teaching. Certainly only a minority of Moslem schools in the empire adopted the 'new method'.

national consciousness among its people. As a result of the labours of an investigating commission of 1884, whose chairman was Count N. P. Ignatyev, the powers of the governor-general were somewhat reduced, more weight was given to the representatives of the normal civil departments of government, and the Russian judicial system was introduced. In 1882 a separate governor-generalship of the Steppes was set up, consisting of the provinces of Akmolinsk, Semipalatinsk, Uralsk, Turgai, and Semirechie. In 1890 Transcaspia was separated from the Caucasus and placed directly under the Ministry of War. In 1898 both Transcaspia and Semirechie were transferred to the governor-generalship of Turkestan. The main material achievements of the last two decades of the century were the introduction of cotton production on a large scale and the building of railways. American upland cotton was planted for the first time in 1883. In 1902 it was grown on an area of nearly 200,000 *desyatin*, and in 1901 nearly 7,000,000 poods of cotton were exported from Central Asia. The first major railway was built from the Caspian coast to Kyzyl Arvat in 1881, was extended to the Amu Darya river in 1886, and reached Samarkand in 1887. In 1900 it was decided to build a railway from Orenburg to Tashkent, and this was completed in 1906.

There was no deliberate policy of russification in Central Asia, but Russian influence was increased by the immigration of Russian civilians and the foundation of some Russian schools. The city of Tashkent already in 1889 had about 20,000 Russian inhabitants in addition to about 100,000 Asians. There was talk of settling Russian peasants in the countryside, but this became serious only in the new century. Schools were set up for the Russian families in the cities—largely officials and railwaymen. The traditional system of Islamic schools was allowed to function as before. There was little demand for modern schools from the Asian population, and little enthusiasm on the part of Russian officials to provide their new subjects with the blessings of modern culture.

The exception was Ilyminsky, who had served from 1858 to 1861 on the Orenburg Border Commission, got to know the Kazakhs, became aware of their mistrust for his old opponents the Tatars and of the unorthodoxy and instability of their Moslem beliefs, and saw an opportunity for his mixture of philanthropy and russification. He was able to arrange for the education of some young Kazakhs in Orenburg and Omsk. One of these, Ibrahim Altynsarin, later became provincial inspector of schools in Turgai province of the governor-generalship of the Steppes, and set up primary schools and a Kazakh teachers' training college. In the next decades two types of school were developed. One was the *aul* school, at elementary level, which moved about with an *aul*, or group of families, during the summer pastoral migrations, and settled in one place during the winter. At a higher level was the two-class 'Russian-Kirgiz school', in which Russian and Kazakh children were taught together, and from which a Kazakh child could graduate to a Russian city school or to the Kazakh Teachers' Training College. In 1897 there were 71 Russian-Kirgiz schools in Turgai province with 2,000 pupils. In the other provinces of the Kazakh Steppes the number was much smaller. But these schools provided the first generation of a modern Kazakh intelligentsia.

In Turkestan the first Russian primary school for Asians was opened in Tashkent in 1884. By 1900 there were 25 such schools in the Syr Darya province with 722 pupils. In 1906 in the whole of Turkestan there were 85 of these schools. However, educational effort was primarily on behalf of resident Russians. Between 1879 and 1904 the Tashkent Teachers' Training College trained 415 teachers, but only 65 of these were Asians.

The population remained obedient and quiet once the conquest had been completed. The only serious outbreak of violence occurred in south-eastern Turkestan in 1898, when a Sufi religious leader, who called himself the Ishan Mohammed Ali, declared a holy war against the Russians, made preparations for an insurrection of which the Russians were unaware, collected a following of about 2,000 persons, and massacred 50 Russian soldiers sleeping in camp in Andizhan. The rising was quickly suppressed and the Ishan hanged.

Not many Moslems in Turkestan had any interest in modern political ideas. But there were just a few who read *Tercümen* and welcomed Gaspirali's 'new method' in education. The first school of this type in Turkestan was opened in Taskhent in 1901, the second in Samarkand in 1903.

XIV

SOCIAL DEVELOPMENT

Agriculture

During the last decades of the century Russian agriculture stagnated. The peasants not only formed the vast majority of those engaged in farming but already in 1880 held more than half the arable land. Improvement in agriculture depended on improvement in the farming methods of the peasants. But progress in these years was negligible. The vast majority of peasants had neither the knowledge nor the resources to improve their farming, and the government made little effort to assist them. The government's economic policy was directed towards industrialization and to such financial measures as would facilitate this aim. The motive for industrialization was itself largely non-economic: it was rightly felt that Russia could not be a Great Power in the modern world unless she were industrialized, and in the views of the Tsar and his ministers Great Power status came before all else.

The peasants therefore received little help from the government: on the contrary, it was felt to be the peasants' duty to help the government by paying taxes, redemption dues, and customs tariffs, in short by paying the main share of the cost of industrialization.

Agriculture thus remained backward. The three-field rotation remained predominant throughout Russia, even if there were some limited areas in which more advanced methods were used. Thus, one-third of the arable land of most of the country was always fallow. Ploughs and other agricultural instruments were primitive, and modern machinery was found only on a few of the most efficiently managed nobles' estates. Fragmentation of holdings increased every year, as each new family had to have pieces of land of different quality in different parts of the village lands. The result was that it was quite frequent in central Russia for holdings to be divided into 30 or 40 strips. There were cases in Yaroslavl province of as many as 120 strips. Much land was also wasted in the form of paths enabling peasants to move between their strips without walking over their neighbours' precious plots.[1]

It was claimed that the average output of grains in the decade 1861–70 was 29 poods per *desyatin* per year, and that this had increased to 39 as an average for the period 1891–1900. The official commission of 1901, quoting this figure, expressed scepticism as to its accuracy.[2] Even if correct, it compares poorly with the increase in agricultural output in a comparable period of time in Japan.[3] The Japanese government, in the decades after the Meiji Restoration, taxed the agricultural population ruthlessly, but it did put some of the money back into agriculture. As an approximate comparison with other countries at the end of the century, we may quote an estimate by an American expert that the average yield per acre in the years 1898–1902 was 8·8 bushels in European Russia, 13·9 in the United States, and 35·4 in Great Britain.[4]

At the turn of the century Russia was suffering from relative rural overpopulation. It is of course obvious that in the most literal sense Russia was very sparsely populated: the greater part of her vast land mass had hardly any inhabitants at all. But if we take the amount of arable land under cultivation, the number of persons employed in agriculture and their dependants, and the output per unit of cultivated land, the result is that more people were producing less per unit of land than in countries of more advanced agriculture with a much higher general density of population, such as Denmark or France. The same output could have been produced by a much smaller

[1] Article by V. Sudeykin in *Brockhaus*, xxxviii. 540–1, on 'cherespolositsa'. Writing at the end of the 1890's, the author noted that there were no general and reliable statistics on this phenomenon.

[2] The commission of 16 November 1901 was charged with investigating the situation of agriculture in the central agricultural region. Quoted in Robinson, *Rural Russia under the Old Régime*, pp. 98, 290.

[3] According to the best available estimate based on Japanese statistics—which were admittedly open to some objections, yet not less satisfactory than the Russian statistics available in the 1880's—the output of all agricultural products more than doubled between 1881–90 and 1911–20, while that of agricultural foodstuffs increased by more than 80 per cent. See W. W. Lockwood, *The Economic Development of Japan* (1955), pp. 85–90.

[4] I. M. Rubinow, in *Bulletin of Bureau of Statistics*, U.S. Department of Agriculture, no. 42, 1906, 'Russia's Wheat Surplus', Robinson, op. cit., p. 290 (footnote reference 24).

number of people. Various attempts were made by Russian agricultural experts to estimate the surplus of labour in Russian agriculture, but they were based on such inadequate evidence and such questionable definitions of terms, and led to such different results, that they are not worth quoting here. It is, however, possible to identify the region in which the pressure of population was greatest. It was the central black-earth area—the south-eastern provinces of Russia proper and the north-eastern Ukraine. Individual provinces with a high pressure of population included Chernigov, Poltava, Kursk, Kharkov, Oryol, and Tambov. It was also clear that this problem was bound to become more serious every year, as the population grew.

In 1905 allotment land amounted to 138,767,587 *desyatin* or 35·1 per cent. of the usable land in 50 provinces of European Russia. Land belonging to the state, Church, municipalities and other institutions amounted to 154,689,513 *desyatin* or 39·1 per cent. Privately owned land totalled 101,735,343 *desyatin* or 25·8 per cent.[1] By far the greater part of the second category consisted of non-arable land, especially forests. Essentially the arable land of European Russia was divided between the first and third categories.

All the allotment land was held by peasants. Its total had increased by 21,000,000 *desyatin* since 1877.

Of the private land, that held by the nobility was now 53,169,008 *desyatin*. Various urban groups held 20,432,871 *desyatin*.[2] Peasants held 13,214,025 *desyatin* in individual ownership, 7,654,006 in the form of ownership by communes, and 3,729,352 as the property of peasant associations. Thus, noble landowners held nearly 20 million *desyatin* less than in 1877, urban groups held nearly 8 million more, and peasants held more than 24 million more. The combined increase of land held by the peasants, in the two categories of allotment land and

[1] These figures come from *Ezhegodnik Rossii 1914*, the annual publication of the Central Statistical Committee (Petrograd, 1915), part vi, pp. 3–5. The figures are not exactly comparable with those for 1877 quoted above, p. 404. For the differences, see Robinson, op. cit., pp. 288–90. It seems most useful in the present context to give the official figures, without attempting to process them or to explain in detail the discrepancies between them. They show the general picture.

[2] Of these, 12,906,795 were held by merchants or 'honoured citizens', 3,763,822 by *meshchane*, and 3,762,254 by commercial and industrial associations.

privately owned land, amounted to over 45 million *desyatin*, nearly as much as all the land still privately owned by the nobility. The total holdings by peasants (allotment, private, and co-operative) amounted to about two-thirds of the arable land.

But these gains did not satisfy the peasants' need for land, or for some means of a living, least of all in the overpopulated provinces. One solution was to rent land from a noble landowner. Competition for land tended over the years to drive rents up, and the peasants, renting small pieces of land in addition to their own small holdings in a desperate struggle to earn enough to support their families and pay off their taxes and redemption dues, were forced to extract the last pound of crops from the soil by the primitive means available to them. These methods were of course bad for the soil. Rents were paid sometimes in cash and sometimes in the form of a share of the crop. The latter was more usual with the poorer tenants, and it was often felt, both by tenants and by outside observers, that this system of 'labour rent' (*otrabotochnaya sistema*) differed but little from the old system of *barshchina* under serfdom.

There were also two other kinds of renting relationship. One was the case of poor peasants, who leased the whole of their holding to a richer neighbour, and went to earn their living as wage-workers in agriculture or in industry. The other was the case of rich peasants who rented large pieces of land from landowners and farmed them together with their own substantial holdings. Such persons became efficient large farmers, making a good living from agriculture on capitalist principles. There were not many of them but their numbers were increasing.

Employment as agricultural labourers on the large estates was an important source of income. The census of 1897 showed 1,837,000 agricultural labourers. With family dependants, this figure would be more than doubled. Agricultural labour was in demand chiefly in the southern and south-eastern provinces, in New Russia, and in the lower Volga provinces, and mostly in the harvest season. Crafts were an important source of income to peasants, chiefly in the central provinces. Casual short-term labour in factories was also available, but was poorly paid. Apart from this, a growing number of children of peasants moved to the cities and became permanent industrial workers.

Search for employment led to large-scale movements of labour within European Russia in two main directions—towards the industrial region around Moscow and towards the expanding agricultural regions of New Russia and the North Caucasus. In the late 1890's these movements were overshadowed by the still larger emigration to Siberia and the Steppes of Kazakhstan.

All opportunities available were used, but the natural preference of the peasant was to acquire more land in his home area. The largest single source of the land was the nobility. The government absolutely refused to consider a redistribution of nobles' land, but it was prepared to go some way in helping peasants to buy land. The Peasants' Land Bank, under the Ministry of Finance, began operations in April 1883, and made loans to individual peasants or communes. It contributed substantially to the purchases made by peasants during the next twenty years. In 1885 the government, alarmed at the amount of land which had passed out of the possession of the nobility since the emancipation, founded a Nobles' Land Bank, also under the Ministry of Finance, which was to make loans to noble landowners at a rate substantially more favourable than that granted by the Peasants' Bank, in order to help them keep their lands. The purposes of the two institutions appeared to conflict with each other, except that both could perhaps try to limit the acquisition by townsmen of nobles' land. In any case, the movement of nobles' land into other hands was not arrested, though possibly it would have been more rapid without the bank's action. By 1904 the Nobles' Bank had advanced loans to the total of 707,000,000 roubles, and a third of the land still held by nobles was mortgaged to it. In 1894 the rate of interest charged by the two banks was equalized.

Unwilling to put more money into agriculture, to lighten the burden of taxation on the peasants, or to redistribute nobles' land, the government had two further possibilities for improving the lot of the peasants. The first was to facilitate colonization in Asiatic Russia. The second was to reconsider the merits or defects of communal and individual tenure.

In the 1880's the government did not favour emigration to Siberia. Permission had to be requested and was not easily obtained. A certain number of illegal migrants, however, found their way across the Urals. On 13 July 1889 a new migration law was published, which required emigrants to obtain permission from the Ministry of the Interior or the Ministry of State Properties, and provided for some small financial aid and for some remission of taxation and postponement of military service. In the next three years the flow of migrants barely increased. With the decision to build the Trans-Siberian Railway,[1] however, the government's attitude changed. As so often in changes of Russian economic policy, a non-economic and strategic factor was decisive. It was now felt necessary to populate Asiatic Russia, especially the region through which the railway was to pass. The senior official A. N. Kulomzin, who as administrator of affairs of the committee on the Siberian railway was in effect in charge of government development policy, made a tour of Siberia in the summer of 1896. On his return the government set up a new office to encourage and supervise colonization—the Resettlement Administration in the Ministry of the Interior. In the next years this organization worked hard to provide accurate information about the available lands in Asia, to facilitate journeys by individual members of families to explore conditions on the spot, and to organize reception for settlers when they arrived. Conditions were certainly rough, the journey was painful, and many bureaucratic muddles occurred. But colonization went rapidly ahead, and most of the families which migrated were able to set themselves up in better conditions than they could have attained at home. In every year from 1896 to 1900 the number of persons migrating surpassed 200,000 and in the next three years it was more than 100,000.

The controversy between supporters and opponents of communal tenure had never died down since the 1850's. In the first decades after the emancipation government policy had not been committed to either view. In the 1880's, however, the Ministry of the Interior, under Tolstoy, became a stronghold of champions of the commune. Their motives were not so much economic as ideological. They maintained that the commune was the centre of loyal conservative peasant feeling, and that the existence of a commune which assured some land to all its members was a guarantee against the formation in Russia of a proletariat. Criticism of the commune came chiefly from the

[1] See below p. 581.

Ministry of Finance, and was advanced mainly on economic grounds. It was held that the economic weaknesses of Russian agriculture were due to communal tenure, and that progress could come only if individual peasant enterprise were encouraged. This line of argument can to some extent also be regarded as ideological since it corresponded to the general doctrine of capitalist free enterprise of which the Ministry of Finance was the exponent in official quarters. The ranks of the revolutionary opponents of the government were also divided in regard to the role of communal tenure. It was in the 1880's that the theoretical arguments between the Populist and Marxist branches of socialism in Russia became clear and were expressed, in muted tones, in the legal press. The Populists upheld the commune, believing, as Chernyshevsky had believed twenty years earlier, that it could be transformed after the coming revolution into the basic organ of socialist government in the countryside. The Marxists opposed the commune as a relic of an obsolete stage of social development. In their view capitalism must triumph in the whole economy before there could be a chance of socialist revolution: they therefore welcomed the development of Russian capitalism, and wished for the speedy disappearance of the commune. There was thus a certain identity of views, for quite contradictory motives, between Populists and officials of the Ministry of the Interior, and between Marxists and officials of the Ministry of Finance. The first two supported it, the second two opposed it. On the other hand the Ministry of the Interior and Marxists agreed that the commune was a bulwark of the old order which caused the former to defend it and the latter to attack it. Conversely, Ministry of Finance and Populists agreed that capitalism would strengthen the autocratic régime, which caused the former to promote it and the latter to resist it. Both Populists and Marxists, of course, rightly regarded the Ministry of the Interior as the main stronghold of the régime which was their enemy, the main fortress of political and social reaction. But the Ministry of Finance fought against the Ministry of the Interior because it believed that its policies, far from strengthening the régime, were undermining it.

Public attention was painfully directed to agriculture in 1891 when there was famine in the provinces of Central Russia. Its immediate cause was a crop failure, but the effects of the poor harvest were made disastrous by the fact that the heavy taxation policy of the previous years had deprived the peasants of such reserves, in cash or in food, as they had had in the early 1880's. The government's reaction was to try further to strengthen the commune. A law of 8 June 1893 tried to meet one of the main criticisms against communal tenure—that the prospect of redistribution deprived peasants of any incentive to improve their holdings—by fixing a minimum of twelve years between general redistributions and forbidding partial redistributions. A further law of 14 December 1893 forbade mortgaging of peasant land, and provided that even privately owned peasant land might be sold only to persons who belonged to the village community, or were willing, if they bought the land, to become members. The same law made more difficult the application of Article 165 of the Emancipation Statute. It laid down that even if a peasant paid off his full redemption debt, he might not claim a consolidated holding of his own unless a two-thirds majority of the village assembly agreed to it. This blow to individual farming was the more unfortunate as in the last years peasants had been making increased, even if not very extensive, use of Article 165: between 1882 and 1887 it had been invoked in regard to 53,678 allotments with an area of 216,504 *desyatin*—substantially more than in the preceding twenty years.[1] In 1894 the Ministry of State Properties was reorganized as the Ministry of Agriculture and State Properties, and its general powers in the encouragement of agricultural improvement were strengthened. However, its authority was still much weaker in areas where serfdom had prevailed than in areas which had been state lands before 1861. The Ministry of the Interior still exercised great power over agricultural Russia through the land commandants who were its subordinate officials.

In 1898, according to the latest information of the Ministry of Agriculture and State Properties, in 50 provinces of European Russia there were 80,160,000 *desyatin* in communal tenure and 22,260,000 *desyatin* in individual tenure.[2] In the northern and central provinces communal tenure was almost universal.

[1] Article 'Vykupnaya operatsiya' in *Brockhaus*, vii. 513–17.

[2] Article 'Pozemel'naya obshchina', by I. Miklashevsky in *Brockhaus*, xxiv. 212–20.

The situation of Russian agriculture did not improve in the last years of the century, criticisms from both central and local government increased, and the evidence of discontent in the countryside and of sporadic revolutionary activity both within Russia and from abroad could not be ignored. Official complacency about the commune began to wear thin. In 1900 a commission was set up, attached to the central administration of the Ministry of the Interior, to examine the situation of the peasantry.[1] On 22 January 1902 the minister of finance, S. Y. Witte, was placed at the head of a Special Commission on the Needs of the Agricultural Industry, and he in turn asked for information from local committees of experts in the *uezd* and provinces. The committees were appointed not by the zemstvos but by the governors, but among their members were many persons active in zemstvo work. Though the whole cumbrous enterprise produced no immediate results of importance, the reports of the committees and of the commission itself contain valuable information on the state of rural Russia and the opinions prevalent about it at the turn of the century.

No clear consensus about communal tenure emerged from the local committees. It could be argued that a majority were in favour if this meant that they were against forcible abolition of the commune, or against if it meant that they were in favour of substantial modification of the institution as it was. It was pointed out that *cherespolositsa* was to be found under both forms of tenure. There was a good deal of support for the argument that redistribution was a disincentive to improvement, though the keenest champions of the commune argued that this was more than compensated by the social justice of the principle. Some opponents of the commune, however, maintained that it did not ensure equality at all, since village assemblies were controlled by the richer and more influential peasants (known as *miroyedy* or 'commune-eaters'), who exacted a tribute of gifts

[1] Other commissions on agriculture appointed in these years included one headed by the vice-minister of finance, V. I. Kovalevsky, on the economic decline of the central provinces (1899); another, under V. N. Kokovtsov, on the relationship of the decline of the central provinces to economic conditions in other parts of the empire (1901); and an examination, from 1902 onwards, by the land department of the Ministry of the Interior, headed by V. I. Gurko, of all existing legislation relating to the peasants. For details see V. I. Gurko, *Features and Figures of the Past* (Stanford, 1939), pp. 207–11.

from the poorer peasants in return for favours.[1] A member of the Samara province committee argued that differentiation between rich and poor was going ahead behind a mask of alleged peasant equality. In fact the poorer peasants would not be worse off if forced out of the village into industry or agricultural wage labour. 'In the sense of the general prosperity of the country . . . open stratification is better than the gradual stratification described above which, with the exception of a small handful of rich, keeps the vast mass of peasants in the position of householders working at a loss.'[2]

One of the subjects discussed at length by the main commission was the separate status of the *volost* court. The minister of justice, N. V. Muravyov, gave it as his opinion that 'the *volost* court in the sphere of civil law creates complete confusion and bewilderment in the juridical ideas of the population: the *volost* court does not make a reality of the rights of the peasants and is not capable of doing so'.[3] The most that could be said in defence of the court was that neither the funds nor the trained personnel were yet available to do what the majority of the commission recognised as desirable—to incorporate the peasants in the general legal system of the country. The commission decided to recommend its abolition and its replacement, wherever and as soon as practical conditions permitted, by an all-class, general, competent, and independent court.

Beneath the discussion of real and important economic, technical, and legal problems was the ideological conflict between the doctrines of capitalism and paternalism. Two quotations may illustrate this.

'Russia in one respect forms an exception among all the countries of the world', said Witte at one session of the commission of which he was chairman. 'Systematically, for more than two generations, the people have been brought up in the absence of any notion of property and legality.' The peasants know the land was once taken from the nobility and given to the commune, now the population has grown and so, they argue, more land must be taken from the nobility and given to the

[1] Observations of Yevreinov, session of 26 Jan. 1905, in *Protokoly po krest'yanskomu delu*, SPB, 1905.

[2] *Trudy mestnykh komitetov o nuzhdakh sel'skokhozyaistvennoy promyshlennosti* (SPB, 1905), *Samarskaya guberniya*, p. 473.

[3] *Protokoly po krest'yanskomu delu*, session of 5 Jan. 1905, p. 7.

commune. 'By emancipating the peasants, the state gave them land, but for their use, not as their personal property. Then the peasantry remained separated from all other classes in administration and in justice. Essentially the peasants had no system of justice granted them but merely got a crude form of settling accounts in the *volost* court.' In areas of individual tenure, however, a sense of property did exist. A governor of one such province said to Witte: 'The peasants reason like this—if they begin to take land away from the landowners, they may take it away from them too.' But in areas of communal tenure, Witte believed, the peasants had but one feeling—we need more land. 'The state itself has, as it were, fostered in the peasants this idea, and it may lead to very dangerous consequences.'[1]

The opposite extreme is expressed by the marshal of nobility of Sergach *uezd* of Nizhnii Novgorod province, P. G. Boboyedov.[2] 'By destroying the Russian people's own concept of law and bringing the people closer to our intelligentsia, which is perverted and has lost its faith, it will be possible to drive the people out of its senses and to destroy all its greatness and its strength—that is to say, its faith, its sense of justice, its historical traditions, its love of country, firmness of spirit, endurance in misfortune, and devotion to the heritage of its fathers and grandfathers, by which Russia lived and was built up, and thanks to which it was able to bear on its shoulders all the internal seditions, the invasions of the Tatars, the French, and so forth.' The same writer defended the institution of land commandants and the principle of paternal tutelage over the peasants by the authorities. 'To abolish administrative supervision and the authority of the land commandant would be to throw the nation into a condition of deprivation of all its rights and to urge it to indulge in lawless, arbitrary, and irresponsible acts.'

Before the commission had completed its work, Russia was in the grip of the violence and disorder of 1905. It was dissolved by the Tsar with its business unfinished. Since it began its labours in 1902, some measures had been passed. An Imperial manifesto of 26 February 1903 had referred ambiguously to the question of land tenure. It mentioned the 'immutability of communal tenure', but also the right of individual peasants to

[1] *Protokoly po krest'yanskomu delu*, session of 12 March 1905, pp. 4–6.

[2] *Trudy mestnykh komitetov . . ., Nizhegorodskaya guberniya*, pp. 580–1.

form their own holdings apart from the commune. More useful was the law of 12 March 1903 which abolished the joint responsibility of the whole commune for the payment of redemption dues and taxes (*krugovaya poruka*), thus at least removing a built-in incentive to bad husbandry in communal villages. The *volost* court continued to exist, but a law of 11 August 1904 deprived it of the right to inflict corporal punishment.

It is not unfair to say that in the forty years since the emancipation the interests of agriculture had been neglected, and the peasants treated as beasts of burden. The backwardness of agriculture was the chief cause of the weakness of the Russian economy, and the discontent of the peasants was the chief cause of the political explosion which followed the defeat of Russia by Japan in 1905.

The National Economy

While agriculture stagnated, the other sectors of the economy made impressive progress at its expense. This was partly the result of private business initiative, but to a much greater extent than in comparable periods of the history of Western countries, it was due to the deliberate policy of the state. The central institution of government economic policy was the Ministry of Finance.

The first man to hold this post under Alexander III, N. K. Bunge, had to clear up Russia's finances after the strains of the war with Turkey. A former professor of economics at Kiev University, he had experience both of university administration and of municipal government, and held relatively liberal political views. He showed himself more concerned than perhaps any of his predecessors or successors at the ministry with the lot of the common people. He introduced Russia's first laws for the protection of industrial labour, abolished the poll-tax and salt-tax, and set up the Peasants' Land Bank. At the same time he substantially raised import duties in order to protect Russian industry, and he reverted to the earlier policy of government intervention in railway affairs by the purchase of some private lines and the construction of new state-owned lines. His resignation was brought about by his reluctance to increase the burden on the taxpayers once more in order to meet new demands for defence in connexion with the Bulgarian crisis of 1886.

His successor, I. A. Vyshnegradsky, the son of a priest and former pupil of a church seminary, began his career as a professor at the St. Petersburg Technological Institute, and later obtained experience of private business as a director of the South-Western Railway Company. He was recruited to the Ministry of Finance as an outside expert by Bunge. Vyshnegradsky set himself both to develop industry and to obtain an improved balance of trade. He had some success in obtaining loans in France, and his tenure of office marks the beginning of the long connexion of Russian state finances with the Paris money market. He increased indirect taxation, put pressure on the agricultural population to sell their crops in order to increase exports,[1] and in 1891 greatly raised import duties, making Russia the most protectionist country in the world at that time. His policies directly contributed to the famine of 1891, for they effectively deprived the peasants of any reserve to sustain them in the face of a harvest failure. Hurried relief measures used up most of the financial gains of the previous five years, and Vyshnegradsky was unable to raise a French loan at this moment owing to indignation in Paris at the recent expulsion of Jews from Moscow. These failures led to his dismissal.

The third minister of finance, Sergei Yulyevich Witte, was one of the outstanding statesmen of the nineteenth century. His father was of German or Dutch origin and Lutheran religion, and married the daughter of a governor, of the well-known Fadeyev family.[2] Sergei was brought up in the Caucasus in a Russian noble environment and in the Orthodox religion. He entered the newly created University of New Russia at Odessa in 1865 and specialized in mathematics. In 1871 he entered government service in the office of the governor-general and became an expert on railway administration. In 1877 when the

[1] By collecting taxes in the autumn, when grain prices were low, he forced the peasants to sell a larger proportion of their crops in order to raise the same amount of cash, thus increasing the amount available for export but leaving them with insufficient food to see them through the next spring. T. H. von Laue, *Sergei Witte and the Industrialisation of Russia* (New York, 1963), pp. 26–7.

[2] The war hero and Pan-Slav propagandist, General Rostislav Fadeyev, author of *Mnenie o vostochnom voprose* (SPB, 1870), was his mother's brother.

Odessa Railway was sold to a private company, he remained with it and became an employee of private business. During the following twelve years he became an extremely successful manager, and also made friends in capitalist circles, including such tycoons as the Jewish financiers Jan Bloch and L. S. Polyakov. In 1889 he accepted Vyshnegradsky's invitation to set up a new railway department within the Ministry of Finance. In 1892 he was made minister of communications, and was specially concerned with the plans for the Trans-Siberian Railway. In August 1892 he was appointed minister of Finance. He held the post until August 1903.

Witte was both a brilliant organizer and a man of broad ideas. He could move among business men and bureaucrats with equal ease, and indeed combined the outlook of both. He was not liked by the aristocracy, who regarded him as an upstart and objected to his marriage to a Jewish divorcee, and he reciprocated the hostility. His political views were uncertain and contradictory. He claimed to be devoted to the principle of autocracy, admired Alexander III, and had no use for parliamentary democracy. At the same time, he was determined to bring Russia into the modern world, and had a respect for efficiency and for rational organization which he could not fail to see were incompatible with the political and social régime of Russia as it was. The motive of his economic policy may be described as essentially non-economic: his aim was the greatness of the Russian state. He could best serve this aim by industrialization, industrialization required foreign loans and foreign investments, these could only be attracted by financial stability, and the best mark of stability was to put the rouble on a gold basis. This he achieved in 1897. He maintained high tariffs and high levels of taxation. The creation of the state spirits monopoly in 1894 proved to be good business for the government. But though he squeezed the taxpayers, Witte believed himself to be a protector of the people's interests. In his view the best thing that could be done for the peasant was to abolish the antiquated communal tenure and force Russian farming to stand up to the operation of economic laws. As for the industrial workers, he introduced in 1897 the most substantial labour laws that Russia had yet known.

The development of the national economy during the two

decades in which these men were in charge can be examined under four main headings—industrial growth, labour policy, state finances, and foreign trade, This brief survey must be concluded with some discussion of the doctrines about Russia's economic future which were current at the turn of the century.

Railway construction went ahead at moderate speed in the 1880's, increasing from 22,865 kilometres in 1880 to 30,596 in 1890. In the next fifteen years the pace was greatly accelerated: by 1904 the total length of railway track in Russia had reached 59,616 kilometres. In each of the four years 1898 to 1901 more than 3,000 kilometres were built, in 1899 5,248.[1] This was the period of the building of the Trans-Siberian Railway, but the main effort went into lines connecting the main industrial regions of European Russia with each other and with the ports.

The new railway boom provided the demand which at last got industrial development in the Ukraine moving fast. This was based not only on the coal of the Donets Basin but also on the iron ore of Krivoy Rog, which began to be thoroughly exploited at the end of the 1880's. Large metallurgical plants grew up not only in the Donets region but at a point between it and Krivoy Rog, at Ekaterinoslav on the Dnieper, served by rail communications from west and east.[2] Coal output in the south was 183,000,000 poods in 1890 and 671,600,000 in 1900. The second most important coal-bearing area in the empire in 1900 was the Dąbrowa Basin in Poland, which in that year produced 251,800,000 poods. Pig-iron production in the south in 1890 was 13,400,000 poods: it was still surpassed by the Urals with a production of 28,200,000. In 1900 the south produced 91,900,000, far ahead of the Urals, whose output had risen to 50,500,000. The same trend was to be seen in iron and steel production. The increase in the south was from 8,600,000 poods in 1890 to 75,800,000 in 1900: the increases in the three other producing areas in the empire were much smaller.[3] Indus-

[1] P. A. Khromov, *Ekonomicheskoe razvitie Rossii v XIX i XX vekakh*, p. 462.

[2] The most important were the Alexander factory on the Dnieper at Ekaterinoslav, which began working in 1887, and the Dnieper factory, in the village of Kamenskoe, 30 versts from Ekaterinoslav, which was built in 1889 and employed about 5,000 workers. R. S. Livshits, *Razmeshchenie promyshlennosti v dorevolyutsionnoy Rossii* (Moscow, 1955), p. 169.

[3] Urals 17,600,000 to 33,800,000, Moscow region 8,300,000 to 19,400,000, and Poland 7,500,000 to 22,700,000. Khromov, op. cit., pp. 456–9.

trial development and the growth of grain exports through the Black Sea ports combined to bring about large increases in the population of the cities of the Ukraine. Between 1886 and 1896 the population of Ekaterinoslav rose from 47,000 to 120,000, of Rostov-on-Don from 80,000 to 150,000, and of Odessa from 200,000 to over 350,000.

Exploitation of the petroleum wells of Azerbaidjan began in the 1880's. In 1890 production was 226,000,000 poods, in 1900 631,000,000. The completion of rail communications from Baku to Tiflis and Tiflis to Batum in 1883 made it possible to sell this petrol in the markets of the world. At the same time the Caspian and Volga waterways provided access for oil fuel to the industrial region of Moscow. Baku, at the beginning of the century the fortress city of a minor Turkish khan, had 46,000 inhabitants in 1886 and 108,000 ten years later. The other great source of mineral wealth in the Caucasus area were the manganese mines of Chiatura in Georgia, which produced more than a third of the world's output. During these years economic progress was also reflected in the growth in population of the administrative capital of the Caucasus, Tiflis, which in 1897 had 159,000 inhabitants.

Textiles still remained the largest branch of Russian industry, employing in 1904 over 600,000 workers, while the number of workers in metallurgy was over 500,000. Textile output was subject to fluctuations, and it suffered a period of depression from 1883 to 1886. But from 1890 to 1900 the production of cotton thread increased from 7,400,000 poods to 14,600,000, and of cloth from 6,700,000 to 11,700,000.[1] The cotton industry was concentrated in the provinces of Moscow and Vladimir. The town of Ivanovo-Voznesensk became the second largest single centre. The importance of St. Petersburg as a centre of the cotton industry declined relatively, though the absolute output of the capital's cotton mills did not diminish. They specialized increasingly in high quality cloths. Another big centre of textile industry in the empire was the Łódź region of Poland, which in 1900 had 14·6 per cent. of the empire's spindles and 15·6 per cent. of its looms. Competition between Moscow and Łódź was fierce. Moscow had an advantage of growing value in its access by waterways to the raw cotton of Central Asia, which in

[1] Ibid., p. 185.

1890 was already providing nearly a quarter of the needs of Russian industry. Polish cotton mills used raw cotton imported from the West.

Development of metallurgy and railways led to the rise of a Russian engineering industry, which was largely concentrated in St. Petersburg, though locomotives and railway wagons were also produced in Moscow, the Baltic provinces, and some centres in the south.

Russian observers noted that as industry grew, production was being concentrated in a small number of very large factories. In this respect Russia, being a latecomer to the process of industrialization, was following the example of more advanced countries at a more rapid pace than they had had at comparable stages of their history. For example, in the metallurgical industry in the Ukraine the average number of workers per factory in 1890 was 1,500, in 1900 4,600. Taking a much longer period, the proportion of the output of the Ivanovo textile region which was produced by factories employing more than 1,000 workers was 22·6 per cent. in 1867 and 82 per cent. in 1913.[1] The exception to this trend was the food industry, whose most important branches were the sugar factories and vodka distilleries.

With the growth of industry, organizations of industrialists came into being. In 1874 the first congress of southern mine-owners was held in Taganrog. From 1880 onwards these were held every year in Kharkov. The congress elected a council to manage affairs until the next yearly meeting. From the 1890's metallurgical factories were represented at the congresses in addition to mines. Government officials attended, and the chairman of the congress was appointed by the minister of finance.[2] In 1884 was founded a congress of petrol industrialists, and in 1887 a Permanent Consultative Office of Iron-masters. A much looser organization, a forum for discussion of matters of common interest rather than a disciplined pressure-group, was the All-Russian Congress of Trade and Industry which met in Nizhnii Novgorod in 1896. Co-operation between

[1] Khromov, op. cit., pp. 303, 304.

[2] A. Ermansky, 'Krupnaya burzhuaziya do 1905 goda' in *Obshchestvennoe dvizhenie v Rossii v nachale XX veka*, ed. Martov, Maslov, and Potresov (SPB, 1909–12), i. 332–47.

the government and industrialists was close. The key position on the government side was the department of trade and industry in the Ministry of Finance, set up in 1881 and greatly expanded during the 1890's. Subordinate to it was the council on factory construction, on which business men were represented. Two other important joint advisory bodies which came under the minister of finance were the council on trade and manufactures and the council on railway tariffs. Committees of trade and industry and stock exchange committees also existed in many industrial cities of the empire.[1]

Consultation between officials and business men was clearly beneficial to Russian industry. But co-operation could be abused, and undue influence could be exerted in either direction. Officials had opportunities to interfere in business, and they had enormous means of patronage in the form of government contracts and protective tariffs. At the same time rich businessmen had the means to induce officials to support their proposals with higher authority. Bribery, whether crude or subtle, direct or indirect, is hard to document, but the belief widespread in Russia at this time, and supported by the bald assertions of Soviet historians, that the wheels of the industrial machine were well oiled with corruption, is unlikely to be quite without foundation.

Another unanswerable question is whether business interests had more influence on government policy than government interests on business policy. The crudest form of Marxist stereotype is that in a period of rising capitalist enterprise the capitalists give the orders and the politicians obey. Government in such periods is 'the executive committee of the *bourgeoisie*'. The purpose is business profit, and political power is a means to attain it. Now there can be no doubt that Russian capitalists, and the numerous foreign capitalists who invested in Russian industry, got big profits. But it does not follow from this that it was they who made the decisions, and the government that obeyed. It is equally arguable that the government set itself certain economic purposes and used the businessmen as its instruments, guaranteeing them high profits as the price of their efforts. The government wished Russia to have big modern industries, for essentially non-economic motives, in order to

[1] See T. H. von Laue, op. cit., pp. 79, 93–94.

make Russia a great military and political force in the world, the equal or superior of the other Great Powers. The Russian bureaucrats did not know how to create industry. The people who knew how to do that were the capitalists, who might be Russians or Jews or foreigners. Let them get on with their job, distasteful to a Russian nobleman but necessary in the modern world. If profits were what they wanted in return, let them have good profits. A similar attitude could be found in Prussia in the mid nineteenth century, though the capitalist ethos had penetrated more deeply into the mentality of the upper class than in Russia in 1900. A better parallel is Japan. The makers of modern Japan were by tradition contemptuous of merchants and all they stood for. But after 1868 they encouraged capitalist enterprise because they understood that if Japan was to be a Great Power it must have modern industries. So the Mitsui, Mitsubishi, and other great business interests were given privileges and subsidies, and allowed to buy valuable resources at very low prices, in order that they should make the industries that Japan needed. Like their Russian colleagues, the Japanese capitalists made fat profits, and in Japan as in Russia the result was military power.[1] To sum up, Russian business and Russian government used and profited from each other, but on balance it was the government which gained the most, and the government which kept the direction of the economy. There was a much closer correlation between the industries which developed most and the industries required for state interests than was the case in countries in which the industrial revolution was a spontaneous process initiated by private invention and private profit-seeking.

One of the most important forms of support given by the government to industry was tariff protection. In 1887 and again in 1891 import duties were raised. Consumption goods suffered most, including articles of wide consumption, but imported raw materials were also taxed. The Russian metal industry did well

[1] It is of course arguable that Japan did better in building up both its economic and its military power than Russia, as was shown in 1904–5. At the time of the Meiji Restoration the capitalist class of Japan was probably more experienced, self-reliant, and enterprising than that of Russia in 1861. The Mitsui family had a couple of centuries of business enterprise behind it before 1868. See William W. Lockwood, *The Economic Development of Japan*, and C. D. Sheldon, *The Rise of the Merchant Class in Tokugawa Japan*, Locust Valley, New York, 1958.

out of this: in 1887 the duty per pood of pig-iron was raised from 5 to 25 kopeks, in 1891 to 30. The Moscow textile industry also did well, since its access to raw material from within the empire caused it to suffer less from duties on imported raw materials than St. Petersburg, which depended on supplies from abroad by sea. Support for protectionism went together with aggressive Russian nationalism, and fitted well with Moscow's traditional rivalry with 'cosmopolitan' St. Petersburg.[1]

At the turn of the century crafts still employed a much larger number of people than factory industry, and produced the greater part of the clothing and household articles and tools used by the people. The growth of factory industry threatened the crafts, and indeed in most forms of textile production the factories drove the craftsmen out of business. But the champions of modern capitalism, whether they were liberals or Marxists, exaggerated the decline of the crafts and have continued to do so retrospectively in historical writing. On the other hand the romantics, whether they were conservatives or Populists, exaggerated not only the extent but the supposed moral and aesthetic values of craft industry. Emotional prejudices on both sides and lack of statistics make it difficult to get a true picture. A commission which investigated craft industry in 1879–80 estimated that 7,500,000 people were employed in this way. Another expert writing a few years later thought that there were nearly 8,000,000.[2] The main areas were the central and northern provinces, especially Moscow province and the provinces to the north and north-east. The most important single field was woodwork, which varied from simple tools of general use to high quality walnut furniture for rich households in Moscow. Some metal goods still sold well, though here factory competition was being felt, for example in the long-established nail manufacture in Tver province. Linen cloth, fur garments, and leather clothing were also made with success. Crafts were an important subsidiary source of income for peasant households, and might keep one or more members of the family

[1] For a discussion by a well-qualified foreign contemporary observer see G. von Schultze-Gävernitz, *Volkswirtschaftliche Studien aus Rußland* (Leipzig, 1899), pp. 260–82.

[2] Article 'Kustar'' in *Brockhaus*, xvii. 125.

occupied for most of the working year. Often their wares were sold to a big merchant from a city, whose relationship to them came to resemble that of an industrial employer to his workmen. Both central government and zemstvos made efforts to help craftsmen and to protect them from exploitation by such merchants. In 1894 a department of rural economy was set up in the Ministry of Agriculture and State Properties, with a small budget to subsidize crafts. It set up several craft schools, and arranged orders from government departments. In 1885 the Moscow provincial zemstvo opened a crafts museum in Moscow and model workshops in several places in the province. The museum helped to sell craft products, took orders from urban customers, and gave subsidies and small loans to craftsmen. Various other zemstvos later set up crafts committees, which arranged exhibitions, small museums, schools, and storehouses and helped in marketing craft goods. A number of schools for special crafts were also founded by rich individuals.

The number of industrial workers is another subject surrounded by doctrinal controversy. Official statistics tended to underrate it, largely as a result of the obsessive desire of the bureaucrats to preserve Russia from the bogey of a 'proletariat'. On the other hand Marxist commentators, both at the time and in restrospect, have exaggerated the number of 'the working class'. The pioneer student of the problem was a Marxist, M. I. Tugan-Baranovsky, whose book *The Russian Factory in Past and Present* appeared in 1900. He estimated the number, on the basis of official statistics available in 1896, as about 2,200,000, but considered that the statistics themselves used incorrect categories and that the number should be higher. He thought that in 1900 there must be at least 3,000,000, including transport workers as well as those strictly employed in factories and mines.[1] At this time approximately 550,000 were employed in textiles, 500,000 in mining and metallurgy, and 400,000 as railwaymen.

In the newest industrial centres a large proportion of the workers were sons of peasants arrived from the villages, with nothing to offer but a pair of strong hands. Their lack of skill could not be expected to command a good wage, and the com-

[1] M. I. Tugan-Baranovsky, *Russkaya fabrika v proshlom i nastoyashchem* (3rd edition reprint, Moscow, 1934), pp. 265, 289–90.

petition of numerous immigrants from overpopulated rural districts enabled the employer to keep wages low. Moreover, many of the workers did not have to support families in the industrial area: they had left them behind in their village, had come to earn some cash to help out the family budget, and could return to the village in case of necessity. These conditions made for miserable wage levels, for the exploitation of the poor which is characteristic of early stages of the industrial process in all lands. In the longer-established centres there was a second or third generation of industrial workers, no longer connected with the villages, possessing industrial skills, able to offer labour that deserved a better wage and desperately needing it. Conditions in practice varied between the four main industrial regions. In the south the unskilled semi-peasant formed the majority, and he was wretchedly paid. In Moscow the proportion of established urban dwellers and of skilled workers was higher, but because Moscow was the centre of an overpopulated district the influx from the countryside was still sufficient to help the employers keep wages down. In St. Petersburg and in the industrial centres of Poland the demand for labour tended to keep pace with the supply, and this pushed wages upwards. In both these areas the proportion of skilled workers was higher than elsewhere in the empire. The employers found that they could best make profits not by producing cheaply with exploited labour but by increasing both productivity and wages, by introducing machines and paying a better price for better work.

The labour laws introduced by Bunge were therefore accepted by the Polish and St. Petersburg industrialists, but resisted by those of Moscow. A law of 1882 forbade labour of children under twelve, limited workers aged twelve to fifteen to an eight-hour day, and obliged employers to let their adolescent employees attend school. In order to enforce the law, a government inspectorate was introduced under the Ministry of Finance. In 1884 and 1885 came further laws, on school attendance for adolescent workers, and forbidding night work in textile factories for women or adolescents. These laws were not immediately enforced, and some years passed before the government inspectorate was efficient, before its officers could stand up to the hostility or persuasion of employers. But by the mid 1890's the labour laws were a reality, and the inspectors proved to be a fine body of honourable men, who made life more tolerable for the workers and brought the light of knowledge into the darker places of Russian industry. An important step further was the law of July 1897, introduced by Witte, which imposed a maximum working day of eleven and a half hours for any worker of either sex or any age, and of ten hours for any workers engaged in nightwork.

Trade unions were forbidden under a provision of the criminal law which prescribed prison or exile for persons organizing a society which would stimulate hatred between employers and workers. Strikes were regarded by the authorities as a form of rebellion. Nevertheless, strikes took place. A landmark was the strike at the Morozov textile factory at Orekhovo-Zuevo near Moscow in 1885. In 1896 about 35,000 cotton mill workers came out in St. Petersburg for a whole month, and when the employers broke the promises they made to settle it, there was a second strike in January 1897. These events undoubtedly contributed to the enactment of Witte's labour law of July 1897.

The political aspects of the labour movement will be discussed elsewhere. But it is worth noting at this point the difference in attitude to labour problems between the Ministry of the Interior and the Ministry of Finance. The Ministry of Finance held to the doctrine, common among European capitalists, that it was possible to achieve a harmony of interests between capital and labour. This harmony was of course interpreted to operate at a level much more favourable to capital than to labour. The Ministry of the Interior was concerned with the more practical task of ensuring public order. Its servants had no special sympathy for either class: if anything, the average Russian general or gendarmerie officer probably disliked the capitalist and felt a certain patronizing affection for the worker. Sometimes policemen considered that the preservation of order included the removal of causes of discontent, even if this were to the material disadvantage of the employers.

The Ministry of the Interior wished its policemen to be stationed inside the factories and to report to them all that was going on: the Ministry of Finance preferred that the maintenance of order be left to the employer, that the police remain outside the factory but be ready to come in when invited by an employer who had lost control of his men. The two ministries competed for control of the factory inspectors, whom the Ministry of the Interior wished to place under its orders. The Ministry of Finance retained control, but was obliged to concede that the inspectors should be locally responsible to the provincial governors. The struggle made the inspectors' own position more difficult. If they took up the workers' grievances, they were liable to be denounced by the employers as subversive elements, but if they co-operated with the employers the workers would refuse to trust them.

The cost of industrial progress was paid by the peasants and the urban poor, on whom fell most heavily the burden of indirect taxation. The most important items of revenue in this category were customs and the spirits monopoly.[1] The spirits monopoly was instituted in 1894. In the first years it brought in about the same as the previous tax on spirits, but in the next years its receipts soared. Other widely consumed objects on which taxes were levied were tobacco, sugar, matches, and petrol. Direct taxes and redemption payments brought in a much smaller revenue, of which the business tax and income-tax, which did not affect the peasants or urban poor, formed about a third. The other main source of government revenue was the railways, but this sum was in fact spent on the administration, repair, or improvement of the state railway network.

The largest items in government expenditure were the armed services, the railway network, and the payment of interest on state loans. The Ministry of the Interior and the Ministry of Finance received substantial sums for various administrative needs. The total grant to the Ministry of Education was less than a tenth of that to the defence ministries.[2]

The value of Russian exports was 498,700,000 roubles in

[1] These two main items accounted for the following sums (in millions of roubles, to the nearest million):

	1880	*1890*	*1904*
Customs	96	142	219
Spirits	223	268	543

Further indirect taxes amounted to 170,000,000 in 1904. Direct taxes and redemption payments together amounted to 143,000,000 in 1890 and 228,000,000 in 1900, of which business tax and income-tax in 1900 provided 86,000,000. (Source: Khromov, op. cit., pp. 494, 498, 504, 598.)

[2] The sums allocated to these purposes were as follows (in millions of roubles, to the nearest million):

1880, 692,000,000 in 1890, and 716,000,000 in 1900. The value of imports was 622,800,000 in 1880, 406,600,000 in 1890, and 626,000,000 in 1900. The structure of exports did not change very much. Grains remained by far the largest item, varying above or below 50 per cent. largely in accordance with the harvest.[1] Among secondary items, flax and linen products declined steadily. Petroleum products, which do not appear in the figures at all in 1880, formed an important item in the 1890's. In imports the dominant position of raw materials was increased, and the share of consumers' goods, already reduced in the 1870's, fell still further. Raw cotton was the largest single item. It was subject to some fluctuation, but was less important in the 1890's than in the 1880's. Raw metals also declined, while imports of machines rapidly increased in the 1890's. The largest single item of imported consumers' goods was tea.[2]

Russia's best customer at the turn of the century was Germany, which in 1901 took 23 per cent. of Russia's exports and delivered 35 per cent. of her imports. The second place was occupied by Great Britain with 20 per cent. of exports and 17 per cent. of imports. No other country approached these two. The third most important buyer of Russian exports was the Netherlands, and the third and fourth most important sources of imports were China and the United States (from which Russia obtained respectively tea and raw cotton).[3]

	1890	*1900*
War and Navy	269	420
Communications	56	367
State debt	263	267
Finance	132	280
Interior	85	88
Education	23	34

(Source: Khromov, op. cit., pp. 518–19, 524.)

[1] In 1880 they made up 46·5 per cent., in most of the 1880's more than 50 per cent. In 1892, the year following the famine, they fell to 34 per cent., in 1894 they rose to 57 per cent., in 1899 and 1900 fell to 41·5 per cent. and 42·8 per cent., in 1904 were 49 per cent. Official figures are reproduced, ibid., pp. 472–4.

[2] The following are some details on individual items. *Exports* (percentage of total): flax and linen products 1880 16, 1890 11·5, 1900 8; petroleum products 1890 4, 1900 6·5. *Imports* (percentage of total): raw cotton from 1881 to 1894 varied between 15 and 20, 1895–1904 between 10 and 15; raw metals from 1881 to 1892 around 6, from 1893 to 1897 around 10, in 1900 less than 6; machines from 1881 to 1893 varied between 3 and 6, in 1899 15, in 1900 12; tea 1880 10, 1890 8, 1900 7·5. (Source: Khromov, op. cit., pp. 476–9.)

[3] Details on the destination of exports and origin of imports ibid., pp. 490–3.

During these years France was the main source of loans to the Russian state. Apart from this, foreign private firms were investing considerable capital in Russian industry and mining. In 1900 there were 269 foreign companies in Russia of which only 16 had existed before 1888. French and Belgian capital was mostly in the southern metallurgical industry and mines, British in petroleum, and German in chemicals and electrical engineering. After the introduction of the gold standard in 1897 the flow of foreign capital increased.

The achievements of what may be called the Witte Era were undeniable, but they aroused plenty of criticism both in conservative circles and among radical opponents of the régime. Common to all criticism was the argument that too much pressure was being put on the peasant taxpayers and too little being done for agriculture. Another charge was that the government's expenditures on industry and communications were wasteful, that the railways were being extravagantly managed and that the prices paid by the government to the metal industry were unnecessarily high. Another line of attack was nationalism. Witte was accused of selling out Russia to rapacious foreign capitalists, who would not only suck up her resources but also bring in all sorts of pernicious foreign habits. Here the main spokesman was Sergei Sharapov, editor in the late 1890's of a weekly paper *Russkii trud*.[1] Witte's supporters would, of course, argue that Russia was using the foreign capitalists at least as much as they were using Russia, and that the industrial development which they were carrying out was making Russia great. But the argument for and against foreign capital has not been and perhaps never will be proved either way, in Russia or in any of the other countries where it has arisen. Least of all will this essentially emotional argument be decided on strictly economic grounds.

These arguments in conservative and official circles had a parallel in the controversies which developed in the 1890's between Marxists and Populists as to the economic future of Russia. Originally the Populists believed that it was possible to preserve Russia from capitalism altogether, to introduce socialism in an essentially peasant country, and then to develop

[1] For a discussion of these views see von Laue, op. cit., pp. 276–90, and Gurko, op. cit., pp. 65–66.

what industry was needed on a socialist basis. The Marxists maintained that capitalism was bound to come to Russia, and that only after it had done its work on Russian society, painful though this might be, would the conditions be created for socialism. The most eminent Russian Marxist was G. V. Plekhanov, who became converted to Marxism after he went into exile, and founded with Vera Zasulich and P. B. Akselrod the 'Liberation of Labour' group in Switzerland in 1883. His most important formulation of the Marxist case against Populism was *Our Differences*, written in 1885. Karl Marx himself had shown great interest in Russia during the last years of his life but had not been sure in his own mind about the future of capitalism or of the village commune in Russia. In a letter to N. K. Mikhailovsky in 1877 he had written that 'if Russia continues to travel along the road she has chosen since 1861, she will miss one of the best chances ever given to a people to avoid all the miseries of the capitalist system'. If revolution did not come soon, Russia would 'fall under the sway of the ineluctable laws' of capitalism. In a reply to a letter from Vera Zasulich Marx wrote in 1881 that 'the commune is the *point d'appui* of social regeneration in Russia'.[1] In 1882, in an introduction to a Russian translation of the *Communist Manifesto*, Marx wrote: 'If a Russian revolution serves as a signal for a workers' revolution in the West, so that both complement each other, then the contemporary Russian form of land tenure may be the starting-point for a communist course of development.'

Whatever the view of the founder of Marxism, by the end of the 1880's economic facts in Russia were supporting Plekhanov's argument. The Populists no longer denied that capitalism existed in Russia, but they believed that the harm it had done to the Russian economy by ruining many small crafts was greater than any good it had done in creating modern industry. The internal market was not expanding, and the Russian people were poorer. The Populist economist N. Danielson, in a book published in 1893 under the pseudonym 'Nikolai-on', wrote: 'The limits of the development of capitalism are set by the growing poverty, which is itself caused by its development, by the growing number of workers who have no employment

[1] *Perepiska K. Marksa i F. Engelsa s russkimi politicheskimi deyatelyami* (Moscow, 1951), p. 301.

and cannot obtain employment.' The solution was 'to develop the productive forces of the population in such a form that they can be used not by an insignificant minority but by the whole people'. The commune must be made the basis of industrial Russia, must be made into 'a suitable instrument to organize big industry and to transform big industry from a capitalistic to a social form'.[1] In 1894 Mikhailovsky wrote a long criticism of Marxism in *Russkoe bogatstvo*, from the moral as much as the economic point of view. In September 1894 appeared the first important economic work from a Marxist point of view, P. B. Struve's *Critical Notes on the Question of the Economic Development of Russia*. It was followed in December 1894 by a full-length exposition of Marxist historical materialism by Plekhanov himself. It was published under the pseudonym of Beltov and passed the censorship with the studiously obscure title *On the Question of the Development of the Monistic View of History*. This was one of the most impressive statements of Marxist doctrine ever made in any language, and made a tremendous impact on the intellectual youth of Russia at the end of the century. Struve's less ambitious book was also extremely influential. It was brilliantly, even provocatively written. After denouncing as 'national vanity' the idea that Russians could 'by the constructions of our own critical thought' escape 'the long difficult cultural work and the efforts of generations, the fierce struggle of social classes, economic forces, and interests', he concluded the book with a phrase which was endlessly quoted for many years afterwards: 'No, let us confess our lack of culture, and go and take a lesson from capitalism.'[2]

By the end of the century industrialization had triumphed in Russia in the form of a mixed private and state capitalism. The people suffered, as the English people suffered in the earlier unplanned English industrial revolution, and as other peoples

[1] Nikolai-on, *Ocherki nashego poreformennogo khozyaistva* (SPB, 1893), pp. 343–4.

[2] P. B. Struve, *Kriticheskie zametki k voprosu ob ekonomicheskom razvitii Rossii* (SPB, 1894), p. 288. Another work of this time that criticized the Populists was *Who are the 'Friends of the People'?* This was illegally circulated in hectographed form, read by few, and therefore had little effect at the time. It became famous as a result of the later career of its author V. I. Ulyanov, better known as Lenin. It is important for an understanding of Lenin's intellectual development. But Lenin's most serious contribution to economic knowledge was his *Development of Capitalism in Russia* (*Razvitie kapitalizma v Rossii*), published in 1899 under the pseudonym V. Ilyin, which is full of valuable information.

have suffered, are suffering, and perhaps have yet to suffer in similar processes. All the suffering can be regarded as justified by those who believe either in the God-given virtue of private capitalist enterprise or in the ineluctable laws of history as interpreted by Marxist science. But the arguments of those who have pleaded for slower and more humane methods, and for more consideration to peasants who, scattered in countless small villages, are unable to combine into strong pressure-groups, cannot be said to have been proved wrong: all that can be said is that their arguments have been disregarded, and their authors vanquished. The controversies between Witte and his critics, between Russian Marxists and Populists, have their relevance in the second half of the twentieth century for many countries which have reached various stages of economic development.[1]

Social Classes

It is possible to get an approximate picture of the class structure of the Russian empire at the turn of the century from the results of the general census of 1897. The census was carefully conducted, and the information it provided was more accurate than any previously collected. Unfortunately, the categories which it enumerated were those traditionally accepted by official Russia, and did not always correspond to the significant social or professional categories of the modern world.

The hereditary nobility, of both sexes and all ages, amounted to 1,220,169. This figure includes the whole noble landowning class, but it also includes many persons who were not landowners. In particular, it covers the highest ranks of the armed forces and the civil bureaucracy, and a considerable portion of the free professions. A further 630,119 persons belonged to the category of 'personal nobles and officials not of the nobility'.[2] Some of these were landowners or professional people, but the great majority of them were in the higher government service, whose numbers approximately doubled between 1880 and 1914.

Ecclesiastics of all religions amounted to 342,927. The overwhelming majority of these were Orthodox. The proportion of

[1] This point is discussed at some length in A. P. Mendel, *Dilemmas of Progress in Tsarist Russia*, Harvard, 1961.

[2] See above p. 15.

Orthodox to the total population was 69 per cent., the next largest group being Catholics with 9 per cent. But as these figures included dependants, and Catholic priests do not have wives or children, the share of Catholics in the total was smaller, and of Orthodox higher, than the proportions in the population as a whole.

The upper classes in the towns, other than the nobility and officials, were covered by the two categories of 'distinguished citizens', who numbered 342,927, and 'merchants', who amounted to 281,179. The first category included a substantial number of professional people, the second essentially covered the business class.

The poorer classes of the towns were lumped together under the traditional but unilluminating heading of *meshchane*. These amounted to a total of 13,386,392. This figure included small shopkeepers, white-collar employees, artisans, and a large part of the urban workers.

Peasants were recorded as 96,896,648 persons. To these must be added a further 2,928,842 persons separately listed as Cossacks. This total of slightly under 100,000,000 is considerably larger than the number given in the census as occupied in agriculture, fishing, and hunting, which was 93,433,044. Moreover, this lower figure included 6,607,409 persons described as having a subsidiary industrial occupation. The explanation is that the category of 'peasants' included a large part of the urban working class, consisting of persons legally belonging to the peasantry but earning their living by manual labour in the towns. The two categories of *meshchane* and peasants together cover the whole working class, not only those regularly employed in factories or transport or mining, but also the large floating population of the unskilled, casually employed, or unemployed urban poor.

A clearer picture of the composition of the urban classes can be obtained from the figures relating to professions and to sectors of the industrial labour force. The following table gives the main professional groups listed in the census. It is useful to distinguish three groups. The first group are government officials, including officers of the armed services.[1] The second

[1] The number of officials, of the fourteen classes of Peter the Great's Table of Ranks, employed in the central government was approximately 23,000 in 1880

are the employees of zemstvos. The third are the professions. These figures are not completely satisfactory. There is certainly some overlapping, since many members of professions were employed by central or local government. The figure for zemstvo employees is particularly unilluminating as it includes clerks and persons in poorly paid positions who would not be regarded as belonging either to the official or to the professional classes. Nevertheless, the figures throw some light on the social structure of Russia at the end of the century.

	Employed persons only	*With their dependants*
Central government		
Administrative and judicial officials	42,034	128,467
Officers of the armed services	44,449	103,952
Officers of the gendarmerie and police	10,425	36,261
Local government		
Zemstvo employees	104,808	299,036
Professions—Teaching		
State School teachers	79,482	173,825
Private teachers	68,173	171,552
Tutors and governesses	10,988	..
Teachers of arts and crafts	7,865	14,841
Total teaching	166,508	360,218
Learned and literary occupations[1]	3,296	8,297
Artists, musicians, and actors	18,254	37,828
Medical		
Directors of hospitals and civil doctors	13,770	38,659
Military and naval doctors	3,186	9,426
Veterinaries	2,902	7,325
Dentists	1,846	3,831
Total medical	21,704	59,241
Engineers and technologists	4,010	11,034
Barristers and attorneys	8,931	30,261

The very rich consisted of some landowners and some business men. The census shows 10,302 households which

and 52,000 in 1914, while those employed in provincial government were approximately 12,000 in 1880 and 16,000 in 1914. The source from which I have made these rather rough calculations is *Adres-kalendar: obshchaya rospis vsekh chinovnykh osob*. This publication, which appeared every year, but whose title was occasionally modified during the nineteenth century (the earliest issue available in the British Museum being for 1828), gives the name of every official and the personnel of every central department and of every provincial governor's office. It is a potential mine of information for 'Namierian' research on Russian political and social history.

[1] This category includes university teachers, professional writers, and all journalists.

employed 11 or more domestic servants and a further 111,939 which employed from 4 to 10.[1] Most of these were probably landowners, who kept several large country-houses as well as a house in the capital, but there were also capitalists who copied this style of life. Conspicuous consumption was most visible in St. Petersburg, with its opulent restaurants, gypsy orchestras, and less reputable forms of entertainment, but other cities also had their attractions to offer. The widespread belief, which also has its parallel in other countries, that the aristocracy showed more discrimination in their choice of luxuries, preferring the more 'cultural' to the more 'animal' pleasures, does not seem to be supported by much evidence. The vulgar parvenu with crude appetites, of course, existed, but when it came to crude appetites impeccable aristocrats could hold their own. On the other hand Russian capitalists were not slow to patronize the arts. Two at least, Morozov and Shchukin, went far beyond the conventional works which it was considered would enhance the social status of a tycoon, and built up the magnificent collections of post-impressionist painting, especially of the early works of Picasso and Matisse, which are one of the artistic glories of Moscow and Leningrad in the 1960's.[2] These two men can certainly hold their own with Mellon and Frick, and may be reckoned apt pupils of Catherine II.

Not all landowners were rich. Of those who were, some spent their time and wealth in the cities or abroad, leaving the management of their estates to bailiffs, while others took an active interest in the technical and economic sides of farming, becoming in fact modern entrepreneurs of agriculture. The smaller landowners, who had to make their living from their land, were forced to be active farmers. From this social milieu came many of the people most active in zemstvo work. Reactionary or liberal, efficient or incompetent, they provided the foundation of provincial public life. Their dealings with the peasants also

[1] In Russia in 1900, as indeed in most of Europe, domestic servants were not the exotic luxury that they had tended to become half a century later. Out of 22,023,474 households recorded in the census, there were 1,769,727 (8 per cent.) which employed at least one servant. These would have covered a large part of the middle classes.

[2] Taken over by the state after the revolution, these paintings were displayed up till the Second World War, but then were banished as decadent and formalistic. In the 1960's they could be seen once more in the Hermitage in Leningrad and the Pushkin Museum in Moscow.

varied greatly. There were landowners who saw their tenants much as their fathers had seen their serfs—as some inferior species, strange and perhaps at times endearing creatures but something less than human. There were others who established a relationship of mutual respect and even of affection.

The vertical divisions between the three middle classes[1]—bureaucrats, intelligentsia, and business men—were clearly visible at the end of the century as they had been at the beginning, but the blurred area between them had grown larger. Yet it was still unrealistic to apply west European categories to Russia and to speak of a *bourgeoisie*, or of a single homogeneous middle class. Russian bureaucrats, business men, and intelligentsia did not share a common ethos. The standards of the bureaucrats were still those derived from the service gentry: the state was placed before the individual, military values above civil values, and the good opinion of the hierarchical superior was preferred to the approval of public opinion. The capitalists of Russia were drawing nearer in outlook to their European or North American counterparts, especially as their business contacts with the latter increased, but they mostly retained their indifference to political rights and liberties and their traditional acceptance of autocracy. Finally, the intelligentsia remained primarily rebellious, rejecting not only the existing political and social system but also what they believed to be the values of the European *bourgeoisie*. For the most part they were not so much liberals as radicals, or even socialists, and though they believed themselves resolutely opposed to autocracy in principle, yet in many cases the objection was to an autocracy which served the existing social system rather than to autocracy as such. The traditional Russian view that oligarchy is worse than absolutism, which we have noticed in such men as Paul Stroganov, Nicholas Milyutin, and Yurii Samarin, remained stronger in the men of the 1890's than they themselves were aware.

The concept of intelligentsia remained extremely hard to define, for it was both a social group and a state of mind. Its nucleus was in the free professions, but there were persons from outside this social category who belonged to the intelligentsia. A member of the intelligentsia must possess a good modern

[1] See above pp. 28–29.

education, yet there were highly educated Russians who would not be considered members of the intelligentsia. An essential feature of all members was preoccupation with general political and social ideas. Such preoccupation was almost bound to lead to opposition to the Russian régime as it was. The defenders of the régime certainly included men of excellent education and first-class minds, but very few who were interested in general ideas. To this there were indeed a few exceptions. Leontyev and Danilevsky might be considered as such. The case of Dostoyevsky is interesting. In his last years he became a champion of the established order, yet retained the rebellious mental attitude of the intelligentsia. One of the most revealing stories about the attitudes of the intelligentsia is the conversation reported by the editor of *Novoe vremya*, A. S. Suvorin, between himself and Dostoyevsky, in which they agreed that if they had knowledge of an impending attempt to murder the Tsar, they could not denounce it to the police, though both were loyal to the Tsar and opponents of revolution.[1] The truth is that in 1900 the word intelligentsia was normally associated with the notion of opposition, and that anyone who considered himself, or was generally considered by others, to belong to the intelligentsia, would normally be against the government and against the social régime.

If in the category of social function the vertical divisions separating the intelligentsia from bureaucrats or business men were rather blurred, in the category of educational attainment the horizontal division separating the intelligentsia from the less well educated was still more blurred. In fact there was a fairly large transitional group which one should perhaps call the 'semi-intelligentsia', people aspiring to the intelligentsia, whose inadequate formal education was compensated either by natural intellectual ability trained by the experience of life, or by such powerful personal ambition or ideological fanaticism as could sweep all barriers aside.

It was from the intelligentsia that most of the political leadership of Russia came in the early twentieth century. This was certainly true of the parties of the left, including the liberals. Even on the right there were persons who, while derived from landed or business backgrounds, yet by their way of life and

[1] A. S. Suvorin, *Dnevnik Suvorina* (Moscow, 1923), pp. 15–16.

their outlook belonged rather to the intelligentsia. It would of course be quite wrong to confuse 'intelligentsia' with 'revolutionary leadership'. The flower, or weed, must be distinguished from the soil in which it grows. What can be said is that the type of professional revolutionary, as imagined and then realized by Lenin or by the Socialist Revolutionaries,[1] was much more easily produced in a society in which the bulk of the best-educated and most thoughtful citizens were alienated from the whole régime.

One of the most famous statements made about Russian society at this time is the passage in Struve's manifesto for the First Congress of the RSDRP in 1898:[2] 'The further to the east one goes in Europe, the weaker in politics, the more cowardly and the meaner becomes the *bourgeoisie*, the greater are the cultural and political tasks that fall to the lot of the proletariat.' Struve was writing about a real problem, but he got his words and his roles wrong. The capitalists in Russia were politically inert because they had no reason not to be: they were doing very well out of the régime, and the question of courage or cowardice did not arise. As for a *bourgeoisie*, a word whose meaning is wider than the capitalists proper, and a phenomenon which only exists when there is a certain minimum homogeneity of the middle classes, the truth is that in 1898 Russia did not possess one. As for the tasks of political leadership, they fell not to the working class but to the intelligentsia.

This is not to deny that the working class was growing both in numbers and in strength. In 1904 there were 1,663,800 workers in factories subject to the inspectorate of the Ministry of Finance. Of these 621,500 were in textiles, and of these 372,136 in cotton. After textiles the most numerous group was metal-working with 235,785 followed by mineral-working with 127,790 and the sugar industry with 118,000. Mining and the industries processing the output of the mines employed a further 599,276 workers, of whom 255,232 were in metallurgical plants and 117,743 in coal mines. A third big group were the workers in transport. Here there were no separate figures for officials, clerical, and manual workers. The total labour force of the railways was 711,922 in 1904, while in 1900 water transport

[1] See below pp. 557–60, 563.

[2] See below p. 552.

employed about 140,000. The overwhelming majority of these were of course workers.[1]

In 1902 more than half the factory workers were employed in factories situated outside large cities. Of those who did work in a big city, more than 80 per cent. in the two capitals stayed the whole year round, but less than half did so in the southern cities of Kharkov and Kiev. This reflects, of course, the more recent origin of southern industry and the lower level of skill of its labour force. Wage rates were notably higher in St. Petersburg than in Moscow or in the south, and metal-workers earned substantially more than textile workers.

Hours of work had been shortened, as we have seen, by the law of 1897. Conditions of work were often unhealthy or dangerous. Regulations of 3 June 1886 had set up provincial offices on factory and mining affairs under the authority of the governors, which were entitled to lay down regulations on medical conditions in places of work. The larger enterprises instituted some sort of medical care for their employees during the 1890's. At the turn of the century these existed in about one-fifth of the factories covered by the inspectorate, and affected about two-thirds of the labour force. Accidents in metallurgical factories were frequent. In 1890 245 persons were killed and 3,508 injured in this branch of industry. In 1904 there were 556 deaths and 66,680 injuries, these casualties amounting to 11 per cent. of the labour force.[2] In 1904 on the railways there were 477 deaths and 5,574 injuries among railway personnel. The law on employers' liability for injuries in the place of work, enacted on 2 June 1903, provided for free medical assistance or payment of medical bills during treatment; payment of the worker at half-pay during his incapacity; a pension to the value of two-thirds of his pay if permanently incapacitated, or correspondingly smaller amounts if the permanent injury were such as to cause only partial incapacity; and a cash contribution to the funeral of workers who were killed.

Housing conditions of Russian workers varied according to

[1] Figures quoted from official statistics of factory inspectors and of the mining and transport departments in K. A. Pazhitnov, *Polozhenie rabochego klassa v Rossii* (Leningrad, 1924), ii. 16–23.

[2] Ibid., pp. 162–5. The increase in 1904 is perhaps in part due to more efficient information. If so, this would not diminish the implications of the figures but merely mean that conditions were no better earlier.

regions, but were normally miserable, as was or had been the case in other countries in similar stages of industrial development. They were relatively best in the Urals, where the workers lived in their own houses, received when they were emancipated from serfdom. In the mining settlements in Siberia, or the petrol areas of Baku, miners were crowded together in barracks with little ventilation or light. In the 1890's in the south they were particularly bad. A type of barracks known as the *zemlyanka* was quite common: it was dug downwards into the earth, and the roof protruded only a short way above ground-level. This type of dwelling was forbidden at the end of the century: the wooden barracks which replaced it were still overcrowded and badly ventilated. An inspector's description of the Bryansk metallurgical factory in 1892 stated that those workers who were allotted family houses were able to preserve a decent standard of cleanliness, but the barracks for unmarried men were another matter:

> These dwellings can be compared without any exaggeration with the quarters of domestic animals: their unwashed and filthy condition cannot recall a human living-place. Even in summer, when the windows and doors are ajar, the air in them is stifling; on the walls and the bunks are traces of slime and mould, and the floors are barely visible for the filth which sticks to them.[1]

In the factory settlements in Central Russia the practice was to provide houses for families, but usually two or three, sometimes even seven families would be squeezed into family houses, and many married couples would be forced to live in the barracks. An exceptional case of good conditions was a Kiev sugar refinery which offered its workers iron bedsteads with blankets and pillows, a small table and cupboard to every two beds, and insisted on rigorous control of ventilation.[2] In the big cities conditions were on the whole better, but there was still a great deal of squalor and poverty. A survey was made in Moscow in 1899 of more than 15,000 habitations, mostly consisting of cubicles separated from each other by boards, several fitted into one normal-sized room of a house. In the accommodation examined, nearly 175,000 persons were living. Nearly 70 per cent. of the dwellings allowed less air per person than the

[1] Quoted in Pazhitnov, op. cit., p. 99. [2] Ibid., p. 111.

medical experts considered to be the minimum necessary for normal health.[1] The investigators found persons of all ages and both sexes thrown together without privacy, in the midst of noise, filth, and foul smells. But the influx of peasants into the cities in search of jobs created an unceasing demand for any living-place, and rents even for these nightmare places were driven up. The remedy of large-scale building by public authorities was not seriously undertaken.

The Russian urban poor suffered not only material exploitation but emotional bewilderment and despair, the result of being uprooted from the village milieu, to which for all its poverty and frustrations they had felt they belonged, and being transplanted into a new, indifferent, or hostile environment. This phenomenon was of course in no way peculiar to Russia. It has been found in the populations of all the hideous urban agglomerations thrown up by industrialization in one country after another. The urban agglomeration is something less than a city, just as the urban poor is something less than a working class. A city has its own character and its own social life: an agglomeration is a collection of uprooted people living like a herd of animals. Cities like Moscow, Kiev, and St. Petersburg of course had their character and social life. But the newcomers from the countryside did not quickly penetrate the barriers and become part of the cities. Mentally, and often physically too, they remained outside the perimeter, in the agglomeration. It was worse in the new cities, which had no civic traditions at all. The phrase 'working class' is somewhat ambiguous. Those regularly employed in factories were only a portion, though a growing portion, of the urban poor. This included also tens of thousands of unskilled, casually employed, or unemployed persons, who managed somehow to keep alive within the agglomerations. Of course the urban poor were discontented: of them it was indeed true that 'they had nothing to lose but their chains'. They were ready supporters of a revolutionary or demagogic movement, as readily of SR's as of Marxists, and—as the pogroms of 1903 in Kishinyov and Gomel showed—of nationalist demagogues and anti-semitic hooligans as of either. The city mob was a factor in

[1] Ibid., p. 116. The minimum was reckoned to be $1\frac{1}{2}$ cubic *sazhen*. A *sazhen* is 7 feet.

Russia at the turn of the century, as it had been in England in the early nineteenth, or as it was in Cairo or Calcutta or Baghdad in the mid twentieth century, and for essentially the same reasons. But when it was a matter of hard, regular work in a political movement, this was not forthcoming from the urban poor as a whole, but only from the working class in the stricter sense. The regular factory workers had better conditions than the rest of the urban poor, but this did not make them contented supporters of the régime. On the contrary, it was the most skilled and best-paid workers, such as the printers and the metal-workers, who were interested in politics and prepared to make the effort of organization. This too has its parallel in the history of the labour movements of other countries.

The peasants continued to form the great majority of the population. One of the subjects which most interested observers of the Russian peasantry was the tendency to economic differentiation, to the formation of a rural *bourgeoisie* and a rural proletariat. This was of special concern to Marxists, such as the Menshevik expert P. P. Maslov, or to Lenin, who made a thorough study of the question. In his *Development of Capitalism in Russia*[1] Lenin used the military survey of horses in Russia in 1888–91 to show the existence of a minority of rich peasants, owning each four or more horses (11 per cent. of the households and 37 per cent. of the number of horses) while more than half had only one horse or none (27 per cent. horseless and 29 per cent. with one horse). Other data from 1889, from four *uezdy* of Voronezh province only, showed that horseless households spent 56 per cent. of their income on food and 14 per cent. on improvements to their land, while owners of five or more horses devoted only 28 per cent. to food, and spent 61 per cent. on improvements. Lenin maintained that a minority of prosperous farmers was appearing, who owned a number of horses and other livestock, employed hired labour, and in some cases possessed minor industrial plants such as distilleries or mills. They were well clothed, wore leather boots, and had a varied diet including plenty of meat. At the other end of the scale, a growing proportion of the peasantry were badly clothed and shod, ate little but rye bread, consumed most of what they

[1] *Razvitie kapitalizma v Rossii* in V. I. Lenin, *Sochineniya*, 5th edition, Moscow, 1958, vol. iii.

produced, and still had to use a large part of their meagre cash income to buy food to get them through the spring. The rest of their income went on a few bare necessities like salt, or kerosene for lamps, and on taxation. There was nothing left for new tools, or improvements to the holding, which deteriorated from bad management. Among the poorer peasants illnesses spread easily, helped by the unhygienic condition of their houses, unwashed earthen floors and poor ventilation.[1]

These two extremes certainly existed, but there was disagreement about how far the mass of medium peasants were being eliminated by the concentration of wealth and poverty. The general trend, as pressure of population increased, at a general low level of output per unit of land, was towards impoverishment. The pessimists could only be proved wrong by a combination of three remedies—increase of agricultural output, settlement of new lands, and increasing opportunities for employment in industry. In the second and third directions something was being achieved, but in the first there was virtually no progress.

The differentiation of the peasantry was taking place, but its social consequences have been exaggerated. In particular, Lenin and his followers, both at this time and retrospectively at a later date, spoke sometimes of a trend towards the formation of a rural *bourgeoisie* and a rural proletariat, and at other times of the existence of these classes. Certainly in the Russian villages at the turn of the century there were rich peasants who exploited their poorer fellows. Certainly there was resentment against such persons, and even a tendency towards jealousy of the richer farmers, whether or not they abused their wealth. This resentment and jealousy was reflected in the widespread use of such opprobrious names as *kulak* (literally 'a fist') and *miroyed* ('commune-eater'). But these rich farmers did not form a *social class*: neither did they feel themselves as such, nor were they so regarded by their fellow villagers. The peasants possessed a class consciousness as peasants, distinct from the gentry and from the people of the towns. Against these they felt a basic solidarity, which affected rich and poor peasants. It was

[1] A classic account of health conditions in two villages in Voronezh province by a zemstvo doctor who became a liberal politician is A. I. Shingaryov, *Vymirayushchaya derevnya*, SPB, 1907.

possible to divide the peasants, on the basis of economic statistics, into rich, poor, and medium, and to show that there were conflicts of interest between these groups. But to conclude from this that there existed three classes among the peasants was to distort the reality. There *was* a class conflict in the countryside, but it was between landowners and peasants, not between sections of the peasantry.

XV

POLITICAL MOVEMENTS

The New Reign

ALEXANDER III died on 20 October 1894 and was succeeded by his son Nicholas. The new emperor was more intelligent and more sensitive than his father. Both those who knew him well, and those who had brief and superficial contact with him, testify to his exceptional personal charm. The charm was, however, apparently associated with weakness and irresolution. Nicholas appeared to agree with the last person he had talked to, and no one could tell what he would do next. Another, and perhaps more plausible, view is that he did not so much lack the ability to make up his own mind as intensely disliked open disagreement: the fact that he treated politely the opinions of his visitors did not mean that he did not have his own views, which were often quite different. In this he may have resembled his greater predecessor Alexander I. That he could be obstinate is shown by his refusal to accept his parents' disapproval of his choice of Princess Alice of Hesse-Darmstadt, a granddaughter of Queen Victoria, as his wife. In the end they gave way, but when the marriage took place, in November 1894, Alexander III was dead. That Nicholas was capable of profound feeling is shown by the depth of his love for the empress, Alexandra Fyodorovna as she became known after conversion to Orthodoxy, which is proved both by the testimony of contemporaries and by the published correspondence and diary of the Tsar. He was devoted to his family, and was happiest when with them or when living the life of a country squire at one of the Imperial estates.

Nicholas was brought up to believe that it was his sacred duty to uphold the principle of autocracy. This he was taught by his father and by Pobedonostsev, who continued to exercise great influence in the first half of the new reign. His wife, who took her conversion extremely seriously, also emphasized the religious obligation to preserve autocracy, but in the first ten years of the reign she took no interest in the detail of politics. As heir to the throne, Nicholas made a journey round the world, visiting Japan, India, and Egypt. This experience aroused in him a genuine interest is Asia and a belief that Russia had a great mission to perform there. In 1893 he was made chairman of the committee on the Trans-Siberian Railway, which enabled him further to develop this interest. Like his father, he favoured such economic modernization as would strengthen the Russian state, and for nine years he supported Witte, the champion of modernization. When Witte was dismissed, it was a result not of mere caprice but of genuine political disagreement. His choice of ministers in the first half of his reign showed reasonable, if not outstanding, judgement. The termination of the careers of several of the most important was not by the emperor's dismissal but by the assassin's bomb or bullet. Nicholas had his irresponsible advisers, as his predecessors had had. One at least of these, Prince V. P. Meshchersky, a reactionary and self-important intriguer, had a bad influence, although he may have exaggerated its extent.[1] Nicholas also had general antipathies and romantic illusions. He distrusted intellectuals, including even persons of aristocratic background who were well educated, and he disliked Jews. At the same time he believed in the innate virtues of the Russian peasant and craved for contact with simple men of the people. This may be variously interpreted as the preference, common enough in history among despotic rulers, for dealing only with stupid people who can be trusted to obey, or as the honourable wish of a good man, surrounded by careerists and flatterers, to escape from the frustrations of the court and to know and help his subjects. In any case, these various characteristics of Nicholas, in the years after 1905, when the memory of revolution was fresh and he was preoccupied with his son's health, contributed to the undoing of himself and his dynasty.

The opening of a new reign aroused among zemstvo leaders the hope that more liberal policies might be considered. This was most strongly expressed in the address of the Tver provin-

[1] His memoirs—V. P. Meshchersky, *Moi vospominaniya*, SPB, 1898—contain some details of interest on political conditions in the third quarter of the nineteenth century. He edited a newspaper entitled *Grazhdanin*, of right-wing complexion and addicted to scandal.

cial zemstvo to the Tsar on the occasion of his accession. In it occurred the passage: 'Sire, we await the opportunity and the right for public institutions to express their opinion on questions which concern them, so that the expression of the needs and thought not only of the administration but also of the Russian people may reach to the very height of the Throne.' The emperor's reply was given at a reception on 17 January 1895 for deputations of the nobility, zemstvos, and cities: 'I am informed that recently in some zemstvo assemblies voices have made themselves heard from people carried away by senseless dreams about participation by representatives of the zemstvo in the affairs of internal government; let all know that I, devoting all my strength to the welfare of the people, will uphold the principle of autocracy as firmly and as unflinchingly as my late unforgettable father.'

Nevertheless, the political climate had changed. The effect of the removal of Alexander III may be compared with that of Nicholas I. People were no longer intimidated by the figure of the new ruler, as they had been by that of the old. The pressure for change was not so obvious or urgent as after the Crimean War, but it was no less real. It took the form not so much of specific demands in high places as of the growth of new social and economic forces whose political consequences could not indefinitely be denied.

During the decade from the accession of Nicholas II to the revolutionary crisis of 1905, four political movements developed. One of these, the nationalism of the non-Russian peoples, has been treated separately. The other three are Marxism, Liberalism, and a revived form of Populism. These will be examined in turn, and the decade will be divided into three distinct though overlapping periods. In the first, which goes approximately to the end of the century, political groups were formed. In the following two years party organizations became consolidated. In the last year or two the pace of events in Russia quickened, leading to a revolutionary phase in 1905. These three phases are only approximate, and the turning-points do not come at exactly the same time in each of the three movements, but they do serve to clarify the course of events.

Marxism

The ideas of Karl Marx were known to Russian intellectuals already in the 1870's. The revolutionaries of *Narodnaya volya* considered Marx one of the great socialists. But it was not until the mid 1880's, when Plekhanov's polemical writings reached Russia, that Russian socialists began to think of Marxism and Populism as different movements, and in fact relations between the two remained friendly for longer than that. A specifically Marxist discussion group existed in St. Petersburg in 1885, led by a Bulgarian student named Dimitar Blagoyev.[1] It communicated with Plekhanov in Switzerland, but its members were arrested in 1886. Other groups in the capital consisted largely of Poles. The most important of these, which functioned from 1889 onwards, included two Russians, M. I. Brusnev and L. B. Krassin.[2] By the end of the 1880's Marxist ideas were becoming very popular among university students, and this process was accelerated with the appearance of Struve's *Critical Notes* and 'Beltov's' *Monistic View* in 1894.[3] The censors were tolerant towards Marxist writings provided that strictly political issues were kept in the background. In 1896 and 1897 the Marxists even published two newspapers, *Samarskii vestnik* in Samara and *Novoe slovo* in St. Petersburg, the latter under the direction of Struve.[4] Marxism came as a revelation to young Russians—as indeed it has come to young intellectuals in many lands since

[1] Blagoyev later founded the social-democratic movement in Bulgaria, split it in 1903, and became the founder of the Bulgarian Communist Party in 1918. He was also the author of a famous book, *A Contribution to the History of Socialism in Bulgaria*, published in Sofia in 1906.

[2] Krassin later became an engineer and an active Bolshevik. He was Soviet ambassador in London in 1924.

[3] See above p. 533.

[4] The phrase 'legal Marxists', with a more or less pronounced accent of contempt, was later applied to Struve and his group. The fact that they made use of 'legal' opportunities to publish Marxist views was surely no fault from the point of view of the cause of socialism. However, Struve and his friends Tugan-Baranovsky, Berdyayev, and Bulgakov did, in fact, form a distinct group. They later moved from Marxism to Liberalism, and three of them returned to the fold of the Orthodox Church. Essentially, they were independent-minded intellectuals of great mental distinction who did not wish to engage in revolutionary party activity, who accepted in large part the Marxist analysis of society without accepting the conclusion that they should work for revolution. That revolutionaries should regard them as traitors to the cause is very easy to understand. But the name 'Legal Marxists' does not seem to me to describe well the political role of these men. The dispute between them and the orthodox Marxists was not primarily about whether or not use should be made of opportunities for 'legal' activity.

then. The specific, concrete, and scientific approach to social problems stressed by Marxists compared favourably with the vague and old-fashioned, if heroic and romantic, slogans of the Populists.

During the same period groups had been forming among the workers of some St. Petersburg factories for study and self-improvement. Their aim was not only political education but education in a wider sense. They were glad to receive help from university students or other educated persons willing to lend them books or to give them oral instruction. At the same time the members of political groups of intellectuals, whether Marxist or Populist, sought contact with the workers. However, there was a certain conflict of aims. In the words of a recent historian, 'The workers wanted to learn in order to escape the monotonous and hopeless condition of the factory worker and to win a place in society. Education was to them the key which opened doors to seemingly unlimited opportunities. . . . The intellectuals on the other hand treated education largely as a means of bringing socialist ideas to the working class. It was the first step in launching the worker on the road to seditious anti-government activity; to them it represented essentially a political device.'[1] This conflict of aims, and a certain instinctive distrust of workers for persons from the upper classes, limited though it did not prevent co-operation. From 1889 there was in St. Petersburg a Central Workers' Circle, of seven or eight members, linking together a number of small groups of workers, and there were several groups of Marxist intellectuals. In August 1893 one of these was joined by Vladimir Ilyich Ulyanov, brother of the revolutionary Alexander Ulyanov executed in 1887. This was the beginning of the revolutionary career of Lenin.[2]

Marxism was also making progress among the Jewish population of Vilna. It was here that a pamphlet entitled *On Agitation* was written in 1894 by Arkadi Kremer. His argument was essentially that Marxists must not confine themselves to propagating their doctrine, but must also make contact with

[1] Richard Pipes, *Social Democracy and the St. Petersburg Labor Movement 1885–1897* (Harvard, 1963), p. 10.

[2] Lenin had been a member of a Marxist group in Kazan organized by N. E. Fedoseyev, but his active career may be said to have started from his arrival in the capital.

the masses, find out what the masses wanted, and gain their confidence by making themselves the exponents of their everyday material grievances.[1] One of Kremer's associates, Julius Martov, came to St. Petersburg in the autumn of 1895. He and Lenin met and became close friends and political allies. Lenin, who in the previous year had been mainly occupied in literary activity, and had gone in the summer to Switzerland to meet Plekhanov, now took up the idea of agitation very seriously. His group and Martov's merged, maintained contact with textile workers at the Thornton mills, and prepared a newspaper for publication on a secret printing press. But in December 1895 most of the group, including Lenin, were arrested, and a month later Martov and several more were rounded up.[2]

With the arrest of the most active St. Petersburg Marxist intellectuals, social democratic activity in the capital passed into the hands of those who thought rather in terms of a working-class organization run by workers than of a conspiratorial organization run by intellectuals. But the surviving groups of both Marxist intellectuals and workers in St. Petersburg, Moscow, Vilna, and Kiev decided to go ahead with their plan to found a party. It was decided to hold a secret congress in Minsk, and it met on 1 March 1898. The new party took the name Russian Social Democratic Labour Party (RSDRP). Controversial questions of organization and discipline were left unsolved. A manifesto, written by Struve, was adopted. The Jewish *Bund*, which had been founded in 1897, was admitted as 'an autonomous organization independent solely in matters of particular concern to the Jewish proletariat'.[3] But a few days

[1] Plekhanov once defined propaganda as presenting many ideas to a few people, and agitation as presenting one idea to many people. Each had its uses.

[2] After Lenin's arrest his group took the name 'League of Struggle for the Liberation of the Working Class'. Pipes argues convincingly (*Social Democracy*, pp. 84–115) that the League had little connexion with the textile strikes of May 1896. At most its surviving members helped the strikers as an editorial and printing centre for leaflets: it certainly did not 'organize' or 'lead' the strike. Still less did Lenin, who had been under arrest for five months. Lenin was fortunate in that the authorities did not know that he was the editor of the secret newspaper, as the captured text was in the handwriting of another of those arrested. Consequently he got a light sentence of exile for three years to Siberia, beginning in 1897. Subject to the normal police restrictions on movement of exiles, Lenin and Martov lived in Siberia in comparatively free and comfortable conditions.

[3] See above p. 496 and n. for the *Bund*, and p. 540 for an extract from Struve's manifesto.

later the police made far-reaching arrests of Social Democrats, and by January 1899 eight out of the nine delegates to the congress were under arrest.

Liberalism

The word 'liberalism' has been used by historians of Russia to describe a wide range of political opinion and activity, extending from rather conservative zemstvo leaders to radical intellectuals who could almost equally well be called 'socialists'.

The most moderate of the zemstvo politicians were not mainly interested in basic political principles. Their aim was to improve public welfare. But for this purpose it was necessary that zemstvo leaders from all parts of the country should help each other with their experience, and that there should be some regular machinery of contact and consultation. The moderates even went so far as to believe that it would be to the good of the country as a whole if there were some central representative body which the central government could regularly consult, in order to inform itself of the wishes of the people's spokesmen. This was not a demand for universal suffrage, still less for parliamentary government: rather it was another version of the old Slavophil doctrine of consultation between Tsar and people. The leading exponent of such views was D. N. Shipov, chairman of the board of Moscow provincial zemstvo. In the summer of 1896 Shipov organized a meeting of zemstvo provincial board chairmen at the Nizhnii Novgorod Fair. The minister of the interior, I. L. Goremykin, was informed beforehand and gave a grudging consent. However, when Shipov proposed to hold a similar meeting the following year in St. Petersburg, he was forbidden to do so.[1]

Some zemstvo leaders were more radical than this. Outstanding among them was the veteran I. I. Petrunkevich, who since his return from banishment had been active in Tver province. More radical as a group than the members of zemstvo assemblies or boards were the expert officials employed by them, who at the end of the century were generally known as the 'Third Element'.[2] The main demands of the Third Element were the abolition of corporal punishment and the

[1] D. N. Shipov, *Vospominaniya i dumy o perezhitom* (Moscow, 1918), pp. 63–85.
[2] See above p. 471 and n. 2.

establishment of universal primary education. They also strongly supported the growing demand from zemstvo boards for the abolition of the separate legal status of the peasantry. This required the disappearance of the *volost* court and the office of land commandant, and the creation of an all-class elective body at *volost* level, the so-called 'small zemstvo unit'. These and similar demands also enjoyed the sympathy of intellectuals in the capitals who were neither members of zemstvos nor zemstvo employees. Such people met the Third Element at professional congresses. There were some societies of great reputation to which provincial intellectuals could belong, and which provided a forum for public discussions. Such was the ancient Imperial Free Economic Society whose president in the late 1890's was Count Peter Heyden, and the Moscow Law Society whose president was Professor S. A. Muromtsev. Another figure of growing importance in the liberal movement was the Moscow historian P. N. Milyukov.

The university students were again becoming interested in politics. In May 1896, at the celebrations for the coronation of Nicholas II in Moscow, a crowd, waiting to see the emperor on the Khodynka field, surged forward across ground interrupted by ditches, thousands of people fell and were crushed by others, and before the movement could be controlled 1,282 people had been killed and more than 500 wounded. Six months later a group of Moscow students organized a demonstrative march to the cemetery where the victims were buried, and some of them were arrested. The next outburst of student feeling was in February 1899, when a tactless announcement by the rector of St. Petersburg University led to student demonstrations in the street, and these ended with a charge by mounted police. This was the first time that violence was used in public against students, and it aroused great public indignation. The Tsar himself was shocked, and made what he believed to be a conciliatory gesture, by appointing the former minister of war, General P. S. Vannovsky, who was hostile to the police, to head an inquiry into the incidents. The students, however, were not appeased. They declared a strike, which spread to other universities. In the summer of 1899 new 'temporary rules' were published, which gave power to special boards, under the regional curators of educational districts, to expel students guilty of political activity, and provided that all those expelled should be sent to serve in the ranks of the armed forces. These repressive measures secured outward order, though there were numerous other student disorders in the following years, especially in Kiev. But the effect was that the universities became centres of bitter hostility to the government up to 1905. The former student P. Karpovich, who on 1 February 1901 murdered the minister of education, N. P. Bogolepov, was not typical, but his action aroused sympathy and even admiration.

At the turn of the century there were two lines of action open to Russian liberals, not mutually exclusive, and both were used. One was to press the government to permit greater public participation in social and administrative policy. Despite discouragement, Shipov and his friends continued their efforts. The government was obstructive, but it was not of one opinion. In 1899 the minister of the interior, Goremykin, who had had some experience of zemstvo work in his earlier career, and did not wish completely to antagonize the zemstvo leaders, proposed that zemstvo institutions should be introduced into more provinces—in Lithuania, White Russia, Western Ukraine, and the Lower Volga. He was strongly opposed by Witte. In a memorandum to Goremykin entitled *Autocracy and Zemstvo*, which became widely known when a copy was published abroad by the opposition,[1] Witte argued that these were incompatible, and that either the autocratic system must give way to constitutional government, or local government must cease to be elective. Witte's language was deliberately ambiguous: his paper could be used in defence of either autocracy or a constitution. The motives for his action seem to have been partly a desire to get the influential Pobedonostsev on his side in the battle of personalities within the government by denouncing zemstvo influence in primary education (which Pobedonostsev wished the Church to control), and partly distrust of regional opinion which he expected would support, from the point of view of agricultural interests, the opponents of his financial and industrial policy. The manœuvre was in any case successful, for Goremykin's proposals were rejected by the Tsar, and he was replaced as minister of the interior by D. S. Sipyagin. Three

[1] *Samoderzhavie i zemstvo*, published in Stuttgart in 1903 by *Osvobozhdenie*, with introduction by P. B. Struve.

years later, however, Witte changed his attitude to the zemstvos and sought to enlist their support for his plans for the reform of agriculture. His decision to set up regional committees in connexion with his Special Conference of 1902 on the needs of agriculture was influenced by one of the outstanding zemstvo leaders, M. A. Stakhovich, the marshal of nobility of Oryol province.[1]

In the first years of the century the government was at last making some effort to understand what was wrong with agriculture in Russia, and even to consider remedies. But it was still determined that all this should be done from above, without participation by any unofficial bodies. Witte's committees were the only partial exception. Even in this case, zemstvo personalities took part only when nominated by governors. The wish of the zemstvos that they might be allowed to elect their representatives to the committees was refused.

The other line of action open to Russian liberals was to set up an illegal political organization, and to make propaganda for a constitution and for democratic liberties. This was the course which appealed to the bolder spirits, especially to the radical intellectuals both in the zemstvos and in the capitals. Their arguments were strengthened by further repressive actions of the government, which in 1899 saw fit to close down the Moscow Law Society, and in the following year interfered with the activities of the Free Economic Society. During 1901 plans were made for the establishment abroad of a newspaper which was to express the views of the moderate opposition to the government. P. B. Struve was chosen as editor of the paper, and it was founded under the name of 'Liberation' (*Osvobozhdenie*) in Stuttgart, where the first number appeared in January 1902. The paper took a strongly radical line. In particular, it insisted that liberals could only claim the right to ask revolutionaries to abstain from violence if they themselves would 'throw political action and civic courage into the scales of history'. The foundation of the newspaper was intended as the first stage towards setting up in Russia an organization which would actually fight for these principles. The second stage was a meeting in Schaffhausen in Switzerland, attended

[1] Gurko, op. cit., pp. 207–11. For the activities of the Commission see above pp. 514–16.

by ten persons each from the zemstvos and from the radical intelligentsia, which founded the Union of Liberation as an illegal oppositional party.[1] The first meeting on Russian soil of most of its leading figures took place in St. Petersburg in January 1904. The programme adopted by this meeting spoke plainly of the abolition of autocracy and the establishment of a constitutional government. The Union of Liberation committed itself to universal, secret, direct suffrage by equal constituencies. It placed political liberty before all else, but it stated that the Union would also in the social and economic field 'follow the same basic principle of democracy, making the direct goal of its activity the defence of the interests of the labouring masses'. It also demanded the restoration of Finland's rights and even upheld 'the right of self-determination of the different nationalities entering into the composition of the Russian state'.[2] Petrunkevich was elected chairman.

The Union of Liberation represented the ideas of the radical intellectuals, but had considerable support even from zemstvo liberals of the old school. Its programme was, however, too strong meat for men like Shipov. The Union thus did not represent all sections of the zemstvo movement. It could, on the other hand, be supported by persons of socialist outlook, and indeed many of its leaders had been socialists. The dividing line between the Union and the true socialist parties was in the field of tactics rather than of doctrine. The Union did not advocate revolutionary violence as a means of seizing power.

The Socialist Revolutionaries

Apart from the 'legal Populists' grouped around *Russkoe bogatstvo*, whose leading figure was N. K. Mikhailovsky, small groups of conspiratorial Populists still existed. There was a People's Will group in St. Petersburg in the early 1890's. It co-operated with the Marxist groups, its members were strongly influenced by Marxist ideas, and were on the point of fusing with the Marxists when they were rounded up by the police in 1897.

[1] George Fischer in his *Russian Liberalism from Gentry to Intelligentsia*, (Harvard, 1958), p. 141, suggests that the 20 should more realistically be divided into 7 gentry liberals, 6 intelligentsia liberals, and 7 intelligentsia socialists. The last group would include the former socialists and so-called 'legal Marxists' Struve, Berdyayev, Bulgakov, and Frank.

[2] I. P. Belokonsky, *Zemskoe dvizhenie* (Moscow, 1914), pp. 191–2.

Other small groups in the provinces called themselves 'socialist revolutionaries'. All were in practice solely concerned with the urban working class: the discouragements of the 1870's had left behind the belief that revolutionary activity among peasants was hopeless. In fact, the main difference between the Marxist and Populist groups at this stage appeared to be one of temperament: the Marxists talked more of the inevitable processes of history, the Populists of revolutionary heroism.

During the 1890's some of those exiled in the 1870's were allowed to return. Among them was Catherine Breshko-Breshkovskaya, a woman of untiring energy and unquenchable revolutionary ardour, who travelled up and down the country seeking disciples and reviving enthusiams, earning thereby the title of 'grandmother of the revolution'. In 1894 another returned exile, the former leader of *Zemlya i volya*, Natanson, tried to create a new organization, under the name People's Right (*Narodnoe pravo*). It had the support of Mikhailovsky, and it produced a manifesto urging the union of all oppositional forces in the country in a struggle for political liberty. Its activities were almost immediately stopped by the police. In the next years, however, three centres developed, from which there emerged a new and important political force, the Socialist Revolutionary movement.

The first was the Union of Socialist Revolutionaries, founded in 1896 in Saratov, which in the following years transferred its activities to Moscow, but had its main following in the Volga valley. In 1898 it published a programme, *Our Tasks*. This paid hardly any attention to the peasants, did not believe that socialism was a practical possibility in the near future, and proposed to devote itself to the struggle for political liberty. It concluded as follows:

> Thus, political liberty in the name of socialist revolution is our immediate aim. The socialist intelligentsia and the most advanced section of the factory proletariat are our main, though not our sole strength. Propaganda, agitation, and the organization of the conditions which will make it possible to begin and carry through the political liberation of Russia, with the help of a systematic terroristic struggle against the autocracy, together with other forms of mass struggle, coming from various strata of the population—such are the tasks of preparatory work at the present time.

A second group arose a little later in the south. There were meetings of Populists in Voronezh in August 1897, in Poltava in November, in Kiev in 1898, and in Kharkov in 1900. The Kharkov meeting ended with a decision to form the southern groups into a Party of Socialist Revolutionaries. Like the Union, the Party put first the struggle against autocracy. 'Putting forward the attainment of a constitution as our immediate demand, we do not renounce the struggle for a further and complete realization of the people's will.' The Party's manifesto paid more attention to work among the peasants than had the Union's *Our Tasks*. It considered it possible to support the peasants' instinctive struggle 'by means of far-reaching agitation and by organizing the struggle in more correct and useful forms—strikes of agricultural workers and small tenants, boycotting of grasping landlords, resistance to . . . unequal taxation, protests against high taxes, and against arbitrary acts of the administration and the government'. The manifesto made no reference to terror.[1]

The third group was established in 1898 in Minsk by Breshko-Breshkovskaya and by a young Jewish chemist and bacteriologist, G. A. Gershuni. In 1900 it published its programme under the title *Liberty*. Its main emphasis was on terror as a weapon of struggle.

These three main sections of the Populist movement made contact with each other. The most effective centre of revolutionary Populism was the Volga valley, and especially the city and province of Saratov. In the winter of 1896–7 Viktor Chernov organized a Populist group among peasants in a village of Tambov province.[2] Other Populists also made propaganda among peasants in Poltava province. Gershuni was the outstanding advocate and practitioner of terrorism, whose attractiveness as a method of political action was notably increased by the assassination of the minister of education Bogolepov. Another talented terrorist organizer was Evno Azeff. At the end of 1901 Gershuni and Azeff went to Berlin,

[1] The quotations are given in S. Slyotov, *K istorii vozniknoveniya partii sotsialistov-revolyutsionerov* (Petrograd, 1917), pp. 71, 82, 83.

[2] For details see V. M. Chernov, *Zapiski sotsialista-revolyutsionera* (Berlin, 1923), chapters 8 and 9. A good brief summary of the origins of the party can be found in O. H. Radkey, *The Agrarian Foes of Bolshevism*, New York, 1958. This book is, however, principally concerned with the events of 1917.

where they met Chernov (who had left Russia in 1899) and the veteran M. R. Gotz, a returned exile from the 1870's who had gone to live abroad. These men were the founders of the united Party of Socialist Revolutionaries, whose formal existence dates from this time.

The Socialist Revolutionaries (or SR's, as they came to be called) were a different kind of party from the Social Democrats. Their formal membership was never large or well disciplined. They became a mighty force at times when the peasants moved into action: then their propaganda, conducted by romantic rebels whose emotions and rhetoric were close to the peasants' own feelings, spread with the speed and power of an epidemic. In quiet times their influence was small. But side by side with the party, formally incorporated in it yet in practice independent of it, was a much smaller and highly disciplined organization, the Combat Detachment (*boevoy otryad*). Of its glories and infamies more will be said later.

In the first years of the century the SR's were a rapidly growing force. The assassination of the minister of the interior Sipyagin on 2 April 1902 by an SR named S. V. Balmashev raised their revolutionary prestige. In March and April 1902 there were peasant riots in Poltava and Kharkov provinces. Peasants invaded landowners' estates, cut their trees, robbed their granaries, drove off their cattle and in some cases burned down their farm buildings or houses. The large number of such outbreaks suggested organization, and indeed the SR's had made propaganda in the area. Both the police and the enemies of the government gave them more credit than they really deserved, and this too raised their morale.[1] Above all the events of 1902 showed them that the Russian peasants were not the stagnant reactionary force that they had feared: great opportunities were there to be used.

Political Parties in Action

The failure of the first attempt to found a Social Democratic Party was followed by bitter divisions among Russian Marxists.

[1] The new minister of the interior, V. K. von Pleve, professed to believe that the revolts were the work of zemstvo statisticians, of whom there were 594 in Poltava province alone, and even obtained from the Tsar powers to forbid statistical zemstvo surveys (Gurko, op. cit., pp. 235–7). There might even be some truth in Pleve's belief, though to 'explain' the revolts in these terms is of course ridiculous.

These appeared most clearly in the free press of the exiles. For some time there had existed a League of Russian Social Democrats Abroad, in which Plekhanov's own Liberation of Labour group had been fused. It published a paper entitled *Rabochii* ('The Worker'). But Plekhanov was now seriously worried by the growth in its ranks of the 'anti-political' heresy, of which he himself had been a champion in *Zemlya i volya* times, but which he had fought, and he had hoped demolished, in his 1883 pamphlet *Socialism and the Political Struggle*. The worst offenders were the married couple S. N. Prokopovich and E. D. Kuskova, who admired the Belgian labour movement, and believed that mass action in pursuit of the workers' material interests was more important than political programmes and ideologies. In 1897 Kuskova visited St. Petersburg and gave a talk to a group of social democrats, who made their notes up into a pamphlet and distributed it, apparently without the speaker's consent. The Marxist exiles in Siberia received copies, and were moved to fierce indignation. So was Plekhanov in Switzerland. The Kuskova lecture was given by its opponents the ironic title of *Credo*, and treated as the expression of a dangerous belief, now thought to be penetrating the social democratic ranks, which was given by its opponents the name 'Economism'. Its essence was supposed to be the doctrine that the political struggle should be abandoned to the *bourgeoisie*, and that the social democratic movement should devote itself solely to the economic struggle for the workers' interests.

It is very doubtful whether 'Economism' existed at all. The views of Kuskova and of Prokopovich (who was at this time under arrest in Russia) may have approximated to this, but they had no significant following. Plekhanov in exile, from 1898 when the *Voraussetzungen* of the German Social Democrat Bernstein appeared, was genuinely preoccupied with the danger of Revisionism to the whole international movement, and wished to prevent it from entrenching itself in the young Russian movement. For Lenin and Martov in Siberia the problem was different. Since their arrest the St. Petersburg movement had fallen into the hands of the school of thought that was derived, not from the intellectual groups but from the workers' circles of the 1890's. Their effective leader, K. M. Takhtarev, published in 1897 two copies of a paper *Rabochaya mysl'* ('The

Workers' Thought') but then felt obliged to go into exile and to continue the paper abroad.[1] He and his friends were certainly not indifferent to the political struggle, but they believed that it should be conducted by the workers themselves, in a mass movement, not by an *élite* of Marxist intellectuals on their behalf. In fact, the conflict between *Rabochaya mysl'* and Lenin was not between the politically minded and the politically indifferent, but between the idea of a mass labour movement and the idea of revolutionary *élitism*. This became the basic issue in the subsequent history of Russian social democracy. It is true that the facts of life in Russia favoured Lenin's view so far as a mass movement was not possible under an autocratic régime, and political action therefore had to be conspiratorial. But the controversy was concerned with more than the best form of tactics or of revolutionary security. It was not only a matter of what each side thought possible, but of what each desired in the future. Lenin never wanted a democratic mass movement: even under conditions of political liberty he would have insisted on an *élitist* organization.

Lenin and Martov were allowed to leave Siberia in 1900. After a short stay in European Russia they went abroad and put into effect the plan they had conceived during their exile of creating a new social democratic newspaper with a clear political programme, round which a restored and unified movement should be built.[2] Though they found Plekhanov personally difficult to handle, they were able to smooth over disagreements, and the first number of the paper *Iskra* ('The Spark') appeared in Germany in December 1900. During the following year, apart from his editorial work and communications with Russia, Lenin worked on a short book which was his greatest contribution to political theory, and is perhaps the most significant single document in the history of modern communism. This book took the title of Chernyshevsky's

[1] Takhtarev published some memoirs on this period in London in 1902, under the pseudonym Peterburzhets, entitled *Ocherki peterburzhskogo rabochego dvizhenia 90-kh godov*. In 1897 the official paper of the League Abroad, *Rabochii*, changed its name to *Rabochee delo* ('The Worker's Cause'): though less 'Economist' than *Rabochaya mysl'*, it too incurred the wrath of Plekhanov.

[2] Lenin had certainly not been idle during his Siberian exile. It was at this time that he wrote *The Development of Capitalism in Russia*, which was published while he was still in Siberia. See above p. 533 n. 2.

utopian novel *What is to be Done?* In it Lenin developed the idea of the 'party of a new type' needed for the revolutionary struggle, the blueprint for his future Bolshevik party and for all the communist parties which came into being in the years after 1917.[1] The party must be based on thorough understanding of Marxist theory and on firm internal discipline. Intellectuals have a decisive role to play, for 'by its own unaided efforts the working class is capable of evolving only a "trade-unionist" consciousness—that is to say, a conviction of the need to form trade unions, struggle with the employers, obtain from the government this or that law required by the workers, and so on'. Only those thoroughly versed in Marxist doctrine can undertake revolutionary leadership of the workers. They can understand the true interests of the workers better than the workers themselves. Lenin did not believe that the existing intelligentsia in Russia was necessarily destined to lead. At first '*bourgeois* intellectuals' would be an important element, because only the upper classes had the opportunity to educate themselves. Marx and Engels themselves had been *bourgeois* intellectuals. But children of peasants or workers who mastered Marxist theory could, of course, enter the *élite*. The essential points were that there must be an *élite*, and that no one could enter the *élite* who had not undergone the intellectual training of learning Marxist theory under the direction of the existing *élite*. The party must become—Lenin himself used the phrase—an organization of professional revolutionaries.

The first years of the century were favourable to the development of the revolutionary movement. In 1899 Russian industry entered a period of depression. Two large mixed industrial concerns, Von Derviz and Mamontov, went bankrupt. In the next years the southern metallurgical industry suffered badly. Many smaller firms were ruined, and unemployment increased. In these conditions the workers were in no position to obtain better working conditions: economic strikes always have poor prospects in slump years. On the other hand the workers' discontent increased, and they were more willing to listen to political slogans. Both Populists and Marxists made use of this more favourable political climate.

[1] A recent English translation, with an introduction and notes by S. V. Utechin, was published by The Clarendon Press, Oxford, in 1963.

These years also saw an unexpected development from the workers' point of view. S. V. Zubatov, head of the defence section (*Okhrana*) of the police in Moscow, tried the experiment of setting up workers' organizations under indirect police control in order to canalize their discontent away from the government and towards their employers. He obtained the consent of the Grand Duke Sergei, governor-general of Moscow, for his plans. In February 1902 was founded the 'Society for Mutual Help of Workers in Mechanical Production'. It organized such harmless activities as demonstrations in favour of the Tsar and communal singing of patriotic songs. The minister of the interior, Pleve, for a time supported the idea, and he pressed for two laws which were passed in June 1903, setting up elected workers' elders to represent them in dealing with employers and obliging employers to compensate injured workers. Zubatov also organized a workers' union in the western provinces. But his unions became to some extent penetrated by social democrats, and in the end probably helped revolutionary activity more than they hindered it. When his union was involved in a general strike in Odessa in 1903, the opposition to Zubatov in government circles, which had been growing ever since he started his enterprise, was strong enough to secure his dismissal from his post. But working-class action was already becoming impressive. Especially alarming to the authorities were a two weeks' strike in Rostov-on-Don in November 1902, which was for some days extended into a general strike, and a strike in Baku in July 1903 which also affected almost all work in the city.

In July 1903 the Second Congress of the RSDRP met, first in Brussels and then in London. This was really the founding congress, for the First Congress in Minsk in 1898 had led to no result. But the second founding congress of 1903 ended in a split. It was clear that the supporters of the *Iskra* line would prevail over the 'Economists', but what was not expected was that the *Iskra* men would themselves split. This came about when Martov decided to oppose Lenin's draft for the party constitution. Lenin wished to confine members of the party to persons who would not only accept the programme but 'support the party by personal participation in one of the party organizations'. Only active revolutionaries were wanted.

Martov wanted a broader definition. On this issue Lenin was outvoted. At a later stage in the congress, in the voting on the composition of the editorial board of *Iskra*, Lenin's supporters were in the majority. It was from the voting on this issue that the names were derived which were later attached to the two sections into which the party split. Lenin called his group the 'majoritarians' (*bolsheviki*), and his opponents the 'minoritarians' (*mensheviki*). Soon afterwards Lenin found himself in a minority again, after Plekhanov had changed his mind about the editorial board. In the summer of 1904 *Iskra* passed under Menshevik control, and Lenin set up his own organization, the Union of Committees of the Majority, with its own central bureau and its own newspaper *Vperyod* ('Forward'). Thus when the revolutionary crisis came in Russia, there were two social democratic parties.[1]

The outbreak of war with Japan in January 1904 produced varying reactions in the Union of Liberation. Struve and Petrunkevich took a patriotic line; Milyukov was against supporting any government-sponsored patriotic activities: and the former Populist Peshekhonov was a defeatist. The attitude of Pleve to even moderate zemstvo liberals remained hostile. He was implacably opposed to any organization on a national scale and saw fit to prevent in April 1904 the re-election of Shipov to the chairmanship of Moscow provincial zemstvo board which he had held for the past eleven years. But Pleve's days were numbered: on 15 July 1904 he was assassinated by the SR E. S. Sazonov.

This event made a tremendous impression on the public, and the government, faced with a war which was not going well, could not afford indefinitely to antagonize its subjects. The new minister, Prince P. D. Svyatopolk-Mirsky, was a man of liberal inclinations. Consciously echoing the appeal of Loris-Melikov a quarter century earlier, he publicly expressed the conviction that 'fertile efforts by the government must be

[1] There can be no place in a general history for the detailed story of the personal, ideological, and other factors involved in the split, or for the manœuvres carried out by the various sections. The full proceedings of the Congresses of the RSDRP are available in many editions. Lenin's own story is in his pamphlet *One Step forward, Two Steps back*. A good recent account by a British historian is J. H. L. Keep, *The Rise of Social Democracy in Russia* (1963), ch. iv.

based on a sincerely benevolent and truly trusting attitude to public and class organizations and to the population in general. Only in such conditions of work is it possible to obtain the mutual confidence without which one cannot expect any solid success in the business of building up the state.' These well-meaning if turgidly bureaucratic phrases were put to the test by the request for permission to hold a congress of zemstvo representatives in St. Petersburg in November. The most that the minister was able to do was to consent to these persons meeting as a private gathering. The congress met, and passed resolutions which included the hope that 'the supreme authority will call together the freely elected representatives of the people', and embark on 'a new path of development of the state, of establishing the principles of law, and of interaction between state and people'. Prince Sergei Trubetskoy was authorized to prepare a memorandum for presentation to the Tsar. In this he argued that the issue of the day was 'the rights and lack of rights not of the village but of all Russian citizens in general', and that the nation needed a statement from the Tsar to express 'the will of the monarch to abolish the police-bureaucratic system and to assemble for creative work the elected representatives of the land'.[1]

No such statement was yet forthcoming. Meanwhile the illegal Union of Liberation had decided to hold a series of public banquets during November, ostensibly to commemorate the fortieth anniversary of the judicial reform but in fact to rally public opinion to press for a constitution. The organizers had in mind the banquets which preceded the downfall of Louis Philippe in France in 1848. The banquets took place, each with hundreds of guests and were fully reported in the press. At the St. Petersburg banquet demands were made for a Constituent Assembly.

[1] Shipov, op. cit., pp. 581–7.

XVI

FOREIGN POLICY

The Franco-Russian Alliance

THE division of the Balkans into Austrian and Russian spheres of influence, carried out by the Treaty of Berlin, corresponded to the conventional wisdom of European diplomacy, but it did not work. The essential reason is that each dominant Great Power antagonized the politically conscious class in the country allotted to it, and each enjoyed sympathy in the corresponding class in the country allotted to its rival. The conflicts between the rulers and the rising middle classes, between the new political parties within each state, and between the rival nationalisms of the states, were not understood by the Russian or Austrian governments. Their failure to handle these problems not only made them unpopular with the Balkan peoples, but damaged their relations with each other.

Serbia's status as a vassal of Austria was formalized by a commercial and a political treaty in 1881. The latter bound the Serbian government not to tolerate any anti-Austrian activity on Serbian soil, and not to conclude an agreement with any other Power without previously consulting Austria. When his ministers objected to the relevant Article 4 of the treaty, Milan (who now assumed, with Austrian approval, the title of king), obtained from the Austrian government a modifying clause, but wrote a letter to the Austrian emperor in which he stated that he personally considered the original article binding. In the following years Milan met with increasing opposition from his subjects, including an armed rising in the north-east in October 1883. Sympathy for Russia, the Slav elder brother and the rival of the hated king's protecting Power, spread in all classes of the Serbian people.

In the new state of Bulgaria there were three political factors—the Conservatives, who stood for economic modernization and rising capitalist interests, the Liberals, who were led by the radical intelligentsia and enjoyed wider peasant support, and the ruler, Prince Alexander of Battenberg, whose inclinations were towards a central European type of monarchy rather than a rough Balkan democracy. Russian policy was ineffective because the Ministry of Foreign Affairs tended to support the Prince and the Ministry of War the Liberals. The most reliable Russophils were the Conservatives, and they were soon alienated by clumsy attempts by Russian business interests to monopolize railway construction in Bulgaria. By September 1883 the three naturally rival forces had been united, by repeated Russian tactlessness, in common opposition to Russian policy.[1]

In 1883 the third Balkan state, Roumania, made an alliance with Germany and Austria. Roumania was, like Serbia and Bulgaria, a territorially dissatisfied state. The Serbian irridenta was in Austria-Hungary and in Turkish territories occupied by Austria (Vojvodina, Bosnia, Hercegovina, and Novi Bazar), the Bulgarian in the Ottoman empire (Macedonia and Thrace). Roumania's irridenta was both in Russia (Bessarabia) and in Austria-Hungary (Transylvania and Bukovina). Roumania was obliged to seek the protection of one of its powerful enemies against the other. An alliance with either Russia or Austria was bound to be unpopular. The saving feature of the alliance which Roumania made in 1883 was that it was guaranteed by the presence of Germany. Roumania had no grievance against Germany. Roumanian admiration for Germany was surpassed only by admiration for France, which was too far away, and at present too weak, to help Roumania. King Carol I of Roumania was a Hohenzollern prince. He and many of his subjects hoped that Germany would press Austria to treat her Roumanian subjects better. In practice this did not happen. The Hungarian authorities were not deterred by any advice from either Vienna or Berlin from their policy of administrative, economic, and cultural 'magyarization', directed in Transylvania against the Roumanians.[2] Thus the alliance of 1883

[1] For details on Bulgaria see C. E. Black, *The Establishment of Constitutional Government in Bulgaria*, Princeton, 1943. There is still no satisfactory work in a Western language on Serbia's politics in the last decades of the century. In Serbo-Croatian, the classic works of Slododan Jovanović, *Vlada Milana Obrenovića* and *Vlada Aleksandra Obrenovića*, are still unsurpassed.

[2] For details see R. W. Seton-Watson, *A History of the Roumanians*, pp. 360–6 and 397–409.

became unpopular in Roumania. At the same time it was, of course, regarded in St. Petersburg as an anti-Russian move, for which Germany no less than Austria was blamed.

During the early 1880's the attitudes of the Powers to the artificial division between Bulgaria and Eastern Roumelia were modified. Alexander III was convinced that Alexander Battenberg was an enemy of Russia and so objected to anything which might strengthen him. For the same reason the British government favoured Battenberg and no longer objected to a union of the two Bulgarian territories. The Austrian attitude was similar.

A serious Anglo-Russian crisis occurred at the beginning of 1885. The Russian conquest of the Turcomans in 1882 had been followed by the occupation of Merv in 1884. On 30 March 1885 Russian troops clashed with Afghan forces at Penjdeh. Russian expansion in Transcaspia had for some time alarmed the British government, and it looked as if the Russians intended to advance still further into an area regarded as essential to the defence of India. Gladstone's ministry demanded increased defence credits, and there was general expectation of war. The British government attempted to persuade the Turks that Russia was threatening their interests, and that the British obligation to defend Asiatic Turkey was involved. At the Congress of Berlin in 1878 Salisbury had stated that Britain considered herself bound only to respect 'the independent determinations' of the Sultan in regard to the closing of the Straits. The implication was that, if ever the Sultan refused a request from the British to pass through the Straits, this would be evidence that he was not 'independent' but was under Russian pressure. In the spring of 1885 the Turks had no desire to go to war with Russia, and were strengthened by a warning from the Great Powers that if they opened the Straits to the British, this would be a breach of the existing international agreement on the Straits. This warning was the work of Bismarck and was in accordance with the obligation of Germany and Austria to Russia under the Three Emperors' League of 1881. Bismarck induced not only Italy but also France to join in the warning to the Sultan. This action put an end to the war crisis. A large-scale war between Britain and Russia in Afghanistan was not practicable, and the Russian government had no serious desire to expand further at this time. In May 1885 a preliminary agreement was made on conditions for arbitration of the frontier dispute, and this was formally agreed on 15 September 1885.[1]

Only three days later Bulgarian nationalists seized power in Plovdiv, the capital of Eastern Roumelia, and proclaimed the unity of the province with Bulgaria. Battenberg accepted the union. The Tsar, infuriated by the prospect that the prince would thus increase his popularity, ordered all Russian officers serving in the Bulgarian army to return to Russia. This left Bulgaria with no officer above the rank of major.

Milan of Serbia, seeing his neighbour greatly increase his territory, demanded compensation. If he could have obtained some Turkish territory to the south-west, he might have been satisfied. But Russia did not wish to see Austria's Serbian vassal strengthened, and Britain did not wish to see Turkey deprived of territory. Milan therefore had no hope of compensation, and decided simply to deny Bulgaria its gains. On 13 November Serbia attacked Bulgaria. However, the Bulgarian army, commanded by native Bulgarian junior officers, defeated the Serbs, and marched into Serbian territory, until ordered to stop by the Austrian minister in Belgrade, who threatened Battenberg with an Austrian occupation of Serbia and a Russian occupation of Bulgaria.

In April 1886 a diplomatic solution was found by the recognition of the prince of Bulgaria as governor-general of Eastern Roumelia. In deference to the Tsar, the name of Battenberg was not mentioned. On 20 August Battenberg was kidnapped by Russian officers and deported to Russian territory, from which he made his way across the Austrian border. Faced with the Tsar's implacable hostility, he decided to abdicate. The Bulgarians, however, showed themselves tougher. Led by the Liberal chief Stambolov, they defied Russian threats, and elected Prince Ferdinand of Coburg as ruler. In November 1886 Russia broke diplomatic relations with Bulgaria. Meanwhile the spectacle of unsuccessful Russian bullying of small Bulgaria produced denunciations of Russia by politicians and

[1] The crisis is discussed in A. J. P. Taylor, op. cit., pp. 298–301. For Russian documents see Baron A. Meyendorff, *La Correspondance diplomatique du baron de Staal 1884–1900* (Paris, 1929), I. 155–262.

journalists all over Europe, especially in Britain and Austria. Austro-Russian tension continued into 1887, and this coincided with a Franco-German crisis, connected with the rise of General Boulanger. Britain also became associated with the Triple Alliance by the Mediterranean Agreements of March and December 1887.[1]

During the crisis of 1886–7 anti-German feeling was loudly expressed in Russia. Katkov was particularly active. As in 1878, Germany was blamed for the actions of Austria. Bismarck worked on the whole for moderation. He always held before him as an aim the restoration of the alliance between the three empires. The Russian foreign minister, Baron Giers, had similar wishes. The Tsar in April 1887 definitely refused to renew the Three Emperors' League, but he was prepared to discuss an agreement with Germany alone. The result of two months' discussions between Bismarck and the Russian ambassador, Count Paul Shuvalov, was the agreement of 18 June 1887, known to historians as the Reinsurance Treaty. It provided for benevolent neutrality in the event of either party being involved in war, with the exception of a war between Russia and Austria or between Germany and France. It recognized the preponderance of Russia in Bulgaria and reaffirmed the closure of the Straits. A secret protocol added that Germany would not consent to the restoration of Battenberg in Bulgaria, and would give diplomatic support to Russia should she find it necessary 'to defend the entrance to the Black Sea'. Essentially, the treaty was incompatible with the Austro-German Alliance, and would not have stood up to the strain of a major war in Europe. Its significance is rather that it indicated to the Russian government Germany's desire for friendly relations. From Bismarck's point of view it was regarded as a first step towards his real aim, the restoration of the Three Emperors' Alliance.

In this same year, however, Bismarck made a mistake which was to have lasting consequences. On 10 November 1887 he forbade the Reichsbank to accept Russian securities as collateral for loans. This action, known to historians as the *Lombardverbot*, was a reprisal for a Russian decree of May 1887 forbidding

[1] There is a vast documentary and secondary literature on this series of crises. For a modern discussion of the whole story, and bibliographical references, see Taylor, op. cit., ch. xiv.

foreigners to hold land in border areas of the empire, which had fallen most heavily on German subjects resident in Russian Poland. The ban, maintained until 1894, had the effect that Russian securities were bought in France, and that the French financial interest in Russia greatly increased.

Bismarck was dismissed by William II in March 1890 at the time when the Reinsurance Treaty was due to be renewed. After some discussion with his new chancellor and senior diplomatic officials, William decided against renewal. This decision was most unwelcome and even alarming to the Russian government. Giers[1] proposed on 15 May 1890 that if the German government felt unable to maintain the specific commitments of the treaty, there should at least be an exchange of letters between the two emperors to the effect that good relations between the two countries were firmly based and did not depend on personalities. But even this modest request was refused by William on the advice of his diplomatic advisers Baron Holstein and Marschall von Biberstein.

During the next years Russia turned towards France and the Franco-Russian Alliance was concluded. France had long desired an ally against Germany, and the crisis of 1887 had made the need seem more urgent. Russia was more cautious. Giers was most unwilling to consider Germany a hostile Power, but the rebuffs received in Berlin pushed him in this direction. His alarm was increased by the fear that Britain was becoming permanently associated with the Triple Alliance. This was not in fact the case, and the only evidence that pointed towards it were statements by Italian leaders on Anglo-Italian friendship at the time of the renewal of the Triple Alliance in June 1891. However, even a slight prospect that Russia's two traditional opponents, Britain and Austria, might combine with the German Empire against Russia, was a reason for seeking friendship elsewhere. Another unpleasant sign was an apparent tendency in Berlin to show a more friendly attitude to the Poles of Prussia:[2] Russo-German friendship had previously been firmest when both governments had kept the Poles firmly in

[1] N. K. Giers (1820–95) served in diplomatic posts, mostly in the Balkans or Middle East, from 1850 to 1875, and then in the Ministry of Foreign Affairs first as head of the Asiatic Department and then as deputy minister from 1875 to 1882, when he succeeded Gorchakov as minister.

[2] See above p. 490.

their place. At the same time the French government had been unsuccessful in its approaches to Britain. An unofficial visit to London by Georges Clémenceau, who had a conversation with Joseph Chamberlain in July 1891, showed that there was little prospect in this direction.[1] Meanwhile Franco-Russian financial co-operation continued. There were important French loans to Russia in December 1888, March 1889, May 1889, and February 1890.

In July 1891 a French naval squadron paid an official visit to Kronstadt. The new relationship between France and Russia was sensationally demonstrated when the Tsar was received on board and stood bareheaded while the *Marseillaise* was played. On 27 August 1891 the first formal agreement was signed. It bound both governments to consult each other if peace was threatened, and to agree on 'the measures which this eventuality would require the two governments to adopt immediately and simultaneously'. A year later the French General Boisdeffre came to St. Petersburg and on 17 August 1892 agreed a draft military convention with the Russian chief of general staff, General Obruchev.[2] If France were attacked by Germany, or by Italy with German help, all available Russian forces would be used against Germany. If Russia were attacked by Germany, or by Austria with German help, all available French forces would be used against Germany. If the Triple Alliance, or one of its members, should mobilize, both France and Russia would mobilize. The French force to be used in support of Russia would be 1,300,000 men. The Russian force to be used in support of France would be from 700,000 to 800,000. The Russian force promised was smaller than the French because in the event of war Russia would have to face two major enemies, Austria as well as Germany, whereas France would be confronted, in addition to Germany, only by the minor military Power Italy. This convention remained in draft form for more than a year. Giers still hoped that the vague *entente* between France and Russia, demonstrated by the Kronstadt visit, would cause Germany to improve her relations with Russia. He was not eager to embark on a full military alliance with France. He made further overtures to the

[1] See J. L. Garvin, *The Life of Joseph Chamberlain* (1933), ii. 458–61.

[2] For Obruchev's earlier career see above p. 453 n. 1.

Germans in April 1893, but there was no response. On 30 December the military convention was confirmed from the Russian side, and on 4 January 1894 from the French.[1]

During the 1890's the most important conflicts between the Great Powers arose in the Far East and Africa, where the main opponent of both Russian and French aims was not Germany but Britain. In the Balkans Austro-Russian rivalry was not as fierce as in the preceding decades, and a limited agreement between the two Powers was even achieved.

The Austro-Serbian treaty expired in 1895 and was not renewed. King Milan of Serbia abdicated in 1888, and his son Alexander, who succeeded him, inclined rather to the Russian than the Austrian side. Bulgarian policy remained anti-Russian as long as Stambolov was in power. In July 1895, however, he was murdered, and in 1896 Russo-Bulgarian diplomatic relations were restored.[2] At the turn of the century Bulgarian foreign policy was Russophil. In 1902 a Russo-Bulgarian military convention was signed, which provided for mutual assistance if either Power were attacked by Roumania.

The affairs of the Ottoman empire were the object of Great Power diplomacy in 1895 and 1896 as a result of terrorist actions by Armenian revolutionaries and reprisals by Turkish troops or mobs against Armenian civilians. The Power which professed greatest sympathy for the Armenian cause was Britain. The Russian government, which was busy repressing Armenian revolutionaries in the Caucasus, did not share this sympathy. It was also alarmed at the prospect of any control over the Ottoman empire by the European Powers. This would be likely to diminish the influence of Russia at Constantinople, which at this time was substantial, and it might even provide an excuse for bringing British warships into the Black Sea. The Russian ambassador, A. I. Nelidov, submitted to the Tsar in

[1] The making of the Franco-Russian Alliance can be studied in *Documents diplomatiques français*, 1st series, vol. viii, ix, x, and xi, and in *Die große Politik*, vol. vii. The best secondary work is Baron B. Nolde, *L'Alliance franco-russe*, Paris, 1936.

[2] These changes were connected with the personal affairs of the rulers. Alexander of Serbia in 1901 married his mistress Draga Mashin, who had close Russian connexions. Prince Ferdinand of Bulgaria at first decided that his heir, Prince Boris, must be brought up a Catholic, as demanded by his wife, Princess Marie-Louise of Parma, in 1893. Three years later he changed his mind, and the child was rebaptized Orthodox. This enabled Nicholas II to recognize Ferdinand as ruler of Bulgaria.

November 1896 a plan for a Russian seizure of the Bosphorus in the event of any British naval action against Turkey.[1] It was, however, decided that a Conference of Ambassadors of the six Great Powers in Constantinople should prepare a new plan of reforms to submit to the Sultan. The conference began its work in December 1896, and in February 1897 its agreed proposals were ready.[2] But before any action could be taken on these, war broke out in April 1897 between Greece and Turkey, as a result of Greek aid to a rebellion in Crete. In the Cretan crisis Britain had sympathized with the Greeks, while Russia, supported by Germany, favoured the Turks. The war brought military victories to the Turks and a reaction of all the Powers in favour of Greece. Peace was made without any gains for the Turkish victors. The Powers' action was bound to encourage the Christian subjects of the Sultan to rebel again, and the small Balkan states to pursue their own aims at Turkey's expense.

The disagreements between Britain and Germany in the Cretan and Armenian questions made it impossible for Austria to achieve her aim of obtaining British co-operation with the Triple Alliance against Russia. The Austrian government was especially weak in 1897 as a result of the bitter political struggle between Germans and Czechs in Bohemia. Germany was strongly encouraging Russia to devote her efforts to Far Eastern affairs, and wished to do as much as possible to clear up Austro-Russian disputes in the Balkans. Austria was therefore pressed by her German ally to reach an agreement with Russia. In May 1897 Franz Joseph paid an official visit to St. Petersburg, and the Foreign Ministers of the two countries signed an agreement on the Balkans. Both Powers declared that they had no intention to annex Balkan territory, and agreed to oppose the acquisition of Balkan territory by any other Power. Both accepted the closure of the Straits. In the event of a disintegration of the Ottoman empire in Europe, Austria

[1] See *Krasny Arkhiv*, no. 1 (1922), pp. 152–63; Count S. Y. Witte, *Vospominaniya* (Berlin, 1922–3, latest edition Moscow, 1960).

[2] The policies of the Powers in the Armenian question are discussed in Taylor, op. cit., pp. 359–60, 368–70. A more recent discussion of Salisbury's attitude to the Straits problem, and of his conversations with Hatzfeld in 1895 and with Nicholas II in 1896, based on a fuller study of the sources, is in J. A. S. Grenville, *Lord Salisbury and Foreign Policy* (1964), pp. 31–53, 78–89.

would have the right to annex the provinces of Bosnia, Hercegovina, and Novi Bazar now occupied temporarily by her. An Albanian state would be set up along the Adriatic coast. The rest of the Ottoman lands in Europe would be divided in such a way as to prevent 'a marked preponderance of any particular Balkan principality to the detriment of the others'.[1]

During the 1890's Bulgaria did not cease to encourage the Slavs of Macedonia, who not only had legitimate grievances against the Turkish régime but increasingly desired either an independent Macedonian state or incorporation in Bulgaria. The Internal Macedonian Revolutionary Organization organized a large-scale insurrection in August 1903. The Turkish armed forces suppressed it, and Bulgaria did not intervene. The Powers, however, were faced with demands from their public opinion for reform and for foreign supervision. The Austro-Russian agreement of 1897 worked well in this crisis. Franz Joseph and Nicholas II met at Mürzsteg, near Vienna, in October 1903, and agreed on a scheme for a European gendarmerie to supervise the execution of reforms.[2]

There is one constant factor in Russo-German-Austrian relations, which was not the occasion for any crisis in these years, yet should not be ignored. This is the Polish problem. The freedom of political activity and propaganda, allowed by Austria to her Polish and Ukrainian subjects, was a source of constant annoyance to the Russian government. Poles from Russia could always find a safe asylum on Austrian territory, and added an additional element of bitterness to the arguments of the Austrian Poles in favour of an anti-Russian foreign policy for the Habsburg monarchy. Austrian toleration of Ukrainians was even more resented in St. Petersburg. Russian statesmen had to admit the right of the Vienna government to decide how to treat its Poles. But they did not admit that an Ukrainian nation existed at all. Little Russians were simply

[1] Full text in A. F. Pribram, *Secret Treaties of Austria-Hungary 1879–1914* (Harvard, 1920), i. 184–90.

[2] Each Power had a sector, in which the gendarmerie officers were to be its nationals—Russia in Salonica, Italy in Bitolj, Austria in Skoplje, France in Seres, and Britain in Drama. The German government, as a friendly gesture towards the Turks, refused to accept a sector. On the background of Macedonian political conditions at this time, see H. Brailsford, *Macedonia*, 1906. A brilliant survey of the Turkish scene at the turn of the century is Sir Charles Eliot ('Odysseus'), *Turkey in Europe*, 1900.

Russians. The Austrian government was maliciously helping to create an artificial nation, whose very *raison d'être* must be hostility to Russia. These resentments undoubtedly influenced the basic attitude of Russian political leaders and public opinion towards Austria. No such problem existed in Russo-German relations. With the partial exception of the first years after Bismarck's dismissal, German policy towards the Poles was completely negative. As for the Ukrainian problem, it was at this time virtually unknown in Germany.

Russian policy in the Far East, the operation of the Franco-Russian Alliance there, and the conflict of interests between Russia and Britain, are discussed separately. If the main concern of Russia in the 1890's was in Manchuria and Korea, the main concern of France was in Africa, and especially in the Nile valley. Here French activities came up against the resistance of Russia's Far Eastern opponent, Britain.

The Russian government became more interested in the Suez Canal as Russian interests in the Far East developed. Russia became an important user of the canal. The Russian representative on the Egyptian Debt Commission supported the French in making difficulties for the British administration in Egypt. At the end of the 1880's there were Russian subjects living in Abyssinia, and there was some interest in the Ethiopian Church in Orthodox circles. In 1894 an Ethiopian mission came to St. Petersburg, led by a former Russian army officer named Leontyev. Some Russian arms were sold to Abyssinia in 1896.

At the crisis of Anglo-French conflict in the Nile valley, after the meeting of Kitchener and Marchand at Fashoda in September 1898, France got no help either from Abyssinia or from Russia. Muravyov[1] was in Paris during the crisis, on 15 October. His advice to the French government was to abandon Fashoda and seek a wider African settlement by negotiation. The Russian war minister, Kuropatkin, some months later told the French military attaché, Lt.-Col. Moulin, that Russia would have supported France if, after she had yielded at Fashoda, Britain had pressed her for further concessions,

[1] Count M. N. Muravyov, after a career in the diplomatic service, became minister in Copenhagen in 1893, and was appointed minister of foreign affairs in 1897, remaining in office until his death in 1900.

but that Russia had absolutely no wish to be involved in the quarrels of France in Africa.[1] The French and Russian governments continued to think about common action against Britain. The two general staffs held discussions on 2 July 1900 and 21 February 1901 on common action in the event of war with Britain alone, or with Britain supported by the Triple Alliance. There was talk of joint Franco-Russian naval action in the Mediterranean, Indian Ocean, and Pacific. As for a Russian invasion of India, it was clearly stated that nothing could be done until the Orenburg–Tashkent Railway was completed.[2]

The truth is that the Franco-Russian Alliance was useful for both Powers against Germany, but inapplicable to Britain. Russia had the advantage over Britain in northern China until the Anglo-Japanese Alliance was made: French aid in the Far East would not be desirable. On the other hand the only thing that Russia could conceivably do to help France in Africa or the Mediterranean would have been to attack in the Middle East. Possibly something useful might have been done in Persia. But any Russian advance through Ottoman territory, whether with or without the consent of the Turkish government, would almost certainly have brought Austria and Germany in against her, and this would not on balance have been to the advantage of France.

In August 1899, when the French foreign minister, Delcassé, visited St. Petersburg, the alliance was extended. The duration of the military convention had been originally made dependent on the duration of the Triple Alliance: now it was to last until denounced by either of the signatories. The aim of the alliance was now stated to be not only the maintenance of peace but the preservation of the balance of power in Europe. The reason for the second change was that it was feared that the Habsburg monarchy, at this time seriously weakened by the German-Czech conflict in Bohemia, might break up, in which case difficult problems of adjustment of the balance of power would certainly arise.

[1] Muravyov's advice is reported by the German ambassador in *Die große Politik*, xiv (2), no. 3893. The conversation between Moulin and Kuropatkin is reported by Moulin to Freycinet in *Documents diplomatiques français*, Series 1, vol. xv, no. 52. The letter is dated 30 Jan. 1889.

[2] Ibid., Series 2, vol. i, p. 146; vol. iii, pp. 601 ff.

The Boer War aroused widespread hostility to Britain on the Continent, and brought up the idea of a Continental League against Britain. This was the subject of a conversation between William II and the Russian ambassador in Berlin, Count Osten-Sacken, on 13 January 1900. On 25 February Muravyov formally proposed to von Bülow that Russia, France, and Germany should jointly mediate between Britain and the Boer republics. Neither the German nor the French government favoured this action, and each in turn saw to it that the British government was informed of its refusal, though the versions differed considerably from each other.[1]

In May 1903 King Alexander and Queen Draga of Serbia were murdered by army officers. Shortly afterwards the rival Karadjordjević dynasty was restored in the person of King Peter. The change was at first expected to diminish Russian and revive Austrian influence. However, the pro-Russian Radical Party was the strongest political force in Serbia, and disputes between Serbia and Austria concerning arms contracts and a proposed Serb-Bulgarian commercial treaty led to an Austrian boycott of Serbian goods—the so-called 'Pig War' of 1906. Russia was too weak to influence Balkan events at this time, but these events strengthened rather than diminished her influence.

The Far East

During the twenty years which followed the Russo-Japanese Treaty of St. Petersburg of 1875, the relations between the two countries were comparatively good. The main potential source of conflict was Korea. In the official Chinese view Korea was a vassal state of China, but Chinese authority was not exercised in practice. The importance of the Korean Peninsula to the security of Japan is obvious from a summary glance at the map. It was also important for Russia's communications by sea to the south. The port of Vladivostok, which had been rapidly developed since its site was acquired in 1860, was frozen for part of the winter. An ice-free port in Korea was an attractive idea to Russian naval planners, but was not at this time a definite object of Russian policy.

[1] See *Die große Politik*, xv. 516–42, and for a discussion of the affair in its general European context Taylor, op. cit., pp. 387–90.

In the first years of the Meiji Era there was a group among the Japanese statesmen who wished to invade Korea, but this policy was not adopted. In 1876, however, Japan signed a treaty with Korea, thus treating it formally as an independent state, and gained access to several Korean ports. Though the Chinese government did not abandon its view that Korea was its vassal, it did not officially object to the treaty. Young Koreans began to go to Japan for education, and when they returned they began to demand the modernization of Korea. The king, and his ambitious queen, were at this time mildly disposed towards reform and on good terms with the Japanese. They were opposed by the traditionalist upper classes, headed by the regent. On 23 July 1882 a mob, inspired by the regent, attacked the palace and the Japanese Legation. The king and queen escaped, and most of the Japanese were able to fight their way out. Chinese troops were sent to Korea, order was restored, some of the leaders of the revolt were executed and the regent deported, and the Japanese diplomats returned with a substantial armed guard. The Korean government now pursued a more friendly policy towards foreign states. The United States signed a treaty with Korea in 1882, Britain and Germany in 1883, Russia in 1884, and France in 1886. All these Powers received the right to trade with Korean ports, and established regular diplomatic missions in Seoul.

In 1883 a German consular official named Moellendorff was appointed director of the Korean customs service. This man decided that the best way to protect his new country against Japanese domination was to interest Russia in it. On his advice the Korean government invited Russian officers to instruct the Korean army, and offered Russia an ice-free port in Korea, to be named Port Lazarev. This action provoked immediate opposition from Britain, and British naval forces occupied an island at the entrance of the Korean Gulf which was called Port Hamilton. This Anglo-Russian crisis was of brief duration: both Powers withdrew their forces, and no Russian port was established.

On 4 December 1884 a group of Korean reformers, led by persons who had studied in Japan, attacked the palace, captured the king, and proposed to introduce a programme of internal reforms and of close co-operation with Japan. However, the commander of the Chinese forces in Seoul, Yuan Shih-kai, recaptured the palace. Riots followed, directed against Japanese and Europeans. Both China and Japan sent troops into Korea. This time hostilities between Japan and China were averted by negotiations. By the Treaty of Tientsin of April 1885 both governments agreed to withdraw their troops, and not to send forces back without mutual consultation.[1]

A new stage in Russia's Far Eastern policy opened with the decision, announced by an imperial rescript of 17 March 1891, to build a railway across Siberia. This could, of course, be justified on general economic and political grounds. Though it would be costly, and would not produce direct material advantages for many years, it was clearly of the greatest importance in developing the natural resources of Siberia. The great famine of 1891 had shown the need to have the means of transporting grain rapidly across the empire. The railway would assist colonization of Siberia by peasants from overpopulated provinces. It was also obviously desirable, from the point of view of general administration, to link the remotest parts of the empire with the centre. But apart from all these general reasons, Witte, the chief advocate of the railway, also had expansionist aims. He believed that the railway would enable Russia to penetrate the Chinese market, and forestall the British, who were believed to be planning railways from the south into Manchuria. He also hoped that a substantial share of trade between the Far East and Europe could be carried by the railway, and thus bring profits to Russia. Witte used various arguments, and any available channels, to influence Alexander III in favour of the enterprise. One channel was a Buryat Mongol doctor named Badmayev, who had fantastic plans for annexing Mongolia and Tibet to Russia. Though hardly likely to take Badmayev seriously, Witte did not hesitate to use his ideas to arouse the imagination of the Tsar. Witte himself used melodramatic language about Russia's destiny in the East. In a memorandum of 1893 to the Tsar, commenting on Badmayev's schemes, he held out the prospect that 'from the shores of the Pacific and the heights of the Himalayas Russia would dominate not only the affairs of Asia

[1] The text of the convention of 1885 is in F. A. McKenzie, *The Tragedy of Korea* (1908), pp. 296–7.

but those of Europe as well'.[1] Whether he himself thought in these terms, or was simply flattering his master with visions of greatness, it is hard to say.

In the spring of 1894 a rebellion in the south of Korea, led by an anti-foreign society called the Tong-Haks, threatened the capital itself. At the request of the Korean government and of Yuan Shih-kai, the Chinese sent troops to help the government, informing the Japanese of their action under the convention of 1885. The Japanese in their turn sent in troops, and presented an ultimatum to Korea, demanding that it should declare itself completely independent of China and should carry out a series of specified reforms. The Japanese in effect occupied Korea, and hostilities developed with the Chinese, which led to a formal declaration of war on 1 August. In the next months the Japanese decisively defeated the Chinese on land and sea.

Russia was now faced in effect with the choice of co-operation with Japan at the expense of China, or defence of China against Japanese claims. The foreign minister, Prince A. B. Lobanov-Rostovsky,[2] wished to avoid a conflict with Japan. When it became known that Japan intended to demand from China the cession of the Liaotung Peninsula, with the port of Port Arthur, the outlet of Manchuria to the sea, his inclination was not to oppose this Japanese gain, but to seek a compensating gain for Russia in Korea. An ice-free port on the Korean coast would more than counterbalance the disadvantage to Russia of the installation of the Japanese in Manchuria. Nicholas II himself at first agreed with this view. But when a conference of ministers was held on 11 April 1895, Witte came out strongly against the Japanese demands. If Japan were established on the mainland, she would quickly build up her power, and Russia would find it extremely difficult to dislodge her later. Witte believed that the main task for Russia must be to gain time until the Trans-Siberian Railway was completed, and Russia able to make her strength felt in the Far East. Until that time, all annexations of

[1] V. P. Semennikov, *Za kulisami tsarizma. Arkhiv tibetskogo vracha Badmaeva* (Leningrad, 1925), p. 80. Badmayev at least did well out of the affair, for the Tsar instructed Witte to grant him a Treasury loan of 2,000,000 roubles.

[2] Prince A. B. Lobanov-Rostovsky (1824–96) served as ambassador in Constantinople (1878–9), London (1879–82), Vienna (1882–94), and Berlin (1894–95). He was appointed minister of foreign affairs in 1896, but died the following year.

Chinese territory by other Powers must be prevented. Meanwhile Russia could pose as the friend of China.[1]

Witte's view prevailed. The Russian government was able to enlist the diplomatic support of both France and Germany. On 23 April 1895 the three Powers intervened in Tokyo. The Japanese government was forced to yield to their pressure, and abandoned the Liaotung Peninsula. It was forced to content itself with the annexation of Formosa and the Pescadores Islands, and a large indemnity.

Russia quickly followed up her advantage. A Russian loan, provided by French banks, enabled the Chinese government to pay the indemnity to Japan. In May 1896 the Chinese statesman Li Hung-chang visited Moscow for the coronation of Nicholas II, and signed a treaty of alliance between China and Russia. Russia was committed to defend China against Japan, and in the event of a Japanese attack on Russia's Far Eastern territory, all Chinese ports would be open to Russian warships. In order to facilitate communication between Russia and China, a new railway was to be built across northern Manchuria, cutting off the Amur salient and linking Vladivostok by the shortest route with Siberia. This was to be called the Chinese Eastern Railway. It was to be financed by a new Russo-Chinese Bank, founded largely with French capital. The Chinese government was to have the right to buy the railway at the end of thirty-six years.[2] The immediate territory through which the railway was to pass was to be a special zone, administered and policed under the authority of the Russian Ministry of Finance.

Russia had advanced in Manchuria, but was not prepared to give up Korea. Here she was helped at first by the clumsiness of the Japanese. The victory over China had made the Japanese the masters of Korea, but they made poor use of their opportunity. Viscount Miura, appointed Japanese representative in Korea in September 1895, overreached himself in his dealings with Korean opposition: on 8 October he had the queen murdered by a gang of professional toughs (*soshi*), and

[1] Witte's own account, which is extremely scanty, is given in his Memoirs, vol. ii, ch. 2. The conferences of Jan.–Apr. 1895 are discussed in Romanov (Russian edition), pp. 67, 81. See next note.

[2] For the financial details see B. D. Romanov, *Rossiya v Man'chzhurii* (Leningrad, 1928), pp. 82–93. (English translation *Russia in Manchuria*, Madison, 1952.)

forced the king to issue a statement completely identifying himself with Japanese aims. However, in February 1896 the king escaped from his palace and took refuge in the Russian Legation. Here he issued a proclamation to his subjects, and was visited by his ministers and by foreign diplomats. Japanese influence rapidly sank. On 14 May 1896 an agreement was signed by the Japanese and Russian ministers, by which both agreed to advise the king to return to his palace, and the Japanese minister formally undertook to 'control the Japanese *soshi*'. Both Japanese and Russian guards on their establishments in Korea were to be limited to small numbers.[1] On 9 June 1896 a further agreement was signed in Moscow by Lobanov-Rostovsky and the Japanese statesman Yamagata. Both governments agreed to advise the Korean government to economize and to balance its budget, but would help with loans if the Korean government should need these for necessary reforms. Both agreed that the raising and maintenance of national armed forces and police should be left to the Korean government. The Japanese were to continue to administer the telegraph lines owned by them on Korean territory, and the Russian government was to have the right to construct a telegraph line from Seoul to the Russian border.[2]

The Russians lost the comparative advantage they had gained over the Japanese in the following year. A new Russian minister, Baron von Speyer, decided to dislodge the British head of the Korean customs, J. McLeavy Brown. He persuaded the Korean government to replace him by a Russian financial adviser, K. Alexeyev. Brown, however, refused to go, and when British ships appeared in the harbour of Chemulpho, the port of Seoul, the Korean government took fright and reinstated Brown.

The next phase of Far Eastern policy came when the German government in November 1897 occupied Kiaochow, on the Shantung Peninsula, as a reprisal for the murder by Chinese of two German missionaries. This action provided an excuse for the seizure of Chinese territory by other European Powers.[3] It was Russia that took the richest spoils. By a treaty of 27 March 1898 the Chinese government ceded the Liaotung

[1] Text in McKenzie, op. cit., pp. 299–301. [2] Text ibid., p. 301.
[3] Britain took Wei Hai Wei, France Kwang Chow Wan.

Peninsula and Port Arthur to Russia for twenty-five years, and granted a concession for a South Manchurian Railway, to be built from Kharbin, on the Chinese Eastern Railway, south to Port Arthur. Thus Russia was taking from China, without war, what she had three years previously prevented Japan from taking as the fruits of victory in war, and she was asserting her supremacy over southern as well as northern Manchuria.

Port Arthur was an ice-free port, but it was separated from Vladivostok by the straits between Korea and Japan, which the Japanese could easily control if they were also established in Korea. Hence the extreme expansionists in Russia, especially in the navy, could argue that not only must Russia not agree to Japanese control of Korea, but that she must herself seek a Korean port. The Japanese government was prepared at this stage to accept a division of spheres with Russia. It was suggested to Baron Rosen, the Russian minister in Tokyo, that Japan should recognize Russian supremacy in Manchuria in return for Russian recognition of Japanese supremacy in Korea. But the government in St. Petersburg could not bring itself to accept this. The most that could be achieved was a convention of 25 April 1898, signed in Tokyo by Rosen and the Japanese foreign minister, Baron Nishi. The two governments agreed to recognize the independence of Korea, and to refrain from interference in its internal affairs. Neither would send military or financial instructors to Korea without consulting the other. Article III provided that 'in view of the large development of Japanese commercial and industrial enterprises in Korea, as well as the considerable number of Japanese subjects resident in that country, the Imperial Russian Government will not impede the development of the commercial and industrial relations between Japan and Korea'.[1]

Russian penetration of Manchuria alarmed Britain. It was not only that British economic interests were excluded from Manchuria. More serious was the danger that Russia, China's neighbour by land, dominating northern China up to a short distance from Peking itself, would eventually be able to make the government of China its vassal, and induce it to pursue policies hostile to British interests in other parts of China. Russia was prepared to make at least a formal concession. In April

[1] Text in McKenzie, op. cit., p. 302.

1899 an Anglo-Russian agreement on spheres of interest provided that Russia would seek no railway concessions in the Yangtze valley, on condition that Britain would seek none 'north of the Great Wall'. This was not of much use to Britain. More was hoped from German support. An Anglo-German agreement of 16 April 1900 stated the desire of both Powers to maintain the open door in China and the integrity of the Chinese empire, but the Germans made it clear to the British that they would take no action against Russia. They were not even prepared to let the Russians fear that they might oppose them. On 15 March 1901 the German chancellor, von Bülow, declared in the Reichstag that the agreement 'was in no sense concerned with Manchuria'.[1]

The truth was that the German government was glad to see Britain and Russia in conflict with each other. Preoccupations in the Far East would make Russia less concerned with the Balkans, and therefore less likely to be involved in hostility with Germany's ally Austria-Hungary, while if the British were tied up in the Far East they might be less able to oppose German plans for naval strength in the North Sea. William II personally encouraged Nicholas II to make Russia a Pacific Great Power. He held out the danger of the Yellow Peril: 'twenty to thirty million Chinese trained and helped by half a dozen Japanese divisions and led by fine undaunted Christian-hating Japanese officers'. He referred also to Korea as a 'tongue of land which may, in an adversary's hand, become a new sort of Dardanelles. These Dardanelles must not threaten your communications. . . . It is evident to every unbiased mind that Korea must and will be Russian.'[2]

The Boxer Rising in China in 1900, and the siege of the diplomatic missions, led to the dispatch of a joint expeditionary force of the European Powers and the Japanese. The Russians used the opportunity to strengthen their forces in Manchuria, and then to demand far-reaching new concessions from the Chinese government in return for their withdrawal. Chinese resistance was strengthened by Japanese diplomatic support.

[1] For the wider background of European diplomacy in connexion with Far Eastern problems, see A. J. P. Taylor, op. cit., chs. xvi to xviii.

[2] *Der Briefwechsel Wilhelms II. mit dem russischen Tsaren* (Berlin, 1920), pp. 328, 334–5.

The Russians finally signed a treaty with China on 8 April 1902, by which Russian troops in Manchuria would be evacuated, in three stages, the process to be completed by 8 October 1903.

The Japanese government, despairing of a settlement with Russia, began in 1901 negotiations for a treaty with Britain. The elder statesman Marquess Ito still hoped to reach agreement with Russia, and visited St. Petersburg in November. He found differing attitudes within the Russian government, but no politeness could conceal the fact that some of the aspirations of some prominent Russians were incompatible with Japan's interests. Ito still wished to negotiate, but the government in Tokyo had no more patience. On 30 January 1902 the Anglo-Japanese Alliance was signed. If either Power were attacked by two other Powers, its ally would come to its assistance. The treaty recognized the special interest of Japan in Korea. Article IV laid down that neither would 'without consulting the other, enter into separate arrangements with another Power to the prejudice of the interests above described'.[1]

During the next two years the conflict between Russia and Japan grew more intense. One of the main factors was the diversity of ideas and aims within the Russian government, which prevented the adoption of any definite policy. Russia could not satisfy, or even reply to, Japanese demands, and drifted into war. For the indecision the Tsar must in the last resort bear the main blame. The foreign minister, Count V. N. Lamsdorff, wished to avoid war, and was more interested in Europe than in the Far East. Witte was also for peaceful methods, though his aims, which amounted to Russian domination of the trade and economic resources of northern China, can hardly be described as 'moderate'. The minister of war, General A. N. Kuropatkin, also wished to avoid war in the Far East, and to keep Russia militarily strong for any dangers which might face her in the West. What he would have liked would have been to ensure the security of the Chinese Eastern Railway and shorten the Russian frontier, by annexing the northern part of Manchuria to Russia, by agreement with Japan. This was of course an 'aggressive' policy, at the expense of China,

[1] For a discussion of the general implications of the Anglo-Japanese Alliance, see Taylor, op. cit., chs. xvi to xviii.

but also a programme of 'minor aggression', intended to avoid war against a substantial opponent.[1]

A further disturbing influence was, however, introduced into Russian policy by various irresponsible persons who obtained access to the Tsar at the end of the century. The man who has received most attention from historians is a retired Guards officer, Captain A. M. Bezobrazov. This man was involved, with various well-connected persons,[2] in a concession for timber in the valley of the Yalu river in northern Korea.[3] The Tsar himself became a large shareholder in the East Asiatic Development Company which these men planned in 1899. Largely owing to the opposition of Witte, the plans were not carried out, and in February 1902 the company was liquidated. However, Bezobrazov remained in frequent contact with the Tsar, made official visits to the Far East, and disposed of large sums of government money. In May 1903 he was promoted to the bureaucratic rank of state-secretary. In June the Yalu concession was revived in the form of the Russian Timber Company of the Far East, with some of the same well-connected shareholders as the earlier project. However, after returning from a conference in Port Arthur, with senior officers, civil officials, and managers of the Chinese Eastern Railway, from 1 to 10 July 1903, Bezobrazov found that his influence with the Tsar was over, and neither he nor his company played any significant part in the subsequent events.

The view once widely held, that Russia was dragged into war by the 'Bezobrazov group' of sinister adventurers, who caused the Tsar to ignore the wise counsels of the statesman Witte, cannot be accepted. But this does not mean that Bezobrazov played no part at all.[4] His indiscreet and self-important state-

[1] Two essential Russian sources on this period are the Diary of Kuropatkin, published in *Krasny Arkhiv*, nos. 2 (1922), 5 (1924), and 8 (1925); and the work of B. B. Glinsky, *Prolog russko-yaponskoy voyny*, SPB, 1906. (French edition P. Marc, *Quelques années de politique internationale*, Leipzig, 1914.) This is based on the papers of Witte.

[2] These included the minister of the court, Count I. I. Vorontsov-Dashkov; a diplomat with long experience of the Far East, N. G. Matyunin; and another retired Guards officer, Colonel V. M. Vonlyarlyarsky.

[3] This had originally been granted by the Korean government in 1896 to a Russian merchant named Y. I. Briner.

[4] The role of Bezobrazov is discussed at length in Romanov, *Russia in Manchuria*. For an excellent brief survey of the evidence see A. Malozemoff, *Russian Far Eastern Policy 1881–1904* (Berkeley, 1958), pp. 179–86, 208–23.

ments on Far Eastern affairs and his much publicized journeys alarmed both Russian and foreign observers, and so increased international tension. His intrigues were certainly a factor in the dismissal of Witte in August 1903, though this must be regarded as largely due to the economic depression which was blamed on Witte's financial policy. Bezobrazov probably also contributed to the Tsar's decision, announced on 13 August, to set up a viceroyalty in the Far East, under Admiral E. I. Alexeyev in Port Arthur, which was to be directly responsible to the Tsar and not subject to the normal chain of command through the ministries. These changes substantially affected the conduct of Russian foreign policy in the critical months which followed. With the removal of Witte, the whole administrative apparatus in Manchuria—the private empire of the Russian Ministry of Finance—was weakened: his successor at the ministry, E. D. Pleske, was a dying man, and the absence of firm direction from the top was soon felt. The creation of the viceroyalty meant that one more authority had to be brought into negotiations with the Japanese or Chinese governments, and delays and suspicions were magnified. The creation on 12 September 1903 of a Far Eastern committee in St. Petersburg with Bezobrazov's cousin the naval captain A. M. Abaza as its secretary-general, further increased the confusion.

The first stage of the evacuation of Russian troops from Manchuria, promised under the Russo-Chinese treaty of 8 April 1902, was punctually completed in October 1902, but when the time came for the next stage, in February 1903, the Russians did not act. The Russian government was determined to extract further advantages from the Chinese, and above all to exclude all other Powers from concessions in Manchuria. The Chinese resisted these demands, with support from Japan, the United States, and Britain. The central issue was now the conflict of interests between Russia and Japan. Between August 1903 and January 1904 proposals and counter-proposals were exchanged, but no agreement could be reached.[1] The Japanese were strengthened

[1] Japanese proposals of 12 Aug., Russian counter-proposals of 3 Oct., Japanese of 30 Oct., Russian of 11 Dec., Japanese of 28 Dec., Russian of 6 Jan., Japanese of 14 Jan. The last Russian proposals, of 2 Feb. 1904, did not reach Tokyo until after the Japanese had started hostilities. Recent secondary sources which contain useful summaries of these negotiations are B. D. Romanov, *Ocherki diplomaticheskoy istorii russko-yaponskoy voyny 1895–1907* (Moscow, 1947), pp. 233–300; Malozemoff,

by the diplomatic support not only of their British ally but also of the United States: the latter was demonstratively expressed by the signature of commercial treaties with China by the United States and Japan on the same day, 8 October 1903, on which the evacuation of Russian forces in Manchuria ought to have been completed under the 1902 treaty. Russia's ally France made efforts to avert war, but the French proposals for mediation of 6 January 1904 were not accepted. On 3 February the Japanese government finally decided for war, on 5 February it broke off diplomatic relations with Russia and on the night of 8–9 February Japanese warships made a surprise attack on Port Arthur.

Essentially, the negotiations had shown that Russia was not prepared to give Japan a completely free hand in Korea, or Japan to give Russia a completely free hand in southern Manchuria. The Japanese were willing only to recognize Russian railway interests, and the Russians made various proposals designed to limit Japanese control over that portion of Korea adjacent to their Manchurian sphere. It is, however, doubtful if war could have been avoided even if 'more moderate' elements had been in charge in both countries. Kuropatkin's plan for annexation of northern Manchuria would hardly have worked, for the Chinese would have refused, and if hostilites had broken out between Russia and China, the other Powers interested in China would have urged Japan to act.

It is certainly reasonable to describe the Russo-Japanese war as a product of 'imperialism'. All the Powers directly or indirectly involved, except the Chinese, were imperialist. It may be argued that British diplomacy was defensive, yet it is also true that the powerful British business interests in China, and the presence of British rule in India (which was at least distantly and indirectly affected by the Far Eastern crises) were obvious examples of imperialism. But the explanation of imperialism solely by economic motives is highly questionable, and it is also doubtful whether historical understanding is increased by righteous indignation against the governments concerned, based on moral assumptions which became almost universal in the 1960's but were certainly not widely accepted at the turn of the century.

op. cit., pp. 237–49; and J. A. White, *The Diplomacy of the Russo-Japanese War* (Princeton, 1964), pp. 95–131.

It can be argued that in the last months of peace it was the Japanese who were pushing towards war, and the Russians who were retreating. Indeed, Russian policy at this time was marked by incompetence and confusion rather than by aggressive intentions. But it is equally arguable that the Russian seizure of the Liaotung Peninsula in 1898 was not only an act of aggression but an unforgivable insult to Japan, from which—despite some temporary relaxation of tension—only war could come. To those living more than half a century later, the most fantastic feature of all was the belief, then held by all concerned, that it would be possible to act as if the Chinese giant did not exist. In 1905 Japan seemed to have prevailed, forty years later Russian supremacy appeared restored, yet it was not long before both victories were shown to be equally illusory.

The two antagonists appeared unevenly matched. An Asian people, from its small islands, was defying one of the European Great Powers, with a population three times as large and a vast territory. But in the area of conflict the advantage was with the Japanese. The Russian land and sea forces available in Manchuria were less than those which the Japanese could quickly bring into action. Land reinforcements depended on the railway through Siberia, which, however impressive the achievement since 1891, was inadequate for transporting large numbers of men and bulky supplies. As for naval reinforcements, the Black Sea fleet could not move owing to the provisions of the Straits Convention in force which closed the Bosphorus to Russian warships while Russia was at war; and the Baltic fleet would have to sail right round Europe, Africa, and Asia.

The viceroy, Admiral Alexeyev, was commander-in-chief for the whole Far Eastern theatre, but General Kuropatkin, who gave up his post as minister of war, was placed in command of the armies in Manchuria. The relations between these two men were bad, and the consequent confusion contributed not a little to Russian difficulties.

The Japanese surprise attack on Port Arthur on 8 February, carried out by 10 destroyers, seriously damaged only one Russian battleship. Next day the main Japanese fleet, commanded by Admiral Togo, appeared before Port Arthur. A Russian force of 5 battleships and 5 cruisers came out to meet them. In the exchange of gunfire which followed, both sides suffered casualties, but the damage to the Japanese ships was greater than to the Russians, and Togo retreated. On the same day the Russians lost a cruiser and a gunboat from a Japanese attack in the Korean port of Chemulpo.

Vice-Admiral S. O. Makarov, who took over command of Port Arthur on 8 March, wished to pursue an offensive strategy, and to challenge Japanese command of the Yellow Sea. The Japanese forces were substantially stronger. Alexeyev, whose headquarters were in Mukden, wished to avoid a major engagement until the Russian land forces were in a position to invade Korea, and the Russian fleet in the Far East had been reinforced from Europe. He therefore urged caution. On 24 March Togo again approached Port Arthur, but when Russian warships came out to engage him, he again retreated. Makarov undertook some reconnaissance and mine-laying operations. On 12 April a Russian cruiser went out to help a minelayer which was under attack by superior forces, and was itself attacked by 6 Japanese cruisers. Makarov, with 2 battleships and 2 cruisers, came out to help the cruiser, but when 6 Japanese battleships and 2 heavy cruisers appeared, he was obliged to return to Port Arthur. In the outer harbour his flagship *Petropavlovsk* blew up on a mine, which Japanese minelayers had laid undetected on the previous night. The admiral and almost the whole crew were killed. This proved a disastrous loss for Russia. Makarov's successors lacked his fighting spirit. The Russian fleet remained within Port Arthur, and the Japanese had the mastery of the sea.

By the end of April 1904 the Japanese 1st Army under General Tamemoto Kuroki, numbering about 60,000 men, was ready to advance across the Yalu river from Korea into Manchuria in the area of Inchou. The Russian advance guard on the north bank, the Eastern Detachment of about 23,000 men under General M. I. Zasulich, had been ordered not to offer large-scale resistance. Instead, he fought a battle at Chiu-lien-chieng, which cost the Russians more than 2,000 casualties and the Japanese half as many. The Japanese crossed the river, and the Russians retreated.

On 5 May the Japanese began landing their 2nd Army, of more than 60,000 men under General Yasukata Oku, at Pi-tzuwo on the Liaotung Peninsula, about sixty miles north-east of Port Arthur. By 10 May the Japanese had established themselves across the isthmus, at this point about ten miles wide, and Port Arthur was cut off from the mainland. Two days later the whole 2nd Army was ashore. Russian warships had made no attempt to interfere with the landings. However, 2 Japanese battleships, in the fleet which was charged with watching the entrance to Port Arthur, were sunk by Russian mines. On 26 May the advancing Japanese attacked Russian positions at Chinchow, some twenty miles from Port Arthur. After fierce resistance, the Russians retreated, and next day evacuated the port of Dairen (Dalny), which the Japanese entered on 1 June.

Alexeyev now urged Kuropatkin to move south, to strike a major blow against either the 1st or the 2nd Japanese Army. Kuropatkin wanted to wait for reinforcements from Russia. The most he would do was to send a force of 2 divisions and 1 brigade, under General G. K. von Stackelberg, to the Liaotung Peninsula. In a battle on the railway seventy miles north-east of Port Arthur, the Russians were driven back with over 3,000 casualties, nearly three times those of the Japanese. Kuropatkin decided to recall Stackelberg's force to the main Russian positions at Liao-Yang and give up for the time being the attempt to relieve Port Arthur.

On 10 August the Russian fleet in Port Arthur attempted to force its way out and engage the Japanese fleet in a major battle. It was defeated. One battleship and 2 cruisers entered neutral ports and were disarmed, 1 cruiser tried to reach Vladivostok but was sunk by Japanese action off Sakhalin, and 5 battleships, 1 cruiser, and 3 minelayers returned to Port Arthur. On 14 August the smaller Russian fleet in Vladivostok came out into the Japan Sea and engaged Admiral Kamimura's forces. The Russians lost a cruiser, two more suffered severe damage, and the fleet was obliged to return to its base.

Between 19 and 24 August General Maresuke Nogi's forces undertook a full-scale attack on the Russian defences of Port Arthur. It was repelled after very heavy fighting, with the loss to the Japanese of 15,000 dead and wounded, a third of Nogi's army.

Meanwhile the Japanese armies in the east were ready for an offensive against Kuropatkin at Liao-Yang. The two armies, each numbering about 150,000 men, met on a front about sixty miles in length. The Russian forces were divided into a southern group, of the 1st, 2nd, and 4th Siberian Corps under Lieutenant-General Zarubayev, and an eastern group, of the 3rd Siberian and the 10th and 17th Army Corps, under General Baron Bilderling. On the Japanese side the commander-in-chief was Field Marshal Iwao Oyama, and his forces were made up of the 1st Army under General Kuroki, the 2nd Army under General Oku, and the 4th Army under General Michitsura Nodzu. Oyama opened the attack on 26 August. The battle lasted for ten days. Both sides gained and lost territory, but on 4 September Kuropatkin ordered a retreat on Mukden. The battle can therefore be regarded as a Japanese victory, though the Russian armies were not decisively beaten. Russian casualties were estimated as over 15,000, Japanese as 24,000.

The next attack by Nogi's army on Port Arthur took place from 19 to 22 September, but it was beaten off by the Russians. At the beginning of October Kuropatkin began a new offensive, on the Sha Ho river south of Mukden. This was an even bigger battle than Liao-Yang. It was fought for twelve days on a front of forty miles, and 350,000 troops and 1,500 heavy guns were involved. Neither side won a decisive superiority, but the Russian purpose, to push the Japanese back and relieve pressure on Port Arthur, was frustrated. Admiral Alexeyev was relieved of his command, at his request, and Kuropatkin became commander-in-chief of the whole theatre. Just before the end of the Battle of the Sha Ho, the Russian Baltic Fleet, under Admiral Z. P. Rozhdestvensky, set out from Libau on its journey round the world on 15 October 1904.

The third general assault on Port Arthur was beaten back on 30 October. There was a lull for a month, but still absolutely no sign of relief for the besieged. At the end of November the last stage of the siege began. From 27 to 30 November the Japanese attacked a hill strongly held and fortified by the Russians, known as Vysokaya Gora. The attack was renewed on 5 December, and on the next day it was abandoned by the remnant of the defenders. In this battle the Japanese had 12,000 casualties and the Russians 4,500. From the hill the Japanese artillery was able to bombard the Russian warships in Port Arthur. Only one battleship escaped into the outer bay. On 15 December

General R. I. Kondratenko, the real organizer of the defence, was killed. Three days later two of the main forts on the landward side of the defences were stormed. The last major battle was from 30 December to 1 January. On 2 January 1905 Port Arthur surrendered, nearly a year after the outbreak of war, and after a direct siege of 156 days. Its defenders showed a bravery and an endurance second only to those of the defenders of Sevastopol fifty years earlier. It is estimated that its capture involved 110,000 Japanese casualties. Russian losses were 9,500 out of 42,000 in the army and 7,700 out of 11,000 in the naval forces afloat or ashore. At the time of surrender there was still ammunition and food available, and it was widely felt that resistance could have continued.[1]

After three months of winter inactivity, Kuropatkin, strengthened by large reinforcements from Russia, took the offensive again. The 2nd Army, under General Grippenberg, attacked Japanese positions south-west of Mukden. The attack was unsuccessful. The battle, which lasted from 25 to 29 January, brought the Russians more than 12,000 casualties.

Three weeks later came the biggest land battle of the war. Generally known as the Battle of Mukden, it lasted from 18 February to 10 March. Each of the antagonists had more than 300,000 men in action. The Japanese had some superiority in numbers of troops, the Russians a more substantial superiority in artillery. The Russian force was divided into three armies, commanded by Generals N. P. Linevich (1st), Kaulbars (2nd), and Bilderling (3rd). The Japanese force was made up of five armies, commanded by Generals Kuroki (1st), Oku (2nd), Nogi (3rd), Nodzu (4th), and Kavamura (5th). Neither Kuropatkin nor Oyama showed himself confident in the handling of such large forces, the largest that had been used in one battle in any war of the nineteenth century, including the American Civil War. But confusion was worse on the Russian side, especially in the 2nd Army of Kaulbars. After three weeks of fierce fighting, Kuropatkin decided to retire north of Mukden. The retreat was for the most part in good order. The Russian

[1] After the war the commander-in-chief of the garrison, General A. M. Stoessel, and three of his senior officers, were tried by courts martial. Stoessel was condemned to death, but this was commuted to ten years' imprisonment, and after serving a year and a half of his sentence he was released.

army was by no means broken as a fighting force, but the abandonment of Mukden was undoubtedly a defeat, and was generally so regarded both in Russia and abroad. Russian losses were heavy: 273 officers and 8,126 men killed, 1,585 officers and 49,426 men wounded, 21,000 of all ranks prisoners, and 8,000 missing. The Japanese admitted 41,000 casualties, but this was certainly less than the true figure.

It was now clear that there could be no Russian victory in Manchuria without reinforcements and reorganization on a vast scale. Meanwhile in Russia the revolutionary movement was growing. The government could not make up its mind to seek peace as long as it could hope for some result from the Baltic Fleet. Rozhdestvensky had had an inauspicious start to his journey in the Dogger Bank Incident of 22 October 1904, when British fishing vessels had been sunk during a panic caused by rumours of the presence of Japanese vessels in the North Sea.[1] After resting for two months in Madagascar, the fleet reached Kamrang Bay in the South China Sea on 13 April 1905. It stayed there a month. The original purpose of the journey, to combine with the Port Arthur fleet and wrest mastery of the seas from the Japanese, had long ceased to be attainable. Rozhdestvensky decided to force his way into Vladivostok, through the Gulf of Korea. On 27 May 1905 the Russian and Japanese fleets met in the Tsushima Straits. They were fairly evenly matched, and the Russian actually had a superiority in heavy guns. The battle was a complete disaster for the Russians. Eight battleships, 3 cruisers, 5 minelayers, an auxiliary cruiser, and 3 transports were sunk; 4 battleships and a minelayer surrendered; and 3 cruisers, 2 transports, and a minelayer were interned in neutral ports. Only 2 cruisers and 2 minelayers managed to reach Vladivostok.

This disaster, together with the mounting revolutionary tide in Russia, convinced the Tsar that he must end the war. For

[1] The Russian government admitted its responsibility, the crisis in Anglo-Russian relations was overcome, and compensation paid. However, fifty years later the Soviet historian, Major-General A. I. Sorokin, sees fit to assert that the presence of British fishermen on the Dogger Bank was a 'provocation', whose 'organizers' intended to hold up the fleet. (*Russko-yaponskaya voyna 1904–1905 gg.*, Moscow, 1956, p. 290.) It is of course 'well known' that Albion is always perfidious, but one cannot help regretting that the major-general does not quote the evidence for his assertion.

their part the Japanese also needed peace. Though brilliantly successful at sea and moderately victorious on land, they knew that their resources and manpower were extended almost to the limit. The offer of President Theodore Roosevelt to mediate was accepted. The peace conference opened in Portsmouth, New Hampshire, on 6 August 1905. The leader of the Russian delegation was Witte. The veteran statesman not only stubbornly resisted Japanese claims, but contrived to make an excellent public impression. American sympathies, which had been with Japan, largely turned towards Russia. Witte accepted the loss of the Liaotung Peninsula and the South Manchurian Railway. These went not to the Chinese, who had remained passively neutral while their territory was fought over by their two powerful neighbours, but to the Japanese victors. Witte also recognized the supremacy of Japanese interests in Korea. For their part the Japanese were perfectly willing to leave the Chinese Eastern Railway, and the dominant position in northern Manchuria, to the Russians. Two problems, however, led to long and tough negotiations. The first was the Japanese demand for an indemnity. This Witte absolutely refused, and in the end he had his way. The second was Sakhalin. In July 1905 Japanese forces had occupied the island, with virtually no resistance from the small Russian forces stationed there. Witte maintained that Russia had not been defeated, and therefore there could be no question of surrender of Russian territory (as opposed to abandonment of Russian interests in foreign territory which had been the object of military operations). In the end the island was divided in two.

In this war Russian officers and men had shown their customary valour, but their generals had not distinguished themselves. The impact of the first victory of an Asian over a European Power in modern times was felt far beyond the theatre of war. Defeat put an end to the designs of the extreme expansionists in Russia, but with the Maritime Provinces and the Chinese Eastern Railway still in its possession, the Russian empire remained a Great Power of the Pacific.

PART VI

FROM REVOLUTION TO REVOLUTION

XVII

THE DAYS OF LIBERTY

The Revolution of 1905

THE public mood in St. Petersburg at the end of the year 1904 was one of political expectancy, following the political banquets of November, and of depression caused by the news that Port Arthur had fallen to the Japanese. In the first days of January there were several strikes in the capital, the immediate cause of which was the dismissal of some workers belonging to the Assembly of Russian Factory Workers. This organization had been created at the end of 1903, with the consent of the authorities, by a priest named Gapon, and a year later had about 8,000 members. Its founder appears to have intended it to be patriotic and non-political, but inevitably it was carried away by the discontent prevalent among the working class. On 9 January 1905 Gapon decided to lead a deputation of workers to present a petition to the Tsar at the Winter Palace. They were followed by a vast, but peaceful and orderly crowd. When the crowd were assembled on the square in front of the palace, the troops opened fire, more than a hundred persons were killed, and several hundreds wounded. This event, one of the landmarks in Russian history, started off the process which has become known as the Revolution of 1905.

First the events of the following ten months may be briefly summarized.

In January there was a general strike in St. Petersburg, and sympathetic strikes in most of the large industrial centres of the empire. On 22 January Svyatopolk-Mirsky was replaced as minister of the interior by the undistinguished bureaucrat A. G. Bulygin. On 4 February the Tsar's uncle, Grand Duke Sergei,[1] governor-general of Moscow, was assassinated by the SR I. P. Kalyayev. On 18 February the Tsar issued a rescript to Bulygin announcing his intention to create an elected consultative assembly, to be composed of 'the most worthy persons, with the confidence of the people, elected by the population to take part in the preliminary consideration of projects of law'. During February peasant revolts broke out in Kursk province, spread to Oryol and Chernigov, and extended widely over the black-earth region. During April the zemstvo movement was active, and professional organizations came forward with radical political demands. At the beginning of June hostilities with Japan came to an end. On 14 June the crew of the battleship *Potyomkin*, of the Black Sea Fleet, mutinied in Odessa, put out to sea, resisted attack from loyal ships but ended by surrendering to the Roumanian authorities in Constanţa. On 6 June the Tsar received a delegation of zemstvo leaders. On 6 July a joint congress of zemstvo and city representatives was held in Moscow in defiance of a police prohibition, and adopted a draft constitution prepared by one of its members as the definite aim of its political activity. On 6 August the proposals of Bulygin for a national assembly were published. It was to be a purely consultative body, elected on an indirect and restricted franchise, and thus was completely unacceptable to any political group except the conservatives. Throughout these months the morale of the armed forces had been deteriorating, peasant revolts had been spreading, violence was especially widespread in the non-Russian provinces, and strikes of varying degrees of intensity occurred at irregular intervals in virtually all industrial areas. No one any longer feared to express his opinions in public, and political meetings, even though still nominally illegal, were ever more frequent. The concession of autonomy to the universities, whose students had been on strike since January, provided a further opportunity for political action. Autonomy was decreed on 26 August, and the student organizations, now under strong socialist influence, decided formally

[1] He was also the Tsar's brother-in-law, having married the elder sister of the Empress Alexandra Fyodorovna. On the assassination see also below p. 646.

to end their strike, and to return to the universities, not in order to study but in order to make the lecture-rooms available for political meetings. This opportunity was fully exploited by the revolutionary parties.

The government had shown itself both weak and politically inept. It still refused the minimum political concessions demanded even by moderate liberals, and it was no longer able to assert its will by force. The crisis came in the autumn. The conclusion of peace did not reduce tension. Another joint congress of zemstvo and city representatives in mid September rejected the Bulygin proposals and reiterated its democratic demands. On 8 October a railway strike was declared, and in the next days there were general strikes in most of the main cities, including St. Petersburg. The whole régime was on the verge of collapse. The Tsar still thought it might be possible to establish a military dictatorship, but no one was willing to take on the assignment. Witte, who had returned from Portsmouth with much increased prestige, advised Nicholas to give a constitution. The Grand Duke Nikolay Nikolayevich, the Tsar's own choice for military dictator, told him that he would shoot himself if the Tsar did not accept Witte's programme.[1] The Tsar yielded, gave Witte what amounted to the status of prime minister, and issued the manifesto of 17 October.

This was in effect a promise of a constitution to be granted from above. It instructed the government to ensure civil liberty, inviolability of the person, and freedom of conscience, speech, meeting, and association. It declared that the franchise for the elected Duma must be so broadened as to bring in 'those classes which are now completely deprived of electoral rights'. It laid down that in future no law would go into force without the approval of the Duma, and that the elected representatives of the people would be enabled to 'take part in supervising the legality of the actions of the authorities established by Us'. This was going a long way towards democratic government, but it still fell far short of the Constituent Assembly demanded by the main political groups.

In all these events the industrial working class, though only a small minority of the population, had played a leading part. The

[1] Witte's own version is in his memoirs *Vospominaniya*, vol. iii., ch. 52.

political consciousness of the workers had developed very fast, influenced by the propaganda of the illegal socialist parties, but still more by the workers' own experience. The sympathetic strikes of January 1905, affecting over 400,000 persons, were a genuine reaction of solidarity. The government's fumbling attempts to conciliate them failed. A mixed commission of officials, employers, and workers was set up at the end of January, with Senator N. V. Shidlovsky as chairman, to investigate the grievances of the workers. The workers of St. Petersburg factories were to elect voters, who were to elect worker delegates to the commission. The voters were elected, to the number of 372, and put forward further demands, including complete freedom of opinion and personal inviolability for the delegates at meetings of the commission, and investigations with the participation of elected worker delegates in other cities besides the capital. The authorities left the demands unanswered, so the worker delegates refused to attend the commission, and it never met. The strike wave of the next months swept along with it even the workers of regions which previously had been little affected by political unrest, such as the textile workers of Ivanovo-Voznesensk or the miners of the Urals. During the summer rudimentary trade unions were organized in several centres, and these entered into contact with each other. The railwaymen's union which organized the October strike was able to make its authority felt over virtually the whole railway network of the country. The culmination of the workers' movement in 1905 was the establishment of the St. Petersburg Soviet of Workers' Deputies. This was not created by order of the political parties, but was the result of action by workers' groups, among which some of the men elected to the Shidlovsky commission in February played a part. On 13 October about 30 deputies from various factories assembled in the Institute of Technology. During the six weeks of its existence, the Soviet's membership increased to about 500 persons. By this time there were 351 delegates of metallurgical workers, 57 of textile workers, and 32 of printers.[1] The socialist parties, of course, quickly realized the importance of the Soviet as an embryonic workers' parliament, and the workers were glad to have the

[1] J. L. H. Keep, *The Rise of Social Democracy in Russia*, pp. 234–5, quoting from *Istoriya soveta rabochikh deputatov* (SPB, 1907), pp. 147, 153.

parties play a leading part. The Soviet was directed by an Executive Committee, established on 17 October. It had a total membership of 31: there were 2 members from each of 7 districts of the city, 2 from each of the 4 largest trade unions, and 3 each from the SR, Menshevik, and Bolshevik organizations in the city. At the time of the publication of the manifesto of 17 October, it is arguable that the Soviet exercised more effective authority in St. Petersburg than the Imperial government.

The peasant revolts were more chaotic than the workers' strikes, but they affected huge numbers in the black-earth provinces and the Volga valley. The SR's made fairly successful efforts to provide leadership, and set themselves to create peasant unions, similar to trade unions, on a nation-wide scale. In May a congress of peasant delegates in Moscow decided to create an All-Russian Peasant Union, with organizations at *volost*, *uezd*, and provincial levels and a central body of five delegates from each province. The founding congress was opened on 31 July, and attended by delegates from 22 provinces. A second congress was held in November, at which 27 provinces were represented. It adopted the watchwords of the SR party, and appealed to the peasants to be ready to use against the landowners the weapon of a general agricultural strike, and if necessary against the government the further weapons of refusal of taxes and military recruits and withdrawal of all savings deposits. The Peasant Union urged the peasants to further revolt in the autumn. Official estimates of the cost of damage from these revolts were 29,000,000 roubles, of which 9,000,000 in the province of Saratov alone.[1]

During the spring new professional unions of the intelligentsia were set up, and existing unions were strengthened and were brought more directly into political action. A meeting in Moscow in May of representatives of the main professional associations set up a central Union of Unions, which chose as its chairman the prominent member of the Union of Liberation Professor P. N. Milyukov.[2] The Union strongly supported the

[1] *Obshchestvennoe dvizhenie*, vol. ii, part 2, p. 260.

[2] The unions were those of professors, teachers, doctors, zemstvo men, barristers, journalists, engineers, veterinaries, pharmacists, accountants, and railway employees, together with the unions for the emancipation of women and emancipation of Jews. Belokonsky, op. cit., p. 271. The union of teachers at this time had

campaign for a Constituent Assembly. Essentially the Union of Liberation, the Union of Unions and the zemstvo movement were controlled by the same persons at this stage, though the membership of the Union of Unions was the most radical in outlook of the three.

The zemstvo movement by mid 1905 was dominated by those who demanded full parliamentary government and a Constituent Assembly based on the so-called 'fourfold' suffrage (universal, secret, and direct in equal constituencies). At the April 1905 zemstvo conference a minority asked only for indirect suffrage. A minority would have been satisfied with the Bulygin proposals in August. At the end of August the zemstvo congress and the Union of Liberation formed a joint commission with the aim of establishing a new Constitutional Democratic Party. The followers of Shipov would not go so far. In effect the old zemstvo movement was broken in two. The majority had combined with the radical professional unions and the 'third element' and accepted a radical political programme, while the minority requested no more than some sort of elected consultative assembly. The founding congress of the Constitutional Democratic Party was in session at the time of the proclamation of the manifesto of 17 October. This was clearly less than the Constituent Assembly which the party demanded. The party leaders thus hesitated for some time as to what attitude to adopt to the manifesto. The former minority of the zemstvo movement, however, at once greeted the manifesto, and decided to form another party, more moderate than the Constitutional Democrats, for which they took the name League of the 17th October. The programme and tactics of both these parties became clear only a few months later.

Right-wing groups, with nationalist and anti-Semitic slogans, made their appearance during 1905. In April the Russian Monarchist Party was founded, with Gringmut, the editor of the *Moskovskie vedomosti*, as its leading figure. A second group was the Union of Russian Men, led by the brothers Sheremetyev and supported by Metropolitan Vladimir of Moscow. Both used traditionalist phrases and had little to offer but resistance

7,500 members, the union of engineers 4,000, the union of barristers 2,250, and the union of doctors 2,000. *Obshchestvennoe dvizhenie*, vol. ii, part 2, pp. 170–82.

to all west European influences and all reforms. More important was the Union of the Russian People, created in the autumn by Dr. Dubrovin and V. M. Purishkevich. This was a more modern party, in the sense that it was not content with a purely reactionary posture but went in for social and political demagogy on a large scale. It aimed at bringing the masses into political life, but in support of the autocracy. It appealed to workers and peasants, extolled the emperor, denounced bureaucracy as a barrier between Tsar and people, and showed special hostility to the intelligentsia. Above all it was anti-Semitic and nationalist. Its support came from those who organized the pogroms of Jewish property in the southern and south-western provinces. It was essentially a forerunner of the fascist movements of the 1930's.

On the left the SR's did well during 1905. Their party rapidly grew into a great mass movement, borne along by the spontaneous peasant revolts, which it had done something to instigate and now sought to lead. Its terrorists too had done well, following up their main killing—Grand Duke Sergei—with numerous assassinations of less eminent officials. It was decided to hold a congress of the party in Finland at the beginning of January 1906.

The Social Democratic organizations in Russia were thoroughly occupied in the work of assistance to the workers' movement in action. But the exiles were still engrossed in their factional rivalries. Lenin in particular was determined to reassert his control over the party. A series of intrigues from the autumn of 1904 to the spring of 1905 resulted in a meeting in London of Bolsheviks and a rival conference in Geneva of Mensheviks. Lenin maintained that the London meeting was 'the Third Congress of RSDRP', but the Mensheviks denied it this status. Strictly speaking, Lenin was wrong, because only twenty-one out of thirty-three committees in Russia were represented, and at a congress three-quarters of all the committees should have been represented. The Bolshevik view was however picturesquely expressed by one delegate: 'We Social Democrats have little in common with the *bourgeois* world. We have our own philosophy, our own law, our own ethics. . . . Begone, *bourgeois* ethics! Begone, *bourgeois* justice!'[1]

[1] J. L. H. Keep, op. cit., p. 210.

Lenin was of course no more exclusively inspired by personal ambition or arrogance than were his rivals. He believed that his ideas for the organization were correct, and that they must be put into practice if the party was to win. He followed events inside Russia with the greatest care, and published in June 1905 one of his most brilliant works, *Two Tactics of Social Democracy in the Bourgeois-Democratic Revolution.* It was in this work that he first formulated the notion of a 'democratic dictatorship of the proletariat and the peasantry', which became one of the basic principles of communist political strategy in later years. Essentially, he maintained that the coming revolution in Russia must be *bourgeois*, and if successful could only lead to the establishment of a *bourgeois* parliamentary system with the type of civil and political liberties which existed in western Europe, but that the Russian *bourgeoisie* was too weak and cowardly to lead a revolution.[1] Leadership could come only from the working class, led by 'its' party, the RSDRP as envisaged by Lenin, and allied with the peasantry. Lenin substituted the peasantry for the *bourgeoisie* as the ally of the working class in the revolutionary struggle, whereas the Mensheviks continued to allocate this role to the *bourgeoisie.* The Mensheviks distrusted the peasantry as a backward, politically ignorant, unreliable, and unpredictable class. Lenin certainly did not deny the faults of the peasantry. He disliked their '*petite bourgeois*' outlook quite as much as the Mensheviks did. But he recognized, more profoundly than the Mensheviks, the revolutionary potential of the peasants' desire for land. The peasant masses could be mobilized for revolution more easily than could the *bourgeois*, who in the last resort had too much to lose. Another aspect of the same problem is that Lenin understood that the political naïvety of the peasants was actually an asset for revolutionary leaders. Peasants could be more easily swayed by a few simple slogans attractively presented than could middle-class intellectuals whose political ideas were already more or less formed. In

[1] Whether even at this time there was anything in Russia that could correctly be called a *bourgeoisie* remains to my mind doubtful. See above p. 538. However, the words *bourgeoisie* and *petite bourgeoisie* were constantly used in the political controversies of these years, and we are obliged to use them too. Though their meaning is not precise, they make at least rough sense. By *bourgeoisie* was meant the urban business and professional classes, by *petite bourgeoisie* the small shopkeepers and other persons of small property, sometimes including the whole peasantry.

Two Tactics is already revealed that preference for partnership between highly sophisticated professional revolutionaries and primitive masses which was characteristic of Lenin's later career and later greatness.

Lenin's aim then was that Bolshevik leadership should control a party which would lead the working class, which would lead the more numerous peasantry. After victory, there would be a dictatorship, in which the party would wield all political power, but the economic and social policies which it would put into effect would not be socialist. Socialism could not become a reality until the Russian social structure had developed a long way, until a much larger part of the population were employed in industry, and until the peasantry had been split into a rural *bourgeoisie* and a rural proletariat. This process had already begun, but its completion would take years yet—nobody would predict how many. Russia's progress to socialism could only be accelerated beyond this if revolution took place in advanced industrial countries in Europe, which would then be able to give both political and economic aid to the Russian democratic government. It was conceivable that a successful '*bourgeois*-democratic' revolution in Russia might provide the spark which would set off the revolutionary conflagration in Europe.

This last idea had already been expressed by a young socialist named Lev Davidovich Bronstein, later better known as Trotsky. He believed that the proletariat might find itself in power in Russia as a result of a '*bourgeois*-democratic revolution'. But if this happened, it could not limit itself to pursuing a *bourgeois* policy. It would have to go on to socialism. In Russia as it was, a socialist revolution would be defeated. But if revolution spread to Europe, socialism might win in both Europe and Russia. These ideas were later formulated by Trotsky in his theory of 'permanent revolution', but the gist of them had appeared already in January 1905 and attracted Lenin's attention.

Trotsky was the only well-known Social Democratic exile who played a leading part in the revolution in Russia. He returned in the spring, took refuge in Finland after some weeks, but was back in St. Petersburg in October, where he became the outstanding figure in the Soviet.

Revolutionary action, apart from the two capitals, was most violent in the non-Russian provinces, where social and national discontents merged. This was especially true of Poland, the Baltic provinces, Georgia, and Finland. Ukrainian nationalism also emerged as a considerable force, mingled with the social aspirations of the peasantry, and Moslem democratic nationalism acquired formal political organization.

The Russian strike movement following the 9 January massacre strengthened the arguments of those Polish socialists who believed in the value of co-operation between the Polish and Russian workers. The SDKPL gained support, and in the much more influential PPS the left wing predominated. At the Eighth Congress of PPS in March 1905 a resolution was passed urging 'the co-ordination of the revolutionary movement of the whole proletariat in all parts of the Russian empire'. PPS supported the demand for a Constituent Assembly of the whole empire, but also asked for a Constituent for Russian Poland within the empire. The leader of the most nationalist wing of the party, Józef Piłsudski, went to Japan in 1904 to discuss Polish action against Russia's war effort. Dmowski, the leader of the National Democrats, also went to Japan, but was not prepared to go so far in co-operation with Russia's enemies, and tried to dissuade Piłsudski. The general tactic of the Polish National Democrats was to avoid violence, but to use every difficulty of the Russian government to press for Polish claims.

Strikes in Poland were numerous and on a large scale. The most serious incidents were in mid June, in the textile city of Łódź, where there was street fighting with barricades for five days. The most important practical concession made to Poles during 1905 was in the field of education. Permission was given to create from private funds schools in which all teaching would be in Polish. There came into being an organization called Mother of Polish Schools (*Polska Macierz Szkolna*) which busily founded schools.

Ukrainians were involved in great numbers both in peasant revolts and in strikes, in which the social and national factors could not easily be separated. The Ukrainian nationalist cause was helped by an event not directly connected with the revolutionary movement. This was a decision of the Academy of Sciences in St. Petersburg in March 1905, to the effect that Ukrainian was not a mere dialect of Russian, but an independent language. During the year the authorities permitted Ukrainian cultural activities. An organization entitled *Prosvita* (Enlightenment) was set up in several Ukrainian cities. It was based on the organization of the same name which had existed in Lwów since 1868. It published books and periodicals in Ukrainian, founded libraries, bookshops, and public reading-rooms and offered prizes and scholarships for students as well as for adult writers and scientists. In 1905 the historian Hrushevsky returned to the Russian Ukraine from Galicia, and during the following years divided his time between Kiev and Lwów, writing prolifically on both historical and political themes.

Ukrainian nationalist politics had grown rapidly both in intensity and in complexity in the first years of the century. From the first Ukrainian party founded on Russian soil, the Revolutionary Ukrainian Party (RUP), at least three parties had evolved by 1905. First was the Radical-Democratic Party, the Ukrainian equivalent of the Russian Constitutional Democrats. To its left was the Ukrainian Social Democratic Party, which combined socialism and nationalism rather in the manner of the Polish PPS. On the right was the People's Party, rather similar in outlook to the Polish National Democrats, extremely nationalist and anti-Semitic. A pamphlet published by this party in 1904, with the title *Ten Commandments*, stated: 'Muscovites, Jews, Poles, Hungarians, and Roumanians are enemies of our people.'[1] In June 1905 a congress of representatives of the People's and Radical Democratic parties demanded a legislative assembly in Kiev, with full powers to make laws on matters affecting only the Ukraine. The congress argued that the St. Petersburg government's authority should be limited to defence, foreign policy, customs, treaties, and such financial matters as affected both Ukraine and the rest of the empire. It also demanded that Ukrainian should be the language of instruction in all schools and government institutions. It was not clear how much support such demands had from the population, but it was certain that no Russian government would

[1] Quoted in article by K. Zalevsky, 'Natsional'nye partii v Rossii', *Obshchestvennoe dvizhenie*, iii. 303.

give them any consideration. Apart from the specifically Ukrainian nationalist parties, the SR's and the RSDRP had strong followings in the Ukraine. Both parties of course operated on an all-Russian basis, but there was a definite undertone of Ukrainian nationalism among their supporters in the Ukraine, even though this was milder than in the case of supporters of the nationalist parties.

In two other western borderlands there were at least mild stirrings of cultural nationalism. Newspapers appeared in the White Russian tongue, and two poets, Yakov Kolas and Ivan Kupala, began to raise it to the level of a distinct literary language, thus performing to some extent the function of Shevchenko sixty years earlier in the Ukraine. A political party was formed in 1903, the White Russian Community (*Belorusskaya gromada*), like the Ukrainian RUP a radical intellectuals' group. In Bessarabia a Moldavian Cultural Society was founded by Dicescu, and the request for schools with instruction in the Moldavian (Roumanian) language was made to St. Petersburg. In 1906 Emanuel Gavrilitsa founded a Democratic Party. Several newspapers appeared in Roumanian. The most that was gained was the introduction, for a few years only, of the Roumanian language as a subject—but not as the language of instruction—in the girls' secondary school and the theological seminary of Kishinyov.

Riga was one of the main centres of working-class action in the empire, and the Social Democrats were extremely strong. It was here that revolutionary activity in the Baltic provinces began, but it soon spread into the countryside. The national struggle against the Baltic Germans was linked with the social struggle against the landowners. Under socialist leadership large-scale revolt developed in Livonia, turning into a civil war. The landowners organized military forces of their own. It was not until the end of the year that the Russian army intervened. In Estland there was less violence, but the movement of national and social revolution was still powerful. Latvian and Estonian nationalist demands were also put forward on peaceful occasions. Such was a conference of 1,000 local officials of Latvian nationality, held in Riga on 19 November, which asked for autonomy for the Latvian lands. At the end of November an 'All-Estonian Congress' was held at Reval, attended by more than 800 persons from all social classes. It demanded the administrative union of all territories of Estonian speech, and the use of Estonian as the official language within this area.[1] During the year a variety of small political parties appeared. In Latvia there were the Latvian People's Party, of conservative nationalists, heirs to the cultural nationalism of the Latvian Association; the Constitutional Democrats, very similar to their Russian counterparts; the Democratic Party, somewhat more radical; and the Latvian Social Democratic League, a socialist and nationalist mixture similar to the PPS among the Poles. The main support of the working class, and a considerable following among poor peasants and agricultural labourers, in the Latvian provinces went to the RSDRP. Among the Estonians the main party was the Free-Thinking Progressive Party, conservative and nationalist and based on the peasantry, with many Protestant pastors among its leaders. A smaller group was the Estonian Democratic Party, more urban in its appeal and led by the more radical section of the intelligentsia.

In Lithuania the strongest political forces were Polish nationalism and Social Democracy, the latter largely Jewish. Two Lithuanian nationalist parties, however, appeared, both appealing to the Lithuanian-speaking peasantry. The Democratic Party, led by Dr. Basanovicius, was moderately liberal in outlook; the Christian Democratic League was more concerned with the rights of the Catholic Church. In November a Lithuanian National Congress was held in Vilna. It asked for autonomy, and for the reorganization of provincial boundaries in such a way that the area of Lithuanian speech should be united. This latter claim was urged with special force by the representatives of Suvalki province, who declared a boycott of taxes, and had to be occupied by Russian troops in 1906. With this exception, Lithuania, in contrast to the Baltic provinces, remained comparatively peaceful during the revolutionary year.

The Russian government decided to conciliate the Finns, and in March 1905 repealed the Conscription Law of 1901 and restored the irremovability of judges. This did not satisfy the

[1] Estonian was spoken in the northern part of Livonia (districts of Dorpat and Pernau) as well as in Estland. Latvian was spoken in the greater part of Livonia and in Kurland.

Finns. The Activist Party continued terrorist attacks on Russian officials, and the Finnish working-class movement developed as rapidly as the Russian. The crisis came at the same time as in Russia, with a general strike in October, co-ordinated with the Russian railway strike. The Social Democrats demanded a Constituent Assembly, while the moderate parties were content with something less. On 4 November the Tsar issued a manifesto, which did not grant a Constituent Assembly, but set up a body called the Constituent Senate, with wide powers to lay down the functions of the reformed Diet. This seemed to the moderates a possible basis for future political development, and they took part in the Senate's labours. The Social Democrats remained in opposition.

The Jews suffered during 1905 from right-wing violence. Pogroms were numerous in the southern and western provinces. In June 1905 fifty Jews were killed in Białystok, and in October more than three hundred in Odessa. The October manifesto offered this much hope to the Jews that at least they would have a vote in the new Duma. But when the year ended, no formal action had yet been taken to remedy the restrictions under which the Jewish citizens of the empire lived. The Jews themselves founded in February 1905, at a meeting in Vilna, the Union for the Attainment of Equal Rights for Jews, which joined the Union of Unions in May.

The Transcaucasian provinces were the scene of some of the most effective revolutionary action in the year. The last months of Golitsyn's governor-generalship were marked by fighting between Armenians and Tatars, largely engineered by the Russian authorities, a Transcaucasian version of the Jewish pogroms in the Ukraine. The new governor-general, Count I. I. Vorontsov-Dashkov, who arrived in May with the old title of viceroy, ended the persecution of the Armenian Church. The *Dashnyaktsutyun* movement in 1905 split into two groups, the Old and the Young. The Young supported the all-Russian movement for a Constituent Assembly, and demanded autonomy for Armenia within the Russian state. The Old, who continued to hope that the Russian empire would liberate the Armenians under Ottoman rule, were anxious not to antagonize the Russian authorities, and therefore much more cautious in their pursuit either of self-government or of political reform.

The conciliatory attitude of Vorontsov-Dashkov did not appease the Georgians. The Social Democrats enjoyed enormous mass support. They were responsible for a peasant revolt in the province of Guria. The peasants boycotted the Russian authorities, withheld taxes and all obligations to the state, and in effect established a republic of their own ruled by the RSDRP. The revolt spread for a time into Imeretia and Mingrelia. The Georgian Church also openly demanded an autocephalous church organization for Georgia. At the request of the Russian exarch, the authorities broke up a meeting of Georgian priests, assembled in Tiflis to formulate this demand. The result was for a time to drive the church into alliance with the revolutionary movement. On 29 August Cossacks attacked a socialist-led demonstration in front of Tiflis city hall, and there were numerous casualties. Thus both town and countryside in Georgia were thoroughly disaffected at the end of 1905.

Political activity also affected the Moslems. In August 1905 a meeting of leading Moslems, held in a ship on the river Oka at Nizhnii Novgorod, set up an All-Russian Moslem League. It announced its intention of uniting all Moslems in the empire in a single political movement. It demanded removal of all forms of legal discrimination against Moslems, and gave rather cautious support to the general democratic movement in Russia. The main impetus undoubtedly came from Volga Tatars, from the new Tatar intelligentsia of school-teachers and disciples of Ismail Bey Gaspirali's modernizing and democratic ideas. Though Islam was of course stressed, as the identifying characteristic, the movement was more secular and nationalist than religious. The notion of the solidarity of the Tatar-Turkish peoples was gaining ground. One of its chief exponents, who played a part in the League in 1905, was a young Tatar, educated in France, named Yusuf Akchura.[1] Another was an older man, Reshid Ibrahimov, who had been an official of the Moslem Spiritual Administration in Ufa in the 1890's and had lived in Turkey from 1895 to 1904.

[1] Akchura was born in 1876. He had published, in the periodical *Türk* edited in Cairo by Ali Kemal, an article entitled 'Three Kinds of Policy' (*Uçtarzi siyaset*), in which the ideas of Ottoman patriotism, Pan Islamism, and Turkish nationalism had been compared with each other.

The First and Second Dumas

The publication of the manifesto of 17 October and the appointment of Witte were followed by a decree of 19 October which revived the institution of the Council of Ministers, and broadened its powers.[1] As president of the council, Witte had a status comparable at first sight to that of a prime minister. The creation of a unified government, with one man at its head, which had been discussed by the Unofficial Committee of 1801, and again in April 1881, but had never been put into effect, seemed at last to be a fact. However, institutions depend on the men who work them, and little could be expected of a weak or compliant prime minister, willing to act at the bidding of irresponsible court cliques. Witte was not such a man, but he owed his position only to the Tsar's good pleasure. He could be removed and replaced by an obedient official. The truth was that a unified government that was not responsible to parliament did not represent much progress, though it was at least likely to be rather more efficient than the system of uncoordinated individual responsibility of ministers to the Tsar.

Even at the beginning of his tenure of office, Witte's position was not strong. General D. F. Trepov resigned his posts of deputy minister of the interior and chief of police, but was appointed commandant of the palace at Tsarskoe Selo. This meant that he was in daily contact with the emperor, had full access to all information, and freely dispensed his advice on political and security problems. Witte had no say in this appointment. But he alone was to blame for the choice of another former policeman, P. N. Durnovo, as minister of the interior. Witte believed he was the best man available, since he was the only high official, with experience of security problems, who was not known to be closely connected with the cliques of Pleve or of Trepov. However, once appointed, Durnovo soon began to intrigue with Trepov against Witte. This did not help him, for when Witte was dismissed six months later, Durnovo lost his job too. But it made Witte's task more difficult.

[1] The institution of the Council of Ministers had existed under Alexander II, but it was a body summoned only occasionally to consider matters of great importance chiefly during the preparation of the reforms of the 1860's. It seldom met in the 1870's, and ceased to exist under Alexander III. The Committee of Ministers continued to exist all through the nineteenth century, but it dealt not with major problems of policy but only with minor matters of routine.

Witte decided to consult some of the leading liberal politicians and see if some could be brought into his government. He invited Shipov to become state controller. Shipov replied that he represented only the minority in the constitutionalist movement, and advised Witte to consult the majority, through F. A. Golovin, the chairman of the bureau of the congress of zemstvo and city representatives. The bureau sent a delegation to see Witte on 21 October. It demanded a Constituent Assembly elected on the fourfold suffrage, immediate establishment of the liberties promised in the manifesto, and a complete amnesty for persons imprisoned for political offences. These were refused, and the conversations came to an end. Witte conferred further with Shipov, A. I. Guchkov, and Prince E. N. Trubetskoy on the possibility of the participation of the moderates in his ministry. These talks too failed, as the moderates were unwilling to join a ministry in which P. N. Durnovo was to be minister of the interior.[1]

For a month and a half the government coexisted with the St. Petersburg Soviet. In November the Soviet conducted a campaign for the introduction of an eight-hour working day. This was naturally supported with enthusiasm by the workers, but made little appeal to the rest of the population. The breach between the Soviet and the non-socialist radical groups widened. A general strike, ordered by the Soviet on 1 November, nominally in defence of the mutineers of the Kronstadt naval base and in protest against the introduction of martial law in Poland, was much less successful than the October strike. It was called off on its fifth day. At the end of November the

[1] Shipov's account is in *Vospominaniya i dumy o perezhitom*, pp. 335–47. Milyukov, who was present at the meeting called by Golovin, which decided to send the deputation to Witte, comments in his own account (*Tri popytki*, Paris, 1921, pp. 12–13) that 'the dividing line between the authorities and the public was not the idea of a Constituent Assembly but the very notion of a constitution'. He reports that he himself met Witte at this time (no precise date given), and advised him to form a Cabinet of practical-minded officials, without representatives of public opinion, simply to get the new political system going. Then elections would be held in due course, and a representative government would come into being. This would of course be a constitution granted from above. 'They will curse you if you act like this, but then they will calm down, and everything will be normal.' Witte, according to Milyukov, replied that he could not do this. 'I can't speak of a constitution, because the Tsar will not have it.' Witte describes his discussions with the moderates in *Vospominaniya*, iii. 102–10, but does not refer to the conversation with Milyukov.

government arrested the chairman of the Soviet, G. S. Khrustalev-Nosar, and on 3 December troops occupied its building and arrested about 190 people, including Trotsky and all other important leaders. The government forces met with no armed opposition in St. Petersburg. In Moscow, however, a general strike was declared, and this led to barricades and fighting in the streets. Large numbers of troops had to be brought in. The Moscow rising lasted from 8 to 20 December, and by the time it was suppressed over a thousand people had been killed, including many who were executed after being taken prisoner.

During December special punitive expeditions of reliable troops were sent to restore order in especially disaffected areas. Major-General A. A. Orlov was in command of the Baltic force, which won a reputation for exceptional ferocity. The repression of the revolt in Georgia was also accompanied by a good deal of bloodshed. An important task was to restore order along the Trans-Siberian line, in order to bring back from Manchuria the demoralized and semi-mutinous troops that had been fighting the Japanese. This was accomplished by two special units, commanded by General P. K. Rennenkampf and General A. N. Meller-Zakomelsky, which started respectively from Kharbin and from European Russia, and met in Chita.[1] From this time onwards the government's authority over the army recovered fairly quickly. The morale of the navy was still extremely low. The *Potyomkin* affair in June 1905 was followed by a mutiny at Kronstadt in October and a still more dangerous mutiny in November in Sevastopol, led by Lieutenant P. P. Shmidt, a revolutionary who was not a regular member of any political group, The navy, however, was a less serious menace to public order than the army, as its influence was limited to a few places.

These months were also marked by disorders organized by counter-revolutionary groups. These were the so-called 'black hundreds', bands of armed persons who purported to defend Russia from the revolutionaries, but in fact devoted most of their efforts to pogroms of Jewish property in the southern towns. Mob violence from the right also occurred in central Russian towns, where the objects of attack were the local intelligentsia, including in some cases secondary school

[1] Witte, op. cit., iii. 152–8.

children. For the most part these actions were local and sporadic, the work of one or two fanatics who made use of the type of hooligan who is always to be found in times of public insecurity. However, the authorities made use of them for their own purposes, and some inflammatory anti-Jewish propaganda was actually printed in the premises of the department of police.[1]

Details of the new electoral system were announced in a further manifesto of 20 February 1906. There were to be two chambers. The upper chamber was to be known as the Council of State, and to be composed in equal number of appointed and elected persons. The elected members were chosen by the Church, provincial zemstvos, nobility, universities, and business organizations.[2] The lower chamber was to be known as the State Duma. Its members were to be elected in separate electoral colleges, according to class or property. In the five largest cities of European Russia the colleges were to elect the members of the Duma directly. Elsewhere, voting was indirect. The electorate elected official voters, who met on an appointed day and cast their votes among the candidates standing for the Duma. The election by peasants was doubly indirect, since their official voters were chosen by *volost* assemblies, themselves elected by peasant householders. Thus peasants who were not householders chose their representatives at two removes. The number of official voters allocated to the different colleges, and to the different urban and rural constituencies, was decided by special regulations, and roughly corresponded to their numerical proportions in the population. The bias of the authorities was rather towards excessive representation for the peasants, since the government expected—wrongly, as it turned out—that peasants would vote for the more conservative candidates.

[1] Witte, op. cit., iii. 84–88, describes how he was informed of these activities by A. A. Lopukhin, who had been director of the department of police from 1903 to 1905, was then appointed governor of Estland, and was dismissed for alleged failure to cope with the disorders there. Lopukhin also informed his brother-in-law, Prince S. D. Urusov, who served under Witte as deputy minister of the interior but was then elected a member of the First Duma, in which he spoke about these anti-Semitic activities of the police. For another exposure of police secrets by Lopukhin, which had more serious consequences, see below p. 646.

[2] The total membership of the Council of State was 196. The original institution of this name continued to perform its previous functions, with persons appointed for the purpose.

In February 1906 the first legally permitted congress of workers' trade unions in Russia met, in Moscow. At this time there were 44 unions in St. Petersburg, with a membership of 35,000, and between 40 and 50 in Moscow with 25,000 to 30,000 members. The congress decided to make use of any forms of organization that might be permitted by the government, but was not prepared to advise its members to abandon existing secret forms. In March 1906 the government published a law on associations under which unions could at least carry on a few innocent collective activities. Strikes remained prohibited, and unions were not permitted to engage in any activities connected with strike action. The value to the workers of the law of March 1906 was very small. But at least the reading-rooms, lectures, and social gatherings which it did allow made it easier for workers to meet, strengthened their sense of solidarity, and gave some opportunity for future workers' leaders to emerge. At the beginning of 1907 the official organ of the unions, *Professionalny vestnik*, claimed that the printers' union included 43 per cent. of all workers employed in that trade. No other union had more than 9 per cent. of its trade members. In the whole empire there were 652 unions with a total of 245,000 members. Poland and the Caucasus together had about a quarter of the membership. There were said to be 52,000 members in St. Petersburg, 48,000 in Moscow, 26,000 in Łódź, 17,000 in Warsaw, 12,000 in Baku, and 10,000 in Odessa.[1]

After the suppression of the Soviet, the industrialists began a counter-offensive against the workers. Employers made agreements not to raise wages except after consulting each other, to circulate black-lists of persons active in strike movements, and to plan lock-out action together. Business organizations were of course concerned not only with action against workers but also with united pressure on the government and with joint promotion of their business interests. In April 1906 was founded the Congress of Representatives of Trade and Industry, organized on an all-Russian scale on a basis of membership not by individual firms but by branches of industry.

In the first months of 1906 the political parties improved their organizations, and decided what should be their attitude to the forthcoming election to the Duma. The Constitutional

[1] V. Grinevich, *Professional'noe dvizhenie rabochikh* (SPB, 1908), pp. 277–85.

Democrats, who became known as 'Kadets',[1] worked out a detailed programme at their Second Congress, held from 18 to 24 January. This included land reform with compensation for landowners, a progressive income-tax, health insurance for workers at employers' expense, and the inclusion among official factory inspectors of persons elected by the workers. The congress decided that the party should take part in the elections, but insisted that the Duma itself must be given the task of drawing up the Fundamental Laws which were to decide the relations between executive and legislative branches of government. Among the party's outstanding leaders were Milyukov and Struve from the Union of Liberation and Petrunkevich and V. A. Maklakov from the zemstvo movement.

The former minority of the constitutionalist movement created the Octobrist Party. Its programme was both more conservative and more cautiously phrased. It did not absolutely reject redistribution of land, but laid greater emphasis on improvements to agriculture, which, whatever its inherent merits, has always been the typical attitude of landowning classes confronted with land reform, not only in Russia and not only in Europe. Apart from the moderates of the zemstvo movement, the Octobrists drew their support mainly from the business class. Their ideas also appealed to mildly liberal elements in the bureaucracy. Shipov was certainly one of the founding fathers of the party, but did not play a leading part in its later activity. Far more important was A. I. Guchkov, son of an eminent Moscow business family of Old Believer background. Guchkov was a man of great ability and great ambition, brave and quarrelsome, devoted to liberty but inclined to interpret it in his own way. A man of combative temperament, ready to use his talents in battle, on the duelling ground, in parliamentary rhetoric, or in backstairs intrigue, he left his mark on Russian history in the next decade.

In January 1906 the Socialist Revolutionaries held their first full congress in Finland. They declared their party to be 'a detachment of the international socialist army', which would

[1] This abbreviation comes from the pronunciation of the letters which form the initials of the name *Konstitutsionno-demokraticheskaya*—Ka-De. To speak of the KD's would, I think, be pedantic, but the often-used 'Cadets' seems to me unsatisfactory, as the word has other associations. I therefore propose to write 'Kadets'.

'pursue its activity in the forms which correspond to the concrete conditions of Russia's present reality'. The SR's were recognized by the Second International as a member party up to 1914. The main emphasis in the party programme was on the land question. It demanded the socialization of the land, its 'conversion from the personal property of individual persons or groups into the general possession of the whole nation'. The arable land that was taken from the landowners would be controlled by elected local authorities, which would allocate it to individual peasant families on a basis of 'labour ownership' (*trudovaya sobstvennost'*). Large forests and fisheries would be administered at the district or provincial level, while the wealth of the sub-soil was to be the property of the state. The political demands of the party programme barely differed from those of other radical parties, with one important exception: the SR's proposed that the Russian state should have a federal structure, with full national self-determination for the non-Russians. In this respect they went much further to meet the needs of the nationalities than any other Russian party. The congress debated terrorism at some length. The more extreme forms of mass terror, such as sabotage of crops, were repudiated. But the congress refused to condemn 'partisan actions' or raids on the property of landowners or public authorities. These were defended, not so much because they enriched the party's funds as because they drew the masses into the revolutionary struggle. The Combat Detachment continued to exist, linked with the main party through its chief, who was automatically a member of the central committee. The Peasant Union ceased to exist during 1906. On the one hand several of its leaders were arrested and its overt organization suppressed by the authorities, on the other hand its members became merged with the SR party. On the right, the *Russkoe bogatstvo* group, being completely opposed to terrorism, split definitely from the SR's and formed the People's Socialist Party. On the left, a group of extreme terrorists, known as the SR Maximalists, operated on their own, until they were broken up by the police. The SR's decided to boycott the coming Duma elections, but the People's Socialists decided to present candidates.

The RSDRP held its Fourth Congress in Stockholm in April 1906. Here formal unity was restored between Mensheviks and

Bolsheviks. Nevertheless, Lenin maintained his own separate organization. Like the SR's, the Social Democrats discussed 'partisan actions'. Lenin defended these as valuable training in revolutionary action, though he admitted that abuses had occurred, and that the party must not be involved in criminal actions which could demoralize its members and get the party a bad name. The Mensheviks objected to partisan actions altogether, and at the congress their view essentially prevailed. The party also had to consider what attitude to adopt to the elections. The general line of the party was to boycott them: the party believed that armed revolutionary action could still succeed, and that to take part in an election to a semi-parliament with no real political power would simply divert the attention of the masses from the real goal. However, some individuals of Social Democratic allegiance had stood for election, and the congress decided that they should be allowed to form a Social Democratic group in the Duma, provided that they operated 'under the constant direction of the central institutions of the party'. In Transcaucasia the election had still not been held at the time of the congress. In Georgia the strength of the RSDRP was overwhelming, and the population certainly wished to elect Social Democrats as its representatives. The congress therefore decided to authorize the party's participation in Transcaucasia.

Meanwhile the prospective powers of the Duma were being drastically limited. The budgetary rules, published on 8 March 1906, exempted the military and naval estimates and the expenditure of the Ministry of the Imperial Court from any control by the Duma. On 23 April were published the Fundamental Laws. These could be modified only by the emperor: there was thus no procedure by which the Duma could initiate a constitutional amendment. Under these laws, ministers were to be appointed by the emperor, and to hold office as long as they enjoyed his confidence: they were definitely not responsible to the Duma. Members of the Duma might put questions to the prime minister or individual ministers, but they were not obliged to give satisfactory replies. The Duma could not overthrow the government, or bring about the resignation of individual ministers, by a vote of censure. It could vote its displeasure, but this remained an empty moral gesture. The president of the Duma, whose functions approximated to those of Speaker in Anglo-Saxon legislatures, had the right to make personal reports to the emperor, and could use these occasions to bring to the ruler's notice the opinions of the Duma. The emperor was in no way obliged to take any action on these reports.

Witte was now on bad terms with the Tsar. Trepov and Durnovo were doing their best to discredit him. Another irresponsible adviser who played some part was Prince Meshchersky. Nicholas expressed his views frankly in letters to his mother. On 12 January he wrote of Witte: 'I have never seen such a chameleon of a man. That naturally is the reason why no one believes in him any more. He is absolutely discredited with everyone except perhaps the Jews abroad.' On 8 February he wrote: 'Trepov is absolutely indispensable to me; he is acting in a kind of secretarial capacity. He is experienced and clever and cautious in his advice. I give him Witte's bulky memoranda to read, then he reports on them quickly and concisely.'[1] The Tsar only kept Witte in office because his prestige was necessary for the conclusion of the huge French loan, on which the recovery of the Russian economy and the freedom of action of the government in regard to its internal enemies so largely depended. At the beginning of April the loan agreement was signed in Paris. On 14 April he resigned, and on 22 April his resignation was made public, five days before the Duma was to assemble. His place was taken by the elderly former minister of the interior, Goremykin. The intriguer Durnovo was also removed from his post. The new minister of the interior was P. A. Stolypin, who had served as governor of Grodno and then of Saratov. In the latter post, at the very centre of the peasant revolts, he had shown a combination of firmness with understanding of the peasants' feelings which had brought him to the attention of the Tsar.

When the results of the election to the Duma were complete, it was clear that radical opinions prevailed throughout the country, no less among the peasants than in the urban classes. The Kadets had by far the largest number of candidates elected. This was due to the nation-wide reputation of many of their leaders, the radicalism of their slogans, and the fact that the

[1] *The Letters of the Tsar to the Empress Marie* (1937), pp. 195, 197, 212.

parties of the extreme left were not competing. Together with some minor groups which co-operated closely with them, they had 179 seats. Though the SR's had not taken part, a large number of persons of SR outlook had stood and had been elected. In the Duma they formed a faction, known as the Labour Group (*Trudoviki*). They were the second largest faction, and numbered 94. On the extreme left were 18 Social Democrats, mostly from Georgia. To the right of the Kadets were 17 Octobrists, and the extreme right wing had 15. The non-Russian nationalities were strongly represented. In Poland the PPS and SDKPL had abstained, and so the National Democrats swept the polls. A Polish Circle (*Koło Polskie*) of 51 members was formed. Ukrainian nationalists of various shades amounted to about 40. About three-quarters of them formed a group of their own which took the name *Ukrainska hromada*.[1] Several members of the Latvian and Estonian democratic parties were elected. There were 30 Moslem members, of whom the majority co-operated with the Kadets, but 6 formed a separate Moslem Labour Group, sympathetic to the *Trudoviki* but distinct from them.

The First Duma included many persons of outstanding abilities, high political ideals, and honourable characters. There were many great issues to be debated, and many important reforms to be carried through. Most important of all was the problem of land reform. Hardly less vital to the future of Russian freedom were the rights of religious dissenters, equality for the Jews, self-government for Poland, and the extension of elementary education. But no progress was made in any of these directions. The Fundamental Laws made a healthy relationship between government and legislature impossible. The Tsar refused to appoint persons who represented the public. Between the ministers and the Duma there was a complete absence of understanding, a complete failure of communication.

The formal inauguration of the Duma took place at a reception in the Winter Palace on 27 April, when the emperor made a polite speech to the new legislators. The Duma began its activities by preparing a reply to this speech from the throne, in which it asked for various reforms including a redistribution

[1] *Obshchestvennoe dvizhenie*, iii. 300–1.

of landed estates and a political amnesty. The Tsar refused to accept the reply from a deputation of the Duma, and insisted that it should be sent to him through the government. On 13 May Goremykin and his ministers appeared in the Taurid Palace, the seat of the Duma, and the prime minister read out a speech in which he rejected all the Duma's proposals and described the redistribution of estates as 'inadmissible'. Several speakers then rose in turn to denounce the government, the ministers withdrew in a body, and the Duma passed a hostile resolution, which had no effect.

Although the debates of the following weeks, on the land question, Poland, the rights of Jews, and other topics, were conducted on a generally high level, they remained perforce quite divorced from political reality. Meanwhile conversations were resumed with some of the political leaders. The initiative seems to have come from Trepov, who met Milyukov, who also saw Stolypin. Shipov was summoned to audience with the Tsar on 28 June. He first saw Stolypin, with whom he discussed the possibility of his forming a coalition government. Shipov's view was that this was impossible unless the Kadets would join. Shipov asked Count P. A. Heyden to see Milyukov, who expressed the view that the only sound solution would be a homogeneous government of Kadets. Shipov himself saw S. A. Muromtsev, who had been elected president of the Duma, and suggested that he might head a government including Kadets. Muromtsev argued that Milyukov should be the head of a government of Kadets. Shipov was then received by the emperor, to whom he recommended that there should be a Kadet government headed by Muromtsev.

But nothing came of these discussions. The Duma had been infuriated by a statement, on 20 June, of the government's agrarian policy, in which compulsory redistribution of landowners' estates was definitely rejected. In reply the Duma issued a proclamation to the people at large, insisting that the land question could not be solved without the Duma's co-operation, and appealed to the people to wait peacefully for an agrarian reform by legislation. This proclamation was regarded, with some legal justification, by the government as an illegal and revolutionary act, and was made the excuse for the dissolution of the Duma. On Sunday 9 July 1906 troops occupied the empty Taurid Palace, and the decree of dissolution was published. Whether the Duma's proclamation had made up the Tsar's mind, or whether he had always intended to dissolve it, and was only playing insincerely with Shipov, remains an open question.[1]

Government was now carried on under Article 87 of the Fundamental Laws. This article authorized the emperor to issue decrees during the recess of the Duma 'if exceptional circumstances call for a measure which requires legislative action'. Such decrees, however, had to be approved by the Duma within two months of its next meeting. The first crisis which confronted the government, of which Stolypin was appointed prime minister in place of Goremykin, did not prove serious. This was the decision of nearly half the members of the dissolved First Duma to cross into Finland, and there issue a statement appealing to the people to offer passive resistance to the authorities, by refusing taxes and recruits to the army. This 'Vyborg

[1] For Shipov's account of the conversations see *Vospominaniya i dumy o perezhitom*, pp. 449–57. Milyukov in *Tri popytki*, Paris 1921, describes his own discussions on pp. 33–41. He expresses the view (p. 54) that the Tsar was insincere throughout his audience to Shipov. He discounts the factor of uncertainty as to the choice of himself or Muromtsev as head of a Kadet Ministry. He argues that those around the Tsar were utterly opposed to any sort of constitutional régime, let alone full parliamentary government. In the eyes of these people 'not only Kutler [a former high government official and expert on agrarian problems, who had joined the Kadets and had been elected to the First Duma] but even Witte were revolutionaries' (p. 60). V. A. Maklakov, at this time a leading Kadet, in his volume of memoirs, *Pervaya gosudarstvennaya duma*, published in exile in Paris in 1938, argues that there were two different plans. One was Trepov's, of a Kadet ministry, the essential purpose of which would have been to trap the Kadets into assuming responsibility in a period of crisis, to use them for a time, and then to restore the power of the old régime. The other was a plan for a genuine division of power between bureaucrats and liberals, a coalition of moderate forces to get the country out of its troubles. Milyukov, so Maklakov argues, was prepared to try the first plan, but the Tsar would not have it. The second plan, which the Tsar would have accepted, Milyukov rejected. Maklakov argues that the second plan should have been adopted, and that the Kadets lost a chance of statesmanship because they could not bring themselves to give up revolutionary demagogy and accept the facts of political life. These arguments are brilliantly presented, but hardly carry conviction. Maklakov is thinking too much in terms of the events of 1917, too little in terms of the situation of 1906 about which he is writing. If Trepov's scheme for an all-Kadet ministry was a trap, still more must the proposal for a coalition ministry have appeared a trap to anyone whose ideas were based on the principles of parliamentary responsible government, as practised in Europe at that time. To enter a government in which they would have no power, and merely give their prestige as a weapon for their enemies to use, can have made no sense to the Kadets. Maklakov, op. cit., pp. 5–15, 187–208.

Manifesto' was signed by about 120 Kadets and most of the Labour Group. The population did not follow its advice. Its main effect was that its signatories were placed on trial in December 1907, sentenced to three months in prison, and disfranchised. The result was that the Kadets were deprived of some of their best parliamentary speakers.

More serious were continuing mutinies, acts of terror, and peasant revolts. There was a serious mutiny in the naval base of Sveaborg in the Gulf of Finland, and further disorders at Kronstadt. At the end of July the Kadet expert on the agrarian question, M. I. Herzenstein, was murdered by right-wing terrorists in Finland. A Finnish court condemned the assassins, but their sentences were commuted by the Tsar. On 12 August SR-Maximalists blew up Stolypin's house. The prime minister was not injured, but 27 persons were killed and his daughter was gravely wounded. On 19 August Stolypin used the powers granted under Article 87 to set up field courts martial, designed specially to deal with peasants engaged in armed rebellion. These courts passed sentence, which might be of death, within twenty-four hours. According to official sources 683 death sentences were carried out by these courts up to April 1907.

Stolypin made another attempt to come to terms with the Octobrists. On 15 July 1906 he saw Shipov and G. E. Lvov to see whether they would consider entering his ministry. Their conditions were that seven out of thirteen ministerial posts should be given to representatives of the public, and that these should be the ministries of the interior, justice, education, agriculture, trade, the procuracy of the Holy Synod, and the state controller. They also demanded that the government should publicly declare its intention of passing a series of reforms, including 'the organization and extension of peasant property'. If local agricultural authorities thought that it was necessary for this purpose compulsorily to acquire landowners' estates, then in such cases the government should agree. They also asked that no more death sentences be carried out, that there be an amnesty for all except persons guilty of assault on life or property, and that the new Duma should assemble not later than 1 December 1906. On 17 July Stolypin replied that these demands could not be accepted, and the discussions came to an end.[1]

[1] The conversations are described in Shipov, op. cit., pp. 463–80.

Stolypin had, however, some constructive plans of his own. A law of 5 October extended the personal freedom of peasants. The choice of peasant representatives to zemstvo assemblies, from the lists of candidates chosen by the peasant voters, was now to be made no longer by the provincial governor but by the persons on the list, who were to meet and choose enough from their number to fill the vacancies. Land commandants were deprived of the power to imprison or fine peasants without a court decision. These were small gains, even if their general intention was plainly benevolent. Much more important was the law of 9 November on individual and communal tenure, which marked the introduction of a radical change in agricultural policy, and will be discussed later. Both these laws were passed under Article 87. Stolypin, however, had made up his mind to hold elections for a new Duma, and these took place in February 1907.

Meanwhile in July 1906 the emperor had signed the new provisions for the Finnish Diet, drafted by the Constituent Senate. There was to be a single chamber of 200 members, elected for periods of three years from sixteen constituencies, by proportional representation and with almost universal suffrage of both sexes. Finland was thus the first country in the world to give the vote to women. Elections took place in 1907. The Social Democrats won 80 seats, the conservative and Russophil Old Finns 59, the radical Young Finns 25, the Swedish People's Party 24, and the newly created Agrarian Party 10.

The government hoped that the Second Duma would be more conservative in composition than the First, but it was disappointed. It is true that the extreme right was stronger, with 63 members, and that the Octobrists increased their strength to 32. But on the left the Labour Group was 101 strong, there were 34 Socialist Revolutionaries (despite the party's official decision to boycott), and 65 Social Democrats. The chief sufferers were the Kadets, whose number fell to 92. This was due partly to the fact that the RSDRP had decided officially to take part in the election, partly to the loss of so many of the Kadets' best candidates because they had signed the Vyborg Manifesto.

The Social Democrats held their Fifth Congress in London in May 1907. This time the Bolsheviks were in the majority. The congress decided to forbid all partisan actions, and to disband the 'fighting groups' of the party. It was clear to the congress that the revolutionary tide in Russia was ebbing. The general difference between Lenin and the Mensheviks on the direction in which the party should look for allies, remained as before. Lenin on the class level preferred the peasants to the urban *bourgeoisie*, and on the political level was less hostile to the SR's than to the Kadets. The Menshevik position was the opposite on both points.

The inability of government and parliament to co-operate was as obvious as in the case of the First Duma. Stolypin was in no hurry to dissolve. He would have been willing to tolerate the Duma's flights of rhetoric if it had been willing to accept his agrarian legislation, which was very dear to his heart and which he sincerely believed essential to the welfare of the peasants. But this the Duma would not do. The Tsar was infuriated by attacks on the Russian army, and was encouraged by messages from the extreme right urging him to dissolve. 'I have been constantly receiving messages from True Russian Men all over Russia', he wrote to his mother, 'expressing their indignation at such disrespectful behaviour in the Duma.'[1] The excuse used by Stolypin was the alleged discovery by the police of a plot against the emperor's life by Social Democrats. The prime minister asked for the cancellation of the parliamentary immunity of 55 of the Social Democratic members of the Duma. The Duma set up a commission of its own to examine the evidence against these members. But instead of waiting for the results of the commission's inquiry, the government on 3 June closed the Taurid Palace and declared the Duma dissolved. The accused Social Democrats were arrested.

As there was no chance of another Duma elected on the existing franchise being more amenable, Stolypin introduced a new electoral law, enormously restricting the franchise.[2] This too was done under Article 87. This action was a clear violation even of the 1906 Fundamental Laws, and Stolypin's whole action can only be regarded as a *coup d'état*.

[1] *Letters of the Tsar to the Empress Marie*, p. 223.

[2] A contemporary German observer estimated that under the new franchise it took 230 landowners to elect an official elector for the Duma, 1,000 rich business men, 15,000 lower-middle-class voters, 60,000 peasants, or 125,000 urban workers. Otto Hoetzsch, *Rußland* (Berlin, 1913), pp. 162–3.

XVIII

THE AGE OF STOLYPIN

Semi-Constitutional Politics

THE restrictive franchise, under which the Third Duma was elected, greatly increased the representation of both the extreme right and the right centre, at the expense of the parties of the left. The largest group in the new Duma were the Octobrists, with 120 seats. To their right was a separate right Octobrist fraction with 11 members. The right wing in the strict sense consisted of the Russian Nationalists with 76 members, the independent Nationalists with 16, and the Right with 53. The moderate left comprised the Party of the People's Liberty (as the Kadets were now called) with 52 seats, and the Progressives with 39. On the far left the Trudoviks and the Social Democrats each had 14 members. The non-Russian national groups were reduced to three—the Polish Circle with 11 seats, the 'Polish-Lithuanian-White Russian Group' with 6, and the Moslem Group with 9. There were some non-Russians in the major party fractions, especially Georgians among the Social Democrats and Baltic Germans among the Octobrists.[1]

The Third Duma was thus an unrepresentative assembly, brought into being by a *coup d'état* and a falsification of the franchise. Nevertheless, it would be wrong to consider the régime which existed under the Third and Fourth Dumas as a simple restoration of the old autocracy. Much had changed since 1904. Political parties not only had elected representatives in the assembly, but had legally recognized organizations throughout the country, and the right to hold public meetings. Political issues could be openly discussed in the press, and the main political groups had their own newspapers. Censorship was much milder. Incitement to violence or insurrection brought reprisals, as was the case in democratic countries in Europe and

[1] These figures apply to the situation in the fourth session, in 1910–11, by which time some slight rearrangements had taken place. *Gosudarstvennaya duma, stenograficheskie otchoty 1906–16, 3 sozyv, 4 sessiya*, pp. 3–18.

America, but mere expression of opinion was not punished. In practice things were not quite as good as this. The borderline between opinion and sedition is not always clear. Freedom of expression was more effective in the capitals than in provincial towns, especially in non-Russian areas. The traditional contempt of police and administration for the law—or, perhaps it would be fairer to say, their inability to understand what the concept of law meant—could not and did not suddenly disappear. From time to time newspapers were fined, or their 'responsible editors'[1] were arrested for a few days. But though these actions of the administration were unpleasant, and would have been considered insufferable in a Western country, it cannot be denied that, in comparison with the systematic suppression of opinion in the age of Pobedonostsev and Pleve, enormous progress had been made.

The Third Duma itself was by no means a servile or reactionary assembly. This already became clear in the debate on the address to the Tsar. The right wished the statement to include the expression 'autocrat of all Russia' (*samoderzhets vserossiiskii*), but were defeated by 212 votes to 146, to the annoyance of the emperor. The right sent a separate statement of their own signed by 114 persons. The right extremists objected in principle to any sort of parliamentary institutions, and essentially used the platform of the Duma to denouce the institution itself. The Nationalists sometimes supported the Right, but more often voted with the Octobrists to form a majority of the centre.

The relations between the Octobrists and the government were at first fairly good. Guchkov and Stolypin respected each other. At a meeting of zemstvo representatives in 1907 Guchkov praised the premier in the following words: 'In the dark times when many were faint-hearted there appeared a man who, in spite of all difficulties, the disaster to his family, and all the slanders against him, understood the situation and took the right road. If we are now witnessing the last convulsions of the revolution—and it is undoubtedly coming to an end—then it is to this man that we owe it.'[2]

[1] It was the practice in some newspapers to appoint as 'responsible editor' an employee whose paid job was in fact to sit in prison when the paper was in trouble with the authorities, while the real editors and writers went on with their jobs.

[2] S. S. Oldenburg, *Tsarstvovanie Imperatora Nikolaya II* (Belgrade, 1939), ii. 12.

After more than half a century, Stolypin remains a controversial figure. He was hated by the moderate left as the man who had dissolved the two Dumas and changed the electoral law. To the revolutionaries, he was the butcher who had set up field courts martial to shoot peasants and workers. The extreme right hated and intrigued against him, because he consented to play the part of a prime minister, thereby diminishing the status of the rightful autocrat, the Tsar. Historical literature has usually represented him either as a bloodthirsty oppressor of the people or as a Russian Bismarck who would have made Russia great by peaceful reforms if the assassin's bullet had not laid him low. It has even been suggested that he was really a liberal.[1] It is better not to try to label this gifted and complex man. He used force brutally, but the situation was brutal. He was certainly not a reactionary. His economic policies were designed to modernize Russia, even at the cost of radical changes. Of his devotion to the peasants there can be no doubt. His famous phrase, that policy must 'take account of the sound and the strong, not the drunken and the weak',[2] has been interpreted as showing concern only for rich peasants and *kulaks* and indifference to the poor peasants. This is not fair to Stolypin. The moralizing tone of the speech in which the phrase occurred reflected his view that the peasant problem was as much moral as economic. He was profoundly concerned with the human, moral, and social future of the peasants, on which he believed that the future of Russia depended. Already as governor of Grodno province, at the time of Witte's commission, he had spoken out strongly in favour of schools for the peasants. 'It is impossible to be afraid of literacy and education, to be afraid of the light .... Universal women's education is essential for the whole of our country. The diffusion of agricultural knowledge, without which an agricultural country cannot exist and is condemned to gradual decay, depends on general education. Develop general education according to a broad programme, in connexion with agricultural instruction, and you will give greater security to the farming class, the most conservative in every country.'[3] Stolypin was a conservative and a narrow

[1] The admirable work of V. Leontowitsch, *Geschichte des Liberalismus in Rußland* (Frankfurt, 1957), seems to me to go too far in this direction.

[2] Speech in the Duma of 5 Dec. 1908.

[3] *Trudy mestnykh komitetov, Grodnenskaya guberniya*, p. 32.

Russian nationalist, but he believed in social reforms and progress. One of his most discerning critics described him as an enlightened absolutist, resolved at all costs to achieve his long-cherished dream of instituting private peasant ownership in Russia.[1] To achieve his aim, he would fight right and left, upper classes and masses. In his statement to the Second Duma he had mentioned the possibility that the state might buy land from private estates, through the Peasants' Bank, to form a land fund for endowing poor peasants. In the Third Duma there was no talk of such daring action. Nevertheless, the Peasants' Bank's purchases were on such a scale as to alarm landowners. At a congress of the nobility in 1909 V. I. Gurko accused the government of 'energetic realization of the programme of the Socialist-Revolutionaries . . . of expelling the landowner element altogether from our villages'. But though Stolypin had enemies in high places as well as low, on the right as well as on the left, he remained both a reformer and an absolutist. He was in favour of co-operating with elected representatives of the people, provided that they did what he wanted. But when his policies met with opposition, he had no respect either for the electorate or for the law. He was a brave and honest man, intelligent and cultured, with a strong personal sense of justice, a devoted servant of his emperor and his country. But his concept of government was paternalist and authoritarian.

The Octobrists were prepared to co-operate with the government to the extent of examining critically but constructively the government's measures, and putting forward proposals for improvements in the major fields of practical policy. This included, as they saw it, problems of national defence. Guchkov himself was especially interested in military matters. The Tsar, however, objected to what he regarded as meddling by irresponsible persons in matters which under the Fundamental Laws were reserved to him. In the summer of 1908 the Duma approved the estimates of the Ministry of the Navy. The Council of State then saw fit to object to the Duma's action, on the ground that the Duma only had the right to grant or refuse the naval or military credits, but was not entitled to express an opinion of the estimates. At the beginning of 1909 the bill came

[1] A. S. Izgoyev, article on Stolypin in *Russkaya mysl'* of Dec. 1907, published in *Russkoe obshchestvo i revolyutsiya*, Moscow, 1910.

back before the Duma, which reiterated its original statement. The government decided, in order that no more time should be wasted, that the Duma's text be accepted, and prevailed on a majority of the Council of State to agree to this. But the Tsar was so angered by what he regarded as the Duma's presumption that he refused to confirm it. He was especially annoyed because Guchkov had spoken critically of the army command in the debate, and the minister of war, General A. F. Rudiger, had not rebuked him. The minister had admitted that the military command needed improvement, but observed that in making appointments to high commands, 'one has to take account of the material and the candidates who are available'. For this lukewarm defence of the army, General Rudiger was dismissed by the emperor. His successor, General V. A. Sukhomlinov, was from the outset on bad terms with the Duma. Guchkov earned the lasting hostility of the Tsar. In March 1911 he was elected president of the Duma, in which office he had regular access to the Tsar. He appears to have hoped that he could convince Nicholas of his devotion, and persuade him both that the Duma was loyal to the throne, and that it was reasonable that the Duma in general, and he himself in particular, should take an interest in defence matters. If this was his hope, he was disappointed. His contacts with the Tsar as president of the Duma only increased the mutual dislike between the two men.

In May 1910 Stolypin put before the Duma a project for the introduction of zemstvo institutions in the western region—the provinces of the old Polish-Russian borderlands. The Duma was in sympathy with both his aims, to develop self-government and to strengthen the non-Polish majorities at the expense of the Polish landowning and educated classes. Stolypin himself declared in his speech to the Duma: 'The purpose of the measure is frankly and without hypocrisy to confirm that the western region is and will be a Russian region, for ever, for all time.' The Duma accepted it by 165 votes to 139. The Council of State, however, disliked the proposal. Class feeling was stronger than nationalism. The majority objected to a policy directed against landowners, even if those landowners were Poles. In March 1911 it rejected it. Stolypin refused to accept the defeat. He asked the Tsar arbitrarily to prorogue the two chambers for three days, and during this interval to pass his measure as an emergency decree under Article 87 of the Fundamental Laws. This article was of course designed to make quick legislative action possible at a time when the chambers were not in session. Its use in 1906 after the dissolution of the First Duma had caused bitterness on the left, but could be theoretically defended. Arbitrarily to interrupt the chambers in the course of a normal session, and then to push through a measure which one of them had rejected, was a monstrous perversion of the existing constitution and an insult to the legislature. Stolypin also demanded that the Tsar should instruct V. F. Trepov and P. N. Durnovo, who had been especially active in the Council of State opposition to his law, and had been motivated by personal hostility to him, to leave the capital and not appear again in the council until the end of the year. He also insisted that the Tsar should give him his written agreement to these actions. The Tsar reluctantly consented. When the decree was announced, the majority in the Duma, which had originally supported Stolypin, turned against him, bitterly indignant at his treatment of the legislature. Stolypin seemed incapable of understanding what he had done, or why those who had been his allies should now oppose him. To him, as to so many prominent Russian public servants, the notions of law and constitutional procedure were meaningless. If he was convinced that his plans were to the advantage of the Russian people, nothing was going to stop him. If the *pays réel* was on his side, as he firmly believed, the *pays légal* should be ignored. On 27 April he himself came to the Duma to explain his action. He argued that Article 87 'gives the Monarch, according to the law, the right to create a way out of a hopeless situation'. He maintained that his action did not violate but 'only strengthened the rights of the still young Russian system of representation'.[1] The Duma rejected his explanation by 202 votes to 82.

Stolypin deeply offended the emperor by placing him in this delicate situation. The previous relations of confidence between the two men were destroyed. Stolypin's enemies on the right, and intriguers such as Prince Meshchersky, plotted against him with renewed energy. At the same time co-operation between him and the moderate majority in the Duma was over.

[1] *Gosudarstvennaya duma, 3 sozyv, 4 sessiya,* columns 2861, 2863.

Guchkov, who of all the Octobrists had most admired him, resigned from the presidency. It is likely that in 1912 Stolypin would have been dismissed. Nicholas was, however, spared the necessity to do this. On 1 September 1911, at a theatrical performance in Kiev, Stolypin was shot and fatally wounded. His assassin, D. G. Bogrov, was both a Socialist-Revolutionary and a former police agent. He had obtained access to the theatre with a police permit. Whether he murdered the prime minister in his capacity as revolutionary or as police agent has never been clearly established.

The next prime minister was V. N. Kokovtsov. A conservative bureaucrat of comparatively enlightened outlook, with a long experience of financial administration, Kokovtsov was a competent but undistinguished head of government. The left of course disliked him, though less bitterly than they had hated the 'executioner' Stolypin. The moderates respected him, but there was no cordiality between them. On the right he was unpopular, among other reasons because he objected to subsidizing their activities from public funds.[1]

In 1912 the figure of Gregory Rasputin became known to the Russian public. This Siberian peasant sectarian was introduced to the Tsar in 1905. In his Diary there is an entry for 1 November 1905, which refers to the meeting.[2] Rasputin became indispensable to the Imperial family because of his ability to hypnotize the Tsarevich, who suffered from haemophilia, and to stop his bleeding.[3] As a result, the Empress Alexandra, permanently and understandably worried for her son's health, became devoted to 'Our Friend'. Rasputin was also a man of dissolute habits, who became involved from time to time in scandalous scenes in public places. The discreditable activities of a man known to be close to the Imperial household naturally gave an opportunity to political opponents of the Tsar. In 1911 Bishop Hermogen of Saratov, a member of the Holy Synod, was banished

[1] For Kokovtsov's version of these matters, and in particular the attempts of the right member of the Duma, N. E. Markov, to extract 960,000 roubles from public funds for his campaign for election to the Fourth Duma, see his memoirs, *Out of My Past* (Stanford, 1935), pp. 284–5, 338–9, 365.

[2] *Dnevnik Imperatora Nikolaya II* (Berlin, 1923), p. 229. The Tsar's words are: 'We have become acquainted with a man of God, Gregory, from Tobolsk province.'

[3] The Tsarevich Alexei, born in August 1904, was afflicted with this disease of the blood, which affects only males but is transmitted only by females.

to his diocese by the Tsar at the request of the procurator. He was on very bad terms with Rasputin, and on one occasion he and a monk named Iliodor had had a fist fight with Rasputin. The bishop claimed that the banishment was due to the influence of Rasputin at court. Guchkov took up the case, and published in his paper *Golos Moskvy* an article by an admirer of Hermogen which accused the synod of tolerance towards the heretic Rasputin. When this issue of the paper was suppressed by the censor, Guchkov introduced the text of the article into an interpellation in the Duma. On 9 March 1912, in the discussion of the funds for the Holy Synod in the budget debate, Guchkov asked how such a person as Rasputin could have become influential, and implied that he could affect appointments and dismissals of public figures. During 1912 hectographed copies of letters from the empress and grand duchesses to Rasputin were circulated in the capital. Guchkov was believed to be responsible for this. The letters could be interpreted by a reader as evidence of intimate relations between the empress and Rasputin, though this was not in fact the case. There are also no grounds for believing that at this time Rasputin had any influence at all on official appointments, though Guchkov may genuinely have feared that he had. It is not surprising that this affair should have strengthened the Tsar's hostility to the Duma politicians in general and to Guchkov in particular, and that the resentment of even the moderate parties against the monarch should have increased.

On 4 April 1912, in the British-owned Lena goldfields in Eastern Siberia, troops fired on a crowd of about 5,000 workers, and 200 persons were killed and as many more wounded. The immediate reaction of the minister of the interior, A. A. Makarov, was to defend the army. When a crowd hurls itself on the soldiers, there is nothing they can do except shoot. 'That is how it has been and that is how it will be in the future.' This unrepentant attitude infuriated the Duma and public opinion at large. The government decided to send a former minister of justice, S. S. Manukhin, at the head of a commission to examine the case. He reported that the workers in this remote place had been exasperated over a long period, not only by the horrible climate and harsh working conditions, but by the inability of the administration of the mines to understand their needs. Pious intentions of improvement were expressed. But the Lena Massacre left a profound impression on the Russian public, and proved to be the starting-point of a new period of working-class militancy in the main industrial regions of the empire. In the next two years the number of strikes grew, and those whose causes were political rather than economic were especially notable.

The Third Duma passed two reforms of some importance. One was the restoration of justices of the peace, as they had been from 1864 to 1889. The land commandants remained as administrative officials, but lost their judicial powers. However, the separation of the peasants from the rest of the people in the judicial system remained a fact right up to the end of the Imperial régime. The *volost* court with its special rules continued to exist. The household, rather than the individual, was still the legal unit. Peasants were liable to punishment for crimes which did not exist for other citizens, such as drunkenness which might have a harmful effect on the economy, punishable by thirty days' imprisonment. Corporal punishment up to thirty strokes could still be ordered for peasants guilty of various vaguely phrased offences involving the disturbance of order or insults to persons in authority. Corporal punishment for all *meshchane* had been ended in 1906.

The other important reform was the introduction, in June 1912, of health insurance for workers. A law of 10 June provided for the establishment of a 'hospital fund' in all enterprises employing more than 100 workers. Smaller enterprises were to share a fund between them. From this fund benefits were paid to sick workers. The funds were based on contributions from employers and deductions from wages. The latter were usually around 2 per cent., and were on no account to exceed 3 per cent. At the same time a new law on accident insurance was published, which expanded the provisions of the law of 1903. To settle disputes arising out of claims for benefits, insurance boards were set up in each province. They were to be composed of the procurator of the district court, two representatives each of workers, employers, and zemstvos, and one representative each of city councils and the Ministry of the Interior.

The composition of the Fourth Duma, elected in the autumn of 1912, differed little from that of the Third. The Right increased its membership to 64 seats. The Nationalists and moderate right numbered 88. The Octobrists had only 99 seats, but the very similar Centre Group had a further 33. The moderate left was slightly stronger than in 1907: there were 57 members of the Party of the People's Liberty and 47 Progressives. On the far left, the Trudoviks had 10 and the Social Democrats 14. The three national groups were somewhat smaller than in the Third Duma: the Polish Circle had 9 seats, the Polish-Lithuanian-White Russian Group 6 and the Moslems 6.

One field in which neither the Third nor the Fourth Duma achieved any notable progress was Church reform.

The revolutionary period had not left the Church untouched. Discontent, which had long been accumulating among the clergy, expressed itself in a movement for reform.[1] The demand came principally from the religious academies, with some cautious support from Metropolitan Antony of St. Petersburg. At the end of 1904 a special conference, headed by Witte (then chairman of the Committee of Ministers), examined the organization of the Church and the relations between Church and state. In a memorandum to the emperor, Witte supported the idea that a council (*sobor*) should be elected by clergy and laymen to discuss reforms. He also urged that steps be taken to broaden the education in Church schools, and to provide priests with a regular salary, so freeing them from their humiliating dependence on the fees which they charged for ministrations to their parishioners. Pobedonostsev opposed these ideas, but the growing pressure could not be ignored. Pobedonostsev resigned his office in October 1905, and was succeeded as supreme procurator by Prince A. D. Obolensky. In January 1906 the Holy Synod decided to convoke a Pre-Conciliar Commission, of ten bishops and twenty-one professors from academies or universities, to prepare for the election of a *sobor*. The conference proposed that the patriarchate, abolished by Peter the Great, should be restored. The patriarch should preside over the synod, and the powers of the supreme procurator be reduced. The patriarch and members of the synod should be elected by the *sobor*, which should meet at regular intervals to discuss general matters of importance to the Church. The *sobor* should be

[1] For a full discussion see J. S. Curtiss, *Church and State in Russia: the Last Years of the Empire 1900–1917* (New York, 1940), ch. 5.

composed of one layman and one priest from each diocese, to be chosen by the bishop from a list put forward by a diocesan conference. The Pre-Conciliar Commission also made various proposals for the improvement of diocesan and parish administration.[1]

The Tsar contented himself with the promise that he would call a *sobor* when times were favourable, but no action was taken. A Pre-Conciliar Consultation was appointed in 1912, but its labours led to no result. The Church remained tied to the state and dependent on a civil bureaucracy. A little was done to help the material situation of the priesthood: state appropriations for payments to parish clergy in 1913 were about 50 per cent. larger than in 1905.[2]

A law of 17 April 1905 promised religious toleration. Change of faith from Orthodoxy to another creed was permitted, and all civil disabilities of schismatics and sectarians were to be removed. But when the Duma tried to give precise legal form to these rights, difficulties arose. In 1909 a bill on changes of religious adherence, and a bill regulating the formation of Old Believer congregations, were passed by the Duma but rejected by the Council of State. Bills on parish reform were introduced in 1908 and 1910, each being a revision of an earlier project, but still further revisions were demanded, and no legislation was passed. In practice the parish clergy remained a depressed class, exercising a substantial but diminishing moral influence on the peasants. In practice also religious discrimination, and even religious persecution, continued in Russia, and continued to receive support from local authorities whatever the central government might wish.

Both the Third and Fourth Dumas took a keen interest in education. A law of 3 May 1908 provided for universal compulsory primary education, to be effective within ten years. It was to consist of four years of school from the ages of eight to eleven for male and female children. The law fixed the salaries and terms of work for teachers. The central government was to provide subsidies for furniture and equipment, but the cost of

[1] J. S. Curtiss, op. cit., pp. 225–7.

[2] The sums were, however, small—12,116,103 roubles in 1905 and 17,932,283 in 1913 (ibid., p. 347). In 1910 there were 2,923 senior priests and 46,633 priests, and 9,950 monks and 14,059 nuns in Russia. *Vsepoddaneyshii otchot ober-prokurora Svyateyshego sinoda po vedomstvu pravoslavnogo ispovedaniya za 1910 god* (SPB, 1913), p. 23.

maintenance of the schools was to be borne by local authorities. The Council of State rejected the law, since its majority objected to the fact that the Church schools were to be separated from the main school system, and also to the provision in the law that non-Russian children might be instructed in their own language in the lower grades of school. However, in many parts of the country the law was in fact carried out, through individual agreements between the Ministry of Education and zemstvos, and through subsidies to individual authorities.[1] Between 1908 and 1914 the number of primary schools increased by nearly 50,000, or by nearly 50 per cent. Teachers' training colleges approximately doubled in number. In 1914 there were rather less than half as many primary schools in the empire as were needed to make primary education universal.[2] The total number of children in primary schools on 1 January 1914 was officially stated as 7,217,433 of whom 2,317,614 were girls.[3] By 1914 most primary schools in Russia were controlled by zemstvos, but some came directly under the Ministry of Education, and the Orthodox Church still maintained a large number of parish schools in which reading, writing, and basic religious instruction were taught.

The number of pupils in secondary schools is difficult to estimate, owing to the variety of institutions falling into this category. But in 1914 there were 442,548 children in gimnazii or pro-gimnazii and 70,221 in real schools. Students undergoing higher education were 71,085 of whom almost 40,000 were at universities, and of the latter number 10,321 were girls. The institutions of higher education other than universities included medical, fine arts, and various professional training colleges. The largest single group after university students were technical students, who numbered 12,484.[4]

The attitude of the government to education had completely changed since the beginning of the century. It was now

[1] By 1914 agreements had been made with 386 out of 426 *uezd* zemstvos and with 257 municipalities. D. M. Odinetz and P. J. Novgorotsev, *Russian Schools and Universities in the World War* (New Haven, 1929), p. 12.

[2] Under the government plan there should have been 149,458 schools in 1914 with 7,478,000 pupils, in which case another 167,542 schools would have been needed to make education universal (ibid., p. 12). Actually the number of primary school pupils in 1914 was slightly less than this.

[3] *Ezhegodnik Rossii 1915* (Petrograd, 1916), part i, p. 119.

[4] All the figures in this paragraph are taken from *Ezhegodnik Rossii 1915*.

understood that if Russia was to be a modern Great Power, the whole nation must be educated. The funds allotted to the Ministry of Education in the budget of 1913 were four times those of 1900.[1] However, the men appointed to the ministry in these years were strong conservatives, out of sympathy with the educated class. They were little liked by the teaching profession, least of all by university students. A. N. Schwarz in the autumn of 1909 forbade the free attendance of women at university lectures, which had been tacitly permitted since 1906, and insisted on the enforcement of the *numerus clausus* for Jewish students, which had never been repealed but had in effect lapsed. He also dismissed some university teachers of socialist opinions. These measures led to a student strike in St. Petersburg in September 1909, which spread to other universities but did not last long. His successor, L. A. Kasso, a year later had more serious trouble. On 7 November 1910 Leo Tolstoy died. As he had been excommunicated by the Orthodox Church, no priest could officiate at his funeral, and the civil authorities refused to be represented. Some thousands of persons attended the burial at his home of Yasnaya Polyana, many of them students. Student organizations in the universities decided to take some action both to commemorate Tolstoy and to protest against the authorities. Demonstrations were held in the two capitals against the death penalty (which Tolstoy had denounced in his lifetime). Kasso decided to take reprisals when the universities reassembled after the Christmas vacation. On 11 January 1911 he forbade any meetings within the universities. This was a violation both of the autonomy of the universities granted in 1905 and of the rights of student organizations. The students replied by declaring a strike for the whole spring term in all institutions of higher education in the two capitals. In Moscow the rector and his two deputies resigned, and the minister then dismissed them from their professorial chairs. Other professors and lecturers were also dismissed. The student strike came to an end by March 1911, but left a bitter atmosphere. The hostility between the government and the educated class, which had been milder for the last few years, had been revived on the nineteenth-century scale.

Relations between the central and local government authori-

[1] See below p. 661.

ties were much better than before 1905. This was partly because zemstvo leaders, alarmed by the events of 1905, were more conservative, partly because the government was more willing to admit that local authorities had a part to play in the progress of the nation. In 1914 government subsidies, mainly for education, formed 20 per cent. of zemstvo revenue. Taxation of land and forests provided 42·4 per cent., urban real estate 6·4 per cent., factories and properties outside the cities 10·8 per cent., and miscellaneous other sources 20 per cent. The total budget of the zemstvos amounted to 336,373,000 roubles. If all trading activities of the zemstvos were included, the total might be as much as 400,000,000 or about one-ninth of the amount of the total Imperial budget.[1] The largest items in their expenditure were education (106,975,000 roubles or about 30 per cent. of all expenditure) and health (82,574,000 roubles or about 25 per cent.). The zemstvos provided three-quarters of the cost of education from their own revenue, and one quarter was covered by central government subsidy. They were in most cases the owners of the school buildings, and some of them also maintained libraries and bookshops. They paid the teachers, but the curriculum in the schools was entirely determined by the Ministry of Education. Public health was organized on the basis of 3,300 medical districts in the territory of 40 zemstvos. There were public health stations for emergency treatment and simpler medical care, and hospitals for serious cases. In the empire as a whole there was one public health station to every 15,000 inhabitants and one hospital to every 40,000. Some zemstvos also had their own pharmacies, where medicines were sold below the normal commercial prices.[2]

Municipal authorites were less enterprising in social welfare than the zemstvos. Their main source of revenue was from municipal enterprises.[3] Taxation was very low, and this un-

[1] T. J. Polner, *Russian Local Government during the War and the Union of Zemstvos* (New Haven, 1930), p. 38.

[2] The total number of doctors in the empire in 1912 was 22,772, of whom 2,088 were women. Compare these with figures given above on p. 536. There were also 28,500 *fel'dshers* (incompletely trained assistant medical personnel), 14,194 midwives, 4,113 dentists, and 13,357 pharmacists. *Ezhegodnik Rossii 1915*, part iii, pp. 1–6.

[3] In Moscow in 1911 54 per cent. of revenue came from municipal enterprises, in Kharkov in 1912 45 per cent., in Ekaterinoslav in 1912 41 per cent., in Odessa in 1912 nearly 37 per cent., P. P. Gronsky and N. J. Astrov, *The War and the Russian Government* (New Haven, 1929), pp. 143–4.

doubtedly reflected the fact that the city franchise was confined to the propertied classes. The budget of St. Petersburg increased from 24,500,000 roubles in 1903 to 46,500,000 in 1913, that of Moscow from 22,300,000 in 1905 to nearly 49,000,000 in 1913. Russian cities resorted widely to loans. In 1914 the average debt of a Russian city amounted to almost twice as much as its annual budget.[1] In 971 cities in 1912 education accounted for 12 per cent. of all expenditure, public health for 12·5 per cent. Moscow in 1901–2 maintained 176 municipal schools with 22,823 pupils, in 1910–11 with 51,099.[2]

A social issue which was much discussed in these years was drunkenness. The spirits monopoly continued to bring in excellent revenues to the government, but its critics argued that the government was debauching the people for its own profit. It was estimated that consumption of vodka increased from 75,000,000 buckets in 1905 to nearly 105,000,000 in 1913.[3] A Russian temperance movement was organized, and M. D. Chelyshev, a self-made millionaire and a teetotaller, brought before the Third Duma a proposal for Prohibition. In the Council of State Witte, particularly sensitive to denunciations of the spirits monopoly which he had introduced, suggested that part of the revenue from the monopoly should be spent on an official campaign against drunkenness. The Tsar himself had some sympathy with the idea, but Kokovtsov was sceptical, partly because as a financial expert he felt that the monopoly revenue was indispensable to the government, partly no doubt because he was sceptical as to the prospect of the Russian peasant renouncing vodka.

Disagreement with the Tsar about temperance propaganda may have contributed to Kokovtsov's downfall. Probably more important were the intrigues of the right and of some of his own colleagues. Chief among these was A. V. Krivoshein, the energetic and ambitious minister of agriculture, who had been hostile to Kokovtsov ever since the latter, as minister of finance, had in 1911 opposed the transfer of the Peasants' Bank to the Ministry of Agriculture. Nicholas kept Kokovtsov in his post until he had concluded an important loan agreement with

[1] Gronsky and Astrov, op. cit., p. 150.

[2] Ibid., p. 156.

[3] *Vestnik finansov* (1914), no. 34, p. 248, quoted in Margaret Miller, *The Economic Development of Russia 1905–1914* (1926), p. 285.

France in November 1913. The French loan, of 500,000,000 francs yearly for five years, was designed for the development of strategic railways in the western regions of the empire. Once the loan was secured, Kokovtsov, like Witte in similar circumstances in 1906, became expendable. He was dismissed in January 1914. Krivoshein had hoped to replace him, but was passed over because he was ill at the time. The Tsar brought back Goremykin. The choice proved disastrous.[1]

During these years the preoccupation of the intelligentsia with revolution and the domination of intellectual life by social utilitarianism were diminishing. The first sensational expression of this trend was a symposium entitled *Vyekhi* ('Landmarks'), published in 1909. The contributors were seven prominent intellectuals who had been active in the Union of Liberation, and had now been converted, or had returned, to religion. Outstanding were the former 'legal Marxists' Struve, Berdyayev, Bulgakov, and Frank, and the literary historian Gershenzon. All agreed in attacking the mystique of revolution and the values of revolutionary utilitarianism in learning and the arts. The most extreme formulation of their criticism was the statement of Berdyayev that 'the love of egalitarian justice, of the public good, and the welfare of the people, has paralysed the love of truth, has almost destroyed any interest in truth'.[2] The article by Struve was concerned with the essentially anarchical attitude of the intelligentsia to the state. Government was regarded as something alien and evil, for which the intelligentsia could accept no responsibility, in which it could have no part. Only when it had been completely transformed and purged of its evil character could the intelligentsia accept any share in it. The result, Struve argued, was to leave no choice but despotism or mob rule.

These articles provoked a storm of indignation. Many persons of liberal outlook understandably felt that the intelligentsia was being blamed for a state of affairs for which the real responsibility should be placed on the autocracy. Others were offended by what seemed to them a pompously pious attitude: the appeal

[1] A curious anecdote is told in Suvorin's Diary for 8 April, 1899. He records that Prince Naryshkin, a friend of the Tsar, begged him, as a death-bed request, to dismiss Goremykin, the minister of the interior. 'This man', said the dying Prince, 'does not love you, and he will destroy your dynasty.' (Suvorin, *Dnevnik*, p. 197.)

[2] *Vyekhi: sbornik statey o russkoy intelligentsii* (Moscow, 1909), p. 8.

of some of the contributors to public 'repentance', and a certain flavour, throughout the volume, of sackcloth and ashes, smacked to them of sanctimonious bigotry. The revolutionary parties reacted extremely sharply. The SR's and Marxists accused the contributors to *Vyekhi* of serving reaction and the 'Black Hundreds', and Lenin sought to identify the whole Kadet party and the whole '*bourgeois* intelligentsia' with the point of view of *Vyekhi*.[1]

It is worth noting that most of those who attacked *Vyekhi* showed special rage at the fact that these men publicly proclaimed themselves to be Christians. That Russians of the intellectual stature of Struve should take religion seriously, should believe that there was any more to be said about the Orthodox Church than had been said in Belinsky's Letter to Gogol, seemed to the anti-religious intellectual Establishment a monstrous betrayal and a monstrous lapse of good taste. In their replies to *Vyekhi* there is something of the tone of a primly respectable cleric denouncing blasphemy.

However, the attitude to religion among educated Russians had begun to change since the turn of the century. The number of educated believers was probably increasing, and there were others who, while not joining any organized religion, nevertheless recognized that Christian and other beliefs should be treated seriously, that they were not just wicked lies devised by ruling classes to sanctify their oppression, but an essential part of human life and of human history. The writers D. N. Merezhkovsky and V. V. Rozanov were responsible for organizing meetings between clergy and lay intellectuals to discuss problems of theology. Several of these discussions, known as religious-philosophical assemblies, were held from 1901 to 1903 in St. Petersburg.[2]

The increased respect for religion may also be regarded as part of a general tendency, certainly not dominant in Russian

[1] Among the replies to *Vyekhi* should be noted a symposium of leading Kadets, including Milyukov himself—*Intelligentsiya v Rossii*, with preface by I. I. Petrunkevich, SPB, 1910. Lenin's view may be found in an article 'O Vyekhakh' published in *Novy den'* on 24 Dec. 1909. It is printed in Lenin, *Sochineniya*, 5th edition (1961), xix. 167–75. For a modern discussion of the controversy see article by L. B. Schapiro, 'The *Vyekhi* group and the mystique of Revolution', in *Slavonic and East European Review* (Dec. 1955), 56–76.

[2] N. Zernov, *The Russian Religious Renaissance of the 20th Century* (1963), p. 90.

intellectual life yet certainly gaining ground, to consider intellectual, spiritual, and aesthetic problems on their own merits rather than exclusively from the point of view of their utility to the radical or revolutionary cause. This trend was to be seen in both literature and the arts. In 1899 the review *Mir iskusstva* ('World of Art') was founded. Its leading figure was S. P. Diaghilev, and closely associated with it were the painter Alexander Benois and the writer Merezhkovsky. In literature the outstanding trend was Symbolism, some of whose practitioners were inclined towards far-ranging religious speculation. Russian Symbolism produced one of Russia's greatest poets, Alexander Blok, together with several lesser yet highly talented writers.[1]

The period was one not only of reaction against social utilitarianism but of great artistic originality and excitement. Russian writers and painters were deeply influenced by contemporary trends in western Europe, especially in France, but they also made their own contributions to these trends. In 1905 Diaghilev founded the Russian Ballet in Paris. This not only had tremendous international success, but also attracted another brilliant Russian, the young composer Igor Stravinsky, who produced the music for *Firebird*, *Petrushka*, and *Sacre du printemps* in the last years before the First World War. Two Russian painters, Marc Chagall and V. V. Kandinsky, also left Russia at this time to settle, the former in Paris and the latter in Germany. Though both may perhaps be said to belong rather to European than to specifically Russian painting, yet the flavour of the small towns of the Russo-Lithuanian borderlands and the Jewish Pale is unmistakable in many of Chagall's paintings. Certainly the contribution of Russia to literature and the arts in the first decade of the twentieth century was not inferior to that of any other great nation.

During these years the revolutionary movements continued to exist. The main leaders were once more in exile. Though the conditions of both workers and peasants in Russia were

[1] Apart from Merezhkovsky these included his wife, Zinaida Hippius (1869–1945), Andrey Bely (1880–1934), Valerii Bryusov (1873–1924), K. D. Balmont (1867–1943), and F. K. Sologub (1863–1927). Two recent works in English which discuss some of these writers are Georgette Donchin, *The Influence of French Symbolism on Russian Poetry*, The Hague, 1958, and Victor Erlich, *The Double Image: Concepts of the Poet in Slavic Literatures*, Baltimore, 1964.

improving, their discontents remained. Indeed, increased prosperity, by making the bare struggle for existence a little easier, enabled them to think more about politics, and thus on balance perhaps increased political opposition to the régime.

The Socialist Revolutionaries suffered a severe blow when it was discovered that the head of their terrorist Combat Detachment, Yevno Azeff, was a police agent. This was revealed to the party's security expert, Vladimir Burtsev, who had for some time been suspicious of Azeff, by a former head of the department of police, A. A. Lopukhin.[1] The party was at first unwilling to admit that this could be true. But a court of honour, appointed by the party in exile, was forced to accept the facts. Azeff managed to escape the vengeance of his former comrades, and died a natural death in Germany in 1918. He remains a mysterious figure. He was undoubtedly a professional police agent for many years, and furnished invaluable information to his masters. But at the same time he was also an active and efficient organizer of terrorism. He informed the police of many revolutionary activities, but he did not inform them of the plans to murder Pleve or Grand Duke Sergei, both of which were directed by him. To explain his action by mercenary motives is hardly convincing. No doubt he liked money and luxury, but among the pleasures which he most savoured were the joys of conspiracy, and the sense of secret power over life and death.

The Social Democrats continued to be torn by factions. The nominal unity restored by the Fourth Congress and maintained by the Fifth proved to be no more than a fiction. Lenin continued to keep his own organization, bound by personal and doctrinal loyalty to him alone. He disregarded the party's official repudiation of 'expropriations' and 'partisan actions'. A sensational bank robbery in Tiflis on 13 June 1907, planned by the Georgian Bolshevik Joseph Djugashvili (later known as Stalin) and carried out by an Armenian named Ter Petrossian (known as Kamo), provided some much-needed funds for the Bolshevik treasury, but unfortunately the notes were traced and could not be used. A guerrilla band in the Urals led by a certain

[1] For Lopukhin's earlier indiscretion see above p. 616. For his indiscretion to Burtsev—which indeed in any country would have been treated as a major offence in a former official—he was in Jan. 1909 condemned to five years' penal labour, which was, however, commuted by the Senate to exile in Siberia.

Lbov was under Bolshevik direction. Lenin's group also became involved in a number of dubious disputes and manœuvres in connexion with the legacies of persons who sympathized with the revolutionary cause.[1] These scandals gave opportunities to Lenin's opponents, and by 1908 the quarrels within the Social Democratic ranks were as fierce as in the first years of the century. A plenary meeting of the central committee in 1909 failed to restore unity. In January 1912 Lenin held a meeting of his followers in Prague which set up the Bolsheviks as a separate party. In August 1912 the followers of Martov and Trotsky held a conference in Vienna, attended also by groups of more moderate outlook. The 'August bloc' which resulted from this conference may be loosely described as a union of Menshevik groups.

In 1913 the Bolsheviks had their own newspaper *Pravda* in St. Petersburg, while the Mensheviks published a separate paper *Luch*. The formal split in the Social Democratic faction in the Fourth Duma came in the autumn of 1913. In the following year it was revealed that the leader of the Bolshevik Duma group, Roman Malinovsky, was a police spy. He had been a regular agent since 1910. He had informed his masters accurately of the divisions in the Social Democratic ranks, and they had done their best to exploit them by giving support to Bolshevik candidates in their rivalry with Mensheviks. Whether this on balance benefited the police or the Bolsheviks the more, is a matter of opinion. The Malinovsky case was less dramatic than the Azeff case, since it did not involve assassinations or terrorism. Malinovsky had continued, for all his police connexions, to play his part as a working-class spokesman. It seems that this annoyed the police, and it was they who revealed his double role to the president of the Duma, M. V. Rodzyanko. Malinovsky resigned his seat in the Duma and went abroad. He was welcomed by Lenin, who long refused to admit his guilt.

It is difficult to judge how much effect the factional disputes had on the working-class movement in Russia. Whether any individual Social Democratic group followed Bolsheviks or Mensheviks depended rather on personal connexions than on

[1] Detailed accusations against Lenin in these matters are found in Martov's pamphlet *Spasiteli ili uprazdniteli* (Paris, 1911). They are discussed at some length in Bertram D. Wolfe, *Three who made a Revolution*, New York, 1948.

deeply felt doctrinal differences. The Mensheviks were stronger in the Ukraine than the Bolsheviks, and they almost completely controlled the labour movement in Georgia. The Bolsheviks were the stronger of the two in most of northern Russia and in the Urals.

During these years a trend appeared in the working-class movement which favoured the abandonment of conspiratorial and highly centralized party organization, and wished to build up in Russia a legal and democratically led labour movement similar to that of European countries. This trend was bitterly attacked by Lenin, who described its leaders as 'Liquidators', on the ground that they were trying to liquidate the party. The Mensheviks were more tolerant towards this trend, and indeed some of the 'Liquidator' leaders took part in the August bloc of 1912. There was of course a good case to be made against the Liquidators. It could reasonably be argued that it was foolish to give up secrecy and conspiracy in a country where government was still so arbitrary, and the newly gained liberties so insecure, as Russia. But Lenin's objection to the Liquidators went deeper than a disagreement about the tactics of the struggle. He recognized in their views a revival of the idea that a workers' movement should be led by workers rather than by professional revolutionaries. This idea he had fought from the beginning of his career, and was to fight all his life. The revolutionary struggle, he remained convinced, could only be led by an *élite* of professional revolutionaries who understood the scientific doctrines of Marxism, who understood the workers' interests better than the workers themselves, who in fact embodied the immanent interests of the working class. In practice Lenin went even further than this, for he acted as if he alone embodied this wisdom. Not only did he break with the Mensheviks, but within his Bolshevik group he could not tolerate persons of independent judgement. Several times he had to purge the ranks of his party. The Bolshevik group was in fact Lenin's group, completely dominated by his brilliant mind and indomitable will.

Constant involvement in factional struggles did not prevent Lenin from conducting a voluminous correspondence with the movement inside Russia, or from thinking and writing on problems affecting the revolutionary cause.

One work of great importance, which must be briefly mentioned, is *The Agrarian Programme of Social-Democracy in the First Russian Revolution*, which he completed at the end of 1907. In this work he came out in favour of the slogan of the Socialist-Revolutionaries—the nationalization of the land. There was a clear tactical motive for this: the peasants' support was essential for the successful revolution, and the peasants could be won if they were offered what they most wanted. But Lenin also offered a theoretical justification. It was essential, he claimed, to liquidate the last remnants of the feudal order by expropriating the landowners. If their land were divided among the peasants, this would lead not, as the SR's believed, to a new social order, but to the development of capitalism in the countryside. This was precisely what Lenin wished to see happen. Inevitably the landowning peasantry would become differentiated into rich and poor, a rural *bourgeoisie* and a rural proletariat. The latter would be the allies of the working class in the later, socialist, stage of revolution. The process would of course take time—how long, he could not foresee. But it would be quicker if all the estates were divided up—if Russia followed what Lenin called 'the American way'—than if the Stolypin policy of preserving the estates while encouraging the more prosperous peasants—which Lenin called 'the Prussian way'—were maintained. The whole process could certainly be accelerated if a 'democratic dictatorship of workers and peasants' could be set up by revolutionary action. But this would be possible only if the workers—by which Lenin meant his own party—could be sure of peasant support.

Economic Development

The most important change introduced into Russian economic life by conscious government action in the last decade of the empire was the legislation designed to favour the establishment of individual peasant holdings in place of communal tenure. The basic act was the law of 9 November 1906. It was supplemented by laws of 14 June 1910 and 29 May 1911.

By the law of 9 November 1906, in a commune where there had been no general redistribution since 1882, any householder might apply to be recognized as the owner of all pieces of land in his possession in 1906 as his private property. Where there had been a more recent redistribution, a householder might claim the same right in regard to all land which he had held before the redistribution; and he could also claim ownership of such further land as he had received by the redistribution, provided that he paid the commune the original redemption price of that land. In either case, the initiative for the conversion of land from communal to private tenure was left to the peasant.

By the law of 14 June 1910 all communes in which there had been no general redistribution since 1861 were declared dissolved. Documents of private ownership would be given to every individual who applied for them. But once the law was in force, the legal position was that the land in all communities affected by this law was no longer communal property but was private property, whether the peasants applied or not.

Apart from this, it remained possible, as it had been before 1906, for a two-thirds majority of the village assembly to decide to replace communal by private ownership for the whole village.

The legislation of 1906–11 was intended not only to encourage conversion of communal into private ownership, but also to encourage consolidation of strips of land into compact holdings. The legislation provided both for consolidation by individual householders and for general consolidations of all strips in a village. General consolidations were to be permitted by a two-thirds majority of the village assembly in villages of either type of tenure. In the case of single consolidations, the procedure remained unchanged in villages of private tenure: the householder who wished to consolidate his holding must obtain the consent of every other householder whose land would be displaced in the process. In villages of communal tenure a new principle was introduced: any householder who had already obtained title to his land as private property might at any time demand from the commune that his strips be consolidated in one place. The commune was then obliged either to grant his request or to pay him compensation in money. The process of consolidation was assisted by expert bodies, known as land organization commissions, set up by a law of 4 March 1906. These existed at both *uezd* and province level. The *uezd* commissions numbered twelve or thirteen persons, of whom three were elected by the peasants and the rest nominated partly by the administration and partly by the zemstvos. The provincial commissions numbered fifteen or sixteen persons, of whom six were elected by the provincial zemstvo assembly on the understanding that three of them should be peasants, and the remainder were nominated by the administration. The laws of 1910 and 1911 extended the right to ask for a consolidated holding even to householders who had not already obtained title to their land, provided that the claim were supported by a commission.

The statistics available on the implementation of these laws up to 1915, and the interpretations of the statistics, are confusing and contradictory. But though a fairly substantial margin of error and uncertainty cannot be eliminated, a general picture does emerge.

According to the official statistical yearbook for 1915, up to 1 May of that year, in 40 provinces of European Russia, applications under the law of 9 November 1906 had amounted to 2,736,172 of which 1,992,387 had been confirmed in their ownership. This latter figure represented 22 per cent. of all householders under communal tenure in these provinces. The land thus converted to private tenure amounted to 13,933,134 *desyatin* which constituted 14 per cent. of the communal land of these provinces. The provinces in which the percentage was well above the average were in the south and south-east, and those in which it was well below were in the north and north-east.[1] Another figure, also based on official statistics possibly from a slightly later date, is of 2,755,633 applications and 2,008,432 confirmations.[2]

Those affected by the law of 1910 amounted in theory to about 3,500,000 households, of whom up to the end of 1915 about 470,000 had received official documents. It is thought by some authorities that in all communes where at least one household had applied, the whole population was officially regarded

[1] *Ezhegodnik Rossii 1915*, part vi, p. 1. Highest percentages were Crimea (64), Mogilev (57), Ekaterinoslav (54), Samara (49), Kiev (49), Kursk (44). Lowest were Perm (4), Vyatka, Astrakhan (5), Vologda (6·5).

[2] N. I. Karpov, *Agrarnaya politika Stolypina* (Leningrad, 1925), p. 81. Karpov based his book largely on the results of an inquiry by the Free Economic Society, which was not available to me: I. V. Chernyshev, *Obshchina posle 9 noyabrya 1906 goda*, Petrograd, 1917.

as being converted to private tenure, and that the number in this category amounted to about 1,700,000. This would leave a further 1,300,000 nominally affected by the law but not regarded even by the officials as having changed their status.[1]

Under the original procedure for dissolution of communes by two-thirds vote of village assembly, the number of households which changed from communal to private tenure up to 1915 was 130,000.[2]

We thus have a minimum figure of 2,600,000 households converted to private tenure, to which may be added with some hesitation the vague figure of 1,700,000. If to these are added the 2,800,000 households which already before 1906 held their land under hereditary private tenure, the total exceeds 7,000,000, which is about half the peasant households in Russia.

Figures of the number of holdings that were consolidated also show some variation. One is that the land organization commissions carried out changes affecting 2,400,000 households, and that up to the end of 1915 1,200,000 had received consolidated holdings. Another estimate puts the number consolidated at 1,303,300.[3] Two main types of consolidated holding appeared: the *otrub*, whose owner lived in the village with the other peasants but had all his land in one place, and the *khutor*, whose owner moved his habitation on to his land, away from the village.

The new legislation led to a good deal of buying and selling of land. It is certain that many of the sellers of allotment land were poor peasants and many of the buyers were prosperous peasants setting themselves up as big farmers. Not all those who sold their land became members of a rural or industrial proletariat: a considerable number sold because they had decided to go as colonists to the new lands of Siberia and the Steppes. Moreover, there were certainly small or medium peasants who bought land from other peasants and lived on small compact

[1] These figures are discussed by Robinson, op. cit., pp. 213–14.

[2] Karpov, op. cit., Table p. 202 (for 35 provinces only).

[3] Robinson, op. cit., p. 225, quoting from P. N. Pershin, *Uchastkovoe zemlepol'zovanie v Rossii* (Moscow, 1922), which was not available to me. The second estimate is in A. N. Antsiferov and others, *Russian Agriculture during the War* (New Haven, 1930), Appendix, and is based on a publication of statistics entitled *O zemle* (Moscow, 1921), which also was not available to me.

holdings and made a success of them. Available figures are not revealing on the problem of the polarization of the peasantry between a rural *bourgeoisie* and a rural proletariat, though in general it seems likely that a process of this sort was taking place to some extent.

Peasants also bought non-allotment land during these years. The best estimate available, based on painstaking study and adjustment of unsatisfactory and not fully comparable official statistics, shows that between 1905 and 1914 noble landowners parted with about 10,000,000 *desyatin* and that state and Imperial land was reduced by about 1,500,000 *desyatin*. Of this land, 9,500,000 *desyatin* were bought by peasants and 2,000,000 *desyatin* were acquired by the Peasants' Land Bank.[1] In 1914 peasants owned more than four times as much land as the nobility: in allotment and private holdings together they had more than 170,000,000 *desyatin*, while noble landowners had less than 40,000,000.

The purpose of Stolypin's agrarian policy was to improve agriculture and to help the most efficient peasants. In these respects it was rather successful. The main criticism of it is that it did not improve the lot of the poorest. There is truth in this, though it is only fair to point out that the settlement of Siberia offered opportunities to many whose prospects in their own villages were bleak. Certainly Stolypin's policy could not 'solve' the problems of rural overpopulation and poverty. But in the mid twentieth century, with the recent experience and present sufferings of so many countries of eastern Europe and Asia before one, it is permissible to doubt whether these problems *can* be 'solved' by any 'correct' policy. Governments have had, and still have, chances to introduce practical improvements, to benefit more or less substantial sections of the population, to make a difficult period of economic transition less painful. Judged from this angle, Stolypin achieved a good deal. The extravagant claims made by some on his behalf that he was a statesman of genius who had placed Russia on the way to a

[1] Robinson, op. cit., p. 270. Readers are referred to Robinson's explanatory notes on the inadequacies of the statistics and the adjustments made. The precise figures given by Robinson for 1905 and 1914 respectively are: (*a*) Nobles: 49,768,000 *desyatin* and 39,558,000; (*b*) State and Imperial: 145,233,000 and 143,736,000; (*c*) Peasants: 160,875,000 and 170,461,000; (*d*) Peasants' Land Bank: 276,000 and 2,281,000.

peaceful happy future from which she was diverted only by a war forced on her by others, may be discounted: but it is equally unjust to treat him as a heartless agent of the urban and rural capitalists and landowners, indifferent to the sufferings of the peasant masses.

The techniques of agriculture unquestionably improved, not only on the large estates but also on peasant holdings, especially of course the bigger compact farms. Sales of agricultural machinery by zemstvo warehouses doubled between 1904 and 1913. Yet many peasants still used primitive instruments. In 1910 there were 6,454,119 wooden ploughs of the traditional type (*sokha*) in use in 50 provinces of European Russia and 4,607,010 iron ploughs.[1] The iron plough was commonly used by peasants only in the southern provinces. In these years peasants learned to pay more attention to fertilization. Livestock manure was used more systematically. Artificial fertilizers also came in to use: though the quantities used were small compared with those of countries of advanced agriculture, the increase in consumption was striking—from about 8,500,000 poods in 1900 to 56,000,000 poods in 1913.[2]

Co-operatives also began to play a part in the Russian village. In 1914 co-operative credit and savings associations had 8,000,000 members throughout the empire, making loans to peasants for the purchase of livestock, tools, fertilizers, and land. Marketing co-operatives were not much developed in European Russia, but grew fast in Siberia. The Russian education system was at last beginning to turn out agricultural specialists (agronomists): there were 2,710 of these in 1909 and 10,000 in 1914. Lecture courses for peasants on agriculture were organized: in 1909 there were 1,964 centres for such lectures, in 52 provinces, attended by 233,981 persons.[3]

Russian agriculture was of course overwhelmingly devoted to grain, both for home consumption and for export. But it is worth mentioning briefly a few other crops and activities. In the year 1913–14 more than half the raw cotton needed by the Russian textile industry was produced within the empire. In

[1] A. Tyumenev, *Ot revolyutsii do revolyutsii* (Leningrad, 1925), p. 160.

[2] Ibid., p. 179, quoting *Torgovo-promyshlennaya gazeta* of 1914, no. 26.

[3] Ibid., pp. 174–5. Both sets of figures from *Torgovo-promyshlennaya gazeta*, the agronomists from No. 26 of 1914, the lecture courses from the issue of 6 Apr. 1911.

that year Central Asia, including the protected khanates, produced 12,617,913 poods and Transcaucasia 1,585,996, while 13,525,000 poods were imported.[1] Sugar-beet continued to be an important crop in Kiev and the south-western provinces. Tobacco was produced in three main areas. Tambov, Chernigov and Poltava provinces grew low-quality tobacco for mass consumption inside Russia; the Caucasus, especially the Kuban and Sukhum areas, specialized in high-quality Turkish-type tobacco; and Bessarabia and Crimea grew smaller quantities of high-quality American tobacco.

Fisheries employed a substantial labour force. In 1914 this amounted to 229,000 workers, of whom almost exactly half were in the Volga–Caspian area, about a fifth each on the Caucasian shore of the Caspian and on the northern coast of European Russia, and 25,000 in the Far East. In the Volga valley there were a few large fishery companies, which owned the rights in certain areas or rented from the state, which was the largest proprietor, but there were also individuals or peasant communities which owned rights. In the spring season, from March to mid May, there was a large influx of seasonal workers, of whom about half were nomad Kalmyks or Kazakhs from the Caspian steppes. The work was very hard, involving seven to nine hours a day with nets, up to the chest in water. Meagre wages were supplemented by a diet of bread and fish. The incidence of malaria was high at the turn of the century.[2]

Hunting was an important occupation in Siberia and in the north-eastern provinces of European Russia, and a useful source of subsidiary earnings in a wider area. The income from the skins and game brought to the market in 1915 was around 1,500,000 roubles, of which about half was accounted for by the three main items of Arctic fox, squirrel, and partridge.[3]

[1] *Ezhegodnik Rossii 1915*, part vii, p. 28.

[2] P. P. Semyonov-Tyanshansky and V. I. Lamansky, *Rossiya — polnoe geograficheskoe opisanie nashego otechestva* (SPB, 1899–1913), vi, pp. 233 ff. The largest item in the fisheries income for 1915 were herrings (13,000,000 poods sold for 26,000,000 roubles). Total output of caviar in 1915 was 34,369 poods valued at 3,581,616 roubles. Three-fifths of this came from the Caucasian coast of the Caspian and the mouth of the river Kura, and two-fifths from the Volga–Caspian area. (*Ezhegodnik Rossii 1915*, part vii, pp. 86–90.)

[3] *Ezhegodnik Rossii 1915*, part vii, pp. 76–85. The figures cover Siberia, Central Asia, and nine European provinces where hunting was important—Vologda, Yaroslavl, Novgorod, Kazan, Archangel, Vyatka, Olonets, Perm, Orenburg.

Progress was made with the conservation and exploitation of Russia's immense forests. Those of Siberia and of the northernmost parts of European Russia were still barely explored, much less exploited. But in the more accessible areas the numbers and training of forestry personnel were improving, wasteful cutting of trees was reduced, and Russia's role as a supplier of timber, though far short of its possibilities, was growing. In 1913 the forest area in European Russia recorded in the official survey was more than 110,000,000 *desyatin*. Of this the state owned almost 61,000,000, the Church and monasteries 1,000,000, peasants 13,000,000, and private owners 35,000,000.[1]

The peak years for colonization of Siberia were 1907, 1908, and 1909 when the numbers were respectively 567,979 and 758,812, and 707,463.[2] In the next four years the tide of migration was reduced by about half, and a growing proportion of the colonists went to Central Asia rather than Siberia proper.[3] Not all these people settled. About 10 per cent. came back in the period 1896–1909, and in the years 1910 to 1914 the proportion was higher. Many of these found a place in some other part of the country, and did not go back to their original villages. Of these 'returners' it is impossible to estimate how many had made a serious effort to settle, and had found they could not manage, and how many had just gone to see what it was like, did not like it, and tried something else.

Colonization was on balance a great success, and some credit should be given to the efforts of the government, as well as to the hard labour of the colonists and the natural resources of at least the better Siberian lands. The main crop produced in the new lands was wheat, and after meeting the needs of the farmers at a considerably higher level of consumption than in European Russia, half the crop was available for export to the rest of the empire or abroad. Livestock farming also did well. Especially successful was the production of butter and eggs for export.

[1] *Ezhegodnik Rossii 1915*, part vii, pp. 92 ff. The state share includes 2,000,000 held by the Department of Mines and almost 5,000,000 by the Appanages. The figure for peasants consists of almost 5,500,000 of peasant allotment and 7,500,000 of peasant communes, The figure for private owners presumably consists mainly of noble landowners and business men, but may include some individual peasants.

[2] D. W. Treadgold, *The Great Siberian Migration* (Princeton, 1957), p. 34.

[3] *Ezhegodnik Rossii 1916* (Petrograd, 1918), pp. 110–11 gives figures for Siberia and Central Asia respectively in each year as follows: 1911, 137,689 and 89,268; 1912, 91,935 and 67,621; 1913, 77,660 and 69,030; 1914, 62,022 and 60,445.

There was growing up in Siberia a different kind of Russian society. There were no noble landowners. The leading people were largely self-made men, farmers or merchants who were proud of their success, and judged others by their merits and not by their social status. It was an individualist, self-reliant society, the only part of the empire in which something like a *bourgeois* ethos prevailed. Stolypin and Krivoshein made a journey round Siberia in 1910. The prime minister was impressed by the material progress, but he did not like the spirit. He wrote to the Tsar of 'an enormous, rudely democratic country, which soon will throttle European Russia'.[1] Russian conservatives distrusted the Siberians. A proposal to introduce zemstvos into Siberia was passed by the Third Duma in May 1908 but rejected by the Council of State. The absence of a noble class seemed to the councillors too dangerous a state of affairs. Zemstvos were in fact not established under Tsardom. But Siberian society went ahead on its own lines. As a British observer noted in 1910, 'just as the English settler in Canada has become a Canadian, so the Russian settler in Siberia has become a Siberian'.[2]

Russian industry was recovering from the depression of 1899–1902 when it was strained by the war with Japan and then more seriously damaged by the disorder of 1905–6. But by 1908 it had again recovered, and in the last years before the First World War its output was higher than ever before. The direction of development was essentially the same as in the 1890's.

Coal output in 1912 was 1,887,000,000 poods, of which about three-quarters came from the southern Donets coalfields. The second largest coal-producing area was the Dąbrowa Basin in Poland. Small but growing quantities were mined in Siberia and Turkestan. About 16 per cent. of Russian coal consumption was covered by imports. Pig-iron output in 1913 was 189,700,000 poods in the south, 55,800,000 in the Urals, 11,000,000 in the Moscow region and 25,600,000 in Poland. Output of iron and steel for the same four regions in 1913

[1] *Krasny Arkhiv* no. 30 (1928), correspondence of Stolypin with Nicholas II, pp. 82–83. I have used the English version of D. W. Treadgold, op. cit., p. 159.

[2] M. Phillips Price, *Siberia* (1912), p. vii.

was 141,000,000 poods, 40,800,000 poods, 11,000,000 poods, and 27,000,000 poods. Output of petroleum in 1913 was 561,300,000 poods. Of this, the Baku oilfields provided four-fifths, and most of the rest came from the new wells at Grozny on the north side of the main Caucasus range.[1]

Manufacturing industry was distributed in the same way as at the beginning of the century. In 1912 the central industrial region provided 35·9 per cent. of the output of manufactures by value, and employed 42·6 per cent. of the labour force; the north-west 11·8 per cent. and 9·9 per cent.; the Ukraine 18·3 per cent. and 16·8 per cent.; and the Urals 3·9 per cent. and 5·5 per cent. Moscow and Vladimir provinces remained the great textile centre. The south, apart from mining and metallurgy, was the centre of the sugar-refining industry, and produced half the Russian output of agricultural machinery. The engineering industry was based on St. Petersburg and to a lesser extent Riga. It provided 28 per cent. of the total value of industrial production in the capital. St. Petersburg also had a substantial textile industry and some chemical, paper, and printing works. Riga had a large rubber factory and a large railway wagon works: other large industrial establishments in the Baltic provinces included shipbuilding in Reval and textiles in Narva.[2]

The branches of factory industry with the largest labour force in 1910 were metal-working with 530,165 workers; cotton with 470,220; mineral-working with 150,678; wool with 134,480; linen, hemp, and jute with 95,139; timber with 92,130; and paper with 86,173.[3]

During these years there was a striking growth of industrial combinations. The most important was *Prodameta*, set up by the southern metallurgical industry. The initiative came from France. The French emissary, Baron Hély d'Oissel, obtained the consent of the government, and the proposal was accepted by the congress of the southern mining industry in Kharkov in November

[1] Khromov, *Ekonomicheskoe razvitie Rossii v XIX i XX vekakh*, pp. 456, 457, 459. Nearly 40 per cent. of Russian pig-iron was produced in three great Southern plants—13·5 per cent. in Dnieper, 13·3 per cent. in Alexandrovsky, and 11·3 per cent. in Petrovsky. Percentages refer to 1913 output. R. S. Livshits, *Razmeshchenie promyshlennosti v dorevolyutsionnoy Rossii* (Moscow, 1955), p. 246.

[2] Ibid., pp. 200, 204–7.

[3] *Ezhegodnik Rossii 1915*, part ix, p. 3.

1901. The organization came into being in 1902. In 1910 members of the group produced 74 per cent. of the pig-iron, 78 per cent. of the sheet iron, and 46 per cent. of the rails of the Russian empire. The group was successful in its pressure to keep both protective tariffs and internal prices high. When zemstvos started to buy iron goods at lower prices from non-member firms, *Prodameta* boycotted the zemstvos. Its policies also conflicted with the interests of other business groups, for instance the Congress of Manufacturers of Agricultural Machines and Instruments, which unsuccessfuly asked *Prodameta* to lower iron and steel prices.[1] Another big combination was *Produgol*, founded in 1904 also at French initiative and including the main coal-mines of the Donets Basin. In 1907–8 Siberian and Transbaikal mines joined it. There were combinations also in the production of iron ore, copper, and railway wagons.

The oldest combination was in the sugar industry. Already in 1887 a syndicate had been set up which included almost all the refineries in Russia, and established precise production quotas for each member. In 1895 the government took over the allocation of quotas, and all refineries were obliged to join. The revenue from the sugar tax was partly used to subsidize exports at low prices. In 1900 the retail price of refined sugar to a Russian consumer was 6·15 roubles per pood, but a pood of Russian sugar was sold in London for the equivalent of 2·38 roubles.[2] Consumption of sugar per head per year in Russia was 4·7 kilograms and in Britain 30 kilograms.

Estimates of foreign investments in Russian industry vary, and the information is not all of the same date. But the chief Russian expert on the subject estimated the total in 1916 as nearly 2,243,000,000 roubles.[3] Of this nearly 55 per cent. was

[1] On the founding of *Prodameta* see Olga Crisp, 'Some Problems of French Investment in Russian Joint-Stock Companies', *Slavonic and East European Review*, xxxv. 222–40. For the activities of *Prodameta* see P. N. Lyashchenko, *Istoriya narodnogo khozyaistva SSSR*, ii. 294–324.

[2] Ibid., 134.

[3] Of the French investments 43 per cent. were in mining and metallurgy, 21·6 per cent. in metal-processing and machinery, and 15·5 per cent. in credit institutions. Of the British investments 33·8 per cent. were in petroleum, 27 per cent. in other branches of mining, and 13·7 per cent. in textiles. Of the German investments 19·8 per cent. were in metal-processing and machinery, 19·2 per cent. in credit institutions, 16·7 per cent. in mining, 16 per cent. in municipal property, and 10 per cent. in textiles. Of the Belgian investments 36·4 per cent. were in mining and metallurgy, 34·9 per cent. in municipal property, and 14·7 per cent.

in mining, metallurgy, and metal-working, about 11 per cent. each was in municipal property and credit institutions, and nearly 10 per cent. was in textiles. Of the total sum the French held 32·6 per cent., British 22·6 per cent., German 19·7 per cent., Belgians 14·3 per cent., and Americans 5·2 per cent. Belgian firms owned the tramways of a large number of Russian cities, and municipal electric power stations were largely German-owned.

Railway construction was slower than in the 1890's. Just under 10,000 versts were built between 1902 and 1911. Two-thirds of the Russian railway network was owned by the state, but the private lines were about 25 per cent. cheaper to manage. Revenue from the state railways steadily increased: in 1908 it was 512,000,000 roubles and 813,000,000 in 1913. At the same time expenditure remained almost constant. Thus the government was able to use its net receipts to pay the large sums due in interest on railway loans, and from 1911 onwards it even had a surplus after paying interest. Criticism in the Duma of extravagance and incompetence in both construction and management kept pressure on the government, and certainly contributed to the improvements which were achieved in the last years of peace.[1] The road system of Russia remained very backward. In 1913 there were 10,672 versts of metalled road under the authority of the central government and 4,675 versts of metalled road managed by zemstvos.

The volume of Russian foreign trade increased, but there was not much change in either its structure or its direction. In 1908 the value of exports was 998,250,000 roubles and of imports 912,630,000. In 1913 these had risen to 1,520,133,000 and 1,374,031,000 roubles. In exports agricultural products predominated, but the share of grain was lower than in the preceding decades (38 per cent. in 1908 and 39 per cent. in 1913), while eggs and butter, which had been negligible items in the 1890's, together formed just over 10 per cent. in both 1908 and 1913. Petrol was less important than at the turn of the century (a little over 3 per cent. in both 1908 and 1913). Timber had grown in

in metal-processing and machinery. Figures are taken from P. V. Ol, *Inostrannye kapitaly v Rossii* (Petrograd, 1922), pp. 8–9, 14, 55, 71, 100.

[1] A discussion of railway policy, and of the views of the committee on railways of the Third Duma in 1912, may be found in Margaret Miller, *The Economic Development of Russia 1905–1914*, pp. 192–201.

importance (around 11 per cent. in both years), and flax and hemp together had continued to decline. In imports the main changes were a continued decline in the share of raw cotton and of tea and an increased share for machinery.[1] At the turn of the century Germany was the best customer for Russian exports, of which she took about 30 per cent., followed by Britain with 17·5 per cent., and Holland with nearly 12 per cent. As a source of Russian imports, Germany was far ahead of all other countries, supplying 47 per cent., followed by Britain with less than 13 per cent. China and the United States accounted for about 6 per cent. each.[2]

The regular budgets of the Russian government showed much the same general picture as at the turn of the century but there were some changes worth noting. Among the direct taxes, the business tax in 1913 amounted to 150,000,000 roubles, more than twice as much as in 1900. Among the indirect taxes the sugar tax reached 149,000,000 and customs brought nearly 353,000,000—increases since 1900 of nearly 150 per cent. and more than 75 per cent. respectively. The spirits monopoly in 1913 brought in 899,000,000 roubles, more than three times as much as in 1900. The main items of expenditure were the same. In 1913 the Ministries of War and Navy together took nearly 826,000,000 roubles, the Ministry of Communications nearly 641,000,000, the Ministry of Finance 482,000,000, and the state debt 424,000,000. The Ministry of Education now received 143,000,000. This was a comparatively small sum, but four times as much as in 1900. Not all expenditure was covered by the budget. 'Extraordinary expenditures' during this period were mainly connected with the Russo-Japanese War, which took 2,600,000,000 roubles between 1904 and 1913. The great bulk of this was spent in the three years 1904, 1905, and 1906, but small sums were being paid up to 1914. The second largest item of 'extraordinary expenditure' from 1904 to 1913 was for railways, and amounted to 763,000,000 roubles. The main item in extraordinary revenue was of course state loans, which between 1904 and 1909 provided 2,700,000,000 roubles.[3]

[1] Raw cotton provided 13 per cent. of imports in 1908 and 8·3 per cent. in 1913; tea 7·4 per cent. in 1908 and 4·5 per cent. in 1913; machinery 8·9 per cent. in 1908 and 12·3 per cent. in 1913; raw metals 2·8 per cent. in 1908 and 4 per cent. in 1913. Khromov, op. cit., pp. 474–5, 478–9.

[2] Ibid., pp. 490–3.

[3] *Ezhegodnik Rossii 1915*, part xii, pp. 14–15.

The law of 1900 limiting the yearly increase in zemstvo taxation to 3 per cent. had provided that this proportion might be made higher if the consent of the provincial governor were given. In practice the governors co-operated with the zemstvos, and the yearly increase in taxation between 1906 and 1913 varied between 4 per cent. and 17 per cent.[1] Between 1908 and 1912 the central government made many grants to zemstvos for education and public health, and on 26 June 1912 a special state board was set up to extend credits to zemstvos and municipalities.

In 1914 the population of the Russian empire, excluding Finland but including Poland, was 148,840,200 rural and 26,297,600 urban. In 1916 there were at least twelve cities of more than 200,000 inhabitants.[2] The voting roll for the municipal councils remained extremely low, usually around 1 per cent. of the whole population. During the last years of peace the cities were spending money much more freely, and amenities were rapidly increasing. They had a long way to go. In 1904 only twenty-seven cities had a modern system of drainage, and it extended only to a minority of the inhabitants. The two capitals were the only cities in which almost all streets were properly paved. Piped water supplies were confined to the biggest cities. All this, however, was changing very fast in the last years.[3]

[1] Details in Miller, op. cit., p. 169, quoted from *Vestnik finansov* (1914), no. 2, p. 46.

[2] In 1916 St. Petersburg had 2,404,530 inhabitants; Moscow 1,853,500; Kiev 615,000; Riga 581,000; Tiflis 330,900; Kharkov 308,790; Tashkent 272,600; Baku 238,900; Saratov 237,800. Kazan was just below the line with 197,000. In 1914 Warsaw had 909,000. (*Ezhegodnik Rossii 1916.*) This list does not include two cities which were not capitals of provinces, but which had large populations. These were Odessa (Kherson province, population in 1904 499,555) and Łódź (Piotrków province, population in 1897 330,000).

[3] The official publication of the Central Statistical Committee of the Ministry of the Interior, *Goroda Rossii v 1910 godu*, has some interesting material. Like all Russian statistics of this time, it has some odd statements which must be due to some sort of mechanical error. It is hard, for example, to believe that there were only 300 private telephone subscribers in Moscow, or only 49 doctors in Odessa in 1910. However, subject to an irreducible element of uncertainty, here are some data taken from a number of the more important towns:

Municipal voters: St. Petersburg 16,000 in a population in 1910 of 1,556,000; Moscow 8,000 in 1,481,000; Saratov 1,884 in 214,000; Kazan 1,501 in 182,000; Samara 1,418 in 141,000; Kiev 3,761 in 497,178.

Electric lighting: St. Petersburg had 2,800 public lanterns lit by electricity,

Nationalism

The years after 1907 were a period of counter-offensive by Russian nationalism against the gains which the nationalities had made in 1905. Stolypin himself was a nationalist, and frequently proclaimed his belief in a Great Russia. He conceived of the Russian empire as a modern centralized state similar to modern Germany or Italy. It was no longer enough that a subject of the empire should be personally loyal to the emperor: it was required of him that he should be a Russian patriot, and that he should refuse to put any other loyalty above his Russian patriotism. At most the peoples of non-Russian language might be allowed the sort of local patriotism that was permitted to Neapolitans or Bavarians, though there could be no question, not even in the case of Finland, of the separate institutional framework that the south German states retained in Bismarck's empire. Stolypin did not object to the existence of other languages and traditions, but essentially he put them on the level of picturesque local folklore, and refused to regard them as objects of serious modern national loyalty. He was a sincere Russian nationalist, but he was also well aware of the value of nationalism as a means of popularizing his régime. Nationalism was the only modern ideology which could compete in demagogic appeal with socialism. Stolypin was not himself an anti-Semite, but he tolerated the anti-Semitism of the extreme right. The appeal of 'the socialism of the imbecile' to the masses, especially in the south-western provinces, town and country, was something which he was not prepared to renounce.

Stolypin was determined to destroy the far-reaching autonomy which the Finns had recovered in 1905, to combat Polish

Kiev 594, Perm 470, Saratov 410, Moscow 322, Tula 120, Kazan 106, Odessa 74, Tomsk 25.

Private telephone subscribers: St. Petersburg had 25,000; Kiev 3,470; Odessa 2,236; Kazan 1,570; Samara 924; Irkutsk 687; Tomsk 678; Tiflis 988; Tashkent 598: Perm 476; Tula 419.

Doctors: St. Petersburg had 1,475, Moscow 1,666, Kiev 711, Kishinyov 511, Tiflis 279, Saratov 138, Samara 123, Kazan 121, Tomsk 89, Tula 58.

Theatres: St. Petersburg had 22, Moscow 10, Tiflis, 5, Saratov 3; Irkutsk, Kishinyov and Tashkent each had 2; most provincial capitals of small population had one.

Brick buildings formed about half the buildings in St. Petersburg and Kiev, a third in Moscow, a quarter in Nizhnii Novgorod and Poltava, a fifth in Kazan.

nationalism not only in the western borderlands but in the Kingdom of Poland itself, and to crush the Ukrainian movement, which he like most Russians regarded as 'Little Russian separatism' organized by foreign forces hostile to Russia. In the Baltic provinces policy was more tolerant than in the 1890's, and in Transcaucasia the struggle was against socialism rather than nationalism. In the relations between Russians and Moslems there was little change.

For the nationalities these years were more difficult than the 1890's in so far as they now felt the hostility not only of the government but also of a large part of the Russian people. On the other hand they were more conscious of their strength as a result of the strong popular movements which had developed in support of nationalism in 1905.

In December 1907 *Macierz Szkolna* was closed, and the situation of schools in Poland more or less reverted to what it had been before 1905. Three measures of the following years which had an outward semblance of democratic reform were in fact directed against Polish nationalism. The first was the introduction of zemstvos in the western provinces. The establishment of elected local government was in principle a progressive reform, but the franchise was so devised as to reduce the influence of the Poles, who were numerically a minority but culturally and politically strong. The second was the formation of a new province of Kholm, with a population in majority Ukrainian, out of the two Polish provinces of Lublin and Siedlce. This was in fact designed not to give democratic rights to the Ukrainians but simply to reduce the amount of Polish territory within the empire. The third was the introduction in 1913 in the Kingdom of Poland of municipal councils in the cities. This proved of little advantage to the Polish city populations, as the franchise was so manipulated as to give the resident Russian bureaucrats disproportionate voting power, and it was laid down that the councils must conduct their business in Russian. A fourth blow to Polish interests was the purchase by the government from a private Polish company of the Warsaw–Vienna Railway. This was followed by the introduction of Russian engineers and workers in place of the former Polish employees.

The attitude of Stolypin was clearly expressed in a Duma debate on 16 November 1907. Dmowski had complained that the people of the border regions and of the Kingdom of Poland felt themselves second-class citizens, and that Poles could never reconcile themselves to this. Stolypin argued that if the Poles had no university, it was because of their refusal—which he clearly considered as unreasonable—to use the Russian language in university instruction. 'First of all come over to our point of view,' he pleaded, 'admit that the greatest blessing is to be a Russian citizen, bear this name with the same pride with which once the Romans bore their citizenship, and then you will call yourselves first-class citizens and you will receive all your rights.'[1] Lack of understanding could hardly have been more complete.

Dmowski, however, persisted in his view that Russia was a lesser evil for the Polish cause than Germany, and that Austria-Hungary was too weak to be of real use as a protector of Polish interests. He also took some part in the movement known as 'Neo-Slavism', a revival of the broader form of Pan-Slavism which thought in terms of friendship and equality between all Slav peoples, Catholic as well as Orthodox, and which had some support within both the Russian and the Austrian empires.

The alternative to Dmowski's policy was for Poles to place their hopes in Austria, and try to get the best terms they could in the future event of a defeat of Russia by the German Powers. This was the course favoured by most Poles in Galicia. It also became the policy of a section of the PPS. With the defeat of the revolutionary movement in Russia, the left wing of the PPS lost ground within the party, and the extreme left SDKPL lost ground among the workers. Trust in the fraternal revolutionary Russian working class seemed less attractive than the pursuit of Polish national aims. It was in these years that Józef Piłsudski, living in exile in Galicia, became the outstanding figure in Polish socialism and in Polish politics as a whole. His Revolutionary Fraction, forming a right wing within the party, became increasingly important.

Polish opinion was also divided in regard to the Ukrainians. In eastern Galicia there was a direct conflict between the two nationalisms. The Poles insisted that Lwów was a Polish city and the whole of Galicia was Polish territory, but some realized

[1] *Gosudarstvennaya duma, 3 sozyv, 1 sessiya,* column 352.

that the Ukrainians would never be polonized, and that they must somehow come to terms with them. The only basis of Polish-Ukrainian co-operation was common enmity to Russia. Those Poles who were most anti-Russian realized that Ukrainian nationalism within the Russian empire could be a powerful weapon against the Russian state, and understood the Austrian policy of making Eastern Galicia a Ukrainian Piedmont. This was especially true of Piłsudski, who had genuine sympathy for the Ukrainian cause. On the other hand Dmowski, convinced of the need to co-operate with Russia, regarded Ukrainian nationalism as an enemy. Not only would any co-operation by Poles with Ukrainians increase the hostility of the Russian government to the Poles, but the Ukrainians were in any case a threat to Polish interests both in Galicia and in the Polish-Russian borderlands of the Russian empire.

For their part the Ukrainians were divided in their attitude to the Poles. The Ukrainians in the Russian empire, though aware of the long tradition of conflict with the Poles, still felt some solidarity with them as fellow victims of russification. In Galicia, three points of view were to be found among Ukrainians. One was willing to compromise and co-operate with the Poles against the common enemy Russia, to accept approximately the views of Piłsudski. The second regarded the Poles as the enemy, and Russia as a protector. This group accepted the view that they were not a separate Ukrainian nation, but were part of the Russian nation. For them the ultimate aim was annexation of Eastern Galicia to Russia. The third point of view considered Poles and Russians as equally enemies, and sought protection from the German Powers, not so much from Austria, whose government seemed needlessly conciliatory to the Poles, as from Germany, whose government treated its Polish subjects in Prussia with much less consideration. It is impossible to say which of these three views was the strongest in Galicia, the only area in which Ukrainian opinion could be freely expressed. All three existed, but in the long term the third was potentially the strongest. It must be emphasized that the basic difference between the Polish and Ukrainian positions was that the Ukrainians, whether in Russia or in Austria-Hungary, had no motive at all to be anti-German.

Within the Russian empire the Ukrainian nationalist movement was strongly repressed. Permission was not given to open new branches of the *Prosvita* cultural organization, and the existing branches were closed down one by one, the last in 1910. The rural co-operative movement, however, was tolerated, as its activities corresponded with the general agricultural policy of the government. In the Ukrainian provinces the co-operative organization was largely in the hands of nationalist Ukrainians. The different political tendencies which had appeared in the Ukraine in 1905 continued to exist, though separate legal Ukrainian parties did not. In 1908 was formed a secret political organization called the Society of Ukrainian Progressives (T.U.P.). It was essentially an intelligentsia party of moderate socialist or radical views.

It is difficult to say how strong Ukrainian nationalism was by 1914 in the Russian Ukraine, though there is no doubt that it was growing. The hard core of the nationalist movement was in the intelligentsia. This point was always stressed by Russian nationalists, who made fun of the Ukrainian language as an uncouth dialect, denied that 'Little Russian peasants' could understand the language used by Professor Hrushevsky, and accused Ukrainian nationalists of serving the cause of polonization of the Russian people, or of taking money from the Austrians.[1] It was true that the Ukrainian social structure was primitive. Of the four nations inhabiting the Ukraine, the proportions engaged in trade, industry and agriculture were as follows: Russians 5 per cent. 20 per cent. and 52 per cent.; Ukrainians 1 per cent. 8 per cent. and 77 per cent.; Poles 2 per cent. 18 per cent. and 53 per cent.; Jews 34 per cent. 38 per cent. and 3 per cent.[2] The working class of the industrial cities of the Ukraine was largely Russian, and in the Black Sea ports it was extremely mixed. Ukrainian was spoken in the countryside. Ukrainian nationalism was potentially a movement of peasants led by intelligentsia. Nevertheless, there was evidence that Ukrainian national feeling was growing also among the workers, and this tendency was likely to continue as the influx of peasants into the cities included a growing proportion who had been

[1] See for example S. N. Shchegolev, *Ukrainskoe dvizhenie kak sovremenny etap yuzhnorusskogo separatizma*, Kiev, 1912.

[2] T. V. Lokot, *Opravdanie natsionalizma* (Kiev, 1910), p. 35. The percentages are based on the 1897 census and refer only to gainfully employed males. They refer to the whole empire, not just to the population of the Ukraine.

affected by Ukrainian nationalism in their village adolescence. The role of the nationally minded Ukrainian school-teacher was of course crucial.

The civil war in the Baltic provinces convinced the government that the Baltic Germans were an element of order, and should be treated with more consideration. Several of the private German schools closed in the 1890's were reopened. There was, however, no change in the status of the university. During the next decade the Baltic provinces were quiet. Nevertheless, it was clear that a new era had come. The former mutual confidence between the German upper classes and the Russian government could never be restored, and the national consciousness of the Estonians and Latvians, directed against both Germans and Russians, could not be wished or talked out of existence.

Stolypin was never prepared to accept the new constitutional situation in Finland. He persisted in the dogmatic though unhistorical assertion that Finland was part of the Russian empire, and that therefore 'all-Imperial' considerations must always take precedence over purely local Finnish interests. His hostility to Finland was greatly increased by the fact that Russian revolutionary parties, including the SR terrorists, had been able to use Finland as a safe refuge, close to St. Petersburg, from which to conduct their operations in Russia. The Finns for their part were prepared to make no concession to Russian susceptibilities. The largest party in the Finnish Diet were now the Social Democrats, who had at least 80 seats out of nearly 200 in all four elections between 1907 and 1910. Their strength was built on the support not only of the industrial workers but of a large part of the peasant small tenants. The only party prepared to co-operate with the Russians were the Old Finns, who held about a quarter of the seats.

Stolypin declared his views in a speech to the Duma on 5 May 1908. Liberal opinion in Finland, he said, spoke of a fight against 'the dark forces of reaction'. These people forgot that 'with the introduction of the new system in Russia another wave of reaction has arisen, the reaction of Russian patriotism and Russian national feeling, and this reaction, gentlemen, is building its nest precisely in all strata of Russian society'. It was not just the Tsar or the government but the whole people that was concerned. 'You, gentlemen, the representatives of the

Russian people, cannot repudiate the heritage of Peter in the Gulf of Finland.' A less exalted tone was adopted by the spokesman of the extreme right, Markov II, deputy for Kursk, who described the Finns as a nation of traitors, who betrayed the king of Sweden in 1809, and would betray Russia too if they got a chance. He appealed to the Duma: 'Cast away all these demands of the Finnish traitors and separatists, and utter a powerful Russian phrase—Russia for the Russians—let all else be subjected to Russia's interests.'[1]

In 1908 a mixed Russo-Finnish commission was set up under P. A. Kharitonov to establish the criteria for distinguishing matters of 'all-Imperial character' from matters of purely Finnish interest. The commission could not agree. In February 1909 the Finnish Diet was dissolved after a speech by the Young Finn leader Svinhufvud criticizing Russian policy. The composition of the new Diet was virtually unchanged. In March 1910 the Duma passed a law based on the recommendation of the Russian members of the Kharitonov Commission. This defined 'all-Imperial' matters in such a way that the competence of the Finnish Diet was reduced to that of a provincial assembly. The Diet was again dissolved, and yet another election took place, with essentially the same results. The new Diet, on a motion of Svinhufvud, refused to consider the agenda submitted to it from St. Petersburg, on the ground that this was based on decisions of the Duma which could not be binding in Finland. The Diet was then dissolved, and Finland was ruled by dictatorial powers. Russian officials and policemen were brought into Finland. A campaign started in the Russian press for the annexation of Vyborg to Finland. Russian subjects were placed by law on an equal footing with Finns for employment in Finland. This led to conflicts between Finnish local authorities, who refused to legalize Russian business firms, and the Russian government, ending in the arrest and imprisonment of some Finnish officials. By 1914 it was clear that the once loyal Finns had been driven into unrelenting hostility to Russia, and that Finland was in effect an occupied enemy country.

The situation of the Jews within the Pale of Settlement

[1] Stolypin's speech is given in the minutes of the Duma for 5 May 1908: *Gosudarstvennaya duma, 3 sozyv, 1 sessiya*, part ii, columns 2919–41. Markov II's speech is in part iii, columns 366–88, the words quoted above being in column 388.

remained much the same as it had been at the turn of the century.

There were no more pogroms, but there was plenty of anti-Semitic propaganda in the south-western and western provinces. The *numerus clausus* on secondary and higher education for Jews was not only reasserted in 1907 but extended: even the practice of studying at home and taking school examinations, as a means of obtaining educational qualifications, was subjected to the ten per cent. limit. Though the governments of Stolypin and Kokovtsov did not pursue active anti-Semitic policies, the general attitude of their members was hostile to the Jews. This was shown particularly clearly by the treatment of the ritual murder trial of the Jewish workman Mendel Beilis in Kiev in October 1913.[1]

In Georgia the revolution and repression left a bitter mood. On 28 August the eminent liberal writer Ilya Chavchavadze was murdered. The Russian authorities removed from their posts and imprisoned a bishop and an archimandrite who continued to demand an autocephalous church. On 28 May 1908 the Russian Exarch Nikon was murdered in Tiflis by a Georgian nationalist. In 1912 the Georgian peasants were at last removed from the state of 'temporary obligation', and began redemption payments for the land they received. The régime of the governor-general, Vorontsov-Dashkov, was more lenient to the Armenians. He valued them as loyal supporters of Russia against Turkey, and believed that their help, and the help of their kinsmen across the Ottoman frontier, would be useful in the event of a war with Turkey. He claimed that the more conservative section of the *Dashnyaktsutyun* were loyal to Russia. Stolypin distrusted all Armenian political groups, and disliked Vorontsov-Dashkov's policy, but did not insist on its reversal.[2]

The competition between Tatars and Russians for the allegiance of the Volga peoples continued, and Russian Orthodox

[1] Beilis was accused of ritual murder of a Christian child. A judicial inquiry produced no evidence of Jewish responsibility for the child's death. The minister of justice then ordered a second inquiry. The affair was protracted for two years. In October 1913 Beilis was acquitted at his trial, but in grudging and insulting terms. See *Krasny Arkhiv*, no. 54 (1932), pp. 162–204.

[2] Some correspondence of Vorontsov-Dashkov with Stolypin and with the emperor is in *Krasny Arkhiv*, nos. 26, 34, and 37.

missionary activities continued to offend Russian Moslems. On the fiftieth anniversary of the Kazan Central Converted Tatars' School in 1913 it was revealed that just under 900 persons had completed their training at the school, and that just under 400 had become teachers. For half a century's effort, this was not an impressive result. The Moslems were holding their own, so much so that the Orthodox Church kept appealing to the government for help, and Stolypin summoned conferences of experts to plan counter-measures.[1]

Another grievance of the Moslem population was the growing immigration of Russian colonists into Moslem territory, mainly in Central Asia but to some extent also in the Caucasus. By 1911 there were more than 1,500,000 Russians in the governor-generalship of the Steppes, forming about 40 per cent. of the total population. Four-fifths of these Russians were rural colonists. In Turkestan the number was much smaller—400,000 of whom nearly 230,000 were rural. However, in 1910 the Turkestan Statute was amended so as to facilitate Russian immigration. All lands in the provinces of Samarkand, Syr Darya, and Fergana which the governor-general decided were in excess of the needs of the nomad population on the basis of 'natural-historical, economic, and statistical investigation', were to be made available for colonization under the Directorate of Land Organization and Agriculture.[2]

Ismail Bey Gaspirali continued to be the most respected figure in Moslem cultural life in Russia. But among the younger Moslems more radical political groups were beginning to appear. A Young Tatar movement in the Crimea, founded by a school-teacher in Karasubazar named Abdurreshid Mehdi, had some contact with the Russian SR's. In Azerbaidjan in 1912 a movement called *Musavat* (Equality) was founded by Mehmed Emin Bey Resul-Zade, who had been a Social Democrat in Baku in 1905, had taken part in the Persian Revolution in Teheran, and returned to Baku in 1910. This movement was part socialist and part nationalist.

The Moslems in the Duma defended their case as best they

[1] Trainees 636 men and 260 women, actual teachers 272 men and 126 women. A. A. Vozkresensky, *O sisteme prosveshchenii inorodtsev*, Kazan, 1913. On Stolypin's conferences, *Krasny Arkhiv*, nos. 35 and 36.

[2] Richard A. Pierce, *Russian Central Asia 1867–1917* (Berkeley, 1960), pp. 135–7, quoting *Aziatskaya Rossiya*, i. 67–68, 87.

could. For example, the Tatar S. N. Maksudov, representing Kazan, complained on 20 February 1910 of the Russian Orthodox missionaries 'who always identify the Christian mission with a policy of russification', and accuse the Tatars always of 'Pan-Islamism', Whatever the Moslems do, they are guilty. If they open schools of their own, or attend Russian schools, seek any sort of education, or publish newspapers, all this proves them to be 'Pan-Islamists'.[1] In another speech on 10 November 1910 the same speaker declared that the 20,000,000 Moslems in Russia, except for a few members of mountain tribes, belong to one race. 'This race is called the Turco-Tatar race.' But the word 'Tatar', he claimed, was an inappropriate name. In fact they were all Turks, with a common language, which 'bears the name all-Turkic' (*obshche-tyurkskogo*)' This common language has four dialects—Azerbaidjani, Dzhagatay, Kipchak, and Steppe-Kirghiz—which are closer to each other than Little Russian and Great Russian. The Russian Moslems wish to join in 'Russian civil culture', but they will not renounce their own nationality or their own language and literature.[2]

The all-Turkic idea had the same weaknesses as the Pan-Slav: there was less unity either of language or of outlook between the brother peoples than the intellectuals hoped. Nomad Bashkirs and Kazakhs distrusted urban, commercially gifted Tatars; Tatars felt that their language was as good as Ottoman Turkish; and the Moslems of Turkestan objected to modernist and secular ideas. But the Tatar democrats were genuine in their willingness to be loyal Russian subjects, provided that they were treated with respect, and genuine in their admiration for Russian culture. A statesmanlike government would have accepted their overtures, and would have tried to win their friendship and to smooth out the friction that inevitably arose between Russians and Moslems in areas of mixed population like Kazan province. Such policies were, however, beyond the comprehension of the politicians of 1910.

Discouraged by Russian policies, some of the Moslem leaders emigrated to the Ottoman empire. Their disillusionment was probably due even more to events in the international field than to internal conditions in Russia. The Young Turkish

[1] *Gosudarstvennaya duma, 3 sozyv, 3 sessiya,* part ii, column 1916.

[2] Ibid. *3 sozyv, 4 sessiya,* part i, columns 1077–84.

Revolution, with its first flush of idealism and fraternization between Moslems and Christians, had aroused their hopes. They began to think in terms of a reconciliation between the new Turkey and Russia, rather as the Neo-Slavists of Austria were thinking of a reconciliation between Austria and Russia. The dream was no less unreal, and this became clear even sooner. The Young Turkish Revolution was followed by the Bosnian crisis, and this in turn led to an active Russian policy in the Balkans which was not at first anti-Turkish yet was bound to become so.[1] The most important of the Moslem emigrés in Constantinople was Yusuf Akchura, one of the organizers of the Moslem Union of 1905. He published in the Ottoman capital a periodical, *Türk Yurdu*, which the censors allowed into Russia. In Turkey Akchura and other Russian-born Moslems exercised an important influence. The growing popularity of Turkish nationalism, which sought to base patriotism on the secular foundation of language in place of the religious foundation of the Moslem faith, was largely due to them, as well as to a few Ottoman-born intellectuals like the poet Zia Gökalp, with whom Akchura was in touch.

Meanwhile in Russia the Tatars developed economically and culturally on the same lines as in previous decades. Their secular intelligentsia and their native business class were becoming influential not only in the Volga valley but further afield, in the Steppes and Central Asia. Kazan was surpassed only by Constantinople and Cairo as a centre of modern Moslem thought.[2]

It has often been claimed that Russian nationalism was something artificial, confined to the politicians of the extreme right but not genuinely acceptable to the Russian people. This is to underrate the phenomenon. It is true that the great majority of liberal and socialist intellectuals were indifferent or hostile to nationalism, and as it was these people who had most contact with Europeans at the time, and who wrote most of the political and historical books and articles at the time or later, it is natural that their interpretation of popular feeling has prevailed.

[1] See below pp. 689–90.

[2] In 1912 466 books in Turkic languages were published in Kazan in 3,200,000 copies. S. A. Zenkovsky, *Pan-Turkism and Islam in Russia*, Harvard, 1960, p. 121.

Yet the potential appeal of nationalism to the Russian people was very great. Like German nationalism, it was most marked in the borderlands.[1] It was in the south-west, where Ukrainian nationalism was strongest, that was also to be found the strongest support for anti-Semitic demagogic Russian nationalism. In fact such organizations as the Union of the Russian People and the League of Archangel Michael were a prototype for some of the semi-revolutionary anti-Semitic fascist movements which flourished in eastern Poland, Roumania and Hungary in the 1930's. It may be argued that this type of nationalist movement is a phenomenon of the area of dense Jewish population, stretching from northern Hungary and Moldavia as far as the Russian Ukraine and Lithuania, that its essence is anti-Semitism, and that it is not indigenous to the Great Russian lands. This is on the whole true. Nevertheless, the ideology and the technique of demagogic organization were becoming known in the Russian regions, and their appeal was considerable. Just as the Austrian type of anti-Semitic nationalism became accepted in north Germany, where it had no historical roots but where circumstances in the 1920's and 1930's made it seem useful to some politicians, so the south-western type of Russian black-hundred demagogy was winning a clientele in Moscow and St. Petersburg. Russian history in the next decades took a quite different course, but that does not justify the historian in writing off as negligible a political trend which, repulsive though its ideas may seem, had great potential popularity.

There was one other nationalist theory expressed at this time which deserves mention. This was the conception of Struve, that a new nation should be created in the Russian empire, with a new national identity and consciousness. 'Russian nationality, just like American, is still being forged, it is, as the Americans say of themselves, *in the making*.'[2] This vast empire, with its tremendous economic development, would be, like America, a melting-pot from which something new would arise. The Poles and Finns, Struve conceded, could not be affected: their nationality was already definitely formed. But

[1] Militant Pan-Germanism, and in a later age, National-Socialism, were strongest in the Bohemian borderlands and Styria.

[2] P. B. Struve, *Patriotica: sbornik statey za pyat' let* (SPB, 1911), p. 300. The italicized words are in English in the original.

all the others could be welded together into something new. The idea is interesting, but hardly convincing. America was built of streams of immigrants from many lands arriving in a country which already had a culture formed by its Anglo-Saxon origins. The immigrants modified the culture, but they never transformed it. In Russia it was not a question of uprooted immigrant groups, but of compact nations living in their own homelands—Georgia, Estonia, Turkestan, and the rest. It was a difficult enough task to forge the American nation out of so many disparate elements, but it would have been immensely more difficult to do this in Russia. None the less, Struve's idea reveals a breadth of vision entirely lacking in the rulers of Russia at this time. They could think of no other way of building Great Russia than physical force and contempt for the nationality of others.

The revolutionary parties paid some attention to the problems of the non-Russian nationalities, but only the Bolsheviks gave it a high priority. The SR's favoured some sort of federal structure for the future Russian republic, but were not very precise. The Mensheviks hardly went beyond generalities: they did not make any effort comparable to the theories elaborated by their colleagues in the Austrian Social Democratic movement, Otto Bauer and Karl Renner. Lenin, however, took the nationality question very seriously, for he was fully aware of the revolutionary potentialities of the national discontents of the non-Russians. Lenin did not himself write the chief exposition of Bolshevik doctrine on the subject, but he directly inspired it. The author was Djugashvili-Stalin, who came to see Lenin in exile in Galicia in the spring of 1913, and wrote at his request an article in the exiled periodical *Prosveshchenie* entitled 'The National Question and Social Democracy'.[1] It was a polemic against the views of Otto Bauer, who sought to combine cultural autonomy, and a guarantee of the personal nationality of every citizen in a multi-national state (such as the Habsburg Monarchy or the Russian empire) with the unity of the state itself. Stalin, at Lenin's bidding, insisted that the state must be centralized, but that any nationality which

[1] This article, together with some later writings, was subsequently published in many editions, in countless languages, as J. V. Stalin, *Marxism and the National and Colonial Question.*

genuinely wished for independence must have the right of 'self-determination up to the point of secession'. Neither the state nor the party must be weakened by institutions designed to ensure cultural autonomy, but a nation must have the right to form a separate state if it wished. The difficulty about this doctrine was, who was to decide which political groups within the nation had the right to decide whether to secede or not? For example, if the Latvians were divided between a '*bourgeois* nationalist' party which wished to create an independent Latvian state which would be a '*bourgeois* democracy', and a 'working-class' party which wished Latvia to remain part of a Russian socialist republic, what should the Russian socialist leaders do? Should they decide between the claimants on the basis of their voting strength in a Latvian election, or on the basis of proletarian solidarity, or on some other grounds? This became a real problem in 1917 and later, but for the time being it was purely theoretical. Meanwhile Lenin's formulation was certainly more attractive to non-Russian nationalists than those of the SR's or Mensheviks.

XIX

FOREIGN POLICY

Russia, France, and Germany

THE Franco-Russian Alliance was not subjected to severe strain by the Russo-Japanese War. Both Britain and France made efforts to avoid being involved in the dispute between their allies. The Anglo-French Agreement on Egypt and Morocco was concluded in April 1904, while the Russo-Japanese War was in its early stage. The French government did its best to help a peaceful settlement of the Dogger Bank incident, without damage to Russian prestige.

The German government, however, attempted to exploit Russia's isolation, and existing bitter feelings towards Britain, to draw Russia towards Germany, either in co-operation with France or at the cost of breaking the Franco-Russian Alliance. The first attempt was a proposal by William II to Nicholas II on 27 October 1904, for a Russo-Franco-German combination against Britain. The Tsar's first reaction was favourable, and on 12 November William sent him a draft of a treaty of alliance. When Nicholas asked that he should be allowed to inform the French government of this proposed Russo-German alliance before signing it, William objected, and replied that it would be better to drop the idea altogether for the time being.[1]

The next attempt was made in the summer of 1905. At this time Franco-German relations were extremely strained in connexion with the Moroccan problem. As a result of German pressure, the French foreign minister, Delcassé, the maker of the *entente* with Britain, resigned on 6 June. Germany appeared to have won a diplomatic victory. The next stage was a new approach to Russia, intended either to align both Russia and France with Germany or to break the Franco-Russian Alliance. On 23–24 July William II and Nicholas II met on the Tsar's yacht in the bay of Björkö in the Gulf of Finland. William

[1] The correspondence is printed in *Krasny Arkhiv*, no. 5 (1924), pp. 6–24.

produced a draft treaty of alliance which he 'happened to have in his pocket'. The first article stated: 'If one of the two empires is attacked by a European Power, its ally will aid it in Europe with all its forces on land and sea.' The fourth article obliged the Tsar, 'after the coming into force of the treaty', to take steps 'to initiate France into the accord' and cause her 'to associate herself with it as an ally'. The foreign minister, Count Lamsdorff, was informed by the Tsar on 30 August.[1] He viewed the treaty with dismay. but was obliged to instruct Nelidov, now ambassador in Paris, to sound the French government on the possibility of a Russo-Franco-German grouping. The French prime minister, Rouvier, objected strongly. Pressed a second time by Nelidov, on instructions from St. Petersburg, on 5 October, he declared flatly that 'Our people would not endure a closer relationship with Germany'.[2] It was now clear to the Tsar that he must choose between the existing Franco-Russian Alliance and a new Russo-German alignment. In the last resort he preferred the old.

The Russian foreign ministry in any case had no desire to abandon the alliance with France. But even if this had been seriously considered, one extremely important objection would at once have arisen—the financial factor. Russia desperately needed a huge loan to restore her economy after the war and the revolutionary disturbances. In December 1905 the finance minister, Kokovtsov, visited both Paris and Berlin. French bankers and political leaders expressed themselves willing to help Russia, but pointed out both that repression of democrats and pogroms against Jews in Russia were making a bad impression on the French public, and that the outlook must remain uncertain until after the forthcoming conference on the Moroccan problem. This was a clear indication to the Russian government that if it wanted a loan it must support French policy in Morocco.[3] In fact at the Algeciras Conference, which met from January to March 1906, France was supported by both

[1] Count V. N. Lamsdorff (1841–1907) served most of his career in the ministry. He was closely associated with Giers, and was deputy minister from 1897 to 1900, when he became minister.

[2] *Krasny Arkhiv*, no. 5 (1924), pp. 46–48. German documents relating to Björkö are in *Die große Politik*, xix. 454–502.

[3] For correspondence on the loan negotiations see *Krasny Arkhiv*, no. 10 (1925), pp. 9–40.

Britain and Russia, and German policy suffered a defeat. After the conference, the French loan was quickly arranged. On 3 April Kokovtsov signed in Paris an agreement which provided for a loan of 2,250,000,000 French francs. Angered by Russian policy at Algeciras, the German government forbade German banks to participate. Witte had hoped for an international loan, but the small British and Dutch participation barely modified the overwhelmingly French character of the enterprise. The Tsar was of course able to use the loan to lessen his dependence on the Duma and to continue repression of the Russian left, to the distress of the left in France. But France's need for a strong military ally in Europe outweighed any ideological sympathies.

Russia and Britain

The next important move of Russian diplomacy was to seek an agreement with Britain. This was the work of Lamsdorff's successor, Izvolsky.[1] The Anglo-Russian conflict in the Far East had been removed by Japan's victory. In the Straits question Britain was less hostile to Russian aims, and Izvolsky hoped in due course to obtain British approval. Meanwhile the main area of conflict was the vast region of Asia lying to the north of India, from Persia through Afghanistan to Tibet. These countries were the subject of discussions between Izvolsky and the British ambassador, Sir Arthur Nicolson, beginning in the summer of 1906. The negotiations were made difficult by the fact that there were really four parties to them. The Russian and British foreign ministries, concerned above all with relations with the European Great Powers, were eager for an agreement. But the British government in India and the Russian governor-general of Turkestan were concerned only with the security of their territory, which each believed to be seriously threatened by the other Power. Thus Curzon, viceroy of India from 1899 to 1905, had been more suspicious of Russian designs, and more insistent on the need for British domination of Persia, than Salisbury or Lansdowne.

[1] A. P. Izvolsky, a professional diplomat, served as minister in Munich 1897–9, in Tokyo 1899–1903, and in Copenhagen 1903–6. He was minister of foreign affairs from 1906–10, and thereafter served as ambassador in Paris until the February Revolution of 1917. He died in 1919.

In Persia 1906 was a year of revolution. Inspired both by nationalism and by radical political ideas, enjoying support among both traditional Moslems and the small new secular intelligentsia, influenced to some extent by the spectacle of events in Russia, the Persian revolutionary movement succeeded at the end of the year in obtaining a constitution from the Shah. The British government had shown some sympathy for the movement, and at a critical stage some hundreds of constitutionalists had been granted asylum (*bast*) in the grounds of the British Legation in Tehran. The Russian government had much less sympathy. Both the British and Russian governments were alarmed at the growth of German influence, the Russians by a project to found a German bank in Tehran, the British by German trade with the Persian Gulf. Neither government, however, was keen to support the other's interest against German penetration in an area of less immediate concern to itself.

In Afghanistan British influence remained supreme, though relations between the government of India and Kabul were sometimes strained. The Russian government had several times, between 1900 and 1903, raised with the British government the question of the establishment, not of full Russo-Afghan diplomatic relations, but of direct contact between the authorities along the Russo-Afghan border. No agreement had been reached before the Russo-Japanese War. On 21 March 1905 the British government made a treaty with Afghanistan. Britain was to give the Emir of Afghanistan a subsidy and to defend him against any other Power. The Emir undertook to deal with other states only through the British government.

Britain had attempted to settle its relations with Tibet by treaties of 1890 and 1893 with China. The Tibetans, however, paid little attention to either Chinese or British wishes, and there were frequent minor incidents on the Tibetan-Indian border. Lord Curzon in 1904 sent an expedition under Colonel Younghusband to Lhasa. On 7 September 1904 a convention was signed, which exceeded Younghusband's original instructions, and pledged the Tibetans to give no concessions on Tibetan territory, and to admit no agents of another Power. It also imposed an indemnity on the Tibetans, which was reduced by one-third as a result of a Russian protest to the British government. In April 1806 the Chinese government recognized the convention.

The Anglo-Russian negotiations ended with the conclusion of an agreement on 31 August 1907. In the case of Persia there was a division of interests. Each Power was to have a zone within which its own subjects might seek economic concessions, and the subjects of the other Power were not to do so. The zone reserved for Russian subjects was very large, including the whole northern part of Persia, its most fertile provinces, the capital Tehran, and the cities of Isfahan, Tabriz, and Meshed. The zone reserved for British subjects was the south-eastern corner, from Bandar Abbas on the Persian Gulf to the Indian border and northwards along the Indian-Persian and Afghan-Persian frontiers, a desert region of some strategic importance but no economic value. Southern and south-western Persia were to be a neutral zone, in which subjects of both Powers might compete.[1] The British government issued a separate statement that it would continue to maintain the *status quo* in the Persian Gulf, and to protect British trade without excluding the legitimate trade of any other Power. In Afghanistan and Tibet the British had things their way. The Russian government recognized that Afghanistan was outside the Russian sphere of interest. Local Russian and Afghan authorities might establish contact with each other to deal with local non-political matters. The Russian government also recognized Britain's special interest in Tibet owing to its proximity to India. Both governments would negotiate with Tibet only through the Chinese government. British commercial agents might have direct contact with the Tibetan authorities, and Buddhist subjects of either Power might have contact with the Dalai Lama in strictly religious matters.

Essentially the convention smoothed away a number of difficulties in the relations between Britain and Russia. It was not an alliance, and it was not directed against Germany. Even in its limited aims it was not entirely successful. The continued internal conflicts in Persia, the counter-revolution of the

[1] The phrase 'partition of Persia', often applied to the convention, is somewhat misleading. The 'zones' were not occupied by the forces of either Power. The convention did not provide for means of forcing the Persian government not to grant concessions to citizens of other Powers in any of the three 'zones'.

Shah and the armed resistance of the constitutionalists, the sympathy of British public opinion for the constitutionalists, and the role of Russian-trained Persian Cossacks and Russian officers in support of the Shah, strained Anglo-Russian relations in Persia. In 1911 there was a further embarrassment when an American financial adviser, Morgan Shuster, was dismissed by the Persian government as a result of a direct military threat from Russia.

Russia, Japan, and America

In the Far East, Russia came to terms with her former enemy Japan. An agreement on fisheries off the Siberian coast, concluded in June 1907, represented a considerable economic loss to Russia. It was followed by a political agreement of 30 July, which contained a secret annexe recognizing Japanese special interests in Korea and Southern Manchuria and Russian special interests in Northern Manchuria and Outer Mongolia. A further treaty of 4 July 1910 recognized the right of each Power 'within its sphere freely to take all measures necessary for the safeguarding and defence' of its interests, and laid down that the two governments would consult each other on 'any matters affecting in common their special interests in Manchuria'. The treaty of July 1907 laid down a line of demarcation between the two spheres in Eastern Manchuria, and a further secret convention, signed on 8 July 1912, extended the line to Western Manchuria and Mongolia.[1]

On 23 August 1910 the Japanese government formally announced the incorporation of Korea in the Japanese empire. A year later the Chinese Revolution gave the Russian government a chance to act in Mongolia. The Mongols, a pastoral Buddhist people numbering about 3,000,000, organized in tribes under hereditary princes, disliked the Chinese traders who lived in their few towns, and resented the growing influx of Chinese peasant settlers into Mongolia. Plans to extend the Chinese railway system into Mongolia were viewed with great alarm. These plans also threatened the small but growing trade from Siberia. This trade from the north was likely to be overwhelmed by an influx not only of Chinese but also of west-

[1] The texts of these treaties are given as appendixes in E. B. Price, *The Russo-Japanese Treaties of 1907–1916*, Baltimore, 1933.

European goods from the south. The overthrow of the Chinese dynasty in 1911 by the republicans provided an opportunity to the Mongols to break away. A Mongol delegation visited St. Petersburg to ask for Russian protection against China. The Foreign Minister was reluctant to become involved, but Stolypin personally received the delegates. Sazonov[1] gave his consent to the delivery of Russian arms from the Irkutsk military district. In November 1911 the Mongols revolted against China, and Outer Mongolia was soon clear of Chinese forces. The Buddhist religious leader, the Hutukhta, was proclaimed the ruler of independent Outer Mongolia in December 1912.

The new state became in fact a Russian protectorate. A Russo-Mongolian treaty of November 1912 confirmed various Russian financial and commercial privileges, including preference for imports from Siberia, permission for Russian subjects to acquire land in Mongolia, and the foundation of a Russo-Mongolian Bank in Urga, the new capital. Russia promised armed assistance in the event of Chinese attempts at reconquest, and the Mongolian government undertook to conclude no treaty with a foreign Power without previous Russian approval.[2]

In November 1913 the Chinese government of Yuan Shih-kai concluded an agreement with Russia, which upheld the principle of Chinese sovereignty in Mongolia, but recognized its autonomy. This was a face-saving device, which did not affect the substance of Russian domination. The Japanese government was perfectly willing to see the Russians established in Mongolia: this was in accordance with the division of spheres of influence under the treaties of 1907–12. The British government could also hardly object, as it had profited from the weakness of China after 1911 to encourage Tibetan aspirations to independence. A separate Anglo-Tibetan agreement of July 1914, which was not recognized by China, had provided for British military instructors and mining prospectors to go to Lhasa, and Britain in fact treated Tibet as a state separate from China.

[1] S. D. Sazonov (1866–1927) succeeded Izvolsky as foreign minister in 1901. Most of his previous career had been spent in diplomatic posts in western Europe.

[2] On these events see documents and commentary in *Krasny Arkhiv*, no. 37 (1929), pp. 3–68.

Russo-Japanese co-operation extended also to common resistance to the attempts of other Powers, especially the United States, to trade or to seek concessions in the northern provinces of China. In 1910 Russia and Japan demanded the right to be included in a group of American, British, French, and German banks which had been formed to offer credits to the Chinese government for industrial development in Manchuria. France and Britain were obliged for political reasons to support this claim. The six-Power consortium thus formed was obstructed by the Russians and Japanese. When Yuan Shih-kai had asserted his authority in China, after the brief revolutionary period of disorder in 1911–12, he concluded a loan agreement with the consortium. Russian and Japanese pressure, however, succeeded in excluding all revenues from Manchuria, Mongolia, or Chinese Turkestan from the securities offered for the loan. On 18 March 1913 the newly elected President Woodrow Wilson withdrew government support from the American banks belonging to the consortium, on the ground that the terms of the agreement with Yuan were not compatible with Chinese independence. The American banks then withdrew, and the consortium broke up in 1914. The relations of Britain with the United States were embarrassed by the behaviour in this affair of Britain's ally Japan and her new friend Russia.[1]

Russia, Germany, and Sweden

Russia concluded agreements with Germany on two important problems during these years.

One was German economic penetration in the direction of the Persian Gulf. The main instrument of this penetration was the projected Berlin-Baghdad Railway. At first the enterprise had had substantial French participation, and several attempts had been made to interest British capital as well, but both the French and the British governments in the end decided not to encourage their subjects to take part. German influence increased in Turkey. The Turkish Revolution of 1908 looked at first as if it would be a set-back for Germany, since the former

[1] These problems are discussed at some length in E. H. Zabriskie, *American-Russian Rivalry in the Far East: a Study in Diplomacy and Power Politics 1875–1914*, Philadelphia, 1946.

Sultan Abdul Hamid had inclined to Germany, and his successors, the Young Turks, hoped, as democrats, to receive French or British support. But British support did not go beyond vague expressions of sympathy, and both in Britain and in France there was more interest in the Christian peoples of the Balkans than in the Turks. The British, French, and Russian governments were alike in their hostility to any form of Moslem nationalism, whether Arabic, Turkish, or Pan-Islamic, whereas Germany had no reason to fear any of these. German bankers were more willing to give loans to Turkey than French or British. For all these reasons German influence was soon re-established in Turkey after the revolution.

The Russian government was, however, anxious not needlessly to antagonize Germany, and was prepared to recognize German interests in the Asiatic provinces of Turkey. In November 1910 a Russo-German Convention was signed at Potsdam. The Germans recognized the predominance of Russian interests in the part of Persia recognized as a Russian zone by the Anglo-Russian Convention. Russia withdrew all opposition to the Baghdad Railway. The Russian government undertook to build a railway from Tehran to Khanikin, on the Persian-Turkish frontier, which would provide a link with the Baghdad Railway and assist German trade in western and northern Persia. If Russian subjects were not able to build this railway, German subjects might later apply for the concession.

The second area concerning which agreement was achieved between Germany and Russia was the Baltic. The Russian government had long wished to abolish the provision of the 1856 Treaty of Paris by which the Åland Islands, which formed part of Finland and dominated the entrance to the Gulfs of Finland and Bothnia, were to be demilitarized. The opportunity came in 1905, when Norway separated from Sweden, and was guaranteed by the Great Powers. The Swedish government proposed a multilateral guarantee by the Powers of the *status quo*. The Russian government felt that this was the time to change the status of the Åland Islands. In August 1907, at a meeting of William II and Nicholas II at Swinemünde, Izvolsky suggested to Bülow a secret Russo-German agreement to guarantee the Baltic *status quo* and to end the demilitarization of the Åland Islands. This was signed in St. Petersburg in

October 1907. However, the British and French governments learned of the protocol, and in order to allay their suspicions the Russian government decided to make a public treaty between Germany, Denmark, Sweden, and Russia. This was signed on 23 April 1908. As a result of Swedish objections to a specific abrogation of the demilitarization of the Åland Islands, a vaguely worded protocol was added to the treaty which could be interpreted by the Russians as entitling them to exercise full sovereignty over the islands, and by the Swedes as signifying that there would be no change.[1]

Relations between Sweden and Russia in these years were correct but hardly friendly. The struggle of the Finns against the russification policy of Stolypin aroused public feeling against Russia in Sweden. But essentially the security of the Baltic depended not on the wishes of the Scandinavian peoples but on the state of Russo-German relations. The Baltic sea route was of great importance to the Russian economy, especially for imports. It was controlled by the Danish Straits. But there was nothing that Russia could do to ensure passage through these Straits. If Germany was her ally, then she could use them even in wartime, but if Germany was her enemy she would be powerless. This is why the Baltic Straits played so small a part in Russian diplomatic history compared with the Black Sea Straits.

Russia, Austria, and the Slavs

The first decade of the twentieth century was a period of unrest among the smaller Slav nations.

The Macedonian Slavs were still under Ottoman rule. The neighbouring Slav states, Serbia and Bulgaria, not only hoped for the final collapse of Ottoman rule in Europe but competed with each other, and with Greece, for the allegiance of the Macedonian Christians, and the three states had territorial ambitions which were not mutually compatible.

In Austria-Hungary there was a whole host of national problems, mostly involving Slav nations, The Czechs sought not only greater self-government for their nation but complete

[1] For details see Baron M. von Taube, *Der großen Katastrophe entgegen* (Leipzig, 1937), ch. 2.

supremacy in the historic lands of Bohemia and Moravia, a third of whose population was German. In northern Hungary the Slovaks were resisting Magyar nationalism with increasing energy, some looking towards association with the Czechs, others hoping for complete Slovak independence. In Galicia the Poles, though reasonably content with their position under Habsburg rule, still hoped for the restoration of a united independent Poland, while the Ukrainians were divided between those who hoped for an Ukrainian independent state, to include the Russian Ukraine, and those who simply wished to be incorporated, as 'Little Russians', in the Russian empire. In south-western Austria the Slovenes of the eastern Alps were conducting a fierce struggle, in the schools and at the lower levels of the administration, against both German and Italian influence. The Croats of Austrian-ruled Dalmatia and Magyar-ruled Croatia wished to be united, but they were divided in turn between those who proclaimed an exclusive Croatian nationhood and those who wished to co-operate with the Serbs in a wider south Slav—or Yugoslav—unity. Further south, in Bosnia the Serbian community, a relative majority of the population, passionately desired union with the kingdom of Serbia, while the Moslems sought restoration of Turkish rule and the Croats an exclusive association with Croatia. Southern Hungary had a vigorous Serbian population, which also sought union with Belgrade, and in north-eastern Hungary there was a Slav population, the most backward in the whole monarchy, whose speech was some sort of Russian dialect, and whose politically conscious minority was divided between Ukrainian and Russian nationalism. Finally, in Hungarian Transylvania and Austrian Bukovina the largest group were the Roumanians, who were becoming increasingly aware of the clash between two loyalties—to the monarchy and to the neighbouring kingdom of Roumania—and increasingly inclined to prefer the second.

In Russia these years, with a comparatively free press and with public debates in the Duma, brought greater public interest in foreign policy in general, and in the affairs of the Slav peoples of neighbouring states in particular.

The extreme right, the heirs to the Russo-Pan-Slav imperialism of the 1870's and 1880's, were concerned chiefly with the

Straits and with the Orthodox Bulgarians and Serbs who lived nearest to them. They were also interested in Eastern Galicia. In their view Russia should, sooner or later, annex this region. This would not only reassert the rights of the Russian Tsar over the last unredeemed portion of the 'Russian land', but would also put an end to the seditious activities directed from Lwów against the empire by 'Little Russian separatists' supported by sinister German or Austrian agencies.

The Octobrists had a wider interest in the Slav world. While the right thought simply in terms of annexing new territories to Russia, the Octobrists were more inclined to think of other Slav peoples as brothers, even as equals, and sympathized also with those Slav peoples who were not Orthodox. The same point of view was to be found among the Kadets, though most of the leading members of this party were less interested in foreign than in internal policy. The exception was Milyukov himself, who had for some years held a chair at the University of Sofia, was well informed on Balkan affairs, and had friends among the Austrian Slavs as well. The revolutionary left was not on the whole interested in foreign policy, and was understandably suspicious of any expansionist tendencies of the Russian government or its supporters. Nevertheless, contact with revolutionaries in the Balkans and in Austria had caused individual SR's and Marxists to learn something about Slav affairs.

In these years there emerged for a short time a movement known as Neo-Slavism. This was a more liberal version of the earlier Pan-Slavism. It originated with the Austrian Slavs. The ideal of a federal republic of Slav peoples was clearly not practicable. Incorporation in Russia was not an attractive prospect to most Slavs, quite apart from the fact that it could only be brought about by war. The aim of the Neo-Slavs was more moderate, though it too proved unrealistic. It was to reorganize the monarchy in such a way as to end magyarization and to give the Slavs and Roumanians a position of real equality with the Germans and Hungarians, and at the same time to associate the monarchy with Russia. The Neo-Slavs argued that Austria should regard itself, not as the second German Power in Europe but as the second Slav Power. The chief exponents of these views were the Pole Roman Dmowski and the Czech Karel Kramář. In 1908 Kramář visited St. Petersburg, and was received by Stolypin. In July 1908 a Slav conference was held in Prague. Among those who attended were the radical Czech professor, T. G. Masaryk, and the Croatian peasant leader, Stepan Radić. Among the Russians were the Octobrist Stakhovich and the right-wing Nationalist Count Bobrinsky, an advocate of the annexation of Eastern Galicia. The Poles included Dmowski. There was talk of the need for Russo-Polish reconciliation. A second conference was held in 1909 in St. Petersburg, at which less attention was paid to the Polish question. A third, which called itself a congress, was held in Sofia in 1910. It was mainly concerned with Balkan problems, especially with Serbo-Bulgarian rivalry.

The Balkan crises of the years 1908–14 showed that the Slav world was hopelessly divided, and the Neo-Slav movement disintegrated. While it had existed, the only real interest of the Russian government in it had been to exploit it for the promotion of Russian aims in the Balkans.

The Balkans and the Great Powers, 1908–1914

In 1906 Baron Aehrenthal was appointed Austrian foreign minister. He had formerly served as ambassador in St. Petersburg, and was thought to be friendly to Russia. In January 1908, however, he annoyed the Russian government by obtaining Turkish permission to build a railway through the *sandjak* of Novi Bazar without previously consulting the Russians. Worse was soon to come.

The Turkish Revolution of 25 July 1908 cast doubt over the Austrian position in Bosnia and Hercegovina. The new Turkish leaders, reformers, and democrats, were likely to argue that, as they were about to make the Ottoman empire a progressive state, the original reasons for placing the two provinces under the rule of a European Power were no longer valid, and they should be restored to them. But for strategic and economic reasons the Austrian government wished to keep Bosnia and Hercegovina. The prince of Bulgaria might also have to face some attempt by the new Turkish rulers to reassert their shadowy sovereignty over Bulgaria. Aehrenthal therefore decided formally to annex the two provinces, and to co-ordinate this action with a declaration of complete independence by Bulgaria. Before doing this he met the Russian foreign minister at the castle of Buchlau in Moravia on 15–16 September.

Russia had already consented to annexation in 1881,[1] but Izvolsky wished, as compensation for this Austrian acquisition, to obtain a revision of the Straits Conventions which would permit Russia to bring warships out of the Black Sea if she were at war but Turkey was not. The Austrian and Russian versions of what was agreed at Buchlau disagreed. Izvolsky believed that he had received Aehrenthal's consent both to a revision of the Straits convention and to the convocation of a formal international conference to decide the new arrangements in the Balkans.

Izvolsky proceeded to London, where he found agreement with his proposal to call an international conference, but opposition to his wishes about the Straits, not so much because the British government objected to Russian aims as because it did not wish to weaken a new government in Constantinople which it expected would be more friendly to Britain, and less subject to German influence, than its predecessor. At the same time the Austrians informed Izvolsky that they would be willing to attend a conference only after the annexation of Bosnia had been agreed. The annexation was of course intensely unpopular in Serbia, where Russian influence was now strong. The Powers vaguely agreed that Serbia should be compensated for the annexation, but the British government objected to such compensation being granted at the expense of Turkey, and Germany insisted that it should not be at the expense of any Austrian territory. The Serbian government attempted to combine with Turkey in opposition to Austrian plans, but the Turks were only interested in a Serbian alliance if it was directed against Bulgaria, which did not interest the Serbs. The Turkish government therefore accepted the action of the Austrians and the Bulgarians, and received some money compensation from each of them.

The situation at the beginning of 1909 was thus that Serbia was denied any compensation, and that Russian prestige was damaged by failure either to obtain its wishes in the Straits or to

[1] See above p. 459.

arrange for an international conference capable of any serious business. To call a conference which would merely endorse the Austrian and Bulgarian actions, and give no satisfaction to either Russia or Serbia, would of course have been a waste of time. Thus at the beginning of 1909 Russia had to choose between swallowing her pride and abandoning Serbia, or supporting Serbian claims and her own demand for a genuine conference, at the risk of a general war. The Russian government decided that Russia was not ready for war, and advised the Serbs to yield. In a note to the Powers of 10 March the Serbian government renounced any claims to compensation from Austria.

But Aehrenthal demanded, in addition to this, a humiliating declaration from Serbia that she 'had decided for the future to fulfil her obligations as a good neighbour towards the monarchy', and the German government insisted that Russia should put pressure on Serbia to this effect. The Russian Council of Ministers on 13 and 20 March discussed the crisis, and decided that Russia must yield. Izvolsky replied to the German note on 20 March in vague terms, arguing that though Russia accepted the German proposal, this 'does not exclude the necessity of a European conference'. This was not enough for the German government, which had now decided to humiliate Russia. The German reply of 21 March demanded 'a precise answer, yes or no'. Any 'evasive, conditional, or unclear answer' would be considered a refusal, in which case 'things would take their course' and Russia would bear the responsibility. Russia and Serbia surrendered, and the Serbs gave the assurance demanded by Austria.

Relations between Russia and Austria were now worse than they had been since the Crimean War, and the German action had caused extreme bitterness. It became the aim of Russian diplomacy to organize all available forces against Austrian influence in the Balkans.

In October 1909 a Russo-Italian agreement was made on the occasion of a meeting between Nicholas II and Victor Emanuel at Racconigi. This stated that if there were any change in the Balkan Peninsula, the two Powers would support the application of the principle of nationality, to the exclusion of any single Power from a dominant position, and neither would conclude a new agreement on the Balkans without consulting the other. Italy was of course still a member of the Triple Alliance, but relations with Austria had long been strained in connexion with Italian claims to Trento and Trieste. The Italian government was also busily preparing to attack Turkey, in order to acquire Libya. It had already obtained the consent not only of the Triple Alliance but also of the French and British to its Libyan plans. At Racconigi the Russians too gave their approval, and in return the Italians promised 'benevolent consideration' to Russian aims in the Straits.

Russian diplomacy also set to work to build an anti-Austrian block among the Balkan states. The original aim was to bind together Serbia, Bulgaria, and Turkey. But it soon became clear that the the only common interest of Serbia and Bulgaria was in opposition to Turkey. As for the Turks, though their relations with Russia at this time were reasonably good, they had no wish to be involved in any anti-Austrian combination. Thus the Russian government was drawn reluctantly into support of a Balkan alliance directed against Turkey. This was of course entirely to the liking of the Pan-Slavs and of the proponents of Russian expansion to the Straits. Sazonov was rather moderate in his aims. The Russian minister in Belgrade, N. G. Hartvig, however, was an enthusiast, who referred, for instance, in a memorandum of 5 November 1911, to Russia's task 'to stand with firm foot on the shores of the Bosphorus, at the gate of entry to the Russian Lake'.[1]

The Italo-Turkish war of 1911 encouraged the Balkan states to combine against Turkey. A Serbo-Bulgarian alliance was signed on 14 March 1912 and a Greek-Bulgarian alliance on 29 May 1912. The Russian government did not inform its French ally of the diplomatic preparations for these alliances, but Sazonov showed the texts to the French prime minister, Raymond Poincaré, when he visited St. Petersburg in August 1912. Poincaré was alarmed by them, and thought that French public opinion would be unwilling to go to war for Balkan interests. However, if a Balkan crisis led to German intervention, France would act. Poincaré confirmed this in conversation with Izvolsky, now serving as Russian ambassador in Paris, a few weeks later. 'If conflict with Austria brought intervention

[1] *Krasny Arkhiv*, no. 8 (1925), pp. 45–48.

by Germany, France would fulfil her obligations.' This was in fact an important extension of the Franco-Russian Alliance.[1]

The Balkan allies, which also included Montenegro, attacked Turkey in October 1912, and their armies were highly successful. The first Great Power crisis occurred in November, when it seemed possible that the Serbs might advance to the Adriatic coast in Albania. Austria was determined to prevent Serbia having access to the sea. During November the Russian and Austrian forces in Poland were increased. As a result of intervention by the Powers, an armistice was signed between the Balkan allies and Turkey on 3 December, and a conference of ambassadors met in London. It agreed that Serbia should be granted facilities for commerce in an Albanian port, to be linked with Serbia by a new railway under international control, but that she should not expand territorially in this direction. In March 1913 the Russian and Austrian forces began to demobilize. The essential fact was that in this crisis Russia and Serbia had, as in 1909, surrendered to Austrian demands.

Russia made a further concession in April 1913 when she reluctantly joined the other Powers in pressing the Montenegrins, who had at last captured the Albanian town of Scutari, not to annex it to Montenegro but to surrender it to the Powers. It was later included in the new state of Albania. The demand of Roumania for territorial compensation from Bulgaria was settled by a convention signed in St. Petersburg on 8 May 1913. Roumania received only the Danube fortress city of Silistria.

The Serbs, Bulgarians, and Greeks were unable to agree as to the division of the large territories in Macedonia and Thrace ceded by Turkey at the Treaty of London of 30 May 1913, which concluded the conference of ambassadors. The Russian government invoked a provision of the Serbo-Bulgarian Alliance of March 1912 that the Russian emperor should arbitrate. The Serbs, who had occupied most of Macedonia in the course of the war against the Turks, intended to keep what they had, and failed to reply to Sazonov's demand of

[1] This phrase is in Izvolsky's report of 12 Sept. 1912 to Sazonov, printed in *Der diplomatische Schriftwechsel Izwolskis 1910–1914* (Berlin, 1925), vol. ii, no. 429, p. 251. For a discussion of the implications of Poincaré's attitude see Taylor, op. cit., pp. 486–9.

19 June that they should unconditionally accept the Tsar's decision. The Bulgarians accepted, but with the insulting proviso that the Tsar must give this decision within a week. This so infuriated Sazonov that he formally repudiated all Russia's obligations to Bulgaria, including the military convention of 1902.[1] This did not bring the Bulgarians to heel: on the contrary, it encouraged them to take the law into their own hands. On 28 June the Bulgarian army attacked the Serbian and Greek forces without declaration of war.

The Bulgarian action might have succeeded if it could have received Austrian support. This was, however, made impossible by the attitude of Roumania. The Roumanians were dissatisfied with the compensation they had received, and alarmed at the prospect of still further gains by Bulgaria. They therefore determined to seize the southern Dobrudja, and invaded Bulgaria. If Austria had helped Bulgaria against Serbia, she would have found herself at war on the opposite side to her own ally Roumania. If it had depended on the Austrians alone, they probably would not have let this deter them. But Austria's ally Germany considered it extremely important that Roumania should remain associated with the Triple Alliance, and insisted that Austria should not take an anti-Roumanian action. Austria therefore had to let things take their course. The combined forces of Serbia, Greece, and Roumania were too much for the Bulgarians, and the Turks even took the opportunity to attack independently and recapture Adrianople.

These events inevitably led to the fall of the Russophil party in Bulgaria, which now became more closely associated than ever with Austria. On the other hand Russia's relations with Roumania improved. Roumanian hostility to Austria continued to grow, as the Hungarian government steadfastly refused to make any concessions to the Roumanians of Transylvania, and Vienna was either unwilling or unable to make the Budapest leaders change their policy. At the same time Roumanian hostility to Russia was reduced by the evidence of ever closer co-operation between Russia and France, which was of all the Powers the most loved and trusted in Roumania. On 1 June 1914 Nicholas II paid a visit to Constanţa, and Sazonov next day accompanied the Roumanian prime minister,

[1] See above p. 574.

Ionel Brătianu, on a drive across the frontier into Transylvania, to the delight of the local Roumanian population and the understandable rage of the Budapest newspapers.

A serious Russo-German crisis developed in the autumn of 1913. The German government had accepted a Turkish request for a German military mission to train the Turkish army. This had been agreed by the Russian and other European governments. The Turkish navy was already being advised by a British mission, and the Turkish gendarmerie by a French. But the head of the German advisory mission, General Liman von Sanders, was appointed commander of the military district of Constantinople. This caused extreme alarm in St. Petersburg. In 1908 Russian hopes of a revision of the Straits Convention had been frustrated, but now there was a prospect of the same Straits being placed in German hands, of the key to Russia's back door being held in Berlin. Russian protests were supported by France and Britain. In January 1914 the crisis was solved by promoting Liman to field-marshal, a rank too senior to permit him to hold a territorial command. But Russian distrust of German intentions remained.

In 1914 Russia was firmly allied to France, and her relations with Britain were closer than they had been since the wars against Napoleon. But it would be wrong to suppose that the Russian political class—ministers, high officials, diplomats, journalists, or members of the Duma—was overwhelmingly anti-German. The Russian right generally preferred Germany to the Western Powers. In their view French and British influence could only strengthen the pernicious forces of democracy. Far better to maintain the principles of autocracy, in association with the German monarchy, against Western Jewish liberalism. The arguments for a German orientation were clearly expressed in a memorandum by the former minister of the interior, P. N. Durnovo, written in February 1914. It maintained that Anglo-German rivalry was the most important existing conflict in the world, and that Russia should keep out of it. The recent support given by Germany to the anti-Russian policies of Austria was explained by German resentment of Russia's association with Britain. 'The vital interests of Russia and Germany are nowhere in conflict. . . . The future of Germany is on the seas, where for Russia, essentially the most continental of all the Great Powers, there are no interests at all.'[1]

Durnovo's arguments essentially refer back to the traditional relationship of Russia and Prussia, based on the mutual respect and sympathy of two monarchies and two landowning classes. But the Germany of 1914 was not traditional Prussia. The Prussian Junkers were still an important agricultural lobby, and still provided the greater part of the German officer corps, but their influence on foreign policy was dwindling. It was being replaced by a heterogeneous middle class, composed of business men, bureaucrats, professors, and journalists, socially and nationally unsure of themselves, full of energy and ability, believing that neither their nation nor their class had yet achieved the power or the status to which they were entitled, reaching out for opportunities in every direction, not stopping to consider the consequences of their action. This restless element, whose mentality was well reflected, despite his impeccably aristocratic Hohenzollern origin, by William II himself, was just as likely to stumble into conflict with Russia in Turkey as with Britain in the North Sea, just as likely to feel enthusiasm for the anti-Slav slogans of demagogues in Vienna or Budapest as for the dreams of *Weltmacht* of Hamburg shipbuilders.

Even so, the war of 1914 was not inevitable. Things could have been different. The crisis might have been postponed for many years, while Russia's economic and military strength grew. The Austro-Russian conflict might have become less bitter, as had been the case for twenty years after 1887. It is just conceivable even that, after the death of Franz Joseph, the monarchy might have been reorganized in some manner more acceptable to its citizens, without provoking either civil or international war.

But none of these things happened. Instead, Gavrilo Prinsip killed Archduke Franz Ferdinand in Sarajevo on 28 June 1914, and the Austrian government decided to take the chance to destroy Serbia. Russia could abandon the Serbs for the third time in five years, accept a status of permanent inferiority to the two German Powers and raise serious doubts in the minds of the

[1] Full text in English in F. A. Golder, *Documents on Russian History 1914–1917* (New York, 1927), pp. 3–24.

French whether she was worth having as an ally, or she could go to war. Judged by the conventional wisdom of international diplomacy in 1914, her decision to go to war was fully justified. Her leaders could hardly foresee the consequences of their decision to all the people of Europe. They did not even foresee that they would destroy the Russian monarchy.

XX

THE END OF THE MONARCHY

The First World War

THE outbreak of war was greeted at least by the articulate portion of the Russian people with patriotic enthusiasm. One expression of this idealist mood was the prohibition of the sale of alcohol, introduced at the end of July and confirmed by a decree of 22 August. This deprived the government of one of its main sources of revenue, and imposed on Russian soldier and civilian alike an unaccustomed form of self-denial. It was, however, accepted at first as both a contribution to the efficiency of the war effort and an assertion of the high moral purpose of the nation.

The zemstvos and city councils were quick to engage in patriotic activities. The board of the Moscow zemstvo called for the formation of an All-Russian Union of Zemstvos for the Relief of the Sick and Wounded. A conference was held in Moscow of the representatives of thirty-five provincial zemstvos: the zemstvo of Kursk, controlled by men of the extreme right, was alone in its refusal to attend. The conference set up the proposed union, which was to have a central committee of ten persons and a conference of two representatives from each member zemstvo, one of these to be elected by the provincial zemstvo assembly, the other by the provincial board. Prince G. E. Lvov was elected chairman. On 25 August the Tsar gave his approval for the formation of the union. The first initiative from the cities was a conference of representatives of cities of Central Russia in Moscow. On 8 and 9 August there was a conference of mayors, from thirty-six provincial capitals and nine *uezd* centres, also in Moscow. As a result of this meeting, application was made to the government for the formation of an All-Russian Union of Cities, and this was authorized on 16 August.

A law of 16 July 1914 laid down that in military zones, whose limits were stated and were modified from time to time, the military commanders should have complete supremacy over civil authorities. This law was later to cause tremendous administrative confusion. Any arrogant and ignorant junior officer could, and often did, throw the economy of a whole region into disorder for weeks on end by some arbitrary order or prohibition. Within the military zones, which stretched well back from the fighting fronts, the care of sick and wounded was to be handled exclusively by the Red Cross. The Zemstvo and Cities Unions were allowed to function only outside the military zones. In practice this distinction could not easily be enforced, and after some months it was ignored.

The Duma was summoned on 8 August for a single day's session, to vote war credits and to sanction the issue of banknotes and the increase of taxes. The Trudoviks and Social Democrats abstained when the war credits were voted. The two Social Democratic groups put forward a resolution condemning the war and the social order which had produced it. The Bolsheviks, however, urged the Russian proletariat to fight against its own government rather than against the official enemy. As a result, five Bolshevik members of the Duma were arrested in November 1914, and in February 1915 they were sentenced to deportation to eastern Siberia.

The workers in the factories and mines were affected by the patriotic enthusiasm which swept the nation at the outbreak of war. Socialist leaders, except for the Bolsheviks, confined themselves to verbal opposition. Among the exiles, a minority of Mensheviks, led by Potresov, went so far as to state that they would prefer the defeat of Germany. The majority, represented by the Menshevik Secretariat in Exile, were equally opposed to all belligerent governments. Lenin's view, however, was that defeat of Russia would be a lesser evil than its victory. He insisted on a breach with the Second International, whose main parties he considered had dishonoured themselves by voting war credits to their respective governments.[1]

The estimated strength of the Russian army at the outbreak of war was 1,423,000. The reserve army, whose mobilization was set in motion at once, amounted to 3,115,000. In addition

[1] In a general history of Russia there can be no place for a discussion of the various arguments for and against the Second International and the creation of a Third, or of the international socialist conferences held at Zimmerwald (1915) and Kienthal (1916), on all of which there is a large and easily accessible literature in west European languages and in Russian.

to this were called up 1,300,000 men from the first-class territorial army (of whom about 400,000 had previously served in the active army) and the reserve, and 715,000 recruits. Thus by the end of December 1914 6,553,000 men had been mobilized.[1] To arm these men only 4,652,000 rifles were available. Another 278,000 were manufactured in Russian factories by the end of the year, and more were ordered abroad.[2] But already at the beginning of the war it was clear that there would before long be a serious shortage of arms.

The commander-in-chief of the Russian armed forces was the Grand Duke Nikolay Nikolayevich, and his chief of staff was General N. N. Yanushkevich. The main commands were the North-Western Front against Germany and the South-Western Front against Austria-Hungary. Apart from these the 6th Army was kept for the defence of the Baltic coast, and there were armies in the Caucasus and at Odessa, in case Turkey or Roumania should join the enemy.

The war began with the massive German attack through Belgium into France. The immediate need was to take the pressure off the French, and for this reason Russian forces invaded East Prussia in August. The army of the Niemen, under General P. K. Rennenkampf, attacked in the direction of Königsberg. The army of the Narew, under General A. V. Samsonov, attacked from Poland northwards. The two armies were separated from each other by the chain of the Masurian Lakes. On 22 August the German emperor appointed Field-Marshal Paul von Hindenburg as commander-in-chief in the east, and General Erich von Ludendorff as his chief of staff. The German commanders decided, at the risk of letting Rennenkampf advance westwards, to take some of their forces away from the north-eastern sector and concentrate them against Samsonov. At the same time two army corps were transferred from the Western Front. This substantially helped the French, and undoubtedly contributed to the victory in the Battle of the Marne. This was indeed the greatest single achievement, and forms the decisive historical justification, of the Franco-Russian Alliance.

[1] Lt.-Gen. N. N. Golovin, *The Russian Army in the World War* (New Haven, 1931), pp. 45–47.

[2] Ibid., p. 127.

On 27 August the German attack against Samsonov was launched. It lasted for three days, and resulted in the complete defeat of the Russians and the encirclement and capture of nearly 100,000 prisoners. Samsonov committed suicide. This great German victory became known as the Battle of Tannenberg, and German nationalists declared that it was a revenge for the other Battle of Tannenberg in 1410, when armies of Poles, Lithuanians, and White Russians had defeated the Teutonic Knights. Having smashed Samsonov's army, Hindenburg reassembled his forces to deal with Rennenkampf. The attack began on 4 September in the Masurian Lakes region and to the north of the lakes. By 13 September the Russian forces were driven eastwards out of German territory. This time there was no large-scale encirclement, but the Russians lost about 45,000 prisoners.[1]

In the south-west the Russian armies were more successful. Galicia was invaded, and the Austrian forces were obliged to retreat. Lwów, the capital of the province, was captured on 3 September. At this stage of the war the Poles in each of the empires supported their governments, though without enthusiasm. At the Duma meeting of 8 August Dmowski and all the Polish members declared their loyalty to Russia. Nikolay Nikolayevich issued a proclamation on the reunion of all Poles under the Russian emperor. Like Alexander I a hundred years earlier, he hoped to win Polish support by the prospect of unity, but there was no word of autonomy, still less of independence. The Central Powers had no more definite alternative. The Austrian foreign minister, Count Berchtold, toyed with the idea of uniting Russian Poland with Galicia and replacing the Dualism, which had prevailed in the Habsburg monarchy since the compromise of 1867 with Hungary, by a Trialism of Austria, Hungary, and Poland. Emperor Franz Joseph expressed mild sympathy for this idea, but it was opposed both by the Hungarian premier, Count Stephen Tisza, who disliked any increase in the Slav subjects of the monarchy, and by the German government, which could not fail to see in any such scheme an unsettling influence on the Poles of Prussia. The Poles of Galicia supported Austria's war effort, and Józef Piłsudski led into

[1] Ludendorff's account is in his book, *My War Memories, 1914–1918* (n.d.), pp. 41–72.

battle the Polish Legions, of Polish exiles from Russia, which he had been forming for some years on Austrian soil.

The Russian authorities were more concerned with the Ukrainian population of Eastern Galicia. The political trend which regarded itself as 'Little Russian', and wished to be incorporated in the Russian empire, was of course delighted with the Russian advance. Count G. A. Bobrinsky, the leading exponent in the Duma of the annexation of Eastern Galicia in the pre-war years, was appointed governor of the newly occupied territories. His authority was, however, diminished by the powers of the military command. These were arbitrarily and sometimes brutally exercised. General Yanushkevich ordered the deportation of large numbers of Galician Jews, and of communities of German peasants which had been settled in Galicia for a century or more. Russian rule soon became generally unpopular. The nationalist-minded section of the Ukrainian population were from the beginning hostile. Their leaders took refuge in Berlin, where they established a centre for propaganda directed equally against Russians and Poles.[1]

The Russian advance caused understandable alarm in Vienna and Budapest. Not only was nearly half Galicia lost, but the Russians had passed the crest of the Carpathians in Ruthenia, the north-eastern corner of the kingdom of Hungary. The inhabitants of this very backward land were Slavs closely akin to the Ukrainians of Galicia and Bukovina, whose national consciousness was hardly developed, but who already before the war had shown a certain pro-Russian inclination. Ruthenia was, however, of greater strategic than political importance. The prospect that the Russian armies would pour down from this height into the Danubian plain had to be taken seriously. The Austrian command appealed for help to its German ally. At the end of September the Germans attacked from Silesia. This did not, however, prevent the Russians from further advance in Galicia, and they also counter-attacked on to German territory in East Prussia north of the lakes. On 12 November another German offensive began in Poland, under

[1] Among them was Dmytro Donzow, whose ideas were an important source of the ideology of extreme Ukrainian nationalism between the world wars. His views at this time were expressed in his pamphlet *Die ukrainische Staatsidee und der Krieg gegen Rußland*, Berlin, 1915.

the command of General von Mackensen, from Thorn and Gnesen eastward and south-eastward. On 23 November Łódź was captured, and the Russians had to retire behind the rivers Bszura and Rawka, tributaries of the Vistula lying some fifty miles west of Warsaw. The Russian advance in East Prussia was stopped, and for the last month of the year the front was comparatively quiet.

Meanwhile, however, Russia had suffered a serious blow with the entry of Turkey into the war on the German side. The Turks of course regarded Russia as their main enemy, and in the event of her defeat by the Central Powers they might hope for gains at her expense as well as for the recovery of some of the territory lost in the Balkan Wars. At the end of July Enver Pasha opened discussions with the Germans, and on 2 August a secret treaty was signed. The Turks, however, insisted that they could not go to war at once, as they needed time to prepare themselves in the Caucasus and the Black Sea. The British government, distrusting Turkey, stopped the delivery of two dreadnoughts that were being built in Britain for the Turkish government. This action, and the entry of Britain into the war on 4 August, caused the Turks once more to hesitate. Their morale was raised again when the two German warships *Göeben* and *Breslau*, then in Mediterranean waters, were ordered by the German Admiralty to the Black Sea, and passed the Dardanelles on 11 August. However, the Battle of the Marne, and the uncertain attitude of Italy, still caused them to hesitate. For its part the British government did not give up hope of Turkish neutrality. When the Greek premier, Eleutheros Venizelos, offered to contribute 250,000 troops and the small but efficient Greek navy to the allies in a war against Turkey, Sir Edward Grey refused the offer. During October German pressure at Constantinople increased, and the Turkish government drifted towards war. The allies could only offer a guarantee of Turkish integrity, while the Central Powers could hold out hopes of territorial gain. In the Turkish Cabinet there was division and confusion, and it is still not clear when, or by whom, the decision to go to war was taken. On 29 October Turkish warships under a German admiral bombarded Odessa. On 31 October Turkey declared war on the allies.

Russia was now cut off from her allies by sea. Imports of

military supplies, and of raw materials for Russian industry, became extremely difficult, and this proved to be one of the main causes of Russia's ultimate downfall. Russia also had a new war front to defend, on the Caucasus. This tied down armies that were needed elsewhere. The overall military disadvantage was not compensated by the fact that the Russian army of the Caucasus won some fine victories.

In the Balkans the situation was for the time being not too bad. The Serbian army beat back the Austrian attack, and invaded Austrian territory in its turn, being welcomed by its fellow Serbs in Bosnia. Roumania and Bulgaria remained neutral. King Carol I of Roumania wished to implement the treaty of alliance with the Central Powers. The majority of the political leaders, however, regarded France as their chief friend, Austria as an enemy, and though none were pro-Russian they recognized that Russian-Roumanian relations had recently improved. The Crown Council held on 3 August 1914 therefore decided for neutrality. Bulgaria was still exhausted from the war of 1913. The Central Powers could offer the Bulgarians territory in Macedonia at the expense of Serbia. But Roumania and Turkey were also potential enemies, and the Bulgarian government did not wish to go to war with the Western Powers or with Russia, for which, despite Sazonov's decision of 1913, popular affection was still strong.

The effects of the war on the Russian economy were complex and contradictory. Peasant agriculture was little damaged. The agricultural labour force in peacetime was far in excess of the needs of production, and so the removal of the conscripts did not lead to a noticeable fall in output. The mobilization laws in any case provided that peasant holdings should not be denuded of labour, or peasant families deprived of support. Large estates were much more adversely affected. The supply of hired labour, necessary for their efficient working, was greatly reduced: 300,000 to 400,000 labourers were called up and not replaced. The result was that the area under cultivation on estates of noble landowners in European Russia fell from 21,800,000 *desyatin* in 1914 to 10,200,000 in 1915.[1] There was not at first any shortage of supplies. As Turkey's entry into

[1] A. N. Antsiferov, *Russian Agriculture during the War*, pp. 143–4.

the war had put an end to grain exports through the Black Sea, the quantities previously exported were available for the home market. Here the main consumer was the army. The rations received by the Russian peasant as a soldier were substantially greater than the amount he had to eat in peacetime, but in 1914 and 1915 enough food was produced and transported to feed both the army at the higher rate of consumption and the civilian population at the pre-war level.

Russian industry was quickly and seriously damaged. Not only was the Black Sea route cut off, but the Swedish government restricted movements of arms and munitions through Swedish territory as a reprisal for interference with Swedish sea-borne trade by the British blockade. Supplies had to be sent by Vladivostok or by Archangel. The industrial labour force was also dislocated by mobilization, and it was some time before steps were taken by the government to ensure the needs of the industrialists. Sudden new demands were also made on industry by the army, not only for arms and munitions but also for clothing and boots. The leather industry in particular was for a time quite unable to satisfy these demands.

The Union of Zemstvos and Union of Cities did their best to help with medical services and with supplies. By 1 October 1914 they had provided 103,635 hospital beds in the rear.[1] They also made great efforts to improve the conditions of transportation of wounded from the front, and to make sure that they were met and cared for at the right time and place. The zemstvos equipped special hospital trains of their own. At the end of 1914 they already had forty of these in operation. They also organized the production of linen, army tents, underclothing, and boots in small enterprises in different parts of the country, largely employing for this purpose the wives or female relatives of serving soldiers.

The central government also set up institutions to deal with the welfare of the soldiers and their dependants. On 11 August 1914 was created the supreme council for the care of soldiers' families and of families of the wounded and war dead. The empress was its president, two grandduchesses were vice-presidents and it included several high officials, besides some members of the Duma chosen not by the Duma itself but by the

[1] Polner, *Russian Local Government during the War*, p. 90.

empress. The committee of the Grand Duchess Tatyana for temporary relief to war sufferers, created on 14 September 1914, was concerned with refugees from the war-stricken areas. The Romanov Committee, which had been set up in 1913 on the third centenary of the dynasty as a philanthropic organization, devoted itself to the care of children of serving soldiers.

The year 1914, despite hardships and difficulties and despite the defeats of Tannenberg and the Masurian Lakes, had gone fairly well for Russia. The year 1915, however, brought military disaster and political crisis.

One of the main aims of the allies was to break through the Black Sea Straits, get Turkey out of the war and re-establish regular communications between Russia and the West. But this task was complicated by the fact that the Russian government included in its war aims the permanent control of the Straits by Russia. Inter-allied diplomacy in the winter of 1914–15 was concerned with the political and military aspects of this problem. On 14 November Grey informed Sazonov that the British government was willing that the question of the Straits and Constantinople should be settled in accordance with the desires of Russia. At this time the Tsar's idea was that Constantinople itself should be an internationally controlled city, but that Russia should possess its immediate hinterland, and have a common frontier with Bulgaria, which should acquire Adrianople and most of eastern Thrace. Meanwhile the British government had decided to try a naval attack on Gallipoli. In the second half of February the attack was made, the Turkish outer forts were silenced but the British force did not get through the narrows.

At this stage the Greek government renewed its offer to the allies of military help, to consist of an army corps of three divisions. The British government welcomed the offer. If an Anglo-Greek army approached Constantinople, it was reasonable to hope that Bulgaria would join the allies in order to get a share of the spoils and recover some of what she had lost in 1913. In this case the threat to Serbia from the east would be removed, and Roumania, no longer obliged to fear for her southern frontier, might perhaps be persuaded to attack Austria. But the Russian government refused. The presence of

Greeks in the neighbourhood of the Straits was unacceptable, for the popular idea of many Greeks that Constantinople should be the capital of a new Greek empire, was well known in St. Petersburg. Sazonov declared that Greek participation in the action against the Straits was something to which the Tsar 'could not in any circumstances consent'. In fact, it was more important that Constantinople should be controlled by Russia after victory than that the victory should be expedited by military operations which Greek action could have helped to win. Russia was to pay dearly for this obstinacy.

In the face of the Russian attitude the Western Powers could not persist. A suggestion by the French government that the Greek army should be used not in Thrace but as a reinforcement to the Serbs against Austria, was reluctantly accepted by Venizelos but refused by King Constantine, who understandably felt that the risks to Greece would be out of proportion to any gains that she could expect. On 4 March 1915 the Russian government put forward its proposals on the Straits question. Russia was to have the city itself, together with the European shore of the Straits and Marmora back to the Enos–Midia line and the Asiatic shore as far as Izmit and the Sakarya river, together with the islands in the Marmara and the islands of Imbros and Tenedos in the Aegean. On 8 March the French government instucted its ambassador in St. Petersburg to accept these terms, and on 12 March the British government did likewise.[1] In return for British consent, the Russian government agreed that the British zone of influence in Persia should be enlarged to include the whole neutral zone of the 1907 convention.

This was apparently a great victory for Russian diplomacy. But the prize still had to be won. As the British naval action against the Straits had failed, it was decided that the enterprise could only be carried out by land forces. On 25 April the expeditionary force, composed of British, Australian, and New Zealand troops, began to disembark. The Turkish forces were in a desperate situation, but were able to hold off the attack until their positions had been strengthened and reinforcements

[1] These documents are in *Documents diplomatiques secrets russes 1914–1917* (Paris, 1928), pp. 252–7. They are French translations of the collection *Konstantinopol i Prolivy*, published by the Soviet government, Moscow, 1926.

received. In August the allies received large reinforcements, but their new attack at Suvla Bay was repelled. From this time there was little hope of success, though the allied armies were not evacuated until January 1916.

The allied failure in the Dardanelles decided Bulgaria to enter the war on the German side. During 1915 both sides wooed the strategically placed Balkan state. The Austrians on 23 May 1915 promised Bulgaria the part of Macedonia taken by Serbia in 1913 in return for her mere neutrality. The allies had less to offer, namely the recovery of Adrianople and Thrace up to the Enos–Midia line, but required in return that Bulgaria should attack Turkey. They also held out vague hopes that, if Serbia acquired Bosnia and a secure access to the Adriatic from a defeated Austria, she might be persuaded to cede some of Macedonia to Bulgaria, and that, if Greece acquired territory in Asia Minor, she might be persuaded to cede Kavalla. The Serbian government, however, objected to being pressed by its allies to yield territory to a still neutral state when it was in a desperate military situation and was receiving very little help. Prime Minister Nikola Pašić refused. The Bulgarians hesitated during the early summer, but the Battle of Suvla Bay in August was decisive. A Bulgarian-Turkish treaty of 3 September recognized that the lower course of the river Maritsa should be the frontier between the two countries. On 6 September 1915 Bulgaria entered a military alliance with Germany and Austria-Hungary. Bulgaria was to receive Serbian Macedonia up to the Kachanik pass and the river Morava, and if either Greece or Roumania joined the allies she was also to receive the territory taken by either or both of them in 1913. On 5 October 1915 Bulgaria declared war on the allied Powers.

Serbia had an alliance with Greece for the event of an attack by Bulgaria. The allies suggested that they should be allowed to land troops at Salonica in order to help Serbia. The Greek government agreed to this, and the forces landed on 5 October. Greek forces did not, however, join the allies, and the pro-allied Venizelos was dismissed by the king of Greece. At the end of October the allied army of 80,000, under the French General Sarrail, attacked northwards, but it was held by the Bulgarians. Meanwhile the Serbs, surrounded on three sides, were overwhelmed. The remnant of their brave army retreated through

Albania and was evacuated on British and French ships. The British government at this stage wished to evacuate Salonica, but the French insisted that this subsidiary front be maintained. The allies therefore remained, and were reinforced by the Serbian army when it had been re-formed and re-equipped.

Apart from the small foothold at Salonica, the allies had lost the whole Balkan Peninsula, and the Straits remained firmly barred against all supplies to Russia. Meanwhile the main Russian armies had suffered disaster.

At the beginning of 1915 the situation was still good. A German offensive in the Masurian Lakes area on 8 February 1915 began with some success in the Augustovo sector, but it was held by the Russians, and no important gain was secured. In Galicia the Russians besieged the important Austrian fortress of Przemysl on the river San, and on 22 March captured it.

Since the outbreak of the war, both sides had been negotiating with Italy. By the spring of 1915 it appeared likely that Italy would not only not fulfil her obligations to her allies of the Triple Alliance, but would come in on the allied side against the Central Powers. This was expected to place Austria in a desperate situation. It became a matter of urgency to deal Austria's other antagonist, Russia, a crippling blow before Italy went to war. It was therefore decided to attempt a massive break-through in the Russian front at Gorlice. The well-prepared offensive was launched on 2 May 1915 by von Mackensen's forces, consisting of the 4th Austrian and 11th German Armies. It was completely successful. Within four days the Russians were in full retreat, and huge numbers of prisoners were being taken. This was the time when the shortage of arms and ammunition in the Russian army had reached its most dangerous point. Units were thrown into battle in which many soldiers had no rifle, and had to wait for a comrade to be killed before they could take his weapon. The Russians were brave, but courage alone was not enough against the deadly German fire. So successful was the offensive that the German High Command decided to continue it at the risk of keeping the new front with Italy inadequately manned. The decision was justified by results. The Italians did not at first make much impression, while the Russian retreat continued. On 22 June the Austrians recaptured Lwów. After a slight pause, the attack was resumed in mid July in three directions—in Lithuania towards Kovno and north-eastwards to the Dvina river at Mitau; from East Prussia southwards to the Narew and towards Warsaw, and from the San valley northwards towards Lublin. On 29 July a further German force attacked eastwards across the Vistula above Warsaw. On 4 August the Russians evacuated the city. In September a new German offensive in Lithuania captured Vilna and reached the lower course of the Dvina. By the end of September the front ran almost due north and south, from a point about fifty miles south-east of Riga (which the Russians still held) down to Kovel, then about one hundred miles eastward and due south again to the river Dniestr to the north-west of Czernowitz. The Russian army had lost all its gains of 1914 on Austrian territory and had had to give up all Russian Poland and a large part of the Polish-Russian borderlands. Casualties had been very heavy. In prisoners alone Russia had lost about a million men in these five months.[1]

The Duma had decided on 9 August 1914 to appoint a Provisional Committee to deal with the affairs of wounded, sick, and victims of the war. It was to consist of all members of the Duma present in Petrograd at any time, and its chairman was the president of the Duma, Rodzyanko. In practice it operated as a permanent standing committee of the Duma, which kept in touch with political and military events, and discussed other matters besides relief. The Duma met formally from 9 to 11 February 1915 to discuss the budget in secret session and to hear a report on the progress of the war from the minister of war, General Sukhomlinov. The members of the Duma were unhappy that the conduct of the war should remain in the hands of the old bureaucratic clique, of whose inefficiency it was not difficult to find evidence. This discontent extended to the zemstvo organization, which despite official approval and financial subsidies from the government, nevertheless met with a good deal of obstruction from officials on the spot. Rumours of treason began to spread. In March a gendarme officer, Colonel Myasoyedov, was executed as an enemy spy. The

[1] Russian prisoners in German hands increased between 10 June and 10 September from 526,100 to 913,172, those in Austrian hands between 31 March and 1 September from 254,842 to 699,254. Golovin, op. cit., p. 92. For the whole period from May to the end of September the total must have been larger.

evidence against him was extremely scanty, and it is highly doubtful whether he was guilty of any offence. He was an enemy of Guchkov, with whom he had fought a duel in 1912, and a friend of Sukhomlinov. The minister made no attempt to save him, but did not thereby save his own position for long.

The news of the German break-through in May intensified the public mood of frustrated patriotic discontent. In Moscow there was a wild explosion of nationalist frenzy from 27 to 29 May. Mobs looted shops and houses belonging to enemy subjects and to persons with foreign names. At first the authorities made no attempt to stop this pogrom: indeed the governor-general appears to have sympathized with it. It was estimated that property to the value of 40,000,000 roubles was destroyed, in 475 business premises and 207 private houses. The persons who suffered these damages were 113 citizens of enemy states, 489 citizens of allied states or Russian subjects with foreign names, and 90 Russian subjects with Russian names.[1]

More constructive was a meeting in May of the Congress of Representatives of Industry and Trade, which proposed that district committees be set up to adapt existing factories to manufacture the articles most urgently needed by the armed forces, and to co-ordinate all business activities to this end. The Congress set up a Central War Industries Committee in Petrograd, with nineteen departments.[2] By the end of 1915 war industries committees existed in 28 provinces and 74 cities. A further meeting of 25 July decided the composition of the Central War Industries Committee. Its total membership was to be 150. This was to include 10 persons elected by workers, 10 nominated by the central government from the ministries concerned with industrial supplies, 3 representatives each of the Union of Zemstvos and the Union of Cities and 2 each of the municipalities of Petrograd and Moscow. The rest were to be persons elected by the Congress of Representatives of Industry and Trade and by local war industries committees. Guchkov was

[1] Oldenburg, *Tsarstvovanie Imperatora Nikolaya II*, ii. 168.

[2] These were: machinery, metal-working, military equipment, chemicals, linen, cotton, wool, leather and boots, transport, food supply, labour, storage, fuel, financial, automobiles and aviation, medical and sanitary, inventions, legal, auditing. S. O. Zagorsky, *State Control of Industry in Russia during the War* (New Haven, 1928), p. 89.

invited at the end of June to become chairman of the central War Industries Committee, and accepted.

The government reluctantly agreed to representation of workers on the committee. It was decided that there should be elections in all factories employing more than 500 workers, and that there should be one voter elected by every 1,000 workers, but every factory with more than 500 workers should elect at least one voter. The Menshevik Secretariat in Exile opposed entry of its supporters into the committee, but the Mensheviks in Petrograd favoured it, in order to exploit the committee for the party's aims. The Bolsheviks, both in Russia and abroad, opposed participation. On 27 September 1915 176 workers' voters, thus elected, met to elect the 10 workers' delegates on the committee, but decided by a small majority to refuse to elect unless certain further demands were granted. The whole machinery was set in motion again, and in November 1915 a somewhat more compliant group of voters duly elected 10 delegates. The mood of the workers, as revealed by these events, did not promise the smooth co-operation of capital and labour for patriotic ends for which the organizers of the committee had hoped. Workers' enthusiasm for the war effort had greatly decreased since August 1914.

The growing discontent with the political leadership was expressed at a conference of the Kadet party, held on 6 June, which demanded the formation of a 'government possessing the confidence of the public'. By this was of course meant a government responsible to the Duma. The Tsar was not prepared to consider such a change. He did, however, remove some of his more unpopular ministers. Sukhomlinov was replaced by General A. A. Polivanov, who had for some years been a friend of Guchkov, and Prince N. B. Shcherbatov, a man of liberal outlook, became minister of the interior.[1] These changes were made in June.

On 5 June simultaneous meetings of zemstvo and city representatives were held to discuss how supplies to the armed forces could be improved. The result was the formation, on 10 July, of the Committee of the All-Russian Unions of Zemstvos and

[1] Other replacements were of the procurator of the synod, V. K. Sabler by A. D. Samarin; and of the minister of justice, I. G. Shcheglovitov by A. A. Khvostov.

Cities for the Supply of the Army, which became generally known by the abbreviated name of *Zemgor*. Its central committee was to consist of the Presidents of the two unions and four representatives of each union elected by its central committee. *Zemgor* undertook to arrange for the placement of government orders in existing factories. It also set up some factories of its own, and organized volunteer labour battalions for emergency jobs.

On 1 August 1915 the Duma met, and remained in session until 16 September. The most important legislative action of this session was the establishment, under a law of 17 August, of a series of special councils intended to improve the co-ordination of the civil and military war efforts and to plan production and supplies. The most important of these was the Special Council of National Defence. It consisted of the presidents of the Duma and the Council of State, nine persons elected by each of the two chambers, one representative each of the Ministries of the Navy, Finance, Transport, Industry and Trade, and of the state controller, five representatives of the Ministry of War, one representative each of the Union of Zemstvos and Union of Cities and four persons elected by the Central War Industries Committee. The other special councils were for Fuel, attached to the Ministry of Industry and Trade; for Food Supplies, attached to the Ministry of Agriculture; and for Transport, attached to the Ministry of Transport. The three other councils also consisted partly of officials and partly of nominees of public organizations. They were empowered to issue regulations fixing prices, deciding transport procedure or allocating goods. The Defence Council had the highest authority, and could veto decisions of the other councils, but the latter could appeal to the Council of Ministers, whose decision was final.

The mood of the Duma continued to be hostile to the government. In August this was given formal expression by the formation of the Progressive block, composed of the Octobrists and Kadets together with some members further to the right and left. The Block had a majority in the Duma. It put forward the demand for a 'government of public confidence'. This slogan was taken up by the zemstvos and cities, and soon became the wish of the great majority of politically conscious Russians, including many in the armed forces and the bureaucratic apparatus itself. But it was not accepted by the Tsar.

The disasters on the front made a change of command essential. Public confidence could not be restored without some changes of senior commanders. Apart from this, something clearly had to be done about the intolerable confusion between civil and military authorities in the military zone. The official intention was to imitate, in the retreat from Galicia and Poland, the scorched-earth policy of 1812. The attempt was made with doctrinaire indifference to the actual conditions, or to the interests of the unfortunate population. The anti-Semitic prejudices of General Yanushkevich were reflected in mass deportations of Galician Jews in brutal circumstances. It was clear that Yanushkevich must go, but Grand Duke Nikolay Nikolayevich was unwilling to part with him. The Tsar therefore decided that the grand duke must be removed, and that he himself must take over his command. A formal justification was the argument that the emperor was the only person of higher rank than the grand duke. The more genuine cause was the Tsar's deep personal conviction that it was his duty to take responsibility and to share the fate of his people. The decision was, however, widely attributed to the empress's dislike of the grand duke and to the influence of Rasputin. Both the acting minister of war, General Polivanov, and Goremykin tried to dissuade the emperor. When the members of the government were informed, they were dismayed. None of them had confidence in the military capacity of Nicholas II, and it was clear that if there were further military disasters the personal authority of the emperor would be damaged, with possibly fatal results for Russia's defence. This point had been understood by Alexander I in 1812, but Nicholas II refused to admit it. At first the ministers bowed to the facts, despite their vigorous objections.[1] However, the general attitude of the Duma, and the development of a campaign, led by the City Council of Moscow, to keep the grand duke in his command, encouraged them to resist. On 3 September—almost three weeks after they had been informed of the Tsar's decision on 19 August, but before it had been officially announced to the public—eight of them signed a letter to the

[1] There is a first-class source of absorbing interest for the discussions among the Ministers in this crisis. This is the record of the proceedings of the Council of Ministers kept by a member of its secretariat, A. N. Yakhontov, published under the title *Tyazholye dni* in vol. xviii of *Arkhiv russkoy revolyutsii*, Berlin, 1926. The discussion following Polivanov's announcement of the news on 3 Sept. is on pp. 52–56.

Tsar begging him to change his mind.[1] The ministers of war and the navy, Polivanov and Admiral Grigorovich, informed Nicholas that though their status as serving officers prevented them from signing the letter, they agreed with it. The effect of the letter was, however, greatly reduced by the firm refusal of Goremykin to support it. He repeatedly assured his colleagues that there was absolutely no chance that the Tsar would change his mind, and that he himself regarded it as his supreme duty to obey the Tsar's wishes, and help him as best he could in a difficult time. Whether this rock-like loyalty served the Tsar well in the end one may doubt. But it pleased Nicholas at the time.[2] He rejected his ministers' advice, and left for the front on 4 September.

Meanwhile on 7 September the Progressive Block produced its programme. It called for a government of public confidence and an end to the duality of military and civil power. Specific demands included an amnesty for political offenders; an end to all religious persecution; concessions to the Poles, Finns, Jews, and Ukrainians; and an end to interference by the administration in the affairs of trade unions and workers' hospital funds.[3] Kharitonov was instructed by the government to meet some members of the Block, and a discussion took place on 9 September. The atmosphere was not unfriendly, and Kharitonov, who reported to his colleagues next day,[4] believed that at least part of the demands could be considered. But Goremykin, in agreement with the emperor, decided to prorogue the Duma without any further consultation. This took place on 16 September.

During the following months most of the more liberal and more able ministers were dismissed. Samarin and Shcherbatov went in September, and the extreme conservative A. N. Khvostov was made minster of the interior. In October it was the turn of Krivoshein, the ablest of them all, who had now convinced himself that co-operation with the Duma was essential, even at the Duma's price of a government responsible

[1] The eight were Bark, Shcherbatov, Shakhovskoy, Kharitonov, Samarin, Ignatyev, Krivoshein, and Sazonov. The text of the letter is reproduced in Yakhontov, op. cit., p. 98.

[2] See above p. 643 n. 1.

[3] The text of the programme is reproduced in Yakhontov, op. cit., pp. 109–110.

[4] Ibid., pp. 119–20.

to it. In January 1916 he was followed by Kharitonov, in March by Polivanov and in June by Sazonov. The foreign minister's fall was caused by disagreement with the Tsar on Poland. Pressed by the allied governments, he urged the Tsar on to grant self-government, but the Tsar would not. In January 1916 Nicholas brought himself to part with Goremykin. The new premier was no improvement. He was B. V. Sturmer, a former provincial governor who had made himself unpopular in liberal circles by his vacillating and opportunist attitude to the zemstvos. In February 1916 the Tsar made a conciliatory gesture by attending the reopening of the Duma. But no actions followed the gesture, and the momentary good will quickly faded.

The emperor now spent most of his time at the front. He was kept informed of events in the capital not only by his officials but by the empress. The correspondence between the Imperial couple, published after the revolution, shows that he placed great confidence in her judgement, and that she attached importance to the views of Rasputin. Whether it is right to conclude that in Nicholas's absence the empress managed—or mismanaged—the political leadership of the empire, and that her choice of advisers was determined by Rasputin, is perhaps more doubtful. The frequent references to 'Our Friend's' approval or disapproval of individuals may prove only that the empress consulted him, not necessarily that his preferences were accepted in all cases by the Tsar, still less that the political initiative came from Rasputin. Apologists for the last emperor maintain that he made up his own mind on the merits of every case, as he saw them, and argue that the legend of the power of Rasputin was created by his enemies, who deliberately exploited the minor misdeeds and discreditable character of the Siberian sectarian in order to smear the reputation of the Imperial family. The least that can be said is that the facts which were known in 1915–16, and the further facts which became known later,[1] lend some plausibility to the theory of Rasputin's influence. At the time it was widely believed.

[1] The most important source are the seven volumes of the proceedings of the Special Commission of Investigation of the Provisional Government, entitled *Padenie tsarskogo rezhima*, published later by the Soviet government, Leningrad, 1925–7. The portions relating to Rasputin are rather fully summarized in Sir Bernard Pares, *The Fall of the Russian Monarchy*, 1939.

Rumours circulated not only of the power of Rasputin over the empress, but of the treasonable actions of this 'German woman'. This last point can be denied with certainty: Alexandra was fanatically devoted to Russia. But the rumours were believed.

The Duma politicians remained bitterly opposed to the régime. Though the Duma was not in session between September 1915 and February 1916, the Committee for Relief provided, as in the previous year, the nucleus of a permanent standing committee. Guchkov was especially embittered and especially active. His position as Chairman of the Central War Industries Committee gave him plenty of opportunities to influence wide sections of the public. In the literature defending the memory of Nicholas, Guchkov is given the role of principal villain. It is argued that he, and the liberal politicians in general, were now so obsessed with their own ambitions that everything, including the country's interests, was subordinated to the aim of power for for the Progressive Block. To this it may be replied that it is equally easy to argue that Nicholas and Alexandra were so obsessed with the dogma of autocracy that they subordinated everything to its maintenance. Certainly there was an ugly element of personal hatred in Guchkov's feelings towards the Imperial couple, which was equalled or surpassed by the empress's hatred of Guchkov. Certainly there were able and loyal men among the officials who carried out the emperor's orders, and certainly the opposition did not give fair credit to the men of the old régime for their efforts to save Russia. Certainly also the politicians were not men of genius, whose advent to power would have delivered Russia from peril. Nevertheless, if one tries to see the reign of Nicholas in perspective, one can hardly maintain that he had made so conspicuous a success of affairs for the last twenty years as clearly to justify the belief that he and his immediate circle could best rule Russia alone without the help, and in direct conflict with the wishes, of the great majority of politically conscious Russians, and indeed of the whole educated part of the nation. If the leaders of the Progressive Block did indeed at times show an almost hysterical antipathy to every act of the government, this was the result of decades of frustration and humiliation, the ultimate responsibility for which must lie with the emperor. The truth is that the insuperable obstacle was his dogmatic devotion to autocracy, which had been deeply implanted in him long before he met Rasputin.

During the first half of 1916 the military situation improved. This was largely because the supply of arms, both from Russian sources and from abroad, greatly improved. On 4 February the Caucasian Army, to which Nikolay Nikolayevich had been transferred when the Tsar assumed the supreme command, entered the Turkish fortress city of Erzurum. On 21 February the great German offensive against Verdun began on the Western Front. The Russian army attacked in Lithuania to relieve pressure on the French. The battle began on 16 March in the area of Lake Naroch. The Russians made some gains but by the end of the month the impetus was exhausted. There was also some fierce fighting further north, around Dvinsk. At the end of April the Germans counter-attacked at Lake Naroch and recovered most of the ground lost earlier.

More serious was a Russian offensive under General A. A. Brusilov against the Austrians in Galicia in June. Considerable Austrian forces were at this time employed in the offensive on the Italian Front. On 4 June the Russian attack began to the east of Lutsk and north of the Dniester. The Russians broke through the Austrian lines at several points, and advanced into Volhynia, Galicia, and Bukovina. Czernowitz was captured, and the Russian troops reached the crest of the Carpathians. Nearly 400,000 Austrian prisoners were taken. In July the bloody Battle of the Somme began on the Western Front, and the Russians attacked the Germans in Lithuania and opposite Riga without success.

Brusilov's victories finally convinced the Roumanian government that the time had come to join the allies. By the treaty of alliance signed on 17 August, Roumania was promised Bukovina, Transylvania, and a large part of the Hungarian plain, stretching westward to the river Tisza. These vast prospective gains, far in excess of the territory inhabited by Roumanians, surpassed anything that the Central Powers could offer. On 27 August 1916 Roumania declared war. The situation for the Central Powers was critical. General von Falkenhayn was replaced as chief of general staff by Hindenburg, and Ludendorff received the post of first quartermaster-general, in which he became the virtual dictator of Germany. Roumania was invaded from the north and south, from Transylvania and Dobrudja. An allied offensive from Salonica in September was resisted by the Bulgarians, and the Russian forces in Bukovina were unable to help the Roumanians. By December 1916 all Roumania south of a line between the Danube Delta and the Carpathians had been lost. The Roumanian Army was regrouped and re-equipped, and received valuable help from a French military mission under General Berthelot. In 1917 it became an efficient fighting force, and won the respect of its opponent General von Mackensen. But from Russia's point of view it was doubtful if the intervention of Roumania had been a gain, since Russian troops had to be used in co-operation with the Roumanians on a new front.

The improvement in supplies was due partly to increased home production and partly to increased imports. By the end of 1916 production of rifles in Russian factories had doubled, while output of machine-guns had increased three times and of heavy guns four times. Imports were improved by an increase in the means of transportation. In 1916 a railway was completed from Petrograd to the Murman coast, while the railway track to Archangel and considerable portions of the Trans-Siberian line were doubled.

Industry had to face great difficulties in regard to raw materials and manpower. Coal-mining output increased from 1,774,000,000 poods (excluding the Dąbrowa region, which was lost through enemy occupation) in 1913 to 2,101,000,000 poods in 1916. Output of petrol also increased from 562,000,000 poods in 1913 to 602,000,000 in 1916. As petrol could not be exported through the Black Sea, more was available for home consumption, and it was used for fuel to a much greater extent than before the war. Output of cotton and wool increased, but was insufficient for demand. Production of both pig-iron and copper absolutely declined. The shortage of leather was especially acute. The army had needed 2,000,000 pairs of boots in peace-time: it now demanded 30,000,000, or nearly as much as the whole peacetime civilian demand for boots and shoes in the empire.

Increased industrial output meant an increase in the labour force. But additional workers could not, as in peacetime, be recruited from the peasantry, for it was estimated that 37 per cent. of the peasants of working age had been called up in the armed forces.[1] A source of manpower was the mass of refugees from Galicia who arrived in the second half of 1915. These were estimated by the committee of the Grand Duchess Tatyana at 3,306,051 but they may have been as many as 6,000,000.[2] Another source was enemy prisoners-of-war. In October 1916 these amounted to 1,545,000. About a third were employed in agriculture, a third in digging trenches and building roads near the front, and a third in miscellaneous industry and construction in the rear. The number of women employed in factories also enormously increased.

Money wages increased between 1913 and 1916 by 133 per cent. However, the value of the rouble on the money market of Stockholm in January 1916 was only 56 per cent. of its value in 1913. Prices had greatly increased. If the 1913–14 level is taken as 100, the level for various commodities in July 1916 was as follows: rye flour 199, sugar 147, meat 332, butter 224, salt 583. Thus real wages in industry as a whole diminished, though the situation was much more favourable in some industries than in others. Metal-, chemical-, and leather-workers were the best paid, and factories working for the armed forces gave better wages than those producing for civilian needs.

The food supply situation became serious by 1916 owing to the combined effect of three factors—decline in output of grain, reduction of railway facilities available for civilian needs, and rapid increase of city populations. Cereal output, for which the average of the years 1909–13 had been 3,234,500,000 poods, was 3,104,000,000 in 1914 and 2,650,000,000 in 1916. The demand of the armed forces for all cereals was 234,000,000 poods in 1914–15 and 686,000,000 in 1916–17. During the war the railways were taken over to a very great extent by the army, and civilian needs received a low priority. At the same time the population of the great cities increased proportionately much faster than that of the nation as a whole. Petrograd had 2,100,000 inhabitants in 1914 and 2,465,000 in January 1917. The population of Moscow increased from 1,600,000 in 1912 to more than 2,000,000 in January 1917. The combination of these factors had the result that by the end of 1916, though

[1] Zagorsky, op. cit., p. 52. [2] Oldenburg, op. cit., p. 184.

Russia was producing enough cereals for her people, the supplies of food to the cities were precarious. The shortage was actually increased by the attempts to fix grain prices. When the revised prices were announced in September 1916 many sellers held back their stocks in the hope that prices would be freed from control later. In November 1916 it was decided to allocate to each province a quota for compulsory levies of grain to be raised for the army, but these were not in fact carried out.[1]

It is difficult to say to what extent these problems were made easier or more difficult by the cumbrous structure of councils and by the activities of such non-official bodies as the *Zemgor* and the Central War Industries Committee. *Zemgor* had some concrete achievements to its credit, such as the evacuation of 150 industrial establishments from Riga in the late summer of 1915, or the establishment of a factory to make field-telephones in September 1915.[2] The relief and hospital work of the Unions of Zemstvos and Cities was undoubtedly of great value, and the army commanders were very grateful for it. Relations between the bureaucracy and the voluntary organizations were, however, often bad. The bureaucrats were jealous of the reputation which the zemstvos were winning, and of the wide popularity of their chairman, Prince Lvov. They accused the zemstvos of providing a shelter for men seeking to escape conscription to the front. There may have been some truth in this charge, but it was certainly levelled in a malicious spirit, and the plight of the armies would certainly have been worse if there had been no Union of Zemstvos.

At the end of 1916 Russia's military situation was surprisingly good, but the political atmosphere was worse than ever. Distrust of the government was almost universal, and was of course consciously increased by the Progressive Block. War weariness was growing. It is true that the greatest losses had been incurred in 1915, but they were still bitterly felt in 1916. According to a later estimate,[3] total Russian casualties, including the year 1917, were 1,300,000 killed in battle; 4,200,000 wounded, of whom 350,000 died from their wounds; and 2,417,000 prisoners. Most of these casualties were incurred before the end of 1916. According to German records, on 10 January 1917 there were

[1] Antsiferov, op. cit., pp. 183, 197–9. [2] Polner, op. cit., pp. 276–80.
[3] Golovin, op. cit., pp. 82–92.

1,231,406 Russian prisoners in German hands. According to Austrian records the number of Russian prisoners in Austrian hands on 1 February 1917 was 853,753.[1]

In September 1916 Nicholas made an appointment of some importance. He chose A. D. Protopopov as minister of the interior. A member of the Fourth Duma and a supporter of the Progressive Block, he was regarded as a moderate liberal and was reasonably well viewed in the Duma. He was a member of a parliamentary delegation which visited France and Britain to try to stimulate good will for a wartime ally. On his return he made a good impression on Nicholas, and also on the empress and Rasputin. Whether he owed his appointment to 'Our Friend' is perhaps not so certain as that he had his support. It seems possible that the Tsar intended this appointment as a gesture towards the Duma. If he had had even a little political sense, he would have understood that a Duma member who entered an irresponsible government, not as a spokesman of the Duma but on his own behalf, would be hated by the Duma as a renegade. In fact, Protopopov was more violently disliked by the Duma than any of his reactionary predecessors. His appointment made the political atmosphere of the capital even worse than it had been.[2]

In the second half of 1916 Central Asia was the scene of a large-scale armed rebellion. Its immediate cause was a plan to mobilize 250,000 persons from Turkestan and 243,000 from the Steppe Region for labour service in the rear of the front. More important as a basic cause was the widespread latent resentment at the growing influx of Russian settlers. The revolt began in Samarkand province in July, spread to Semirechie in August, and was not suppressed until the end of the year. Nearly 3,000 Russian civilians were killed or missing. The number of Moslem casualties is unknown, but may have amounted to several hundred thousand, and those who fled to Chinese territory were still more numerous. The revolt had no repercussions on the political situation in European Russia.

[1] Golovin, op. cit., pp. 90, 91.

[2] The grotesque record of Protopopov as minister is recounted in *Padenie tsarskogo rezhima,* especially in his own long statement which forms the greater part of vol. iv.

The Duma reasssembled at the beginning of November in an atmosphere of general discontent with the Sturmer government, in which circumstantial reports of mismanagement of the war effort and of intrigues in high places mingled with irresponsible rumours of enemy espionage. In the session of 14 November Milyukov made the most sensational speech of his career. He listed the misdeeds and failings of the government one by one, and after each point exclaimed, 'Is this stupidity or treason?' He produced no more solid ground for the second hypothesis than an article in an Austrian newspaper, but his words set off a new flood of rumours and disaffection in the capital.

On 22 November the Tsar at last brought himself to dismiss Sturmer. In his place was appointed the decent but unremarkable bureaucrat A. F. Trepov. The new premier made some improvements in the ministry, but was unable to get rid of Protopopov, whom the empress defended with a zeal worthy of a better cause.

The next noteworthy event was the murder of Rasputin on 29 December 1916. The crime, the true story of which was more macabre than the numerous attempts made by Hollywood in subsequent years to dramatize it, was the work of Prince Felix Yusupov, the right-wing Duma member Purishkevich, and the Grand Duke Dmitri Pavlovich. These misguided enthusiasts no doubt saw themselves as saviours of their country. On balance, their action probably made the situation a little worse. The empress was distracted with grief, the emperor returned from headquarters to Petrograd, and Trepov was dismissed. With him resigned the only remaining member of the government who was a man of both honour and ability, the minister of education, Count N. P. Ignatyev. The last premier of the monarchy was Prince N. N. Golitsyn, who had neither qualifications nor desire for the job. In so far as there still was a government in Russia, it was conducted by Nicholas, the empress, and Protopopov.

Increasing difficulties in the food supplies of the capital increased the discontent of the working class, which was already strongly influenced by anti-war propaganda. On 22 January

1917 the illegal socialist organizations called for strikes in commemoration of the massacre of January 1905. In Petrograd about 300,000 workers responded, in Moscow about a third of the factories stopped work, and there were some strikes in Kharkov.[1]

The date of the reassembly of the Duma was fixed for 27 February. The Workers' Group of the Central War Industries Committee published an appeal to Petrograd workers to leave their work on that day, and march to the Taurid Palace to give the Duma the demands of the working class. The illegal Bolshevik committee urged its followers to ignore the Duma, but to strike and demonstrate on 23 February, the anniversary of the trial of the Bolshevik Duma members.[2] The military commandant of Petrograd gave orders for the arrest, on 8 February, of the leading members of the Workers' Group. This action led to acrimonious correspondence between Guchkov and the police, removed the only official body which represented the workers, and somewhat increased the total volume of opposition to the government. It did not, however, lead to any concrete reaction. Neither on 23 nor 27 February was there any noticeable increase in the number of strikes, and only a few hundred persons appeared outside the Taurid Palace. On 7 March there was a lock-out at the big Putilov Works. The same day the Tsar returned to headquarters.

The following day, 8 March, saw the beginning of the final crisis of the Imperial régime. It began with demonstrations in celebration of International Women's Day, a socialist occasion. About fifty factories, with about 90,000 workers, were on strike at this time.[3] Their workers, and discontented housewives queuing for goods in short supply, swelled the demonstrations. The streets filled with marching workers and with police. On 9 March there were 200,000 on strike, and the crowds in the streets were bigger. The authorities issued a statement that there

[1] N. Avdeyev, *Revolyutsyia 1917 goda: khronika sobytiy* (Moscow, 1923), i. 8.

[2] Lenin was at this time in Switzerland, He kept fairly regularly in touch with Russia by correspondence. Apart from this he had been engaged on writing his famous work *Imperialism, as the Highest Stage of Capitalism*, completed in the spring of 1916 but not published until his return to Russia a year later. The Russian Bureau of the Central Committee, which directed Bolshevik activity in Russia, was led by A. M. Shlyapnikov, V. M. Molotov, and P. A. Zalutsky.

[3] Avdeyev, op. cit. i. 32.

were now ample bread supplies in the shops, but this had no effect. On 10 March the strike was general. The commandant of Petrograd received telegraphic instructions from the Tsar to put an end to the disorders immediately. His threat to mobilize into the army all workers who did not return to their jobs, was completely ineffective. There were some clashes between demonstrators and soldiers. On 11 March a company of the Pavlovsky Regiment mutinied, but later returned to its barracks. Rodzyanko sent a telegram to the Tsar demanding that a person possessing the confidence of the country be asked to form a new government. This request was supported by two army commanders, General Brusilov and General Ruzsky. The Tsar's reaction was to instruct the government to prorogue the Duma until April. On 12 March Rodzyanko sent another telegram with the same request. The Tsar commented to his loyal friend, the minister of the court Baron Frederiks: 'That fatty Rodzyanko has sent me some nonsense, which I shan't even answer.'

12 March was the decisive day, and it was decided by the mutiny of the Volhynian, Lithuanian, Pavlovsky and Semyonovsky Regiments. From this time the soldiers had joined the workers, and together they proved a match for the armed police forces, which continued to fight a hopeless battle. Soldiers and workers captured the Peter Paul Fortress and various prisons, releasing political prisoners. Among these were the arrested Workers' Group leaders, who proceeded to the Taurid Palace, where, together with representatives of trade unions and co-operatives, they set up a Provisional Committee of the Soviet of Workers' Deputies.[1] In the same building the Duma deputies had elected a Provisional Committee of the Duma,[2] to act according to the needs of the situation. The government was by now incapable of governing, and sent a telegram to the Tsar begging to be dismissed. The Tsar refused. In the evening the Tsar's brother, Grand Duke Michael, at the request of the government, telegraphed the suggestion that Prince G. E. Lvov, chairman of the Union of Zemstvos, be made premier. The only reply was that the Tsar was on his way

[1] Ibid., pp. 40–41.

[2] Its members were V. Shulgin (Nationalist); Dimitryukov (Octobrist); P. N. Milyukov and Nekrasov (Kadets), Chkheidze (Menshevik); A. F. Kerensky (Trudovik); and V. Lvov, Karaulov, Rzhevski, Konovalov, and Shidlovsky (members of the Progressive Block from conservative groups).

to Petrograd, and would then decide. In the same evening the Soviet held its first meeting. It was composed of workers elected in the factories and of active members of the revolutionary parties available in the city. Representatives of the mutinous regiments asked to be included, and it was decided to change its name to Soviet of Workers' and Soldiers' Deputies.

On 13 March the Tsar's train was turned back when it was learned that the lines to Petrograd and Moscow were held by the revolutionaries. On the evening of 14 March he arrived in Pskov, the headquarters of General Ruzsky, commanding the Northern Front. On the same day in Petrograd the Provisional Committee of the Duma and the Executive Committee of the Soviet reached agreement. The Soviet was to support the government to be formed from the Duma, for as long as it pursued an agreed political programme. This provided for a complete and immediate amnesty, covering all political and religious offences, including terrorist attempts and agrarian crimes. It promised freedom of speech, press, meeting, association and strike to all, including even military personnel within the limits of 'military-technical conditions'. All restrictions based on class, religion, and nationality were to be abolished. Immediate preparations were to be made for the election of a Constituent Assembly, by universal direct franchise with secret ballot and equal constituencies. There were also to be elections to local authorities. The police was to be replaced by a People's Militia, whose officers were to be elective. The programme also promised the military units which had taken part in the revolution that they would not be disarmed or sent out of the capital.[1]

On 15 March the Provisional Government was formed. It was led by Prince G. E. Lvov, Foreign Affairs were entrusted to Milyukov and War to Guchkov. The Ministry of Justice went to Kerensky, who thus formed a personal link between the government and the Soviet, of whose leadership he was also a member. The most important remaining posts were held by Kadets.

On the same evening Guchkov and Shulgin reached Pskov as emissaries of the government to accept the abdication of the Tsar. Nicholas had at first intended to hand the Crown to his

[1] Full text in Avdeyev, op. cit. i. 189–90.

son, but he later decided that he could not part from him, nor leave the frail child to face the unknown future. He therefore abdicated in favour of his brother. Next day in Petrograd Michael met the members of the government. Milyukov and Guchkov begged him to accept the throne, but their colleagues disagreed. The Grand Duke himself decided to decline. Russia became a republic.

This was the end of the Romanov dynasty, which had ruled Russia a little more than three hundred years, and of the Russian monarchy, which was as old as the Russian state. Fifteen months more were to pass before Nicholas and his wife, with their five teenage children, two servants, and the family doctor, were done to death with revolvers and bayonets in a cellar in Ekaterinburg. In March 1917 Russia was swept by hope and joy. Mighty floods of benevolence and rhetoric covered the land. The politicians prepared themselves for glorious roles as great statesmen, brushing up their memories of 1789. The peasants, in the villages and in the trenches, believed that the land would soon be theirs. The workers at the factory bench and in the street, and the women of all classes and in all parts of the empire, rejoiced that peace was in sight. And in Switzerland Vladimir Ilyich Ulyanov heard with interest the news from Petrograd. The ineluctable processes of History, expounded by the founders of Marxism, were speeding up, and Lenin's hour of destiny was drawing near.

CONCLUSIONS

NINETEENTH-century Russia was, to use the terminology of the mid twentieth, an 'underdeveloped' society. Its mineral resources were only partly exploited, its agriculture primitive, its people unskilled and uneducated, its social structure unbalanced, yet all these things were changing, and the speed of change was faster at the end of the century than at the beginning.

The process to which the Russian people was subjected, and which was responsible for many of the social strains and political troubles of the period, can be described as deliberate modernization. The societies of western Europe, and those derived from them in North America and the South Pacific, had gone through the process, but it had taken longer. Modernization in the West happened: in Russia it was willed by the ruler. Peter the Great is not only a great figure in the history of Russia: he is the first, and perhaps still the outstanding, example of a type which subsequently appeared in many countries of Asia and Africa. He was followed by Mohammed Ali and Mahmud II, the Meiji Era statesmen and Kemal Atatürk, and dozens of lesser figures in more recent times. For the great majority of the human race modernization has been a deliberate, not a spontaneous process: Western experience is not typical but exceptional.

Deliberate modernization has three aspects—military, economic, and cultural. Peter the Great was concerned with all three, in the order of importance stated above, and although under his successors the pace varied the priorities did not change.

At the end of the eighteenth century the gap between Russia and western Europe was narrower than in Peter's time. In the military field there was no gap at all. Russian armies could not only beat the armies of the declining Ottoman or Persian empires, but hold their own against the best in the world. Suvorov's campaigns in Italy showed what the Russian commander and the Russian soldier could do. The economy was still backward, but some sectors, such as the Ural iron industry, had achieved great success. Cultural advance had been small:

some thousands affected a style imitated directly from France, while the vast majority lived in primeval ignorance.

In the first half of the nineteenth century the gap again widened. It is true that this period saw the greatest triumphs yet achieved by Russian arms, the highest prestige of the Russian state, and the first splendid flowering of Russian literature. The generation which destroyed Napoleon also received the poems of Pushkin and the stories of Gogol, and Alexander I for a time was greeted as the benefactor of all Europe. But in comparison with the economic upsurge of Britain and other Western countries, Russia remained almost stagnant, and the new ideas that swept across Europe won but few disciples in Russia. Europe's dual revolution, industrial and political, did not pass Russia by, but its impact was much diminished by the Restoration of 1815. In the general attempt to petrify Europe after the defeat of Napoleon, Russia was petrified at an earlier stage, a stage which included serfdom. The tragedy of the Decembrists made things worse. The numbers of the enlightened in Russia in 1825 were not large, but in quality they were equal to any in the world. Their ranks were decimated by the disaster, and the survivors were silenced. The elimination of the intellectual and moral *élite* was something which Russia could less afford at this time than any other great nation.

The extent of the gap was revealed by the Crimean War. The Russian colossus, the sinister gendarme hated by lovers of freedom within the empire and throughout Europe, was shown to be a scarecrow. The age of Nicholas was followed by the transitional period of Alexander II. The reign began with a lost war and ended with a war won and a peace lost. The defeat of 1856 was not so definite as to break the régime, yet alarming enough to make change necessary. The great reforms were carried out by the old bureaucratic team, and after a few years the original impetus was lost: the reforms carried out in the same years in Japan were the work of new men, their scope wider and their effect more lasting. The victory of 1878 was not so brilliant, still less was the peace which concluded it so glorious, as to restore the prestige of a régime which had disappointed so many hopes. The bomb which killed the Tsar Liberator was thrown by one of his own subjects. But

Russia paid a heavy price for this triumph of *Narodnaya volya.* It had essentially the same effect as the failure of the Decembrists—a deliberate choice by government of political and social stagnation.

In the last fifty years of Tsardom the priorities of modernization changed, in practice if not in intention. In military strength Russia fell behind: the wars against Japan and Germany demonstrated the customary Russian valour but were marked by no Russian victories.[1] In the economic field, by contrast, Russia made tremendous progress. By 1914 Russia had become an important industrial Power, and even in agriculture, so long neglected by government and hampered by antiquated social institutions, progress was at last being made. In the cultural field, the gap between Russia and Europe had been closed at the highest level, in the sense that Russia could stand comparison with any other country in the world in its output of writers, artists, scientists, or original thinkers; but the gap between the educated *élite* and the people, within Russia, was still wide. In education the last two decades of the nineteenth century were the most reactionary of all. At a time when Russia had the human and financial resources to educate the whole nation, the policy of class privilege was artificially maintained. What was understandable, and perhaps even justifiable by the standards of the time, in the days of Uvarov, was indefensible and immensely harmful to Russia in the days of Delyanov. This policy was reversed after 1905. Real efforts were made at last to educate peasant boys and girls, and they were continued right up to the collapse of Tsardom: Count P. N. Ignatyev, Imperial Russia's penultimate minister of education, was one of its best.

Thus in the last years before 1914 the gap between the intellectual *élite* and the people was narrowing, and the obsession of the *élite* with social and political revolution was diminishing. A Russian *bourgeoisie* with a genuinely *bourgeois* ethos was beginning to form, and the vertical compartments between the three middle classes—business, government service, and the free professions—were beginning to break down. But all this was at an early stage. The alienation of the intelligentsia from the whole social and political régime was still a more important

[1] Victories were won against lesser foes—Austrians and Turks.

fact than the growth of *bourgeois* values, and the Russian political mind was still different from the Western.

At the beginning of the nineteenth century the Russian intellectual *élite* had received the ideas of the European Enlightenment. But the experiences from which the Enlightenment had developed had not been felt in Russia, and the foundation of traditions and habits on which the Russian disciples sought to build a new structure of ideas was quite different from that which had existed in the West.

The long struggle in the West for freedom of judgement in religious belief, from which had evolved the claim for freedom of judgement in politics, and the still longer struggle between social classes, none of which was strong enough completely to dominate the others, had no parallel in Russia. For a time Novgorod had taken part in the process of sea-borne trade which trained the burgher class of medieval Europe in capitalist enterprise. After Novgorod fell, these skills virtually disappeared, and Russians had no part in the later flowing of European trade across the oceans. In Russia, as in every organized society in human history, objects were made, bought, and sold, but this added up to a good deal less than the trading capitalism of early modern Europe.

The place of law in society, and the attitude of the subject to law, were also quite different in Russia and in Europe. The whole tradition which continued from the Roman republic through the Catholic Church into the secular age of the West was missing in Russia: what little had reached Kievan Russia from Byzantium was lost in the following centuries. Law in Russia meant the will of the ruler or the consensus of the community. The importance of exact definition and predictability, essential to the Western concept of law, was not recognized. The task of interpreting the law was not valued: persons who dealt with such things were regarded at best as soulless formalists buried in dusty papers, at worst as tricksters who made a living from deceiving honest people.

Political power and leadership belonged to the autocrat. The great changes in Russian history had come by action from above. This was true not only of Peter the Great's transformation, but also of the Great Schism of the seventeenth century.

The movements which brought about the Reformation in Europe came from below: they had their origin in the troubled consciences of priests and laymen. The Russian Schism was not a movement of this kind. It was started by a decision of the patriarch to introduce reforms which he thought would benefit the Church, and it provoked the hostility of a conservative priesthood and laity.

In the nineteenth century the Russian political mind was still dominated by the principle of autocracy. This was true not only of the supporters of the established order but of its opponents.

Those opponents who were not revolutionaries wished to see the power of the autocrat and his ministers preserved or strengthened, but used against the privileged and for the benefit of the people. Examples of this attitude have been given in the preceding pages: Paul Stroganov and Nicholas Milyutin are the most obvious. The opposite point of view, which preferred the European example of limiting the monarchical power, institutionalizing the liberties of individuals and groups, and giving initiative to society as well as to government, had its supporters, but they fought a losing struggle from Catherine II herself (in her earlier phase) down to moderate liberals of the type of V. A. Maklakov.

As for those who sought salvation through revolution, they seem at first sight to be bitter enemies of autocracy, but the appearance is somewhat deceptive. Many intended from the beginning to replace the autocracy of the Tsar by a revolutionary dictatorship. It is true that they declared, no doubt sincerely, that the dictatorship would be temporary, and its aim would be true government by the people, or the peasants, or the working class. But in matters of dictatorship, the provisional has a way of lasting, and of this Pestel, Tkachov, and Lenin, to take three outstanding cases, were certainly aware. The other trend among the revolutionaries, which was most strongly represented within the Socialist Revolutionary Party, was towards popular anarchy, the absence of any authority or institutions, and trust in the democratic instincts of the people. This trend was inevitably less effective than the Jacobin trend, but it was not less widespread. Both trends were far from the predominant trend of the nineteenth-century European left, which recognized the importance of institutions and law. In the Russian revolutionary camp the only group which had this outlook were the Mensheviks—or at least, a section of them—and they were as permanently doomed to minority status within the camp of revolution as were the moderate liberals within the camp of reform.

The demand for a free society, based on civil liberties, representative institutions and due process of law, was ineffective because the social forces which supported it were too weak. It is true that the government made some important concessions to this demand: the judicial reform, the zemstvos, and—too late—the State Duma. It is also true that revolutionaries made use of these concessions for their own purposes. But the government did not respect its own institutions. Officials of the central ministries, provincial governors, and even the Tsar himself ignored or despised the law. This practice of illegality by the authorities did much to strengthen the contempt for law among the people as a whole, and played havoc with the efforts of whose few officials, lawyers, writers, or politicians whose aim was to implant in the Russian public an understanding of the concept of law. The belief that only violent revolution could solve Russia's problems could be upheld by powerful arguments. Even in periods of comparative calm and prosperity it had its devoted organized champions. Repeated unsuccessful wars gave them their chances.

In the complex history of revolutionary movements in Russia three stages can be distinguished.

In the first stage small groups of conspirators operated without mass support. The first were the Decembrists. The type of action they planned belongs to the eighteenth-century tradition of Guards mutinies, but they themselves were men of the nineteenth century, of the world of modern political ideas. Their failure was followed by three decades without revolutionary action: under Nicholas I men of radical ideas could only meet and talk, and even this was savagely punished. At the end of the 1850's radical opinions could be more boldy and publicly expressed, and conspirators not only talked about action, but tried to act. The period of groups, or 'circles', of intellectuals (*kruzhkovshchina*) merges imperceptibly into the second stage, of limited mass action.

Socialist ideas arose in western Europe as a result of social and economic development, but they reached Russia ready-made at a time when the social conditions to which they related hardly existed. In England, France, and Germany labour movements were the result in part of leadership by socialist intellectuals and in part of action by the workers themselves in defence of their interests: in the English case the second factor was especially important. In Russia socialist movements were created entirely by socialist intellectuals: it was not so much that the masses were looking for leaders as that the intellectuals were looking for masses to lead. In an agrarian country just emerging from serfdom, the suffering masses were in the first instance the peasants. In the second half of the century peasant discontent was frequently expressed in minor riots and acts of violence. But the attempts of the revolutionary intelligentsia to organize peasant support were not successful. The first mass base for the revolutionary movement was found not in the countryside but in the cities, among the urban poor and the growing industrial working class. This is not hard to understand: large numbers herded together in the inhuman conditions of the urban agglomerations of early industrialization are both more inclined to listen to revolutionary doctrines, and more accessible to revolutionary organizers, than peasants scattered over wide areas, living a traditional life and largely accepting traditional values. In the 1870's the Populists attracted at least hundreds of urban workers, and Khalturin's Northern Workers' Union is a landmark in the history of the Russian working class. In the 1890's, when industry was more advanced and the working class more numerous, the mass base for the revolutionary movement in the cities was much stronger. In the interval, thanks to the works of Plekhanov, the specific doctrinal emphasis of Marxism on the role of the working class, in contrast to the earlier Populist concern with the peasants, had become largely accepted among the politically conscious younger generation in Russia.

A leadership from the revolutionary intelligentsia and a limited mass following among the working class were sufficient to create a strong political movement, but they were not sufficient to take power in an agrarian country ruled by a bureaucratic, police, and military régime. The mass assault on the autocracy would become possible only when the peasant masses were drawn into the struggle. This was the third stage.

It is an interesting lesson of Russian experience (and also of other countries in modern times) that the involvement of the peasants in a mass revolutionary movement has been not the cause but the result of the disintegration of the régime. It was when the Russian autocracy was dangerously shaken by the war with Japan that peasant action developed from the stage of scattered riots and disorders into the more advanced stage of mass revolutionary movement. In 1906 this movement was checked and then crushed. In 1917 the same thing happened again on a larger scale: the decisive moment came when the peasants in uniform, in the Petrograd garrison, joined the workers demonstrating in the streets. In the months which followed the February Revolution, the disintegration of the army and civil government, and the involvement of the peasants in mass revolutionary action, went ahead together and interacted on each other.

The importance of lost wars should not be underrated. The connexion of the revolutions of 1905 and 1917 with military disasters is obvious, and it is no disparagement of the talents of the revolutionaries to point this out. Clearly revolution was not *caused* by defeat, but equally clearly it was defeat which weakened both the material strength of the government and the will of the men at the top, and made them vulnerable to the revolutionary assault. The limited defeat of 1856 showed the dangerous weakness of the Russian state and the need for reform, but was not serious enough to shake either the will of the rulers or the obedience of the armed forces. In 1878 patriotic zeal was followed by national frustration: on balance this probably made the public mood more sympathetic to the action of the revolutionaries, but the régime was even less endangered than in 1856. On the other hand the decisive victory of 1815 increased both the power and the will of the rulers; there was a widespread desire among the intellectual *élite* for a new order, but the holders of power would not yield, and the Tsar would not force them.

During the century the territories of the Russian empire were greatly increased: in Europe it acquired central Poland

and eastern Moldavia, in Asia Transcaucasia up to Batum and Kars, Transcaspia, Turkestan, the mouth of the Amur, and the coastal strip down to Vladivostok. Apart from this, in 1913 Finland was well on the way towards absorption in the Empire, Khiva and Bukhara were protectorates, northern Manchuria was virtually a Russian colony, and Mongolia seemed destined for the same fate. Russian ambitions had been frustrated in Roumania, southern Manchuria and Korea, and two small territories to which historical or moral claims were advanced by pressure groups—Eastern Galicia and Turkish Armenia—were still beyond Russian reach. More important, Constantinople was still held by the Turks. But in the general scramble of the Powers for territory, Russia had not done badly.

In the nineteenth century the governments of the Great Powers did not think it wrong to make conquests: they were ashamed only when their efforts were defeated. Disapproval of imperialism was not yet part of the common fund of respectable opinions. There was as yet no need to argue that expansion is only wrong if it is made across salt water, or to substitute the bland phrases 'fusion' and 'unification' for the old-fashioned word 'conquest'.

Less than half the subjects of the empire were Russians. A broad distinction can be made between two types of situation, corresponding approximately to the distinction between the peoples of the European and the Asiatic provinces—the nationalities problem and the colonial situation.

In the European territories from the 1890's—with a temporary reversal from 1905 to 1907—the government increasingly pursued a policy of russification. Essentially, this was an attempt to introduce a new secular ideology of state, to supplement the traditional basis of legitimacy—the claim to loyalty of a monarch divinely sanctioned—with a new principle—the sovereignty of the Russian nation. The closest parallel to russification was the policy of magyarization adopted in Hungary after 1867. Both were 'modern' policies by contrast with those of the Ottoman or Habsburg monarchies, which made no attempt to change the basis of legitimacy.[1] But both were

[1] The Habsburg dynasty of course ruled over Hungary too. But in Hungary the government based its policy on official nationalism, while in the rest of the Habsburg lands (often, though inaccurately, described as 'Austria'), this was not the

unsuccessful: Poles, Balts, and even Ukrainians refused to become Russians, and Slovaks, Serbs, and Roumanians refused to become Hungarians.

In the Asiatic territories no attempt was made to russify. In principle the conquered peoples were allowed to live as they wished, provided that they obeyed the Tsar's authorities: there was no doctrinaire desire to interfere with their social organization or customs, religion, culture, or language. In practice, however, the conquest had far-reaching economic and social effects on the subject peoples. This was especially clear in the areas where massive colonization by Russian peasants or Cossacks took place: the Kazakh steppes, Bashkiria, and parts of Turkestan and the north Caucasus. Russian colonial rule was essentially similar to colonial rule by other European Powers. Its exponents had the same combination of arrogance and benevolence, the same sense of superiority based on ignorance of other cultures, the same well-meaning but complacent belief that they were bringing order and progress to barbarians. Russian administrators shared the mentality of their British or French colleagues: the mentality of 'taking up the White Man's Burden', or of the *mission civilisatrice*.

By far the most important of the nationality problems in the Russian empire was the Polish. Its place in Russian political history may be compared with the place of the Irish Question in British. In both cases there is a conflict lasting for hundreds of years, marked on both sides by much savagery and very little generosity. In both cases the religious chasm and religious fanaticism are decisive factors. In both cases there is a dispute about a territory in which the rival cultures mix: Lithuania may be called Russia's Ulster. In both cases the stronger antagonist was obsessed by fear that the weaker would be used by his enemies against him, and in both cases these fears were more than once justified. In both cases a section of the intellectual *élite* of the stronger antagonist was obsessed by its bad conscience at the wrongs inflicted on the weaker. This factor is more striking in England than in Russia. Though Alexander I may be set against Gladstone, it cannot be said that Russian practising

case: *Kaisertreue* was all that was required of them. There is no brief form of words that can make these distinctions correctly and clearly. But I trust that my over-simplified phrases may rather enlighten than mislead the reader.

politicians were much worried by the injustices done to the Poles. Herzen and Bakunin, Vyazemsky and Chaadayev, even Chicherin and Valuyev, are honourable witnesses that Russians had a conscience, but they can hardly compare with the volume of protest poured out by generations of English radicals. It is not that Russians were silenced by the censorship: far from being silent, they trumpeted forth their rage against the Poles, and their hatred of European friends of the Poles, and the chorus was led by Pushkin.

The differences are as important as the similarities. The Irish never conquered England. The Poles conquered large stretches of the Russian Land, and for centuries they invaded or threatened Muscovy. Moreover the relationship of Poland to the religious conflict was not the same as that of Ireland. To Russians, Poland traditionally appeared not only a Catholic nation, but the spearhead, directed against Holy Russia, of the hosts of Rome which ruled the lands that lay beyond her. Beyond Ireland was only the Atlantic Ocean, which the British navy ruled. Poland to Russians was as King Philip's Spain to the Elizabethan English. Fear, distrust, and hatred of Polish power, originating in religious hatred, formed the Russian attitude to the Poles, which lasted long after Poland had ceased to be a Great Power and after religious passions had calmed.

Another difference is that, whereas the English were more advanced, in culture and in material skills, than the Irish, the Russians were in all these things more backward than the Poles at the time when they conquered their land. In Polish hostility to Russia, the element of contempt for barbarism has always been strong. This is the other side to the Russian fear of Western aggression spearheaded by Poles: Poles have seen themselves as champions of Europe against Eastern hordes. This factor barely diminished during the nineteenth century. There were Poles who got to know the achievements and the qualities of the Russian *élite*, and were enamoured of the splendid culture of St. Petersburg. This was especially the case at the beginning of the century, and the friendship of Mickiewicz and Pushkin is its symbol, but the events of 1830 reversed the trend. It was visible again at the turn of the nineteenth and twentieth centuries: perhaps the last two decades of the Imperial régime were the period in which Russian culture had most attraction for educated Poles.[1] But at no time were more than a small minority so affected. Most Poles, educated or not, viewed Russia with a mixture of indifference, contempt, and dislike, based on vivid if distorted memories of the past and much ignorance of the present. The typical Russian view of Poles was not a whit more magnanimous.

After the Poles, the people whose fate was most closely linked to the Russians were the Turks. In this context is meant not so much the Ottoman Turks as the whole family of Turkic peoples stretching from the Crimea, the Volga Basin, and Azerbaidjan across the Kazakh steppes to Turkestan. Here too there were memories of aggression and religious fanaticism on both sides. The Russians, like the Christian Balkan peoples, suffered centuries of rule by Moslem Turkic rulers, and when their turn came they imposed their rule by force on Turks or Tatars. Geography was unfavourable to those Turks living north of the great mountain barrier which extends from the Black Sea to Mongolia. As the people of the north gathered strength, and pressed southwards and south-eastwards upon them, there was none to help. The Ottoman empire was above all a Mediterranean Power, The Persians looked no further than the Caspian and Afghanistan, and both India and China were under assault from the sea. Yet under Russian rule the Volga Tatars did not lose their vigour: they were ahead of any Moslem people in their assimilation of modern ideas, and in their determination to build a democratic life for themselves. Geography and numbers were against them, but at the moment of the collapse of Tsardom they were holding their own, and they had bright hopes for the future.

The people of Turkestan had been almost untouched by modern ideas at the time that the Russians conquered them. It is one of the strange mysteries that the peoples of this ancient land of civilization, which for millennia past has provided rulers for great empires in other lands, never themselves achieved national identity, not even in the pre-modern sense in which the Persians achieved and preserved it. The people of

[1] There was also some revival of the guilt complex of the Russian intelligentsia about Poland. See the great poem by Blok, *Vozmezdie*, and the penetrating essay on it by Lednicki, *Russia, Poland and the West*.

Turkestan never 'entered history' as a nation in their own right. Under Russian rule they fared about as well or as ill as the Moslem peoples ruled by the French or the British. In some ways Russian rule resembled French, particularly in the influx of agricultural settlers from Europe. The problems of administration were similar to those which faced the British in India. It is worth noting, however, that the Russian forces maintained in Central Asia after its conquest were never less, and sometimes a good deal more, than those maintained by the British in India 'although the Central Asian local population only amounted to one thirtieth of that of the Indian sub-continent'.[1] The Russian generals did not believe that they were loved. It is easy to assert that hatred was directed only against the Tsar's reactionary government, and that the Russian people loved, and was loved by, the peoples of Central Asia. Unfortunately there is little evidence to support this comfortable view, and a good deal to oppose it. The revolt of 1916 was due above all to resentment at Russian colonization. The Russian peasants who settled in Central Asia hardly distinguished themselves by the respect or understanding they showed for Moslem ways of life and culture. The truth is that many though not all Russian administrators, like many though not all British administrators in India or Africa, gave honourable service to their subjects, improved their conditions, and regarded them with a genuine though condescending affection; whereas the Russian peasants in the Steppe Region and the Russian railwaymen in Tashkent, like the British workers in the Rhodesian Copper-Belt and other 'poor whites' or *petits blancs* elsewhere, felt little but hostility and contempt.

There can hardly be another country or period in which writers and thinkers were so obsessed with the destiny or the historical mission of their nation as was the case in Russia in the nineteenth century. Russian literature is full of striking images on these themes. One need only recall the unfortunate Evgeny confronted with the idol on the bronze horse, or Gogol's *troyka* rushing ahead, none knew whither: 'She flies past everything that is on earth, and other peoples and states step squinting aside, and make way for her.'

[1] Geoffrey Wheeler, *The Modern History of Soviet Central Asia* (1964), p. 70.

Chaadayev saw Russia as a 'gap in the intellectual order'. In his speech on Pushkin, delivered almost fifty years after Chaadayev wrote his *Philosophical Letters*, Dostoyevsky claimed that Russian culture incorporated European culture in itself.

> Yes, the vocation of the Russian man is indisputably an all-European and a world-wide vocation. Perhaps indeed to become a genuine, complete Russian can only mean (in the last resort, let me emphasize) to become the brother of all men, to become, if you like, a universal man . . . . Oh, the people of Europe do not know how dear they are to us. And I believe that we (that is to say, of course, not we but the Russians of the future) will all eventually understand, every single one of us, that to become a real Russian will mean precisely this: to strive to bring conciliation to the contradictions of Europe, to show a way out of the sorrows of Europe in our own Russian soul, universally human and all-uniting; to find a place in it, with brotherly love, for all our brothers, and finally perhaps to speak the final word of the great harmony of all, of the brotherly unison of all the nations according to the law of the gospel of Christ.[1]

Of Dostoyevsky's burning sincerity there can be no doubt, but his delight in the brotherly nature of the Russian people could only provoke irreverent reactions from members of many nations which had had practical experience of this brotherhood. Some might ruefully recall lines in another tongue:

> Und willst du nicht mein Bruder sein,
> So schlag' ich dir den Schädel ein.

Christian humility was also a virtue not always conspicuous in the behaviour of Russians either towards other nations or among themselves. None the less, those who deny the imprint of Christianity on the Russians, whether they be Christian enemies of Russia or anti-Christian spokesmen for the Russian people, have left out a whole dimension of its history, something which in the mid twentieth century few Russians and probably no foreigners could understand, something which historians a hundred years hence may see more clearly, which may, however, be lost to human view for ever.

The mission which the later revolutionaries had in mind for

[1] F. M. Dostoyevsky, *Dnevnik pisatelya za 1877 god* (Berlin, 1922), pp. 597–9. Though the title of the volume is as above, the Pushkin speech is included as *Dnevnik pisatelya za 1880 god*, ch. 2. The speech was delivered on 8 June to a meeting of the Society of Lovers of Russian Speech.

Russia was definitely secular. Already in 1861 Zaichnevsky had written of 'the glorious future of Rusia, to whose lot it had fallen to be the first country to achieve the glorious work of socialism'. In March 1917 there can have been few who recalled these words, but there were many who were determined to make them a reality.

In the hundred-odd years since the Russians had driven out Napoleon, their country had come a long way. The nineteenth century was a great age for Russia, as for other countries, but it was not a happy age. It is full of heroism and achievement, but it is the suffering rather than the joy that one remembers. Imperial Russia built great armies, great factories, and great prisons, it conquered vast lands in Asia and it ruined thousands upon thousands of human lives. There are heroism and genius in abundance on one side of the balance, human wastage and frustration on the other: the long years torn out of the lives of Shevchenko and Chernyshevsky, the unending struggle against intrigue and stupidity that blighted the careers of the Milyutin brothers, and of countless lesser officials who toiled on in the countless dreary little offices of which the great government machine of the Russian empire was composed, doing their duty and perhaps in the long run doing more good than harm.

In March 1917 it seemed to many that the sufferings had been worth while, because now at last the chance of true liberty and true greatness had come. Great things were done in the years that followed, and these, together with the great inventions that have caused the earth to shrink and given man power to abolish his species, have truly merged the destiny of Russia with the fate of the whole human race, though not in the sense in which Dostoyevsky foretold it. Indeed, no sooner are prophecies fulfilled than they turn out to have been false. Yet the belief that social and political prophecies can be, or have been, replaced by an exact science of human society and human history, is only another in the long line of human myths, and its spokesmen will not escape the fate of earlier myth-makers.

BIBLIOGRAPHY

THE following short bibliography lists the works which have been most useful to me, and those which are likely to be most accessible to residents of English-speaking countries. In the case of books, especially the collected works of well-known writers, which have been published many times, I have given either the edition which I have myself used, or that which is most accessible. As even the best Western libraries sometimes do not contain editions, or have individual volumes missing, my choice may be unhelpful to some readers. For this defect, which is probably unavoidable, I ask indulgence.

The bibliography is divided in time, subject, and type of book. In time, the divisons are: (1) works which cover the whole or most of the period with which this book is concerned; (2) those which provide the historical background up to the end of the eighteenth century; (3) the reign of Alexander I, 1801–25; (4) the reign of Nicholas I, 1825–55; (5) the reign of Alexander II, 1855–81; (6) the reign of Alexander III and the first half of that of Nicholas II, 1881–1905; (7) the last years of the Imperial régime, 1905–17. In subjects the divisons are: (i) government and politics; (ii) political and social ideas; (iii) economic and social development; (iv) nationalities; (v) diplomacy, war and foreign relations. The main types of material are (*a*) official documents; (*b*) published private papers, memoirs, and correspondence; (*c*) contemporary political or other works; (*d*) biographies; (*e*) specialized secondary works; (*f*) general surveys.

The divisions between these categories are inevitably blurred, and no attempt has been made to maintain them in doctrinaire rigidity. Many works listed in one period contain material relating to the preceding or the following period. Many works which deal mainly with politics contain also a great deal of economic material. The distinction between biographies and specialized secondary works is difficult to maintain, and some of the biographies contain such an abundance of original documents as to justify their being placed in the category of official documents. I ask pardon for the view that, when in doubt, it is less important to uphold in its purity the distinction between 'primary' and 'secondary' sources sanctified by historical pedantry than to provide a guide which may help persons who wish to pursue further studies.

The place of publication of all works published abroad is stated unless unidentified. If published in Great Britain, the place is only stated where there might otherwise be confusion. SPB is an abbreviation for St. Petersburg. In the case of the works published in that city between 1914 and 1924 the name Petrograd is used, and for works published after 1924 the name Leningrad. In the case of a series of volumes begun when the city had one name and completed when it had another, the name in use at the beginning of the series is normally retained.

With a few exceptions, I have not listed articles in this bibliography. Readers should, however, note that articles in learned journals are an extremely important source. I would mention especially the Soviet journals *Istorik marksist*, *Istoricheskie zapiski*, *Voprosy istorii*, and *Istoria SSSR*; the English-language *Slavonic and East European Review* and *American Slavic and East European Review*; the French *Le Monde slave* and *Cahiers du monde russe et soviétique*; and the German, *Osteuropa* and *Jahrbücher für die Geschichte Osteuropas.*

I have also not listed works of imaginative literature. Of these there are of course many easily accessible editions. But it should be clearly stated that it is hardly possible to have much understanding of Russian nineteenth-century history without having some knowledge of the works—preferably in Russian—of Pushkin, Lermontov, Gogol, Turgenev, Tolstoy, Dostoyevsky, Chekhov, and Blok, not to mention other lesser yet outstanding writers.

I. THE WHOLE PERIOD

Pride of place must be given to three periodical publications which are an inexhaustible source of primary material for the historian. First are the collections of the Imperial Russian Historical Society, published in 148 volumes from 1867–1916—*Sbornik Imperatorskogo russkogo istorischeskogo obshchestva*—referred to hereafter as *SIRIO.* Individual volumes covering specific subjects are mentioned below in their context. Second is the monthly *Ruskaya Starina,* founded and managed by the Semevsky family. It published large quantities of memoirs, private papers, and correspondence and some public documents between 1870 and 1917. Third is *Russkii Arkhiv,* founded in 1863 by P. I. Bartenev and published by him until 1912, and after his death up to 1916. It published material of the same sort. These periodicals will be quoted below as *RS* or *RA* respectively.

The texts of laws may be found in the Collection of Laws, codified by Speransky in 1830 and subsequently enlarged. This has three editions—*Polnoe sobranie zakonov Rossiiskoy Imperii 1649–1825,* in 45 volumes, nos. 1–30,600, SPB, 1830; *Sobranie vtoroe* from 12 December 1825 to 28 February 1881, in 55 volumes, nos. 1–61,928, completed SPB, 1884; and *Sobranie tretye* from 1 March 1881 to 31 December

1908, in 28 volumes, nos. 1–31,329, completed SPB, 1911. They are well indexed, and easy to use. Only occasional references have been given to them in footnotes. A reader can easily check the text of any law from the date.

Another useful source is the yearly list of persons holding senior official posts, *Mesyatsoslov s rospisyu chinovnykh osob*, published from 1776 onwards. From 1828 to 1915 it bore the title *Adres-kalendar', obshchaya rospis nachal'stvuyushchikh i prochikh dolzhnostnykh list po vsem upravleniyam v Rossiiskoy Imperii*. It was published by the Department of Heraldry of the Senate.

Two general surveys by Russians, available in English, may be recommended: A. A. Kornilov, *Modern Russian History*, New York, 1924, and Michael T. Florinsky, *Russia: A History and an Interpretation*, New York, 1953. Florinsky's book is the best single comprehensive work in English, showing admirable balance in the selection of facts and subjects, and all the more stimulating for one or two rather bizarre individual judgements. To these should be added the short book by Michael Karpovich, *Imperial Russia 1801–1917*, New York, 1932, essentially a long essay, of the quality one expects from this outstanding Russian historian, who left his main memorial in the school of young historians he trained, but unfortunately so little in the form of his own published works. Of general surveys by Soviet historians, mostly by the collaboration of several authors, a recent accessible example is *Istoria SSSR, uchebnik dlya pedagogicheskikh institutov*. Volume 2, which was published in Moscow in 1964, deals with the period 1859–1917.

Four general reference works contain an enormous amount of information. First is the detailed geographical survey of the Russian empire at the end of the nineteenth century, containing social, economic, and historical material going back into past epochs, P. P. Semyonov-Tyanshansky and V. I. Lamansky, *Rossiya: polnoe geograficheskoe opisanie nashego otechestva*, SPB, 1899–1914, 19 volumes. Second is the *Entsiklopedicheskii slovar'*, published in St. Petersburg jointly by F. A. Brockhaus (Leipzig) and I. A. Efron (St. Petersburg). There are 86 volumes (41 volumes, mostly in more than one part, making up 82 bound books, together with four supplementary volumes) between 1890 and 1907. This work is referred to in my footnotes as 'Brockhaus Encyclopaedia'. Third is the *Bolshaya Sovetskaya Entsiklopediya*, of which there are two editions, the first in 65 volumes, appearing between 1926 and 1931, the second in 50 volumes, appearing between 1949 and 1957. To these may be added the incomplete but useful biographical dictionary *Russkii Biograficheskii Slovar'*, in 25 volumes, SPB, 1896–1913.

In 1902, to commemorate the centenary of the foundation by Alexander I of the central ministries in their modern form, a series of official histories were published in St. Petersburg. The most valuable are those dealing with the Committee of Ministers—*Komitet Ministrov, istoricheskii obzor 1802–1902* by S. M. Seredonin, in 5 volumes, and with the Ministry of Education—*Istoricheskii obzor deyatel'nosti Ministerstva narodnogo prosveshcheniya 1802–1902*, 1 volume, by S. V. Rozhdestvensky. Also useful are those on the Ministries of Finance, War and Foreign Affairs—*Ministerstvo finansov 1802–1902*, 2 volumes, edited by N. K. Brzhesky; *Stoletie Voennogo Ministerstva*, 13 volumes, chief editor Lieutenant-General D. A. Skalon; and *Ocherk istorii Ministerstva inostrannikh del 1802–1902*, edited by S. A. Byelokurov, F. F. Martens and others. The volume on the Ministry of the Interior, *Ministerstvo vnutrennikh del, istoricheskii ocherk 1802–1902*, 3 volumes, is rather sketchy, but still contains some interesting information. In 1911 a bicentenary official history of the Senate was published—*Istoria Pravitel'stvuyushchego senata 1711–1911* in 5 volumes, edited by A. N. Filippov, S. F. Platonov, N. D. Chechulin, and E. N. Berendts.

The following works cover different aspects of history during the whole period, and in some cases also earlier periods.

Economic and Social

BERLIN, P. A. *Russkaya burzhuaziya v staroe i novoe vremya*, Moscow, 1922.

BLUM, JEROME. *Lord and Peasant in Russia*, Princeton, 1961.

KHROMOV, P. A. *Ekonomicheskoe razvitie Rossii v XIX i XX vekakh*, Moscow, 1950.

KORF, Baron S. A. *Dvoryanstvo i ego soslovnoe upravlenie za stoletie 1762–1855 godov*, SPB, 1906.

LYASHCHENKO, P. I. *Istoriya narodnogo khozyaistva SSSR*, Moscow, 1948, 2 volumes.

ROMANOVICH-SLAVYATINSKY, A. *Dvoryanstvo v Rossii ot nachala XVIII-go veka do otmeny krepostnogo prava*, Kiev, 1912.

TUGAN-BARANOVSKY, M. I. *Russkaya fabrika v proshlom i nastoyashchem*, SPB, 1900; 3rd edition Moscow, 1934.

Khromov and Lyashchenko are well-known Soviet text-books. The work of Romanovich-Slavyatinsky on the nobility and of Tugan-Baranovsky on the Russian factory are pioneering studies which are still of great value.

Education

HANS, NICHOLAS. *History of Russian Educational Policy*, 1931.

Religion

AMMANN, A. M., *Abriß der ostslawischen Kirchengeschichte*, Vienna, 1950.

CONYBEARE, F. C. *Russian Dissenters*, Harvard, 1921.

FLOROVSKY, G. *Puti russkogo bogosloviya*, Paris, 1937.

Nationalities

DUBNOW, S. M. *History of the Jews in Russia and Poland*, Philadelphia, 1916, 3 volumes.
HRUSHEVSKY, M. *Abrégé de l'histoire de l'Ukraine*, Paris, 1920.
Istoryia Uzbekskoy SSR. Academy of Sciences of Uzbek SSR, Tashkent, 1956.
KIRIMAL, EDIGE. *Der nationale Kampf der Krimtürken*, Emsdetten, 1952.
LANG, D. M. *A Modern History of Georgia*, 1962.
SENN, A. R. *The Emergence of Modern Lithuania*, New York, 1959.
TÖRNE, P. O. von. *Finland under etthundratrettio år 1809–1939*, Helsinki, 1943.
UUSTALU, E. *The History of the Estonian People*, 1952.
VAKAR, N. P. *Belorussia, the Making of a Nation*, Harvard, 1956.
WHEELER, G. *The Modern History of Soviet Central Asia*, 1964.
WITTRAM, R. *Baltische Geschichte*, Munich, 1954.

The following three works, on subjects not easily classifiable, extend over the whole or most of the period, and all three are contributions of high quality and originality, covering ground largely unexplored.

ALLEN, W. E. D. and MURATOV, P. *Caucasian Battlefields: A History of the Wars on the Turco-Caucasian Border 1828–1921*, 1953.
LENSEN, G. A. *The Russian Push towards Japan 1697–1875*, Princeton, 1959.
LEONTOWITSCH, W. *Geschichte des Liberalismus in Rußland*, Frankfurt, 1954.

II. HISTORICAL BACKGROUND UP TO END OF EIGHTEENTH CENTURY

The best introduction to Russian history is still the five-volume work of the outstanding historian of the nineteenth century, V. O. Klyuchevsky. This was published, largely posthumously, as *Kurs russkoy istorii*, from 1904 to 1921, another edition in Moscow in 1936. There is an English translation of poor quality, last volume published 1931. A new and good translation, by Mrs. Lilian Archibald, of volume 4, dealing with Peter the Great, was published in 1958. Another great work is P. N. Milyukov's *Ocherki po istorii russkoy kul'tury*, 3 volumes, SPB, 1904. Part of it has been translated as *Outlines of Russian Culture*, edited by M. Karpovich, Philadelphia, 1942, 3 volumes. Another important historian is the Marxist M. N. Pokrovsky, whose posthumous reputation has been subject to some fluctuation in his own country. Apart from his magnificent work as editor and publisher of historical documents, three of his own books deserve attention—*Russkaya istoriya s drevnyeyshikh vremyon*, 4 volumes, Moscow, 1918; *Ocherk istorii russkoy kul'tury*, in 2 parts, Moscow, 1922; and *Russkaya istoriya v samom szhatom ocherke*, Moscow, 1933.

The pioneer modern work in English, on which generations of students have been brought up, is Sir Bernard Pares's *History of Russia*. The latest edition, with an Introduction by his son, the late

Professor Richard Pares, a still more distinguished historian though not a specialist in Russian history, appeared in 1955. The finest English scholar in the field of Russian history, the late B. H. Sumner, apart from his specialized studies, published in 1944 a *Survey of Russian History*. This was essentially an attempt to explain to the English-speaking public their wartime ally in the light of its past. Its presentation is original, dividing the subject into main themes, and examining each first in the present or immediate past and then going back into history. It remains a stimulating work with many valuable insights. Of a number of text-books published in recent years in English, the two best seem to me to be N. V. Riasanovsky, *A History of Russia*, New York, 1963, and Richard Charques, *A Short History of Russia*, London, 1959. The first is the more profound and shows an unusual balance of judgement in the allocation of space to different periods. The second is indeed short, but very clear and sound.

The following works, dealing with aspects of Russia in the eighteenth century, provide a good immediate background.

Economic and social

PORTAL, R. Article entitled 'Manufactures et classes sociales en Russie au 18e siècle', in *Revue Historique*, July–Sept. 1949.

—— *L'Ourale au 18e siècle*, Paris, 1950.

SEMEVSKY, V. I. *Krest'yane v tsarstvovanie Imperatritsy Ekateriny II*, SPB, 1901–3, 2 volumes.

—— *Krest'yanskii vopros v Rossii v XVIII i pervoy polovine XIX veka*, SPB, 1905.

Cultural

LARIVIÈRE, CHARLES DE. *La France et la Russie au 18e siècle*, Paris, 1909.

MOHRENSCHILDT, D. VON. *Russia in the Intellectual Life of 18th Century France*, New York, 1936.

ROGGER, HANS. *National Consciousness in 18th Century Russia*, Harvard, 1960.

Foreign Policy

ANDERSON, M. S. *Britain's Discovery of Russia 1553–1815*, 1958.

GERHARD, DIETRICH. *England und der Aufstieg Rußlands*, Munich, 1933.

LANG, D. M. *The Last Years of the Georgian Monarchy 1658–1832*, 1957.

LORD, R. H. *The Second Partition of Poland*, Harvard, 1915.

MADARIAGA, ISABEL DE. *Britain, Russia and the Armed Neutrality of 1780*, 1962.

Many volumes of *SIRIO* contain official documents relating to the eighteenth century, including proceedings of Catherine II's Commission of 1767 and of the supreme political authorities under her predecessors. Of the unofficial literature of the period the most important single work, for the understanding of the following century, is perhaps A. N. Radishchev's *Journey from St. Petersburg to*

Moscow, which appeared in 1790, and has been published since in many editions and has been translated.

On the reign of Paul there is the official biography by N. K. Shilder, with documentary appendices, *Pavel Pervy — istoriko-biograficheskii ocherk*, SPB, 1901, and a good later study, M. V. Klochkov, *Ocherki pravitel'stvennoy deyatel'nosti vremeni Imperatora Pavla I*, Petrograd, 1916.

III. THE REIGN OF ALEXANDER I, 1801–1825

Government and Politics

The most valuable official documents are included in the two main biographies of Alexander I. Each of the 4 volumes of N. K. Shilder, *Imperator Aleksandr I, ego zhizn' i tsarstvovanie*, SPB, 1897, contains very large documentary appendices, and 2 of the 3 volumes of the Grand Duke Nikolay Mikhailovich, *Imperator Aleksandr I*, SPB, 1912, consist entirely of documents. The Grand Duke's three volumes on *Le comte Paul Stroganov*, SPB, 1905, also consist overwhelmingly of documents: the second volume contains the Minutes of the Unofficial Committee, and the third volume relates to foreign policy. Two other similar publications by the Grand Duke are *Perepiska Imperatora Aleksandra I s sestroy velikoy knyaginey Ekaterinoy Pavlovnoy*, SPB, 1910, and *L'Impératrice Elisabeth, épouse d'Alexandre Ier*, SPB, 1908–9, 3 volumes. It should be noted that the bulk of the documents in all these works is in French.

The most convenient collection of Speransky's political memoranda is *M. M. Speransky: proekty i zapiski*, ed. S. N. Valk, Moscow, 1961. Speransky's financial project is in *SIRIO* vol. 45, pp. 1–73. The papers of the duc de Richelieu, during his period of office as governor-general of New Russia, are collected in *SIRIO* vol. 54. A rich source of materials on the reign of Alexander I, and to some extent also of Nicholas I, are the Vorontsov Archives—*Arkhiv knyaz'ya Vorontsova*, 40 volumes, Moscow, 1870–95. Also useful are the Mordvinov Archives—*Arkhiv grafov Mordvinovykh*, ed. V. A. Bilbassov, SPB, 1901–3, 10 volumes. Also of interest are the writings of Karazin—*Sochineniya, pis'ma i bumagi V. N. Karazina*, ed. D. I. Bagaleyev, Kharkov, 1910. Some of the writings and correspondence of Rostopchin are contained in *Matériaux en grande partie inédits pour la biographie du comte Théodore Rostaptchine, rassemblés par son fils*, Brussels, 1864.

Among memoirs of contemporaries the following deserve mention: *Mémoires du prince Adam Czartoryski*, Paris, 1887, 2 volumes, for both internal and foreign policy; G. R. Derzhavin, *Zapiski*, ed. P. I. Bartenev, Moscow, 1860; I. I. Dmitriev, *Vzglyad na moyu zhizn'*,

Moscow, 1866; *Mémoires de la comtesse Edling*, Moscow, 1888; A. S. Shiskov, *Zapiski, mneniya i perepiska*, ed. N. Kiselyov and Y. F. Samarin, Berlin, 1870, 2 volumes; F. F. Vigel (Philippe Wiegel), *Zapiski*, Moscow, 1928; *Avtobiografiya Yuryevskogo Arkhimandrita Fotia*, in instalments in *RS* between March 1894 and August 1896. Karamzin's *Memoir on Ancient and Modern Russia* was published in Russian and English, with an interesting introductory essay by Richard Pipes, Harvard, 1954.

The documents relating to the Decembrists have been published in successive volumes since 1925, under the editorship first of Pokrovsky and later of M. V. Nechkina. Eleven volumes have appeared in the series, which is entitled *Dokumenty po istorii vosstaniya dekabristov*. A small but useful anthology of Decembrist writings is *Dekabristy, otryvki iz istochnikov*, ed. Y. G. Oksman, Moscow, 1926.

The following are secondary works relating to aspects of internal politics and social problems during the reign.

BARYATINSKY, Prince V. *Le Mystère d'Alexandre Ier*, Paris, 1925.

DUBROVIN. 'Nashi mistiki-sektanty', articles in *RS*, Sept. 1894–Nov. 1895.

KIZEVETTER, A. A. *Istoricheskie ocherki*, Moscow, 1912.

—— *Istoricheskie otkliki*, Moscow, 1915.

MAZOUR, ANATOLE G. *The First Russian Revolution 1825*, Berkeley, 1937.

NECHKINA, M. V. *Dvizhenie dekabristov*, Moscow, 1955, 2 volumes.

PIPES, RICHARD. 'The Russian Military Colonies 1810–1831', in *The Journal of Modern History*, vol. xxii, Sept. 1950.

PYPIN, A. N. *Obshchestvennoe dvizhenie v Rossii pri Aleksandre I*, SPB, 1900.

—— *Religioznye dvizheniya pri Aleksandre I*, Petrograd, 1916.

—— *Russkoe masonstvo, XVIII i pervaya chetvert XIX veka*, Petrograd, 1916.

RAEFF, MARC. *Siberia and the Reforms of 1822*, Seattle, 1956.

RAUCH, G. VON. *Rußland: staatliche Einheit und nationale Vielfalt*, Munich, 1954.

SEMEVSKY, V. I. *Politicheskie i obshchestvennye idei dekabristov*, SPB, 1909.

SUKHOMLINOV, M. I. *Izsledovaniya i stati*, vol. i, *Materialy dlya istorii obrazovaniya v Rossii v tsarstvovanie Imperatora Aleksandra I*, SPB, 1889.

TURGENEV, N. I. *La Russie et les Russes*, Paris, 1847.

VERNADSKY, George. *La Charte constitutionelle de l'Empire russe de 1820*, Paris, 1933.

Of these, the outstanding works are those by Kizevetter and Pypin. The book by Turgenev, a Decembrist who left Russia before 1825, made a great impression in Europe in its time. The book by Nechkina is very learned and valuable.

The following biographies are useful. The best is that by Raeff, which can in fact serve as an excellent one-volume survey of the whole reign for persons who can only read English.

KORF, BARON M. A. *Zhizn' grafa Speranskogo*, SPB, 1861, 2 volumes.

LEY, FRANCIS. *Madame de Krudener et son temps*, Paris, 1961.
RAEFF, MARC. *Michael Speransky, Statesman of Imperial Russia 1772–1839*, The Hague, 1961.
VENTURI, FRANCO. *Il moto decabrista e i fratelli Poggioli*, Turin, 1956.
WALISZEWSKI, K. *Le Règne d'Alexandre Ier*, Paris, 1923–5, 3 volumes.

A view by a foreign observer is Robert Pinkerton, *Russia: or Miscellaneous Observations on the Past and Present State of that Country and its Inhabitants*, London, 1833. The author was an active organizer of the Bible Society.

On Poland in this reign, apart from Czartoryski's memoirs, may be recommended the chapters in *The Cambridge History of Poland*, vol. 2, 1941, by M. Handelsman on 'The Duchy of Warsaw' and by General Marian Kukiel on 'Polish Military Effort in the Napoleonic Wars', and the latter's book *Czartoryski and European Unity 1770–1861*, Princeton, 1955.

Foreign Policy and the Napoleonic Wars

Volumes 21, 70, 77, 82, 83, 88, and 89 of *SIRIO* contain diplomatic reports from Russian representatives in Paris between 1800 and 1811. Volumes 112, 119, and 127 cover the years 1814 to 1820. The reports of Caulaincourt and his successor Lauriston during their service as ambassador in St. Petersburg were published by Grand Duke Nikolay Mikhailovich under the title *La France et la Russie*, SPB, 1905, in seven volumes. A memorandum by Capodistrias on his service as a Russian diplomat and foreign minister is published in *SIRIO*, volume 3. The first three volumes of *Lettres et Papiers du chancelier comte de Nesselrode 1760–1850*, Paris, undated, relate to this reign. There are important documents on foreign policy in Czartoryski's memoirs and in the appendixes of Shilder's biography.

The Soviet Ministry of Foreign Affairs has recently begun a valuable collection of documents under the title *Vnyeshnyaya politika Rossii XIX i nachala XX veka*. Four volumes in the First Series, covering the early part of the century, have appeared, the first 3 covering 1801–5 and the fourth 1812.

An invaluable source is the collection of treaties of Russia with the European Powers, published by F. Martens under the title *Sobranie traktatov i konventsiy, zaklyuchonnykh Rossiey s inostrannymi derzhavami*, SPB, various dates. The volumes touching this period for each foreign country are: Britain, vol. 11 up to 1831, vol. 12 1831–95; France, vol. 13 up to 1807, vol. 14 1807–20, vol. 15 1820–1906; Austria, vol. 2 1762–1808, vols. 3 and 4 up to 1878; Germany (chiefly Prussia), vols. 6–8 1762–1888. The summaries and comments on events between the various treaties, based on the author's knowledge of unpublished documents, are of great value, though his judgements cannot be accepted without reservations.

No attempt will be made here to list diplomatic documents from non-Russian sources. There is already a large literature, with adequate bibliographies, on this period in west European languages.

Documents relating to the occupation of parts of the Russian empire by Napoleon's armies were published in volumes 128, 133, and 139 of *SIRIO*. The Academy of Sciences of the Soviet Union published in 1962, on the 150th anniversary of the invasion, a collection of documents relating to the mobilization of the Russian people to meet it, entitled *Narodnoe opolchenie v otechestvennoy voyne 1812 goda*. Two years later it followed with a collection relating to the liberation of Europe by the Russian army, entitled *Pokhod russkoy armii protiv Napoleona v 1813 godu i osvobozhdenie Germanii*.

Memoirs of participants in the war of 1812, and later accounts of them by persons with direct experience, include the following:

BOUTOURLINE, GÉNÉRAL. *Histoire militaire de la campagne de Russie en 1812*, Paris, 1814.

CLAUSEWITZ, GENERAL CARL VON. *The Campaign of 1812 in Russia*, 1843.

DAVYDOV, DENIS. *Voennye zapiski*, ed. V. Orlov, Moscow, 1940.

LABAUME, EUGÈNE. *Relation circonstanciée de la campagne de Russie en 1812*, Paris, 1814.

LANGERON, GÉNÉRAL DE. *Mémoires*, Paris, 1902.

SÉGUR, GÉNÉRAL COMTE DE. *Histoire de Napoléon et de la Grande Armée pendant l'année 1812*, Paris, 1825.

WILSON, SIR ROBERT. *The Invasion of Russia*, 1860.

The works of General A. I. Mikhailovsky-Danilevsky about the wars of this reign, including his own memoirs of some of these campaigns, are also a useful source. They are: *Opisanie pervoy voyny Imperatora Aleksandra s Napoleonom v 1805 godu*, SPB, 1843; *Opisanie vtoroy voyny Imperatora Aleksandra s Napoleonom v 1806 i 1807 godakh*, SPB, 1846; *Opisanie tyuretskoy voyny s 1806 do 1812 goda*, SPB, 1843; *Geschichte des vaterländischen Krieges im Jahre 1812*, Leipzig, 1840; *Zapiski o pokhode 1813 goda*, SPB, 1834; *Zapiski 1814 i 1815 godov*, SPB, 1832.

Among later works on the war of 1812 must be mentioned the collective effort in seven volumes, *Otechestvennaya voyna i russkoe obshchestvo*, edited by A. Dzhivelegov, S. P. Melgunov, and V. I. Picheta, to celebrate the centenary, Moscow, 1912. A later study by a distinguished Polish military historian is General Marian Kukiel, *Wojna 1812 roku*, Kraków, 1937. Louis Madelin, *La Catastrophe de Russie*, Paris, 1949, is a useful survey from the French point of view. The well-known and much-translated work of E. V. Tarle, *Napoleon's Invasion of Russia*, cannot be recommended: the discrepancies between the two editions are clearly due to factors other than the historian's own judgement.

Outstanding among all secondary works on diplomacy in this period is the classic of Albert Vandal, *Napoléon et Alexandre Ier*, Paris, 1893–6, 3 volumes. The following may also be recommended, on subjects directly affecting Russian policy:

CRAWLEY, C. V. *The Question of Greek Independence*, 1930.
HECKSCHER, ELI F. *The Continental Blockade*, 1922.
KRAEHE, ENNO E. *Metternich's German policy*, Princeton, 1963.
OKUN, S. B. *Rossiisko-amerikanskaya kompaniya*, Moscow, 1939.
TARLE, E. V. *Kontinental'naya blokada*, first published 1913, reprinted as vol. 3 of his collected works, *Sochineniya*, Moscow, 1957–62, 12 volumes.
YAKCHITCH, G. *L'Europe et la résurrection de la Serbie*, Paris, 1917.

For the large secondary literature on the diplomacy of the European Powers in general in the Napoleonic era, the reader is referred to the numerous well-known general works and bibliographies.

IV. THE REIGN OF NICHOLAS I, 1825–1855

Government and Politics

Volumes 74 and 90 of *SIRIO* contain the proceedings of, and many of the papers placed before, the Committee of 6 December 1826. Volume 98 contains 'Materials for the biography of Nicholas I'—various papers relating to his life and policies. Volume 113 contains documents relating to the organization of the Orthodox Church during the reign. Volumes 131 and 132 contain the correspondence between Nicholas I and Grand Duke Constantine in the years 1825–31, relating mainly to Polish affairs.

Two biographies which contain a great deal of documentary material are Shilder, *Imperator Nikolay I, ego zhizn' i tsarstvovanie*, SPB, 1903, 2 volumes, and Prince A. G. Shcherbatov, *General-fel'dmarshal knyaz' Paskevich, ego zhizn' i deyatel'nost'*, SPB, 1888–1904, 7 volumes. The first only goes as far as 1830. The second contains numerous letters from the Tsar to Paskevich, who was one of his closest friends. There are also documents in the large-scale work of the German historian Theodor Schiemann, *Geschichte Rußlands unter Kaiser Nikolaus I*, Berlin, 1904–9, 4 volumes.

Some interesting reports of the Third Department on the state of public opinion early in the reign were published in nos. 37 (1929) and 38 (1930) of *Krasny Arkhiv* (see below p. 760) under the title *Graf A. Kh. Benkendorf o Rossii v 1827–1830 godakh*. The reports were the work not of Benckendorff but of his assistant von Fock. Uvarov's famous report of 1832 is in *Sbornik postanovleniy po Ministerstvu narodnogo prosveshcheniya—tsarstvovanie Imperatora Nikolaya I*, SPB, 1875. His report on his first ten years as Minister was published under the title *Desyatiletie ministerstva narodnogo prosveshcheniya 1833–1843*, SPB, 1864.

Three volumes of documents relating to the Petrashevsky Circle were published by the Academy of Sciences of the Soviet Union under the title *Delo Petrashevtsev*, Moscow, 1937–51, 3 volumes. The official report on the Cyril and Methodius Society is in *RA*, 1892, no. 7, under the title *Ob ukraino-slavyanskom obshchestve*.

The memoirs of Baron M. A. Korf, which appeared in instalments in *RS*, volumes 99–102, throw light on the higher bureaucracy, as do those of P. A. Valuyev for the years 1847–60 in *RS* in instalments from 1890 onwards. The memoirs of A. V. Nikitenko, which throw light on the bureaucratic, academic, and literary worlds, appeared first in instalments in *RS*, but were later published as a whole. A recent edition is A. V. Nikitenko, *Dnevnik*, Moscow, 1955–6, 3 volumes. Two instalments of the memoirs of N. I. Kostomarov, concerning his involvement with the Cyril and Methodius Society, appeared in the review *Russkaya mysl'* in 1885, in nos. 5 and 6.

The following secondary works on government and politics in the reign are of value. The last contains documents. A combination of Polievktov and Riasanovsky is the best short introduction to the whole reign that can be recommended.

MONAS, SYDNEY L. *The Third Section: Police and Society in Russia under Nicholas I*, Harvard, 1961.

POLIEVKTOV, M. *Nikolay I, biografiya i obzor tsarstvovaniya*, Moscow, 1918.

RIASANOVSKY, N. V. *Nicholas I and Official Nationality in Russia 1825–1855*, Berkeley, 1959.

ZABLOTSKY-DESYATOVSKY, A. P. *Graf P. D. Kiselyov i ego vremya*, SPB, 1882, 4 volumes.

Political and Social Ideas

The essential primary sources are the Works of the great political writers of the period. The following editions may be mentioned.

BAKUNIN. *Izbrannye sochineniya*, Petrograd, 1919–21, 5 volumes.

BELINSKY. *Polnoe sobranie sochineniy*, by Soviet Academy of Sciences, 1953–9, 13 volumes. An earlier attempt at a complete collection, starting in St. Petersburg in 1900, came to an end after producing 10 volumes.

CHAADAYEV. *Sochineniya i pis'ma P. Y. Chaadaeva*, ed. M. Gershenzon, Moscow, 1913, 2 volumes. Further unpublished Philosophical Letters appeared, translated from the original French into Russian, in *Literaturnoe nasledstvo*, 1935, nos. 22–24.

HERZEN. *Polnoe sobranie sochineniy i pisem*, ed. M. K. Lemke, Petrograd, 1919–25, 22 volumes.

KHOMYAKOV, A. S. *Polnoe sobranie sochineniy*, Moscow, 1911, 8 volumes. The set in the British Museum is not complete. A new useful selection of some of his more important writings is *Izbrannye sochineniya*, ed. N. S. Arsenyev, New York, 1955.

Outstanding among biographies of the writers of the period is the monumental work of M. P. Barsukov, *Zhizn' i trudy M. P. Pogodina*, SPB, 1888–1910, 22 volumes. It contains long quotations from letters and writings not only of Pogodin but of his contemporaries, is a mine of both political and literary information, and should really be considered as a primary source. Another useful work is an anthology of a few important Slavophil writings, not easily obtainable elsewhere—N. L. Brodsky, *Rannye slavyanofily*, Moscow, 1910. Some letters of Westernizers, especially Granovsky and Belinsky, are contained in F. F. Nelidov, *Zapadniki 40-kh godov*, Moscow, 1910. A valuable work of memoirs by a contemporary who belonged to the Westernizers' Circle is P. V. Annenkov, *Literaturnye vospominaniya*, SPB, 1909.

The following secondary studies of the lives and ideas of the intelligentsia of the age of Nicholas I are recommended.

BERLIN, SIR ISAIAH. *The Marvellous Decade*—four articles on the years 1838–48, especially brilliant on Belinsky, published in *Encounter* in 1953.

CARR, E. H. *The Romantic Exiles*, 1933.

—— *Michael Bakunin*, 1937.

GRATIEUX, A. *A. S. Khomiakov et le mouvement slavophile*, Paris, 1939, 2 volumes.

HARE, RICHARD. *Pioneers of Russian Social Thought*, 1951.

LAMPERT, E. *Studies in Rebellion*, 1957.

MALIA, MARTIN. *Alexander Herzen and the Birth of Russian Socialism*, Harvard, 1961.

QUÉNET, CHARLES. *Tchaadaev et les lettres philosophiques*, Paris, 1931.

STANKEVICH, A. *T. N. Granovsky, biograficheskii ocherk*, Moscow, 1869.

Economic and Social Development

A contribution by N. A. Milyutin to a collection of articles edited by P. I. Bartenev, editor of *Russkii Arkhiv*, in Moscow, 1872, under the title *Devyatnadtsaty vek*, vol. 2, contains a summary, of great interest because from so authoritative a source, of various proposals for the abolition of serfdom made in the first part of the century. Three outstanding secondary studies of later date are the following:

DRUZHININ, N. M. *Gosudarstvennye krest'yane i reforma P. D. Kiselyova*, Moscow, 1958, 2 volumes.

GRYNDZYUNSKY, P. G. *Gorodskoe grazhdanstvo doreformennoy Rossii*, Moscow, 1958.

STRUVE, P. B. *Krepostnoe khozyaistvo*, Moscow, 1913.

Nationalities

On the relations between Poland and Russia there are two valuable recent works:

LESLIE, R. F. *Polish Politics and the Revolution of November 1830*, 1956.

LEDNICKI, W. *Russia, Poland and the West: Essays in Literary and Cultural History*, 1954.

On relations with Asian peoples the following may be noted:

BADDELEY, J. F. *The Russian Conquest of the Causasus*, 1908.

BEKMAKHANOV, E. V. *Prisoedinenie Kazakhstana k Rossii*, 1957.

SMIRNOV, N. A. *Myuridizm na Kavkaze*, Moscow, 1963.

Foreign Observers

There are two very well-known accounts by foreign visitors, both of which had considerabe influence in their day. One is by the Marquis de Custine, *La Russie en 1839*, Paris, 1843. More than a century later an English abbreviated translation was published under the title *Journey for Our Time*, with an introduction by General W. Bedell Smith, former American ambassador in Moscow, London, 1951. The other is the description by Baron Haxthausen, whose English edition was published under the title *The Russian Empire, its People, Institutions and Resources*, London, 1856.

Foreign Relations

This is no place to review the large literature on the diplomacy of the Eastern Question. Exception may be made for three secondary works which contribute directly to knowledge of Russian policy in the 1830's—G. H. Bolsover, 'Nicholas I and the Partition of Turkey', article in *Slavonic and East European Review* (1948), no. 68, pp. 115–45; Philip E. Mosely, *Russian Diplomacy and the Opening of the Eastern Question*, Harvard, 1934; and Florescu, R. N., *The Struggle against Russia in the Roumanian Principalities 1821–1854*, Munich 1962. Apart from the later volumes of the papers of Nesselrode (vols. 4–8), the main Russian diplomatic source is *Peter von Meyendorff, ein russischer Diplomat an den Höfen von Berlin und Wien—politischer und privater Briefwechsel 1826–1863*, edited by Otto Hoetzsch, Leipzig, 1923, 3 volumes. A good collection of documents on the Russian invasion of Hungary in 1849, published in the original French or German, is Erzsébet Andics (ed.), *A Habsburgok és Románovok szövetsége*, Budapest, 1961. As Roumania played an important part, hitherto somewhat underestimated by historians writing in English, in Russian foreign policy and in the 'Eastern Question' during this period, mention should here be made of the excellent collection of documents published by the Roumanian Academy, *Documente privind istoria României: răscoala din 1821*, Bucarest, 1959–60, and to the third and fourth volumes of the collective work, based on profound research and knowledge, *Istoria României*, also published by the Academy, Bucarest, 1964.

The literature of the Crimean War is also vast and well known. The four volumes of A. M. Zayonchkovsky, *Vostochnaya voyna*, SPB, 1908–12, contain many important documents. The work of E. V. Tarle, *Krymskaya voyna*, republished as volumes 8 and 9 of his *Sochineniya*, is extremely useful, perhaps still more on the military operations than on the diplomacy. The reader may be referred to the classic works of the participants—A. W. Kinglake, *The Invasion of the Crimea*, 9 volumes, many editions; Baron de Bazancourt, *L'Expédition de Crimée, jusqu'à la prise de Sévastopol*, Paris, 1856, 2 volumes; and General E. I. Totleben, *Opisanie oborony Sevastopolya 1863–1872*, 2 volumes. A recent brief and clear survey, based almost wholly on British military sources, is W. Baring Pemberton, *Battles of the Crimea*, 1962.

V. THE REIGN OF ALEXANDER II, 1855–1881

There are two essential collections of documents relating to the emancipation of the serfs: *Pervoe izdanie materialov redaktsionnykh komissiy dlya sostavleniya polozheniy o krest'yanakh vykhodyashchikh iz krepostnoy zavisimosti*, SPB, 1859; and *Krest'yanskoe delo v tsarstvovanie Imperatora Aleksandra II*, ed. A. Skrebitsky, Bonn, 1862. Valuable collections of documents relating to peasant risings in the 1850's and 1860's have been published in Moscow recently, under the title *Krest'yanskoe dvizhenie v Rossii*. Three volumes cover respectively the years 1850–6 (published 1962), 1857–May 1861 (1963), and 1861–9 (1964).

The following are editions of the main political writers of this reign:

CHERNYSHEVSKY. *Polnoe sobranie sochineniy*, edited by V. Y. Kirpotin, B. P. Kozmin, and others, Moscow, 1939–51, 15 volumes.
DOBROLYUBOV. *Sobranie sochineniy*, Moscow–Leningrad, 1961–3, 9 volumes.
PISAREV. *Sochineniya*, Moscow, 1956, 4 volumes.
SAMARIN. *Sochinenya*, ed. D. Samarin, Moscow, 1878–90, 8 volumes.
TKACHOV. *Izbrannye sochineniya*, ed. B. P. Kozmin, Moscow, 1933.

A valuable source of information on the economic condition of the peasantry nearly twenty years after emancipation is the volume published by the Imperial Free Economic Society and the Russian Geographical Society, on the basis of a joint inquiry—*Sbornik materialov dlya izucheniya sel'skoy pozemelnoy obshchiny*, SPB, 1880.

The following are Memoirs by officials of the government or persons close to it, whether conservatives or moderate liberals. Outstanding are the diaries of Milyutin and Valuev, major primary sources for the reign. The Memoirs of Chicherin, a leading scholar also active in zemstvo affairs, of the veteran Slavophil Koshelyov and of the German ambassador Schweinitz are also especially useful.

CHICHERIN, B. N. *Vospominaniya*, Moscow, 1929, 4 volumes.
FIRSOV, N. A. *Studencheskie istorii v Kazanskom universitete*, in instalments in *RS* between Mar. and Aug. 1890.
KOSHELYOV, A. I. *Zapiski A. I. Koshelyova*, Berlin, 1884.
LEVSHIN, A. I. *Dostopamyatnie minuty v moey zhizni*, in *RA*, 1885, vol. ii.
MESHCHERSKY, V. P. *Moi vospominaniya*, SPB, 1898, vol. 2.
MILYUTIN, D. A. *Dnevnik D. A. Milyutina*, Moscow, 1947–50, 4 volumes.
PONOMARYOV, N. K. *Vospominaniya mirovogo posrednika pervogo prizyva 1861–1863* in *RS* Feb. 1891.
SCHWEINITZ, GENERAL VON. *Denkwürdigkeiten*, Berlin, 1927.
SHESTAKOV, P. D. Various articles of recollections on university life, published in *RS* in Oct., Nov., and Dec. 1888, Jan. 1889, Feb.–Apr. 1891, Dec. 1896, Jan. 1897.
SOLOVYOV, Y. A. 'Zapiski senatora Solovyova o krest'yanskom dele 1857–1858', articles in *RS* Feb.–May 1880 and Jan.–March 1882.
TOLSTOY, D. N. *Zapiski grafa D. N. Tolstogo*, in *RA*, 1885, vol. ii.
VALUYEV, P. A. *Dnevnik P. A. Valueva, ministra vnutrennikh del*, vol. i, 1861–4, vol. 2, 1864–76, Moscow, 1961.

The following are memoirs by revolutionaries, or accounts of the actions of persons with whom the authors were closely connected:

APTEKMAN, O. V. *Obshchestvo 'Zemlya i volya'*, Moscow, 1919.
DEBAGORY-MOKREVICH, V. *Vospominaniya*, SPB, 1904.
FIGNER, VERA. *Zapechatlyonny trud*, Moscow, 1920.
—— and PRIBYLEVA-KORBA, A. P. *A. D. Mikhailov*, Moscow, 1925.
PANTELEYEV, L. F. *Iz vospominaniy proshlogo*, ed. S. A. Reiser, Moscow, 1934.
STEPNYAK, S. *Underground Russia*, London, 1883.

The following biographies are of value. Leroy-Beaulieu's is slight, but throws light on its subject, the great N. A. Milyutin, of whom no major study, and no collection of papers, has yet been published. Footman's short but brilliant book is concerned mainly with Zhelyabov, but also with *Zemlya i volya* in general, and has a good short bibliography. The life of the Tsar by Tatishchev is a more or less official biography, based on a wide knowledge of the official sources.

COQUART, A. *Dmitri Pisarev (1840–1868) et l'idéologie du nihilisme russe*, Paris, 1946.
FOOTMAN, D. J. *Red Prelude*, 1944.

LAMPERT, E. *Sons against Fathers: Studies in Russian Radicalism and Revolution*, 1965.
LEROY-BEAULIEU, A. *Un homme d'état russe*, Paris, 1884.
NEVEDENSKY, S. *Katkov i ego vremya*, SPB, 1888.
NOLDE, BARON B. E. *Yury Samarin i ego vremya*, Paris, 1926.
TATISHCHEV, S. S. *Imperator Aleksandr II, ego zhizn' i tsarstvovanie*, SPB, 1903, 2 volumes.

The following secondary studies include works on economic problems. Lemke contains the texts of the 'Young Generation' and 'Young Russia' proclamations. Venturi's book is the most comprehensive survey of the revolutionary movement in this reign yet published in any country. The two works by the contemporary Soviet historian Zayonchkovsky are outstanding contributions.

DZANSHIEV, G. A. *Epokha velikikh reform*, Moscow, 1900.
GESSEN, I. V. *Sudebnaya reforma*, SPB, 1905.
KORNILOV, A. A. *Krest'yanskaya reforma*, SPB, 1905.
—— *Obshchestvennoe dvizhenie pri Aleksandre II*, Moscow, 1909.
KOSHELYOV, A. I. *Ob obshchinnom zemlevladenii v Rossii*, Berlin, 1875.
LEMKE, M. K. *Ocherki osvoboditel'nogo dvizheniya 60-kh godov*, SPB, 1908.
—— *Politicheskie protsessy v Rossii 1860-kh godov*, Moscow, 1923.
VENTURI, FRANCO. *Il popolismo russo*, Turin, 1952, 2 volumes. English translation in one volume under title *Roots of Revolution*, 1960.
YARMOLINSKY, A. *The Road to Revolution*, 1957.
ZAYONCHKOVSKY, P. A. *Otmena krepostnogo prava*, Moscow, 1954.
—— *Krizis samoderzhaviya na rubezhe 1870–1880 godov*, Moscow, 1964.

One of the main sources for the revolutionary movement are the articles, including both recollections and official documents, published in the two periodicals *Byloe*, which appeared in St. Petersburg (Petrograd) in 1906–7 and again between 1917 and 1926, and *Katorga i ssylka*, which appeared in Moscow from 1921 to 1935.

Nationalities

On the Polish Rebellion of 1863 the most useful secondary work is R. F. Leslie, *Reform and Insurrection in Russian Poland*, 1963, which also includes a comprehensive bibliography. Two contemporary sources of great interest on the relations of the Baltic Germans to Russia in this reign are *La Correspondance de Yu. Samarin avec la baronne de Raden*, Moscow, 1894, and Pastor Carl Schirren, *Livländische Antwort an Herrn Juri Samarin*, Leipzig, 1868.

Foreign Observers

Two first-class works by contemporary foreign observers are Anatole Leroy-Beaulieu, *L'Empire des Tsars et les Russes*, Paris, 1881–9, 3 volumes, and Sir Donald Mackenzie Wallace, *Russia*, first published 1877, revised in 1912, and republished in paper-back form, with an Introduction by Cyril E. Black, in New York in 1961.

Foreign Relations

The papers of Meyendorff cover the first years of the reign. For the documentation of European diplomacy in this period, see the volume in the present series by A. J. P. Taylor, *The Struggle for Mastery in Europe 1848–1918*. The following secondary works are related to Russian foreign policy in the reign. The works of Leontyev and Danilevsky are of course classics of political ideas which had great influence on public opinion in relation to foreign policy. The studies by Petrovich and Thaden discuss these and similar ideas. Sumner's book, apart from its outstanding merit as a study in diplomatic history, contains an extremely useful bibliography of Russian foreign policy in the 1870's.

DANILEVSKY, N. Y. *Rossiya i Evropa: vzglyad na kul'turnie i politicheskie otnosheniya slavyanskogo mira k germano-romanskomu*, SPB, 1956.
BELYAEV, N. I. *Russko-tyuretskaya voyna 1877–1878 godov*, Moscow, 1956.
GORIAINOV, S. *Le Bosphore et les Dardanelles*, Paris, 1910.
KHALFIN, N. A. *Politika Rossii v Sredney Azii*, Moscow, 1960.
LEONTYEV, K. N. *Vizantizm i slavyanstvo*, Moscow, 1876.
MEDLICOTT, W. N. *The Congress of Berlin and after*, 1963.
MOSSE, W. E. *The European Powers and the German Question 1848–1871*, 1958.
PETROVICH, M. B. *The Emergence of Russian Panslavism*, New York, 1956.
RUPP, G. *A Wavering Friendship: Russia and Austria 1876–1878*, Harvard, 1941.
SETON-WATSON, R. W. *Disraeli, Gladstone and the Eastern Question*, 1935.
STOJANOVIC, M. D. *The Great Powers and the Balkans*, 1939.
SUMNER, B. H. *Russia and the Balkans 1870–1880*, 1937.
THADEN, E. C. *Conservative Nationalism in 19th century Russia*, Seattle, 1964.

VI. THE REIGNS OF ALEXANDER III AND NICHOLAS II, 1881–1905

An essential source for this and the following period is the periodical *Krasny Arkhiv*, published in Moscow between 1922 and 1941. It was mainly concerned with foreign affairs, but also contained a great deal of valuable documentation on internal affairs in the last decades of the Imperial régime.

Some useful information on agriculture is contained in an official publication of the Ministry of State Properties, Department of Agriculture and Village Industry, entitled *Sel'skoe i lesnoe khozyaistvo Rossii*, SPB, 1893. Government regulations on the peasantry in the last years of the century are contained in *Sbornik uzakoneniy o krest'yanskikh i sudebnykh uchrezhdeniyakh*, SPB, 1901, published by the land department of the Ministry of the Interior. The Minutes of Witte's commission on the peasant problem were published as *Protokoly po krest'yanskomu delu*, SPB, 1905. The reports of the local committees investigating the peasant problem were published, one volume for each province, as *Trudy mestnykh komitetov o nuzhdakh sel'skokhozyaistvennoy promyshlennosti*, SPB, 1905.

Witte's famous memorandum on the zemstvos was published under the title *Samoderzhavie i zemstvo* in Stuttgart in 1903.

Information on education may be found in *Materialy po shkolnomu obrazovaniyu v Rossii*, SPB, 1906, and in the report of the Holy Synod, *Obzor deyatel'nosti vedomstva pravoslavnogo ispovedaniya za vremya Aleksandra III*, SPB, 1901.

The essential results of the census of 1897 are in the official publication *Obshchii svod po imperii rezul'tatov razrabotki dannykh pervoy vseobshchey perepisi naseleniya*, SPB, 1905, edited by N. A. Troynitsky. Further statistical information may be found in the yearly publication of the Central Statistical Committee of the Ministry of the Interior, *Ezhegodnik Rossii*, published from 1904 onwards.

An essential primary source for this period is the correspondence of K. P. Pobedonostsev, of which two series have been published—*K. P. Pobedonostsev, i ego korrespondenty*, Moscow, 1923, 2 volumes, and *Pis'ma Pobedonostseva k Aleksandru III*, Moscow, 1925–6, 2 volumes.

Collected works of political writers include the following:

LENIN. 5th edition, published in Moscow from 1958 onwards. The first 8 volumes deal with this period. The most important individual works of the period are *Razvitie kapitalizma v Rossii*, which forms volume 3; *Chto delat'* (vol. 6); and *Shag vperyod, dva shaga nazad* (vol. 8). These have been frequently translated into English. A modern edition of the second, which may be specially recommended, is *What is to be Done?* with introductory essay by S. V. Utechin, Oxford, 1963.

PLEKHANOV. *Sochineniya*, edited D. Ryazanov, Moscow, 1923, 24 volumes.

VLADIMIR SOLOVYOV. *Sobranie sochineniy Vladimira Sergeevicha Solovyova*, edited by S. M. Solovyov and E. L. Radlov, SPB, no date, 10 volumes.

The following are important memoirs, or reflections by contemporaries. Gurko's memoirs are exceptionally well edited and indexed, with useful biographical notes on the personalities mentioned.

CHERNOV, V. M. *Zapiski sotsialista-revolyutsionera*, Berlin, 1923.

GERSHUNI, G. *Iz nedavnego proshlogo*, Paris, 1908.

GURKO, V. I. *Features and Figures of the Past: Government and Opinion in the Reign of Nicholas II*, Stanford, 1939.

MAKLAKOV, V. A. *Vlast' i obshchestvennost' na zakate staroy Rossii*, Paris, no date.

KIZEVETTER, A. A. *Na rubezhe dvukh stoletiy: vospominaniya 1881–1914*, Prague, 1929.

MARTOV, Y. O. *Zapiski sotsial-demokrata*, Berlin, 1922.

PETERBURZHETS (K. M. Takhtarev). *Ocherki peterburzhskogo rabochego dvizheniya 90-kh godov*, London, 1902.

PETRUNKEVICH, I. I. *Iz zapisok obshchestvennogo deyatelya*, forming vol. xxi of the periodical *Arkhiv russkoy revolyutsii*, Berlin, 1934.

POBEDONOSTSEV, K. P. *Moskovskii sbornik*, 5th edition, Moscow, 1901 (translated as *Reflections of a Russian Statesman*, London, 1898).

SHIPOV, D. N. *Vospominaniya i dumy o perezhitom*, Moscow, 1918.

SUVORIN, A. S. *Dnevnik Suvorina*, Moscow, 1923.

WITTE, S. Y. *Vospominaniya*, 3 volumes, Berlin, 1922–3, latest edition, Moscow, 1960.

The history of the Russian Social Democratic Labour Party and its successors has a vast polemical literature. An earlier survey, from the Menshevik point of view but still worth reading, is Martov, Y. O. and Dan, F., *Geschichte der russischen Sozialdemokratie*, Berlin, 1926. A recent survey, from a non-Marxist point of view, which to most non-Marxists will appear admirably clear and scholarly, is L. B. Schapiro, *The Communist Party of the Soviet Union*, 1960. In the Soviet Union there have been not only untold numbers of detailed studies, both scholarly and polemical, but also a number of comparatively brief histories of the party, all of course from the point of view of the Bolshevik claimants to its succession. The differences among these various versions are due not so much to scholarly considerations as to fluctuations in the Party line of the CPSU. They are, of course, essential reading not only for students of the Soviet period but also for those who specialize in the early history of Russian Marxism. For students of Russian history as a whole in the period covered by the present work, they may be regarded as of marginal importance. Readers may perhaps confine themselves to the latest version of the intra-party polemic, which is *Istoria Kommunisticheskoy partii Sovetskogo Soyuza*, Moscow, 1962, English version *History of the Communist Party of the Soviet Union*, edited by Andrew Rothstein and Clemens Dutt, Moscow, no date (?1962).

The following are useful secondary works on internal politics during these years:

BARON, S. H. *Plekhanov, the Father of Russian Marxism*, Stanford, 1963.

BELOKONSKY, I. P. *Zemskoe dvizhenie*, Moscow, 1914.

BILLINGTON, J. H. *Mikhailovsky and Russian Populism*, 1958.

FISCHER, GEORGE. *Russian Liberalism, from Gentry to Intelligentsia*, Harvard, 1958.

GARDENIN, Y. (V. M. Chernov). *K pamyati N. K. Mikhailovskogo* (? Geneva), 1904.

HAIMSON, LEOPOLD. *The Russian Marxists and the Origins of Bolshevism*, Harvard, 1955.

KEEP, J. H. L. *The Rise of Social Democracy in Russia*, 1963.

KINDERSLEY, RICHARD. *The First Russian Revisionists: a Study of Legal Marxism in Russia*, 1962.
MENDEL, A. P. *Dilemmas of Progress in Tsarist Russia*, Harvard, 1961.
PIPES, RICHARD. *Social Democracy and the St. Petersburg Labour Movement*, Harvard, 1963.
RADKEY, O. H. *The Agrarian Foes of Bolshevism*, New York, 1958.
SLYOTOV, S. *K istorii vozniknoveniya partii SR*, Petrograd, 1917.
SPIRIDOVICH, Général. *Histoire du terrorisme russe 1886–1917*, Paris, 1930.
VESELOVSKY, B. *Istoriya zemstva za sorok let*, SPB, 1909–11, 4 volumes.

The following works on economic problems, some contemporary and some recent, deserve attention:

LAUE, T. H. VON. *Sergei Witte and the Industrialisation of Russia*, New York, 1963.
LIVSHITS, R. S. *Razmeshchenie promyshlennosti v dorevolyutsionnoy Rossii*, Moscow, 1955.
MIGULIN, P. P. *Russkii gosudarstvenny kredit*, Kharkov, 1899–1904, 3 volumes.
MASLOV, P. P. *Agrarny vopros v Rossii*, SPB, 1908.
NIKOLAI-ON (N. Danielson). *Ocherki nashego poreformennogo khozyaistva*, SPB, 1893.
PAZHITNOV, K. A. *Polozhenie rabochego klassa v Rossii*, Leningrad, 1924.
ROBINSON, G. T. *Rural Russia under the Old Regime*, 1929.
SCHULTZE-GÄVERNITZ, G. VON. *Volkswirtschaftliche Studien aus Rußland*, Leipzig, 1899.
STRUVE, P. B. *Kriticheskie zametki k voprosu ob ekonomicheskom razvitii Rossii*, SPB, 1894.

The following works are concerned with the non-Russian nationalities. Some of them also cover the years after 1905.

DMOWSKI, ROMAN. *Myśli nowoczesnego Polaka*, Lwów, 1904.
CHICHERINA, S. V. *O privolzhskikh inorodtsakh i sovremennom znachenii sistemy N. I. Il'minskogo*, SPB, 1906.
FELDMAN, J. *Geschichte der politischen Ideen in Polen seit dessen Teilungen*, Munich, 1917.
KALNINS, BRUNO. *De baltiska statornas frihetskamp*, Stockholm, 1950.
LUXEMBURG, ROZA. *Die industrielle Entwicklung Polens*, Berlin, 1898.
MENDE, G. VON. *Der nationale Kampf der Rußlandtürken*, Berlin, 1930.
PAASIVIRTA, J. *Arbetarrörelsen i Finland*, Stockholm, 1949.
PERL, F. *Dzieje ruchu socjalistycznego w zaborze rosyjskim*, Warsaw, 1910.
PIERCE, R. A. *Russian Central Asia 1867–1917*, Berkeley, 1960.
VOZNESENSKY, A. A. *O sisteme prosveshcheniya inorodtsev*, Kazan, 1913.
WUORINEN, J. H. *Nationalism in Modern Finland*, New York, 1931.
ZENKOVSKY, S. A. *Pan-Turkism and Islam in Russia*, Harvard, 1960.

For diplomatic sources on Russian foreign policy in this period the reader is referred to Taylor, op. cit. Here only a few works are mentioned which could be of use to a reader.

On Russian policy in Europe, two primary sources must be noted. One is the diary of Lamsdorff, dating from before his period of office as foreign minister. It appeared in two parts—V. N. Lamsdorff, *Dnevnik 1886–1890*, Moscow, 1926, and *Dnevnik 1891–1892*, Moscow, 1934. The second source are the papers of Baron de Staal, for many years Russian ambassador in London, edited by Baron A. von Meyendorff—*La Correspondance diplomatique du baron de Staal 1884–1900*, Paris, 1929, 2 volumes.

An outstanding secondary work is S. Skazkin, *Konets avstro-russko-germanskogo soyuza*, Moscow, 1928, which deals with the disintegration of the Three Emperors' Alliance. The best secondary work on the making of the alliance with France is Baron B. E. Nolde, *L'Alliance franco-russe*, Paris, 1936. The mature views of a great French historian on Franco-Russian relations are contained in the article by the late Professor Pierre Renouvin, 'Les relations franco-russes à la fin du 19e et au début du 20e siècle', in *Cahiers du monde russe et soviétique*, no. 1 (May 1959), pp. 128–147. Two valuable recent studies which throw light on Russian foreign policy are R. L. Greaves, *Persia and the Defence of India 1884–1892*, (1959) and J. A. S. Grenville, *Lord Salisbury and Foreign Policy: the Close of the Nineteenth Century*, (1964). Three outstanding books on the Balkan background, the first by a later historian and the others by contemporary observers, must be recommended—C. E. Black, *The Establishment of Constitutional Government in Bulgaria*, Princeton, 1943; H. N. Brailsford, *Macedonia*, 1906; and Sir Charles Eliot, *Turkey in Europe*, 1900.

The following is a short list of books on Russian policy in the Far East and on the Russo-Japanese War. Mackenzie contains the texts of treaties with Korea. Semennikov is documentary, and most useful. Glinsky is based on Witte's papers and opinions. Rosen's memoirs were written many years after his service as a Russian diplomat in the Far East. Kuropatkin's diary is a valuable primary source; his book on the war is an apology for his own record but is also important. The late Field-Marshal Sir Ian Hamilton was attached to the Japanese army during the war.

CONROY, H. *The Japanese Seizure of Korea: 1868–1910*, Philadelphia, 1960.

GLINSKY, B. B. *Prolog russko-yaponskoy voyny*, SPB, 1906. There is a French version under the name of P. Marc, *Quelques années de politique internationale*, Leipzig, 1914.

HAMILTON, SIR IAN. *A Staff-Officer's Scrap-Book during the Russo-Japanese War*, 1907, 2 volumes.

KUROPATKIN, GENERAL A. N. *Dnevnik Kuropatkina*, published in *Krasny Arkhiv*, no. 2, 1922 and covering Dec. 1902–Feb. 1904.

—— *The Russian Army and the Japanese War*, 1909, 2 volumes—abridged translation from the Russian original.

MacKenzie, F. A. *The Tragedy of Korea*, 1908.
Malozemoff, A. *Russian Far Eastern Policy 1881–1904*, Berkeley, 1958.
Romanov, B. D. *Rossiya v Man'chzhurii*, Leningrad, 1928. There is a rather unsatisfactory English translation, *Russia in Manchuria*, Madison, 1952.
—— *Ocherki diplomaticheskoy istorii russko-yaponskoy voyny 1895–1907*, Moscow, 1947.
Rosen, Baron R. *Forty Years of Diplomacy*, New York, 1922, 2 volumes.
Semennikov, V. P. *Za kulisami tsarizma, arkhiv tibetskogo vracha Badmaeva*, Leningrad, 1925.
Sorokin, Major-General A. I. *Russko-yaponskaya voyna 1904–1905 godov*, Moscow, 1956.
Sumner, B. H. *Tsarism and Imperialism in the Middle and Far East*, London, 1940.
White, J. A. *The Diplomacy of the Russo-Japanese War*, Princeton, 1964.

VII. THE LAST YEARS, 1905–1917

One of the main primary sources for this period are the proceedings of the Duma—*Gosudarstvennaya duma, stenograficheskie otchoty 1906–1916*, published in St. Petersburg (Petrograd) until the revolution. Another are the periodical publications by the political parties of the proceedings of their congresses and other meetings. Of these, the proceedings of the RSDRP are easily obtainable, as they have been published in several editions in the Soviet Union. The others are much harder to come by, but some at least of them are obtainable in the major European and North American libraries. For further details the reader may be referred to the excellent bibliographies in the works by Fischer, Keep and Radkey listed in the preceding section.

A great deal of material, largely but not wholly of a scandalous type, is to be found in the seven volumes of the report of the commission set up by the Provisional Government in 1917 to investigate the affairs of the last stage of the previous régime—*Padenie tsarskogo rezhima*, Leningrad, 1925–7. A valuable source on the proceedings of the Council of Ministers in 1915 are the notes kept by its secretary, A. N. Yakhontov, and published under the title *Tyazholye dni* in volume xviii of *Arkhiv russkoy revolyutsii*, Berlin, 1926.

Some of the papers of the Tsar and the Empress have been published. These are his diary—*Dnevnik*, Berlin, 1923; and his correspondence with his wife and his mother—*The Letters of the Tsaritsa to the Tsar 1914–1916* (1923); *The Letters of the Tsar to the Tsaritsa* (1929); and *The Letters of the Tsar to the Empress Marie* (1937).

The following memoirs are of interest:

Kokovtsov, V. N. *Out of My Past*, Stanford, 1935.

MAKLAKOV, V. A. *Pervaya gosudarstvennaya duma*, Paris, 1939.
—— *Vtoraya gosudarstvennaya duma*, Paris, 1946.
MILYUKOV, P. N. *Tri popytki*, Paris, 1921.
—— *Vospominaniya 1859–1917*, posthumously edited by M. Karpovich and B. I. Elkin, New York, 1955, 2 volumes.
SUCHOMLINOW, GENERAL W. A. *Erinnerungen*, Berlin, 1924.

The extracts from the diaries and reminiscences of General A. A. Polivanov—*Iz dnevnikov i vospominaniy po dolzhnosti voennogo ministra i ego pomoshchnika 1907–1916 godov*, Moscow, 1924, is also a valuable source.

Three political publications from this period must be noted as especially important. *Obshchestvennoe dvizhenie v Rossii v nachale XX veka*, SPB, 1909–12, 4 volumes, edited by Martov, Maslov and Potresov, is a survey by a number of Menshevik writers of the economic, social, and political events and trends of the first years of the century. The material on the nationalities is particularly useful. The second work is *Vyekhi: sbornik statey o russkoy intelligentsii*, Moscow, 1909, the well-known controversial symposium, most of whose contributors were former Marxists returned to Christian beliefs. The third work is the reply to *Vyekhi* from the orthodox Kadet point of view—*Intelligentsiya v Rossii*, with a preface by I. I. Petrunkevich, SPB, 1910.

The following works by contemporary foreign observers are in many ways revealing:

HOETZSCH, O. *Rußland*, Berlin, 1913.
KRAMÁŘ, KAREL. *Die russische Krisis*, Munich, 1925.
MASARYK, T. G. *The Spirit of Russia*, 1918.
PARES, SIR BERNARD. *Russia and Reform*, 1907.
—— *My Russian Memoirs*, 1931.
WILLIAMS, HAROLD. *Russia of the Russians*, 1914.

The two most important works by Lenin in this period were *Two Tactics of Social Democracy* (*Sochineniya* 5th edition, vol. 11, and numerous translations into English) and *The Agrarian Programme of Social Democracy in the First Revolution 1905–1907* (ibid., vol. 16, also easily accessible in English). For the large polemical literature within the Social Democratic movement, see the bibliographies in the secondary works listed in this and the preceding section.

The following secondary works on political history are of value:

NIKOLAEVSKY, B. *Azeff, the Russian Judas*, 1934.
OLDENBURG, S. S. *Tsarstvovanie Imperatora Nikolaya II*, Belgrade, 1939, 2 volumes.
OWEN, L. *The Russian Peasant Movement*, 1937.
PARES, SIR BERNARD. *The Fall of the Russian Monarchy*, 1939.

SLYOZBERG, G. B. *Dorevolyutsionny stroy Rossii*, Paris, 1933.
TREADGOLD, D. W. *Lenin and his Rivals*, 1955.

The following deal with aspects of social and economic development, mainly in the last decade of the régime.

CRISP, OLGA. 'Some Problems of French Investment in Russian Joint-Stock Companies,' in *Slavonic and East European Review*, vol. 35, pp. 222–40.
GRINEVICH, V. *Professional'noe dvizhenie rabochikh*, SPB, 1908.
KARPOV, N. I. *Agrarnaya politika Stolypina*, Leningrad, 1925.
MILLER, MARGARET. *The Economic Development of Russia 1905–1914*, 1926.
OL, P. V. *Inostrannye kapitaly v Rossii*, Petrograd, 1922.
OZEROV, I. K. *Politika po rabochemu voprosu v Rossii za poslednie gody*, Moscow, 1906.
PASVOLSKY, L., and MOULTON, H. G. *Russian Debts and Russian Reconstruction*, New York, 1924.
PAVLOVSKY, G. *Agricultural Russia on the Eve of the Revolution*, 1930.
PROKOPOVICH, S. N. *Kooperativnoe dvizhenie v Rossii*, Moscow, 1913.
SHINGARYOV, A. I. *Vymirayushchaya derevnya*, SPB, 1907.
TIMOSHENKO, V. P. *Agricultural Russia and the Wheat Problem*, Stanford, 1932.
TREADGOLD, D. W. *The Great Siberian Migration*, Princeton, 1957.
TYUMENEV, A. *Ot revolyutsii do revolyutsii*, Leningrad, 1925.

The following deal with the Church and religious life:

CURTISS, J. S. *Church and State in Russia: the Last Years of the Empire 1900–1917*, New York, 1940.
FEDOTOV, G. P. *Novy grad*, New York, 1952.
ZERNOV, N. *The Russian Religious Renaissance of the Twentieth Century*, 1963.

The following deal with the nationalities and with aspects of the ideology of Russian nationalism and russification:

AMES, E. O. F. *The Revolution in the Baltic Provinces*, 1907.
BENNIGSEN, A., and QUELQUEJAY, C. *Les Mouvements nationaux chez les musulmans de Russie: le Sultangalievisme au Tataristan*, Paris and The Hague, 1960 (the first part covers these years).
—— and —— *La Presse et le mouvement national chez les musulmans de Russie avant 1920*, Paris and The Hague, 1964.
DONZOW, D. *Die ukrainische Staatsidee und der Krieg gegen Rußland*, Berlin, 1915.
HAYIT, BAYMIRZA. *Türkestan im XX. Jahrhundert*, Darmstadt, 1956 (the first chapter covers this period).
Iz istorii natsionalnoy politiki tsarizma. Two instalments of documents relating to the policy of the Stolypin government towards the Volga Tatars, *Krasny Arkiv*, nos. 35 and 36, 1929.
KOVALEVSKY, P. I. *Russkii natsionalizm i natsionalnoe vospitanie*, SPB, 1912.
LOKOT, T. V. *Opravdanie natsionalizma*, Kiev, 1910.
MAZEPPA, I. *Pidstavy nashoho vidrozhdennya*, Augsburg, 1946.
PAHLEN, COUNT K. K. *Mission to Turkestan*, 1944 (a translation of the memoirs of a former high official, relating to 1909, previously unpublished.)

RESHETAR, J. *The Ukrainian Revolution*, Princeton, 1952 (first chapter).
RESUL-ZADE, M. E. *Das Problem Aserbaidschan*, Berlin, 1938.
SHCHEGOLEV, S. N. *Ukrainskoe dvizhenie kak sovremenny etap yuzhnorusskogo separatizma*, Kiev, 1912.
STRUVE, P. B. *Patriotica*, SPB, 1911.

For the literature of the diplomatic origins of the First World War the reader is referred to the bibliography in Taylor, op. cit. Here we will mention two books of memoirs by leading Russian diplomats—S. D. Sazonov, *Les Années fatales*, Paris, 1927; and Baron M. von Taube, *Der großen Katastrophe entgegen*, Leipzig, 1937. An interesting discussion of Russia's international situation on the eve of the war is Prince G. Trubetskoy, *Rußland als Großmacht*, Stuttgart, 1913.

Two useful secondary works on Russia in the Far East after the Russo-Japanese War are E. B. Price, *The Russo-Japanese Treaties of 1907–1916*, Baltimore, 1933 (which contains the texts of the treaties in Appendixes); and E. H. Zabriskie, *American-Russian Rivalry in the Far East*, Philadelphia, 1946.

On the end of the régime there are two important works by allied diplomats—Sir George Buchanan, *My Mission to Russia*, 1923, 2 volumes; and Maurice Paléologue, *La Russie des Tsars pendant la guerre*, Paris 1921–3, 3 volumes. The chronology of the last days is competently summarized in *Revolyutsiya 1917 goda, khronika sobytiy*, edited by A. Avdeyev, Moscow, 1923, volume I. A series of monographs on Russia during the First World War was published by Yale University Press between 1929 and 1931. This series included the following volumes:

ANTSIFEROV, A. N. *Russian Agriculture during the War.*
FLORINSKY, M. T. *The End of the Russian Empire.*
GOLOVIN, N. N. *The Russian Army in the World War.*
GRONSKY, P. P. and ASTROV, N. *The War and the Russian Government.*
ODINETZ, D. M. and NOVGOROTSOV, P. J. *Russian Schools and Universities during the World War.*
POLNER, T. I. *Russian Local Government during the War and the Union of Zemstvos.*
ZAGORSKY, S. O. *State Control of Industry in Russia during the War.*

Map 1. The provinces of European Russia

MAP 2. The main regions of European Russia

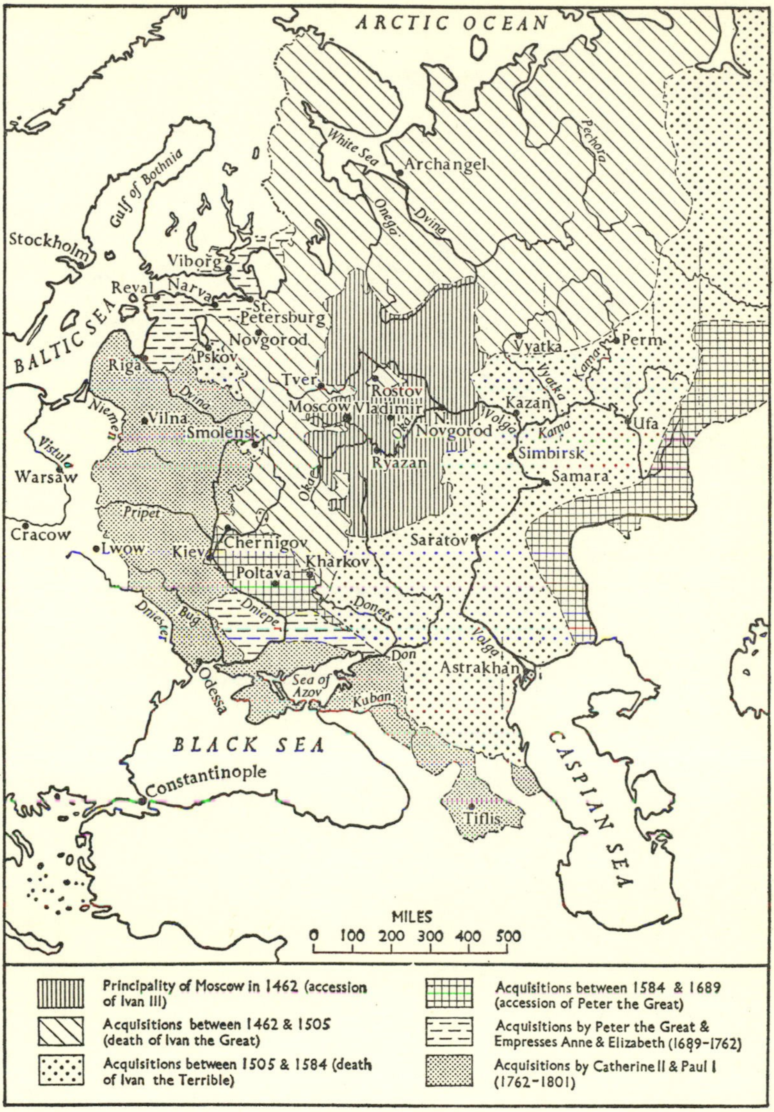

MAP 3. European Russia up to 1800

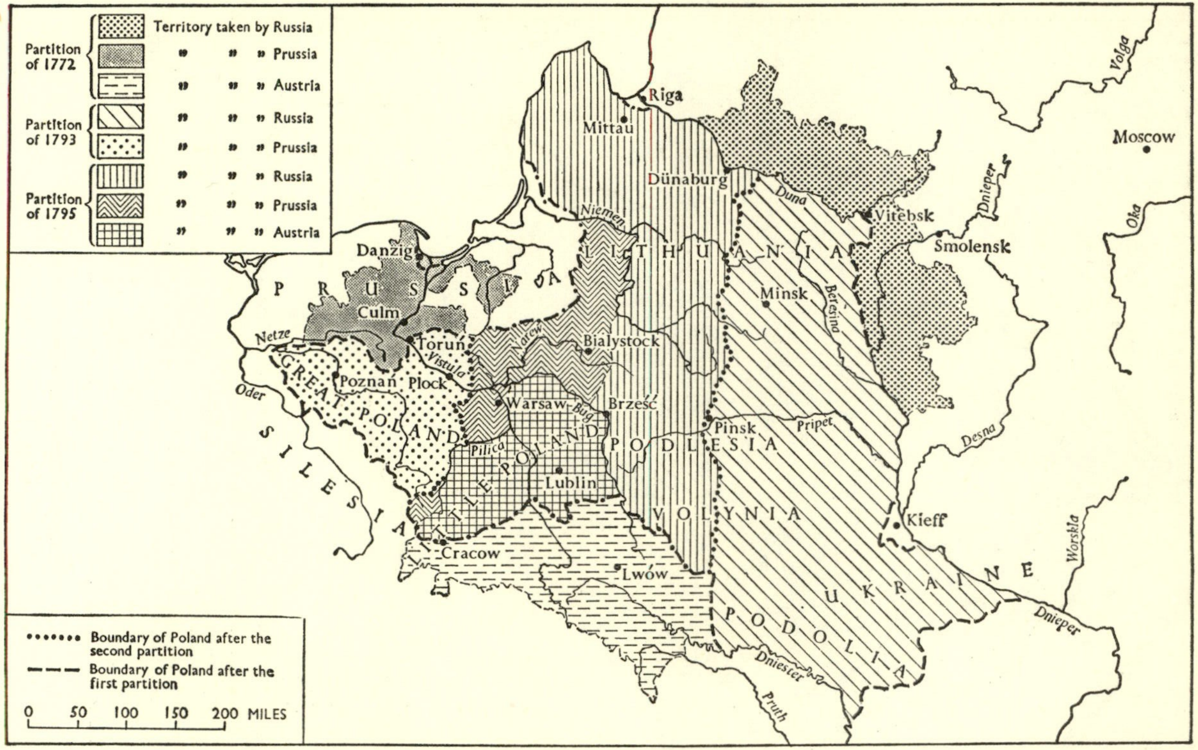

MAP 4. The Russo-Polish borderlands to 1795

BALTIC SEA
Danzig
Kovno
PRUSSIA
Vilna
Poznań
Minsk
Warsaw
RUSSIA
Łódz
POLAND
Breslau
Pinsk
Lublin
Cracow
GALICIA
Lwów
Tarnopol
AUSTRIAN EMPIRE
Budapest
Danube
Czernowitz
BUKOVINA
Dniester
MOLDAVIA
Bessarabia
(To Russia 1812)
Iaşi
TRANSYLVANIA
Danube
WALLACHIA
Grand Duchy of Warsaw 1809–1817
Ceded by Prussia to Russia 1807, included in the Kingdom of Poland 1815
Ceded by Austria to Russia 1809, restored to Austria 1815
Eastern border of the Kingdom of Poland 1815
Russian boundary 1815
0 50 100 150 Miles

Map 5. Russia's western border 1809–1917

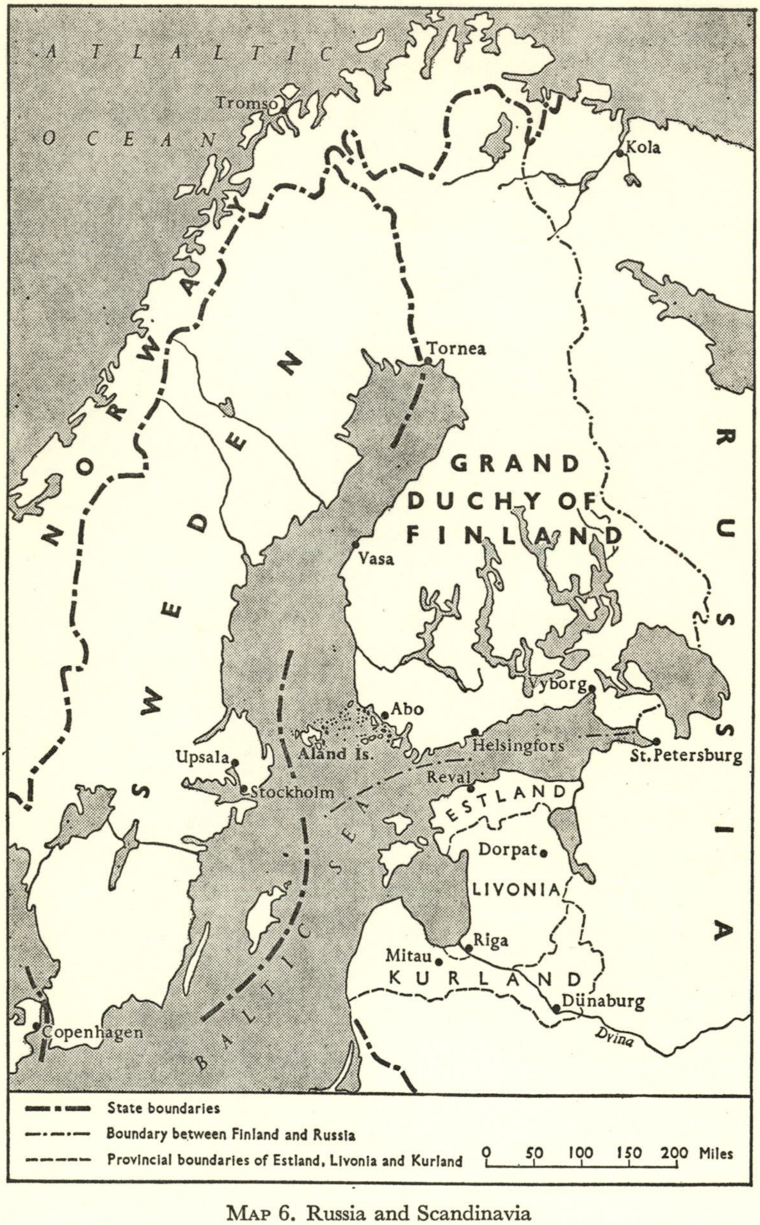

MAP 6. Russia and Scandinavia
(Swedish-Norwegian frontier 1905, other frontiers 1809–1917)

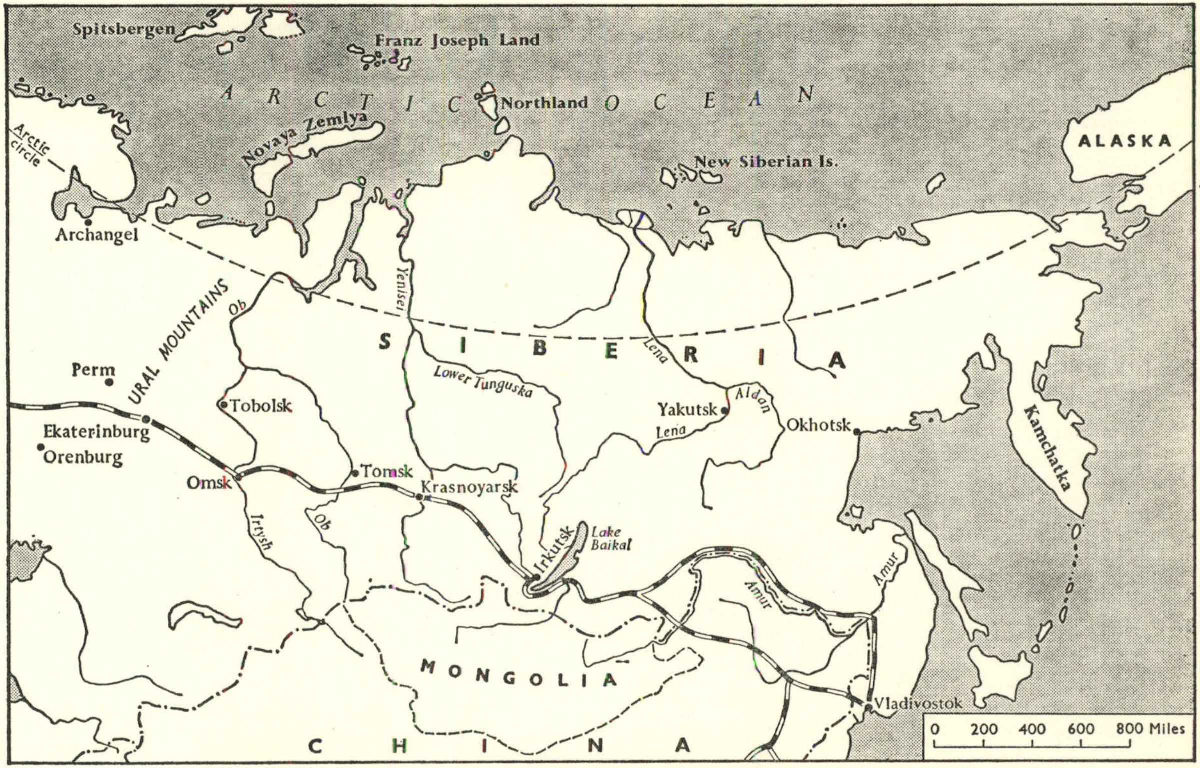

MAP 7. Siberia and the Trans-Siberian Railway

Kuban
Stavropol
Maykop
Kuma
Georgiyevsk
Pyatigorsk
Kizlyar
Mozdok
Malka
Terek
Terek
Grozny
Makhachkala
Sukhumi
RUSSIA
CAUCASUS
CASPIAN SEA
BLACK SEA
Poti
Akhaltsikh
Kura
Derbend
DAGHESTAN
Batum
Tiflis
Akhalkalaki
Artvin
Ardahan
Trebizond
Aleksandropol
Shemakha
Kars
Yelizavetpol (Gandzha)
Baku
Yerevan
Erzurum
TURKEY
Aras
Aras
Kura
Nakhichevan
PERSIA
Astara
Acquired from Persia 1813
Acquired from Persia 1828
Acquired from Turkey 1829
Acquired from Turkey 1878
0 20 40 60 80 100 Miles

MAP 8. The Caucasus and Transcaucasia

MAP 9. Russia as a Pacific Power

MAP 10. The conquest of Turkestan and Turkmenia

Map 11. Russia, Austria, and the Balkans, 1856–1914

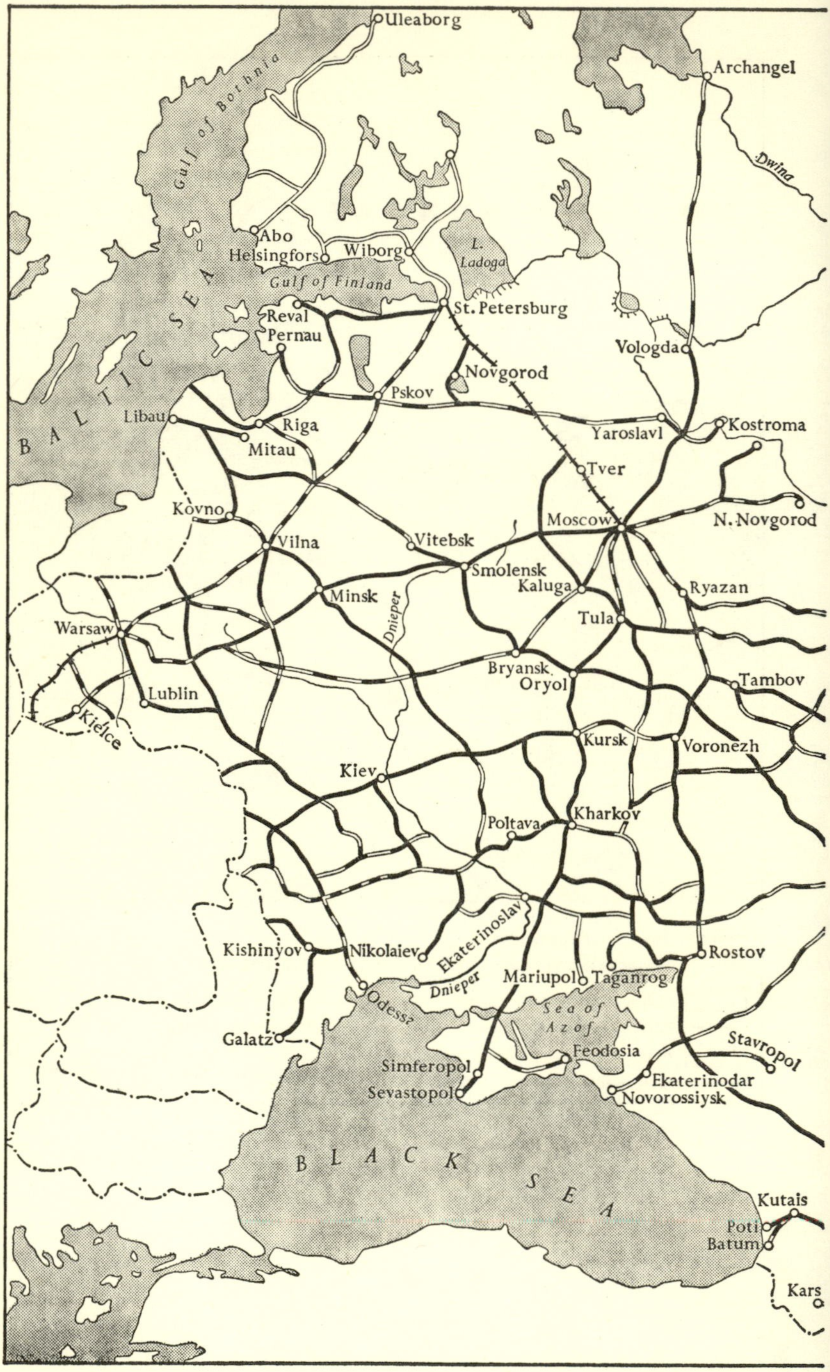

Map 12. Railways in European

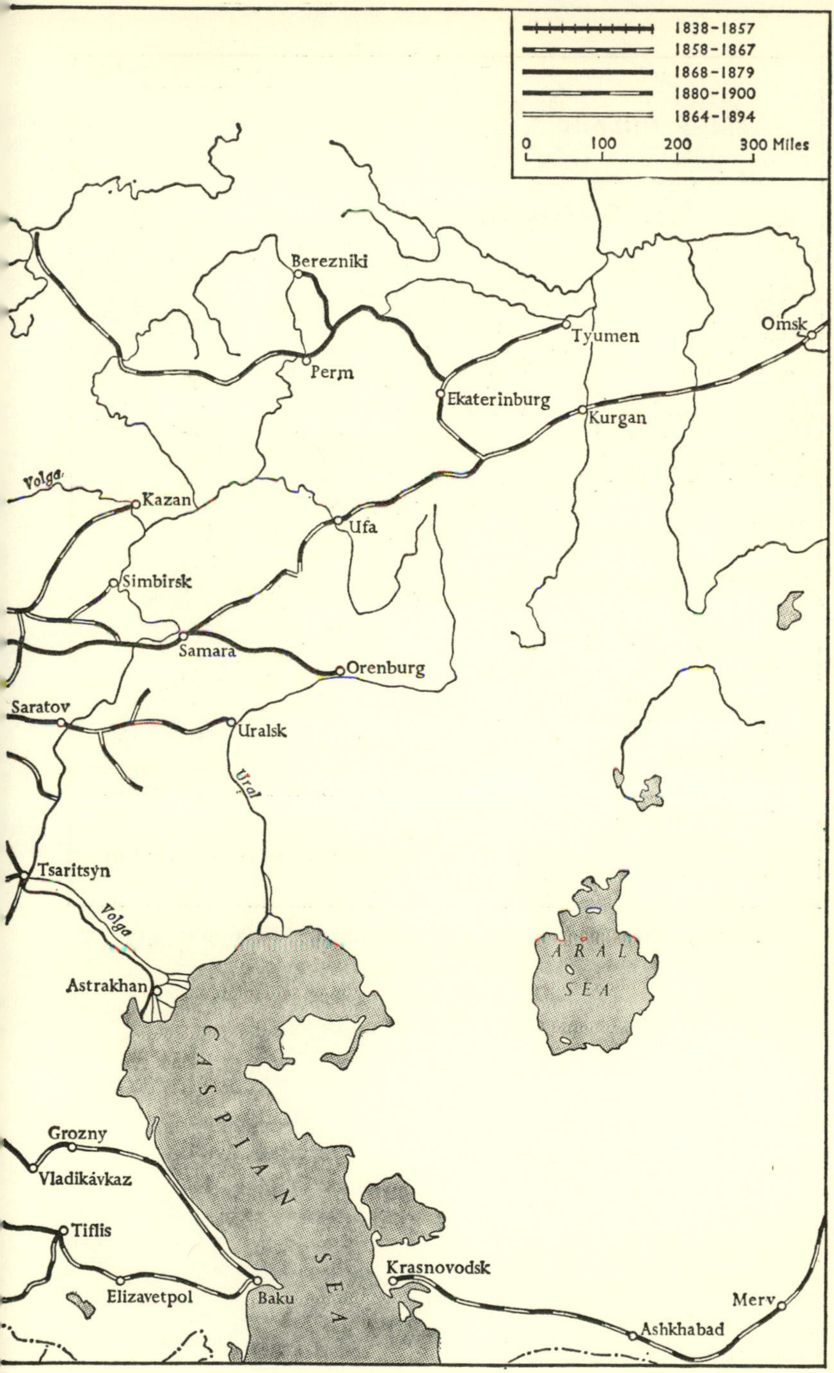

1838-1857
1858-1867
1868-1879
1880-1900
1864-1894
0 100 200 300 Miles
Berezniki
Perm
Tyumen
Omsk
Ekaterinburg
Kurgan
Volga
Kazan
Ufa
Simbirsk
Samara
Orenburg
Saratov
Uralsk
Ural
Tsaritsyn
Volga
Astrakhan
ARAL SEA
CASPIAN SEA
Grozny
Vladikávkaz
Tiflis
Elizavetpol
Baku
Krasnovodsk
Merv
Ashkhabad

Russia up to 1917

MAP 13. The main industrial areas in European Russia up to 1917

INDEX OF PERSONS

The dates of birth and death of all the persons listed are given, except for those who were rulers of countries other than Russia, where only the dates of reigns are given. Where dates of birth and death were not available, a short description of the individual is given, and the date at which he or she appears in the text. For those whose dates of birth and death are given, a description has been added only in certain cases where there might be confusion between several persons of the same name.

INDEX OF PLACES AND SUBJECTS

PRINTED IN GREAT BRITAIN
AT THE UNIVERSITY PRESS, OXFORD
BY VIVIAN RIDLER
PRINTER TO THE UNIVERSITY